PSYCHOLOGY OF EMOTIONS, MOTIVATIONS AND ACTIONS

HANDBOOK OF PSYCHOLOGY OF EMOTIONS

RECENT THEORETICAL PERSPECTIVES AND NOVEL EMPIRICAL FINDINGS

VOLUME 1

PSYCHOLOGY OF EMOTIONS, MOTIVATIONS AND ACTIONS

Additional books in this series can be found on Nova's website under the Series tab.

Additional e-books in this series can be found on Nova's website under the e-book tab.

PSYCHOLOGY OF EMOTIONS, MOTIVATIONS AND ACTIONS

HANDBOOK OF PSYCHOLOGY OF EMOTIONS

RECENT THEORETICAL PERSPECTIVES AND NOVEL EMPIRICAL FINDINGS

VOLUME 1

CHANGIZ MOHIYEDDINI
MICHAEL EYSENCK
AND
STEPHANIE BAUER
EDITORS

nova publishers
New York

NOTICE TO THE READER

The Publisher has taken reasonable care in the preparation of this book, but makes no expressed or implied warranty of any kind and assumes no responsibility for any errors or omissions. No liability is assumed for incidental or consequential damages in connection with or arising out of information contained in this book. The Publisher shall not be liable for any special, consequential, or exemplary damages resulting, in whole or in part, from the readers' use of, or reliance upon, this material. Any parts of this book based on government reports are so indicated and copyright is claimed for those parts to the extent applicable to compilations of such works.

Independent verification should be sought for any data, advice or recommendations contained in this book. In addition, no responsibility is assumed by the publisher for any injury and/or damage to persons or property arising from any methods, products, instructions, ideas or otherwise contained in this publication.

This publication is designed to provide accurate and authoritative information with regard to the subject matter covered herein. It is sold with the clear understanding that the Publisher is not engaged in rendering legal or any other professional services. If legal or any other expert assistance is required, the services of a competent person should be sought. FROM A DECLARATION OF PARTICIPANTS JOINTLY ADOPTED BY A COMMITTEE OF THE AMERICAN BAR ASSOCIATION AND A COMMITTEE OF PUBLISHERS.

Additional color graphics may be available in the e-book version of this book.

Library of Congress Cataloging-in-Publication Data

ISBN: 978-1-62808-053-7

Published by Nova Science Publishers, Inc. † New York

CONTENTS

Preface   ix

Part I: Emotions, Action and Culture   1

Chapter 1   What Is an Emotion?   3
                   Changiz Mohiyeddini and Stephanie Bauer

Chapter 2   Emotional Action: An Ideomotor Model   11
                   Andreas B. Eder and Klaus Rothermund

Chapter 3   Culture and Conceptual Contents of Emotion   39
                   Stacey N. Doan

Part II: Emotions in Developmental and Educational Settings   61

Chapter 4   Research on Emotions in Developmental Psychology Contexts:
                   Hot Topics, Trends, and Neglected Research Domains   63
                   Günter Krampen and Lisa Trierweiler

Chapter 5   Social Referencing in Infancy: Important Findings and
                   Future Directions   81
                   Lindsay E. Vandivier and Matthew J. Hertenstein

Chapter 6   Anxiety and Cognitive Performance   87
                   Michael W. Eysenck

Chapter 7   Psychology of Emotion and Its Application in Educational Settings   101
                   Kristin Bitan, Anna Haep and Gisela Steins

Chapter 8   Emotionality in Mathematical Problem Solving   115
                   Alex M. Moore and Mark H. Ashcraft

Chapter 9   The Self-conscious Emotions of Guilt,
                   Shame and Pride in Education   143
                   Shaalan Farouk

Part III: Emotions, Psychopathology and Health   159

Chapter 10   Emotion and Psychopathology   161
                   Stephanie Bauer and Changiz Mohiyeddini

Chapter 11   Emotion and Genetics   **171**
                  Christian Montag, Brian W. Haas
                  and Martin Reuter

Chapter 12   Rumination and Emotions   **187**
                  Susan Nolen-Hoeksema, Vera Vine and Kirsten Gilbert

Chapter 13   Strengthening Positive functioning in Children Growing
                  Up Amidst Political and Military Violence:
                  The Role of Emotions in Adjusting to Trauma   **211**
                  Guido Veronese and Marco Castiglioni

Chapter 14   Emotion and Obesity   **235**
                  Allan Jones

Chapter 15   Differential Effects of Negative Metacognitions and Positive
                  Metacognitions and Meta-Emotions on Anxiety and Depression   **249**
                  Nils Beer

Chapter 16   Sensation Seeking and Emotion   **273**
                  Nico Liebe and Marcus Roth

Chapter 17   The Influence of Light on Mood and Emotion   **297**
                  Elisabeth M. Weiss and Markus Canazei

Chapter 18   Affective Reactions to Physical Activity, Exercise
                  and the Activities of Daily Living: A Review   **307**
                  Wolfgang Schlicht, Annelie Reicherz and Martina Kanning

Chapter 19   Emotions and Performance:
                  Valuable Insights from the Sports Domain   **325**
                  Sylvain Laborde, Markus Raab and Fabrice Dosseville

Chapter 20   Mindfulness and Emotions   **359**
                  Sara LeBlanc and Changiz Mohiyeddini

Chapter 21   Emotions and Creativity   **377**
                  Jessica D. Hoffmann

Chapter 22   The Psychobiology of Disgust   **407**
                  Sonja Rohrman and Anne Schienle

Part IV: Emotions and Emotional Competences   **429**

Chapter 23   Self-Leadership, Self-Regulation and Emotion Regulation:
                  Is There a Common Regulatory Core?   **431**
                  Marco R. Furtner and Laura N. Hiller

Chapter 24   Improving Emotional Competence in Adults   **453**
                  Moïra Mikolajczak, Ilios Kotsou and Delphine Nelis

Chapter 25   Emotional Intelligence   **465**
                  Marc Brackett and Nicole Elbertson

Chapter 26   Adaptive Emotional Functioning: A Comprehensive
                  Model of Emotional Intelligence   **469**
                  Nicola S. Schutte and John M. Malouff

Chapter 27   Regulating the Impact of Emotions to Improve Decisions **489**
                  Kathleen E. Darbor and Heather C. Lench

Short Communication One and Two   **503**

Chapter 28   Sleep, Memory and Emotions   **505**
                  Małgorzata Wisłowska, Gabriela G. Werner,
                  Tina Moeckel, Dominik P.J. Heib,
                  Kerstin Hoedlmoser and Manuel Schabus

Chapter 29   Oxytocinergic Modulation of Emotional
                  Processes in Social Interactions   **517**
                  Anthony Lane, Olivier Luminet and Moïra Mikolajczak

Index   **527**

PREFACE

"The Handbook of Psychology of Emotions" is a timely, comprehensive, and authoritative edition consisting of chapters by an eminent group of international emotion researchers who provide a cutting-edge overview of all major aspects of human emotions. In addition to reviewing the current state of the art in a number of main research areas related to the topic of emotion, the authors present squarely an outlook for the future research on emotion.

Volume 1 is divided into four sections. Section One covers a brief discussion on the question of "What is an emotion?", the general theoretical issues concerning the link between emotions and action as well as the link between culture and conceptual contents of emotion. Section Two focuses on the impact of emotions in developmental and educational settings providing a chapter on research hot topics, trends, and neglected research domains in developmental psychology contexts, and a chapter on social referencing in infancy. In addition, it provides four chapters comprehensively reviewing the link between anxiety and cognitive performance, the application of psychology of emotion in educational settings, the role of emotionality in mathematical problem solving, and the impact of self-conscious emotions in education. Section Three contains chapters on specific psychopathological and health related issues. It provides a chapter on emotion and genetics, a chapter on rumination and emotions, and a chapter on the role of emotions in adjusting to political and military violence. Furthermore it comprises a chapter on emotion and obesity, a chapter on meta-emotions, anxiety and depression, a chapter on sensation seeking and emotion. In addition the influence of light on mood and emotion, affective reactions to physical activity, emotions and performance as well as emotions and mindfulness is reviewed in separate chapters.

Finally, Section Four contains chapters on improving emotional competences in adults, emotional intelligence, self-leadership and emotion regulation, adaptive emotional functioning and regulating the impact of emotions in order to improve decisions. These are followed by two short communications on the link between sleep, memory, and emotions and oxytocinergic modulation of emotional processes in social interactions.

Chapter 1 - William James has raised this question in 1884 in the 9th volume of Mind, i.e. almost 130 years ago. 158,905 articles later we are in the position to answer this question with: "We don't know". Although from the beginning of time immemorial, great masters of the human mind have made philosophical, phenomenological, anthropological, sociological, and psychological attempts to comprehend humans' emotions, emotions still maintain their enigmatic nature and "the language of emotions" remains highly cryptic. At the same time the human quest for knowledge about emotions seems to be steady. Whereas for some philosophers, such as Seneca and Ryle, emotions are irritating and inconvenient divergences from rationality that instigate our cognitive capacity, others, such as Aristotle and Hume, have characterized emotions in a more positive light, as a component of functional reasoning. Further dichotomies that are discussed in the literature relate to ongoing debates regarding whether emotions are "states or reflect a process", "disorganizing vs. organizing", "adaptive vs. maladaptive", "conscious vs. unconscious", "positive vs. negative". On one hand, these theoretical approaches have made valuable input to accelerate our understanding of emotions. Yet on the other hand, they have contributed to the complexity of the language of emotions. Already thirty years ago Kleinginna and Kleinginna have identified 92 definitions of emotions! Most obviously this impressive amount of definitions could be acknowledged as symptoms of the same issue that they aim to contribute to, its solution. This can be seen as a marked sign of an essential uncertainty about the theoretical foundation of the topic and signals of a pre-paradigmatic state of the development of psychology of the emotions as a discipline. Considering that "a definition emerges only at the end of a long discussion, and even then it is always tentative and appropriate only within a limited context and certain models of culture and personal character" it is obvious that the probable function of William James' question is to raise further questions about the nature, meaning and impact of emotions rather than expecting a comprehensive answer.

However, there is a surprising degree of consensus on a number of fundamental points regarding the meaning, function and impact of emotions. These include:

1) Emotions are essential aspects of human nature comprising multiple components such as cognitive, behavioural, expressive, experiential and physiological/neuroendocrinological systems that operate in a relatively coordinated and synchronized manner. It has been acknowledged that emotions generally shape the basis for temperament and personality and have a profound influence on perception, cognition, action, cognitive and physical performance, physical activity and problem solving. However, there is a controversial debate regarding whether different emotions possess unique, distinguishable and cross-situational consistent recurrent patterns of behavioural and/or physiological processes.

2) It has been widely acknowledged that as complex psychological phenomena, emotions have emerged through the course of evolutionary history in order to increase the adaptability of human responses to ontogenetic and developmental challenges in a constantly rapidly changing environment a significant portion of which entail social relations and interactions. Consequently, emotions are crucial and have arisen to increase and maintain the human-environment fit. Therefore, the diversity of humans' emotions mirrors different adaptive challenges. Accordingly, the investigation of human emotion as a crucial part of our evolutionary-biological and cultural heritage may facilitate our understanding of the history of human evolution and adaptation to both the physical and social environment.

3) Emotions are generated and maintained in a dynamic transactional process between organism and environment. On the one hand environmental clues stimulate emotional responses, yet on the other the emotional responses themselves influence the person–environment transaction. Put simply, activated emotions, as a component of the (psychological) environment, trigger cognitive processes which in turn, launch new emotional responses that may focus, as meta-emotions, the initial emotion as target.

4) In addition to their psycho-physiological functions, emotions are a social entity and serve various social functions. In this line of research the constructivist theory maintains that

the social function of emotions is a key point in understanding the function of emotions. Accordingly, emotions script our social behavior, shape social referencing and play a fundamental role in sympathy and empathy, thus they form the basis for conscience and moral behavior and facilitate prosocial behavior. Self-conscious social emotions such as guilt, shame and pride are crucial to regulate social interaction and reciprocity. The activation of emotions sensitizes us to the relevant and challenging features of our social environment informing us about others' behavioral intentions, while also providing us with valuable information as to whether something is good or bad. Hence, the sustainability of social interactions and relationships throughout the life span require an accurate decoding and encoding of socio-culturally (partly) determined emotional signals. Therefore initiation, maintenance and expansion of functioning social networks require adequate socioemotional competences.

5) It has been widely acknowledged that cultures lay out the possibilities for emotions and in that regard, guide the act of recognizing an emotion. Hochschild emphasizes that apart from what we think an emotion is, we also have socio-culturally colored ideas about what it should be.

Accordingly, emotions are influenced by cultural ideas and images, and shaped through socio-cultural roles and norms regarding what we feel, what we should feel (feeling rules) and how an emotion should be expressed (display rules).

6) An increasing evidence base indicates that the dysregulation of emotions contributes to various forms of psychopathology, and plays a prominent role in the development of depression, aggression and violence, obesity; self-regulation.

Whereas it has been established that an optimal and appropriate regulation of emotions- in terms of fitting with social standing, social rules, performance expectations and individual goals – enhances health and well-being .

Chapter 2 - This chapter presents a new model of emotional action that emphasizes an anticipatory control of emotional actions. It begins by reviewing existing hypotheses about a causal relationship between emotions and action. Then, findings and hypotheses of an ideomotor model are discussed about how an emotional action is learned, represented, activated, selected, and expressed. Finally, the model is applied to an analysis of emotional fight-and-flight behaviors.

Chapter 3 - The extent to which culture shapes the experience of emotion has been a central concern for psychologists and anthropologists alike. The topic is potentially important not only for understanding the role that cultures play in giving meaning to inner experience and shaping psychological processes, but also for our conceptualization and understanding regarding the nature of emotion, itself. Perhaps, because of its complexities, researchers examining cross cultural differences and similarities in emotion has often focused on specific components of emotion (e.g. facial expressions, causes of emotion, emotion recognition) in their studies. Furthermore, the specific aspect of emotion that is considered often depends on the researchers' theoretical assumptions regarding what constitutes emotions. Emotions have either been seen as biological, a product of evolution or a social construction, a product of culture. The purpose of the following paper is to present how emotions have been conceptualized in the literature and how this conceptualization has influence the way in which researchers examine the role of culture. The authors then review the cross-cultural literature on emotion under the lens of the conceptual act model of emotion, and conclude with implications for research and clinical practice.

Chapter 4 - This chapter presents bibliometric analyses of the representation of emotions in psychology research from a developmental perspective across a four-decade time span and across developmental age groups. After an overview on the frequency of the topic of emotions in developmental psychology research in general, the authors focus on the overrepresentation (popularity) and underrepresentation (neglect/ disregard) of certain emotions in developmental psychology research. Using the classification codes and descriptor terms of the *Thesaurus of Psychological Index Terms* and the data from the psychology literature database PsycINFO of the American Psychological Association (APA), bibliometric analyses are performed on the frequency of concepts of emotional development in general and on the frequencies of specific emotions in developmental psychology research. These analyses examine both cumulative findings and time trends across four decades (1970-2010). Findings reveal that, overall, negative emotions dominate research on emotions, and that the highest relative frequency of emotions across four decades of research in developmental psychology is found for childhood. In conclusion, neglected research domains as well as new topics and trends in research on emotions in developmental psychology are discussed.

Chapter 5 - Social referencing occurs when infants use adult emotional displays to regulate their behavior toward environmental objects, people, and situations. Social referencing provides infants with opportunities' to learn about their environments. The present chapter highlights five areas in which future investigation should focus in social referencing and the strides that have been made in each: (a) the importance of naturalistic studies, (b) the development of social referencing, (c) individual differences, (d) neural underpinnings, and (e) atypical populations.

Chapter 6 - There has been much interest in understanding the adverse effects of anxiety on cognitive tasks. One of the main theories in this area is attentional control theory. According to this theory, it is important to distinguish between performance effectiveness (the quality of performance) and processing efficiency (the relationship between performance effectiveness and the use of processing resources). A major prediction (which has been supported strongly by recent research involving the use of functional magnetic resonance imaging (fMRI) and event-related potentials (ERPs) is that there are greater adverse effects of anxiety on processing efficiency than on performance effectiveness.

Another major assumption within attentional control theory is that adverse effects of anxiety mostly revolve around the central executive component of the working memory system. More specifically, anxiety impairs the efficiency of specific functions of the central executive including the inhibition and shifting functions. Research has provided reasonable empirical support for these assumptions.

Finally, the chapter concludes by considering some ways in which future research might develop and extend the theoretical reach of attentional control theory.

Chapter 7 - The aim of this chapter is to point out the relevance of insights from emotion psychology for interaction designs in the school context. The authors chose three different levels on which to demonstrate this relevance. The first level deals with the pupils themselves and takes into consideration those insights from emotion psychology, which should be taught and shown to pupils in order to help them to establish a positive and helpful design of interaction. The second level deals with those findings from emotion psychology which should be an integral part of teacher training for the benefit of a constructive interaction design between teachers and pupils and a successful classroom management. The third and last level deals with leadership in educational contexts and the management of schools, especially concerning headmasters. The authors are going to point out and report research results from all three levels of school interaction (pupil-pupil; pupil-teacher; headmaster-teacher), which in total show that fundamental knowledge of emotion psychology contains valuable conclusions for a positive design of life in schools.

The authors' research primarily focuses on forming the ability of the protagonists to understand and realize the interdependence of their own belief systems, emotions and actions. They should thus be enabled to develop sensitivity for the social effects which their own behavior has on the beliefs, emotions and actions of their social environment. In order to develop this ability, important theories and concepts to consider are cognitive models of emotion and emotion regulation as well as the foundation of rational-emotive behavior therapy, completed by theories of emotional contagion and models of emotion categorization.

Chapter 8 - For some, doing mathematics is enjoyable, and represents an opportunity to learn and excel. For others, the mere thought of doing mathematics can induce anxiety, fear, and avoidance. What are the factors behind such emotions, and how do they affect math learning and performance?

This chapter explores the positive and negative avenues through which attitudes and emotions about mathematics can influence math learning and performance, a topic of considerable importance in an era of widespread math achievement testing in educational settings. The authors discuss the influence of attitudes and emotions on learning and understanding math, with particular attention to math anxiety. The authors explore the cognitive mechanism central to most mathematical problem solving, the working memory system, and then describe how that system is compromised during problem solving when emotions are aroused. The chapter ends with a discussion of some new research directions on this topic, including some strong hints about possible causal relationships in math anxiety.

Chapter 9 - The experience of self-conscious emotions is associated with a person's evaluations of the self and his or her conduct in a particular situation. In particular an individual is expected to experience guilt, shame and pride when they perceive themselves to have succeeded or failed to abide by internalised values and moral standards. Hence an examination of how and when individuals experience self-conscious emotions can provide considerable psychological insight into their personal values and moral imperatives. Moreover, the different self-conscious emotions a person experiences do not remain inert within the confines of their body. Instead, they have a prevailing influence on an individual's thoughts and their behaviour. With this in mind substantial psychological and some educational research has been conducted on the self-conscious emotions. In this chapter, a brief review of the literature on the development of self-conscious emotions is followed by a detailed examination of guilt, shame and pride as experienced by school children and adolescents. The analysis of each emotion will include an exploration of how it is experienced by learners and its potential influence on their behaviour and their ability to learn. Furthermore, each self-conscious emotion is examined as an achievement emotion, which learners experience in relation to their work, or as a social emotion, which students experience in their social interactions. At the end of the chapter the circumstances under which teachers experience guilt and pride are also described and discussed. The purpose of research in this field has been to study teachers' self-understanding and moral purpose by examining their self-conscious emotions.

Chapter 10 - Emotions are intrinsically tied to mental health and mental well-being as well as to various forms of psychopathology. In this chapter the authors give an overview on the role that emotions and emotional processing play in different mental disorders. Specifically the authors review key approaches and empirical findings related to depression, anxiety disorders, and eating disorders. For each of these conditions there is a considerable evidence base documenting the relevance of emotions, emotion processing and emotion regulation for the development and maintenance of psychopathology. These findings are of immediate relevance to clinical sciences and intervention research as they offer opportunities to develop new interventions or to enhance existing treatment approaches by addressing the relationship between emotions, emotional processing, and emotion regulation on the one side and psychopathological symptoms and impairment on the other side. However, more research is needed in order to better align treatment approaches to evidence from basic research. To that end the authors outline priorities for such future research related to emotion and psychopathology.

Chapter 11 - This chapter gives a brief overview on the genetics of emotions. After an introduction into historical aspects of the field followed by insights on the topic derived by animal models, two lines of research will be highlighted, which both successfully investigated the genetic aspects of emotions. First, Williams Syndrome will be in the focus of the present review. This neurodevelopmental condition is of great interest in the context of genetics and emotions, because here 26-28 genes on chromosome 7 are missing in humans and this condition is associated with abnormal emotional behavior. Second, a molecular genetic approach to emotionality is presented, in which individual differences in emotion-related-personality dimensions are investigated. This chapter closes with a short outlook on future research leads.

Chapter 12 - Emotions typically have informational value, arising when there are important changes in the environment and/or changes in progress toward one's goals. Thus, when emotions arise, particularly negative emotions that may signal threat or loss in the environment or lack of progress toward goals, people tend to reflect on or evaluate the causes, meanings, and consequences of these emotions. Martin and Tesser referred to such reflection and evaluation as *rumination*. They argued that rumination is functional when it leads people to take action to reduce the discrepancies between their current state and a desired state, or to give up unattainable goals. If rumination does not lead to such outcomes, and instead persists and focuses a person's attention on unattained goals and negative emotions, it can become maladaptive.

For example, if a woman has the goal of a positive relationship with her husband, but has been having frequent arguments with him, she will experience negative emotion, and this may lead her to ruminate on the discrepancy between her goal (a positive relationship) and her current state (hostility between the couple). If she ruminates on the discrepancy in an instrumental, problem-solving way, then her ruminations will end when she either takes action to overcome the discrepancies (e.g., she initiates a conversation with her husband in an effort to repair the relationship) or when she relinquishes the desired goal (e.g., she decides her husband is impossible to live with and files for divorce). The consequence of such an instrumental approach is positive or neutral affect. In contrast, if her ruminations simply perseverate on the discrepancies between the current state and a desired state, the discrepancy will remain, and she will continue to experience negative affect.

The authors' research has focused on maladaptive forms of rumination, their consequences and mechanisms of action, and sources of individual differences in maladaptive rumination. In the Response Styles Theory, Nolen-Hoeksema defined maladaptive rumination as a perseverative focus on the causes, meanings and consequences of negative affect in the absence of instrumental behavior to relieve that negative affect. She argued that such a perseverative focus maintains and exacerbates negative mood by (a) enhancing negative mood-congruent thinking, (b) interfering with problem-solving, and (c) inhibiting instrumental behavior. Nolen-Hoeksema and Davis argued that rumination also damages social relationships, as supportive others grow weary of the ruminator's inability or unwillingness to take action on, or "let go" of, ruminations, and subsequently become hostile and/or withdraw their support. Thus, the ruminator not only fails to solve the problems behind the original negative mood, but also develops new problems that may inspire new negative emotions, such as loss of social support.

Most of the research on maladaptive rumination has focused on rumination in the context of sadness or depression, and that will be reviewed here. The authors will also review work supporting the mechanisms by which rumination has is deleterious effects. However, in recent years, rumination has been conceptualized as a transdiagnostic process occurring in multiple disorders, and exacerbating any emotional state that is present. Thus, the authors will review work on rumination in the contexts of anxiety and anger, as well as recent work on rumination in the context of positive emotions. The authors will conclude with questions for future research.

Chapter 13 - Mainstream clinical studies on children living and growing-up in war-affected areas appear to emphasize the symptoms and dysfunction that can arise when children are exposed to political and military violence. This focus may reflect Western preconceptions regarding the fragility and vulnerability of children, which also inform diagnostic and intervention programs.

The very construct of resilience is too closely related to pathological frameworks, accounting for the successful adaptation of only a small minority of the population affected by trauma. In fact, resilience does not explain why the greater part of the child population does not develop symptoms in the aftermath of war despite multiple exposures to traumatic events.

To gain a better understanding of functioning factors and positive adjustment in children affected by war, a change of framework is required. Positive emotions, optimism and life satisfaction are pivotal factors that can affect children's well-being, enabling them to overcome traumas and psychological suffering.

In this chapter the authors present two quantitative cross-sectional studies carried out in the Palestinian Occupied Territories, which show that despite adverse life conditions and the ongoing chronic conflict affecting the area, Palestinian children remain optimistic, satisfied with their lives and able to deal with environmental constraints via positive emotions. The children completed self-reported measures before receiving psycho-educational interventions aimed at reinforcing positive emotions as protective factors in coping with trauma. Ecological dimensions promoting positive emotions and life satisfaction in children are discussed.

Chapter 14 - Obesity has reached epidemic proportions and is today one of the most costly chronic diseases in terms of morbidity, mortality and healthcare consumption. Obesity carries with it numerous serious health related consequences including type II diabetes, cardiovascular diseases, neuropathy and cancer. It has previously been estimated that over half a million people die each year in the United States alone due to obesity related health problems, with obesity related healthcare costs estimated to be over 100 billion dollars (report published by the U.S. Department of Health and Human Services, 2007). In a study by Kelly et al., it was estimated that in 2005 9.8% of the world's adult population, approximately 400 million people, were obese. In the same period (2005-2006) the National Health and Nutrition Examination Survey estimated that 34.3% of the adult population in the United States had excess body weight in the obese range. It is therefore of considerable concern that the prevalence rates in obesity are on the rise. Within the next decade it is estimated that prevalence rates in obesity will be as high as 40% in the United States, while by the year 2030 it is estimated that 573 million to 1.12 billion people worldwide will suffer from obesity.

A person is defined as obese if their excess body fat exceeds 30 on the body mass index (BMI = weight in kilograms divided by height in meters squared), and morbidly obese if excess body fat reaches 40 or more on the BMI. In simplistic terms obesity is a result of an energy imbalance. In overweight and obese individuals more energy is consumed than is expended. The aetiologies of energy imbalance are however potentially numerous and multifaceted, as such biological, physiological and psychosocial risk factors need to be considered. The increase in prevalence rates of obesity are unlikely to be explained by changes in our biology (for example genetic), as prevalence rates have increased rapidly over a relatively short period of time. The increase in obesity can most likely be explained by changes in behaviour, lifestyle and nutrition, such as decreases in physical activity, easier access to inexpensive food high in fat and sugar and significantly larger portion sizes compared to 30 years ago, leading to significant increases in consumption of unhealthy food and increases in energy imbalance (for a debate on the respective contribution of physical activity vs. nutrition in explaining the global increase in obesity see Biddle and Dovey, 2009). Specific causal and contributing factors leading to individual differences in weight gain are less clear. Factors that determine increases in unhealthy eating habits and sedentary behaviours are being explored, and it appears that emotions may play an important role in explaining the growing rates of obesity in the global population. Moreover, obesity may be a risk factor not only in relation to somatic health but also in relation to mental health, for example obese individuals may be more vulnerable to adverse changes in affective state compared to normal weight individuals. The current chapter aims to explore the relationship between emotion and obesity. The associations between emotion and energy imbalance will be examined in an attempt to explain individual differences in weight gain and to identify potential determinants of the obesity epidemic. The chapter will also explore pathways that attempt to explain how emotional distress and obesity are linked, as well as take a critical look at current treatment practices for obese individuals.

Chapter 15 - This study attempts to derive and investigate adaptive metacognitive and meta-emotional self-regulatory processes by partially reversing and, moreover, extending Wells and Matthews' and Wells' metacognitive model of psychological and emotional disorders within a positive psychology framework. The assumption of this study is that adaptive metacognitive and meta-emotional self-regulation, specifically in the light of challenge, unpredictability or ambiguity, should contribute to state emotional equilibrium, measured as absence or low levels of state depression and comorbid state anxiety. Investigating the metacognitive and meta-emotional etiology of (state) depression and anxiety appears to be valuable in light of steadily increasing prevalence rates of both disorders in Western societies. Depressive disorders are the predominant mental disorders affecting an estimated 340 million people worldwide with increasing tendency. The current economic crisis with increased job insecurity necessitates even more pronounced adaptations to challenge and change to maintain psychological stability.

Examining both maladaptive metacognitions and adaptive metacognitions and meta-emotions in terms of their effects on anxiety and depression sheds light on the core question: Is mere absence of maladaptive metacognitions sufficient for buffering potential (state) depression and anxiety and subsequent successful problem-solving in situations of challenge? The assumption of the present study is that pure absence of dysfunctional metacognitions is a necessary but not sufficient precondition for successful resolution of challenge. In addition to the absence or low levels of maladaptive metacognitions, psychological stability and success in challenging or unpredictable situations requires high levels of adaptive metacognitions and meta-emotions.

The present study explores the linear relationships between dysfunctional metacognitions, positive metacognitions and meta-emotions as independent variables and anxiety and depression as outcome measures. A mixed sample of 212 worker and student participants was utilized and completed the following battery of questionnaires: the five dimensions comprising Meta-Cognitions Questionnaire 30 (*MCQ-30*, Wells and Cartwright-Hatton, 2004), the three-dimensional Positive Metacognitions and Positive Meta-Emotions Questionnaire (*PMCEQ*, Beer and Moneta, 2010) and the Hospital Anxiety and Depression Scale (*HADS*, Zigmond and Snaith, 1983). A cross-sectional design was employed and data analysis comprised correlation analysis and subsequent structural equation modeling (SEM) analyses. PMCEQ-F1 – Confidence in Extinguishing Perseverative Thoughts and Emotions – was negatively predictive of Anxiety and Depression. PMCEQ-F2 – Confidence in Interpreting Own Emotions, Restraining from Immediate Reaction and Mind-Setting for Problem-Solving – also negatively predicted state Anxiety and state Depression but to a far lesser extent than PMCEQ-F1. This can be explained in the light of what these factors measure: PMCEQ-F1 reflects an inverse construct of Wells and Matthews' (1996) Self-Regulatory Executive Function (S-REF) perseveration and rumination as assessed by the MCQ-30, specifically by the MCQ-F2 subscale "Negative Beliefs about Worry concerning Uncontrollability and Danger". Above and beyond the perseveration-inhibiting PMCEQ-F1, the PMCEQ-F2 factor also incorporates problem-focused or agentic properties. The ability to quickly terminate worry and rumination cycles as assessed by the PMCEQ-F1 items has by nature more pronounced decreasing effects on (state) Anxiety and Depression than the agency-related constructs as measured by some of the PMCEQ-F2 items. This argument was further supported by the finding that the even more agency-related PMCEQ-F3 factor – Confidence in Setting Flexible and Feasible Hierarchies of Goals – was a non-significant predictor of both (state) Anxiety and Depression in the SEM model. As expected and in line with a plethora of previous studies, the MCQ-30 construct, comprising the five MCQ-30 subscales utilized as indicators in this study, was strongly and negatively predictive of state Anxiety and state Depression. Comparing the relative contributions of PMCEQ-F1 and MCQ-30 to (state) Anxiety and Depression in absolute terms revealed that the predictive power of the MCQ-30 was slightly higher than the one of the PMCEQ-F1 subscale.

The study findings suggest that absence of psychological distress, here assessed by (low levels of) anxiety and depression, not only requires the absence of maladaptive metacognitive traits as measured by the MCQ-30 but also the presence of adaptive metacognitions and adaptive meta-emotions as assessed by the PMCEQ. Compared to the MCQ-30, the PMCEQ instrument covers a more encompassing range of psychological dimensions by assessing problem-focus and goal-setting as positive traits, beyond the worry- and rumination-related maladaptive traits measured by the MCQ-30. It is therefore concluded that potential self-empowering coaching applications of the PMCEQ should be wider in scope than the corresponding, however inverse and clinical, ones of the MCQ-30. This has already been reflected in Beer and Moneta's study with PMCEQ factors having significant negative effects on maladaptive coping and perceived stress and significant positive effects on adaptive coping.

In terms of interventions it is argued that potential clinical and coaching interventions aimed at development and cultivation of PMCEQ-F1 "skills" would reduce anxiety and depression. Cultivation of the agentic psychological constructs measured by PMCEQ-F2 and PMCEQ-F3 is hypothesized to increase problem-solving, self-determination and goal-setting. This in turn should have enhancing impacts on academic and professional performance measures, potentially enhancing happiness and life satisfaction above and beyond merely buffering against anxiety and depressive states. It conclusion, it can be argued that PMCEQ-F1 better informs potential clinical interventions whereas PMCEQ-F2 and PMCEQ-F3 could be at the focus of self-empowering coaching practices.

Chapter 16 - The following chapter addresses the concept of *sensation seeking* and its wide-reaching connections to emotions. The first part introduces the conceptualization and measurement of sensation seeking and presents a chronological overview of its development. For a better understanding of the construct of sensation seeking, different conceptual perspectives and their implications are considered and discussed. The second subchapter follows and elaborates on a number of links that connect sensation seeking to a wide range of emotions (e.g., excitement, curiosity, depression, anger, fear, disgust, and frustration) and tries to embed the reported results into a neurophysiological framework. The third part presents their own study in which the authors investigated the moderating effect of sensation seeking on affect caused by stress to prove the stress-buffering effects of sensation seeking and to look for differences between high vs. low sensation seekers in the strategies they use and in their abilities to self-regulate emotion.

Chapter 17 - In the 7th century William Shakespeare wrote "A sad tale's best for winter." However, he was not the first who understood the power of light on our psyche. 2000 years ago Hippocrates, the father of modern medicine, already acknowledged that the absence of light, particularly in winter, can produce diseases. Since then, the impact of light on mood and the use of bright light as a treatment-option for affective disorders have been studied extensively by scientists. Light is the major zeitgeber for human circadian rhythms, much more powerful than social zeitgebers eg. work or school schedules. Non-visual effects of light include hormone regulation, the synchronization of the circadian system, the regulation of body temperature, but also the regulation of cognition and alertness. Bright light treatments are dating back to Lewy et al. who could demonstrate that exposure to bright white light (a mixed spectrum of wavelengths similar to day light) can adjust circadian rhythms and suppress melatonin. The most extensive clinical trials on bright light therapy have focused on seasonal affective disorders suggesting that light can modulate mood in the long term. Today light therapy is used to treat different disorders like sleep disorders, affective disorders, dementia etc.. This chapter will give an overview about the neurobiological basis for light therapy and discuss different mood disorders responsive to light therapy. Additionally, the influence of light on normal brain emotional processing will be discussed.

Chapter 18 - This narrative review deals with the association between physical activity or exercise and affective reactions. It outlines what is known about affective reactions, accompanying or following increasing exercise intensities. It also summarizes the results of ambulatory assessment studies. Those studies monitor the individuals' activity levels in daily routine and their reactions to it.

Chapter 19 - Emotions not only color our lives and give meaning to them but also have a strong impact on human performance. Why is it so important to consider the relationship between emotions and performance? From an evolutionary perspective, emotions have been at the core of our struggle to survive and, more prominently in today's world, to perform. The authors chose to study this relationship in sports, a high-pressure domain that reflects, to some degree, survival fights and contests. In addition, sports is an applied field that is concerned with enhancing performance.

In this chapter, the authors will use sports examples to illustrate (a) a select set of theories that have been developed to explain the emotion–performance relationship, (b) the methodologies used to study this relationship, and finally (c) the applied interventions that can be derived from previous theoretical considerations. The authors' hope is that the chapter will improve comprehension of the role of emotions in performance.

At the theoretical level, the authors will draw on two foundational works of the early 2000s: the work of Hanin and Lazarus, as well as on the more recent work of Jones and colleagues, to see how the field has evolved over the last decade. At the methodological level, the authors provide a guide to eliciting and assessing emotions. The authors stress the fact that sports researchers are increasingly considering the mind–body interaction. In the last section, the authors discuss practical interventions that have been inspired by the theories reviewed. For example, following Lazarus's theory, recognized that it is possible to change cognitions to change the emotional state, and following Hanin's theory, others recognized that changing emotions alters choices in risky tasks.

Chapter 20 - Mindfulness is a technique that evolved from Budhism that is now making a positive impact on western psychotheraputic practices. Mindfulness is a type of self control that involves paying attention to the current moment without judgment or further cognitive processing. A meta-analysis by Baer Smith, Hopkins, Krietemeyer, and Toney determined that mindfulness is a multifaceted construct that consists of the following factors, describing, non-judging, acting with awareness, non-reacting and observing. From an emotional standpoint, the objective of mindfulness is to increase a person's awareness of their emotions without avoidance or judgment. This promotes a healthy interaction with both thoughts and emotions, enabling people to cultivate a new perspective whereby they interpret serious life events as challenges, rather than overwhelming threats. Mindfulness has been shown to have a positive impact on numerous health issues from physical health complaints such as chronic pain to mental health problems such as depression. Over the past thirty years there has been a growing interest in the mindfulness construct and it's utility for treating a multitude of mental and physical health problems. To date, a wide variety of training programs have now incorporated mindfulness as an integral part of their treatment due to the pronounced impact it has been shown to have on health and well-being.

Chapter 21 - Emotions and moods are inextricably linked to creative potential and creative production. This chapter begins by outlining the psychological definitions of creativity and detailing common ways of measuring creativity. The differential impacts of positive and negative moods on creativity are reviewed. The majority of empirical studies to date suggest that positive feelings can enhance creativity; theoretical models such as the broaden-and-build model and the dopaminergic theory of positive affect support the empirical findings by suggesting that positive mood leads to greater cognitive flexibility and access to more ideas. A smaller, but significant group of studies have suggested that negative moods can also enhance creativity in some circumstances. Theories have also been put forth to explain these findings, including the mood-as-input model and the feelings-as-information theory which both suggest in part that people in a negative mood may persist longer at a task and reach more original solutions to problems. The chapter also discusses other factors that might impact the creativity-mood relationship: the duration and intensity of the affective state, the level of emotional activation, and the type of creative task are all explored. The relationships between affective disorders and creativity are reviewed, most notably the enhancing effects of mania on creative production. It is noted that while the quantity of ideas produced during mania may be high, the quality of the ideas may be low. Finally, a limited number of studies have explored the effects of creative production of subsequent mood states, suggesting both benefits and risks of a creative lifestyle. Artists are often reinforced for their emotionality and most aspiring artists experience much frustration, which can lead to substance abuse or affect regulation problems. Alternatively, true creative achievement may lead to pride or elation, and intrinsic motivation to embark of other creative endeavors, making the creative process itself enjoyable.

Chapter 22 - This chapter on disgust provides a concise overview about central aspects of this basic emotion. According to bio-evolutionary approaches, disgust evolved from a distaste response, and acquired multi-faceted functions such as disease prevention, and transmission of socio-moral standards over time. The disgust response is a brief state of loathing which is accompanied by changes in three loosely coupled response systems of overt behavior, verbal report, and somatic activation, including characteristic neuro-immunological reactions. Individuals greatly differ in the degree they experience disgust. Disgust proneness constitutes a temporally stable personality feature that is already present in childhood, and can be considered a vulnerability factor of specific mental disorders, such as specific phobias of the animal and blood type, obsessive-compulsive disorders, and hypochondriasis. Several questionnaires have been developed for the assessment of overall as well as domain-specific disgust proneness.

Chapter 23 - Though, self-leadership, self-regulation, and emotion regulation are all related to regulatory processes, they have not yet been related to each other on a conceptual level. Self-leadership is about regulatory processes in order to influence one's own thoughts and behavior. Self-regulation aims to change one's own behavior and emotion regulation to influence one's own emotions. In this chapter, the central question will be whether the different regulatory systems have a common and unifying core. Therefore, the central differences and similarities between self-leadership, self-regulation and emotion regulation are highlighted. The different regulatory systems have in common that they all refer to self-influencing processes. The conceptual analysis shows that goals and (self-) observation are central keys in all self-influencing, self-regulatory, and emotion regulatory processes.

Chapter 24 - Emotional competence (EC)— i.e. the ability to identify, express, understand, regulate and use one's own and others' emotions flexibly and constructively — has important consequences for adaptation. Specifically, people with greater EC have greater mental and physical well-being, better social relationships and greater career success. The current chapter focuses on what can be done for people suffering from a deficit in EC and answers the four following questions: (1) Is it still possible to improve one's competencies as adults? (2) How? (3) Do the changes last? (4) And, crucially, which benefits—in terms of well-being, health, social relationships and work success— can be expected from such EC improvement?

Chapter 25 - A book on the psychology of emotions would be incomplete without mention of emotional intelligence (EI). Though the specific concept of EI was introduced formally just over two decades ago, the idea that individuals vary in their ability to understand, leverage, and manage their own and others' emotions is common sense to many and something that ancient philosophers pondered well before the psychological sciences brought the issue to the fore.

The first formal and scientific introduction of EI occurred in 1990, when social psychologists, Drs. Peter Salovey and Jack Mayer, proposed a model of EI that delineated people's emotion-related abilities into four separate areas. This four-branch model described EI as the set of abilities required to perceive, use, understand, and manage emotions. Accordingly, *perception* of emotion involves identifying emotions in oneself, others, and even objects and processes. For instance, emotion may be perceived from one's own physiology, such as heart rate, breathing, or bodily tension; another's tone of voice or gestures; the sound of a symphony; or the colors and shapes in a painting. *Use* of emotion involves leveraging feelings to guide cognitive activities, including decision making, creativity, and communication. For instance, one may take advantage of upbeat, motivated feelings by seeing them as an opportunity to tackle a daunting task list, or one may wait until a calm and relaxed moment before dealing with an irritating coworker or family member. *Understanding* of emotion refers to knowing the causes and consequences of one's own and others' emotions. For instance, some people may be more attuned to and better able to predict how certain situations make them feel or how certain feelings may make them think or act. *Management* of emotion involves making conscious efforts to prevent, reduce, initiate, maintain, or enhance emotions in oneself or others. For instance, a friend's frustration may be reduced by offering to help; warm feelings toward loved ones may be maintained by focusing on their positive attributes.

The four EI abilities are interdependent and hierarchical to some extent, such that one must be able to perceive emotions in order to use them or understand them. Similarly, in order to manage emotion effectively, one must be able to perceive, use, and understand emotion well. EI develops over the lifespan and varies as a function of one's genetics and environment.

The general public as well as academics were mostly unaware of EI until 1995, when Daniel Goleman, writer for the New York Times, popularized the construct in his book, *Emotional Intelligence: Why it can Matter more than IQ*. With the release of this book, Goleman captured the attention of much of the world. Yet, within the book's pages were overzealous claims about EI, embellishing its importance and extending its definition to include a broad range of character traits and skills related to achieving success in life. Numerous self-help and professional development books as well as self-report measures of EI were developed based on Goleman's and many others' conceptualizations of EI. A number of studies have shown that self-report measures of EI are highly redundant with measures of personality and mostly unrelated to performance-based assessments of EI.

According to the ability model, individual differences in EI are measured best by performance tests. Performance tests address the limitations of self-reports of EI, which often are inaccurate. The Mayer-Salovey-Caruso Emotional Intelligence Test for adults and the Mayer-Salovey-Caruso-Emotional Intelligence Test, Youth Version (MSCEIT-YV) for adolescents (ages 12 to 17) are tests designed to measure the four abilities of EI. The MSCEIT is considered an objective, performance test because responses are evaluated based on comparison to responses made by either emotion "experts" or a normative sample. For example, the ability to manage emotions is assessed with vignettes describing emotion-laden situations. Participants read the vignettes and rate possible strategies for managing the emotional aspects of the situations on a scale ranging from "very ineffective" to "very effective." Their ratings are compared to responses made by a normative sample (of 5,000 individuals) or by a group of scientists and psychologists who have dedicated their careers to studying human emotion. MSCEIT scores are correlated somewhat with (correlations ranging from .3 to .4) but distinct from general and verbal intelligence.

EI, as assessed with MSCEIT scores, is associated with a wide range of outcomes. Individuals with higher MSCEIT scores report higher quality friendships and are rated as more socially skilled by peers. Dating and married couples with higher MSCEIT scores report having more satisfying and happier relationships with less conflict. College students with higher MSCEIT scores report lower levels of drug and alcohol use and less stealing, gambling, and fighting. Higher MSCEIT scores also are associated with decreased levels of anxiety and depression. In terms of workplace outcomes, MSCEIT scores are correlated positively with performance indicators such as company rank and merit pay increases. Business professionals with high MSCEIT scores are rated by their supervisors as effective at both managing stress and creating satisfying work environments.

With growing recognition of the potential role of EI in the success of individuals and organizations, questions have shifted from "What is EI and how can it be measured?" to "Can EI be taught, and if so, how?" As EI is a set of abilities associated with specific knowledge (e.g., one's ability to manage emotion likely depends on the repertoire of strategies one accumulates with experience), it is probable that EI is malleable and can be expanded with training. Indeed, increasing evidence indicates that emotional skills can be learned, in particular, in educational settings. In fact, over the last decade, a school-based program grounded in the ability model of EI has been developed and tested. This program, The RULER Approach, focuses on the development of EI skills in both the adult stakeholders in students' education (i.e., teachers, parents, administrators, and other school staff) as well as the students themselves. Adults are educated on the role of emotion skills in enhancing their own relationships at school and the academic, social, and personal lives of students. Adults develop their own EI and learn how to foster emotionally supportive learning environments. Then, classroom teachers are trained on a vocabulary-based program aimed at helping children from kindergarten through high school to identify, evaluate, and understand their own and others' feelings and behavior, and develop strategies for managing emotions in their lives. Research on RULER has shown that the program enhances academic performance, promotes well-being among teachers and students, and helps teachers to create more socially and emotionally intelligent classroom communities.

Since its inception in 1990, EI has received much attention in scientific, educational, professional, and psychological communities. Research investigating its underlying theory and its application has shed light on the significance of EI in personal, professional, and social settings. Still, there is much to learn about the construct, its measurement, its development, and its impact.

Chapter 26 - Emotional intelligence describes adaptive emotional functioning. Perceiving, understanding and managing emotions effectively in the self and others are core elements of emotional intelligence. The model of emotional intelligence presented in this chapter organizes the numerous promising categories of research findings on emotional intelligence through a dimensional framework that describes aspects of emotional intelligence, possible antecedents of emotional intelligence, and likely consequences of emotional intelligence.

Aspects of emotional intelligence are the core dimension of the model and include ability emotional intelligence, emotional self-efficacy, and trait emotional intelligence. Ability emotional intelligence is the potential to show emotional competency. Emotional self-efficacy is the expectation that one can bring about good outcomes in emotional functioning. Trait emotional intelligence describes the extent to which individuals actually show emotional competence in their daily lives.

The dimension of antecedents of emotional intelligence consists of the categories of individual difference characteristics and situational factors. Possible individual-difference antecedents of emotional intelligence include genetically and neurologically determined dispositions, cognitive abilities, emotion-related mastery experiences, processing style, characteristic states of consciousness such as mindfulness, and motivation. Antecedent situational factors include priming and social networks.

The dimension of consequences of emotional intelligence consists of categories reflecting functioning in different realms of life. These realms of life include subjective well-being, mental and physical health, relationships, work, and personality. Several intervention studies designed to increase emotional intelligence provide evidence for the causal role of emotional intelligence in bringing about improvements in these realms of life.

The dimensional model of emotional intelligence provides a framework for understanding discoveries already made regarding emotional intelligence as well as a guide for future research.

Chapter 27 - Emotions influence decisions, often without our awareness. They affect how information is processed, whether a risk is perceived, the ability to regulate decisions and behavior, and the desire to act on a decision. Through these processes emotions impact almost every choice made in daily life. New research suggests that people have the ability to recognize and regulate the impact of emotions on their decisions, improving their choices, and that certain skills and knowledge are required in order to do so. This chapter will review recent evidence about the situations that encourage people to regulate the impact of emotions and the strategies that people employ to reduce emotional biases in decisions. The authors will also review evidence about the individual qualities that promote regulation. These findings have implications for helping people 1) make unbiased judgments of risk involved in future activities such as gambles and health choices, 2) avoid the use of stereotypes when evaluating new people and situations, and 3) improve their ability to make decisions by reducing tendencies to avoid the decision for fear of regretting the outcome.

Chapter 28 - Every day we learn. The question is how can we memorize and sort out the relevant bits of the vast amounts of information encountered each day. Today it is believed that sleep and "offline consolidation" do play a crucial role in this process. Consolidation is a process occurring as soon as fresh information has been encoded by the brain. It depends on the brain's plasticity that is the function to form new memories and integrate that new information into long-term memory according to subjective needs at a neuronal level. From everyday experience we know that emotional content has some advantage when it comes to forming a memory with specific "offline" benefits overnight. On average, people can remember almost twice as much of text when it is emotionally charged as compared to neutral information. The growing number of studies on sleep-dependent memory consolidation both confirm the benefits of various memory systems from specific sleep stages or sleep patterns but also reveal accumulating discrepancies and open issues. At the end, the success story of sleep and memory appears much less straightforward than originally believed.

Chapter 29 - Oxytocin (OT), a polypeptide hormone is, by far, one of the most studied hormones in the field of psychological science. For more than two decades now, many researchers have token, and still take, an interest in the effects of OT on human behaviours. Their findings show that OT is involved in many social and interpersonal processes. For those reasons, the scientific community has described OT as a social hormone *par excellence*, and as we will see in this chapter, OT influence social behaviours by acting on both emotions and cognitions involved in social interactions. Oxytocin does this particularly by acting on emotional recognition, on trust and on social sharing of the emotions.

PART I: EMOTIONS, ACTION AND CULTURE

In: Handbook of Psychology of Emotions
Editors: C. Mohiyeddini, M. Eysenck and S. Bauer

ISBN: 978-1-62808-053-7
© 2013 Nova Science Publishers, Inc.

Chapter 1

WHAT IS AN EMOTION?

Changiz Mohiyeddini[*1] *and Stephanie Bauer*[2]
[1]University of Roehampton
[2]Centre for Psychotherapy Research, University Hospital Heidelberg, Germany

INTRODUCTION

William James has raised this question in 1884 in the 9th volume of Mind, i.e. almost 130 years ago (see also James, 1894). 158,905 articles later (according to Medline research on 30th of October 2012) we are in the position to answer this question with: "We don't know". Although from the beginning of time immemorial, great masters of the human mind have made philosophical, phenomenological, anthropological, sociological, and psychological attempts to comprehend humans' emotions, emotions still maintain their enigmatic nature and "the language of emotions" (Plutchik, 2003, p. 4) remains highly cryptic. At the same time the human quest for knowledge about emotions seems to be steady. Whereas for some philosophers, such as Seneca (trans., 1963) and Ryle (1949), emotions are irritating and inconvenient divergences from rationality that instigate our cognitive capacity, others, such as Aristotle (trans., 1941) and Hume (1739/1969), have characterized emotions in a more positive light, as a component of functional reasoning. Further dichotomies that are discussed in the literature relate to ongoing debates regarding whether emotions are "states or reflect a process", "disorganizing vs. organizing", "adaptive vs. maladaptive", "conscious vs. unconscious", "positive vs. negative" (for a discussion see Plutchik, 2003). On one hand, these theoretical approaches have made valuable input to accelerate our understanding of emotions. Yet on the other hand, they have contributed to the complexity of the language of emotions. Already thirty years ago Kleinginna and Kleinginna (1981) have identified 92 definitions of emotions! Most obviously this impressive amount of definitions could be acknowledged as symptoms of the same issue that they aim to contribute to, its solution. This can be seen as a marked sign of an essential uncertainty about the theoretical foundation of

---

[*]Corresponding author:Professor Changiz Mohiyeddini, habil, Ph.D., MSc. Professor of Personality Psychology and Research Methods, Department of Psychology, University of Roehampton, Whitelands College, Holybourne Avenue, LONDON SW15 4JD, Tel. +44 (0)20 8392 3616; E-mail:c.mohiyeddini@roehampton.ac.uk.

the topic and signals of a pre-paradigmatic state of the development of psychology of the emotions as a discipline (see Brandtstädter, 2001). Considering that "a definition emerges only at the end of a long discussion, and even then it is always tentative and appropriate only within a limited context and certain models of culture and personal character" (Solomon, 2008, p.3-4) it is obvious that the probable function of William James' question is to raise further questions about the nature, meaning and impact of emotions rather than expecting a comprehensive answer.

However, there is a surprising degree of consensus on a number of fundamental points regarding the meaning, function and impact of emotions. These include:

1) Emotions are essential aspects of human nature comprising multiple components such as cognitive, behavioural, expressive, experiential and physiological/neuroendocrinological systems that operate in a relatively coordinated and synchronized manner (Buck, 1994; Izard, 1993; Lang, Bradley, and Cuthbert, 1990; MacLean, 1993; Nesse, 1990). It has been acknowledged that emotions generally shape the basis for temperament and personality (Goldsmith and Campos, 1982; Izard, Libero, Putnam, and Haynes, 1993; Malatesta, 1990) and have a profound influence on perception, cognition(e.g., Campos, Mumme, Kermoian, and Campos, 1994; Damasio, 1994, 1998;Frijda, 1986; Lazarus, 1991a; Sroufe, 1984), action (Eder and Rothermund in this volume), cognitive (Eysenck, in this volume) and physical performance (Laborde, Raab and Dosseville, in this volume), physical activity (Mohiyeddini and Bauer, 2007;Mohiyeddini, Pauli and Bauer 2009; Schlicht, Reicherz and Kanning, in this volume) and problem solving (Moore and Ashcraft, in this volume). However, there is a controversial debate regarding whether different emotions possess unique, distinguishable and cross-situational consistent recurrent patterns of behavioural (Ekman, 1994; Frijda, 1986) and/or physiological (Levenson, 1992) processes.

2) It has been widely acknowledged that as complex psychological phenomena, emotions have emerged through the course of evolutionary history in order to increase the adaptability of human responses to ontogenetic and developmental challenges (Trierweiler and Krampen, in this volume) in a constantly rapidly changing environment (Lazarus, 1991b; Toobyand Cosmides, 1990) a significant portion of which entail social relations and interactions (Bitan, Haepand and Steins, in this volume). Consequently, emotions are crucial and have arisen to increase and maintain the human-environment fit (Darwin, 1872/1965; Hamburg, 1963; Izard, 1971, 1977; James, 1890/1950; Levenson, 1994; Plutchik, 1980; Tomkins, 1962, 1963). Therefore, the diversity of humans' emotions mirrors different adaptive challenges (e.g. Ekman, 1992; Izard, 1977; Plutchik, 1980). Accordingly, the investigation of human emotion as a crucial part of our evolutionary-biological and cultural heritage may facilitate our understanding of the history of human evolution and adaptation to both the physical and social environment (Darwin, 1872/1965; Ekman and Friesen, 1971; Hamburg, 1963; Izard, 1971; Plutchik, 1980).

3) Emotions are generated and maintained in a dynamic transactional process between organism and environment (Lazarus, 1966). On the one hand environmental clues stimulate emotional responses, yet on the other the emotional responses themselves influence the person– environment transaction (Campos et al., 1994; Kagan,1994; Saarni, Mumme, and Campos, 1998). Put simply, activated emotions, as a component of the (psychological) environment, trigger cognitive processes which in turn, launch new emotional responses (Arnold, 1960; Ekman, 1972; Gross, 1998a,b; 1999; Izard, 1977; Lazarus, 1991a; Levenson,

1994; Leventhal, 1984; Plutchik, 1980; Scherer, 1984; Tomkins, 1962) that may focus, as meta-emotions, the initial emotion as target (Mohiyeddini and Bauer, in prep).

4) In addition to their psycho-physiological functions, emotions are a social entity (Hochschild, 1975, 1983) and serve various social functions. In this line of research the constructivist theory maintains that the social function of emotions is a key point in understanding the function of emotions. Accordingly, emotions script our social behavior (Averill, 1980; Keltner and Buswell, 1997), shape social referencing (Vandivier and Hertenstein, in this volume) and play a fundamental role in sympathy and empathy, thus they form the basis for conscience and moral behavior (Eisenberg and Fabes,1998; Eisenberg and Miller, 1987; Hoffman, 1978, 2000) and facilitate prosocial behavior (Isen, Daubmen and Nowicki, 1987). Self-conscious social emotions such as guilt, shame and pride (Farouk, in this volume) are crucial to regulate social interaction and reciprocity. The activation of emotions sensitizes us to the relevant and challenging features of our social environment informing us about others' behavioral intentions (Fridlund, 1994), while also providing us with valuable information as to whether something is good or bad (Walden, 1991). Hence, the sustainability of social interactions and relationships throughout the life span require an accurate decoding and encoding of socio-culturally (partly) determined emotional signals (Hobson, 1995; Izard and Ackerman, 1997). Therefore initiation, maintenance and expansion of functioning social networks require adequate socioemotional competences (Brackett and Elberston, in this volume; Mikolajczak, Kotsou and Neils, in this volume; Schutte and Malouffin this volume).

5) It has been widely acknowledged that cultures lay out the possibilities for emotions and in that regard, guide the act of recognizing an emotion (Hochschild, 2009). Hochschild (2009) emphasizes that apart from what we think an emotion is, we also have socio-culturally colored ideas about what it should be.

Accordingly, emotions are influenced by cultural ideas and images, and shaped through socio-cultural roles and norms regarding what we feel, what we should feel (feeling rules) and how an emotion should be expressed (display rules) (Darwin, 1872/1965; Doan, in this volume; Ekman, 1971, Hochschild, 1975, 2009; Izard, 1971; Markusand Kitayama,; Miyamoto and Ryff, 2011; Tsai et al., 2007; Uchida, Townsend, Markus, and Bergseiker, 2009).

6) An increasing evidence base indicates that the dysregulation of emotions contributes to various forms of psychopathology (e.g. Bauer and Mohiyeddini, in this volume; Montag, Haas and Reuter, in this volume; Nolen-Hoeksema, Vine and Gilbert, in this volume; Veronese and Castiglioni, in this volume), and plays a prominent role in the development of depression, aggression and violence (Beer, in this volume; Cicchetti and Cohen, 1995; Dodge and Somberg, 1987; Hubbard and Coie, 1994; Lochman and Lenhart, 1993), obesity (Jones, in this volume); self-regulation (Furtner and and Hiller, in this volume; Liebe and Roth, in this volume).

Whereas it has been established that an optimal and appropriate regulation of emotions-in terms of fitting with social standing, social rules, performance expectations and individual goals – enhances health and well-being (LeBlanc and Mohiyeddini, in this volume).

EMOTIONS AND RELATED PHENOMENA

Many attempts have been made to systematically differentiate between the various definitions and concepts that have been postulated in emotion research over time, such as affect, emotion, emotional episodes, and mood. While frequently, emotion and affect are used interchangeably, there are other contexts in which the latter is used to refer to the experiential (MacLean, 1990) or behavioral (Kaplan and Sadock, 1991) components of emotion. Scherer (1984) suggests to consider affect as a higher-ranking category for various valenced states such as emotions, moods, traits, and emotional episodes. According to Gross (1998) in this context it is essential to differentiate between emotion, emotional episodes, and mood. While emotions typically relate to specific objects, develop over relatively short time periods and may fluctuate significantly, moods are more diffuse, enduring, and less fluctuating. Emotions tend to trigger behavioral response tendencies more likely than moods which are less object-focused and affect cognition more than behavior. Put simply, in contrast to moods, emotions are shorter and more intense, more frequent, have a specific trigger and activate response tendencies. Whereas moods are less intense, do not need a specific trigger, last longer and may not activate response tendencies. Emotional episodes are also more enduring than emotions and they emerge as part of ongoing interactions causing not only changes in facial expression, posture, voice, verbal expression, and experience, but also include the social context, relevant events, and people in the environment (Averill, 1982). However, it has been recently suggested to integrate moods and emotions in a hierarchical order (Diener, Smith, and Fujita, 1995; Watson and Clark, 1992). Accordingly, emotions are subordinate part of a higher order valenced mood category (see Gross, 1998)

What is an Emotion?

Certainly a mystery of the human mind, a fundamental aspect of human nature, a gateway to disentangle the secrets of evolution, a to ran to understand free will[1] and an exciting field for scientific activity and obviously not "a" simple question with "a" straightforward answer.

Of course, in his famous public discourse on "The Oration on the Dignity of Man" pronounced in 1486, Pico della Mirandola, the influential philosopher of the Renaissance, was right to emphasize "the idea that men could ascend the chain of being through the exercise of their intellectual capacities is a profound endorsement of the dignity of human existence". However, the history of the ongoing debate on humans' emotion as "one of the most confused and difficult topics in all of psychology" (Plutchik, 1994, p. 1) makes it obvious that this exercise of intellectual capacities for the sake of the dignity of human existence is heavily related to individual emotional capacities and is a highly perplexing and emotional adventure itself.

---

[1]Although The existence of free will and its exact nature and definition have long been debated in philosophy (van Invagen, 1983; Richards, 2001) and psychology (Baer, Kaufman, and Baumeister, 2009), most human emotional experiences are based on the assumption of free will: anger occurs more likely when we believe that the perpetrator was in control of his action, had a choice to act differently, has done that intentionally and on purpose.

REFERENCES

Aristotle. (1941). *The basic works of Aristotle* (R. McKeon, Ed.). New York: Random House.

Arnold, M. (1960). *Emotion and personality.* New York: Columbia University Press.

Averill, J. R. (1980). A constructivist view of emotion. In R. Plutchik and H. Kellerman (eds.), *Emotion: Theory, research and experience: Vol. I. Theories of emotion* (pp. 305-339). New York, NY: Academic Press.

Averill, J. R. (1982). *Anger and aggression: An essay on emotion.* New York: Springer.

Baer, J., Kaufman, J. and Baumeister, R. (eds.) (2009). *Psychology and Free Will.*Oxford University Press.

Brandtstädter, J. (2001). *Entwicklung – Intentionalität – Handeln.* Stuttgart: Kohlhammer (development - intentionality - action).

Buck, R. (1984). *The communication of emotion.* New York: Guilford Press.

Campos, J. J., Mumme, D. L., Kermoian, R., and Campos, R. G. (1994). A functionalist perspective on the nature of emotion. *Monographs of the Society for Research in Child Development*, 59(2-3), 284-303.

Cicchetti, D., and Cohen, D. J. (Eds.). (1995). *Developmental psychopathology: Vol. 2. Risk, disorder, and adaptation.* New York: Wiley Interscience.

Damasio, A. R. (1998). Emotion in the perspective of an integrated nervous system. *Brain Research Reviews, 26,* 83–86.

Damasio, A. R. (1994). *Descartes' error: Emotion, reason, and the human brain.* New York: Grossett.

Darwin, C. (1965). *The expression of the emotions in man and animals.* Chicago: University of Chicago Press. (Original work published 1872).

Diener, E., Smith, H., and Fujita, F. (1995). The personality structure of affect. *Journal of Personality and Social Psychology, 69,* 130-141.

Dodge, K. A., and Somberg, D. R. (1987). Hostile attributional biases among aggressive boys are exacerbated under conditions of threats to self. *Child Development, 58,* 213–224.

Eisenberg, N., and Fabes, R. A. (1998). Prosocial development. In W. Damon (Series Ed.) and N. Eisenberg (Vol. Ed.), *Handbook of child psychology: Vol. 3. Social, emotional, and personality development* (5th ed., pp. 701–778). New York: Wiley.

Eisenberg, N., and Miller, P. (1987). Empathy and prosocial behavior. *Psychological Bulletin, 101,* 91–119.

Ekman, P. (1994). Moods Emotions And Traits. In P. Ekman & R. Davidson (Eds.) *The Nature of Emotion: Fundamental Questions.* New York: Oxford University Press. Pp. 15-19.

Ekman, P (1992). "Are there basic emotions?". *Psychological Review, 99,* 550–553.

Ekman, P. (1972). Universals and cultural differences in facial expressions of emotion. In J. Cole (Ed.), Nebraska Symposium on Motivation, 1971 (Vol. 19, pp. 207–282). Lincoln: University of Nebraska Press.

Ekman, P. (1971).*Universal and cultural differences in facial expressions of emotion.* Lincoln: University of Nebraska Press.

Ekman, P., and Friesen, W. V. (1971). Constants across cultures in the face and emotion. *Journal of Personality and Social Psychology, 17,* 124–129.

Fridlund, A. (1994). *Human facial expression.* San Diego, CA: Academic Press.

Frijda, N. H. (1986). *The emotions.* Cambridge, England: Cambridge University Press.

Goldsmith, H. H., and Campos, J. J. (1982).Toward a theory of infant temperament. In R. N. Emdeand R. J. Harmon (Eds.), *The development of attachment and affiliative systems* (pp. 231–283). Hillsdale, NJ: Erlbaum.

Gross, J. J. (1999). Emotion regulation: Past, present, future. *Cognition and Emotion, 13*, 551-573.

Gross, J.J. (1998a). Antecedent- and response-focused emotion regulation: Divergent consequences for experience, expression, and physiology. *Journal of Personality and Social Psychology, 74*, 224-237.

Gross, J.J. (1998b). The emerging field of emotion regulation: An integrative review. *Review of General Psychology, 2*, 271-299.

Hamburg, D. A. (1963).Emotions in the perspective of human evolution. In P. H. Knapp (Ed.), *Expression of emotions in man* (pp. 300–317). New York: International Universities Press.

Hobson, R. P. (1995). Apprehending attitudes and actions: Separable abilities in early development? *Development and Psychopathology, 7*, 171–182.

Hochschild, A.R. (2009). Introduction: An Emotions Lens on the World. In. D.R. Hopkins, J. Kleres, F. Helena and H. Kuzmics (Eds.). *Theorizing Emotions: Sociological Explorations and Applications* (pp. 29-37). Frankfurt am Main, New York. Campus

Hochschild, A. R. (1983). *The managed heart.* Berkeley, CA: University of California Press.

Hochschild (1975). The Sociology of Feeling and Emotion: Selected Possibilities. *Sociological Inquiry, 45*, 280–307.

Hoffman, M. L. (2000). *Empathy and moral development: Implications for caring and justice.* New York: Cambridge University Press.

Hoffman, M. L. (1978). Empathy, its development, and prosocial implications. In C. B. Keasey (Ed.), *Nebraska Symposium on Motivation* (Vol. 25, pp. 169–218). Lincoln: University of Nebraska Press.

Hubbard, J. A., and Coie, J. D. (1994). Emotional correlates of social competence in children's peer relations. *Merrill-Palmer Quarterly, 40*, 1–20.

Hume, D. (1969). *A treatise on human nature.* London: Fontana/Collins. (Original work published 1739).

Isen, A. M., Daub man, K. A., and Nowicki, G. P. (1987). Positive affect facilitates creative problem solving. *Journal of Personality and Social Psychology, 52*, 1122-1131.

Izard, C. E. (1993). Four systems of emotion activation: Cognitive and noncognitive processes. *Psychological Review, 100*, 68–90.

Izard, C. E. (1977). *Human emotions.* New York: Plenum.

Izard, C. E. (1971). *The face of emotion.* New York: Appleton-Century-Crofts.

Izard, C. E., and Ackerman, B. P. (1997). Emotions and self-concepts across the life span. In K. W. Schaie and M. P. Lawton (Eds.), *Annual review of gerontology and geriatrics: Vol. 17. Focus on emotion and adult development* (pp. 1–26). New York: Springer.

Izard, C. E., Libero, D. Z., Putnam, P., and Haynes, O. M. (1993). Stability of emotion experiences and their relation to traits of personality. *Journal of Personality and Social Psychology, 64*, 847–860.

James 1890/1950

James, W. (1884). What is an emotion? *Mind, 9*, 188-205.

James, W. (1894).The physical basis of emotion. *Psychological Review, 101*, 205-210.

Kagan, J. (1994). On the nature of emotion. In N. Fox (Ed.), The development of emotion regulation: Biological and behavioral considerations. *Monographs of the Society for Research in Child Development,59* (2–3, Serial No. 240), 7–24.

Kaplan, H. I., and Sadock, B. J. (1991). *Synopsis of psychiatry* (6th ed.). Baltimore: Williams and Wilkins.

Keltner, D. and Buswell, B. N. (1997). Embarrassment: Its distinct form and appeasement functions. Psychological Bulletin, 122, 250-270.

Kleinginna, P. R., and Kleinginna, A. M. (1981). Cognition and affect: A reply to Lazarus and Zajonc. *American Psychologist, 40,* 470-471.

Lang, P. J., Bradley, M. M., and Cuthbert, B. N. (1990). Emotion, attention, and the startle reflex. *Psychological Review, 97,* 377-395.

Lazarus, R. S. (1991a). *Emotion and adaptation.* Oxford, England: Oxford University Press.

Lazarus, R. S. (1991b). Progress on a cognitive motivational-relational theory of emotion. *American Psychologist, 46,* 819-834.

Lazarus, R. (1966). *Psychological stress and the coping process.* New York: McGraw-Hill.

Levenson, R. W. (1994). Human emotions: A functional view. In P. Ekman and R. J. Davidson (Eds.), *The nature of emotion: Fundamental questions* (pp. 123-126). New York: Oxford University Press.

Leventhal, H. (1984). A perceptual-motor theory of emotion. *Advances in Experimental Social Psychology, 17,* 117-182.

Lochman, J. E., and Lenhart, L. A. (1993). Anger coping intervention for aggressive children: Conceptual models and outcome effects. *Clinical Psychology Review, 13,* 785–805.

MacLean, P. D. (1993).On the evolution of three mentalities. In J. B. Ashbrook (Ed.), *Brain, culture, and the human spirit: Essays from an emergent evolutionary perspective.* (pp. 15-44). Lanham, MD England: University Press of America.

MacLean, P. D. (1990). *The triune brain in evolution: Role in paleocerebral functions.* New York: Plenum.

Malatesta, C. Z. (1990). The role of emotions in the development and organization of personality. In R. Thompson (Ed.), *Nebraska Symposium on Motivation: Vol. 36. Socioemotional development* (pp. 1–56). Lincoln: University of Nebraska Press.

Markus, H. R., and Kitayama, S. (1991). Culture and the self: Implications for cognition, emotion, and motivation. *Psychological Review, 98,* 224—253.

Miyamoto, Y. and Ryff, C (2011). "Cultural differences in the dialectical and non-dialectical emotional styles and their implications for health". *Cognition and Emotion, 25,* 22–30.

Mohiyeddini, C. and Bauer, S. (in prep.). *What is a "meta-emotion"?*

Mohiyeddini, C., Pauli, G. and Bauer, S. (2009). The role of emotion in bridging the intention–behaviour gap: The case of sports participation. *Psychology of Sport and Exercise. 10,* 226-234.

Mohiyeddini, C. and Bauer, S. (2007). Intentions-Verhaltens-Lücke bei sportlichen Aktivitäten: Die Bedeutung von Emotionen. *Zeitschrift für Sportpsychologie, 14,* 3-13. (Intention-Behaviour Gap in physicalactivity. Journal of Sport Psychology).

Nesse, R. M. (1990). Evolutionary explanations of emotions. *Human Nature, 1,* 261-289.

Plutchik, R. (2003). *Emotions and life: Perspectives from psychology, biology, and evolution.* Washington, DC US: American Psychological Association.

Plutchik, R. (1994). *The psychology and biology of emotion.* New York, NY US: Harper Collins College Publishers.

Plutchik, R. (1980). *Emotion: A psychoevolutionary synthesis*. New York: Harper and Row.

Richards, J. (2001). *The root of the free will problem: kinds of non-existence. Human Nature after Darwin: A Philosophical Introduction*. Routledge.

Ryle, G. (1949). *The concept of mind*. London: Hutchinson.

Saarni, C., Mumme, D. L., and Campos, J. J. (1998). Emotional development: Action, communication, and understanding. In W. Damon (Series Ed.) and N. Eisenberg (Vol. Ed.), *Handbook of child psychology: Vol. 3. Social, emotional, and personality development* (pp. 701–767). New York: Wiley.

Scherer, K. (1984). On the nature and function of emotion: A component process approach. In K. R. Scherer and P. E. Ekman (Eds.), *Approaches to emotion* (pp. 293-317). Hillsdale, NJ: Erlbaum.

Seneca. (1963). On anger (J. W. Basore, Trans.). In *Moral essays*. Cambridge, MA: Harvard University Press.

Solomon, R. C. (2008). The philosophy of emotions. In M. Lewis, J. M. Havil and-Jones and L. F. Barrett (Eds.), *Handbook of emotions* (3rd ed.). (pp. 3-16). New York, NY US: Guilford Press.

Sroufe, L. A. (1984). The organization of emotional development. In K. Scherer and P. Ekman (Eds.), *Approaches to emotion* (pp. 109–128) London: Erlbaum.

Tooby & Cosmides 1990

Tomkins, S. S. (1962). *Affect, imagery, consciousness: The positive affects* (Vol. 1). New York: Springer.

Tsai, J. L.; Louie, J. Y., Chen, E. E., and Uchida, Y. (2007). "Learning what feelings to desire: Socialization of ideal affect through children's storybooks". *Personality and Social Psychology Bulletin, 33*, 17–30.

VanInvagen, P. (1983). *An Essay on Free Will*. Oxford: Clarendon Press.

Uchida, Y., Townsend, S.S.M., Markus, H.R., and Bergseiker, H.B (2009). "Emotios as within or between people? Cultural variations in lay theories of emotion expression and inference". *Personality and Social Psychology Bulletin, 35*.1427–1438.

Walden, T. A. (1991). Infant social referencing. In J. Garber and K. A. Dodge (Eds.), *The development of emotion regulation and dysregulation* (pp. 69-88). Cambridge, England: Cambridge University Press.

Watson, D., and Clark, L. A. (1992). Affects separable and inseparable: On the hierarchical arrangement of the negative affects. *Journal of Personality and Social Psychology, 62*, 489-505.

In: Handbook of Psychology of Emotions
Editors: C. Mohiyeddini, M. Eysenck and S. Bauer

ISBN: 978-1-62808-053-7
© 2013 Nova Science Publishers, Inc.

Chapter 2

EMOTIONAL ACTION: AN IDEOMOTOR MODEL

Andreas B. Eder[1,] and Klaus Rothermund[2]*
[1]University of Würzburg, Germany
[2]University of Jena, Germany

ABSTRACT

This chapter presents a new model of emotional action that emphasizes an anticipatory control of emotional actions. It begins by reviewing existing hypotheses about a causal relationship between emotions and action. Then, findings and hypotheses of an ideomotor model are discussed about how an emotional action is learned, represented, activated, selected, and expressed. Finally, the model is applied to an analysis of emotional fight-and-flight behaviors.

Keywords: Emotional action, ideomotor theory, instrumental learning, aggression

INTRODUCTION

Emotion is typically conceptualized as a set of orchestrated responses to a significant event, consisting of (a) a *cognitive response*, corresponding to the evaluation or appraisal of the stimulus, (b) a *motivational response*, corresponding to the activation of a specific action or, at least an inclination to act, (c) a *somatovisceral response*, supporting the preparation and execution of muscular responses, (d) an *expressive response*, consisting of facial and vocal expressions and gross body postures, and (e) a *feeling or experiential response*.

According to contemporary emotion theories, the first stage of an emotion is the affective encoding or emotional appraisal of a stimulus event (Ellsworth and Scherer, 2003). The

---
* Corresponding author: Andreas B. Eder, Department of Psychology, University of Würzburg, Röntgenring 10, 97070 Würzburg, Germany. E-mail: andreas.eder@psychologie.uni-wuerzburg.de; Phone: +49 931 31 83336; Fax: +49 931 31 82812.

output of this encoding process then generates a motivation to act, which is accompanied by physiological and behavioral changes (Frijda, 1986). A feeling or emotional experience emerges when aspects of the cognitive, motivational, physiological, and motor responses permeate into consciousness (Scherer, 2009).

According to a component model of emotions, emotions are thus intimately related to motivation and action. Some theorists even argue that emotions exist for the sake of action, for dealing with recurrent challenges of the environment (e.g., Tooby and Cosmides, 1990). Yet, the relationship between emotion and action is variable. There is much emotion without action, and much action without obvious emotion (Mauss, Levenson, McCarter, Wilhelm, and Gross, 2005).

Furthermore, the same emotion may lead to different actions depending on the affordances of a situation (Frijda, 2004). Scared to death, you may rush from the building if the fire bell rings, but you may seek shelter under the next desk if an earthquake shakes the building. How to understand these variable relationships?

The present chapter focuses on this question. We first discuss existing hypotheses about a causal relationship between emotion and action. After that, we will present an ideomotor model of emotional action that emphasizes an anticipatory control of emotional behavior.

Then, central hypotheses of this model are described about how an emotional action is learned, represented, activated, selected, and expressed.

Finally, the model is applied to an analysis of fight-or-flight behaviors in aversive emotional situations.

THE RELATIONSHIP BETWEEN EMOTION AND ACTION

Emotion theorists agree that emotions allow a simple interface between sensory inputs and behavior systems (Scherer, 1994). However, they disagree about the flexibility of this interface: While Darwin-evolutionary theory proposes a very rigid link between emotions and a set of hardwired responses, emotional decision theory, by contrast, suggests a highly flexible integration of emotional information in a behavior decision process. In between are emotional motive theories that assume a fixed relation between emotions and motive states but a variable translation of the motive state into a concrete behavior. In the following, we will present each hypothesis in more detail.

The Hard Interface: Evolutionary Theory

Evolutionary theory proposes that emotions are associated with dispositions for actions that have increased the fitness of the species in recurring, challenging situations in the past. In his classic book "The expression of the emotions in man and animals", published in 1872, Charles Darwin was the first who proposed the existence of multiple emotions that differ in their (expressive) response patterns, functions, and evolutionary history. Darwin suggested that a feeling state (corresponding to an emotion) evokes an automatic tendency to perform movements that are associated with this emotional state, as he illustrated elegantly with an anecdote about how he reacted to a snake at the London Zoo as if his life were in danger: "I put my face close to the thick glass-plate in front of a puff adder in the Zoological Gardens, with the firm determination of not starting back if the snake struck at me; but, as soon as the blow was struck, my resolution went for nothing, and I jumped a yard or two backwards with astonishing rapidity. My will and reason were powerless against the interpretation of a danger which had never been experienced." (Darwin, 1872, p. 38).

For evolutionary theorists, emotions are 'problem-solving devices' that have increased the probability of successfully dealing with a few basic, ubiquitous problems in the ancestral past (Ekman, 1992; Levenson, 1999; Plutchik, 2001). Emotional action dispositions are therefore inherited and they were object to natural selection presses in the past.

For example, if withdrawing rapidly from a snake saves an animal from being bitten, this fear reaction surely aids survival of the fearful animal (Öhman and Mineka, 2003). As a consequence, a genetic transmission of the underlying biological structure is more likely. Shaped by natural selection, each emotion is thus associated with a different set of behavior responses that were functional for solving a specific problem in the ancestral past.

Even though an evolutionary analysis of emotional action is intuitively appealing, it is not without problems. One problem is that a functional analysis of emotional reactions is typically a post-hoc enterprise. Given that there are no established principles and procedures for identifying the function of a behavior of our Pleistocene ancestors, one can make many plausible suggestions of adaptations (Gray, Heaney, and Fairhall, 2003). For instance, evolutionary psychologists have related joy and happiness to basic need satisfaction (Frijda, 1994), goal pursuit (Nesse, 2004), resource-building (Fredrickson, 1998), social bonding (Panksepp, 2000), and social facilitation (Buss, 2000). In retrospection, it is difficult to tell apart which adaptive explanation is true and which is not.

A second problem is that most emotional actions are not as uniform as one would expect on the basis of evolutionary theory (Barrett, 2006). According to a strong version of this hypothesis, each kind of emotion should elicit its own pattern of stereotypic responses that is hardwired at birth. However, few emotional actions, at least in mammals, are truly fixed action patterns in the sense that they are not learned and uniform across different situations (Moltz, 1965). For instance, flight is clearly a behavioral response away from a source of danger, but depending on the affordances of a situation there could be very many ways of fleeing from a threat. As noted by Frijda (2004): "Evolutionary psychologists talk too easily about emotions as patterns of stimulus-elicited behaviors [...] without wondering about the mechanisms these actions might presuppose" (p. 161). A powerful theory of emotional action thus must additionally specify the processes that adjust a behavioral response to the affordances of an emotional situation.

The Hot Interface: Emotional Motive Theory

Emotional motive theories identify these processes in motivational states that are evoked by emotional events. McDougall (1926) was one of the first emotion theorists who proposed an intimate link between emotions and some motivational concept; he suggested that emotions correspond with the distinctive feeling tone and the bodily changes that are aroused by powerful instincts.

For him, instincts were more than biologically hardwired responses or inherited action dispositions; rather, he assumed that instincts involve mental processes that correspond with "a knowing of some thing or object, a feeling in regard to it, and a striving towards or away from that object" (p. 27). These processes are most aptly described as motivational processes that direct attention, thought, and behavior to a particular class of objects that have significance for the person.

McDougall (1926) suggested that each emotion is linked to a different instinct, and through this motive disposition, to a specific action inclination. For instance, anger was coupled with aggression, fear with an inclination for flight, disgust with a motivation for repulse, and tender with a motivation for parental care. By relating emotions to different instincts, McDougall distinguished seven primary emotions, each of which is characterized by a different action inclination.

Using a different terminology, subsequent theorists refined the basic idea that emotional behavior is directed and aroused by 'central motive states' (e.g., Bindra, 1969; Frijda, 1986; Roseman, 2008). For instance, Frijda proposed that emotional events, as appraised by the individual, elicit changes in motive states that he called states of action readiness. Such states of action readiness may consist "(a) in readiness to go at it or away from it or to shift attention; (b) in sheer excitement, which can be understood as being ready for action but not knowing what action; or (c) in being stopped in one's tracks or in loss of interest" (Frijda, 1988, p. 351). Thus, the idea is that an emotion evokes a readiness to behave in a general way that is functional for dealing with a significant event, rather than being associated with a specific behavior. So, for example, fear might trigger a readiness to flee or hide, but depending on the circumstances there could be very many ways of fleeing and hiding. Accordingly, many different behaviors can be displayed in emotional episodes that have a label in common (anger, fear, and so on), and what behavior is actually produced is determined conjointly by the nature of the motive state, the perceived affordance in the eliciting event, and the individual's action repertoire.

With motivational states as flexible translators between environmental input and behavioral output, motive theories thus can account for the variability and richness of emotional action. Yet, this theoretical approach has several shortcomings. One problem is that little is known about the inner structure of emotional motives and how motive states interact with perceptual systems in the generation of an emotional response. Frijda (2010), for instance, proposed that emotional motives have a specific aim (e.g., the aim to avoid loss and harm), and that an action schema is automatically selected that may be appropriate for fulfilling the aim. However, it is not clear how a motive state comes to select an action schema, and what kind of behavior is actually controlled by an action schema. Just take as an example the simple situation of a caged rat that is frightened by a painful electric shock. By knowing that the rat is motivated to escape from her torture, it is difficult to predict whether the rat will fight (Ulrich and Azrin, 1962), take flight (Blanchard and Blanchard, 1968), or show no activity at all (i.e., freeze; Fanselow, 1980). As a matter of fact, behavior analysts had hard times to account for the appearance of these mutually exclusive fear responses (e.g., Blanchard, and Blanchard, 1990; Gray, 1994), meaning that behavior prediction is poor even with a fair knowledge of the motive state, the action schema, and the environmental situation.

One could of course argue that all these behaviors that occur in threatening situations are "defensive" or suppose the existence of an action readiness to avoid. As noted by Russell (2009), however, doing so creates additional problems.

First, there are counterexamples (e.g., predator inspection and threat-sensitive foraging; Blanchard and Blanchard, 1990). Second, labeling a variety of different behaviors as "defensive" adds nothing to their explanation, because the particular behavior that actually occurs remains to be explained (i.e., fight, flight, or freeze). And, third, one cannot classify an isolated behavioural act as defensive except in the context of an interpretation of the situation as dangerous. For example, to interpret doing nothing as freezing, and not as being startled, disoriented, or disinterested, requires knowledge of the context. Thus, the inference of a defensive reaction to a threatening event is sometimes close to circularity.

Another problem concerns the number of hypothesized motive states and how they are related to different emotions. McDougall (1926) provided an explicit list of seven basic emotions, each of which is characterized by its own distinct motive state (instincts). Modern theorists, however, refrain from making such lists (or they do so more in the secret), and often without assuming a direct correspondence between emotions and motive states. For instance, a readiness to approach has been linked to eleven different emotions, including distinct states such as sorrow, boredom, surprise, and joy (Frijda, Kuipers, ter Schure, 1989).

Thus, at least some emotions may be associated with several, sometimes even conflicting, tendencies to act. Complicating things further, alternative theories proposed that behaviors associated with anger, sadness, fear, and so on are aroused by more fundamental emotional properties such as *valence* and *arousal* (Russell and Barrett, 1999), *positive* and *negative activation* (e.g., Watson, Wiese, Vaidya, and Tellegen, 1999), or *appetitive* and *aversive motivations* (e.g., Lang, 1995). Thus, at present it is not clear what emotional motives are, how many of them exist, what motives are associated with which emotions, and whether motive states can be reduced to more basic properties of emotional episodes.

The Loose Interface: Emotional Decision Theory

These ambiguities caused some theorists to question the assumption that emotions can cause actions directly; instead, they proposed that emotions influence action control indirectly by providing feedback on the consequences of actions and by stimulating retrospective appraisals of behavior decisions.

When making a decision, people anticipate the emotions they might experience as a result of the outcomes of their choices, and they select those actions that they expect will make them feel better rather than worse (Baumeister, Vohs, DeWall, and Zhang, 2007; Mellers and McGraw, 2001; Schwarz, 2012; Slovic, Finucane, Peters, and McGregor, 2007). Thus, an emotion is here the goal, and not the cause of an action.

There is indeed strong evidence that anticipated emotional states can have a powerful influence on action tendencies. For instance, sad people help others more readily when they believe that helping will cheer them up (Manucia, Baumann, and Cialdini, 1984), angry people aggress others more when they hope that acting aggressively reduces their emotional distress (Bushman, Baumeister, and Phillips, 2001), and people anticipating guilt make more generous offers (Nelissen, Leliveld, van Dijk, and Zeelenberg, 2011).

However, for many of these studies it is not clear how emotions become integrated in action decisions.

For instance, some researchers proposed that people weight anticipated feelings by the perceived chances of their occurrence in a rational decision process, choosing the action that maximizes subjective pleasure (e.g., Mellers, Schwartz, and Ritov, 1999), whereas other researchers pointed out that experienced emotions can have a direct hedonic impact on action control without conscious cognitive mediation (e.g., Loewenstein, 1996).

Furthermore, emotions may influence action control via multiple routes, as proposed by dual-process theories that distinguish between an automatic route that is based on associative processes and a controlled route that is based on conscious thinking and reasoning processes (e.g., Clore, and Ortony, 2000; Strack and Deutsch, 2004).

Even though a multiple-route conception is a powerful approach for an explanation of many phenomena, they cannot hide the fact that they are fairly silent about how an action is selected and initiated in the first place.

Summary

To summarize, existing models seem to trade precision for generality in the explanation of emotional behavior. While evolutionary approaches make very specific predictions about a limited set of hardwired emotional responses and their underlying biological circuitry, they are too narrow to account for the richness and complexity of the behavior that is typically displayed in emotional situations.

Emotional motive theory and emotional decision theory, on the other hand, have the potential to account for this behavioral complexity; however, they lack precision of the processes that generate an action when referring to vague and ill-defined constructs like aims, action decisions, and action schemas. What is consequently most needed is a framework that specifies in more detail how complex emotional actions are learned, represented, initiated, and expressed. Such a framework is described next.

AN IDEOMOTOR MODEL OF EMOTIONAL ACTION

A distinctive feature of the present framework is that it integrates emotions into an existing theory of action control, which is ideomotor theory. While traditional theories of emotional action often distinguish an emotional system from an action system, with the emotion system adjusting operations of a separate action system, the present approach pursues the idea that affective processes are always part of the mental machinery that generates an action, with 'emotional actions' being only particular instantiations of a more general class of affectively motivated actions.

This integrative approach has the advantage that it allows to derive hypotheses about emotional effects on action control processes on the safe ground of an established action theory that is well-supported by many independent strands of evidence.

A central hypothesis of the present model is that an action is initiated, selected, and controlled by an anticipation of sensory action effects, which include affective consequences of actions (ideomotor hypothesis).

From this reference of actions to sensory events, it is hypothesized that perceiving an object and generating an action are represented by codes in a common representational domain (common-coding hypothesis). Affective processes influence the action generation process by a hedonic weighting of the anticipated action effect that primes actions with desired effects (hedonic hypothesis). Furthermore, stimulus events can generate emotional action tendencies by activating emotional outcomes that are associated with a behavioral response (affordance hypothesis).

It should be noted that each of these hypotheses is not new but only their combination and the extension to emotional action is new. In fact, much of the empirical work that is described below tested ideomotor theory and/or instrumental learning theory, while our own work only filled some gaps between both approaches (and certainly not all of them). In the following sections, we will present each hypothesis in detail. First, however, we must additionally clarify the target of our inquiry, which is emotional action.

What Is an "Emotional Action"?

This question must be answered in two parts: First, what is an "action"? Second, what makes an action "emotional"? We want to reserve the term "action" for those body movements that are performed for their effects on the environment. These effects can be many and varied. Some of these effects may be intended, such as the loud honk following a push of my car horn, but other effects may be not, such as the awkward position of my arm joints. Some effects may be desired, such as the cars moving out of my way, and others may be undesired, such as the angry looks of the passengers nearby. Some effects may be achieved through a complex movement sequence, while other effects may require only a single response. The point is that movements make a difference in the perceived world, and that people anticipate making a difference when they perform a movement. They certainly do so when they select an action voluntarily; however, they may also do so when performing an action involuntarily, as we will argue later in this chapter.

Emotional actions are then those movements that make a difference with respect to emotional states of affairs (for a related argument see Averill, 1994). For instance, if a spider phobic is spotting a big, ugly spider on the floor, she may cry for her husband, or suck the spider up with a vacuum cleaner, or smash it with a shoe. All these actions may have the same effect: removing the spider from sight and with it the source of emotional tension.

As our spider example shows, the cause of the emotional action thus may lie not only in the present (i.e., in the spider) but, also, in the future (i.e., in the removal of the spider). Of course, only a spider that is present can be removed. However, removing and avoiding bad and unpleasant things is only one side of emotional actions. The other side is approaching and attaining positive and pleasant objects or states. For example, our spider phobic person may give her husband an affectionate hug after he had bravely removed the spider, expressing gratitude and affection to him. Again, the cause of the emotional action may not only lie in the presence of a stimulus (i.e., in the presence of the husband) but in the anticipated consequence of the action (i.e., the expression of gratitude).

Emotional actions may thus be performed for their consequences, whether these consist in attaining desired consequences (i.e., rewards), such as a praise and a smiling face, or in the avoidance of undesired consequences (i.e., punishments), such as an insult and an angry face.

Following Rolls (2005), it is thus assumed that anticipations of rewarding and punishing consequences, as appraised by an individual, can elicit emotional states, and that different emotional states can be described depending on whether a reward or punishment is obtained, omitted, or terminated (see Figure 1). These emotional states may then motivate actions to attain a positive outcome (i.e., a reward or the omission of a punishment) and to avoid a negative outcome (i.e., a punishment or the omission of a reward) in a given situation.

The present conceptualization of emotional action thus draws a very thin line between emotion and motivation. The very same motivational systems that propel behavior towards desired end-states and away from undesired end-states in more mundane settings may also motivate actions in emotional settings.

While emotions may recruit domain-general motivation systems for controlling actions, this does not mean that a distinction between emotional and motivational states is not meaningful. In fact, the present approach posits that not all emotional states may generate an action inclination, but only those that involve anticipations of behavior outcomes.[1]

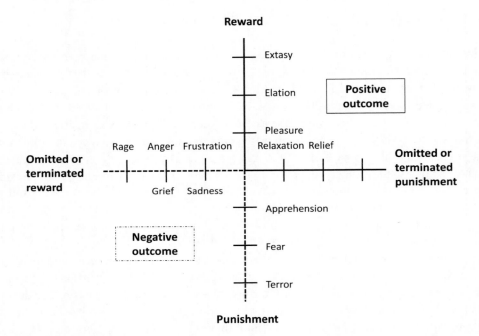

Figure 1. Classification scheme of reward and punishment contingencies, affective outcomes, and some emotions. The vertical axis describes emotions that are typically associated with the expectation or delivery of a reward (up) or a punishment (down). The horizontal axis describes emotions that are typically associated with the omission or termination of an expected reward (left) or punishment (right). Figure taken and adapted from Rolls (2005).

Furthermore, emotional states may elicit more reactions than just a motivational response (see the component model described above). For example, our spider phobic person may spontaneously widen her eyes, frown, and shriek at the sight of the spider (Dimberg, 1986), exhibiting a full set of expressive behaviors that are dissociable from the motivational response (for evidence see e.g., Landis, 1924; Mauss, Wilhelm, and Gross, 2004; Reisenzein

---

[1] An example emotion is *surprise* that is, by definition, elicited by an unexpected event. Surprise interrupts ongoing action, rather than producing an action (Horstmann, 2006; Reisenzein, Bördgen, Holtbernd, and Matz, 2006), which is in line with the present hypothesis that anticipatory processes are required for the initiation of a specific action.

et al., 2006). Despite intimate links between emotion and motivation, there are thus good reasons to keep both constructs separate.

The Ideomotor Hypothesis

The ideomotor hypothesis proposes that actions are represented in memory by their sensory effects, and that in turn these sensory effects are used to select, initiate, and control a motor activity (Greenwald, 1970; Hommel, Müsseler, Aschersleben, and Prinz, 2001; Kunde, Elsner, and Kiesel, 2007).

William James (1890) has elegantly illustrated the basic principle underlying ideomotor theory more than a century ago (see Figure 2 for a reprint). When a hypothetical motor neuron M moves a muscle, either induced externally by sensory stimulation or internally by random motor babbling, the movement produces a kinesthetic feedback that is registered by the neuron K. Anticipating Hebb's postulate of "what fires together, wires together", the kinesthetic sensation K will then become associated with the active motor neuron M, closing a 'motor circle'. On the basis of this cirlce, the motor activity controlled by M is then selected by activating K—that is, "the idea of the movement M's sensory effects will have become an immediately antecedent condition to the production of the movement itself" (James, 1890, p. 586). After falling in disgrace during the reign of behaviorism (Thorndike, 1913), ideomotor theory was rediscovered by modern cognitive psychology (for an historical review see Stock and Stock, 2004). Since then, numerous studies were conducted that examined assumptions of modern ideomotor theory empirically (for recent reviews see Hommel, 2013; Nattkemper, Ziessler, and Frensch, 2010; Shin, Proctor, and Capaldi, 2010).

Behavioral and neuroimaging studies have shown more specifically (i) that perceptions of action consequences become associated with the producing movements in memory (e.g., Elsner and Hommel, 2001; Elsner et al., 2002), (ii) that knowledge of the sensory effect is automatically retrieved from memory during response selection (e.g., Kunde, 2001; Kühn, Keizer, Rombouts and Hommel, 2011), and (iii) that anticipation of sensory effects is causally involved in the production and control of a motor response (e.g., Greenwald, 2003; Kunde, Koch, and Hoffmann, 2004; Melcher, Weidema, Eenshuistra, Hommel and Gruber, 2008).

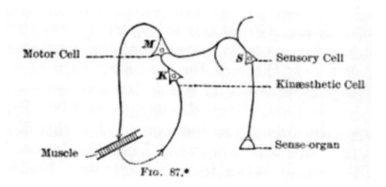

Figure 2. The motor circle underlying ideomotor action as illustrated by William James (1890, p. 582).

Most important for our present concern, ideomotor theory was extended to affective action effects (Eder and Hommel, in press; Eder and Klauer, 2009; Lavender and Hommel, 2007). According to ideomotor theory, a movement should become associated with any consequence that is perceived after its execution. This should also include affective sensations that are registered after a behavioral response.

In support of this idea, several strands of evidence have shown that affective consequences of actions can be learned, consolidated, and retrieved from memory like other, nonaffective sensory effects.

Learning of Affective Action Effects

Most evidence for a learning of affective action consequences comes from the rich animal and human research literature on reinforcement learning.

Since Thorndike's classic formulation of the law of effect (1911), it is well known that 'satisfactory' consequences of a behavior influence the motivation for a behavioral response. While early theories of reinforcement learning proposed that a reinforcer passively "stamps in" an association between a stimulus and a response without being itself included in the associative structure, modern research showed that this early conception is incorrect (Hall, 2002). Instead, it turned out that the consequence becomes an integral part of the cognitive structure that controls the behavioral response.

Evidence for this conclusion comes from devaluation studies in which a pleasant consequence of an action is devalued after sufficient instrumental training. The logic behind these studies is straightforward. If the action outcome merely cements an association between a situation and a response, subsequent changes to the value of that outcome should have no impact on subsequent performance of that action because the relation between the action and the outcome is not represented within the S-R structure. If, however, consequences of actions are learned during instrumental training, any subsequent change in the value of the outcome should be directly manifested in behavior performance. In fact, exactly this result has been observed in studies with animals and humans (e.g., Adams and Dickinson, 1981; Gámez and Rosas, 2007). For instance, Colwill and Rescorla (1985) trained rats to carry out two different responses, each produced a different food reward. After sufficient training, one outcome (but not the other) was paired with a toxin, inducing a negative affective state (nausea). When the animals could freely decide between the two responses in a subsequent extinction test, they no longer showed a preference for the response whose outcome had been devalued. The rats had learned to anticipate specific food rewards after the instrumental training, and they used this knowledge to avoid an outcome that is associated with a negative affective state.

Memory for Affective Action Effects

Devaluation studies clearly show that movements become associated with their rewarding consequences in memory. However, they do not show that the affective value of the effect was memorized. Such evidence is provided by incentive learning studies that show that memories of affective action effects require an updating if the value of the outcome has changed (Dickinson and Balleine, 1994, 2002).

A dramatic example comes from a study of sexual motivation. Everitt and Stacey (1987) trained male rats to press a lever for access to and mating with a sexually receptive female at the end of the session. After sufficient instrumental training, the rats were then castrated. Although the castration produced an immediate reduction in the sexual responsiveness to the female herself, it had no impact on the rate at which the males pressed the lever in the first postoperative session. As argued by Dickinson and Balleine, because the male rats had not been exposed to a female while in the castrated state, their behavioral performance was presumably controlled by the high incentive value assigned to her during training in the intact state. Exposure to the female at the end of the first postoperative session, however, allowed the males to learn about her reduced incentive value, and, indeed, they pressed at a significantly lower rate than controls in all subsequent sessions.

Incentive learning studies suggest that animals develop memories of the affective outcomes of their actions, and that they use these memories to respond advantageously in future situations. Interestingly, a very similar idea was proposed for emotions in human decision making. Damasio (1994) suggested that somatic responses to emotional action outcomes are stored in memory, and that in turn these somatic states (or brain representations thereof) can signal costs and benefits of a response choice when automatically reinstated in a choice situation (the so-called *somatic marker hypothesis*). For a test of this idea, Bechara, Damasio, Damasio, and Anderson (1994) introduced the Iowa Gambling Task to simulate real-life decision-making as affected by uncertain rewards and punishments. In this task, participants could freely select cards from four decks, with each card indicating that the participant has won or lost a specific amount of play money. Unbeknownst to the subject, cards from two decks yield a net gain in the long run (good desks), while drawing cards from the other two decks produces a net loss in the long term (bad decks). Normal participants learn after several trials of selecting from all four decks which are the risky or "bad" decks. Furthermore, before they choose from the risky desk they exhibit an anticipatory emotional reaction (indexed by a change in skin conductance level), and they start to avoid selecting cards from these decks.

In contrast, patients with bilateral damage to the ventromedial prefrontal cortex do not exhibit an anticipatory emotional reaction. They also refrain from picking from the bad decks immediately after a punishment (loss of money), but unlike the healthy controls, they later revert to selecting from the bad decks. The authors concluded that these patients are insensitive to future consequences of their choices because they lack the ability to integrate emotional (somatic) signals about the costs and benefits of their choices (for a thorough review see Dunn, Dagleish, and Lawrence, 2006).

Automatic Retrieval of Affective Action Effects

Several strands of evidence thus converge in the conclusion that affective consequences of actions are encoded in memory structures. Ideomotor theory additionally proposes that this knowledge is retrieved automatically during action selection. Supportive evidence for this claim comes from two studies in which affective action effects were completely irrelevant for the task at hand (Beckers, De Houwer, and Eelen, 2002; Eder, Rothermund, De Houwer, and Hommel, 2012).

In a first learning phase, participants could freely choose between two responses, each response produced a different affective outcome (e.g., the presence or absence of an electric shock or a presentation of pleasant and unpleasant pictures).

In a subsequent test phase, the same actions were emitted in response to a neutral feature of affective stimuli (e.g., whether a picture shows an animal or a person). Responses with affectively congruent effects were emitted faster than responses with affectively incongruent effects, irrespective of whether the produced effect was pleasant or unpleasant. These results support the claims that (a) affective effects become automatically associated with their eliciting movements, and that (b) the affective consequence is automatically retrieved during response selection, even when they are not useful for the task at hand.

Furthermore, given the relative facilitation of a response that produced an unpleasant consequence (e.g., an aversive shock), it is obvious that the process responsible for the affective congruency effect was not hedonically motivated; rather, this finding provides strong evidence for an ideomotor approach, which assumes that the priming of a response effect in memory directly excites the corresponding response (even in the case of an unpleasant effect).

Functional Role of Affective Action Effects

Our review has shown that there is substantial evidence that movements become associated with their affective effects in memory, and that this knowledge is automatically activated during response selection. However, it is possible that this knowledge affects action control only indirectly, so that we need to ask whether an anticipation of affective effects is directly connected with action control. Hence, do we have evidence that anticipatory representations of affective action effects play a causal role in initiating and controlling a behavioral response?

Affirmative evidence comes from an unpublished study that investigated an influence of affective compatibility relations on processing bottlenecks that are related to response selection (Van der Goten, Caessens, Lammertyn, De Vooght, and Hommel, 2001; cited in Hommel et al., 2001). A typical finding in dual-task performance is that latencies in a secondary task (Task 2) increase dramatically when the secondary task overlaps in time with the selection of a response in a primary task (Task 1) (see Pashler, 1994, for a review). This latency increase is typically explained with capacity restrictions of a serial S-R translation stage that can translate only one stimulus into its corresponding response at a time—a processing bottleneck that all other translations have to await (Pashler, 1984; Welford, 1952).

Van der Goten and colleagues however showed that selection of a neutral response to a stimulus in Task 1 is facilitated if the stimulus (e.g., the word 'grave') is affectively compatible with the response that is selected for Task 2 (e.g., a response that produced a grumpy on the screen). This backward compatibility effect suggests that affective features of the response in Task 2 were activated before the selection of a response in Task 1 was completed—a finding that is problematic for the assumption of a serial S-R translation stage (see also Ellenbogen and Meiran, 2011; Hommel, 1998; Watter and Logan, 2006).

Instead, this study shows that the affective effect of a response may play a role when selecting the response for execution, which means that response selection considers codes that represent and, thus, predict these consequences.

The Common Coding Hypothesis

If one agrees with ideomotor theory that connections between actions and sensory effects are mutually formed by a Hebb-like mechanism, one has to face the problem that sensory and motor parameters have to be represented in a way that allows the system to "wire" together different types of representations. This problem is addressed by the common-coding hypothesis that proposes that representations of perceived events and planned actions have a common format (Prinz, 1990, 1997). According to Prinz (1992), a commensurate coding of action and perception originates in a common reference to events in the distal environment— events that are registered as a given state in the case of perception and events that are anticipated as a future state in the case of action planning. "Perceiving and action planning are functionally equivalent, inasmuch as they are merely alternative ways of doing the same thing: internally representing external events" (Hommel et al., 2001, p. 860).

Given a commensurate format, representations of actions and perceptions may mutually influence each other on the basis of their overlap in a common-coding domain. Consistent with this assumption, numerous studies have shown that stimuli can prime the execution of 'compatible' responses (i.e., responses that share one or more features with stimuli) and that responses can prime the perception of 'compatible' stimuli (for reviews see Hommel, 2009; Thomaschke, Hopkins, and Miall, 2012; see also Kornblum, Hasbroucq, and Osman, 1990). More important for the present discussion, such compatibility effects were also observed between affective stimuli and responses. Eder and Rothermund (2008), for instance, showed that the cognitive representation of a pushing or pulling lever movement becomes associated with a different affective meaning depending on how the movement was instructed by the experimenter. When a lever pull was instructed as a movement 'towards the body', for example, the lever was pulled faster in response to positive than to negative stimuli; in contrast, exactly the reverse pattern of facilitation was observed when pulling the lever was instructed as a movement in a 'downward' direction. Presumably, the cognitive representation of the lever movement became associated with the positive implication of moving something towards oneself (Neumann and Strack, 2000) or with the negative implication of moving something downwards (Meier and Robinson, 2004). The affective 'response code' then interacted with the affective 'stimulus code' in a shared representational domain.[2]

A commensurate event coding can also create confusion, especially if a feature is shared by different events. For an illustration of this problem, take as an example a social situation in which several persons are smiling simultaneously. In order to distinguish the smiles pertaining to different persons, the perceiver's brain must relate perceptual features encoding a smile to feature bundles that represent different persons. This 'binding problem' is solved by a feature integration process that binds the information to the relevant events and that distinguishes it from features pertaining to other events (Treisman, 1996). Given a commensurate coding of perception and action, a need for feature integration should thus apply to action planning and sensorimotor processing as well (Hommel, 2004).

An interesting hypothesis about the feature binding process is that access to integrated action features is temporarily blocked for other representational purposes after completed action planning, so that other cognitive processes cannot interfere with action control (for a thorough discussion of this assumption see Thomaschke et al., 2012). Binding a code to an action plan should hence impair both planning another action and perceptions requiring that code, which was indeed observed (e.g., Müsseler and Hommel, 1997; Stoet and Hommel, 1999). Conclusive evidence for an analogous occupation of affective codes through action planning was provided by Eder and Klauer (2009). They had participants prepare an

---

[2] Following Schyns, Goldstone, Thibaut (1998), a feature code is defined as "any elementary property of a distal stimulus that is an element of cognition, an atom of psychological processing" (p. 1). Given that positive and negative affect is "a fundamental, psychologically irreducible property of the human mind" (Barrett, and Bliss-Moreau, 2009, p. 167), properties of distal events that have the capacity to elicit affective states thus meet all criteria for a "code".

approach-related lever pull (assumed to be coded as positive) or avoidance-related lever push (assumed to be coded as negative) in every trial and asked them to indicate whenever they were ready by pressing a button. The button press triggered the presentation of a briefly flashed positive or negative stimulus, which participants were to identify. Hence, the stimulus appeared after the planning of the lever action was completed but before it was carried out. If the planning would involve integrating a positive or negative code, participants would be expected to have difficulties identifying a stimulus that shares this particular code. In other words, planning a "positive" action should impair the identification of positive stimuli, while planning a "negative" action should impair the identification of negative stimuli. Indeed, Eder and Klauer consistently observed this outcome pattern in several experiments: identifying affectively response-compatible stimuli was more difficult than identifying response-incompatible stimuli. Analogous interference effects were observed with responses that were affectively neutral originally but became extrinsically associated with a positive or negative meaning through task procedures (Eder and Klauer, 2007), or if an evaluative response is selected during the preparation of another evaluative response (Eder, Müsseler, and Hommel, 2012).

As these studies show, perceiving an affective event and planning an affective action (or more precisely, an action that produces an affective event) thus seem to make use of the same type of affective codes, at least to some degree.

The Hedonic Hypothesis

The ideomotor hypothesis suggests that affective action consequences become associated with the producing movements in memory just like other, nonaffective effects. People associate positive and negative action outcomes with the producing movements, and thinking of the consequence automatically reinstates the associated behavior.

The intriguing implication is that the cognitive anticipation of a negative outcome, once learned as a behavioral effect, should prime the associated behavior that generates this outcome (Beckers et al., 2002; Eder et al., 2012). It is clear that this priming process is highly dysfunctional for an action control system that is aimed at an avoidance of undesired outcomes. Thus, for a motivational control of behavior, ideomotor action must be constrained by an additional process that is sensitive to the needs and desires of the person.

In the present framework, this motivational process is covered by the hedonic hypothesis: the anticipation of a positive action effect potentiates an evoked response tendency, while the retrieval of an unwanted, negative effect inhibits an associated action.

Motivational evaluations of anticipated action effects are thus hypothesized to constrain behavioral impulses induced by ideomotor processes, enhancing responses that result in desired effects while suppressing those that generate undesired effects.

Suggestive evidence for the existence of such a motivational process comes from a study of Beckers and colleagues (2002). In their experiment, a movement that generated an aversive shock was executed faster in response to negative stimuli than to positive stimuli, suggesting that the negative stimulus has primed the response via activation of the aversive outcome (indexing an ideomotor process). However, in addition to this priming effect, the shock-generating movement was also initiated more slowly than the alternative movement that was not followed by a shock. The relative suppression of the response that produced an aversive effect suggests that the hedonic implication of the response effect had an additional motivational effect on action control.

The study design of Beckers and colleagues (2002) can however not rule out the possibility that the participants have postponed the experience of the aversive shock strategically (see e.g., Hineline, 1970). More conclusive evidence for an automatic response suppression comes from an experiment of Eder and colleagues (2012) that measured a response preference in a free-choice test situation. Participants first learned to associate one response with pleasant visual effects and another response with unpleasant visual effects. In a subsequent test phase, affective stimuli were presented as go stimuli for a free decision between both responses. In support of the hedonic hypothesis, responses associated with pleasant effects were preferred over responses producing unpleasant effects. This motivating effect was observed in addition to, and independently of, an affective congruency effect between stimuli and response effects. More important for our present concern, a preference for the response associated with a pleasant effect was observed even when no response-effects were presented in the test (i.e., in extinction) and when participants were unable to verbalize the action-outcome contingency. Latter finding suggests that the hedonic implication of a behavioral effect can influence action selection automatically, even in the absence of a conscious expectation and evaluation of the affective consequence.

The Affordance Hypothesis

Our review has shown so far that the cause of an emotional action may not lie so much in the present situation but, rather, in the anticipated consequences of the behavior. However, this model would be insufficient if it would fail to take motivational properties of stimuli into account. In fact, one reason why researchers feel so compelled of emotional action tendencies is that voluntary behavior is often so difficult to control in the presence of emotional stimuli—just take the examples of being afraid to approach a snarling dog or a harmless spider. Without doubt, stimuli can have a powerful influence on action control in these situations, which must be accounted for. The present model accounts for these action tendencies by the assumption that representations of outcomes are not only aroused by internal processes (during action planning) but also by associations with external stimuli.

This idea is based on a standard model of associatve learning that describes classical conditioning processes as learning about predictive relations between an originally neutral event (the conditioned stimulus; CS) and a biologically significant event (the unconditioned stimulus; US) (Rescorla, 1988). Numerous studies have convincingly demonstrated that after several pairings a CS comes to activate a detailed representation of the US that encodes sensory and affective properties of the outcome (Delamater, 2012).

Furthermore, a Pavlovian priming of an internal outcome representation has been shown to trigger a specific action tendency—a phenomenon that is known as outcome-specific Pavlovian-to-instrumental transfer of control (specific PIT; Trapold and Overmier, 1972).[3]

---

[3] There is also a second form of transfer, termed "general PIT," in which a Pavlovian cue increases the vigor of an ongoing operant response when both contingencies involve appetitive or aversive stimuli, whereas it decreases the response strength when one of the contingencies is aversive and the other is appetitive (Rescorla and Solomon, 1967). Thus, general PIT affects the strength of an ongoing response, but not the selection of a response.

In a typical demonstration of specific PIT, relations between stimuli and differential outcomes (Pavlovian learning: S1-O1, S2-O2) and relations between responses and outcomes (instrumental learning: R1-O1, R2-O2) are established in separate training sessions. In a transfer test, both responses are then made available in extinction (i.e., without a presentation of outcomes), and the preference for a specific response is measured in the presence of each conditioned stimulus (i.e., S1: R1 vs. R2; S2: R1 vs. R2). The typical result is a preference for the response whose outcome is signaled by the Pavlovian cue (for a review see Urcuioli, 2005).

Overmier, Bull, and Trapold (1971) showed in an early study with dogs that PIT processes may play an important role for emotional action selection. In their study, one stimulus warned of a shock delivered to one leg, while a second stimulus warned the dogs of a shock to the other leg (Pavlovian learning). The dogs could however avoid the shock by pressing different pressure plates in response to each stimulus (avoidance learning). Results showed that the dogs learned faster to avoid the shocks in this condition relative to a control condition in which the warning stimuli were followed by shocks to either leg. The dogs have obviously learned to predict which leg will be shocked in the presence of which stimulus, and they used this knowledge to figure out more quickly which action is necessary to avoid a shock.

Another example for action tendencies induced by PIT comes from a study on human drug seeking (Hogarth, Dickinson Wright, Kouvaraki, and Duka, 2007). In this study, regular smokers first learned to discriminate between a stimulus that signaled a tobacco reward and another stimulus that signaled a money reward (Pavlovian learning). In a subsequent training session, they learned which of two different motor responses earned which outcome (instrumental learning). Finally, they had the opportunity of making either of the two instrumental responses in the presence of either stimulus (transfer phase). Results showed a preference for the response that shared an outcome with the current stimulus: The tobacco-seeking response was selected more frequently in the presence of the tobacco cue, while the money-seeking response was produced more often in the presence of the monetary cue. Given that the Pavlovian and instrumental associations were established in separate sessions, it is clear that this finding cannot be explained with habitual responding to the reward cues (i.e., stimulus-response associations). Furthermore, the preference for a specific reward in the transfer phase cannot be explained with a general priming of affective outcomes that should prime all appetitive responses indifferently (i.e., general PIT). Rather, the specific influence on action selection suggests that a Pavlovian cue can evoke a motor response by priming the representation of the outcome that is associated with this response.

Stimuli thus may trigger a behavioral reaction by activating the representation of an outcome, which then promotes, via ideomotor processes, the selection and initiation of the response that operates on this outcome.

Affective properties of the outcome should then influence the motivational strength of the evoked response in line with the hedonic hypothesis, which was indeed observed (Eder and Dignath, 2012; see also Allman, DeLeon, Cataldo, Holland, and Johnston, 2010). Tasting the flavor of drinks, participants first learned in separate training sessions to associate particular ingredients and responses with two different drinks (lemonades). In a first transfer test, participants worked harder for a lemonade when the picture of an associated ingredient was shown (i.e., they exhibited specific PIT). Before a second transfer test, the taste of one drink was devalued using bad-tasting Tween20.

Importantly, the outcome devaluation treatment selectively reduced working for the devalued drink in the presence of stimuli that were associated this lemonade, eliminating the specific PIT effect. Responding for the non-devalued drink was however not affected by the devaluation treatment. This finding shows that both the outcome and its value were represented during the transfer test, and that the capacity of a stimulus cue to motivate a specific response depended on the current value of the shared outcome.

SOLVING THE PUZZLE: FIGHT OR FLIGHT?

In the following, we will apply our framework to a discussion of fight-or-flight responses that are involved in fear and anger episodes. Several eminent emotion theorists have related fear to an action inclination to escape or avoid and anger to an inclination to attack (e.g., Cannon, 1929; Frijda, 1986; McDougall, 1926; Izard, 1977; Plutchik, 2001; Roseman, 2008). Although there is little doubt that people often flee in a fearful state and respond aggressively in an angry state, it has also been repeatedly observed that frightened people 'fight' and that angry people take 'flight' (see Berkowitz, 2012; Berkowitz and Harmon-Jones, 2004). How to understand this variable relationship?

In their search for an answer, experimental psychologists have analyzed the antecedent conditions, the behavioral characteristics, and the outcomes of aggressive actions in fear and anger situations (Berkowitz, 1988; Hutchinson, 1983). These studies soon made clear that there is no simple answer. As a matter of fact, aggressive behaviors were observed in response to a variety of different aversive events, such as physical blows, electric shocks, loud noises, or intense heat, exposure to foul odors, irritable cigarette smoke, unpleasantly high room temperatures, immersion in cold water, and viewing disgusting or frightening scenes. Furthermore, it was observed that intense aversive stimuli elicit intraspecific attack, interspecific attack, and attack of inaminate objects. In short, studies failed to identify distinct sets of environmental cues that can account for the occurrence of fight or flight responses in aversive situations.

Looking beyond objective situation characteristics, appraisal theorists proposed that aggressive behavior is caused by the cognitive appraisal of a negative event or outcome as "frustrative" (Dollard, Miller, Doob, Mowrer, and Sears, 1939), as "illegitimate" (Averill, 1982), or as being due to someone else "blameworthy" actions (Ortony, Clore, and Collins, 1989). Furthermore, it was suggested that in addition to these appraisals a person must see some potential for coping with the frustrative event (Ellsworth and Smith, 1988).

However, it is not clear which appraisals are necessary or sufficient for aggressive behavior in anger situations (Kuppens, Van Mechelen, Smits, and DeBoeck, 2003). For example, several experiments found that even supposedly "legitimate" frustrations can give rise to aggressive tendencies, and if someone else is not blamed for an unpleasant outcome (for a review see Berkowitz, 1989, 2010).

Viewing different appraisal-patterns as causes of fight and flight tendencies thus does not receive much support.

The by far most important predictor of aggressive action tendencies is instead the learning history of an individual. Numerous studies showed that humans and animals can learn to respond aggressively in aversive situations (Bandura, 1973).

For instance, when shocked rats learned that their attacks terminate the shocks, they attack more frequently (Knutson, Fordyce, and Anderson, 1980); in contrast, if shocks increase after an attack, subsequent attack become less probable (Azrin, 1970; Follick and Knutson, 1978). Terminating an aversive shock thus enhances aggression, whereas producing an aversive shock reduces aggression, showing that the motivation for a fight response is controlled by its consequence. A negative reinforcement of aggressive behavior should of course be also effective if a person views another person as a source of their uncomfortable feelings.

In line with the hedonic hypothesis, it is thus hypothesized that people respond aggressively if they believe that aggressive behavior improves their situation. Several strands of evidence are in line with this hypothesis. For instance, Bushman and colleagues (2001) showed that provoked people do not exhibit increased aggression when they believed that venting their anger has no effect on their feeling state. Thus, at least some aggressive behaviors may aim at a mood-repair.

Other studies showed that outcomes of aggressive actions have reinforcing properties, suggesting a more subtle influence. One study examined whether mouse killing can reinforce key pressing by rats that habitually kill mice. Offered a choice between a key that granted access to mice and one that did not, the rats preferred the key that yielded mice (Van Hemel, 1972).

Sebastian (1978) reported that human participants who were provoked by a confederate experienced greater pleasure the more intense the suffering they supposedly had inflicted on their provocateur. Latter finding is also in line with a modern brain imaging study showing that punishing defectors in a social trust game activates reward circuits in the brain (de Quervain et al., 2004).

A reinforcing role of aggressive action consequences is also suggested by a study of Verona and Sullivan (2008). They observed that aggressive behavior reduced physiological tension (indexed by a heart rate decrease), and that lowered physiological tension actually strengthened the angered participants' urge to attack another person. In contradiction to the catharsis-hypothesis (Feshbach, 1984), acting aggressively thus seems to enhance an aggressive action inclination rather than reducing it.

To summarize, there is substantial evidence that many aggressive actions of angered people are instrumental in the sense that they are being performed because of their consequences.[4]

In the current framework, an instrumental control of aggressive behavior does however neither presuppose a conscious decision to act nor a rational weighting of costs and benefits of aggressive actions. Rather, it is proposed that thinking of the consequences of inflicting injury on another person may automatically instigate a tendency to perform this action (ideomotor hypothesis), and that external cues may do the same if they activate these thoughts (affordance hypothesis).

---

[4] Note that the present conception of an "instrumental" aggressive response is different from that proposed in dichotomies between affective (hostile) and instrumental aggression, in which instrumental aggression is typically defined as an intentional action that inflicts injury to some person or object but which, nonetheless is "directed towards the achievement of nonaggressive goals" (i.e., whose primary aim is not to do harm) (Feshbach, 1964, p. 258). Let aside the fact that this dichotomy is difficult to maintain for a number of reasons (for which see Bushman and Anderson, 2001), we define instrumental acts as those movements that are controlled by their consequences, which may (or may not) consist in the aggressive destruction of an aversive source of stimulation.

Consistent with this theorizing, many studies showed that aggressive action inclinations are indeed enhanced in the presence of situational aggression cues (e.g., Berkowitz, 1974; Berkowitz and LePage, 1967; for a meta-analysis see Carlson, Marcus-Newhall, and Miller, 1990). In one particular study (Swart and Berkowitz, 1976), participants were first tormented by a confederate. Then, they learned that their tormenter suffers if a light was turned on (Pavlovian learning). Finally, they were given the opportunity to aggress against another confederate, with whom they have not interacted before, in the presence of the previously conditioned light. Participants responded with more aggression in the presence of the light that was associated with their tormentor's pain relative to a condition in which the light was paired with an affectively neutral event. Cues of a victim's suffering thus seem to have the capacity of eliciting impulsive aggressive reactions under special circumstances. Even though there exist several explanations for the effect of situational aggression cues on aggressive inclinations (for which see Carlson et al., 1990), this sort of aggression transfer is remarkably similar to the specific transfer effects that were described above in the discussion of the affordance hypothesis.

An ideomotor analysis of aggressive behavior thus proposes that people learn to anticipate attractive outcomes of aggressive behaviors, and that situational cues can elicit a spontaneous aggressive response by activating its controlling outcome. With this emphasis on learning and cognitive priming processes, the present approach has much in common with the cognitive-neo-associationist model of aggressive behaviors (Berkowitz, 2012; Berkowitz and Harmon-Jones, 2004), while there are also some notable differences (e.g., the idea of emotion networks vs. the present idea of affectively infused response-outcome associations). Rigorous hypothesis testing will show whether the present analysis has some merits above and beyond these approaches.

CONCLUSION

Many emotional action theories are based on the idea that emotions prime cognitive action structures, which in turn activate body movements. The present ideomotor approach lends credibility to this idea. Thinking about the consequences of a movement may indeed produce the movement itself, and emotions may prime thoughts of particular consequences of actions. Many of these consequences may be functional for coping with an emotional event, but others may be not, or even be outright dysfunctional. In either case, having a closer look at the consequences of actions, rather than at their antecedents, may be the key for a better prediction of how people will respond in an emotional situation.

However, it is also clear that the range of possible action outcomes is constrained by the characteristics of the emotional situation. A frightened person may anticipate very different outcomes depending on whether she feels threatened by making contact with a dental drill, by the neighbors' aggressive dog, or by the diagnosis of a cancer disease. As a consequence, she may prepare very different actions to cope with each threat. Furthermore, not all situations are controllable to the same degree, and context cues are used to estimate which action outcomes can be achieved in a given situation (Kiesel and Hoffmann, 2004). Analyzing the characteristics of an emotional situation thus provides important clues about what people hope, fear, and aspire for their immediate future, and how they will act in this situation.

The present approach also has some limitations. One limitation is that all behaviors are treated equally. At least in lower animals, however, avoidance responses that are closer to species-specific defense reactions (SSDRs) are learned faster than arbitrary responses (Bolles, 1970; Crawford and Masterson, 1982), suggesting that characteristics of the behavioral response may play a role as well. Another limitation is that the present model does not clarify the impact of emotional arousal on action control. One possibility is that emotional arousal intensifies the motivational response that is evoked by anticipatory processes. Another possibility is that emotional arousal affects the generation of a motivational response directly, by influencing the processes that encode the value of an outcome (see e.g., Eder and Rothermund, 2010). Further research is necessary that evaluates these possibilities.

Perhaps the biggest challenge is however the question of how emotional actions are connected to and influenced by other emotional response components (i.e., cognitive, physiological, expressive, and experiential responses). It should have become clear from our review that emotional actions involve more than just "doing" something and require complex cognitive, affective, and physiological preparations. According to the present approach, emotion may not be the crucial element that binds together multiple response systems but, rather, the action that is afforded by an emotional situation. Analyzing emotional actions may then not only enhance our understanding of how emotions make us behave, but also how they make us feel in the way they do.

REFERENCES

Adams, C. D. and Dickinson, A. (1981). Instrumental responding following reinforcer devaluation. *The Quarterly Journal of Experimental Psychology B: Comparative and Physiological Psychology*, 33B, 109–121.

Allman, M. J., DeLeon, I. G., Cataldo, M. F., Holland, P. C., and Johnson, A. W. (2010). Learning processes affecting human decision making: An assessment of reinforcer-selective Pavlovian-to-instrumental transfer following reinforcer devaluation. *Journal of Experimental Psychology: Animal Behavior Processes*, 36, 402–408.

Averill, J. R. (1982). *Anger and aggression: An essay on emotion.* New York: Springer-Verlag.

Averill, J. R. (1994). Emotions are many splendored things. In: P. Ekman and R. J. Davidson (Eds.), *The nature of emotion: Fundamental questions* (pp. 99-102). New York: Oxford University Press.

Azrin, N. H. (1970). Punishment of elicited aggression. *Journal of the Experimental Analysis of Behavior*, 14, 7–10.

Bandura, A. (1973). *Aggression: A social-learning analysis.* Oxford, England: Prentice-Hall.

Barrett, L. F. (2006). Are emotions natural kinds? *Perspectives on Psychological Science*, 1, 28–58.

Barrett, L. F. and Bliss-Moreau, E. (2009). Affect as a psychological primitive. *Advances in experimental social psychology*, 41, 167–218.

Baumeister, R. F., Vohs, K. D., DeWall, C. N., and Zhang, L. (2007). How emotion shapes behavior: Feedback, anticipation, and reflection, rather than direct causation. *Personality and Social Psychology Review*, 11, 167–203.

Bechara, A., Damasio, A. R., Damasio, H., and Anderson, S. W. (1994). Insensitivity to future consequences following damage to human prefrontal cortex. *Cognition*, 50, 7–15.

Beckers, T., De Houwer, J. and Eelen, P. (2002). Automatic integration of non-perceptual action effect features: The case of the associative affective Simon effect. *Psychological Research*, 66, 166–173.

Berkowitz, L. (1974). Some determinants of impulsive aggression: Role of mediated associations with reinforcements for aggression. *Psychological Review*, 81, 165–176.

Berkowitz, L. (1988). Frustrations, appraisals, and aversively stimulated aggression. *Aggressive Behavior*, 14, 3–11.

Berkowitz, L. (1989). Frustration-aggression hypothesis: Examination and reformulation. *Psychological Bulletin*, 106, 59–73.

Berkowitz, L. (2010). Appraisals and anger: How complete are the usual appraisal accounts of anger? In: M. Potegal, G. Stemmler and C. Spielberger (Eds.), *International handbook of anger* (pp. 267–286). New York: Springer-Verlag.

Berkowitz, L. (2012). A different view of anger: The cognitive-neoassociation conception of the relation of anger to aggression. *Aggressive Behavior*, 38, 322–333.

Berkowitz, L. and Harmon-Jones, E. (2004). Toward an anderstanding of the determinants of anger. *Emotion*, 4, 107–130.

Berkowitz, L. and LePage, A. (1967). Weapons as aggression-eliciting stimuli. *Journal of Personality and Social Psychology*, 7, 202–207.

Bindra, D. (1969). A unified interpretation of emotion and motivation. *Annals of the New York Academy of Sciences*, 159, 1071–1083.

Blanchard, R. J. and Blanchard, D. C. (1968). Escape and avoidance responses to a fear eliciting situation. *Psychonomic Science*, 13, 19–20.

Blanchard, R. J. and Blanchard, D. C. (1990). An ethoexperimental analysis of defense, fear, and anxiety. In: N. McNaughton and G. Andrews (Eds.), *Anxiety* (pp. 124–133). Dunedin, New Zealand: University of Otago Press.

Bolles, R. C. (1970). Species-specific defense reactions and avoidance learning. *Psychological Review*, 77, 32–48.

Bushman, B. J. and Anderson, C. A. (2001). Is it time to pull the plug on hostile versus instrumental aggression dichotomy? *Psychological Review*, 108, 273–279.

Bushman, B. J., Baumeister, R. F. and Phillips, C. M. (2001). Do people aggress to improve their mood? Catharsis beliefs, affect regulation opportunity, and aggressive responding. *Journal of Personality and Social Psychology*, 81, 17–32.

Buss, D. M. (2000). The evolution of happiness. *American Psychologist*, 55(1), 15–23.

Cannon, W. B. (1929). *Bodily changes in pain, hunger, fear, and rage* (2nd ed.). New York: Appleton-Century.

Carlson, M., Marcus-Newhall, A. and Miller, N. (1990). Effects of situational aggression cues: A quantitative review. *Journal of Personality and Social Psychology*, 58, 622–633.

Clore, G. L. and Ortony, A. (2000). Cognition in emotion: Always, sometimes, or never? In: R. D. Lane and L. Nadel (Eds.), *Cognitive neuroscience of emotion.* (pp. 24–61). New York: Oxford University Press.

Colwill, R. M. and Rescorla, R. A. (1985). Postconditioning devaluation of a reinforcer affects instrumental responding. *Journal of Experimental Psychology: Animal Behavior Processes*, 11, 120–132.

Crawford, M. and Masterson, F. (1982). Species-specific defense reactions and avoidance learning: An evaluative review. *Integrative Physiological and Behavioral Science*, 17, 204–214.

Damasio, A. (1994). *Descartes' error: emotion, research and the human brain*. New York: Avon.

Darwin, C. (1872). *The expression of the emotions in man and animals*. London: John Murray.

De Quervain, D. J.-F., Fischbacher, U., Treyer, V., Schellhammer, M., Schnyder, U., Buck, A., and Fehr, E. (2004). The neural basis of altruistic punishment. *Science*, 305, 1254–1258.

Delamater, A. R. (2012). On the nature of CS and US representations in Pavlovian learning. *Learning and Behavior*, 40, 1–23.

Dickinson, A. and Balleine, B. (1994). Motivational control of goal-directed action. *Animal Learning and Behavior*, 22, 1–18.

Dickinson, A. and Balleine, B. (2002). The role of learning in the operation of motivational systems. In: H. Pashler and R. Gallistel (Eds.), *Steven's handbook of experimental psychology, Vol. 3: Learning, motivation, and emotion* (pp. 497–533). Hoboken, NJ: John Wiley and Sons Inc.

Dimberg, U. (1986). Facial reactions to fear-relevant and fear-irrelevant stimuli. *Biological Psychology*, 23, 153–161.

Dollard, J., Miller, N. E., Doob, L. W., Mowrer, O. H., and Sears, R. R. (1939). *Frustration and aggression*. New Haven, CT: Yale University Press.

Dunn, B. D., Dalgleish, T. and Lawrence, A. D. (2006). The somatic marker hypothesis: A critical evaluation. *Neuroscience and Biobehavioral Reviews*, 30, 239–271.

Eder, A. B. and Dignath, D. (2012). [Reinforcer-selective Pavlovian-to-instrumental transfer following reinforcer devaluation]. Unpublished raw data.

Eder, A. B. and Hommel, B. (in press). Anticipatory control of approach and avoidance: An ideomotor approach. *Emotion Review*.

Eder, A. B. and Klauer, K. C. (2007). Common valence coding in action and evaluation: Affective blindness towards response-compatible stimuli. *Cognition and Emotion*, 21, 1297–1322.

Eder, A. B. and Klauer, K. C. (2009). A common-coding account of the bidirectional evaluation–behavior link. *Journal of Experimental Psychology: General*, 138, 218–235.

Eder, A. B., Müsseler, J. and Hommel, B. (2012). The structure of affective action representations: temporal binding of affective response codes. *Psychological Research*, 76, 111–118.

Eder, A. B. and Rothermund, K. (2008). When do motor behaviors (mis)match affective stimuli? An evaluative coding view of approach and avoidance reactions. *Journal of Experimental Psychology: General*, 137, 262-281.

Eder, A. B. and Rothermund, K. (2010). Automatic influence of arousal information on evaluative processing: Valence-arousal interactions in an affective Simon task. *Cognition and Emotion*, 24, 1053–1061.

Eder, A. B., Rothermund, K., De Houwer, J., and Hommel, B. (2012). *Directive and incentive functions of affective action effects: An ideomotor approach*. Manuscript submitted for publication.

Ekman, P. (1992). An argument for basic emotions. *Cognition and Emotion*, 6, 169–200.

Ellenbogen, R. and Meiran, N. (2011). Objects and events as determinants of parallel processing in dual tasks: Evidence from the backward compatibility effect. *Journal of Experimental Psychology: Human Perception and Performance*, 37, 152–167.

Ellsworth, P. C. and Scherer, K. R. (2003). Appraisal processes in emotion. In: R. J. Davidson, K. R. Scherer and H. H. Goldsmith (Eds.), *Handbook of affective sciences* (pp. 572–595). New York: Oxford University Press.

Ellsworth, P. C. and Smith, C. A. (1988). From appraisal to emotion: Differences among unpleasant feelings. *Motivation and Emotion*, 12, 271–302.

Elsner, B. and Hommel, B. (2001). Effect anticipation and action control. *Journal of Experimental Psychology: Human Perception and Performance*, 27, 229–240.

Elsner, B., Hommel, B., Mentschel, C., Drzezga, A., Prinz, W., Conrad, B., and Siebner, H. (2002). Linking actions and their perceivable consequences in the human brain. *NeuroImage*, 17, 364–372.

Everitt, B. J. and Stacey, P. (1987). Studies of instrumental behavior with sexual reinforcement in male rats (*Rattus norvegicus*): II. Effects of preoptic area lesions, castration, and testosterone. *Journal of Comparative Psychology*, 101, 407–419.

Fanselow, M. (1980). Conditional and unconditional components of post-shock freezing. *Integrative Physiological and Behavioral Science*, 15, 177–182.

Feshbach, S. (1964). The function of aggression and the regulation of aggressive drive. *Psychological Review*, 71, 257–272.

Feshbach, S. (1984). The Catharsis Hypothesis, aggressive drive, and the reduction of aggression. *Aggressive Behavior*, 10, 91–101.

Follick, M. J. and Knutson, J. F. (1978). Punishment of irritable aggression. *Aggressive Behavior*, 4, 1–17.

Fredrickson, B. L. (1998). What good are positive emotions? *Review of General Psychology*, New Directions in Research on Emotion, 2, 300–319.

Frijda, N. H. (1986). *The emotions*. New York: Cambridge University Press.

Frijda, N. H. (1988). The laws of emotion. *American Psychologist*, 43, 349–358.

Frijda, N. (1994). Emotions are functional, most of the time. In: P. Ekman and R. J. Davidson (Eds.), *The nature of emotion: Fundamental questions* (pp. 112-122). New York: Oxford University Press.

Frijda, N. H. (2004). Emotions and action. In: A. S. R. Manstead, N. Frijda and A. Fischer (Eds.), *Feelings and emotions: The Amsterdam symposium* (pp. 158–173). New York: Cambridge University Press.

Frijda, N. H. (2010). Impulsive action and motivation. *Biological Psychology*, 84, 570–579.

Frijda, N. H., Kuipers, P. and ter Schure, E. (1989). Relations among emotion, appraisal, and emotional action readiness. *Journal of Personality and Social Psychology*, 57, 212–228.

Gámez, A. M. and Rosas, J. M. (2007). Associations in human instrumental conditioning. *Learning and Motivation*, 38, 242–261.

Gray, J. A. (1994). Three fundamental emotion systems. In: P. Ekman and R. J. Davidson (Eds.), *The nature of emotion: Fundamental questions* (pp. 243-247). New York: Oxford University Press.

Gray, R. D., Heaney, M. and Fairhall, S. (2003). Evolutionary psychology and the challenge of adaptive explanation. In: K. Sterelny and J. Fitness (Eds.), *From mating to mentality: Evaluating evolutionary psychology* (pp. 247-269). New York: Psychology Press

Greenwald, A. G. (1970). Sensory feedback mechanisms in performance control: With special reference to the ideo-motor mechanism. *Psychological Review*, 77, 73–99.

Greenwald, A. G. (2003). On doing two things at once: III. Confirmation of perfect timesharing when simultaneous tasks are ideomotor compatible. *Journal of Experimental Psychology: Human Perception and Performance*, 29, 859–868.

Hall, G. (2002). Associative structures in Pavlovian and instrumental conditioning. In: H. Pashler and R. Gallistel (Eds.), *Steven's handbook of experimental psychology, Vol. 3: Learning, motivation, and emotion.* (pp. 1–45). Hoboken, NJ: John Wiley and Sons Inc.

Hineline, P. N. (1970). Negative reinforcement without shock reduction. *Journal of the Experimental Analysis of Behavior*, 14, 259–268.

Hogarth, L., Dickinson, A., Wright, A., Kouvaraki, M., and Duka, T. (2007). The role of drug expectancy in the control of human drug seeking. *Journal of Experimental Psychology: Animal Behavior Processes*, 33, 484–496.

Hommel, B. (1998). Automatic stimulus–response translation in dual-task performance. *Journal of Experimental Psychology: Human Perception and Performance*, 24, 1368–1384.

Hommel, B. (2004). Event files: Feature binding in and across perception and action. *Trends in Cognitive Sciences*, 8, 494–500.

Hommel, B. (2009). Action control according to TEC (theory of event coding). *Psychological Research,* 73, 512-526.

Hommel, B. (2013). Ideomotor action control: On the perceptual grounding of voluntary actions and agents. In: W. Prinz, M. Beisert and A. Herwig (Eds.), *Action science: Foundations of an emerging discipline* (pp. 113-136). Cambridge, MA: MIT Press.

Hommel, B., Müsseler, J., Aschersleben, G., and Prinz, W. (2001). The Theory of Event Coding (TEC): A framework for perception and action planning. *Behavioral and Brain Sciences*, 24, 849–937.

Horstmann, G. (2006). Latency and duration of the action interruption in surprise. *Cognition and Emotion*, 20, 242–273.

Hutchinson, R. R. (1983). The pain-aggression relationship and its expression in naturalistic settings. *Aggressive Behavior*, 9, 229–242.

Izard, C. E. (1977). *Human emotions.* New York: Plenum.

James, W. (1890). *The principles of psychology* (Vol. 2). New York: Holt.

Kiesel, A. and Hoffmann, J. (2004). Variable action effects: Response control by context-specific effect anticipations. *Psychological Research*, 68, 155–162.

Knutson, J. F., Fordyce, D. J. and Anderson, D. J. (1980). Escalation of irritable aggression: Control by consequences and antecedents. *Aggressive Behavior*, 6, 347–359.

Kornblum, S., Hasbroucq, T. and Osman, A. (1990). Dimensional overlap: Cognitive basis for stimulus-response compatibility--A model and taxonomy. *Psychological Review*, 97, 253–270.

Kühn, S., Elsner, B., Prinz, W., and Brass, M. (2009). Busy doing nothing: Evidence for nonaction—effect binding. *Psychonomic Bulletin and Review*, 16, 542–549.

Kunde, W. (2001). Response-effect compatibility in manual choice reaction tasks. *Journal of Experimental Psychology: Human Perception and Performance*, 27, 387–394.

Kunde, W., Elsner, K. and Kiesel, A. (2007). No anticipation–no action: the role of anticipation in action and perception. *Cognitive Processing*, 8, 71–78.

Kunde, W., Koch, I. and Hoffmann, J. (2004). Anticipated action effects affect the selection, initiation, and execution of actions. *The Quarterly Journal of Experimental Psychology Section A*, 57, 87–106.

Kuppens, P., Van Mechelen, I., Smits, D. J. M., and De Boeck, P. (2003). The appraisal basis of anger: Specificity, necessity and sufficiency of components. *Emotion*, 3(3), 254–269.

Landis, C. (1924). Studies of emotional reactions. I. A preliminary study of facial expression. *Journal of Experimental Psychology*, 7, 325–341.

Lang, P. J. (1995). The emotion probe: Studies of motivation and attention. *American Psychologist*, 50, 372–385.

Lavender, T. and Hommel, B. (2007). Affect and action: Towards an event-coding account. *Cognition and Emotion*, 21, 1270–1296.

Levenson, R. W. (1999). The intrapersonal functions of emotion. *Cognition and Emotion*, Functional accounts of emotion, 13, 481–504.

Loewenstein, G. (1996). Out of control: Visceral influences on behavior. *Organizational Behavior and Human Decision Processes*, 65, 272–292.

Manucia, G. K., Baumann, D. J. and Cialdini, R. B. (1984). Mood influences on helping: Direct effects or side effects? *Journal of Personality and Social Psychology*, 46, 357–364.

Mauss, I. B., Levenson, R. W., McCarter, L., Wilhelm, F. H., and Gross, J. J. (2005). The tie that binds? Coherence among emotion experience, behavior, and physiology. *Emotion*, 5, 175–190.

Mauss, I. B., Wilhelm, F. H. and Gross, J. J. (2004). Is there less to social anxiety than meets the eye? Emotion experience, expression, and bodily responding. *Cognition and Emotion*, 18, 631–662.

McDougall, W. (1926). *An introduction to social psychology* (Revised edition). Boston: John W. Luce and Co.

Meier, B. P. and Robinson, M. D. (2004). Why the sunny side is up: Associations between affect and vertical position. *Psychological Science*, 15, 243–247.

Melcher, T., Weidema, M., Eenshuistra, R. M., Hommel, B., and Gruber, O. (2008). The neural substrate of the ideomotor principle: An event-related fMRI analysis. *NeuroImage*, 39, 1274–1288.

Mellers, B. A. and McGraw, A. P. (2001). Anticipated emotions as guides to choice. *Current Directions in Psychological Science*, 10, 210–214.

Mellers, B., Schwartz, A. and Ritov, I. (1999). Emotion-based choice. *Journal of Experimental Psychology: General*, 128, 332–345.

Moltz, H. (1965). Contemporary instinct theory and the fixed action pattern. *Psychological Review*, 72, 27–47.

Müsseler, J. and Hommel, B. (1997). Blindness to response-compatible stimuli. *Journal of Experimental Psychology: Human Perception and Performance*, 23(3), 861–872.

Nattkemper, D., Ziessler, M. and Frensch, P. A. (2010). Binding in voluntary action control. *Neuroscience and Biobehavioral Reviews*, 34, 1092–1101.

Nelissen, R. M. A., Leliveld, M. C., van Dijk, E., and Zeelenberg, M. (2011). Fear and guilt in proposers: Using emotions to explain offers in ultimatum bargaining. *European Journal of Social Psychology*, 41, 78–85.

Nesse, R. M. (2004). Natural selection and the elusiveness of happiness. *Philosophical Transactions of the Royal Society of London. Series B: Biological Sciences*, 359, 1333–1347.

Neumann, R. and Strack, F. (2000). Approach and avoidance: The influence of proprioceptive and exteroceptive cues on encoding of affective information. *Journal of Personality and Social Psychology*, 79, 39–48.

Öhman, A. and Mineka, S. (2003). The malicious serpent: Snakes as a prototypical stimulus for an evolved module of fear. *Current Directions in Psychological Science*, 12, 5–9.

Ortony, A., Clore, G. L. and Collins, A. (1988). *The cognitive structure of emotions*. New York: Cambridge University Press.

Overmier, J. B., Bull, J. A. and Trapold, M. A. (1971). Discriminative cue properties of different fears and their role in response selection in dogs. *Journal of Comparative and Physiological Psychology*, 76(3), 478–482.

Panksepp, J. (2000). The riddle of laughter: Neural and psychoevolutionary underpinnings of joy. *Current Directions in Psychological Science*, 9, 183–186.

Pashler, H. (1994). Dual-task interference in simple tasks: Data and theory. *Psychological Bulletin*, 116, 220–244.

Plutchik, R. (2001). The nature of emotions. *American Scientist*, 89, 344-350.

Prinz, W. (1990). A common coding approach to perception and action. In: O. Neumann and W. Prinz (Eds.), *Relationships between perception and action: Current approaches* (pp. 167–201). New York: Springer-Verlag.

Prinz, W. (1992). Why don't we perceive our brain states? *European Journal of Cognitive Psychology*, 4, 1–20.

Prinz, W. (1997). Perception and action planning. *European Journal of Cognitive Psychology*, 9, 129–154.

Reisenzein, R., Bördgen, S., Holtbernd, T., and Matz, D. (2006). Evidence for strong dissociation between emotion and facial displays: The case of surprise. *Journal of Personality and Social Psychology*, 91, 295–315.

Rescorla, R. A. (1988). Pavlovian conditioning: It's not what you think it is. *American Psychologist*, 43, 151–160.

Rescorla, R. A. and Solomon, R. L. (1967). Two-process learning theory: Relationships between Pavlovian conditioning and instrumental learning. *Psychological Review*, 74, 151–182.

Rolls, E. T. (2005). *Emotion explained*. Oxford: Oxford University Press.

Roseman, I. J. (2008). Motivations and emotivations: Approach, avoidance, and other tendencies in motivated and emotional behavior. In: A. J. Elliot (Ed.), *Handbook of approach and avoidance motivation*. (pp. 343–366). New York: Psychology Press.

Russell, J. A. (2009). Emotion, core affect, and psychological construction. *Cognition and Emotion*, 23, 1259–1283.

Russell, J. A. and Barrett, L. F. (1999). Core affect, prototypical emotional episodes, and other things called emotion: Dissecting the elephant. *Journal of Personality and Social Psychology*, 76, 805–819.

Scherer, K. (1994). Emotion serves to decouple stimulus and response. In: P. Ekman and R. J. Davidson (Eds.), *The nature of emotion: Fundamental questions* (pp. 127-130). New York: Oxford University Press.

Scherer, K. R. (2009). The dynamic architecture of emotion: Evidence for the component process model. *Cognition and Emotion*, 23, 1307–1351.

Schwarz, N. (2012). Feelings-as-information theory. In: P. Van Lange, A. Kruglanski and E. Higgins (Eds.), *Handbook of theories of social psychology* (pp. 289-309). London: Sage Publications Ltd.

Schyns, P. G., Goldstone, R. L. and Thibaut, J. P. (1998). The development of features in object concepts. *The Behavioral and brain sciences*, 21, 1–17.

Sebastian, R. J. (1978). Immediate and delayed effects of victim suffering on the attacker's aggression. *Journal of Research in Personality*, 12, 312–328.

Shin, Y. K., Proctor, R. W. and Capaldi, E. J. (2010). A review of contemporary ideomotor theory. *Psychological Bulletin*, 136, 943–974.

Slovic, P., Finucane, M. L., Peters, E., and MacGregor, D. G. (2007). The affect heuristic. *European Journal of Operational Research*, 177, 1333–1352.

Stock, A. and Stock, C. (2004). A short history of ideo-motor action. *Psychological Research*, 68, 176–188.

Stoet, G. and Hommel, B. (1999). Action planning and the temporal binding of response codes. *Journal of Experimental Psychology: Human Perception and Performance*, 25, 1625–1640.

Strack, F. and Deutsch, R. (2004). Reflective and impulsive determinants of social behavior. *Personality and Social Psychology Review*, 8, 220–247.

Swart, C. and Berkowitz, L. (1976). Effects of a stimulus associated with a victim's pain on later aggression. *Journal of Personality and Social Psychology*, 33, 623–631.

Thomaschke, R., Hopkins, B. and Miall, R. C. (2012). The planning and control model (PCM) of motorvisual priming: Reconciling motorvisual impairment and facilitation effects. *Psychological Review*, 119, 388–407.

Thorndike, E. L. (1911). *Animal intelligence: Experimental studies.* New York: Macmillan.

Thorndike, E. L. (1913). Ideo-motor action. *Psychological Review*, 20, 91–106.

Tooby, J. and Cosmides, L. (1990). The past explains the present: Emotional adaptations and the structure of ancestral environments. *Ethology and Sociobiology*, 11, 375–424.

Trapold, M. A. and Overmier, J. B. (1972). The second learning process in instrumental learning. In: A. H. Black and W. F. Prokasy (Eds.), *Classical conditioning II: Current theory and research* (pp. 427-452). New York: Appleton-Century-Crofts.

Treisman, A. (1996). The binding problem. *Current Opinion in Neurobiology*, 6(2), 171–178.

Tudor, S. (2001). Accepting One's Punishment as Meaningful Suffering. *Law and Philosophy*, 20, 581–604.

Ulrich, R. E. and Azrin, N. H. (1962). Reflexive fighting in response to aversive stimulation. *Journal of the Experimental Analysis of Behavior*, 5, 511–520.

Urcuioli, P. J. (2005). Behavioral and associative effects of differential outcomes in discrimination learning. *Learning and Behavior*, 33, 1–21.

Van der Goten, K., Caessens, B., Lammertyn, J., De Voght, G., and Hommel, B. (2001). *Affective backward compatibility: Selecting „good" and „bad" primes the perception of congruent words.* Unpublished manuscript, University of Ghent, Belgium.

Van Hemel, P. E. (1972). Aggression as a reinforcer: Operant behavior in the mouse-killing rat. *Journal of the Experimental Analysis of Behavior*, 17, 237–245.

Verona, E. and Sullivan, E. A. (2008). Emotional catharsis and aggression revisited: Heart rate reduction following aggressive responding. *Emotion*, 8, 331–340.

Watson, D., Wiese, D., Vaidya, J., and Tellegen, A. (1999). The two general activation systems of affect: Structural findings, evolutionary considerations, and psychobiological evidence. *Journal of Personality and Social Psychology*, 76, 820–838.

Watter, S. and Logan, G. D. (2006). Parallel response selection in dual-task situations. *Perception and Psychophysics*, 68, 254–277.

Welford, A. T. (1952). The „psychological refractory period" and the timing of high-speed performance—a review and a theory. *British Journal of Psychology*, 43, 2–19.

AUTHOR NOTE: Preparation of this chapter was supported by a German Research Foundation Grant ED 201/2-1 to Andreas Eder.

In: Handbook of Psychology of Emotions
Editors: C. Mohiyeddini, M. Eysenck and S. Bauer

ISBN: 978-1-62808-053-7
© 2013 Nova Science Publishers, Inc.

Chapter 3

CULTURE AND CONCEPTUAL CONTENTS OF EMOTION

Stacey N. Doan
Boston University, Boston, USA

ABSTRACT

The extent to which culture shapes the experience of emotion has been a central concern for psychologists and anthropologists alike. The topic is potentially important not only for understanding the role that cultures play in giving meaning to inner experience and shaping psychological processes, but also for our conceptualization and understanding regarding the nature of emotion, itself. Perhaps, because of its complexities, researchers examining cross cultural differences and similarities in emotion has often focused on specific components of emotion (e.g. facial expressions, causes of emotion, emotion recognition) in their studies. Furthermore, the specific aspect of emotion that is considered often depends on the researchers' theoretical assumptions regarding what constitutes emotions. Emotions have either been seen as biological, a product of evolution or a social construction, a product of culture. The purpose of the following paper is to present how emotions have been conceptualized in the literature and how this conceptualization has influence the way in which researchers examine the role of culture. We then review the cross-cultural literature on emotion under the lens of the conceptual act model of emotion, and conclude with implications for research and clinical practice.

Keywords: Emotion, culture, ethnicity, social construction, conceptual act model of emotion

CULTURE AND CONCEPTUAL CONTENTS OF EMOTION

The extent to which culture shapes the experience of emotion has been a central concern for psychologists and anthropologists alike. The topic is potentially important not only for understanding the role that cultures play in giving meaning to inner experience and shaping psychological processes, but also for our conceptualization and understanding regarding the nature of emotion, itself. Perhaps, because of its complexities, researchers examining cross cultural differences and similarities in emotion has often focused on specific components of emotion (e.g. facial expressions, causes of emotion, emotion recognition) in their studies. Furthermore, the specific aspect of emotion that is considered often depends on the researchers' theoretical assumptions regarding what constitutes emotions. Emotions have either been seen as biological, a product of evolution or a social construction, a product of culture. The purpose of the following paper is to present how emotions have been conceptualized in the literature and how this conceptualization has influence the way in which researchers examine the role of culture. We then review the cross-cultural literature on emotion under the lens of the conceptual act model of emotion, and conclude with implications for research and clinical practice.

The Great Emotion Debate

The concept of emotion has flourished and thrived among psychologists, anthropologists, philosophers and linguists. Emotions affect memory, judgment and decision-making . It mediates cognitive and social processes, and plays a fundamental role in well - being and interpersonal functioning (Barrett, 2006). Interestingly, despite the popularity of "emotion" in a wide range of research arenas, there lacks a clear consensus on what the term emotion actually entails. In the past several decades, two contrasting theories have emerged. In one perspective, basic emotions theory, emotions are seen as a small number of discrete mechanism or set of mechanisms that have a biological basis and are genetically encoded (Ekman, 1984; Izard, 1992, 1994; Johnson-Laird and Oatley, 1992). Contrary to this perspective, the social constructivists argue that emotions are not natural kinds, but socially constituted syndromes whose very existence depends on social concepts (Averill, 1980; Harre, 1986; Lutz, 1988). Out of these two polar perspectives, two very distinct lines of research have emerged.

Basic Theory of Emotion

"The brain states and bodily responses are the fundamental facts of an emotion, and the conscious feelings are the frills that have added icing to the emotional cake," LeDoux, 1996, p. 302.

Heavily influenced by the work of Darwin (1872), psychologists supporting the basic view of emotions argue that across all human cultures, a small set of biologically hardwired emotions have evolved to deal with universal human predicaments such as achievements, failures and losses (Ekman, 1980, 1992, 1993; Izard, 1971, 1992; LeDoux, 1996). Emotions come with a set of responses which mobilized the individual to react in the most adaptive manner. Each emotion is associated with a specific set of brain states and bodily responses. According to differential emotions theory (DET), discrete basic emotions emerge in infancy according to a maturational timetable, and each emotion has a corresponding set of prototypic facial expression (Izard, 1992). Originally, in its strong form, DET argues that since infants, unlike adults and older children, do not modify their expressions and behavior due to social norms or display rules, there exists a one to one correspondence with expression and experience, such that if and only if an infant experience an emotion will the corresponding expression occur.

The basic theory of emotion in essence argues that emotions (at least those defined by western culture) are natural kinds, entities that exist outside of our perception, each emotion having their own unique neurological and physiological patterns. The tasks of researchers then are to discover the properties of these emotions, their mechanisms, and causal role in cognitions and behaviors. The role of culture then is somewhat constrained, relegated to influencing emotion through determining events and situations that may trigger emotions, and creating norms for display rules and behavioral responses. This line of study has focused on examining universality in emotion expression and recognition across cultures.

Culture and Emotion Recognition

Indubitably the driving force behind the study of emotional expressions, Paul Ekman and Carroll Izard conducted two separate programs of research in an attempt to see if facial expressions were indeed universally understood. In these early studies, photographs depicting individuals expressing a single emotion were presented to people from a range of literate and illiterate societies (Ekman, 1972; Ekman and Friesen, 1971; Izard, 1971). Among literate cultures agreement was above chance for six emotion words, anger, disgust, fear, happiness, sadness and surprise. With regards to the least literate culture, the Fore of New Guinea were able to identify most of the emotions with the exception that fear and surprised were often confused.

Further research elaborated on the idea that recognition was equated with expression. Ekman and Friesen (1971) collected data in two preliterate cultures. Participants were asked to express on their face the felt emotion elicited by simple stories. Pictures of these expressions were then presented to American subjects who were able to recognize the facial expressions (although once again fear and surprise were often confused). These results were further replicated when spontaneous emotion expressions were used (Ekman, 1972). Japanese and American participants were videotaped with a hidden camera while watching video clips eliciting extreme disgust. When the participants across the two cultures thought themselves to be alone the types and frequencies of their facial expressions were identical.

For Ekman and his colleagues cultural differences emerged in two aspects 1) antecedents of emotions and 2) display rules. The former focused on examining how cultures may influence the way in which different events may elicit different emotions. Display rules on the other hand, referred to the social norms and learned cultural scripts for emotion regulation and management. Evidence for the influence of culture on expression was provided by empirical research documenting that Japanese participants only responded differently from their American counterparts when the experimenter was in the room, suggesting that it is the presence of others that activated the display rules (Friesen, 1972 cited in Kupperbusch et al, 1999). Despite the similarity found across cultures, a recent meta-analysis have suggested that cultural values do seem to predict differences in emotion recognition and expression, despite small effect sizes after controlling for statistical and methodological artifacts (van Hemert, Poortinga, and van de Vijver, 2007). Furthermore, others have suggested an in-group bias for recognizing emotions (Elfenbein and Ambady, 2002), prompting the researchers to argue that while there was a universal basis for emotion, cultures add "accents", their own "grammar" and "vocabulary" (Marsh, Elfenbein, and Ambady, 2003).

From the basic emotions perspective, culture can highlight or deemphasize certain emotions, and influence the way in which emotions are suppressed or expressed. Emotions may be evoked by social interactions, but are not seen as an index of social relationship; they are reflective of internal physiological states (Lutz, 1988). Emotions are thus discrete, physiological entities that are universal, thus leaving culture with very little or no leeway to influence how it is experienced. Reacting to this perspective, the social constructivists present a contrasting view, they argue for the notion that emotions are not concrete, natural, elements, but cognitive constructions, which are heavily influenced by cultural values and systems, and that emotional expressions are merely the tip of the iceberg when it comes to understanding the experience of emotion.

Social Construction of Emotion

"Psychologists have always had to struggle against a persistent illusion that …there is something there, the emotion, of which the emotion word is a mere representation." (Harre, 1986. p. 4)

Proponents of the social constructivist approach argue that there is no one reality in which all humans simultaneously experience (Berger and Luckman, 1980). From this perspective, humans are not passive recipients, but active participants who construct their understanding of the world using the framework given by culture (Gergen, 1985). The process of socialization than is to teach children how to use the shared common framework to understand and interpret ambiguous events in the world.

With regards to emotions, social constructionists maintain that specific emotion words (e.g. anger, sadness, love) do not match onto anything more concrete then a vague, bodily felt perturbation. These felt sensations do not align to discrete emotions and can thus can be felt in many different emotions (e.g. James-Lange theory of emotion). Emotions are more complex than biological entities, instead they depend upon social concepts (Averill, 1980; Harre, 1986; Lazarus, Kanner, and Folkman, 1980; Lutz, 1988; Ratner, 1989, 2000; Shweder and Levine, 1984). Emotions, from this perspective, are seen as schemas, internal representations of social norms or rules that guide the interpretation of a situation, organization of a response and interpretation of a behavior. While some of these components may be biologically based, these biological bases are not themselves emotions, instead emotions are polythetic, where no single component is essential to the whole. Emotions in this case are seen as constituted syndromes, interrelated response elements (physiological changes, expressive reactions, responses, and subjective experiences), which have been primarily determined by social forces. According to Averill the relationship between emotions and culture is that "the emotions are viewed here as transitory social roles, or socially constituted syndromes. The social norms that help to constitute these syndromes are represented psychologically as cognitive structures or schemata. These structures -- like the grammar of a language -- provide the basis for the appraisal of stimuli, the organization of responses, and the monitoring of behavior." (Averill, 1980, p. 305-306). In sum, emotions for the social constructivists are not fixed, natural states, but instead are social products.

Evidence for the social constructivists view point has come from the work of anthropologists who have suggested that emotions are conceptualized differently, are not always felt the same way across cultures, and even that certain cultures and epochs "create" emotions that may not felt in another place or time. For example, one of the first social constructivists Finck (1887 as cited in Johnson, Laird and Oatley, 2000) argued that romantic love, a complex of feelings, attitudes and sentiments did not exist in classic times, instead romantic love is a unique construction that depends on currently cultural beliefs. This thesis has been defended by recent researchers as well (Beall and Sternberg, 1995). Some researchers have argued that grief is an experience of meaning making, an exchange between cultural models, individual mental models, and social interactions (Stroebe and Schut, 1999). In her work with the Utku, Briggs (1970) has argued that anger as we know it does not exist. Morsbach and Tyler (1986) argues that the Japanese have a unique feeling, *amae*, that does not seem to have an equivalent in other culture. Lutz's (1988) work with the Ifaluk argues for the notion that emotions are not conceptualized as internal states, but as historically and culturally shaped ways of understanding the self in the context of social relationships.

In sum, depending on the theoretical orientation of any given researcher and how they define what constitutes emotion, the research that follows often focuses on specific components of the emotion process. Some psychologists have made attempts to integrate the two polar stances, arguing that perhaps some emotions are basic, while more complex emotions (which are built from the basic emotions) are socially constructed (Oatley and Johnson, 2000). Others deemphasized the subjective experience and the corresponding physiological and expressive components, instead focusing very successfully on how different situations elicit certain emotions through the process of interpretation or evaluation (e.g. appraisal theory), and how culture may play a role in determining how any given situation is interpreted and given its emotional quality (Lazarus, 1991; Lazarus et al., 1980; Scherer, Shorr, and Johnstone, 2001). These different theories however have generally presupposed the idea that discrete emotions (at least some of them) exist as entities on some basic level.

The Conceptual Act Model of Emotion

However, as early as 1962, Schacter and Singer argued that emotions (e.g. sad, happy, fear) are the byproducts of contextually driven cognitive processes which interpret and give meaning to basic physiological processes, rather than distinct entities that exist outside of perception. This perspective has been further built upon and elaborated by a host of researchers, convinced that there is nothing fundamental about basic emotions (Barrett, 2006; Barrett, Mesquita, Ochsner, and Gross, 2007; Ortony and Turner, 1190; Russell, Bachorowski, and Fernandez-Dols, 2003). Recently, Barrett (2006, 2007) presented a perspective which argues that the basic building block of emotion is core affect, "a constantly changing stream of transient alterations in an organism's neurophysiological state that represents its immediate relationship to the flow of changing events" (Barrett, 2007, p. 377). Core affect is a basic affective state that is either positive or negative, dimensions which have been shown to be universal (Mesquita, 2003; Scherer, 1997).

Core affect can be influenced by physical factors (hormonal changes, pharmacological agents etc), but more often by appraisals, evaluations of the self in relation to an object or situation. It is important to note that appraisal in this context is not merely seen as a causal factor, but a description of a state, such that core affect influences and constrain the appraisal which in turn may influences core affect. It is important to note that appraisal in this context is thought of as descriptions rather than causes (Fridja, 1993; Frijda, 2007). Core affect than is categorized into specific emotions based on one's learned conceptual knowledge of emotion. Thus, for example, instead of an event (seeing a bear) triggering a specific fear mechanism leading to a host of physiological and behavioral changes, seeing a bear may through automatic or conscious evaluation lead to a general change in core affect (increase in arousal, and negative valence) which then is categorized as fear based on past experiences and one's conceptualizations of fear. This categorization process has often been compared to the way in which colors and phonemes are perceived and categorized.

The state of physiological and cognitive effects (e.g. attributions) are not necessarily conscious, and context plays a heavy role in how emotion is experienced (Barrett, 2006). Specific emotions (e.g. fear, anger) in this model do not exist outside of our mind. Instead, what we conceive of as emotions are emergent properties of core affect (valence) and categorization based on conceptual knowledge about emotion. This account acknowledges the variability in the phenomenological experience of individual emotions (i.e. fear when encountering a snake, fear while watching a scary movie etc.) as well as within individuals, and across cultures. "Variation in the conceptualizing an instance of core affect, whether because of language use, context, culture, or individual differences in prior experience, will produce variation in whether emotions are experienced, which emotions are experienced, and how they are experienced," (Barrett, Mesquita, Ochsner, and Gross, 2007, p. 387). The conceptual act model of emotion in essence puts culture back into the fore front of determining what constitutes emotions.

While core affect accounts for similarities in emotional experience across culture, it does not explain differences in emotion experience. Core affect interacts with and mutually constrains perceptions of situations. Our perceptions and categorization of any given affective event is influenced by our conceptual knowledge of emotion, which in turn is influenced by past experiences (memory), culture and language. Emotion is thus a constructed mental representation, which includes "current perceptions, cognitions, actions and core affect" (Barrett, Mesquita, Ochsner, and Gross, 2007, 386). From this perspective, there are no natural kinds of emotions, in fact the basic emotions are not necessarily universal, and cultural variation in emotion experiences are inherently determined by cultural differences in emotion concepts (Barrett, 2006). Barrett et al (2006) argued that mental representations of emotions hold at least three additional components, arousal content, relational content and situational content. In the following paper, I review the cross-cultural research in these arenas in order to answer the question, in what ways does culture influence the way we conceptualize emotion and hence shape our very experience of it?

Arousal and the Experience of Emotion

Arousal also coined activation, energy, tension and activity is the subjective feeling relating to energy. A person subjectively senses being somewhere on a continuum drowsiness and excitement. While originally conceptualized as part of core affect (Russell et al., 2003; Russell and Barrett, 1999), and directly driving the experience of emotion (Schacter and

Singer, 1962) debate still lingers with regards to the extent that arousal is integral to the experience of emotion since research suggests that most, but not all individuals conceptualize emotion as having an activation/deactivation component (Barrett, 2004). One possible explanation for this individual difference is that people vary in their awareness of somatovisceral changes, which in turn influence their experience of emotion (for a review see Weins, 2005). It seems individuals who are sensitive to their bodily states are more likely to focus on the activation/deactivation component when reporting on emotional experiences (Barrett, 2004; Barrett, Quigley, and Bliss-Moreau, 2004)

Studies examining the relationship among intereoceptive sensitivity and emotion have found that individuals categorized as good heartbeat perceivers (high on intereoceptive sensitivity) were more likely to rate emotional film clips ((Wiens, Mezzacappa, and Katkin, 2000)), and affective images (Pollatos, Kirsch, and Schandry, 2005) more arousing. In addition to self reported ratings, results from studies using EEG have found higher levels of activation in the P300 time window among better heartbeat perceivers (Herbert, Pollatos, and Schandry, 2007; Pollatos et al., 2005)It is important to note that these findings held true during presentation of affective stimuli and not neutral ones. Thus, it seems sensitivity to bodily states in the presence of an affective situation may influence how an emotion is experienced such that individuals, who are perceptive of their somatic states, are more likely to experience an emotion-laden situation as more arousing.

To the best of the author's knowledge no studies have directly examine intereoceptive awareness using the standard heart beat detection, across cultures. However, there is evidence to suggest that cultures may differ to the degree that emotions are experience on the dimension of activation and deactivation. In a study utilizing participants from 35 countries, researchers found that the participants' country of origin played an effect on participants' self reported feelings of ergotropic symptoms such as changes in breathing, heart beating faster, muscles tensing and trophotropic symptoms, such as lump in throat, and stomach troubles, during affective experiences (Scherer and Wallbott, 1994). Participants from Asian countries in particular seem to report lower levels of arousal. Scherer and his colleagues ask participants from Japan to recall situations in which they felt any of four emotions (happy, sad, fear/anxiety, and anger). Results from the study showed that the strongest intercultural difference was the fact that Japanese respondents only rarely indicated specific physiological responses or even unspecific sensations (pleasant or unpleasant arousal or rest states) in their description of varying emotion experience (Scherer, Matsumoto, Wallbott, and Kudoh, 1988).

Emotion perception studies provide further evidence for the idea that arousal may not be conceptualized as part of emotion in the same way (or to the same degree) across all cultures. In emotion perception studies, participants are presented with slides of faces displaying several different emotions, participants are then asked to rate how faces are perceived on levels of emotional arousal (Matsumoto, 1990, 1993; Matsumoto and Ekman, 1989). Overall, the results from several studies seem to suggest country differences in perceived arousal.

Cultural values may predict the extent to which feelings of activation and deactivation are perceived. Specifically, power distance, or the extent to which cultural values endorse a hierarchical or more democratic system of relating, may lead to the suppression of negative emotions as they may have a negative impact on the social order. In a cross-national study of emotion perception, Matsumoto (1989) found a negative correlation between the intensity ratings of negative facial expressions and the power distance ranking of each country. The results seem to suggest that individuals coming from a hierarchical society tend to perceive negative emotions as being less intense. Asian cultures, which tend to be high on power distance, seem to consistently rate emotional facial expressions as lower in intensity than Western cultures (Ekman et al, 1987). This difference seems to hold true regardless of race or gender of the poser being judged (Matsumoto, 1990; Matsumoto and Ekman, 1989).

African Americans, on the other hand, tend to perceive certain emotions such as fear and disgust more intensely than Asians and Caucasians (Matsumoto, 1993). These differences have been attributed to social and cultural experiences of different ethnic groups. Matsumoto posits for example, that the history of subjugation and discrimination of African Americans may lead them to attribute more intensity to emotional expressions such as anger. Asian cultures, on the other hand, tend to be collectivistic in nature, and collectivistic cultures are thought to suppress emotions and favor control in order to avoid confrontation. These cultural norms may lead to lower experiences of emotional arousal and lower judgments of intensity. Indeed, anthropological accounts suggest East Asians are seen as less emotional and less expressive, more inhibited in their expression of emotion (for a review see Russell and Yik, 1996). Within emotion perception studies however, it is unclear whether individuals from different cultures actually experience lower levels of physiological arousal or that physiological arousal is decoupled from the experience of emotion, such that these physiological reactions are not necessarily conceptualized as emotional. The latter seems more plausible since studies examining cross-cultural differences in emotion experience have consistently reported cross-cultural similarities in measures of physiological responding (Drummond and Quah, 2001; Levenson, Ekman, Heider, and Friesen, 1992; Tsai, Levenson, and Carstensen, 2000; Tsai, Levenson, and McCoy, 2006).

Physiological Responses

In one of the first studies to look at emotional differences in physiological response across cultures, researchers compared the emotional experience of Minankabua participants from West Sumatra, a culture that stresses the masking and controlling of strong negative emotional displays, to Western samples (Levenson et al., 1992). Using the Directed Facial Action Task, wherein participants were systematically instructed to structure their facial expressions to conform to standardize conceptions of happiness, sadness, disgust, fear, and anger, the researchers recorded seven measures of physiology -- heart rate, skin conductance, finger pulse transmission time, finger pulse amplitude, respiratory period and respiratory depth. These measures were compared to baseline measurements in which participants were told to maintain a neutral face unrelated to emotion. Participants were also asked to report any emotions, memories, or physical sensations that occur while making the facial configurations. In addition to rating the difficulty of making the expression, subjects was asked to rate the intensity of any emotion reported. Results from the study demonstrate that across most of the physiological measurements, the facial configurations resulted in similar patterns across both cultures, with the exception of respiratory depth.

Recent studies by Tsai and her colleagues have confirmed that with regards to physiology, there seems to be very little cultural differences. Using a standardized emotion-induction procedure, she examined potential ethnic differences in emotional responding in first generation Chinese Americans and European Americans, while viewing affective film clips. Physiological measures were drawn from cardiac, electrodermal, respiratory, and somatic systems. Participants also reported how they felt in response to the film clips, online, through continuous reports of positive and negative affect while watching the clips, as well as retrospectively rating how intensely they experienced specific emotions after all the films have been viewed. There were no significant culture differences across all physiological and experiential measures.

The lack of cross-cultural difference with regards to physiology has also been demonstrated in more ecologically valid tasks, such as discussing past conflict (Tsai, Levenson, McCoy, 2006), reliving past emotional experiences (Tsai, Chentsova-Dutton, Friere-Beabeau, and Przymus, 2002) and experiencing loud noises (Soto, Levenson, and Ebling, 2005). In sum, the evidence seems to suggest that objective measurements of physiology seem to differ very little across cultures (for a recent review see Levenson, Soto, and Pole, 2007). It is interesting to note however, that Tsai and her colleagues found significant physiological differences between Caucasians and Hmong Americans, a Southeast Asian group during a relived experience of love, (Tsai, Chentsova-dutoon, bebeay, Pryzymus, 2002) an emotion that is, on many aspects, considered a recent Western construction (Beall and Sternberg, 1995). This finding suggests that the consistency in which physiology is observed across cultures may be due to methodology at hand. Eliciting emotions which tend to have more similar conceptions across culture may elicit similar physiology. Future studies should examine emotions which vary dramatically across cultures, such as the concept of shame. Socially more complex emotions may possible reveal more interesting interactions regarding culture and physiology.

While physiological measurements seem to be similar across cultures, cultural differences abound with regards to behavioral and experiential facets. For example, the Mingankabua reported having more difficulty making the appropriate configurations, raters also judged the quality of the configurations as lower in quality, in addition the Mingankabua were less likely to report experiencing the target emotion. Recent studies have further demonstrated that while physiology remains relatively consistent, emotional behavior and self-reported experiences of emotional experience vary across cultures, (Soto et al., 2005; J. Tsai et al., 2002; J. Tsai and Levenson, 1997). European American couples have been shown to display more positive and less negative behavior during discussions of past conflict than Chinese Americans (Tsai, Levenson, McCoy, 2006), exhibiting more social smiles when reliving happy events than Hmong Americans, (Tsai, Chentsova-Dutton, Friere-Bebeau, and Przymus, 2002) and overall, reporting significantly more emotion (Soto, Levenson, Ebling, 2000).

How do we reconcile the idea that on an objective, physiological level individuals from different cultures seem to respond very similarly, yet report different emotional experiences? One possibility, if we were to endorse the universal's stance that emotions have their reality at the physiological level, with each emotion characterized by a specific physiological response, then we must concede that the self-reports are flawed, somehow inaccurate or that culture is influencing the way that people respond, but that the experience of emotion itself is essentially the same. However, research has shown that emotions do not seem to have distinct autonomic signatures (Cacioppo, Berntson, Larsen, Poehlmann, and Ito, 2000). In addition, to say that self-reported experience is somehow flawed takes away the authenticity of the individual experience. Intuitively, when some one says they do or do not "feel" a certain way, we necessarily must give credit to the individual's perspective since we must assume that the individual has direct access to their experience to the extent in which an outsider does not.

Being that "there is no known objective, external measure of the subjective, internal events that we experience as anger, sadness, fear, and so on. If we want to know whether people feel these emotions, we have to ask them," (Barrett, 2004, p. 266). Finally, there is no evidence to suggest that physiological arousal necessarily is interpreted and weighed the same way across culture. However, if we were to understand emotions as conceptual acts, a byproduct of categorization, we can necessarily argue that arousal/physiology may or may not be incorporated, or emphasized to varying degrees in the context of emotions across cultures.

What possible differences in emotional experience may account for differences in experiencing arousal? In addition to the cultural values, discussed above the differing levels of intensity reported across cultures may be due to cultural differences in emotional expression. Research has demonstrated that when individuals act in accordance with a certain emotion, they tend to feel that emotion even more (Duclos et al., 1989; Laird, 1974). For example, in two studies Laird (1974) find that individuals who were instructed to adopt facial expressions of certain emotions reported feeling the emotion more. In study 2, participants were instructed to smile or frown while watching cartoons; the group who was instructed to smile found the cartoons more humorous, suggesting that emotional behavior plays an important role in influencing emotion experience.

Certain cultures, specifically Eastern cultures have more rules restricting the open experience and expression of emotions (Argyle, Henderson, Bond, Lizuka, and Contarello, 1986). In addition whereas individuals from European American cultures believe that emotional expression is healthy and improves one's relationships with others, members of Chinese culture believe just the opposite(Potter, 1988; Russell and Yik, 1996; Zheng and Berry, 1991). In addition in many Asian cultures the open display of emotion in social interaction is considered undesirable, and expressing one's feelings overtly is regarded as an admission of weakness (Cheung, Lau, and Waldman, 1980). We would expect that individuals from these cultures may regulate their feelings, resulting in a less intense emotional experience. At an extreme end, cultures that de-emphasize emotion may also foster alexithymia that is difficulty in identifying one's feelings and distinguishing them from bodily sensations. Alexithymia have been found to be higher in Asians and Asian Americans as compared to their Western counterparts (Dion, 1996; Le, Berenbaum, and Baghavan, 2002). Cultural differences in alexithymia have been found to be partially mediated by differences in emotional socialization (Le, Berenbaum, and Raghavan, 2002). Specifically, Le and her colleagues found that based on participants' retrospective reports, parents who were more likely to avoid negative emotional situations and displayed less physical affection have children who reported more difficulty in identifying emotions. The notion that emotional socialization may play an important role in the understanding of emotion is further supported by research examining emotional understanding across cultures. Wang and her colleagues have demonstrated that Chinese children score lower on emotion understanding scores as well as showing slower progress in emotion knowledge over time (Wang, 2003; Wang, Hutt, Kulkofsky, McDermott, and Wei, 2006). This difference in emotional understanding is partially mediated by cultural differences in discussing internal states (Doan and Wang, under review). Finally, individuals from cultures that de-emphasize the experience of affect may be less likely to categorize any given event as affective. For example, researchers examining the daily emotion experiences between Japanese and American participants found that, Japanese respondents were more likely to indicate that that they did not experience any emotional content (Mesquita and Karasawa, 2002).

Cultures differ in the way that emotions are socialized and hence cognized, in addition to holding different prescriptions and values regarding emotion expression. These differences in cultural practices and values play a fundamental role in influencing the felt phenomenological experience of emotion. While physiology seems to differ little across cultures, how it is incorporated into our experience of emotion does not appear to be universal, suggesting that emotion contains a broad spectrum of components that may be emphasized or de-emphasized. In the next section, we look at how relational content, may influence not only the mental contents of felt emotion, but where it is localized as well.

Relational Self-construal and Its Effects on Emotion

"When it comes to the human mind-heart (*renxin*), one must locate it in human life, and human life is not so much realizable in the individual body (geti) as in the collective body (qunti) . . . otherwise known as society."
-Liang Shuming

Relational content within the context of an emotional experience represents an individuals' construal of the self in relation to others. Individualism and collectivism measures reflect the extent to which the self is defined in relation to others (Triandis, 1995). Among individualistic cultures (usually Western) the locus of behavior is thought to lie in attributes of the person, such as attitudes, preferences and motives (Choi, Nisbett, and Norenzayan, 1999), and the self is defined as an autonomous and unique individual. Collectivism on the other hand, sees the individual as an entity embedded within a larger social structure, and where behavior is explained by interactions between the individual and the society. Individualism and collectivism are viewed by some as two opposite ends of a continuum (Hofstede, 1980), while others see them as separate dimensions that can coexist (Triandis, 1995; Triandis and Gelfand, 1998).

Specifically, one way in which cultures have been differentiated on the basis of the self is variance on the dimension of independence-and-interdependence, a social orientation that refers to the degree to which individuals are encouraged to focus on themselves (i.e., independence) or on other people (i.e., interdependence) (Marcus and Kitayama, 1991). Although both independence and interdependence can co-exist in any one culture (Mascolo and Li, 2004), different cultures prized and valued different attributes (such as individuality versus communality), which in turn, influence how the self is socialized and hence constructed. This self-construal influences the emotion experience in a wide variety of ways, including the extent to which social and relational implications of emotional events are realized, the type of emotions experienced, engaged or disengaged, what constitutes good feelings and where emotion is localized, within the privacy of the self or in the context of interactions.

Social and Relational Components of Emotion

Since the status of relationships with others tend to be more central in interdependence than independent cultural contexts, appraisals, "psychological representations of emotional significance" (Clore and Ortony, 2000, p. 32), differ in their focus on whether the perceived impact of the situation is fundamental to individual or interdependent goals (Mesquita and Leu, 2007). In cultural models which focus on interdependent self concepts, the social and relational implications of emotional events are emphasized such that they constitute an important dimension of emotional experience (Kitayama, Marcus, and Kurokawa, 2000). For example, when presented with a standard list of emotion words and indigenous Japanese words, Kitayama, Markus and Negishi (1989, as cited in Marcus and Kitayama, 1991) found that Japanese students' ratings of similarity between words yielded a dimension of interpersonal engagement in addition to the standard dimensions of valence and arousal. Specifically, the emotion words range along socially disengaged emotions such as pride and anger, to socially engaged emotions such as shame, and feelings of connection with others. Emotions in a collectivistic context seem to be more grounded in social worth and shifts therein, as well as belonging to the self-other relationship rather than within the psyche of one individual (Mesquita, 2001).

To test the notion that individuals from Asian cultures would make interdependent themes more salient and thus facilitate socially engaging emotions whereas Americans would emphasized socially disengaging emotions in order to emphasize the individual self, researchers had Japanese and American college students briefly describe at the end of each day (for two weeks) the most affective episode of that day (Kitayama, Mesquita, and Karasawa, 2006). Furthermore, the respondents were asked to rate how strongly they experience each of 27 emotions. The list of emotion terms contained four types, which were defined by their valence (positive and negative), and social orientation (engaging and disengaging) in addition to emotion terms indicative of well being (calmness, elation), and negative well being (depression, boredom). For the analysis, the emotional situations were divided into positive and negative events. Results revealed that in a positive situation, the Japanese reported experiencing engaging emotions more strongly than disengaging emotions. In contrast, Americans reported experiencing more strongly disengaging emotions in positive situations. In negative situations, disengaging emotions were experienced more intensely than engaging emotions in both cultures, but the tendency was more pronounced for Americans. Furthermore, disengaging emotions were experienced more intensely by Americans than Japanese. In examining, how engaging or disengaging emotions relate to well being, regression analyses indicated that engaging positive emotions predicated happiness in both cultures. However, the effect of engaging emotions was stronger for the Japanese than the Americans. On the other hand, the effect of disengaging positive emotions was much stronger for Americans than for the Japanese. Similar results were found when in a second study participants from both cultures were asked to respond to a pre-selected, diverse set of emotional events.

In another experience sampling study, Japanese students residing the U.S., Japanese students in Japan and American students where given an emotion questionnaire four times a day (Mesquita and Karasawa, 2002). The questionnaire asked participants if they had experienced any emotion in the past three hours, and if so what the last emotion was and to describe the event that elicited the emotion, as well as rating how pleasant the events were. In addition, participants described how the events related to interdependent and independent concerns. Specifically, for independent concerns participants were asked the extent to which they felt the self in control, their ability to cope, and how harmful or beneficial the event was to their self esteem. Interdependent concerns focused on social distance, did the event bring the person closer or further away from people, whether they lost face, and whether or not they though the other person's behavior signal immoral or improper behavior. Results of their analyses suggested that interdependent concerns were more predictive of pleasantness than independent concerns in the Japanese groups. However, independent concerns were not more predictive of pleasantness than independent concerns for Americans.

Mesquita (2001) tested the idea that several components of emotions, specifically appraisal for connectedness of respect, perceived source of appraisal, action readiness, social sharing and belief changes would differ across indigenous Dutch group in the Netherlands, a group classified as individualist, African Suranmese and Turkish groups in the Netherlands, classified as collectivist (Hofstede, 1980). The author made the following arguments for the five different components of emotion: 1) *appraisal:* in collectivist cultures, the social worth of people are considered interconnected, thus a collectivistic individual who lose respect will think that his offender was acting intentionally 2) *perceived source of appraisal:* the meaning of emotional situations in collectivistic cultures should be seen as more obvious as compared to individualistic cultures, where emotions are considered subjective phenomenon 3) *action readiness:* the relational character of emotions from collectivistic cultures would result in more outward changes or action tendencies 4) social sharing: social sharing in collectivistic cultures would be more elaborate than just exchanging of information as is often found in individualistic cultures 4) *belief changes*: individuals from collectivistic cultures are more likely to let emotions change their beliefs.

Participants in the study were asked to report an instance from their past that reflected six emotion laden situations: success, positive attention, offense-by-non-intimate (acquaintance or stranger offended you), offense-by-intimate, intimate immoral behavior, self immoral behavior. Cultural differences regarding the five aspects of emotion experience were tested for three different combinations of the stimulus situations, positive (success and positive attention), offense situations (offense by non-intimate, and intimate other), and immoral situations (intimate immoral and self immoral). Results from the analyses revealed that relational concerns were indeed more relevant to collectivistic groups, that in situations of harm by another person, individuals from collectivistic groups were more likely to perceive higher levels of connectedness of respect. Furthermore, with respect to positive and offense situations, individuals from collectivistic cultures are more likely to think that the meaning of the emotional situation being appraised was more obvious (group consensus). Finally, the data seems to suggest that members from collectivistic cultures are like to interpret the meaning of emotional situations in terms of their social position and social status of their own group.

In sum, this line of research suggests large cultural difference in the way that emotions are understood. Across cultures, individuals from a more interdependent culture tend to appraise situations in terms of implications for the group, their happiness is more related to engaged emotions, in addition to seeing emotional situations as involving the group, and relationships with others rather than emotions as a personal internal state.

Locating Emotion

In English, the term emotion represents a psychological state, while as the previous section has suggested, bodily sensations play an important role, physiological sensations, and affective situations are subsumed under feelings. Emotions by their very nature are considered private, internal states, and emotion words label and reference these internal states ((Davitz, 1969). However, these conceptions of emotions are emerge from within American ethnopsychological themes of what it means to be a person (Levine, 1980; Lutz, 1982). This notion of emotion belonging within the psyche of the individual is not universal across cultures. Indeed, for some cultures inner experience play less of an important role in defining feelings as compared to interactionally situated experiences.

In their research on the Minangkabau, Levenson and his colleagues found a reduction in emotional experience produced by the Directed Facial Action task. One possible explanation for this was that "for Minangkabua, the state produced by the Directed Facial Action task would be much less likely to be labeled as emotion because, for them, the task is missing the critical element for emotional experience as defined by their culture, namely, the meaningful involvement of another person," (Levenson et al., 1992, p. 985). For Americans, the facial configuration and subsequent ANS activation may be enough to characterize the experience as emotion, however for the Minangkabua, since the experience lacked any meaningful interaction, the experience is not labeled as emotional. Indeed anthropological accounts have suggested that the internal experience of emotion so evident in Western culture does not necessarily hold true across cultures. In discussing the Minangkabua, Heider (1991) argues that the emphasis of emotion is focused on the implications of emotion for interpersonal interactions and relationships rather than internal feelings.

Anthropological accounts provide further evidence. For example, research on the Ifaluk of Micronesia showed that emotion words were defined not through introspection of internal states but referring to external circumstances (Lutz, 1988). The Ifaluk have values that are interdependent in nature. People are expected to share labor and food, and even children. The society is hierarchical in nature, thus awareness of one's place in relation to another is fundamental. Lutz argues that this way of relating structures the way in which emotional words are cognitively organized. She presented the Ifaluk with emotion words and asked them to sort them into clusters (Lutz, 1982). Participants were then asked to justify their classifications. Hierarchical clustering analyses revealed that the most common aspect on which words were sorted and defined was situation. In addition, multidimensional scaling procedures revealed that the emotion words vary on two levels, valence – specifically the pleasant or unpleasantness of the situation for the self and dominance, the strength of the self in relation to the other. Lutz argues that the focus of perception on the external renders emotions as public and social products, differing dramatically from the Western perception of emotions which focuses on internal experience (comfort/discomfort, as well as physiological arousal or activation).

This emphasis of emotion being characterized as part of the external rather than the internal is also described among the Chinese. Sun (1991) argues that personality is less psychologized in Chinese culture as compared to the West, "what would be personal and emotional problems for Westerners are either somatized into physical ailments or externalized into interpersonal or moral issues by the Chinese... Chinese are prone to re-describe what would be, in Western narratives, 'psychological' phenomena in terms of shame, social morality, social roles, and interpersonal relationship" (Sun, 1991, p. 6). In contrast to Westerners conceptualization of depression as intrapsychic, among the Chinese psychological problems are often describe with bodily symptoms, and in terms of social morality, roles and interpersonal relationships.

Somatic complaints, often described as altered expressions of emotional distress (Kirmayer and Young, 1998; Kleinman, 1987), are in fact, higher among individuals from Asians as compared to their Western counterparts (Hong, Lee, and Lorenzo, 1995; Kleinman and Kleinman, 1985). Similarly, Levy (1973) has reported that the Tahitaians treat sadness, longing, and depression not as emotion but something closer to a physical illness.

Studies looking at the way in which people use language to describe emotions in a variety of cultures, have found supporting evidence for the idea that cultures may differ regarding how emotion is conceptualized and where it is localized (Kovesces, 2003; Pavlenko, 2002; J. Tsai, Simeonova, and Watanabe, 2004; Ye, 2002). Tsai and her colleagues conducted two studies to examine whether it was cultural conceptions of emotion or linguistic variation that was driving the cultural difference. In the first study, using the Adult Attachment Interview, researchers interviewed in participants from three different groups (European American, more acculturated Chinese Americans, and less acculturated Chinese Americans) about their early family situation, relationships with parents, and instances of rejection and loss. The researchers summed the amount of times the participants referred to social words (e.g. friend, mother, give), positive emotion words (e.g. happy, fun, bright), negative emotion words (e.g. angry, sad) and somatic words, which include physical states and functions (e.g. ache, sleep) as well as sensory and perceptual processes (e.g. saw, sound). Results from this first study demonstrated that less acculturated Chinese Americans used significantly more somatic and social words than European Americans. There were no differences with regards to reference to positive and negative emotion words. The researchers concluded that since all the interviews were conducted in English, the cultural differences found could not be attributed to linguistic variation. In study 2, a more naturalistic emotion eliciting task was used. European American and Chinese American couples were asked to discuss two events 1) what happened to them during the day and 2) an area of conflict in their relationship. Results were consistent with the first study; less acculturated Chinese Americans used more somatic and social words than European Americans. In addition, group differences were also more pronounced during discussion of the emotional task as compared to the neutral one.

These results suggested that in certain cultures, emotion is not necessarily seen as existing within the psyche of the individual, but in the context of the self (the body) situated in social interactions. In sum, culture plays a large role in influencing the specific aspects of how bodily sensations and social interactions are incorporated into emotional experience. When the individual, and hence his/her preferences, attitudes, ideas are subsumed under the larger collective identity, the private self becomes hypocognized, and the social self more fundamental in giving meaning to affective experiences. In collectivistic cultures, emotions are not seen as private, internal experiences, but relational, dyadic social experiences. From this perspective, emotions as internal states are less meaningful as compared to emotions as index of the self in relation to other.

Situational Contents

Mental representations of emotions in addition to physiological experiences and relational representations include meaningful perceptions of a situation, particularly as it relates to core affective feelings (Barrett, Mesquita, Ocshner and Gross, 2007). This section focuses on components of emotional experience that most directly relates the individual with his or her context, particularly how a situation is evaluated and to the extent that the situation, including the presence of other people is taken into account.

The events that elicit emotions are not universal across cultures, due to the cultural meaning that is brought to bear upon the situation. In an early study, Scherer and his colleagues ask Americans, Europeans and Japanese to describe the situations in which they experienced anger, sadness, happiness and fear. Although expecting high similarity across cultural groups, they actually found significant cultural differences especially with the Japanese. Joy was associated with births, bodily pleasures and achievement more so for the Europeans and Americans than for the Japanese. Death and separation were more associated with sadness for Americans while the Japanese were more saddened by relationship problems. Fear was more associated with relationships for the Japanese than for Americans or Europeans. With regards to anger, Europeans experienced most anger within close relationships, while the Japanese were more likely to experience anger among strangers. Injustice also caused anger more often among European Americans as compared to the Japanese. These differences are attributed to the way in which culture shapes experience and meaning-making. For example, the authors argued that since the Japanese have differing ideas of death, and hierarchy, thus would invariably feel different when confronted with these situations.

The extent to which affective experiences are more context dependent was examined using an experience sampling (Oishi, Diener, Scollon, and Biswas-Diener, 2004). In this study, American, Hispanic, Japanese and Indian college students were administered a mood questionnaire consisting of positive and negative scales. In addition to mood, participants also reported whether they were alone, with a friend, with a classmate/coworker, with a romantic partner, stranger or with family. Cross-situational consistency was found across all four cultures. However, affect was more dependent on the type of situation among the Japanese and Hispanics than Americans. Specifically, the mean level of positive affect experienced in a family context was not correlated with positive affect in a number of other situations. There was more cross-cultural consistency with regards to negative affect, Hispanics were the only group to report different mean levels of affect in family contexts than for other situations. In addition, the standard deviation of mean positive and negative affect across all six situations was computed. Results indicated that there was greater variation for positive and negative events. Furthermore, the standard deviation was lager for in interdependent than in independent cultures providing further support of the idea that the specific situations seems more important in determining affective experiences in interdependent cultures.

How the interpretation of facial expressions may be influenced by context also seem to differ across cultures. . Reflecting individualistic values, Westerners tend to think of emotional expressions as a manifestation of the internal state of the individual. The face in particular is important -- most Americans agree that emotion can be infer from an individual's face (Carroll and Russell, 1996). However, Asians on the other hand conceptualize the self in terms of interpersonal relationships. Emotional expressions should be suppressed or adapted to be harmonious with that of the group (Rothbaum, Pott, Azuma, Miyake, and Weisz, 2000). Because of this difference, Masuda and his colleagues argue that the Japanese would be more likely to consider the context (other people's expression) when judging the expression of a central figure. They presented cartoon images of a central figure portraying happiness, sadness, or anger, at two levels, moderate or intense (Masuda et al., 2008). In the background were four other faces which either showed the same expression, a different expression (all at moderate levels) or a neutral expression. Japanese and American participants were presented with the images and asked to rate the emotion on a 10 point scale. In addition, a recognition memory test was administered in which participants were exposed to old and new images. In the new images, the emotions displayed by the central and peripheral figures were different or the figures were wearing different clothes. Results of their data demonstrated that the differences between matched and unmatched images were significantly higher for the Japanese than for Americans across all three emotions. In addition, Japanese participants were more accurate in identifying the new images when the peripheral facial expressions were changed. There were no cultural differences in recognition memory for the original images, images where the central figure's expressions were changed, or images where the clothes were changed. These results suggest that the cultural difference was not just due to the Japanese participants overall sensitivity to context. In addition, measurements of eye movement showed that the Japanese spent less time looking at the main character, and shifted from the main character to the background quicker than Americans. In sum, results suggested that for the Japanese emotional expressions are understood not as an individual expression of an internal state, but as a construction that is inter-related between self and other such that individual feelings cannot be separated from the feelings of the social group.

Some Concluding Thoughts

The complexity of the concept of emotion and lack of definition within psychological and anthropological research has somewhat muddled the way in which we understand its universality or cultural specificity. Indeed, the different theoretical perspectives of researchers in the field, have somewhat constrained how they have attempted to study culture and its effects or lack thereof on the experience of emotion. Construing emotion as biologically fixed modules relegates the role of culture to a minor moderator of emotional expression. On the other hand, seeing emotion as a complex cluster of cognitions and social constructed roles focuses the role of culture in determining the very experience of emotion.

In our review of the research, we have focused heavily on how the cognitive contents of affective experiences differ dramatically by culture. Specifically, using the conceptual act model of emotion as a guiding framework we found cultural differences in arousal, relational and situational contents across cultures. While we do not deny that there exists a sense of universality with regards to certain aspects of emotion, after all humans across all cultures share very similar experiences of sadness, and joy, we do propose that it seems most conservative and parsimonious to accept that while concrete aspects of emotion, specifically core affect, negative or positive, is the basis for any emotion experience, it is not enough to fully describe the rich interplay of cognitions, physiology and feelings that become involved when individuals have emotional episodes.

From this perspective, we can naturally see that culture, a powerful collection of loosely organize meanings, socializations practices and values, which shape individuals beliefs and values, also plays a fundamental role in how they experience the world. We believe that understanding how emotion is experienced differentially across cultures is important for both clinicians and researchers alike.

REFERENCES

Argyle, M., Henderson, M., Bond, M., Lizuka, Y., and Contarello, A. (1986). Cross-cultural variations in relationship rules. *International Journal of of Psychology, 21*, 287-315.

Averill, J. (1980). A constructivist view of emotion. In R. Plutchik and H. Kellerman (Eds.), *Emotion theory research and experience*. New York: Academic Press.

Barrett, L. (2004). Feelings or words? Understanding the content in self-reported ratings of experienced emotion. *Journal of Personality and Social Psychology, 87*(2), 266-281.

Barrett, L. (2006). Are emotions natural kinds? *Perspectives on psychological science., 1*(1), 28-58.

Barrett, L., Mesquita, B., Ochsner, K. N., and Gross, J. J. (2007). The experience of emotion. *Annual Review of Psychology, 58*, 373-403.

Barrett, L., Quigley, K., and Bliss-Moreau, E. A., K. (2004). Arousal focus and interoceptive sensitivity. *Journal of Personality and Social Psychology, 87*, 684-697.

Beall, A., and Sternberg, R. (1995). The social construction of love. *Journal of Social and Personal Relationships, 12*(3), 417-438.

Berger, P. L., and Luckman, T. (1980). *The social construction of reality*. New York: Irvington.

Briggs, J. (1970). *Never in Anger*. Cambridge, MA: Harvard University Press.

Carroll, J., and Russell, J. A. (1996). Do facial expressions signal specific emotions? Judging emotion from the face in context. *Journal of Personality and Social Psychology, 70*(2), 205-218.

Cheung, F., Lau, B., and Waldman, E. (1980). Somatization among Chinese depressives in general practice. *International Journal of Psychiatry and Medicine, 10*(4), 361-374.

Choi, I., Nisbett, R. E., and Norenzayan, A. (1999). Causal attribution across cultures: Variation and universality. *Psychological Bulletin, 125*, 47-63.

Clore, G., and Ortony, A. (2000). Cognition in emotion: Always, sometimes, or never. In L. Nadel, R. Lane. and G. L. Ahern (Eds.), *The cognitive neuroscience of emotion*. New York: Oxford University Press.

Davitz, J. (1969). *The language of emotion*. London: Academic Press.

Dion, K. L. (1996). Ethnolinguistic correlates of alexithymia: Toward a cultural perspective. *Journal of Psychosomatic Research, 41*, 531-539.

Drummond, P. D., and Quah, S. H. (2001). The effect of expressing anger on cardiovascular reactivity and facial blood flow in Chinese and Caucasians. *Psychophysiology, 38*(2), 190-196.

Duclos, S., Laird, J., Schneider, E., Sexter, M., Stern, L., and Van Lighten, O. (1989). Emotion-Specific Effects of Facial Expressions and Postures on Emotional Experience. *Journal of Personality and Social Psychology, 57*(1), 100-108.

Ekman, P. (1972). Universal and cultural differences in facial expressions of emotions. In J. Cole (Ed.), *Nebraska Symposium of Motivation*. Lincoln, NE: University of Nebraska Press.

Ekman, P. (1980). *The Face of Man*. New York: Garland.

Ekman, P. (1984). Expression and the nature of emotion. In K. Scherer and P. Ekman (Eds.), *Approaches to emotion* (pp. 319-344). New Jersey: Lawerence Erlbaum.

Ekman, P. (1992). An argument for basic emotions. *Cognition and emotion, 6*, 169-200.

Ekman, P. (1993). Facial expression of emotion. *American Psychologist, 48*, 384-392.

Ekman, P., and Friesen, W. V. (1971). Constants across cultures in the face and emotion. *Journal of Personality and Social Psychology, 17*(2), 124-129.

Elfenbein, H., and Ambady, N. (2002). On the universality and cultural specificity of emotion recognition: A meta-analysis. *Psychological Bulletin*(128), 203-235.

Fridja, N. (1993). The place of appraisal in emotion. *Cognition and emotion, 7*(3), 357-387.

Frijda, N. (2007). The Laws of Emotion. In. Mahwah, NJ: Laurence Erlbaum Associates.

Gergen, K. J. (1985). The social constructionist movement in modern psychology. *American Psychologist, 40*(3), 266-275.

Harre, R. (1986). *The social construction of emotions*. New York: Basil Blackwell.

Heider, K. (1991). *Landsacapes of emotion. Three cultures of emotion in Indonesia.* Cambridge, England: Cambridge University Press.

Herbert, B., Pollatos, O., and Schandry, R. (2007). Interoceptive sensitivity and emotion processing: An EEG study. *International Journal of Psychophysiology, 65*(3), 214-227.

Hofstede, G. (1980). *Culture's consequences: International differences in work related values.* Newbury Park, CA: Sage.

Hong, G., Lee, B., and Lorenzo, M. (1995). Somatizatin in Chinese American clients: Implications for psychotherapeautic services. *Journal of Contemporary Psychotherapy, 25*(2), 105-118.

Izard, C. (1971). *The face of emotion.* New York: Appleton-Century-Crofts.

Izard, C. (1992). Basic emotions, relations among emotions, and emotion-cognition relations. *Psychological Review, 100*, 561-565.

Izard, C. (1994). Innate and universal facial expressions: Evidence from developmental and cross-cultural research. *Psychological Bulletin, 115*, 288-299.

Johnson-Laird, P., and Oatley, K. (1992). Basic emotions, rationality, and folk theory. *Cognition and emotion, 6*, 201-223.

Kirmayer, L., and Young, A. (1998). Culture and somatization: Clinical, epidemological and ethnographic perspectives. *Psychosomatic Medicine, 60*, 420-430.

Kitayama, S., Marcus, H., and Kurokawa, M. (2000). Culture, emotion, and well being: Good feelings in Japan and the United States. *Cognition and emotion, 14*, 93-124.

Kitayama, S., Mesquita, B., and Karasawa, M. (2006). Cultural affordances and emotional experience: socially engaging and disengaging emotions in Japan and the United States. *Journal of Personality and Social Psychology, 91*(5).

Kleinman, A. (1987). Anthropology and psychiatry: The role of culture in cross-cultural research on illness. *British Journal of Psychiatry, 151*, 447-454.

Kleinman, A., and Kleinman, J. (1985). Somatization: the interconnections in chinese society amogn culture, depressive experiences and the meanings of pain. . In A. Kleinman and B. Good (Eds.), *Studies in the anthropology and cross-cultural psychiatry of affect and disorder.* Berkeley, CA: University of California Press.

Kovesces, Z. (2003). *Metaphor and emotion.* Cambridge: Cambridge University Press.

Laird, J. (1974). Self-attribution of emotion: The effects of expressive behavior on the quality of emotional experience. *Journal of Personality and Social Psychology, 29*(4), 475-486.

Lazarus, R. S. (1991). *Emotion and adaptation.* New York: Oxford University Press.

Lazarus, R. S., Kanner, A., and Folkman, S. (1980). Emotions: a cognitive-phenomenological analysis. In R. Plutchik and H. Kellerman (Eds.), *Theroies of emotion* (pp. 189-217). New York: Academic.

Le, H., Berenbaum, H., and Baghavan, C. (2002). Culture and alexithymia: Mean levels, correlates and the role of parental socialization of emotions. *Emotion, 2*(4), 341-360.

LeDoux, J. (1996). *The emotional brain.* New York: Simon and Schuster.

Levenson, R., Ekman, P., Heider, K., and Friesen, W. V. (1992). Emotion and autonomic nervous system activity in the Minangkabau of West Sumatra. *Journal of Personality and Social Psychology, 62*(6), 972-988.

Levenson, R., Soto, J., and Pole, N. (2007). Emotion, biology, and culture. In S. Kitayama and D. Cohen (Eds.), *Handbook of Cultural Psychology.* New York: Guilford Press.

Levine, R. (1980). Anthropology and child development. In C. M. Super and S. Harkness (Eds.), *Anthropological perspectives in child development.* (pp. 71-86). San Francisco: Jossey Bass.

Levy, R. (1973). *Tahitians: mind and experience in the Society Islands.* Chicago: University of Chicago Press.

Lutz, C. (1982). The domain of emotion words on Ifaluk. *American Ethnologist, 9*(1), 113-128.

Lutz, C. (1988). *Unnatural emotions: everyday sentiments on a micronesian attol and their challenge to western theory.* Chicago: University of Chicago Press.

Marcus, H., and Kitayama, S. (1991). Culture and self: implications for cognition, emotion, and motivation. *Psychological Review, 98,* 224-253.

Marsh, A., Elfenbein, H., and Ambady, N. (2003). Nonverbal "accents": Cultural difference sin faical expressions of emotion. *Psychological Science, 14,* 373-376.

Mascolo, M. F., and Li, J. (2004). Culture and developing selves: Beyond dichotomization. . In W. Damon (Ed.), *New Directions in Child and Adolescent Development Series.* San Francisco, CA: Josey-Bass.

Masuda, T., Ellsworth, P. C., Mesquita, B., Leu, J., Tranida, S., and van de Veerdonk, E. (2008). Placing the face in context: Cultural differences in the perception of facial emotion. *Journal of Personality and Social Psychology, 94,* 365-381.

Matsumoto, D. (1990). Cultural similarities and differences in display rules. *Motivation and Emotion, 14,* 192-214.

Matsumoto, D. (1993). Ethnic differences in affect intensity, emotion judgments, display rule attituddse, and self-reported emotional expression in an American sample. *Motivation and emotion, 17*(2), 107-123.

Matsumoto, D., and Ekman, P. (1989). American-Japanese cultural differences in intensity ratings of facial expressions of emotion. *Motivation and emotion, 13,* 143-157.

Mesquita, B. (2001). Emotions in collectivist and individualist contexts. *Journal of Personality and Social Psychology, 80*(1), 68-74.

Mesquita, B. (2003). Cultural differences in emotions: A context for interpreting emotional disturbances. *Behaviour Research and Therapy, 47*(7), 777-793.

Mesquita, B., and Karasawa, M. (2002). Different emotional lives. *Cognition and emotion, 16*(1), 127-141.

Mesquita, B., and Leu, J. (2007). The cultural psychology of emotion. In S. Kitayama and D. Cohen (Eds.), *The handbook of cultural psychology.* New York: Guilford Press.

Morsbach, H., and Tyler, W. (1986). A Japanese emotion: Amae. In R. Harre (Ed.), *The Social Construction of Emotion.* Oxford: University Press.

Oishi, S., Diener, E., Scollon, C., and Biswas-Diener. (2004). Cross-situational consistency of affective experiences across cultures. *Journal of Personality and Social Psychology, 86*(3), 460-472.

Ortony, A., and Turner, T. J. (1190). What's basic about basic emotions? *Psychological Review, 97*, 315-331.

Pavlenko, A. (2002). Emotions and the body in Russian and English. *Pragmatics and Cognition, 10*(1-2), 201-236.

Pollatos, O., Kirsch, W., and Schandry, R. (2005). On the relationship between interoceptive awareness, emotional experience, and brain processes. *Cognitive brain research, 25*, 948-962.

Potter, S. (1988). The cultural construction of emotion in rural Chinese social life. *Ethos, 16*(2), 181-208.

Ratner, C. (1989). A social constructionist critique of naturalistic theories of emotions. *Journal of Mind and Behavior, 10*, 361-372.

Ratner, C. (2000). A cultural psychological analysis of emotions. *Culture and Psychology, 6*, 5-39.

Rothbaum, F., Pott, M., Azuma, H., Miyake, K., and Weisz, J. (2000). The development of close relationships in Japan and the United States: Paths of symbiotic harmony and generative tension. *Child Development, 71*(5), 1121-1142.

Russell, J. A., Bachorowski, J. A., and Fernandez-Dols, J. M. (2003). Facial and vocal expressions of emotion. *Annual Review of Psychology, 54*, 329-349.

Russell, J. A., and Barrett, L. (1999). Core affect, prototypical emotional episdoes, and other things called emotion: Dissecting the elephant. *Journal of Personality and Social Psychology, 76*, 805-819.

Russell, J. A., and Yik, M. (1996). Emotions among the Chinese. In M. H. Bond (Ed.), *The handbook of Chinese psychology* (pp. 166-188). Hong Kong: Oxford University Press.

Scherer, K. (1997). Profiles of emotion-antecedent appraisal. *Cognition and emotion, 11*(2), 113-150.

Scherer, K., Matsumoto, D., Wallbott, H., and Kudoh, T. (1988). Emotional experience in cultural context. A comparison between Europe, Japan and the United States. In K. R. Scherer (Ed.), *Facets of emotion, recent research* (pp. 5-30). Hillsdale, NJ: Lawrence Earlbaum.

Scherer, K., Shorr, A., and Johnstone, T. (2001). *Appraisal processes in emotion: theory, methods, research.* Canary, NC: Oxford University Press.

Scherer, K., and Wallbott, H. (1994). Evidence for universality and cultural variation of differential response patterning. *Journal of Personality and Social Psychology, 66*(2), 310-328.

Shweder, R., and Levine, R. (1984). *Culture theory: Essays on mind, self, and emotion.* New York: Cambridge University Press.

Soto, J., Levenson, R., and Ebling, R. (2005). Cultures of moderation and expression: Emotional experience, behavior, and physiology in Chinese Americans and Mexcan Americans. *Emotion, 5*(2), 154-165.

Stroebe, M., and Schut, H. (1999). The dual process model of coping with bereavement: Rationale and description. *Death Studies, 23*(3), 197-224.

Sun, L. (1991). Contemporary Chinese culture: Structure and emotionality. *The Australian Journal of Chinese Affairs, 26*, 1-141.

Triandis, H. C. (1995). *Individualism and collectivism*. Boulder, CO: Westview Press.

Triandis, H. C., and Gelfand, M. J. (1998). Converging measurement of horizontal and vertical individualism and collectivism. *Journal of Personality and Social Psychology, 74*(1), 118-128.

Tsai, J., Chentsova-Dutton, U., Friere-Beabeau, L., and Przymus, D. (2002). Emotional expression and physiology in European Americans and Hmong Americans. *Emotion, 2*(4), 380-397.

Tsai, J., and Levenson, R. (1997). Cultural influences on emotional responding: Chinese American and European American dating couples during interpersonal conflict. *Journal of Cross-cultural Psychology, 28*, 600-625.

Tsai, J., Levenson, R., and Carstensen, L. (2000). Autonomic, expressive and subjective responses to emotional films in younger and older adults of European American and Chinese descent. *Psychology and Aging, 15*, 684-693.

Tsai, J., Levenson, R., and McCoy, K. (2006). Cultural and temperamental variation in emotional response. *Emotion, 6*(3), 484-497.

Tsai, J., Simeonova, D., and Watanabe, J. (2004). Somatic and social: Chinese Americans talk about emotion. *Personality and Social Psychology Bulletin, 30*(30), 1226-1238.

van Hemert, D., Poortinga, Y. H., and van de Vijver, F. (2007). Emotion and culture: A meta-analysis. *Cognition and emotion, 21*(5), 913-943.

Wang, Q. (2003). Emotion situation knowledge in American and Chinese preschool children and adults. *Cognition and emotion, 17*, 725-746.

Wang, Q., Hutt, R., Kulkofsky, S., McDermott, M., and Wei, R. (2006). Emotion situation knowledg eand autobiographical memory in Chinese, immigrant Chinese and European American 3-year olds. *Journal of Cognition and Development, 7*(1), 95-118.

Weins, S. (2005). Interoception and emotional experience. *Current opinion in neurology, 18*, 442-447.

Wiens, S., Mezzacappa, E., and Katkin, E. (2000). Heartbeat detection and the experience of emotion. *Cognition and emotion, 14*, 417-427.

Ye, Z. (2002). Different modes of describing emotions in Chinese. *Pragmatics and Cognition, 10*(1), 307-339.

Zheng, Z., and Berry, J. (1991). Psychological adaptations of Chinese Sojouners in Canada. *International Journal of Psychology, 26*, 451-470.

Part II: Emotions in Developmental and Educational Settings

In: Handbook of Psychology of Emotions
Editors: C. Mohiyeddini, M. Eysenck and S. Bauer

ISBN: 978-1-62808-053-7
© 2013 Nova Science Publishers, Inc.

Chapter 4

RESEARCH ON EMOTIONS IN DEVELOPMENTAL PSYCHOLOGY CONTEXTS: HOT TOPICS, TRENDS, AND NEGLECTED RESEARCH DOMAINS

Günter Krampen[*] *and Lisa Trierweiler*[†]
Leibniz-Institute for Psychology Information (ZPID),
University of Trier, Germany

ABSTRACT

This chapter presents bibliometric analyses of the representation of emotions in psychology research from a developmental perspective across a four-decade time span and across developmental age groups. After an overview on the frequency of the topic of emotions in developmental psychology research in general, we focus on the overrepresentation (popularity) and underrepresentation (neglect/ disregard) of certain emotions in developmental psychology research. Using the classification codes and descriptor terms of the *Thesaurus of Psychological Index Terms* (Gallagher Tuleya, 2007) and the data from the psychology literature database PsycINFO of the American Psychological Association (APA), bibliometric analyses are performed on the frequency of concepts of emotional development in general and on the frequencies of specific emotions in developmental psychology research. These analyses examine both cumulative findings and time trends across four decades (1970-2010). Findings reveal that, overall, negative emotions dominate research on emotions, and that the highest relative frequency of emotions across four decades of research in developmental psychology is found for childhood. In conclusion, neglected research domains as well as new topics and trends in research on emotions in developmental psychology are discussed.

---

[*] Günter Krampen. E-mail: krampen@uni-trier.de.
[†] Lisa Trierweiler. E-mail: lisa.trierweiler@zpid.de.

INTRODUCTION

Psychology of emotions is a historically classical and lasting significant research domain in developmental psychology. Early contributions referred nearly exclusively to affective and emotional development in infancy, childhood, and—somewhat less—in adolescence (e.g., Piaget, 1932; Watson and Rayner, 1920; Wundt, 1900). After the analyses, conception and discussion of complex and ambitious emotions and morale in ethics and in the philosophy of morality (e.g., in the classical tradition of Aristotle [384-322 BC] as well as in the philosophical traditions of the Enlightenment), at the least since the implementation and spreading of life-span developmental psychology (see, e.g., Baltes, 1968; Baltes and Brim, 1978-1984; Baltes and Schaie, 1973; Schaie, 1965), emotions have become a topic of empirical investigation in adulthood and old age as well. In fact, one may observe an accumulation of research on emotional development in the elderly, with rather less for early and middle adulthood. In evaluating the recent status of developmental research one may conclude that there are still up to now classical hot topics in research on emotions in infancy and childhood as well as some newer hot topics in research on emotions which refer to the elderly. Thus, it can be supposed that there is a rather long life-span gap for research on emotions in young and middle adulthood development.

Before presenting the results of bibliometric analyses, which allow empirical testing of these hypotheses on different representations of emotions in developmental psychology research in different age groups, a comprehensive overview on the frequency of the topic of emotions in developmental psychology research will be given. Firstly, we do this with the focus on theoretically based concepts and constructs with reference to emotional development. Secondly, we change the perspective to certain affects and emotions and their popularity (overrepresentation) or neglect/disregard (underrepresentation) in developmental psychology research. Both bibliometric analyses, that is, the first on the frequency of concepts of emotional development and the second on the frequencies of analyzing specific emotions in developmental psychology research, are implemented in general, cumulative analyses as well as in analyses on time trends for the last four decades (i.e., developmental psychology research in the time span from 1970 to 2010). All bibliometric analyses were performed with the data available in PsycINFO, the psychology literature database of the *American Psychological Association (APA)*, which is accessible online in the Internet (www.apa.org/pubs/databases/psycinfo). The scope of PsycINFO ranges from the beginnings of psychology in the 19th century up to now and includes approximately 3 million records of psychology publications with an exhaustive focus on the Anglo-American research community and publications in the English language. However, contributions in other languages and by authors from non-English-speaking countries are underrepresented; currently less than 5% of all documents in PsycINFO refer to these (see Arnett, 2008, 2009; Krampen, 2009; LoSchiavo and Shatz, 2009). In bibliometric analyses, the classification codes (CC) and the descriptor terms (DE) in PsycINFO were used. CC and DE are listed and defined in the *Thesaurus of Psychological Index Terms* (Gallagher Tuleya, 2007). All bibliometric analyses presented in the following are restricted to the classification codes (CC) for the category "Developmental Psychology". Descriptor terms, which are significant for research on emotions (see Table 1 and Table 2), are analyzed bibliometrically for this CC, which is exhaustive for research in developmental psychology.

Initial analyses were performed to gain insight into the overall total frequency of emotion terms assigned in PsycINFO. In the present bibliometric analysis, the absolute frequency of 21 emotion concepts and 43 emotional states listed in the *Thesaurus of Psychological Index Terms* (Gallagher Tuleya, 2007) was determined.

In a second step, the relative frequency of these terms in the content classification category "Developmental Psychology" (with the CC – 2800, and including the subcategories 2820 – Cognitive and Perceptual Development, 2840 – Psychosocial and Personality Development, and 2860 – Gerontology) was calculated. Time trends for the use of these descriptors were determined for four decades of research: 1970-1979, 1980-1989, 1990-1999, and 2000-2009.

As a starting point for our journey, Figure 1 illustrates the development of the use of emotion descriptors (i.e., emotion concepts and emotional states) across the four decades.

In the 1970s, emotion descriptors made up 5.7% of the total number of descriptors assigned in the content classification category "Developmental Psychology". This number increased each decade, to 7.9% in the 1980s, 11.1% in the 1990s, and a slight increase to 11.7% in the 2000s. Building on these findings, time trends are presented for the relative frequency of these descriptors across developmental age groups. In the following, the findings for the emotion concepts will be presented first followed by those for the emotional states.

Next, time trends of the emotion concepts and emotional states will be presented with a specific focus on the representation of emotions in different age groups in developmental research.

Based on the results presented here, we conclude with a discussion of the hot topics, trends, and neglected research domains in research on emotions in developmental psychology.

METHOD

Frequency of Concepts of Emotional Development in Developmental Psychology Research

As a starting point, we were interested in determining how often the 21 emotion concepts have been assigned to documents in the PsycINFO database, and more specifically, how often these terms have been assigned together with the content classification code for "Developmental Psychology". Table 1 presents the year of inclusion into the *Thesaurus of Psychological Index Terms* (Gallagher Tuleya, 2007) and the absolute frequencies of the 21 emotion concepts used in PsycINFO.

In addition, the absolute frequency of each term and its percentage of occurrence in "Developmental Psychology" are given in descending order for the absolute frequencies. As can be seen in Table 1, the relative frequency of the emotion concepts (in percent) ranges from 55.8 for emotional development to 3.0 for emotional abuse.

Taking the relative frequencies into consideration, we selected four terms with high percentages to illustrate their development across four decades of research in the next section.

These are emotional development (55.8%), emotional security (32.3%), emotional control (23.1%), and emotional adjustment (17.8%).

Table 1. Absolute and Relative Frequencies of Descriptors on "Emotion" within the Classification Codes "Developmental Psychology" in PsycINFO (220,074; Date of Search: March 2012)

Descriptor - Emotion	Year of inclusion	Total frequency f	Developmental Psychology (CC)	
			f	%
emotional development	1973	5,292	2,953	55.8
emotions	1967	26,147	2,433	9.3
emotional adjustment	1973	13,518	2,411	17.8
emotional states	1973	25,780	1,914	7.4
emotional responses	1967	13,186	1,306	9.9
emotional control	1973	2,532	584	23.1
emotionality (personality)	1973	2,751	455	16.5
emotional regulation	2007	2,265	429	18.9
emotional content	1973	3,117	288	9.2
emotional security	1973	1,083	350	32.3
emotional maturity	1973	808	284	35.1
emotional disturbances	2007	7,432	251	3.4
morale	1978	1,875	219	11.7
emotional intelligence	2003	2,473	206	8.3
emotional stability	1973	888	150	16.9
expressed emotion	1991	1,067	54	5.1
emotional abuse	1991	1,681	50	3.0
emotional instability	1973	370	25	6.8
emotional immaturity	1973	99	22	22.2
emotional inferiority	1973	170	18	10.6
emotional superiority	1973	94	7	7.4

Note: The specific content classification codes for the subcategories of Developmental Psychology (2800) are Cognitive and Perceptual Development (2820); Psychosocial and Personality Development (2840); and Gerontology (2860).

Time Trends in the Representation of Emotional Development Concepts in Developmental Psychology Research

After determining that the use of emotion descriptors has increased steadily across four decades of psychological research in "Developmental Psychology" (see Figure 1), the question remains regarding the specific developmental trajectories of the emotion concepts and emotional states during this time. To examine this more closely, relative frequencies of the descriptors selected above were calculated for each of the four decades.

We begin with the four selected emotion concepts: emotional development, emotional control, emotional security, and emotional adjustment. Figures 2 and 3 depict the frequencies over time. Emotional development had the highest percentage of relative frequency (55.8%), and this is mirrored in its trajectory across four decades although its development has reached a plateau from the 1990s onward (remaining at 1.6% relative frequency in developmental psychology research throughout the first decade of 2000).

Emotional control, in contrast, started rather slowly at 0.01% relative frequency in the 1970s, and doubling in the 1980s, with an even bigger jump in the 1990s to 0.3%, and continuously growing to 0.5% in the 2000s. Emotional adjustment increased steadily across three decades, reaching a maximum of 1.6% relative frequency in developmental psychology research, and during the final decade has fallen back to slightly above the rate in the 1980s.

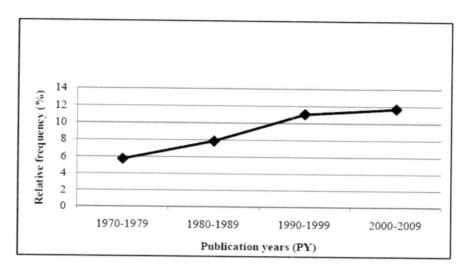

Figure 1. Relative frequency of all emotion concepts and emotional states (21 emotion concepts and 43 emotional states) in developmental psychology research across four decades.

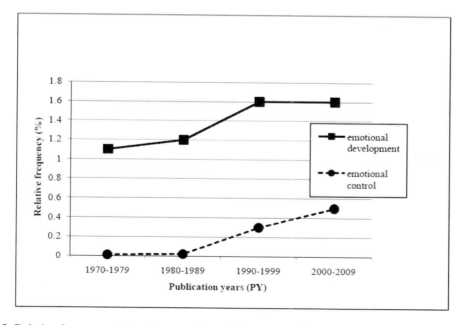

Figure 2. Relative frequency of developmental psychology research on the two emotion concepts 'emotional development' and 'emotional control' across four decades.

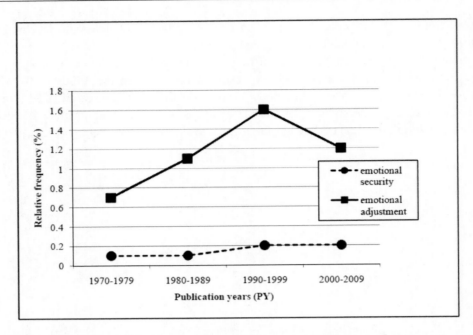

Figure 3. Relative frequency of developmental psychology research on two emotion concepts 'emotional security' and 'emotional adjustment' across four decades.

The graph representing the trajectory of emotional security is rather flat. This term's relative frequency in developmental psychology research did increase twofold from the 1980s to the 1990s, but compared to the other three emotion concepts, the absolute numbers are relatively low to begin with (only 2 assignments of this term in the 1970s to 355 in the 2000s).

Frequency of Specific Emotions in Developmental Psychology Research

How do the specific emotional states fare over the four decades of research in developmental psychology? For each of the 43 terms, Table 2 presents the year of inclusion in the *Thesaurus of Psychological Index Terms* (Gallagher-Tuleya, 2007), the absolute frequencies in PsycINFO, and their relative frequencies in the content classification category "Developmental Psychology".

An interesting finding, in terms of absolute frequency, is that the first eight descriptors deal with negative emotions. Happiness is the first positive emotion to make its appearance, in ninth place. The relative frequencies of these terms in "Developmental Psychology" are generally lower than the emotion concepts mentioned above, but this is to be expected due to the specificity of the terms.

The relative frequencies of the emotional states (listed in the table in descending order) range from 24.7% for loneliness to 0.2% for mania. Again, after reviewing the relative frequencies, we selected eight negative emotional states and four positive emotional states to illustrate the research trends on their usage in developmental psychology across four decades (see next section).

The negative emotional states are anxiety (5.5%), depression—emotion (6.7%), grief (9.9%), distress (6.9%), loneliness (24.7%), alienation (7.6%), sadness (11.9%), and dissatisfaction (10.4%). The positive emotional states that will be examined in further analyses are happiness (10.6), pleasure (7.0%), hope (8.0), and optimism (8.0%).

Research on emotions in general and in the context of developmental psychology as well is engaged to the larger extent in analyses of negative, aversive emotions (see Table 2).

Reason for this is not only the simple fact that more negative than positive or ambivalent emotional states are listed in the APA's *Thesaurus of Psychological Index Terms* (Gallagher Tuleya, 2007). Because of their direct significance for survival of an individual, his or her community and mankind (which is analyzed in evolution theory and evolution psychology), all languages differentiate between many more words for negative, aversive emotions (being alarm reactions) than for positive ones.

This is reflected in the *Thesaurus*, in which 30 negative emotional states (ranging from alienation to suspicion) in contrast to only 10 positive emotional states (e.g., affection, enthusiasm, happiness, hope, optimism, and pride) and only 2 ambivalent emotional states (ambivalence and mania) are listed (see Table 2).

These negative index terms dominate research on emotions not only because of their relevance for psychopathology (almost all mental disorders imply disrupted emotions), stress research, and clinical psychology.

In addition, the negative ones are of significance for the processes and regulation of individual and social development.

Developmental psychology and clinical psychology focus this in contexts of psychopathological, delayed, or dangerous individual developments which are either manifest or anticipated and should both be treated by adequate measures.

This traditional deficit-oriented approach, which is in the primary search for treatment methods, is supplemented by humanistic psychology (see, e.g., Bühler and Allen, 1972; Maslow, 1967), health psychology (e.g., Krampen and Montada, 1998; Rodin and Salovey, 1989; Schwarzer, 2009) and positive psychology (e.g., Seligman, 2002; Seligman and Csikszentmihalyi, 2000) by an explicit normative approach referring to criteria for and processes of optimal human development.

Especially the revival of this normative approach in the conceptualization of positive psychology has given (or may give in the near future) an impulse to analyze positive emotions like optimism, happiness, love, and pleasure more frequently, which are listed as personal strengths in the *Values in Action Classification of Strengths* (VIA-IS; Peterson and Seligman, 2004) in studies on personality development.

Time Trends in the Representation of Specific Emotional States in Developmental Research

With the exception of six emotional states that were added in more recent years (2 positive and 4 negative), all others in the analysis have a longstanding status in the *Thesaurus of Psychological Index Terms* (Gallagher Tuleya, 2007), dating back to 1973 and even earlier. The only emotional state descriptor included in the decade analyses that does not date back to the initial set of terms is hope. This term was included in 1991; therefore, its trajectory will be presented across two decades.

Table 2. Absolute and Relative Frequencies of Descriptors on "Emotional States" within the Classification Codes "Developmental Psychology" in PsycINFO (222,741; Date of Search: April 2012)

Descriptor – Emotional states	Year of inclusion	Total frequency f	Developmental Psychology (CC)	
			f	%
anxiety	1967	38,732	2,120	5.5
depression (emotion)	1967	20,264	1,348	6.7
fear	1967	12,184	969	8.0
grief	1973	9,493	938	9.9
distress	1973	12,780	880	6.9
loneliness	1973	2,551	629	24.7
anger	1967	6,309	564	8.9
emotional trauma	1967	13,417	559	4.2
happiness	1973	3,767	399	10.6
love	1973	4,587	330	7.2
frustration	1967	2,125	260	12.2
optimism	1973	2,523	201	8.0
guilt	1967	3,364	196	5.8
affection	1973	1,198	196	16.4
pleasure	1973	2,654	185	7.0
shame	1994	2,276	169	7.4
sadness	1973	1,272	151	11.9
alienation	1971	1,960	148	7.6
hope	1991	1,733	139	8.0
dissatisfaction	1973	1,171	122	10.4
sympathy	1973	694	98	14.1
hopelessness	1988	1,342	91	6.8
jealousy	1973	1,277	81	6.3
ambivalence	1973	986	67	6.8
aversion	1967	1,563	63	4.0
suffering	1973	2,194	58	2.6
pessimism	1973	892	56	6.3
pride	1973	449	55	12.2
embarrassment	1973	482	45	9.3
helplessness	1997	403	36	8.9
boredom	1973	510	34	6.6
gratitude	2006	283	31	11.0
disgust	1994	620	24	3.9
mental confusion	1973	689	23	3.3
doubt	1973	186	21	11.3
apathy	1973	583	20	3.4
disappointment	1973	203	17	8.4
homesickness	1994	82	14	17.1
suspicion	1973	410	12	2.9
restlessness	1973	287	12	4.2
enthusiasm	1973	221	11	5.0
mania	1967	4,191	7	0.2
euphoria	1973	207	1	0.5

Note: The specific content classification codes for the subcategories of Developmental Psychology (2800) are Cognitive and Perceptual Development (2820); Psychosocial and Personality Development (2840); and Gerontology (2860).

The trajectories of the negative emotion terms within developmental psychology research across four decades are depicted in Figures 4 and 5. Specifically, Figure 4 illustrates that anxiety and distress both have steady upward growth within developmental psychology research across the four decades.

The trajectory of distress makes clear the fact that this emotional state has gained in importance from the 1970s (0.1%) to the 2000s (0.6%). Depression has a rather steep ascent from 0.2% relative frequency in the 1970s to 0.9% in the 1990s, but dropping back to 0.8% in the 2000s. Grief became a research focus in the 1980s (0.5%), topping off at 0.6% relative frequency in the 1990s and remaining at this level since.

Figure 5 reveals the stellar ascent of loneliness, and this is especially clear when viewed together with the three trajectories of alienation, sadness, and dissatisfaction within developmental psychology research. With rather level paths until the 1990s, both sadness and dissatisfaction have gained in research interest during the last decade. Alienation, in contrast, has declined steadily across the four-decade period, having reached its peak in the 1970s with a relative frequency of 0.15% and dropping to 0.05% in the 2000s. This might be related to the superficially viewed relationship of the term "alienation" with the political ideology of the Eastern bloc states in the 1990s.

The relative frequencies of the four positive emotions are presented in Figure 6. Two of the three emotions that have been in the Thesaurus since 1973 have fluctuating trajectories. The positive emotion appearing most frequently in developmental psychology research is happiness.

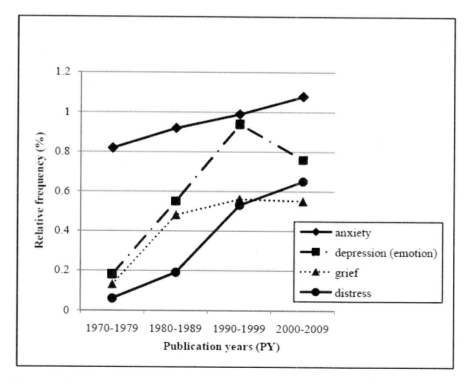

Figure 4. Relative frequency of negative emotions in developmental psychology (anxiety, depression-emotion, grief, distress) across four decades of research.

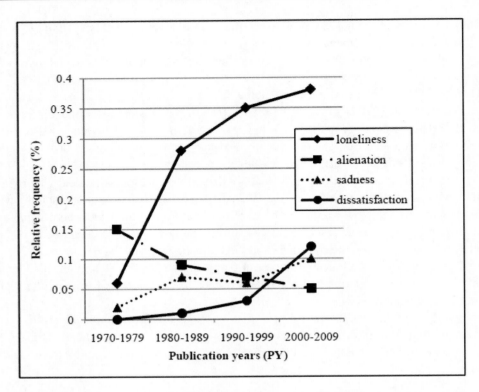

Figure 5. Relative frequency of negative emotions in developmental psychology (loneliness, alienation, sadness, dissatisfaction) across four decades of research.

However, its ascent has been turbulent. Its frequency doubled in the 1980s to 0.2% only to drop back down to 0.12% in the 1990s to double once again to 0.24% in the 2000s. Similarly, pleasure has followed an up and down pattern across the four-decade time span, beginning with 0.06% in the 1970s and ending with 0.08% in the 2000s.

In contrast, optimism has steadily increased across the four-decade period, beginning with a relative frequency of 0.01% within developmental psychology research in the 1970s to 0.17% in the 2000s. Hope shows signs of positive development since its inclusion two decades ago.

Representation of Emotions in Developmental Research on Different Age Groups

In the *Thesaurus of Psychological Index Terms* (Gallagher Tuleya, 2007), developmental age groups are divided into three main categories of childhood (birth-12 years), adolescence (13-17 years), and adulthood (18 years and older).

Of these, only childhood and adulthood are further differentiated into subcategories. These are neonatal (birth-1 month), infancy (1-23 months), preschool age (2-5 years), and school age (6-12 years) for childhood, and young adulthood (18-29 years), thirties (30-39 years), middle age (40-64 years), aged (65 years and older), and very old (85 years and older) for adulthood.

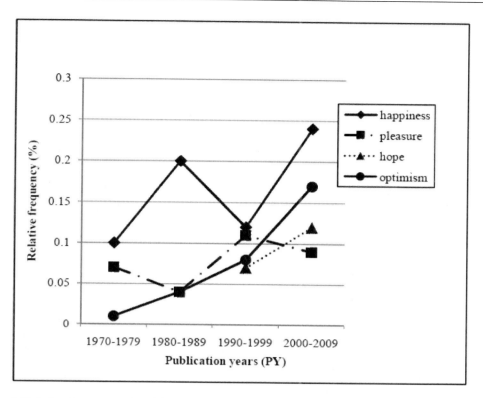

Figure 6. Relative frequency of positive emotions in developmental psychology (happiness, pleasure, hope, optimism) across four decades of research with the exception of the term 'hope' which was introduced in 1991.

Figure 7 shows the relative frequencies of the four selected emotional concepts and 12 emotional states in developmental psychology publications according to the three main developmental age groups. The relative frequencies of these emotions across four decades of research in developmental psychology are highest for childhood, a finding that could be presumed and is described in more detail below.

Interesting is the finding that the relative frequency has experienced a very slight decrease from the 1990s to the 2000s of 0.1% (from 3.7% to 3.6% relative frequency).

In spite of this, childhood still receives most attention in the research on emotions in developmental psychology. The trajectory of adolescence follows a similar, albeit slightly lower, pattern of development. This topic received increased attention in the 1980s, having grown from 0.7% relative frequency in the 1970s to 2.3%.

With only a very slight increase to 2.6% in the 1990s, adolescence has also leveled out with a slight decrease to 2.5% in the 2000s. Having begun with the lowest relative frequency (0.6%) of all three developmental age groups, adulthood has increased steadily across the four decades, with its final position (3.0%) situated between childhood and adolescence in the 2000s.

This latter finding led us to examine the trajectories of research on emotions in adulthood more closely, specifically paying attention to the subcategories young adulthood, thirties, middle adulthood, and aged and very old (see Figure 8).

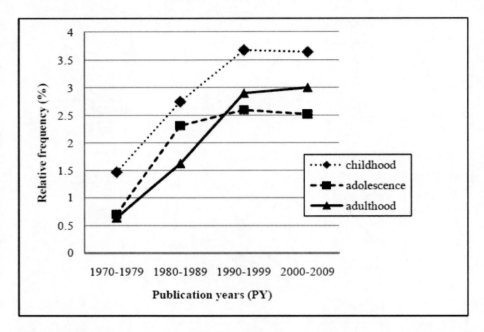

Figure 7. Relative frequencies of selected emotional concepts and states in developmental psychology according to developmental age group across four decades of research.

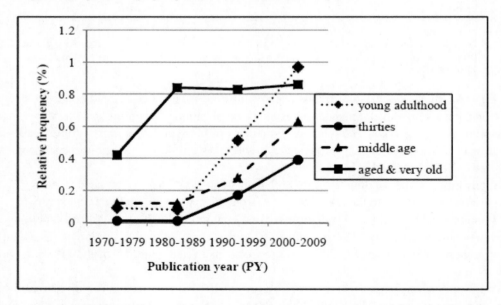

Figure 8. Relative frequencies of selected emotional concepts and states in developmental psychology across four stages of adulthood and four decades of research.

Initially, the group of aged and very old received the most attention in research on emotions in developmental psychology, climbing to more than 0.8% relative frequency in the 1980s, an amount significantly higher than for the other three adult groups during this time. While this level has been maintained throughout the 2000s for the aged and very old developmental age group, the other three groups began to climb higher in the 1990s, with the steepest rise in the young adulthood group from 0.08% relative frequency to almost 1.0% relative frequency in the 2000s. Similar, albeit lower trajectories, are found for the middle age group with a relative frequency of 0.63% in the 2000s, and the research focus for the thirties, although relatively neglected during the 1970s and 1980s, began its ascent in the 1990s up to almost 0.4% in the 2000s.

CONCLUSION

Hot Topics, Trends, and Neglected Research Domains in Research on Emotions in Developmental Psychology

A long-lasting hot topic of research on emotions in developmental psychology is the ontogenetic differentiation of affect and emotions in infancy and childhood. Affective utterances and emotional expressions of the newborn with its dominant functions in interpersonal regulations are supposed to be the starting points of emotional development.

Very early, in infancy and early childhood, those affects and emotional expressions are quickly consolidated and differentiated by conditioning and modeling to full functioning emotions not only regulating interpersonal interactions, but intrapersonal states and processes, too. Interpersonal as well as intrapersonal regulation functions of affects and emotions are, up to now, frequently described in developmental stages reaching from disgust, distress, and arousal (in the 1st month of life) to pleasure (2nd month), anger (7th month), grief, fear, and surprise (9th month), embarrassment (18th month), pride (24th month), shame (30th month), and guilt (36th month).

These functionalistic approaches to the development of emotions (see, e.g., Barrett, 1998) highlight the social functions of emotions, the social canalization of emotional expressions and its internalization in preschool age children. However, the intrapersonal functions of emotions are mentioned as well, but this is not explicitly differentiated and theoretically founded.

Somewhat like a bridge between the interpersonal and intrapersonal functions of emotions is the differentiation between "hot" and "cold" emotions: Hot emotions refer to spontaneous emotional expressions in a rather reflex manner, cold emotions are dependent from cognitive processes, for example, causal attributions and/or appraisals and reappraisals. This is in the focus of the attributional approach to emotional development (Weiner and Graham, 1985) and to stress theoretical models (Lazarus and Launier, 1978). Both approaches refer directly to the questions on emotion-cognition relationships and the development of these.

Since the 1960s it is hypothesized that hot emotions are present from infancy to old age, but cold (cognitive) emotions develop in connection with cognitive, language, and social development in early to middle childhood (Izard, 1985; Brandtstädter, Krampen, and Vesely, 1985).

A rather independent, newer, but age synchronous line of developmental research has emerged with reference to the development of empathy in infancy and early childhood. This newer hot topic focuses joint attention, emotional infection, and developmental differentiations in interpersonal perception skills (Moore and Dunham, 1995).

A second newer research trend refers to analyses of the development of emotional regulations within action contexts, that is, volitional regulation of (intentional) actions and reflexive emotional regulation. Functions of volitions are described and tested empirically mostly in cross-sectional, somewhat less in longitudinal, and up to now not at all in cross-sequential designs.

The same is true for analyses of the connected developmental transitions (1) from verbal instructions by others to verbal instructions by the child himself/herself and (2) from speaking aloud to inner self-instruction as means of action regulation in specific situations. Analyses of emotional regulation refer to the development of actions and/or (self-) instructions with the goal to regulate the quality, duration, intensity, or expressions of emotional states and emotions which are manifest or anticipated. Beside the older concept of delay of gratification (Mischel, Ebbesen, and Raskoff-Zeiss, 1972), some other processes (direct instructions, suggestions for reframing of situation and/or causes, modeling, and/or discourse about emotions with and by others, e.g., parents) are described, by which children learn strategies of emotional regulation and coping (see, e.g., Thompson, 1991, 1994).

These concepts may be multiple and converging or multiple and contradictory. They refer not only to childhood, but to adolescence and adulthood as well.

Thus, taken together, the classical and the new hot topics on emotional development in infant and childhood development are complementary in theory and research on development: Brought together are the developmental concepts of differentiation of affects and emotions on one hand and of integration of these emotions into larger conceptualizations of emotional regulation, action regulation, and coping on the other hand. This is in agreement with the "orthogenetic principle of development" in the tradition of Gestalt psychology originally formulated by Heinz Werner (1957).

Further on, this extends research on emotional development and emotion regulation from the classic and lasting focus on infant and (early) childhood development to the newer hot topic of research on emotion regulation, action regulation, and coping of adolescents and adults, thus building a bridge over the whole life-span. The bibliometric results presented confirm this convincingly.

These developmental concepts of emotions as well as emotion and action regulation are widely used in gerontopsychological research, that is, in action and control theoretical models on development in adulthood, especially in the elderly and successful aging (for an overview see, e.g., Brandtstädter and Lerner, 1999; Krampen and Greve, 2008).

Negative emotions (e.g., depressive outlook, resignation, dissatisfaction, and hopelessness) as well as positive emotions (e.g., life satisfaction, happiness, optimism, and hope), which refer to self-perceptions of own development and the development of significant, codeveloping others, are conceptualized and empirically analyzed in their interrelations with more or less strong efforts of intentional self-development, that is, the conception of "individuals as producers of their own development" (Lerner and Busch-Rossnagel, 1981, p. 1).

Control- and action-theory developmental models, which focus on emotions and emotion regulation refer, for example, to the theories of primary and secondary control (Rothbaum, Weisz, and Snyder, 1982), of personal control and emotional evaluation of own development (Brandtstädter, Krampen, and Heil, 1986), of assimilative, accommodative, and immunization modes of coping and intentional self-development (Brandtstädter, 2001) as well as of selective optimization by selection and compensation (Baltes, 1997).

Results confirm not only the heuristic value of these control theory models, but their empirical validity for the description of (emotional) development in adulthood, too. This hot topic of recent research on emotion regulation in developmental psychology is restricted up to now mostly to empirical analyses of developmental processes in the elderly and aged.

Its potential for applications on developmental processes in middle and early adulthood as well as in adolescence and (late) childhood is supposed, but rarely empirically investigated (Freund, 2001, 2007). This may be a hot future path of research on emotions in developmental psychology.

REFERENCES

Arnett, J. J. (2008). The neglected 95%: Why American psychology needs to become less American. *American Psychologist, 63*, 602-614.

Arnett, J. J. (2009). The neglected 95%, a challenge to psychology's philosophy of science. *American Psychologist, 64*, 571-574.

Baltes, P. B. (1968). Longitudinal and cross-sectional sequences in the study of age and generation effects. *Human Development,* 11, 145-171.

Baltes, P. B. (1997). On the incomplete architecture of human ontogeny: Selection, optimization, and compensation as foundation of developmental theory. *American Psychologist, 52*, 366-380.

Baltes, P. B. and Brim, O. G. Jr. (Eds.). (1978-1984). *Life-span development and behavior* (Vol. I -VI). New York, NY: Academic Press.

Baltes, P. B. and Schaie, K. W. (1973). *Life-span developmental psychology: Personality and socialization.* New York, NY: Academic Press.

Barrett, K. C. (1998). A functionalistic perspective to the development of emotions. In: M. F. Mascolo and S. Griffin (Eds.), *What develops in emotional development?* (pp. 109-133). New York, NY: Plenum.

Brandtstädter, J. (2001). *Entwicklung, Intentionalität, Handeln* [Development, intentionality, action]. Stuttgart (Germany): Kohlhammer.

Brandtstädter, J. and Lerner, R. M. (Eds.). (1999). *Action and self-development.* Thousand Oaks, CA: Sage.

Brandtstädter, J., Krampen, G. and Heil, F. E. (1986). Personal control and emotional evaluation of development in partnership relations during adulthood. In: M. M. Baltes and P. B. Baltes (Eds.), *The psychology of aging and control* (pp. 265-296). Hillsdale, NJ: Erlbaum.

Brandtstädter, J., Krampen, G. and Vesely, H. (1985). Attribution und sprachliche Kompetenz: Zur Bewährung attributionstheoretischer Annahmen bei Grundschülern mit unterschiedlichem Entwicklungsstand [Attribution and language competence: On the confirmation of attribution theory assumptions in elementary school students with different developmental levels]. *Sprache und Kognition*, 4, 130-138.

Bühler, C. and Allen, M. (1972). *Introduction to humanistic psychology.* Belmont, CA: Brooks/Cole.

Freund, A. M. (2001). Developmental psychology of life-management. In: N. J. Smelser and P. B. Baltes (Eds.), *International encyclopedia of the behavioral and social sciences* (Vol. 13, pp. 8827-8832). Oxford, UK: Elsevier.

Freund, A. M. (2007). Differentiating and integrating levels of goal representations: A life-span perspective. In: B. R. Little, K. Salmela-Aro and S. D. Phillips (Eds.), *Personal project pursuit* (pp. 247-270). Mahwah, NJ: Erlbaum.

Gallagher Tuleya, L. (2007). *Thesaurus of psychological index terms* (11th ed.). Washington, DC: American Psychological Association.

Izard, C. E. (1985). Emotion-cognition relationship and human development. In: C. E. Izard, J. Kagan and R. B. Zajonc (Eds.), *Emotions, cognitions, and behavior* (pp. 17-37). New York, NY. Cambridge University Press.

Krampen, G. (2009). Introduction and some ideas as well as visions on an Open Access European Psychology Publication Platform. *Psychology Science Quarterly,* 51 (Suppl. 1), 3-18.

Krampen, G. and Greve, W. (2008). Persönlichkeits- und Selbstkonzeptentwicklung über die Lebensspanne [Personality and self-concept development in the life-span]. In: R. Oerter and L. Montada (Hrsg.), *Entwicklungspsychologie (Developmental psychology)* (6th ed., pp. 652-686). Weinheim (Germany): Beltz.

Krampen, G. and Montada, L. (1998). Health psychology: Bibliometrical results on the emergence and rapid consolidation of a new field of research and application. *Psychology and Health,* 13, 1027-1036.

Lazarus, R. S. and Launier, R. (1978). Stress-related transaction between person and environment. In: L. A. Pervin and M. Lewis (Eds.), *Perspectives in interactional psychology* (pp. 287-327). New York, NY: Plenum.

Lerner, R. M. and Busch-Rossnagel, N. A. (1981). *Individuals as producers of their own development: A life-span perspective.* New York, NY: Academic Press.

LoSchiavo, F. M. and Shatz, M. A. (2009). Reaching the neglected 95%. *American Psychologist,* 64, 565-566.

Maslow, A. H. (1967). A theory of metamotivation: The biological rooting of the value-life. *Journal of Humanistic Psychology,* 7, 93-127.

Mischel, W., Ebbesen, E. B. and Raskoff-Zeiss, A. (1972). Cognitive and attentional mechanisms in delay of gratification. *Journal of Personality and Social Psychology,* 21, 204-218.

Moore, C. and Dunham, P. J. (Eds.). (1995). *Joint attention.* Hillsdale, NJ: Erlbaum.

Peterson, C. and Seligman, M. E. P. (2004). *Character strength and virtues: A handbook and classification.* Washington, DC: American Psychological Association.

Piaget, J. (1932). *Le jugement moral chez l'enfant* [Development of moral judgment in childhood]. Paris (France): Alcan.

Rodin, J. and Salovey, P. (1989). Health psychology. *Annual Review of Psychology,* 40, 533-579.

Rothbaum, F., Weisz, J. R. and Snyder, S. S. (1982). Changing the world and changing the self. *Journal of Personality and Social Psychology,* 42, 5-37.

Schaie, K. W. (1965). A general model for the study of developmental problems. *Psychological Bulletin,* 64, 92-107.

Schwarzer, R. (2009). Gesundheitspsychologie [Health psychology]. In: G. Krampen (Ed.), *Psychologie: Experten als Zeitzeugen* [Psychology: Experts as Contemporary Witnesses] (pp. 240-249). Göttingen, Germany: Hogrefe.

Seligman, M. E. P. (2002). *Authentic happiness: Using the new positive psychology to realize your potential for lasting fulfillment.* New York, NY: Free Press.

Seligman, M. E. P. and Csikszentmihalyi, M. (2000). Positive psychology: An introduction. *American Psychologist, 55,* 5-14.

Thompson, R. A. (1991). Emotional regulation and emotional development. *Educational Psychology Review, 3,* 269-307.

Thompson, R. A. (1994). Emotion regulation: A theme in search of definition. *Monographs of the Society for Research in Child Development, 59,* 250-283.

Watson, J. B. and Rayner, R. (1920). Conditional emotional reactions. *Journal of Experimental Psychology, 3,* 1-14.

Weiner, B. and Graham, S. (1985). The attributional approach to emotional development. In: C. E. Izard, J. Kagan and R. B. Zajonc (Eds.), *Emotions, cognitions, and behavior* (pp. 167-191). New York, NY. Cambridge University Press.

Werner, H. (1957). The concept of development from a comparative and organismic point of view. In: D. B. Harris (Ed.), *The concept of development* (pp. 135-148). Minneapolis, MN: University of Minnesota Press.

Wundt, W. (1900). Bemerkungen zur Theorie der Gefühle [Remarks on the theory of emotions]. *Philosophische Studien, 15,* 149-182.

In: Handbook of Psychology of Emotions
Editors: C. Mohiyeddini, M. Eysenck and S. Bauer

ISBN: 978-1-62808-053-7
© 2013 Nova Science Publishers, Inc.

Chapter 5

SOCIAL REFERENCING IN INFANCY: IMPORTANT FINDINGS AND FUTURE DIRECTIONS

Lindsay E. Vandivier and Matthew J. Hertenstein[*]
DePauw University, Greencastle, IN, US

ABSTRACT

Social referencing occurs when infants use adult emotional displays to regulate their behavior toward environmental objects, people, and situations. Social referencing provides infants with opportunities' to learn about their environments. The present chapter highlights five areas in which future investigation should focus in social referencing and the strides that have been made in each: (a) the importance of naturalistic studies, (b) the development of social referencing, (c) individual differences, (d) neural underpinnings, and (e) atypical populations.

Keywords: Infant communication, emotional communication, social referencing

SOCIAL REFERENCING IN INFANCY: IMPORTANT FINDINGS AND FUTURE DIRECTIONS

Social referencing, a major developmental milestone in infancy, refers to the process in which infants use adult emotional displays to regulate their behavior toward environmental objects, people, and situations (Campos & Sternberg, 1981). In a typical social referencing paradigm, infants are placed in a situation of uncertainty or ambiguity, usually involving a stranger, a novel toy, or a visual cliff (Walden & Ogan, 1988). When infants encounter one of these objects or events, an adult expresses a negative or positive emotional display in response. Successful social referencing takes place to the degree to which infants regulate their behavior toward one of these objects or events in accordance with the adult's emotional

[*] Send correspondence to: Matt Hertenstein, DePauw University, 123 Harrison Hall, Greencastle, IN 46135, mhertenstein@depauw.edu, 765.658.4609.

displays. Social referencing plays a vital role in infants acquiring information and learning about themselves and their environments (Walden & Ogan).

Although there is a general consensus that social referencing plays a key role in development, disagreement remains in defining the exact conditions under which social referencing takes place. One perspective argues that social referencing can occur only in situations of uncertainty where infants actively seek information about the situation (Bretherton, 1984; Sorce, Emde, Campos & Klinnert, 1985). A second perspective proposes that social referencing is not limited to infants' seeking information, but can also occur when caregivers are willing to provide information about a situation (Feinman, 1992). From this perspective, infants still must understand and use the information to regulate behavior when it is presented to them (Bretherton).

Whether infants are active solicitors or passive recipients, most agree on the importance of behavior regulation in response to adults' emotional displays. Below, we shall briefly address five areas in the field of social referencing that are deserving of future attention by researchers and the strides that have been made in each.

FUNDAMENTAL QUESTIONS AND SUGGESTIONS FOR FUTURE RESEARCH NATURALISTIC STUDIES

One limitation of the social referencing literature is that most studies have been conducted almost exclusively in laboratory settings, which limit the external validity of this area of research (Feinman, 1992). To advance the field of social referencing more studies should be conducted in children's natural environments. By conducting studies in infants' natural environment, researchers can focus on how caregivers and infants actually emote, as opposed to manipulating displays in the lab. More naturalistic studies will lead to a more comprehensive understanding of social referencing and add to the ecological validity of the field of study.

One such approach was employed by Karasik, Tamis-LeMonda, Adolf and Dimitropoulou (2008) who used a semi-naturalistic design to examine mothers' expressive communication with their infants during a typical social referencing paradigm involving a sloped walkway. The slope was designed to be somewhat risky, so the mothers would use natural gestures and emotional commands (Karasik et. al). Karasik et al. found that mothers in both discouraging and encouraging conditions favored using more positive emotional displays and gestures. Even when mothers discouraged their infants, they rarely, if ever, displayed purely negative emotionality. Furthermore, the researchers found that mothers' emotional communication was linked to infants crawling and walking experience, as well as their age. Although this study was performed in a laboratory, the mothers were encouraged to behave naturally and portray their typical expressions allowing researchers to examine how mothers use their emotions to encourage and discourage infants in certain situations (Karasik et. al.). This contrasts with most previous laboratory work in which adults are instructed how to respond to infants (e.g., Hertenstein & Campos, 2001). Future naturalistic and semi-naturalistic studies should be conducted to better understand how social referencing operates in infants' natural ecologies.

DEVELOPMENT OF SOCIAL REFERENCING

Of course, social referencing does not emerge in children in a mature fashion, but develops over time. Moreover, it's important to identify the developmental processes that enter into the unfolding of social referencing. Unfortunately, few studies examining social referencing have taken a truly developmental perspective (although, see Walden & Ogan, 1988). One recent and promising approach was taken by Tamis-LeMonda and Adolph (2005) who investigated the role that motor development plays in social referencing. In this study, experienced walkers were more likely to go against their mothers' discouraging emotional displays if their perceptual information suggested that the slope was safe. That is, if the slope appeared not risky to the skilled walker, they continued down the slope against their mother's discouraging displays. In contrast, inexperienced walkers did not traverse the slopes when their mother used discouraging displays (Tamis-LeMonda & Adolph). Thus, experienced walkers relied primarily upon the perceptual information in the environment to regulate their approach behavior, whereas inexperienced walkers relied on their mothers' displays to regulate their behavior. In this case, one developmental process – i.e., locomotor activity – enters into the development of social referencing.

INDIVIDUAL DIFFERENCES

Researchers have identified individual differences in the degree to which social referencing occurs for infants (Blackford & Walden, 1998). That is, some infants regulate their behavior in accordance with the emotional displays of an adult and others do not, or do so to varying degrees. There has been preciously little research conducted that has identified the variables that explain these differences between infants. The work that has been done most often implicates temperament, level of motor skills, and the perception of ambiguity (Tamis-LeMonda & Adolph, 2005; Feinman & Lewis, 1983)

Feinman and Lewis (1983), for example, found that temperament may play a role in social referencing temperamental differences in 10-month-old infants. Ten-month-old infants with "easy" temperaments were more likely to approach a stranger following a positive display of emotion from their mother compared to a neutral display. Infants with "difficult" temperaments did not differ depending on the displays from their mother.

Children perceive ambiguity in the environment differently and these differences may then also lead to individual differences in social referencing. That is, some infants may perceive a particular environmental event as risky, but others may perceive it as safe. These perceptions may then drive differences in social referencing. Tamis-LeMonda and Adolph (2005) describe researchers' lack of attention to this difference in infants as the "one size fits all" approach. That is, much research is predicated on the assumption that infants perceive a particular stimulus as equally ambiguous or uncertain. Tamis-LeMonda and Adolph argue, however, that a toy or sloped walkway may be perceived as dangerous, safe, or ambiguous depending on the individual infant. If researchers establish a test to gauge ambiguity, individual differences can be better assessed and social referencing studies will yield more informative results. In sum, the investigation of individual differences in social referencing is central to our understanding of the phenomenon.

NEURAL UNDERPINNINGS OF SOCIAL REFERENCING

Researchers have begun to investigate the neural underpinnings of social referencing. For example, Carver and Vaccaro (2007) invited 12-month-olds into the lab for a two phase experiment. In the first phase, infants' caregivers displayed positive, negative, and neutral displays toward novel objects and researchers observed subsequent infant behavior. In phase two, the researchers recorded infants' brain responses via Event-Related Potential (ERP) as infants viewed images of the objects to which their caregivers emoted in phase one. The researchers found that objects associated with negative emotionality resulted in greater ERP brain response in infants. In addition, infants who looked at adults in phase one less quickly demonstrated a decrease in ERP amplitude to negatively associated objects compared to infants who looked more quickly in phase 1. This study constitutes one of the first to identify brain states with social referencing. It will be important to further investigate the neural underpinnings of social referencing in infancy.

SOCIAL REFERENCING PARADIGM WITH ATYPICAL POPULATIONS

One crucial area of study that has received a limited amount of attention deals with social referencing in atypical populations. One population that has been investigated to some degree is children with Down syndrome. In two studies, researchers compared typically developing toddlers to those with Down syndrome in social referencing paradigms. They found that infants with Down syndrome expressed negative affect in response to parental positive emotional displays, an atypical emotional response in a social referencing context (Knieps, Walden, & Baxter, 1994). In addition, infants with Down syndrome look less often to their parents when presented with ambiguous objects compared to typically developing children (Kasari, Freeman, Mundy, & Sigman, 1995). Unfortunately, no studies to our knowledge report whether there are differences between children who are typically developing and those with Down syndrome in terms of the degree to which they regulate their behavior toward objects as a function of an adult's emotional displays. Future research should focus not only on this question, but also extend to other atypical populations such as children with autism and neurodevelopment disorders, as well as maltreated infants.

CONCLUSION

Social referencing is crucial for infants' development and their learning about their environment. We have identified five areas in which researchers may consider focusing their attention and some of the progress that has been made in each. We look forward to learning what is discovered about social referencing in the years to come.

REFERENCES

Blackford, J. U., & Walden, T. A. (1998). Individual differences in social referencing. *Infant Behavior and Development, 21*(1), 89-102.

Bretherton, I. (1984). Social referencing and the interfacing of minds: A commentary on the views of Feinman and Campos. *Merrill-Palmer Quarterly: Journal of Developmental Psychology, 30*(4), 419-427.

Campos, J. U., & Sternberg, C. (1981). Perception, appraisal and emotion: The onset of social referencing. In M.E. Lamb & L.R. Sherrod (Eds.*), Infant social cognition: Empirical and theoretical considerations* (pp.273-314). Hillsdale, NJ: Erlbaum.

Carver, L. J. & Vaccaro, B. G. (2007). 12-month-old infants allocate increased neural resources to stimuli associated with negative adult emotion. *Developmental Psychology, 43*(1), 54-69.

Feinman, S. (1992). In the broad valley: An integrative look at social referencing. In S. Feinman (Eds.), *Social referencing and the social construction of reality in infancy* (3-13). New York: Plenum Press.

Feinman, S. (1992). What do we know and where shall we go? Conceptual and research directions for social referencing. In S. Feinman (Eds.), *Social referencing and the social construction of reality in infancy* (371-405). New York: Plenum Press.

Feinman, S. & Lewis, M. (1983). Social referencing at ten months: A second-order effect on infants' responses to strangers. *Child Development, 54*, 878-887.

Karasik, L. B., Tamis-LeMonda, C. S., Adolph, K. E., & Dimitropoulou, K. A. (2008). How mothers encourage and discourage infants' motor actions. *Infancy, 13*(4), 366-392.

Kasari, C., Freeman, S., Mundy, P., & Sigman, M. (1995). Attention regulation by children with down syndrome: Coordinated joint attention and social referencing. *American Journal on Mental Retardation, 100*(2), 128-136.

Knieps, L. J., Walden, T. A., & Baxter, A. (1994). Affective expressions of toddlers with and without down syndrome in a social referencing context. *American Journal on Mental Retardation, 99*(3), 301-312.

Sorce, J. F., Emede, R. N., Campos, J.J., & Klinnert, M.D. (1985). Maternal emotional signaling: Its effect on visual cliff behavior of 1-year olds. *Developmental Psychology, 21*(1), 195-200.

Tamis-LeMonda, C. S. & Adolph, K. E. (2005). Social referencing in infant motor action. In B. Homer & C. Tamis-LeMonda (Eds.), *The development of social cognition and communication* (145-164). Mahwah, NJ: Lawrence Erlbaum Associates.

Walden, T. A. & Ogan, T. A. (1988). The development of social referencing. *Child Development, 59*, 1230-1240.

In: Handbook of Psychology of Emotions   ISBN: 978-1-62808-053-7
Editors: C. Mohiyeddini, M. Eysenck and S. Bauer   © 2013 Nova Science Publishers, Inc.

Chapter 6

ANXIETY AND COGNITIVE PERFORMANCE

*Michael W. Eysenck**

Department of Psychology, University of Roehampton, Whitelands College, London, UK

ABSTRACT

There has been much interest in understanding the adverse effects of anxiety on cognitive tasks. One of the main theories in this area is attentional control theory (Eysenck, Derakshan, Santos, & Calvo, 2007). According to this theory, it is important to distinguish between performance effectiveness (the quality of performance) and processing efficiency (the relationship between performance effectiveness and the use of processing resources). A major prediction (which has been supported strongly by recent research involving the use of functional magnetic resonance imaging (fMRI) and event-related potentials (ERPs) is that there are greater adverse effects of anxiety on processing efficiency than on performance effectiveness.

Another major assumption within attentional control theory is that adverse effects of anxiety mostly revolve around the central executive component of the working memory system. More specifically, anxiety impairs the efficiency of specific functions of the central executive including the inhibition and shifting functions. Research has provided reasonable empirical support for these assumptions.

Finally, the chapter concludes by considering some ways in which future research might develop and extend the theoretical reach of attentional control theory.

INTRODUCTION

Over the past 50 years or more, there has been considerable interest in the effects of anxiety on performance. Most of this research literature has been concerned with anxiety as a personality dimension. Some researchers have focused on individual differences in trait anxiety in the sense of a very general susceptibility to anxiety and have used measures such as the State-Trait Anxiety Inventory (Spielberger et al., 1983). Other researchers have focused

---

* Department of Psychology, University of Roehampton, Whitelands College, Holybourne Avenue, London, SW15 4JD, UK, email: Michael.Eysenck@roehampton.ac.uk

on individual differences in test anxiety (e. g., the Test Anxiety Scale, Sarason, 1978). This is more specific dimension than trait anxiety in that its focus is on susceptibility to anxiety in test situations. Test anxiety and trait anxiety correlate moderately highly with each other and their effects on performance are typically comparable.

Different types of performance can be identified. Perhaps the most obvious distinction is between cognitive performance (e.g., verbal reasoning; mathematical problems; decision making) on the one hand and motor or sport performance on the other hand. The emphasis in this chapter is very much on anxiety and cognitive performance. For those interested in anxiety and sport performance, Wilson (in press) has provided an excellent review of theory and research. It is undoubtedly the case that the underlying processes responsible for the effects of anxiety on sport performance differ somewhat from those responsible for anxiety's effects on cognitive performance. However, there is considerable evidence that the adverse effects of anxiety on both sport performance and cognitive performance depend in part on impaired attentional control and processing inefficiency (Wilson, 2008).

Many years ago, Hembree (1988) carried out a meta-analysis to assess the general relationship between anxiety (trait or test) and cognitive performance. He reported that the mean correlation over hundreds of studies was -0.29. This indicates that there is a negative association between anxiety and cognitive performance, but obviously fails to address the causality issue. Some clarification on this issue can be obtained by considering intervention studies in which systematic attempts are made to reduce people's test anxiety levels. Schwarzer (1990) reviewed the literature available at that time. He found that individuals who had received treatment designed to reduce test anxiety outperformed those not receiving treatment on both test performance and academic achievement (grade point average).

As suggested already, the main focus in this chapter is on individual differences in anxiety construed as a personality dimension. However, there is an important distinction between anxiety as a semi-permanent disposition and anxiety as a transient state (state anxiety) determined jointly by personality and by the situational context. It is a matter of theoretical importance whether trait or test anxiety on performance affects cognitive performance directly or whether its effects are mediated indirectly by state anxiety.

The above issue could be addressed most appropriately by carrying out research involving different levels of test or trait anxiety and different levels of situational stressfulness. However, surprisingly little research based on this paradigm has been carried out. Accordingly, I will focus on the effects of trait or test anxiety on performance. It must be acknowledged in the present state of knowledge that it is not currently possible to arrive at a definitive conclusion regarding the extent to which these effects depend on the prevailing level of state anxiety.

In what follows, I will initially consider various related theories of anxiety and cognitive performance that I and my colleagues have put forward. After that, I will evaluate these theories in the light of the available evidence and suggest directions for future theory and research.

THEORIES OF ANXIETY AND PERFORMANCE

Most theorists have argued that at least some of the negative effects of anxiety on cognitive performance are due to attentional mechanisms. For example, consider the influential cognitive interference theory put forward by Sarason (e.g., 1988). In essence, Sarason argued that anxiety is associated with excessive worry and self-concern or, more generally, with self-preoccupation on one's inadequacies and shortcomings. All of these cognitive activities require attention which is thus not available for task performance.

Sarason's (1988) cognitive interference theory takes us part of the way to an understanding of the effects of anxiety on performance. However, it is limited in part because of its failure to consider the specific cognitive mechanisms involved. It is easiest to clarify this in terms of a concrete example. Eysenck's (1979) theory of anxiety and performance was based in large measure on the working memory model of Baddeley and Hitch (1974). Within the original version of the model, there were three processing components. First, there was the central executive, which is an attention-like, limited capacity, modality-free system. Second, there is the phonological loop, which is used for simple verbal processing and brief storage (e.g., rehearsal). Third, there is the visuo-spatial sketchpad, which is used for simple visual and spatial processing and storage. There have been subsequent developments of the working memory model (Baddeley, 1986, 2001).

An obvious issue within the context of the working memory model is to identify the component or components that are most heavily used for worry and self-preoccupation generally. The answer provided by Eysenck (1979) was based on the assumption that worrying typically involves extensive processing of a verbal nature. As a consequence, it was assumed that worrying mostly involves the central executive component of working memory and can also involve the phonological loop.

The prediction that anxiety has a greater adverse effects on the central executive than on the other components of the working memory system was tested by Eysenck, Payne, and Derakshan (2005). In their study, the participants carried out a visuo-spatial task (designated as the primary task) concurrently with a secondary task imposing demands on one of the components of working memory. As predicted, high-anxious participants performed the primary task worse than low-anxious participants when the secondary task involved use of the central executive. However, the adverse effects of anxiety on the primary task were non-significant when the secondary task involved use of the visuo-spatial sketchpad or the phonological loop.

Christopher and MacDonald (2005) tested the same theoretical prediction but used a very different methodology. They assessed the capacity of each component of the working memory system in individuals high or low in anxiety. As predicted, anxiety reduced the capacity of the central executive but had non-significant effects on the capacity of either the phonological loop or the visuo-spatial sketchpad.

Two further versions of Eysenck's (1979) original theory were put forward subsequently. First, there was processing efficiency theory that was proposed by Eysenck and Calvo (1992). Second, there was attentional control theory. This was proposed by Eysenck, Derakshan, Santos, and Calvo (2007) and subsequently revised slightly by Derakshan and Eysenck (2009).

For the purposes of this chapter, I will focus mostly on two major theoretical assumptions incorporated within attentional control theory. These assumptions are of major importance for two reasons. First, they are at the core of the theory. Second, they are distinctively different from the assumptions made by other theories. It is also worth mentioning briefly another distinguishing feature of attentional control theory compared to other theories concerned with anxiety and performance. There is consensus that anxiety affects attentional processes by increasing attentional bias for threat-related stimuli and subsequent difficulties in disengaging from such stimuli (see review by Bar-Haim, Lamy, Pergamin, Bakemans-Kranenburg, M., & van Ijzendoorn, 2007), and this is incorporated within attentional control theory. In addition, however, it is assumed within attentional control theory that anxiety impairs attentional control even in the absence of threat, and this assumption is uncommon in other theories. In other words, attentional control theory assumes that anxiety produces a general rather than a threat-specific impairment of attentional control.

PROCESSING EFFICIENCY VS. PERFORMANCE EFFECTIVENESS

The first core assumption (which was also incorporated within the early versions of the theory) is that there is a fundamental distinction between performance effectiveness and processing efficiency. Performance effectiveness can be defined straightforwardly as the quality of performance. It is typically assessed by dependent variables such as the percentage of responses that are correct. Processing efficiency is more complex. It can be defined as the relationship between performance effectiveness on the one hand and the effort or processing resources used to achieve that level of performance on the other hand.

The single most important prediction of attentional control theory is that any adverse effects of anxiety are typically greater on processing efficiency than on performance effectiveness. This prediction depends on two assumptions. First, it is assumed that worries and other task-irrelevant thoughts utilise some of the resources of the central executive, which causes reduced processing efficiency. Second, anxious individuals frequently try to compensate for these adverse effects of anxiety on processing efficiency by additional motivation involving greater use of processing resources.

Nearly all other theories concerned with anxiety and cognitive performance focus on the effects of anxiety on performance effectiveness and there is no distinction between performance effectiveness. Why is this distinction important? There are several reasons. However, the most consequential one is that occurs when there is a non-significant difference in performance quality (performance effectiveness) between groups high and low in trait or test anxiety.

Within the confines of traditional research, the experiment would be regarded as a failure and the findings discarded. Within attentional control theory, in contrast, it would still be worth obtaining evidence about processing efficiency because the theory predicts that anxiety typically impairs processing efficiency even in the absence of any effects of anxiety on performance per se. As we will see, there are numerous studies in which non-significant effects of anxiety on performance are coupled with significant adverse effects of anxiety on processing efficiency.

EXECUTIVE FUNCTIONING

The second core assumption contained within attentional control theory represents a development of earlier versions of the theory. According to the original version of the theory (Eysenck, 1979) and processing efficiency theory (Eysenck & Calvo, 1992), the main effects of anxiety are on the central executive component of the working memory system.

As we have seen, the assumption that anxiety impairs the efficiency of the central executive has received reasonable empirical support. This assumption was necessarily vague at the time it was proposed because there was a dearth of clear evidence concerning the various executive functions associated with the central executive. However, as the number and nature of the executive functions we possess has become clearer, it became increasingly important to try to identify those executive functions most affected by anxiety.

The precise predictions made by attentional control theory with respect to the effects of anxiety on executive functioning will be discussed after an analysis of the number and nature of such functions.

Executive Functions

In spite of the progress that has been made, there is still controversy and disagreement concerning the nature of our executive functions. However, the approach adopted by Miyake, Friedman, Emerson, Witzki, Howerter, and Wager (2000) has the advantage over competing approaches that it was based squarely on empirical research. In essence, they presented their participants with many different executive tasks. This was followed by using latent-variable analysis to analyse the data in order to identify statistically the number and nature of the executive functions assessed by the tasks.

The analyses used by Miyake et al. (2000), and subsequently extended by Friedman and Miyake (2004), indicated the existence of three functions. First, there is the inhibition function, which involves making use of attentional and/or response control to minimise or prevent disruption or interference from task-irrelevant stimuli or responses.

Second, there is the shifting function. The essence of this function is that it is used to shift or switch attention flexibly in order to maintain optimal focus on the most currently relevant task or aspects of it.

Third, there is the updating function. This function is used to update and also to monitor information that is currently active within the working memory system.

Before proceeding, it is worth noting that there is support for Miyake et al.'s (2000) tripartite view of executive functions. For example, Collette, van der Linden, Laureys, Delfiore, Degueldre, Luxen, et al. (2005) found using positron emission tomography (PET) that each of the three executive functions was associated with a partially distinctive brain-activation pattern. In addition, however, there was also evidence that all three executive functions shared common brain areas of activation involving the right intraparietal sulcus, the left superior parietal gyrus, and the left lateral prefrontal cortex.

The article by Miyake et al. (2000) has been extremely influential (over 1400 citations by mid-2012). However, other researchers who have conducted their own latent-variable analyses of data from executive tasks have not always concurred with the conclusions of

Miyake et al. (2000). For example, there is the research of Fournier-Vicente, Larigauderie, and Gaonac'h (2008) in which their participants carried out a range of different cognitive tasks. Latent-variable analyses indicated the presence of five executive functions rather than the three of Miyake et al. (2000). More specifically, they identified executive functions that they labelled verbal storage and processing co-ordination; visuo-spatial storage and processing co-ordination; shifting, selective attention; and strategic retrieval. Some of these functions are clearly different from those postulated by Miyake et al. (2000), but there is overlap in that shifting corresponds to Miyake et al.'s shifting function and selective attention may correspond approximately to their inhibition function.

It is not entirely clear why Fournier-Vicente et al. (2008) identified more executive functions than Miyake et al. (2000). However, Fournier-Vicente et al. argued that their empirical approach was more fine-grained and thus produced more executive functions.

There is a final plausible candidate for an executive function. Collette, Oliver, van der Linden, Laureys, Delfiore, Luxen, et al. (2005a) compared brain activation when two tasks were performed singly and when they were performed under dual-task conditions. In essence, there was clear evidence for a parieto-frontal network that was associated with dual-task co-ordination but that was not involved in performance of single tasks. The implication of these findings is that dual-task co-ordination may well be an important executive function.

In sum, there is probably more empirical support for the inhibition, shifting, and updating functions than for any other executive functions. However, a case can also be made for the addition of dual-task co-ordination as an executive function. A key issue still awaiting complete resolution is that of overlap among the various executive functions. For example, it is arguable that dual-task co-ordination is not a separate function but rather involves in large measure the inhibition and shifting functions.

Theoretical Predictions

According to attentional control theory (Eysenck et al., 2007), it is assumed that high levels of anxiety have greater adverse effects on attentional control than on other aspects of cognitive functioning. That overarching assumption leads to the prediction that high anxiety impairs the efficiency of the inhibition and shifting functions. These functions involve different types of attentional control. The inhibition function involves negative attentional control in the sense that it is used to prevent attention being directed towards task-irrelevant stimuli or responses. In contrast, the shifting function involves positive attentional control in that it is used to permit the optimal allocation of attention within and between tasks.

The updating function appears to be rather different in nature in that it mostly reflects the capacity of a short-term memory system. Within attentional control theory, it is assumed that anxiety does not impair the efficiency of the updating function under non-stressful conditions but does do so under stressful conditions.

Eysenck et al. (2007) reviewed the relevant research literature, most of which was consistent with these assumptions. In subsequent research, Walkenhorst and Crowe (2009) used the N-back task, which is generally assumed to utilise the updating function. On this task, participants are presented with several items in a sequence of unpredictable length, after which they have to indicate which item was presented a given distance back in the sequence (e.g., 4 back). Individuals high in trait anxiety performed verbal and spatial N-back tasks faster and as accurately as those low in trait anxiety, suggesting that anxiety in the absence of stress does not impair the updating function.

Attentional control theory does not explicitly consider the possible effects of anxiety on dual-task co-ordination. However, it is very likely that successful dual-task co-ordination requires good attentional control, and so high anxiety may well impair such co-ordination. There is insufficient evidence at present to evaluate that suggestion. However, recent unpublished research in our laboratory with Paul Miguel provides tentative support for the notion that anxiety impairs dual-task co-ordination.

PERFORMANCE EFFECTIVENESS VS. PROCESSING EFFICIENCY

Much research over the years has investigated the prediction that anxiety has a greater adverse effect on processing efficiency than on performance effectiveness and the findings have been predominantly supportive (see Eysenck et al., 2007, for a review). However, most of the evidence is somewhat inconclusive. The single most important reason is that it is difficult to assess and measure processing efficiency. Until fairly, recently, there was almost exclusive reliance on behavioural measures to assess processing efficiency, but these measures mostly can only be regarded as providing very indirect evidence concerning underlying processing efficiency.

Derakshan and Eysenck (2010) considered what would be required in order to provide a stringent and robust test of the prediction. They identified three major criteria. First, it is more straightforward to interpret the evidence in an unequivocal fashion if the effects of anxiety on performance effectiveness are non-significant. Why is this criterion included? In essence, it could be complicated to decide whether the effects of anxiety on processing efficiency were greater than its effects on performance effectiveness if both effects were negative.

Second, any attempt to contrast the effects of anxiety on processing efficiency and performance effectiveness should ideally focus on tasks involving the inhibition function or the shifting function rather than the central executive more broadly construed. The reason is that those two executive functions are the ones specifically identified within attentional control theory as being most susceptible to the adverse effects of anxiety.

Third, it is important when assessing processing efficiency to focus on internal processes and mechanisms rather than on the indirect behavioural reflections of those processes and mechanisms. In principle, measures of brain functioning (especially functional magnetic resonance imaging or fMRI and event-related potentials or ERPs) can provide more direct measures of processing efficiency. If individuals high in anxiety have less processing efficiency than those low in anxiety, we would expect to find evidence of greater brain activation during task performance for the former than for the latter group.

How can we ensure that research involving fMRI or ERPs is maximally informative with respect to the prediction from attentional control theory? It is essential for researchers to predict *a priori* precisely where in the brain (in the case of fMRI) and when (in the case of ERPs) that differences between high- and low-anxious groups will occur. As we will see, this is becoming increasingly feasible as more is discovered about where and when various executive processes occur in the brain.

Findings

Several studies have been reported in the literature that approximate to the above desiderata for a study to test the prediction that anxiety impairs processing efficiency more than performance effectiveness. I will start by considering some studies that have focused on anxiety and the inhibition function.

Savostyanov, Tsai, Liou, Levin, Lee, Yurganov, et al. (2009) investigated the inhibition function in an experiment using the stop-signal paradigm. On the great majority of trials, participants need to make an appropriate response as rapidly as possible. On a small number of crucial trials, however, a stop signal is presented, which indicates that participants must inhibit their response.

There were no effects of anxiety on performance effectiveness. Significant effects of anxiety were obtained, however, when Savosyanov et al. focused on event-related perturbations of EEG spectral power, with the key measure being EEG desynchronisation. On stop trials, participants who were high in anxiety had much greater EEG desynchronisation than those low in anxiety throughout the time period between the onset of the stop signal and 600 ms later. Since the inhibition function was needed to prevent the response being produced, this finding strongly suggests that high anxiety is associated with reduced efficiency of the inhibition function.

It is unlikely that this greater EEG desynchronisation associated with high anxiety reflects other cognitive processes because there were practically no effects of anxiety on EEG desynchronisation prior to the stop signal.

There is further support for the prediction from attentional control theory that the effects of anxiety on the inhibition function are greater on its efficiency than on performance effectiveness from other fMRI studies using various other paradigms. For example, Bishop (2009) used a task in which a target letter had to be detected under high perceptual load in the presence or absence of distraction (resisting distraction requires the inhibition function). There was no effect of trait anxiety on either response speed or accuracy in either condition, indicating that anxiety did not affect performance effectiveness. However, the key findings related to activation within the dorsolateral prefrontal cortex, an area associated with attentional control generally and the inhibition function in particular. As predicted by attentional control theory (but diametrically opposed to the prediction from Bishop's own theory), high-anxious participants had greater activation within this area than low-anxious ones under distraction compared to the no-distraction control condition.

Basten, Stelzel, and Fiebach (2011) used the Stroop task in which the task is to say out loud the colours in which words are printed. On crucial trials, there is a conflict between the word (e.g., RED) and the colour in which it is printed (e.g., blue). It is generally assumed that the inhibition function is required to inhibit saying the colour word rather than naming the colour. There were small or non-significant effects of anxiety on performance effectiveness on the Stroop task. As predicted, high-anxious participants showed greater activation than low-anxious ones in the dorsolateral prefrontal cortex, which is strongly associated with attentional control.

As indicated earlier, an alternative way of testing predictions from attentional control theory is to use event-related potentials. This was done by Righi, Macacci, and Viggiano (2009). They used the Sustained Attention to Response Task in which participants must respond to inhibit or withhold a response when the digit 3 is presented but to respond when any other digit is presented. Individuals high and low in trait anxiety did not differ in performance effectiveness whether a response was or was not required. The key finding was that high anxiety (but not low anxiety) was associated with a larger N2 response on NoGo trials (i.e., when 3 was presented and the inhibition function was required) than on Go trials (i.e., when any other digit was presented). This anxiety-specific N2 response was found in the anterior brain, and its timing and location both suggest that it reflects inhibitory processes within the prefrontal cortex.

Sehlmeyer, Konrad, Zwiterserlood, Arolt, Falkenstein, and Beste (2010) carried out a similar study using a GoNogo paradigm. There were small differences in performance effectiveness between the high- and low-anxious groups. They replicated the findings of Righi et al. (2009) in that the only significant effect of anxiety on event-related potentials was that high-anxious individuals had a stronger N2 component in the NoGo condition in which the inhibition function was required.

In sum, there is convincing evidence that the adverse effects of anxiety are greater on processing efficiency than on performance effectiveness on a range of tasks requiring use of the inhibition function. As yet, there is much less evidence relating to the effects of anxiety on efficiency and effectiveness on tasks requiring the shifting function. The most directly relevant study was carried out by Santos, Wall, and Eysenck (unpublished). A digit was presented on a screen and there were three possible simple tasks (e.g., is the digit odd or even?). They assessed the shifting function by varying the extent to which the required task changed during any given block of trials.

What did Santos et al. (unpublished) find? First, there were no effects of anxiety on performance effectiveness on any task regardless of whether or not the shifting function was required. Second, there were effects of anxiety when they compared brain activation in the high-switching and no-switching conditions. As predicted, the increase in brain activation in the high-switching condition compared to the no-switching condition was greater for individuals high in anxiety than for those low in anxiety. Thus, high anxiety was associated with impaired processing efficiency but not performance effectiveness.

Of importance, the brain areas that showed the greatest differentiation between those high and low in anxiety were those (mainly BA 9/46) that are known to be associated with attentional control and the shifting function (Wager, Jonides, & Reading, 2004). It would be valuable for future research to replicate and extend these promising findings.

EXECUTIVE FUNCTIONS

There has been much research of relevance to the prediction that anxiety impairs the efficiency of the inhibition function. The basic experimental approach in most of the literature was to compare performance under two conditions, in one of which distracting, task-irrelevant stimuli were presented and in the other of which no distracting stimuli were presented. The prediction from attentional control theory is that high-anxious individuals should be significantly more distractible than low-anxious ones. Eysenck et al. (2007) reviewed the literature available at that time and found that the great majority of relevant studies reported empirical support for the prediction.

There is additional support for the prediction that anxiety impairs the efficiency of the inhibition function in a recent study by Moser, Becker, and Moran (2012). In their study, they assessed the inhibition function by assessed the extent of attentional distraction to a colour singleton presented on a visual search task. Those high in trait anxiety showed significantly more attentional distraction than those low in trait anxiety. In addition, the evidence suggested that the mechanism involved in this effect did not involve worry.

One of the greatest difficulties in research designed to assess the effects of anxiety on a given executive function is to find 'process pure' tasks. Most tasks involve various different functions, which makes it hard to identify the process or processes most affected by anxiety. A task that seems to provide a relatively process-pure measure of the inhibition function is the antisaccade task. This task is very simple conceptually. Participants are presented on each trial with a peripheral cue that is visible to the left or the right of the fixation point and their task is to look on the other side of the fixation point. Various dependent variables can be measured, but the single most useful measure is the latency of the first saccade in the correct direction. Typically, use is also made of a control condition known as the prosaccade task. On this task, participants simply look at the cue and so there is no conflict between the natural direction of gaze and that required by the instructions.

Much research in recent years has used the antisaccade and prosaccade tasks. As predicted, it has typically been found that high-anxious individuals show impaired performance (i.e., slower latency of first correct saccade) with the antisaccade task but not with the prosaccade task. That pattern of findings indicates that anxiety is associated with impairments of the inhibition function. Precisely this pattern of findings was reported by Derakshan, Ansari, Shoker, and Eysenck (2009).

It also follows from attentional control theory that the negative effects of anxiety on speed of the first correct saccade on the antisaccade task should be greater when the cue is threat-related (e.g., an angry face) than when it is not (i.e., a neutral or happy face). This prediction was tested by Reinholdt-Dunne et al. (2012). They found that individuals high in trait anxiety showed slower performance than those low in trait anxiety when angry faces were presented as cues but not when other types of faces were presented.

There has been much less research on the effects of anxiety on the shifting function than on the inhibition function. The most thorough attempt to investigate the shifting function was by Derakshan, Smyth, and Eysenck (2009). They studied task switching, which is the most direct approach to investigating the shifting function. At a basic level, the task-switching paradigm involves two tasks (A and B). Some blocks of trials involve frequent switches between the two tasks (e.g., alternating trials on task A and task B). That is the switching condition. Other blocks of trials involve only one of the two tasks (A or B), and that is the no-switching condition. The most consequential difference between the two conditions is that the shifting function is required in the switching condition but not in the no-switching condition. In their study, Derakshan et al. (2009) used pairs of arithmetical tasks (e.g., multiplication and division).

What did Derakshan et al. (2009) find? The most important finding was that there was a highly significant interaction between anxiety and task switching. In this interaction, individuals high in anxiety performed much more slowly on blocks requiring task switching than on no-switching blocks. In contrast, the performance of individuals low in anxiety was relatively unaffected by the presence or absence of task switching.

Ansari, Derakshan, and Richards (2008) used the antisaccade and prosaccade tasks to explore the effects of anxiety on the shifting function. They did this by comparing performance when antisaccade and prosaccade trials were blocked (i.e., no-switching condition) or mixed (i.e., switching condition). The findings were complicated, but suggested that the shifting function was used less efficiently and effectively by high-anxious than by low-anxious participants.

In sum, there is substantial support for the prediction that anxiety impairs the inhibition function. There is also accumulating support for the prediction that anxiety impairs the shifting function.

Conclusion

The major assumptions of attentional control theory have been confirmed numerous times in research using a wide range of different paradigms and dependent variables. More specifically, there is an increasing range of research (much of it involving the use of fMRI and ERPs) that indicates the importance of the theoretical distinction between performance effectiveness and processing efficiency. There are many studies in which there were no effects of anxiety on performance but nevertheless anxious individuals used greater effort and resources and so displayed significantly less processing efficiency.

There is also considerable support for the assumption that the major adverse effects of anxiety depend on the central executive component of Baddeley's working memory system. Initial research showed in a general way that anxiety impairs the efficiency of the central executive. More recent research has focused on the specific functions of the central executive. There is now accumulating evidence that anxiety impairs the inhibition function and the shifting function. This more recent research has served to clarify more precisely the ways in which anxiety influences the functioning of the cognitive system.

Three avenues of future research in this area will be mentioned briefly. First, the use of measures such as fMRI and ERPs has greatly increased our ability to assess individual differences in processing efficiency, and has already provided several exciting findings. However, there is still a need for more theoretically driven research in which the precise brain areas that should be more activated in high anxiety are predicted in advance of the research.

Second, one of the important assumptions within attentional control theory is that high anxiety is often associated with a high level of motivation and use of processing resources. There is much indirect evidence supportive of that assumption, but there is as yet a strange dearth of experimental research in which motivational factors are considered explicitly.

Third, it is arguable that the emphasis in research to date has been too much on the effects of anxiety on task processing and not enough on the effects of task processing on anxiety. For example, Vytal, Cornwell, Arkin, and Grillon (2012) found recently that increasing the cognitive load on a task led to a reduction in anxiety. More sophisticated research is needed to elucidate the precise dynamic patterns of anxiety on cognitive processing and of cognitive processing on anxiety.

REFERENCES

Ansari, T. L., Derakshan, N., & Richards, A. (2008). Effects of anxiety on task switching: Evidence from the mixed saccade task. *Cognitive, Affective & Behavioral Neuroscience*, *8*, 229-238.

Baddeley, A. D. (1986). *Working memory*. Oxford: Clarendon Press.

Baddeley, A. D. (2001). Is working memory still working? *American Psychologist*, 56, 851–864.

Baddeley, A. D., & Hitch, G. J. (1974). Working memory. In G. H. Bower (Ed.), *The psychology of learning and motivation*, Vol. 8. London: Academic Press.

Bar-Haim, Y., Lamy, D., Pergamin, L., Bakemans-Kranenburg, M. J., & van Ijzendoorn, M. H. (2007). Threat-related attentional bias in anxious and nonanxious individuals: A meta-analytic study. *Psychological Bulletin*, *133*, 1-24.

Basten, U., Stelzel, C., & Fiebach, C. J. (2011). Trait anxiety modulates the neural efficiency of inhibitory control. *Journal of Cognitive Neuroscience*, *23*, 3132-3145.

Bishop, S. J. (2009). Trait anxiety and impoverished prefrontal control of attention. *Nature Neuroscience*, *12*, 92-98.

Christopher, G., & MacDonald, J. (2005). The impact of clinical depression on working memory. *Cognitive Neuropsychiatry*, *10*, 379-399.

Collette, F., Oliver, L., van der Linden, M., Laureys, S., Delfiore, G., Luxen, A., et al. (2005a). Involvement of both prefrontal and inferior parietal cortex in dual-task performance. *Cognitive Brain Research*, *24*, 237-251.

Collette, F., van der Linden, M., Laureys, S., Delfiore, G., Degueldre, C., Luxen, A., et al. (2005b). Exploring the unity and diversity of the neural substrates of executive functioning. *Human Brain Mapping*, *25*, 409-423.

Derakshan, N., Ansari, T. L., Shoker, L., & Eysenck, M. W. (2009). Anxiety, inhibition, efficiency, and effectiveness: An investigation using the antisaccade task. *Experimental Psychology*, 56, 48–55.

Derakshan, N., & Eysenck, M. W. (2009). Anxiety, processing efficiency, and cognitive performance: New developments from attentional control theory. *European Psychologist*, 14, 168–176.

Derakshan, N., & Eysenck, M. W. (2010). Introduction to the special issue: Emotional states, attention, and working memory. *Cognition & Emotion*, *24*, 189-199.

Derakshan, N., Smyth, S., & Eysenck, M W. (2009). Effects of state anxiety on performance using a task-switching paradigm: An investigation of attentional control theory. *Psychonomic Bulletin & Review*, *16*, 1112-1117.

Eysenck, M W. (1979). Anxiety, learning, and memory: A reconceptualisation. *Journal of Research in Personality*, *13*, 363-385.

Eysenck, M. W., & Calvo, M. G. (1992). Anxiety and performance: The processing efficiency theory. *Cognition & Emotion*, 6, 409–434.

Eysenck, M. W., Derakshan, N., Santos, R., & Calvo, M. G. (2007). Anxiety and cognitive performance: Attentional control theory. *Emotion*, 7, 336–353.

Eysenck, M. W., Payne, S., & Derakshan, N. (2005). Trait anxiety, visuo-spatial processing and working memory. *Cognition and Emotion*, *19*, 1214–1228.

Fournier-Vicente, S., Larigauderie, P., & Gaonac'h, D. (2008). More dissociations and interactions within central executive functioning: A comprehensive latent-variable analysis. *Acta Psychologica*, 129, 32-48.

Friedman, N. P., & Miyake, A. (2004). The relations among inhibition and interference control functions: A latent-variable analysis. Journa*l of Experimental Psychology: General, 133*, 101-135.

Hembree, R. (1988). Correlates, causes, effects, and treatment of test anxiety. *Review of Educational Research*, 58, 47–77.

Miyake, A., Friedman, N. P., Emerson, M. J., Witzki, A. H., Howerter, A., & Wager, T. D. (2000). The unity and diversity of executive functions and their contributions to complex 'frontal lobe' tasks: A latent variable analysis. *Cognitive Psychology*, 41, 49–100.

Moser, J. S., Becker, M. W., & Moran, T. P. (2012). Enhanced attentional capture in trait anxiety. *Emotion*, *12*, 213-216.

Reinholdt-Dunne, M. L., Mogg, K., Benson, V., Bradley, B. P., Hardin, Liversedge, S. P., et al. (2012). Anxiety and selective attention to angry faces: An antisaccade study. *Journal of Cognitive Psychology*, *24*, 54-65.

Righi, S., Mecacci, L., & Viggiano, M. P. (2009). Anxiety, cognitive self-evaluation and performance: ERP correlates. *Journal of Anxiety Disorders*, *23*, 1132-1138.

Santos, R., Wall, M., & Eysenck, M. W. (unpublished). *Anxiety and task switching: A functional neuroimaging study.*

Sarason I. G. (1978). The test anxiety scale: Concept and research. In C. D. Spielberger, & I. G. Sarason (Eds.), *Stress and Anxiety, Vol. 5*. Washington DC: Hemisphere; 1978:193–216.

Sarason, I. G. (1988). Anxiety, self-preoccupation and attention. *Anxiety Research*, *1*, 3-7.

Savostyanov, A. N., Tsai, A. C., Liou, M., Levin, E. A., Lee, J.-D., Yurganov, A. V., & Knyazev, G .G. (2009). EEG correlates of trait anxiety in the stop-signal paradigm. *Neuroscience Letters*, *449*, 112–116.

Schwarzer, R. (1990). Current trends in anxiety research. In P. J. D. Drenth, J. A. Sergeant, & J. R. Takens (Eds.), *European perspectives in psychology* (pp. 225–244). Oxford: John Wiley & Sons.

Sehlmeyer, C., Konrad, C., Zwitserlood, P., Arolt, V., Falkenstein, M., & Beste, C. (2010). ERP indices for response inhibition are related to anxiety-related personality traits. *Neuropsychologia*, *48*, 2488-2498.

Spielberger, C. D., Gorsuch, R. L., Lushene, R., Vagg, P. R., & Jacobs, G. J. (1983). *Manual for the State-Trait Anxiety Inventory*. Palo Alto, CA: Consulting Psychologists Press.

Vytal, K., Cornwell, B., Arkin, N., & Grillon, C. (2012). Describing the interplay between anxiety and cognition: From impaired performance under low cognitive load to reduced anxiety under high load. *Psychophysiology*, *49*, 842-852.

Wager, T. D., Jonides, J., & Reading, S. (2004). Neuroimaging studies of shifting attention: A meta-analysis. *Neuroimage*, 22, 1679–1693.

Walkenhorst, E., & Crowe, F. (2009). The effects of state worry and trait anxiety on working memory processes in a normal sample. *Anxiety, Stress, & Coping*, 22, 167-187.

Wilson, M. R. (2008). From processing efficiency to attentional control: A mechanistic account of the anxiety-performance relationship. *International Review of Sports Exercise Psychology*, *1*, 184-201.

Wilson, M. R. (in press). Anxiety, attention, the brain, the body and performance. In S. Murphy (Ed.), *Handbook of sport and performance*. Oxford: Oxford University Press.

In: Handbook of Psychology of Emotions
Editors: C. Mohiyeddini, M. Eysenck and S. Bauer

ISBN: 978-1-62808-053-7
© 2013 Nova Science Publishers, Inc.

Chapter 7

PSYCHOLOGY OF EMOTION AND ITS APPLICATION IN EDUCATIONAL SETTINGS

Kristin Bitan[*], Anna Haep[†] and Gisela Steins[‡]

Faculty of Educational Science, Institute of Psychology,
University of Duisburg-Essen, Germany

ABSTRACT

The aim of this chapter is to point out the relevance of insights from emotion psychology for interaction designs in the school context. We chose three different levels on which to demonstrate this relevance. The first level deals with the pupils themselves and takes into consideration those insights from emotion psychology, which should be taught and shown to pupils in order to help them to establish a positive and helpful design of interaction. The second level deals with those findings from emotion psychology which should be an integral part of teacher training for the benefit of a constructive interaction design between teachers and pupils and a successful classroom management. The third and last level deals with leadership in educational contexts and the management of schools, especially concerning headmasters. We are going to point out and report research results from all three levels of school interaction (pupil-pupil; pupil-teacher; headmaster-teacher), which in total show that fundamental knowledge of emotion psychology contains valuable conclusions for a positive design of life in schools.

Our research primarily focuses on forming the ability of the protagonists to understand and realize the interdependence of their own belief systems, emotions and actions. They should thus be enabled to develop sensitivity for the social effects which their own behavior has on the beliefs, emotions and actions of their social environment. In order to develop this ability, important theories and concepts to consider are cognitive models of emotion and emotion regulation as well as the foundation of rational-emotive behavior therapy, completed by theories of emotional contagion and models of emotion categorization.

---

[*] Corresponding author: Kristin Bitan, Universität Duisburg-Essen, Fakultät für Bildungswissen- schaften, Institut für Psychologie, D-45117 Essen, Germany. E-mail: Kristin.bitan@uni-due.de.
[†] E-mail: Anna.haep@uni-due.de.
[‡] E-mail: Gisela.steins@uni-due.de.

INTRODUCTION

1. Psychology of Emotion and Education

Our research particularly focuses on the effects of interaction designs between pupils on the one hand and teachers and pupils on the other, in order to understand which ones serve and encourage the pupils' cognitive and social-emotional development best. It has been shown that the interaction design has a significant effect on the social-emotional as well as the cognitive development of individuals (Pianta, 2006; Hattie, 2009). In order to understand the significance of interactions between human beings, developmental and social psychological foundations are traditionally used and considered helpful. But in order to understand the hindering or conducive conditions of interaction designs, the psychology of emotion comes into play. Since our research results are actively incorporated into the education of teachers, they are settled alongside the interface of social and emotional psychology in the school context.

The aim of this chapter is to point out the relevance of insights from emotion psychology for interaction designs in the school context. We chose three different levels on which to demonstrate this relevance. The first level deals with the pupils themselves and takes into consideration those insights from emotion psychology, which should be taught and shown to pupils in order to help them to establish a positive and helpful design of interaction. The second level deals with those findings from emotion psychology which should be an integral part of teacher training for the benefit of a constructive interaction design between teachers and pupils and a successful classroom management. The third and last level deals with leadership in educational contexts and the management of schools, especially concerning headmasters. The leadership of a group has got effects on its commitment, motivation and its actual performance. Here, emotion psychology offers valuable insights for an understanding and positive way of influencing these processes.

We are going to point out and report research results from all three levels of school interaction (pupil-pupil; pupil-teacher; headmaster-teacher), which in total show that fundamental knowledge of emotion psychology contains valuable conclusions for a positive design of life in schools. The potential, which knowledge of emotion psychology offers in this context, could be used for the constructive design of school life. But indeed, it is currently used very rarely, since it neither plays a big role in the education of teachers, nor in the advanced training of headmasters. This represents a gap, which can be found when it comes to psychological knowledge concerning designs of interaction in teacher training in general (Evertson& Weinstein, 2006) and which shows an urgent need to be closed.

Our research primarily focuses on forming the ability of the protagonists to understand and realize the interdependence of their own belief systems, emotions and actions. They should thus be enabled to develop sensitivity for the social effects which their own behavior has on the beliefs, emotions and actions of their social environment. In order to develop this ability, important theories and concepts to consider are cognitive models of emotion and emotion regulation as well as the rational-emotive behavior therapy by Ellis (1994; David, Lynn & Ellis, 2010), completed by theories of emotional contagion and models of emotion categorization (Hatfield, Cacioppo & Rapson, 1994). Besides, according to our opinion, Ellis' theory already completely contains all elements of the metacognitive therapy, which Wells (2000) declares as new.

Findings from interaction research, which was conducted at schools, can be used to clarify how the above mentioned insights relate to the interaction design of certain protagonists and how they can be used in the school context. A compilation of numerous meta-analyses significantly shows the strong effects, which the teacher-pupil-interaction has got on the cognitive development of pupils (Hattie, 2009, p.118-119). Further research clearly shows that the way in which teachers organize their interactions with pupils considerably affects their social-emotional development (Steins, 2011). According to Hattie, a successful and ideal design of interaction especially includes the teacher's ability of being non-directive, empathetic, affectionate and encouraging. These are characteristics concerning the behavior of teachers which are likewise helpful and important for the social-emotional development of pupils (Steins, 2011; Haep & Steins, 2011).

But similarly to the way, in which a pupil's motivation or his willingness to work hard and act disciplined cannot always be controlled in an ideal way, the behavior of teachers also often underlies extreme variations, which cannot be explained by exclusively drawing on knowledge and research from social psychology alone. Here, important insights from emotion psychology come into play, especially those models, which deal with the development and regulation of emotions. School reluctance, boredom, stress, fear, anger and jealousy or envy are emotions, which make it hard for pupils as well as teachers to establish a constructive and learner-friendly interaction design. Without awareness for the development of emotions and knowledge about the possible consequences, the only solution which is left for teachers as well as pupils is to pull themselves up, adjust or to trick. An important premise of our research is that they will not be able to deeply work on complex conflicts or solve other occurring problems satisfyingly this way.

In the following, we are going to present three levels of school life interaction and we are going to show how insights from the above named areas of emotion psychology can be transferred to these levels.

2. The Pupil-pupil-interaction: Social Education at School

Schools have an educational mandate, which comprises the goal to educate pupils cognitively as well as socially. We claim that it is of great significance to combine both fields. Schools should focus on creating a social, learner-friendly environment and should thus systematically establish strategies to prevent antisocial and problematic behavior. But, in practice, schools very rarely focus on the social-emotional development of their pupils. Furthermore, the interaction design of all participants is likely to be neglected by teachers, because they are mostly not aware of its importance and significance.

The Teaching Subject "Emotional Education"

We developed a special teaching subject within the framework of the research project "Emotional Education". This teaching subject focuses on supporting pupils to develop and refine their social competencies. They learn to act more responsibly towards themselves and towards others. The foundations of the concept are the main assumptions of Albert Ellis' rational-emotive behavior therapy. In this program, we particularly focus on the cognitive models of emotions and emotion regulation.

The subject has been implemented into the school life of our partner schools as follows: The subject has been developed for grades 7 and 8 (which means, that participating students are between 13 and 15 years old). It is taught two lessons a week and is a mandatory subject for all participating students for the duration of one school year. Comments concerning the students' performance in the teaching subject can be found on their school certificate. The lessons are taught by teacher trainees who are being trained at the University of Duisburg-Essen and who are being prepared and supported by a special seminar.

Outsider:
Rational and irrational components

iB: No one likes me! I'm not worth being loved. I don't belong here. And I absolutely need other children to be my friends, I can't stand it the way it is now!

rB: I really would like to play with the other children. There really should be something I can do about this situation. But until I find a solution, I am able to stand being alone, although it's not the nicest thing on earth!

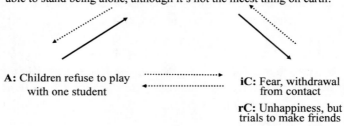

A: Children refuse to play with one student

iC: Fear, withdrawal from contact

rC: Unhappiness, but trials to make friends

Figure 1. A-B-C Outsider.

The Teaching Concept

The teaching concept consists of three different elements: Firstly, pupils learn how to recognize their emotions and how to differentiate them. Then, they learn about anger and the side effects that go along with this emotion. And thirdly, they practice and are coached in role-plays in order to deepen their knowledge (Haep & Steins, 2011; Haep, Steins & Wilde, 2012).

With the help of Albert Ellis' ABC-model, students learn the connection of (activating) events (A), thoughts or beliefs (B) and consequences (C) (Ellis & Hoellen, 2004). Ellis states that it most notably depends on how a person estimates an event and that this person will feel and act according to the estimation (see Figure 1). Thus, a very important insight for students is to realize, that not the activating events, but the beliefs and thoughts of a person are central to our emotional reactions. Beliefs can be divided into two categories: irrational, not helpful thoughts and rational, helpful thoughts. Beliefs about certain events therefore also have a big influence on the code of interaction with different persons (see Figure 1). The students are trained to realize this by analyzing many different examples and ABC-models. A person's individual beliefs (B) about activating events (A) have a large influence on the emotional reactions and the behavior (C). A trigger for irrational thoughts and beliefs can be absolutistic demands, which persons tend to have implemented in their belief system. Absolutistic demands are divided into three categories by Ellis: Demands concerning the world

("Everything should work out the way I want it to."), demands regarding others ("Other students should act exactly as I want them to.") and self-demands ("I should perform better at school. Without good marks, I'm a useless person.").

After having figured out the whole ABC-model, in a second step, pupils then learn about the connection of beliefs and feelings. They are helped to internalize why some beliefs and thoughts, emotions and behaviors are not helpful for them (Haep & Steins, 2012). By understanding and accepting the B-C-connection, they are enabled to take over responsibility for their thoughts, beliefs and emotions and do not have to blame others any longer.

The third step provides sufficient time to practice the new insights with the help of many exercises, such as role-plays, in order to achieve and intensify the intended change.

It was relevant to us, to create a concept which focuses on the individual and its characteristic attributes. Every single student is repeatedly focused on and the concept particularly tries to point at specific topics and examples stemming from the everyday experience realm of pupils aged 13 to 15. Pupils are practicing by talking about single matters of importance, but also by participating in role-plays and other student-focused activities. Among other situations, we also try to include real-life situations from the students' school experiences. For example, students may report a conflict situation with one of their teachers. This situation is then used as an example and students are asked to differentiate this situation into an A-B-C-model. The whole group, under the supervision and with the support of the trainee teachers, then tries to work out rational solutions for a positive interaction.

A very important component of the concept is a binding sanction system for the lessons. This sanction system is established by agreeing on rules of communication and cooperation together with the students and by establishing consequences for possible infringements against these rules but also for adhering to the rules. In order to practice the self-perception of the participating students the concept includes an evaluation sheet, which is used to comment on and explain every student's behavior from their own point of view as well as from the point of view of their "Emotional Education" teachers. At the end of the school year, the teaching unit closes with a reward for those pupils, who more often got a + than a − in the course of their behavioral evaluation.

Results

Our results, which were measured by using a standardized questionnaire, showed the development of positive effects on the disposition to empathy after half a school year already in the pilot phase. The new knowledge, which was taught to the students in their new subject "Emotional Education" was correctly reproduced and used in every-day life even half a year later (Haep, Weber, Welling & Steins 2011).

For the main research phase (2009/2010) lessons in "Emotional Education" took place in four different school classes (N = 85).

- Social climate aspects of class and school life from a point of view of the pupils were measured with a questionnaire relating to social climate in school classes by Eder and Mayr (2000) at the beginning and at the end of the project. Our research findings are that the values increase significantly. But it has to be mentioned that in some school classes apart from the increase in the willingness to learn and the social climate, other aspects such as rivalry and disturbances increased as well. It can be stated that specific characteristics can be found in every class, but also that the positive dimensions increased significantly in every class.

- Another questionnaire was used in order to measure the amount of anger. Pupils were asked to fill in the questionnaire at the beginning and the end of their training, in which they had to indicate how often they would feel angry while being at school and how often and how many other students were treated well/ badly by them. A very strong effect can be found in the results regarding the amount of persons treated badly and the frequency of this behavior: Here, the amount of persons as well as the frequency decreased significantly.

- Every week, the trainee teachers, who were conducting the lessons in "Emotional Education", evaluated the lessons according to the following parameters: Loudness and attention of the pupils, contentment with their team teaching performance, the achievement of their learning objective and the confidence in the fact, that their lessons would affect the students in a positive way. The findings show, that within the course of a school year, the estimated loudness decreased and the other parameters increased, although not strongly.

- The weekly evaluations were analyzed according to the participation in the reward event. If the pupils increased their emotional competency, the number of participants should have increased as well, in analogy to the comment on their school certificate. Here, the numbers and comments were analyzed after half a school year and compared to those at the end of the whole school year. In all school classes the participation increased significantly. (End of half year term: 47: participation/ 40: no participation; End of full school year term: 69: participation/ 18: no participation).

Classroom disturbances:
rational and irrational components

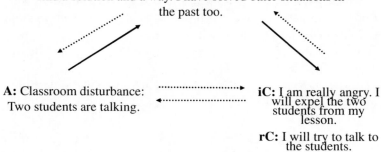

iB: I just can't do this. I will never manage to make the pupils listen to me. I'm incapable of doing this job.

rB: I can't do this right now. But I'm sure I will be able to find a solution and a way. I have solved other situations in the past too.

A: Classroom disturbance: Two students are talking.

iC: I am really angry. I will expel the two students from my lesson.

rC: I will try to talk to the students.

Figure 2. A-B-C Classroom disturbances.

The Teacher as a Model

In the framework of the subject "Emotional Education" it is not only important to teach students about the content, but also to use the proper teaching method. If rational-emotive education is taught, this means in the first place, that teachers will need to be rational models for their students themselves (Steins, 2011). An irrational model would weaken the effects (for the project). A person, who teaches rational-emotive education, should have internalized rational philosophies and should thus act accordingly. In this regard, it is also important that teachers are interested in their students and ready to listen to them. Dysfunctional thinking (iB) and acting (iC) or, on the other hand, functional thinking (rB) and acting (rC) of teachers have a strong and direct influence on students (see Figure 2). If teachers act irrationally, by, for example, interpreting a situation with non-attentive students in such a way that they are incapable of teaching children and as a consequence expel them from the lesson, as shown in the example below, this will lead to different reactions and effects with the students.

Noisy group of pupils

iB: These pupils are really getting on my nerves. They absolutely have to adhere to my rules and do what I'm telling them.

A: The class is loud and noisy.

iC: I will punish the whole class.

Figure 3. A-B-C: Irrational beliefs and irrational actions.

Children and adolescents are able to develop rational (and irrational) belief systems through observation and reinforcement. Findings from deVoge (1979) show that irrational belief systems can be dominated by rational ones if they are consequently reinforced over a longer period of time. In this regard, it is crucial to consider the important role of language. Language is eminently affected by role models. In order to support a beneficial development it is important that models, in this case teachers, use rational language and statements when talking to students. Irrational statements, which are made by students, should also be a matter of discussion in order to create learning opportunities.

3. Professionalization of Trainee Teachers at University Level

In our project, every trainee teacher is prepared for teaching the subject "Emotional Education" at our partner schools by participating in a special seminar. First of all, every participant is informed about the principles of rational-emotive behavior therapy and learns how to apply them to concrete problems and situations. The seminar furthermore emphasizes a rational mode of communication. Trainee teachers, who start teaching at a new school during their university education, are in a very demanding situation: They are a new part of the school as a system, teaching pupils is new to them as well, they are supposed to act as role models and overall impart knowledge and the content of certain subjects. The trainee teachers in our project are regularly supported by supervision and sitting in on classes, which is supposed to help them to develop a rational belief system. The participants of the project furthermore regularly write reports once a week, in which they summarize the main events of every lesson. These reports often convey irrational thoughts or behavior, which again helps the supervisor to detect aspects, which are still problematic and need to be discussed (see Figure 3).

Trainee teachers definitely need the conjunction of theory and professional practice and therefore the seminar is being accepted by them as a great opportunity to gain experiences. There are plenty of situations, in which the participating trainee teachers have to learn that it cannot be their aim, to make each and every student happy, but that it is most important to be consistent and transparent in their behavior (see Figure 4).

The depicted situation in the A-B-C (Figure 4) was reported by the students in the forefront of the lesson. For the conduction of the seminar, a trustful atmosphere, in which everybody can express assertions openly, is crucial. In this case, the irrationals thoughts of the trainee teachers were discussed within an A-B-C and then later transformed into rational thoughts. Furthermore, their function as a role model for the students was discussed in this context.

Reward event

iB: This will cause a scene. The pupils will demand that everyone can go. We should ignore the rule and let everybody participate.

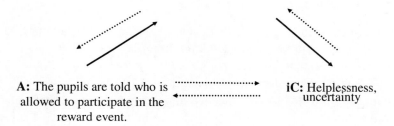

A: The pupils are told who is allowed to participate in the reward event.

iC: Helplessness, uncertainty

Figure 4. A-B-C: Reward event.

Schools as Systems

The above mentioned example shows that it is often hard for teachers to stick to (their own) rules consistently. Therefore, schools should operate with a consistent sanction system. If schools do not possess a consistent sanction system, difficulties will arise for all participants. Establishing clarity concerning rules and sanctions will definitely help to improve the interaction of all parties involved.

This was also found in our research: The principles of education at our cooperating schools differed widely, because no consistent sanction system had been established. The rules, which some of the teachers established, varied tremendously and this was also true regarding the sanctions, which followed the infringements of certain rules. The described situation caused numerous problems between teachers and students. On the one hand, students never knew which of the inconsistent rules to apply and on the other hand, teachers constantly complained about the students' misconduct. Again, the miscarriage of interaction influenced the whole school atmosphere (Haep et al., 2011).

The Education of Trainee Teachers

What do these findings imply for the education of trainee teachers? It is crucial to teach them how important a positive and successful interaction in everyday school life is and which components play a vital role. While they are being trained at university, they can learn that they are important models for their students and that they therefore thoroughly need to reflect their behavior and emotions.

4. Becoming a Teacher: Prospective Teacher Training and Emotion Psychology

While the above stated research findings particularly dealt with interactions between pupils as well as teachers and pupils and the professionalization of trainee teachers by participating in one of our university projects, this part of the chapter looks at the second and practical part of teacher education in Germany and later comes to talk about the importance of emotion psychology for the leadership in educational contexts.

Following teacher training at university, prospective teachers take part in a practical education phase, which is currently being reduced from two to one and a half years in the federal state North Rhine-Westphalia (NRW). This second teacher education phase is regarded as very stressful and exhausting by many prospective teachers (Daschner et al., 2007). In case of the practical teacher training, too, we bring forward the argument that the above depicted principles of dealing cognitively with emotions and their regulation, as proposed by Ellis' rational-emotive behavior therapy (Ellis, 1994; David, Lynn & Ellis, 2010), offer rewarding possibilities, to deal with the demands and challenges of this education phase. For example, possible stress factors are related to classroom observations by training instructors or headmasters. Dealing with feedback and the frequency of teaching evaluations are also described as stressful and applying pressure. In this case, too, it depends on the belief and assessment concerning the situation, whether one is able to deal with it constructively.

It might be useful to depict this situation within an A-B-C based on Ellis' theory (compare Figure 5). A prospective teacher could, while expecting a classroom observation (activating event, A), think the following: "I absolutely cannot stand being criticized by my training instructor. He always picks at my lessons and my teaching abilities. I will never become a good teacher; everything I do is wrong." Such an irrational assessment of the situation (beliefs, B) again might lead to emotional consequences (C) such as fear of the next classroom observation or depressive episodes, which again may lead to withdrawal and avoidance on a behavioral level. Furthermore, feedback could be rejected as a form of self-protection, which means, that valuable learning opportunities would be missed out on.

Classroom observation

iB: I absolutely cannot stand being criticized by my training instructor. He always picks at my lessons and my teaching abilities. I will never become a good teacher; everything I do is wrong.

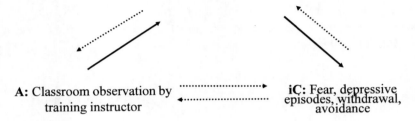

Figure 5. A-B-C: Classroom observation.

School inspection

iB: I have to prepare hundreds of documents for this inspection all alone. This is too much work! I cannot let anyone treat me like that! I don't deserve this!

rB: This inspection certainly is a good deal of work, but I can plan and handle this work together with my staff of teachers. Once we have finished, we will be able to use our work for the development of our school!

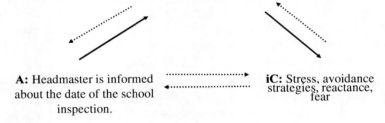

Figure 6. A-B-C: School inspection.

A rational assessment of the described situation would lead to a more open and relaxed approach to feedback. Moreover, prospective teachers could then use their practical education as well as the judgment of professionals as valuable support for professionalization.

From this very short insight it is clearly recognizable, that prospective teachers can superficially finalize their education on a successful level and become teachers, but this still does not mean that feedback has been accepted and that suggestions for improvements have been implemented at all.

This poses problems, since teachers do not receive much feedback from professional instructors once they finished their education, since classroom observations are still very rare phenomena in Germany. Therefore, we argue that specific knowledge concerning models from emotion psychology and the ability to rationally work on one's thoughts and behavior could lead to more acceptance and usage of highly valuable learning opportunities and have positive influences on the professionalization of future teachers. Findings from the field of emotion psychology therefore need to be implemented more thoroughly into practical teacher education as well.

5. The Higher Level: Psychology of Emotion and Its Use in School Leadership

The last part of this chapter deals with the relevance of implementing knowledge from emotion psychology and the thus resulting helpful way of dealing with emotions on a leadership level in education, in this special case, when it comes to headmasters of schools. In the last years, a school's self-reliance and image have become more and more important. This also led to a new role of a school's headmaster: from being a sole administrative board to becoming a leadership personality, who actively shapes everyday school life (Warwas, 2009; Rosenbusch, 2005; Dubs, 2005). A headmaster significantly determines, in which direction a school – including its teaching staff and students – develops and which beliefs and attitudes are prevailing.

Our research regarding leadership in education has concentrated on the attitudes of headmasters towards a newly introduced evaluation instrument: the school inspection, which is called Qualitätsanalyse in NRW (Haep & Steins, 2010; Steins & Haep, 2012). Within the scope of the study, headmasters were interviewed concerning their acceptance, expectancies and attitudes towards school inspection, before they were visited by the inspectors. Many headmasters regarded the external evaluation quite positively (40%) or at least in a neutral way and expected a learning opportunity for their own school, which would help them to adapt and develop competences. But still, 30% regarded an evaluation of the quality of their schools in a very sceptical up to hostile way. These headmasters voiced notably many irrational, not helpful thoughts and beliefs concerning the external evaluation instrument and some even strictly refused it. Very often aspects such as a high work amount, low expectancies concerning the instruments' efficiency, negative feelings of external control, not enough support, a lacking qualification of the evaluators and severe scepticism were expressed. This also shows the high uncertainty, which is a side effect of a new situation such as a mandatory external evaluation for all schools.

In the situation described above (compare Figure 6), it would be more functional and reasonable for headmasters as well as the teaching staff, on which the headmaster's attitude is transferred, to adopt a rational attitude concerning the evaluation (activating event, A). It makes a significant difference, whether headmasters judge this event in a dysfunctional way, such as in the following example (beliefs, B): "I have to prepare hundreds of documents for this inspection all alone. This is too much work, which I do not even get paid. I cannot let anyone treat me like that; it really makes me furious." On the other hand, the same event could be evaluated in a rational way, such as in this example (beliefs, B): "This inspection certainly is a good deal of work, but I can plan and handle this work together with my staff of teachers. Once we have finished the portfolio which the inspectors need, we will be able to use it productively and on its basis develop the quality of our school." Different consequences (C) arise on the basis of the thoughts and beliefs the headmasters have concerning the external evaluation. This will include a much higher stress level in case of the irrational headmaster, which again will influence the commitment and attitude of the teaching staff and the whole school. This lack of acceptance towards the evaluation is likely to lead to avoidance strategies in teachers, an unrealistic, euphemized depiction of the school itself, reactance (Brehm, 1966) and fear of the inspection.

The results of our study have shown that by no means every headmaster deals with evaluation and feedback situations concerning their schools constructively. This leads us to the conclusion, that the school sector has a considerable demand concerning functional behavioral repertoire when it comes to dealing with one's own emotions such as stress, fear, insecurity, reactance or shame. These feelings have to be taken seriously, even when they are highly irrational. They show that leaders have not necessarily learned to deal with their beliefs, interpretations and emotions concerning certain situations in appropriate ways. Our suggestions are that it would be helpful to appropriately prepare headmasters for their position. We suggest that preparation could be most effective through a profound psychological basis and a training, in which they learn to adequately deal with their emotions and such situations.

Principles stemming from Ellis' rational-emotive behavior therapy (Ellis 1994; David, Lynn & Ellis, 2010) could be very supportive in this regard. Also, substantiated offers for professional development from the area of (emotion) psychology are going short, although they hold an essential role in the development of schools and leadership in education. As already described while referring to the other levels of school, it is essential to include knowledge from emotion psychology in order to redefine the approach to the protagonists' own fears, concerns but also resistance more rationally and thus create a productive learning opportunity for the whole school.

Schools, as complex systems including different levels of demands can only work productively and future-oriented if they do not close their minds to their learning opportunities. Complex problems will hence only be solved in the long term if leaders of schools take an academic look at the emergence of emotions, their meaning and ways of emotion regulation. The resulting effects will again positively influence teaching staff and pupils and, therefore, the whole school and its atmosphere as a system. A headmaster who does not realize the impact and importance of a rational way of dealing with his or her emotions is furthermore less likely to rate the social and emotional learning field highly, which again influences teaching staff and pupils. This is, as our above stated findings show, a point of view which reduces school to cognitive knowledge production only and ignores that every individual, regardless of its position in the school system, needs a stable emotional base, which is the precondition for cognitive learning processes.

CONCLUSION

Our current efforts of implementing insights of emotion psychology into different levels of the school context are received with high interest by all participants. This results in many offers to organize and conduct advanced education and further training on all levels dealing with findings from emotion psychology and the transmission of these into the school context. This can be regarded as an indicator for the confirmation of our assumption that there is a relevant knowledge gap in this area.

Research insights from emotion psychology are not the only relevant sources of knowledge for a constructive and positive interaction in educational contexts. Fundamental theories from social psychology (and the application of this knowledge to the school context) play an equal role in our work: Power and authority as well as conformity processes, findings from research about group dynamics as well as concerning reactance, resistance and dissonance or attributions and self-awareness, to name just a few aspects. All these processes, which are relevant for the interaction designs, can be integrated into models in emotion psychology without problems. We are currently working on and designing a multi-annual educational program at university, which is dealing with classroom management. This program focuses on teaching psychological knowledge to teacher trainees in such a way, that their knowledge can directly be used in the interaction with pupils at school. The above mentioned rational-emotive behavior theory plays a crucial role in this concept as a basis for self-reflection and the reflection of others.

A central question in the discussion concerning emotions is focusing on health aspects: How harmful are certain emotions and are they harmful at all? Also, influenced by discourses in emotion psychology, complex discussions emerge concerning the relation between emotion regulation, the adjustment to adverse conditions and the dissociation of unwanted conformity processes. One example can exemplify this point: Would it not be better (and healthier?) to be angry about adverse circumstances at school than to take them calmly? In the discussion of these questions concerning everyday life in school, research findings from emotion psychology can further a sense of reality and stimulate self-efficacy with teachers (cp. Gross, 1998).

We are focusing our research on getting a deeper insight into processes which are relevant from an emotion psychological viewpoint through qualitative analysis, in order to understand positive and negative, successful and miscarrying interactions better.

REFERENCES

Brehm, Jack Williams (1966). *A Theory of Psychological Reactance.* New York: Academic Press.

Daschner, P. and Drews, U. (2007). *Teacher Traineeship Guide.* (Kursbuch Referendariat.) Weinheim: Beltz Verlag.

David, D., Lynn, S. J., & Ellis, A. (2010). *Rational and Irrational Beliefs.* Oxford: Oxford University Press.

de Voge, C. (1979): *A Behavioral Therapy Approach to Teaching Rational-Emotive Principles to Children.* (Ein verhaltenstherapeutischer Ansatz zur Vermittlung von rational-emotiven Prinzipien bei Kindern.) In: Ellis, A. & Grieger, R. (Hrsg.): Practice of Rational-Emotive Therapy (Praxis der rational-emotiven Therapie) (S.276-282). München.

Dubs, R. (2005). *The Leadership of a School.Leadershipand Management.* (Die Führung einer Schule. Leadership und Management.) (2.,überarb. Aufl.). Zürich: SKV.

Ellis, A. (1994). *Reason and Emotion in Psychotherapy.* New York: Birch Lane Press.

Ellis, A. und Hoellen, B. (2004): *Rational-Emotive Behavior Therapy*: Reflections and Redefinitions. (Die Rational-Emotive Verhaltenstherapie-Reflexion und Neubestimmung.) Stuttgart: Pfeiffer bei Klett-Cotta.

Evertson, C. M. & Weinstein, C. S. (2006). *Classroom Management as a Field of Inquiry*. In: Evertson, C. M. & Weinstein, C. S. (Ed.), Handbook of Classroom Management (3-16). NJ: Mahwah: Lawrence Erlbaum Associates.

Gross, J. J. (1994). Antecendent-and Response-focused Emotion Regulation: Divergent Consequences for Experience, Expression, and Physiology. *Journal of Personality and Social Psychology, 74,* 224-237.

Haep, A., & Steins, G. (2010). *Attitudes of Headmasters towards the School Inspection QA NRW*. (Einstellungen der Schulleiter/innen zur QA NRW.) Unpublished report/ Unveröffentlichter Bericht.

Haep, A. & Steins, G. (2011). Rational-Emotive Education as Social Education in the School Context: Effects and Implementation. (Rational-emotive Erziehung als Sozialerziehung im schulischen Kontext: Effekte und Implementierung.) *Zeitschrift für Rational-Emotive & Kognitive Verhaltenstherapie, 22,* 18-37.

Haep, A. und Steins, G., & Wilde, J. (2012): *Social Education SEK1*. (Sozialerziehung SEK1.) Donauwörth: Auer.

Haep, A., Welling, V., Weber, P. & Steins, G. (2011): *Psychopathology of Children and Adolescents, the Role of the Parents and School and the Relevance of a Social Psychological Perspective*. (Psychopathologisierung von Kindern und Jugendlichen, die Rolle des Elternhauses und der Schule und die Relevanz einer sozialpsychologischen Perspektive.) In: Witte, E. H. & Doll, J.: Social Psychology, Socialization and School. (Sozial- psychologie, Sozialisation und Schule. Lengerich: Pabst Science Publi- shers.

Hatfield, E., Cacioppo, J. T., &Rapson, R. L. (1994). *Emotional Contagion*. Paris: Cambridge University Press.

Hattie, J. (2009). *Visible Learning. A Synthesis of over 800 Meta-analyses Relating to Achievement*. London: Routledge.

Pianta, R. C. (2006). *Classroom Management and Relationships between Children and Teachers: Implications for Research and Practice*. In Evert- son, C. M. & Weinstein, C. S. (Ed.), Handbook of Classroom Manage- ment (685-710). London: Routledge.

Rosenbusch, H. S. (2005). *Organisational Pedagogic at Schools.Fundamental Principles of Pedagogic Leadership*. (Organisationspädagogik der Schule. Grundlagen pädagogischen Führungshandelns.) Neuwied: Luchterhand.

Steins, G. (2011). *Belief Systems of Teachers and the Social Behavior of students*. (Bewertungssysteme von Lehrkräften und das Sozialverhalten von Schülern und Schülerinnen.) In Limbourg, M. & Steins, G. (Eds), Social Education at School (Sozialerziehung in der Schule) (499-522). Wiesbaden: Verlag für Sozialwissenschaften.

Steins, G. &Haep, A. (2012). Why is it so Difficult for Schools to Change? ExplanationsfromSocialPsychology. (Warum sind Veränderungen in der Schule so schwierig? Erklärungen aus der Sozialpsychologie.) *Lehren & Lernen, 38,* 28 - 31.

Warwas, J. (2009). Professional Self-conceptionand Stress in School Administration. (Berufliches Selbstverständnis und Beanspruchung in der Schulleitung.) In: *Zeitschrift für Erziehungswissenschaft, 12:* 475 – 498.

Wells, A. (2000). *Emotional Disorders and Metacognition: Innovative Cogni-tive Therapy*. Chichester, UK: Wiley.

In: Handbook of Psychology of Emotions
Editors: C. Mohiyeddini, M. Eysenck and S. Bauer

ISBN: 978-1-62808-053-7
© 2013 Nova Science Publishers, Inc.

Chapter 8

EMOTIONALITY IN MATHEMATICAL PROBLEM SOLVING

Alex M. Moore and Mark H. Ashcraft*
University of Nevada Las Vegas, US

ABSTRACT

For some, doing mathematics is enjoyable, and represents an opportunity to learn and excel. For others, the mere thought of doing mathematics can induce anxiety, fear, and avoidance. What are the factors behind such emotions, and how do they affect math learning and performance?

This chapter explores the positive and negative avenues through which attitudes and emotions about mathematics can influence math learning and performance, a topic of considerable importance in an era of widespread math achievement testing in educational settings. We discuss the influence of attitudes and emotions on learning and understanding math, with particular attention to math anxiety. We explore the cognitive mechanism central to most mathematical problem solving, the working memory system, and then describe how that system is compromised during problem solving when emotions are aroused. The chapter ends with a discussion of some new research directions on this topic, including some strong hints about possible causal relationships in math anxiety.

INTRODUCTION

In 1992, the creators of a popular line of dolls, Mattel, introduced the "Teen Talk Barbie," designed for an older demographic of Barbie enthusiasts. This version of the doll was built to play recordings scripted to represent the teenage voice of the United States at the time. The recordings seemed harmless enough, including lines such as "Let's go shopping!", or "Want to have a pizza party?" However, one line in particular, "Math class is tough!"

---
* Corresponding Author: Mark H. Ashcraft, Email address: Mark.Ashcraft@unlv.edu.

enraged women's advocacy groups. Critics alleged that Mattel was reinforcing negative attitudes and stereotypes directed at young women, undermining involvement in science, technology, engineering, and mathematics (STEM). Mattel removed the offensive line from future Teen Talk Barbie dolls, and offered to swap out these controversial dolls for the improved versions, which made no mention of mathematics (*The New York Times*, 1992).

Mattel is not the only culprit involved in marketing negative stereotypes to young women and teens. Retailer Forever 21 produced magnets with pink lettering that read, "I'm too pretty to do math!", and department store JC Penny stocked their shelves with sweatshirts that read, "I'm too pretty to do my homework so my brother has to do it for me." Both products were withdrawn from stores shortly after their debut due to the backlash from women's organizations and the general public. Many people felt that these instances of "math bashing" might promote apathy or dislike regarding mathematics, and schoolwork in general, however innocuous they might appear on the surface. As we will explore in this chapter, these kinds of attitudes and beliefs are damaging. They have the potential to foster pervasive, negative emotions related to math, influencing students even to the point of fear and avoidance of mathematics.

Contrast such attitudes and beliefs with the growing appreciation of the importance of math proficiency throughout life, and the relationship between higher education and employment. Bynner & Parsons (1997) report that deficits in basic mathematical understanding are more detrimental to future career opportunities than are reading deficits, and others have also noted that underdeveloped math skills are associated with negative educational outcomes in children (Ma, 1999) and adults alike (Hembree, 1990). Indeed, our work with elementary school children demonstrates that those students who fail to develop mastery in even basic math principles lag behind their peers longitudinally on standardized assessments of math achievement (Ashcraft & Moore, 2012; Moore & Ashcraft, 2012a). Understanding the degree to which individuals' affective reactions influence their math performance and achievement is an important topic, with potentially broad implications in academic and career settings.

In this chapter, we will explore the impact these attitudinal and affective states have on math achievement and performance. We will review the evidence on educational outcomes related to attitudes about mathematics, and discuss the cognitive mechanism most strongly impacted by affective reactions. We then examine the literature demonstrating online mathematics performance deficits observed under the influence of these emotional factors.

MATHEMATICS MOTIVATION, INTEREST, SELF-EFFICACY, AND MATHEMATICS ANXIETY

To frame our discussion of attitudinal, belief, and emotional factors in mathematics, consider Geary's distinction between biologically primary and secondary competencies (Geary, 1995; 2000). In this view, mental abilities can be categorized as those that emerge early in development without explicit training, the biologically primary abilities, and those that develop later and only with explicit, usually effortful, learning, the biologically secondary abilities. In the domain of number, Geary argued that basic mathematical abilities such as recognizing the numerosity of sets, small number counting, and even basic arithmetical relations like addition and subtraction are biologically primary. That is, regardless of culture or level of education, these basic competencies are demonstrated without significant variation in expression, and are found quite early in development. Conversely, large number computation, and more complex arithmetical and mathematical operations, are learned only through explicit instruction, and require significant effort on the part of the individual to practice and master the principles involved; these are biologically secondary.

The idea of biologically primary capacities is supported by results showing that infants and young children are sensitive to numerical properties of the environment; they can discriminate between sets of objects that differ in number, if the sets have at least a 2:1 ratio (e.g., 8 vs. 4 dots), and they display rudimentary forms of addition and subtraction (Gelman & Gallistel, 1978; Wynn, 1992, 1996). To further support these primary abilities, consider the capacities observed in the Mundurucu, an indigenous tribe located in the Amazonian jungle. Without formal instruction and with only limited exposure to more developed cultures, these people are able to grasp basic ideas of counting and number words, but their understanding only allows for precise enumeration of small sets of objects (no more than about 5); for larger collections, the set is described as being "many". Interestingly, these individuals perform in number tasks at a level comparable to kindergarten or first grade children in western cultures (Dehaene, Izard, Pica, & Spelke, 2008; Siegler & Booth, 2004).

The lack of precision and mastery seen in unschooled mathematics highlights the importance of formal instruction for the development of sophisticated math abilities. Geary (1995) stresses that the presence of a biologically primary capacity does not translate into adequate development of the biologically secondary understanding in that domain. For example, the inherent ability for learning language does not translate into the ability to read and write without training. Mathematics follows the same pattern. So, for example, Mundurucu children do not progress further in their numerical development, since they are not formally schooled (see Zebian & Ansari, 2012, for supportive evidence with groups of literate and illiterate adults). Relevant to this chapter then is the idea that mastery in math-related topics is a learned skill, and requires the individual to expend large amounts of effort to fully grasp the concepts found in mathematics. Throughout years of education, children are expected to develop certain attitudes regarding this education, namely that the domain of number and mathematics is important to learn, and that the individual will develop the self-efficacy and motivation to practice the principles and develop adequate understanding. Simply put, math takes effort.

With these ideas in mind, we will begin reviewing the literature related to the educational outcomes associated with adherence to these beliefs, as well as discuss what the literature indicates if these beliefs are essentially rejected by the individual. Specifically, we speak of high interest, motivation, and self-efficacy in mathematics, and their role in what we call an approach constellation of factors – or in the case of low interest, motivation, and self-efficacy, an avoidance constellation (Ashcraft & Moore, 2009; Moore, Rudig, & Ashcraft, 2012).

Interest and Motivation

At the beginning of formal education, children report overall positive attitudes towards mathematics. From a pool of first and fifth graders, Stevenson et al. (1990) found that 72% of the students reported having these positive views toward the domain. Our own data corroborate these claims. For example, 87% of our first grade sample expressed "very good" feelings when doing math and 74% of these same children were quite pleased with their mathematical abilities, expressing that they were "very good' in math overall (Ashcraft & Moore, 2009). Stevenson et al. (1990) did report a general decline in affect towards mathematics with increasing age, however, a phenomenon thought to be particularly due to the fact that mathematics content and procedures increase in complexity and difficulty across grades, thus requiring increasing effort to master the concepts.

Despite this overall decline, both self-reported interest and motivation are still strongly related to success in mathematics; high interest and motivation correlate with a student's current success in the area, and with continued engagement and success in later math-related pursuits. Köller, Baumert, and Schnabel (2001) examined interest in math, along with standardized math scores and math course enrollment, longitudinally with a sample of 600 7th, 10th, and 12th grade students. Not surprisingly, their results showed that those students who reported higher interest adopted a stronger belief that mathematics is important to learn, tended to enroll in more advanced math courses, and ultimately achieved higher grades in those courses compared to their less interested and less motivated peers (see also Leuwerke, Robbins, Sawyer, & Hovland, 2004). This is a prime example of how interest contributes to the approach constellation of attitudes, essentially that the positive correlations demonstrates an overall disposition to approach or pursue mathematics.

Motivation to learn and pursue mathematics, likewise, is correlated with a variety of positive outcomes. Studies have found that high levels of motivation in mathematics are associated with overall better math performance, thus higher achievement, and the tendency to seek out future math-related experiences or courses. High levels of self-reported motivation have been found to be predictive of math-related college majors and career goals (Simpkins, Davis-Kean, & Eccles, 2006), and to bolster mathematics self-efficacy (Berger & Karabenick, 2011; Lopez, Lent, Brown, & Gore, 1997). High motivation is also positively associated with higher math achievement scores ($r = .31$), and negatively associated with math anxiety ($r = -.72$; Zakaria & Nordin, 2008).

Although high motivation is illustrated here as contributing to an approach outlook of mathematics, a distinction needs to be made clear regarding the source of the motivation; that is to say, if the individual is intrinsically or extrinsically motivated. Intrinsic motivation is believed to involve a genuine interest in increasing one's knowledge and understanding within the domain, a perception of mathematics being objectively important, and the tendency to persevere through more advanced math topics in accordance with these beliefs. Extrinsic motivation, conversely, is believed to drive the individual to achieve in order to gain recognition in the form of good grades or praise from teachers or parents, rather than for one's own benefit. Extrinsically motivated students are expected to seek less help from their teachers and avoid situations in which negative feedback or judgments are likely. In the event of receiving such negative consequences for their efforts, extrinsically motivated students disengage from the situation, and discontinue their pursuit of achievement (e.g. National Mathematics Advisory Panel, 2008; Ryan & Pintrich, 1997).

Self-efficacy

Ashcraft & Rudig (2012) adapted Bandura's (1977) definition of self-efficacy to the domain of mathematics, suggesting that "self-efficacy is an individual's confidence in his or her ability to perform mathematics and is thought to directly impact the choice to engage in, expend effort on, and persist in pursuing mathematics" (p. 249). To examine the impact of high self-efficacy, Pietsch, Walker, and Chapman (2003) measured a general form of self-efficacy (how confident are you at doing math?) as well as specific aspects self-efficacy within mathematics (e.g. how confident are you at computing percentages?) in a sample of 416 9th and 10th graders. The results demonstrated a positive relationship between general self-efficacy and performance, showing that this measure predicted end-of-year performance on a comprehensive math exam. Furthermore, the specific content self-efficacy measures predicted exam scores more strongly than the general score (both self-efficacy measures predicted above and beyond a measure of math self-concept). Similarly, Lee (2009) found, in an extensive sample (n = 250,000; across 41 countries) that the average correlation between math performance and math self-efficacy was .42, and that the average correlation between math performance and math anxiety was -.65 (for data on incoming university students, see Cooper & Robinson, 1991).

Given that the definition of self-efficacy seems to imply a strong motivational component, it is not surprising that the two factors have been found to jointly affect performance. In a 9th grade sample, Berger and Karabenick (2011) found that high motivation coupled with high self-efficacy was associated with the belief that math is intrinsically valuable. Interestingly, the coupling of high motivation and high self-efficacy was also associated with more sophisticated learning strategies (e.g. elaboration) when students were learning new math procedures. This was in contrast to students with low self-efficacy, who relied on simple rehearsal and memorization strategies for learning. In other words, those with high self-efficacy were heavily engaged in the learning process, and were more willing to expend greater effort in mastering the material. It is likely that students using more elaborative learning methods are doing so because of their positive pursuit of the subject matter, and it is likely that the prior success of these students is due, in part, to their more effortful approaches to understanding the material (Berger & Karabenick, 2011). With these ideas in mind, it becomes quite transparent as to why high self-efficacy is associated with positive educational outcomes in a similar manner as described for motivation. Both factors seem to underlie the drive to fully commit the effort required for mastery of the information of this biologically secondary domain of knowledge.

Although the results here are correlational, and thus do not demonstrate causal relationships, it is the case that these three approach factors—high interest, high motivation, and high self-efficacy—are quite reliably associated with positive educational outcomes and lifelong benefits for individuals. Again, high levels of these factors are associated with higher success in current and continued math courses, continued engagement in mathematics, and stronger beliefs that mathematics is an important and useful domain of study; this is the approach constellation.

On the opposite end of the continuum, of course, are low interest, low motivation, and low self-efficacy, the avoidance constellation. Here, individuals tend to demonstrate low levels of persistence in the domain, disengagement in the learning process when challenges or negative feedback are present and, most importantly, lower overall math achievement. Again, although causal mechanisms cannot be addressed, a fourth factor tends to accompany the avoidance attitudes, one that is rarely present in the approach constellation. This fourth factor can be quite debilitating, and is related to impaired math learning and performance. This factor, of course, is mathematics anxiety.

Mathematics Anxiety

Mathematics anxiety was originally defined by Richardson and Suinn (1972) as "a feeling of tension and anxiety that interferes with the manipulation of numbers and the solving of mathematical problems in a wide variety of ordinary life and academic situations" (p. 551). Its effects can be seen both in everyday situations (awkwardness when trying to calculate a tip on a restaurant bill) and in important testing situations (students' nervousness when taking important college entrance exams). We can observe its effects in the laboratory, using tasks as simple as digit comparison and rapid counting of objects (e.g. Maloney, Ansari, & Fugelsang, 2010a). Some researchers have claimed its effects to be quite similar to, if not the equivalent of, a phobic disorder (Faust, 1988). We have observed participants display a variety of anxiety-related behaviors in the lab when doing simple arithmetic, including bursting into tears (Ashcraft, 2002).

The classic approach to investigating math anxiety is to examine how it is associated with other important measures, both educational outcomes such as math grades and standardized math achievement scores, as well as other personality variables, such as other forms of anxiety. Predictably, high levels of math anxiety are correlated with a host of negative beliefs and attitudes relating to math. The two meta-analyses on math anxiety (Hembree, 1990; Ma, 1999) report that high math anxiety is negatively correlated with the approach constellation factors; -.37 for perceived usefulness of math, -.64 for motivation to excel in or pursue math, -.82 with mathematics self-efficacy in grades 6-11 (-.65 for college samples), and -.75 for pre-college enjoyment in math (-.47 in college samples). The most disturbing of these correlations are those concerning educational outcomes. Math anxiety correlates -.34 with math achievement scores in pre-college individuals (-.31 in college), and -.30 with high school grades (-.27 in college). Not surprisingly, then, university students' math anxiety correlates -.32 with the intent to enroll in future math courses (see also Cooper and Robinson, 1991 and Lee, 2009 for the inverse relationships between self-efficacy and math anxiety). Thus, high math anxiety co-occurs with low interest, low motivation, and low self-efficacy, the avoidance constellation; in fact, they go hand in hand (Ashcraft, Krause, & Hopko, 2007; Ashcraft & Moore, 2009; Moore et al., 2012).

As stated previously, this information was obtained using classic correlational methods to examine the role of affect in mathematics. More recently, the field has turned to the laboratory, to better understand the cognitive mechanisms impaired by this negative affective condition, and the nature of the impairment. As a preview, it is now widely believed that affective reactions have their strongest impact on the working memory system. Before reviewing the work on how affect leads to disruption in the functioning of working memory, we discuss the normal functioning of this working memory mechanism briefly, and its important role in mathematics calculation.

WORKING MEMORY AND MATHEMATICS

Solve the following problem, bearing in mind the several steps involved in the entire process as you work through the problem:

$$(44 - 28) / (32/8)$$

Subtracting $44 - 28$ is, for most people, a computation, that is a calculation rather than a matter of retrieving an answer directly from memory. Once completed, you then have to hold the result of 16 in memory for a few moments while simultaneously computing 32/8, before performing the final division ($16 / 4 = 4$). The multiple steps, and the necessity of holding values in memory while simultaneously performing other steps – and keeping track of the sequence of steps – illustrates the kind of situation confronting an individual in math computation tasks. Critically, the system responsible for keeping track, for coordinating multiple steps, and for performing the intermediate computations, is the working memory system.

Consider being asked to solve – or even to estimate the answer to – a second problem:

George walks into the grocery store with the five dollar bill his mother gave him to buy candy. George decides that he wants to buy as many jaw breakers as possible. If each jaw breaker costs 38 cents, how many jaw breakers can George buy with $5.00?

Assuming that George understands the problem, and realizes that he needs to divide $5.00 by .38 – important steps that are not at all guaranteed, of course – it is quite unlikely that he will mentally compute the answer via division, or even that he will compute by repeatedly adding .38; both of these would surely overwhelm the capacity of working memory to maintain intermediate values, keep track of place in the sequence of procedures, and the like. George will probably rely on an approximation strategy for problem solution if he must rely on mental processing alone. But even that solution requires substantial effort, with multiple steps and heavy reliance on keeping track of intermediate solutions; for example, round 38 cents to 40 cents, count by 40s up to 200 to realize that 5 jaw breakers will cost $2.00, multiply by 2 to get 10 jaw breakers for $4.00, etc. – not to mention the processing required to generate the estimation strategy itself. The difficulty, as research described in this section illustrates, is often attributable to the computational effort required by the problem, effort applied through one's working memory.

Thought of as the online blackboard or workbench of the mind (Ashcraft, 1995; Baddeley, 2000; DeStefano & LeFevre, 2004), working memory is commonly believed to be a limited-capacity mechanism, responsible for the manipulation, integration, and storage of information at the forefront of a person's attention (see also Engle, 2002; Miyake & Shah, 1999; Raghubar, Barnes, & Hecht, 2010). This mechanism has been shown to contribute to a wide array of mental abilities, such as memory, learning, and language comprehension, and has been associated with overall fluid intelligence (Engle, 2002). It has not been until recently, however, that researchers have begun to demonstrate its role in mental arithmetic processing (DeRammelaere, Stuyven, & Vandierendonck, 1999; Imbo & LeFevre, 2010; Imbo & Vandierendonck, 2007a, 2008; Ramirez, Gunderson, Levine, & Beilock, in press;

Seyler, Kirk, & Ashcraft, 2003; see DeStefano & LeFevre, 2004 and Raghubar et al., 2010 for extensive reviews). From implicating this mechanism in simple procedures like counting (Camos & Barrouillet, 2004; Hecht, 2002) through more complex procedures like addition (Ashcraft & Kirk, 2001), and multiplication (Imbo & Vandierendonck, 2007b), these investigations have clearly shown that working memory resources are crucial to the successful completion of almost any math task. In this section, we will review the body of literature establishing working memory as being a crucial component in mental arithmetic. In the final section, we describe how affective reactions—math anxiety, choking under pressure, and stereotype threat—impact this mechanism, and thus math performance.

Although there are several existing models of working memory (Miyake & Shah, 1999), a common theme shared among the frameworks is that the mechanism is constrained in processing due to its limited capacity for storing and manipulating information, a long-noted limitation (e.g., James, 1890/1981). Past this agreement, a major distinction between the models is whether the mechanism's resources are available for domain-general abilities, like attentional processes (e.g. Engle, 2002), or operate within sub-components that process specific types of information. Many studies in math cognition have investigated working memory by way of the latter model description, more specifically the multi-component model proposed by Baddeley and colleagues (Baddeley, 1996, 2000; Baddeley & Hitch, 1974; Baddeley & Logie, 1999).

The multi-component model describes the roles of three distinct subcomponents that work in concert to store, manipulate, and process information. One of these components, the central executive, is thought to manage the entire system, actuating processes like attention and task switching, performing calculations, and integrating stored information held by the other two subcomponents, often referred to as slave systems. One of the slave systems, the phonological loop, is exclusively engaged in semantic-based information processing such as active rehearsal of information in short-term memory, and storage of verbal or semantic information. The other slave system, the visuospatial sketchpad, is engaged when the task at hand requires storage or manipulation of visual- or imagery-based information (Baddeley & Logie, 1999). Note that a fourth component proposed by Baddeley and colleagues, the episodic buffer, is not discussed here as it has not been investigated thoroughly within math cognition (Baddeley, 2000).

Two general paradigms are in common use in studies of working memory's role in cognitive processing. In the first, the individual difference approach, participants are pre-tested on a working memory span task, and assigned to groups based on their scores. Performance on some cognitive task is then evaluated as a function of group membership, usually showing that inferior performance is characteristic of the low span group.

In the second paradigm, the dual task procedure, a primary task (some math task) is performed concurrently with a secondary task known to rely on working memory; both tasks are also performed in isolation, to obtain baseline information. If the secondary task interferes with primary task performance (or vice versa), the conclusion is that the primary task also relies on working memory, and was disrupted when resources were diverted by the secondary task. If there was no interference between the tasks, of course, this suggests that the primary task can be completed without working memory's involvement. This dual task approach can be a fruitful way of understanding math processing, especially working within the multi-component model of working memory. For example, by using a secondary task known to rely on phonological processing, we can determine if the math task under consideration also relies on phonological processes. The same logic applies to secondary tasks known to involve the visual-spatial system, or indeed the central executive.

A clear example of both approaches was demonstrated in a study on simple mental subtraction, by Seyler et al. (2003). Participants showed a pronounced problem size effect in Experiment 1, a pronounced increase in latencies for problems with a two-digit minuend (for 11 − 4, the minuend is 11). The pattern of latencies suggested strongly that the larger problems relied heavily on relatively slow procedures for solution, rather than more rapid retrieval from memory. On the hypothesis that such slower procedures demand the resources of working memory, Seyler et al. conducted another test (Experiment 4). They pre-tested the participants on a working memory span task, and categorized them into low, medium, and high span groups. They then tested them on simple subtraction facts in the dual-task procedure. The secondary task required them to hold either 2, 4, or 6 randomly selected letters in working memory, then report them in order after solving the subtraction problem.

The results were very straightforward. First, errors in letter recall increased more sharply in the dual task when the load on working memory increased, compared to the errors observed in the control task (letter recall only). Thus, mental subtraction indeed seemed to rely on the resources of working memory. Second, individuals with lower working memory spans made far more errors in the dual task than in the control condition, whereas the difference between dual and control conditions was much smaller for the high span group. Thus, low span participants were particularly disadvantaged at doing subtraction when their working memory resources were diverted by the dual task setting. And finally, this disadvantage for the low span group depended on how heavily working memory was loaded; when the load was light (2 letters), there were no group differences, but when the load was heaviest (6 letters), the low span group made almost twice as many letter recall errors (56%) as the high span group (31%). Clearly, working memory resources were necessary for these adults to perform even elementary subtraction. Depriving them of sufficient resources degraded their performance significantly.

Having illustrated both the general importance of working memory to arithmetic processing and the typical design of studies used to investigate such effects, we turn to the research involving the sub-components of the working memory system. The majority of findings suggest that the resources of the sub-components are allocated for the efficient completion of calculation strategies. That is, working memory is called for when processing requires some strategy or procedure, which requires the maintenance of semantic or visual information in the case of slave systems, and general attentional resources in the case of the central executive.

Slave Systems

Much work has been dedicated to understanding the responsibilities of the two slave systems during mathematical calculation, specifically the phonological loop. Although it has been reported that the evidence supporting the functions of the slave systems seems inconsistent, we believe that the results thus far have honed in on the unique characteristics of the systems' roles (DeStefano & LeFevre, 2004; Raghubar et al., 2010). As noted by DeStefano and LeFevre (2004), the evidence supporting either sub-component relies on many factors, such as presentation format (Imbo & LeFevre, 2010; Trbovich & LeFevre, 2003), modality of presentation (Heathcote, 1994; Logie, Gilhooly, & Wynn, 1994), as well as the mathematical operation under scrutiny (Lee & Kang, 2002; Seyler et al., 2003).

Phonological Loop

It is generally appreciated that the phonological loop's role in mental arithmetic is related to the storage and maintenance of the verbal and/or semantic qualities of number. A typical way to load this system has already been described in our discussion of Seyler et al. (2003); the participant is asked to memorize a string of randomly ordered letters, presumably taxing a verbal rehearsal mechanism. Variations exist, including repetitive verbalization of letters (Hecht, 2002), or remembering non-words instead of letters (Trbovich & LeFevre, 2003).

The interfering nature of a phonological load is often associated with procedural strategies of calculation, such as counting to arrive at the correct sum if retrieval is not used (Hecht, 2002; Imbo & Vandierendonck, 2007a; Seyler et al., 2003), transformation in addition and subtraction (Imbo & Vandierendonck, 2007a), or storage and maintenance of intermediate values of more complex problems, such as multi-digit addition or multiplication (Ashcraft, 1995; Heathcote, 1994; Imbo & Vandierendonck, 2007b; Logie et al., 1994; Seitz & Schumann-Hengsteler, 2002). In all such cases, maintaining a phonological load while performing such math procedures leads to degraded performance. As an example, holding letters of the alphabet in working memory so they can be reported later interferes with maintaining intermediate sums in a running total task (e.g., Logie et al., 1994).

Visuospatial Sketchpad

The visuospatial sketchpad is thought to store and manipulate visual or imagery-based information. Loading this system typically involves remembering spatial information from visual arrays, for example remembering the sequence of locations an object moved through on a computer screen. The evidence supporting the involvement of this sub-component is less abundant than that of the phonological loop, but existing literature suggests that it is implicated in procedural strategies that rely on memory for physical calculation of problems. For example, visuospatial load tends to interfere with subtraction calculation, due to the pervasive use of visually based calculation strategies (imagining the borrow operation in column format).

In contrast, it is not strongly implicated in multiplication calculation, presumably because multiplication procedures rely on stored verbal associations of numbers, allowing for direct recall of answers (Imbo & LeFevre, 2010; Lee & Kang, 2002). These observations are supported developmentally as well, revealing that younger children have a more difficult time in calculation when under a concurrent visuospatial load, because the math facts have not been stored in memory sufficiently enough for direct recall. As children age, however, both visuospatial and phonological loop secondary tasks result in interference, because their calculation strategies have shifted to incorporate both visual aspects of the problem, as well as fact retrieval (McKenzie, Bull, & Gray, 2003; see Siegler, 1996 for an account of calculation strategy shifts).

Central Executive

Unlike the role of the slave systems, the evidence supporting the involvement of the central executive is rather cohesive. The general role of the central executive in mathematics is to coordinate and manipulate the information stored in the two slave systems, primarily that of the phonological loop. The coordination and manipulation referred to here seem to include processes such as general inhibition of irrelevant information, task switching, and the completion of problem solving algorithms. (Baddeley & Logie, 1999). To load this component of working memory, the secondary task requires the participant to generate responses during calculation. Two common methods are random letter generation (speaking strings of letters from the alphabet in a random order; Hecht, 2002) and the continuous choice reaction time task (response keys are pressed to indicate the presence of high or low tones; Imbo & Vandierendonck, 2007b; Szmalec, Vandierendonck, & Kemps, 2005). The goal of these types of secondary tasks is to diminish the executive's limited capacity calculation resources without loading the storage capacity of the phonological loop or visuospatial sketchpad.

It seems that the central executive is involved with almost any level of mental computation. Evidence supporting this claim comes from studies investigating single-digit calculation, across all operations (DeRammelaere et al., 1999; Hecht, 2002; Imbo & Vandierendonck, 2007a, 2007b; Lemaire, Abdi, & Fayol, 1996; Seitz & Schumann-Hengsteler, 2000). Naturally, with its implication in such low level calculation, it is not surprising that the central executive is also associated with such low level procedural strategies as counting, in coordination with the phonological loop (Camos & Barrouillet, 2004; Hecht, 2002). For example, Hecht (2002) tested the role of working memory in the selection and execution of calculation strategies within an addition verification task. The primary task was verification of the basic addition facts, while two secondary tasks were used. One loaded the phonological loop, requiring the participants to repeat one letter of the alphabet, articulatory suppression, while verifying the addition problems, while the other loaded the central executive, requiring participants to generate letters of the alphabet in a random order while verifying the veridicality of the problems. Participants verified the addition equation while performing the secondary task, and after each verification response indicated which strategy they used to solve the equation.

Hecht (2002) did not find evidence linking available working memory resources to strategy selection, but did find that these resources were crucial for efficient strategy execution, specifically counting. The data showed that although both articulatory suppression and random letter generation impaired accurate responding across all strategies, the presence of the random letter generation secondary task alone caused reaction time to slow verification when the counting strategy was used.

Beyond a simple counting strategy, executive resources have been shown to be involved in transformation strategies (e.g., transforming $7 + 9$ to $7 + 10 - 1$), as well as any calculations requiring a carry operation, such as addition (Fürst & Hitch, 2000; Imbo, Vandierendonck, & DeRammelaere, 2007; Seitz & Schumann-Hengsteler, 2002) and multiplication (Seitz & Schumann-Hengsteler, 2000, 2002). These resources also gain importance in calculations that require an increasing number of carry operations (Imbo, Vandierendonck, & Verguewe, 2007), as well as being involved the continuous maintenance of intermediate sums during calculations (Fürst & Hitch, 2000).

Although seemingly easy and well learned for the average, educated adult, even fairly simple arithmetic is demanding of a significant amount of mental capacity. Although all of the details have yet to be investigated concerning how math performance relies on working memory, it is clear that it plays a crucial role in mental calculation. With this in mind, factors that might interfere with the proper functioning of this system, such as affect and emotion, deserve special consideration.

EMOTIONAL IMPACT ON PERFORMANCE

We turn now to the issue of how affective reactions influence online performance, not performance in the sense of achievement and expertise accumulated during education, as discussed in the first section, but ongoing performance on math tasks, in the moment it happens. As noted above, a major finding in the math cognition literature is that non-trivial problem solving, i.e., math processing that involves conscious processing, relies quite heavily on working memory. This turns out to be a major locus of disruption when negative emotional reactions influence online performance – anxiety and emotion consume important resources from working memory, thus depriving the individual of adequate resources for successful problem solving. We discuss the three major forms of emotional or affective disruptions that have been studied, and describe how they impair otherwise normal functioning in the cognitive system. Specifically, we will speak about the impairments in math performance associated with math anxiety, choking under pressure, and stereotype threat.

Mathematics Anxiety

Our original research was exploratory, intended to see if math anxiety truly had any online effects on cognitive processing. We used a standard laboratory task, asking for timed verification (true/false judgments) to problems in the four arithmetic operations of addition, subtraction, multiplication, and division (Ashcraft & Faust, 1994; Faust, 1988; Faust, Ashcraft, & Fleck, 1996; see Ashcraft, 1995 and 2002 for reviews). We obtained four promising effects across the several studies. First, there was no particular evidence of a math anxiety effect on the basic facts of addition or multiplication, i.e., one-digit operand problems like 3 + 7 or 4 X 8. For the most part, these problems seem to be solved via fairly straight-forward retrieval from long-term memory, with little or no involvement of working memory.

For problems even slightly more difficult than these, e.g., for two-digit addition problems, the results began to reveal differences between the low and high math anxious groups. Routinely, the low math anxious participants were the fastest to complete the problems, and also showed high levels of accuracy. The high math anxious participants often showed equally rapid responding, but with far more errors. Basically, the high math anxious participants seemed to demonstrate a strategy of trying to complete the tasks as rapidly as possible, without putting much effort into producing accurate responses. This seemed to us a deliberate use of a speed/accuracy tradeoff, and was our first clue that the avoidance characteristics associated with math anxiety might also apply to their online performance.

The third effect observed was that high math anxious participants showed more difficulty in rejecting the false problems presented, even when the problems were given dramatically inaccurate answers (e.g. $8 + 7 = 38$). The typical result when false answers depart further and further from the correct value is a decline in latencies and errors (e.g., Ashcraft & Stazyk, 1981). This was the pattern we observed for our low anxious participants; their errors declined from 8% to 2% as the stated answers grew more and more distant from the correct value. The high math anxious participants' errors remained in the 7% to 13% range of errors, however (Faust, et al., 1996). These results seem to us now to reflect something about people's intuitive sense about number and arithmetic, their "number sense" in Dehaene's (1997) term. It's as if our low math anxious participants could easily reject $8 + 7 = 38$ by knowing that 38 was unreasonable, "out of the ball park," but this sense of approximate magnitude was faulty in the high math anxious participants, possibly a kind of low level deficit in knowledge of number. The low level deficit hypothesis has been followed-up on more recently by Maloney and colleagues, who showed that those with high math anxiety suffer associated deficits in tasks as simple as number comparison (deciding which of two presented Arabic numerals is larger or smaller: Maloney et al., 2010a), as well as in simple counting procedures within a subitizing task (visual enumeration of objects: Maloney et al., 2010b). The authors speculated that math anxiety might actually be a product of these low level deficits, a possibility that needs to be explored more thoroughly in future research.

The fourth and final effect observed from the early exploratory studies was increased difficulty observed in more complex, two-column addition problems. In these tasks, high math anxious participants were quite slow to produce their answers, and made a large number of errors. This was especially true if the problems required a carry operation. Because of the increased load on working memory to calculate problems that included a carry operation, we hypothesized that the processing deficit observed in high math anxious samples might be due to decreased functionality of the working memory mechanism.

An ideal theoretical home for such a hypothesis was provided by Eysenck's Processing Efficiency Theory, a theory concerned with the effects of generalized anxiety on cognitive performance (Eysenck & Calvo, 1992; Eysenck, Derakshan, Santos, & Calvo, 2007). Eysenck's theory suggests that an individual's anxiety triggers negative ruminations and worry, and these ongoing, conscious ruminations consume some of the resources of working memory. Thus, when the individual is called upon to perform a cognitive task that requires working memory processing, task performance will be compromised due to lowered working memory resources; obviously, if the cognitive task is automatic, or requires no working memory for its completion, there should be no decrement in performance. We reasoned that math anxiety should function much like generalized anxiety, at least when math anxious individuals are placed in a math task. Thus we predicted decrements in their performance when the math task they were performing relied on working memory.

To test the hypothesis, we conducted a dual-task experiment, using one- and two- column addition as the primary task, and letter recall as the secondary task. Participants were shown either 2 or 6 letters, and had to remember them while solving the subsequent additions; they then had to recall the letters in order. We tested groups of low, medium, and high math anxious participants, asking them to solve both carry and non-carry problems. Because of the dual-task paradigm, we reasoned that those trials that required two-column addition with the carry operation would be most demanding of working memory resources, especially when a six-letter recall load was imposed on processing. And following Eysenck's reasoning, we predicted that those who had the highest levels of math anxiety would show the largest impairment in this condition, due to their anxiety-limited working memory resources.

The results from this investigation supported our predictions. Interference was present for all groups when carrying was required, and when a high letter load was present. Importantly, we also found the predicted three-way competition for working memory resources, the condition in which high math anxious participants had to perform a carry operation while also having to hold six letters in memory. This condition yielded a 39% error rate for the high math anxious group, versus only a 20% error rate for the low anxious group. We now refer to this especially difficult, three-way competition for resources as an "affective drop" in performance, a noticeable impairment in performance due in large part to the negative affect experienced by high math anxious individuals (Ashcraft & Moore, 2009). We suspect strongly that the same affective drop occurs in any online situation that involves math and working memory, e.g., classroom math tests, standardized math tests, and the like.

Equivalent results have been found in two-column subtraction with borrowing (Krause, Rudig, & Ashcraft, 2009) as well as in an experiment testing a novel math procedure, modular arithmetic, explained below (Krause, 2008). In these results, it was found that high anxious participants showed stronger impairments than their low anxious peers. Interestingly, Krause also found that the high anxious participants required much more practice to achieve mastery in the novel math procedure, supporting the idea that math anxiety is closely linked to the ability to learn mathematical information.

Since the emergence of this initial research, the field has moved forward to explore two more situational factors that lead to affective drop, i.e., emotion-based interference in performance. Importantly, in both cases, the impact of these situational factors is on the working memory system.

Choking under Pressure

The first of the two situational factors is an effect referred to as choking under pressure. This construct, also referred to simply as "choking", describes the phenomenon in which a person performs much more poorly than anticipated in contexts of high expectation and pressure. Almost counter-intuitively, this phenomenon is encountered in situations in which the individual desires to excel, and this desire is thought to exacerbate the effect. The effect is especially pronounced among those who have demonstrated exceptional ability, or the potential for exceptional ability, although in principle it is not limited to such individuals.

The initial evidence of this impairment in mathematics was provided by Beilock and colleagues (e.g. Beilock & Carr, 2005; Beilock, Kulp, Holt, & Carr, 2004; DeCaro, Rotar, Kendra & Beilock, 2010). In this work, participants have been given a novel math task to perform, one that places heavy demands on working memory. The task is modular arithmetic, a calculation procedure in which the problem such as $20 \equiv 15$ (mod 5), stated as "20 is congruent to 15 modulo 5," is solved by subtracting the second number from the first (20 − 15), then dividing the result by the third number (5/5); if the division produces a whole number, then the equation is said to be true; if a remainder exists, then the problem is false (Gauss, 1966). After an initial block of trials, participants solved a second block of these problems in one of two contexts. One group was told merely to continue doing as best as they could; this was the low pressure condition. In the high pressure condition, participants were told that they and a (fictitious) team mate would receive a monetary reward only if they improved their performance by 20% during the second block of trials. They were also told that their performance would be videotaped, and the tapes would be viewed by other students and teachers.

The results from this experiment showed that participants' performance deteriorated significantly when they were placed under pressure to perform; in contrast, the low pressure condition actually improved somewhat on the second block, due to practice. Importantly, the deterioration found in the high pressure group was only evident on the difficult problems, i.e., those problems with large numbers requiring a borrow in the subtraction, e.g., $43 \equiv 17$ (mod 4). These, of course, are the problems that require a substantial amount of working memory for their solution. Simpler problems, like $8 \equiv 4$ (mod 2) were unaffected by pressure, since such problems rely very little on working memory. Thus, similar to the original working memory and math anxiety studies, impairments in performance were only found in those problems where a heavy demand was placed on working memory processing (Beilock et al., 2004).

To examine choking further, Beilock and Carr (2005) grouped their participants into high and low working memory capacity groups, as determined by a working memory pre-test. The reasoning for this was simple: if choking under pressure is an impairment of working memory function, and the deficits are found in the difficult, demanding problems, then high and low working memory capacity participants should demonstrate differential decrements in performance. What they found was that the high working memory capacity participants outperformed the low working memory participants under standard testing conditions. But when placed under pressure, the high capacity group's performance dropped on difficult problems, to the point of resembling the performance of the low capacity group. Essentially, Beilock and Carr found that choking is almost exclusively an impairment for those who are most likely to succeed in the task, given their higher capacity for information manipulation and processing. Their explanation for this selective deficit (as confirmed in Beilock & DeCaro, 2007) was that those participants who have larger working memory capacities use their augmented processing potential to generate more sophisticated problem solving strategies. When deprived of their full working memory resources, they end up relying on the less demanding heuristic processes characteristic of low capacity individuals. Thus, the low capacity group showed no decrement in performance under pressure, since their solutions never relied on strategies that depended heavily on working memory (see also Beilock & Ramirez, 2011).

Finding this selective impairment, both in terms of the situational factor of pressure, and as an individual difference factor, raises some important questions about the validity of high-stakes testing in educational settings (e.g. standardized math exams). These data suggest that the situation, not the actual ability of the individual, could be a major determining factor in the success achieved on these kinds of tests. Furthermore it seems to suggest that the high-stakes testing situations might be working against those individuals who are most able to excel in upper level courses, for example, but for reasons related to testing rather than ability (Ashcraft & Moore, 2009).

Stereotype Threat

The third emotional factor that has been investigated in the literature is stereotype threat. Stereotype threat has been investigated using math tasks largely because it is a convenient topic for these investigations – rightly or wrongly, several relevant stereotypes exist concerning math performance, gender, and ethnicity. Briefly, stereotype threat is thought to occur when an individual belongs to a group that is subject to a negative stereotype. The individual's anxiety arises out of fear that negative performance would reflect poorly on the group being targeted by the stereotype, thus confirming the negative stereotype.

Steele and Aronson (1995) examined verbal problem solving performance in groups of African-American and European-American college students in their original demonstration of stereotype threat. To elicit the threat, two task instructions were devised. The control instructions described the purpose and task in a neutral way, not mentioning group differences. Performance under these instructions did not show group differences. To induce the stereotype threat, the second set of instructions described the task as being diagnostic of intellectual ability. The results showed significantly lower scores in the threat group for African-Americans, compared to African-Americans in the control condition (and compared to the European-American groups). Thus, the threat manipulation seemed to arouse anxiety in the African-American group, presumably because they did not want to confirm negative stereotypes about their group's intellectual capacity.

More recent work in this domain has shown that almost any individual can fall victim to threat-induced decrements in performance, as long as there is a plausible negative stereotype and the individual identifies with the group (Schmader, 2002) and the domain being tested (i.e. domain identity, Spencer, Steele, & Quinn, 1999). In line with this description is the idea that a low sense of domain or group identity lessens the strength of this effect. Thus, this affective reaction is strongly influenced by the individual's social identity, even to the point that if a positive stereotype is used in place of a negative one, participants demonstrate a stereotype lift (Schmader, Johns, and Forbes, 2008).

Relevant to the topic of this chapter, however, are the findings that mathematics is a domain that clearly reveals this effect. Aronson, Lustina, Good, Keough, Steele, and Brown (1999) elicited the stereotype threat effect in Caucasians. Their instructions to the threat group indicated that the purpose of the study was to understand why Caucasians perform worse in math than Asians; the no threat group heard neutral instructions. The results showed that the threatened group of Caucasian men performed worse than the group that was not reminded of the stereotype. Simlarly, Beilock, Rydell, and McConnell (2007) investigated the effect based on gender identity. In this experiment, one group of women was told that the researchers were trying to investigate why women perform worse in math than men, while the other group was told that the purpose was to investigate problem solving. The no threat group demonstrated a modest improvement from baseline to post-test, from 86% to 92% accuracy, due to practice. The threatened group, however, showed the predicted drop in performance, from 89% to 79% accuracy, from baseline to post-test. As in the choking studies mentioned earlier, the decline in performance was obtained only on the difficult problems. Thus, the fact that the impairment of stereotype threat was only observed in the difficult problems suggests that, similar to choking and math anxiety, working memory resources were compromised with the presence of the induced anxiety.

In an important extension of such work, neuroimaging results suggest that the stereotype effect is associated with raised awareness of social identity, resulting in the engagement of emotional regulation mechanisms in the brain. Krendl, Richeson, Kelley, and Heatherton (2008) investigated math performance with and without stereotype threat using fMRI technology. The experimental sessions began with a neutral implicit association test (IAT: Greenwald, McGhee, & Schwartz, 1998), followed by a math ability pre-test, including complex math statements (e.g., Is $19 \times 6 - 6^2 = 78$?), and modular arithmetic. The participants had 5 seconds to make true/false judgments about each problem; performance was at chance levels in a pilot experiment. After baseline performance was measured, stereotype threat was induced for half of the participants, and then participants completed another IAT, with the threat group making paired judgments about gender and math/arts fields (Nosek, Banaji, & Greenwald, 2002a), while the control group completed the liberal/conservative political IAT (Nosek, Banaji, & Greenwald, 2002b). Participants completed a math post-test after the second IAT, with similar problems as described for the pre-test.

The behavioral results showed that from Test 1 (T1) to Test 2 (T2), the control group's performance improved, presumably due to practice, while the threat group's performance decreased, creating a significant interaction. Reaction time analyses showed a significant decrease in response time from T1 to T2 in the control group, but no significant differences between tests in the threat group. Thus, the behavioral evidence suggested that the threatened group failed to profit from practice with the math statements.

The neuroimaging results showed differential activation of neural circuits from T1 to T2. In the control group, there was stronger activation of prefrontal and parietal structures (e.g., Angular Gyri) in T2 compared to T1, whereas the threat group showed greater activation in the ventral anterior cingulate cortex (vACC) in T2 compared to T1. Subsequent region of interest (ROI) analyses revealed a double dissociation of neural circuits recruited over time.

The control group showed significant increases in the left inferior prefrontal cortex, left inferior parietal cortex, and bilateral angular gyri. This network has previously been associated with numerical computation and increasing expertise in math tasks (Dehaene, Spelke, Pinel, Stanescu, & Tviskin, 1999; Delazer, et al., 2003; Menon, Rivera, White, Glover, & Reiss, 2000). Critically, this network did not show greater activation over time in the threat group. Instead, the threat group demonstrated greater activation in the vACC, activation that was not observed in the control group. The vACC has previously been shown to be active when assessing the emotional salience of stimuli, and plays a role in emotion regulation (Bush, Luu, & Posner, 2000; LeDoux, 2000). Studies have further implicated this region in evaluating social feedback (e.g. social rejection: Somerville, Heatherton, & Kelley, 2006).

It seems very likely from these data that stereotype threat is affecting performance in math processes by altering the neural circuits and regions that are active during processing. Non-threatened participants appear to be activating the normal neural mechanisms associated with numerical processing and math knowledge. Threatened participants, in contrast, show activation in emotional processing regions, as if they were being tested in an emotional rather than mathematical task.

The behavioral similarities among the three emotional effects discussed here, math anxiety, choking under pressure, and stereotype threat are compelling; all three appear to compromise working memory, detracting from the individual's ability to successfully solve difficult math problems. It is now gratifying to see neurological evidence, in the form of fMRI data, that corroborates this view. The normal math processing regions and circuits are inappropriately inactive under stereotype threat, and presumably under math anxiety and choking, whereas the emotional processing circuits and regions – essentially the fear system – are inappropriately active. The "affective drop" in math performance (Ashcraft & Moore, 2009) appears to be accompanied by a boost in neural activity related to negative affect.

CONCLUSION: CURRENT AND FUTURE DIRECTIONS

We conclude with brief discussion of three questions that deserve further attention in studies of emotionality in mathematical problems solving; When does math anxiety appear, and are there other manifestations of it aside from working memory deficits?; What is it that consumes working memory during an emotional reaction?; and What are the causal factors for these emotional reactions?

A very recent study demonstrates that young children can exhibit math anxiety, and further draws the clear connection between math anxiety and neurological mechanisms. Young, Wu, and Menon (2012) published results on the first investigation to measure neural response in math anxious children. They had 2nd and 3rd grade children complete simple and more difficult addition and subtraction verification problems while collecting fMRI scans. In separate sessions, the children also completed measures of intelligence, working memory, math and reading achievement, as well as trait and math anxiety scales. Critically, the high and low math anxious groups showed no significant difference on scores other than the math anxiety scale.

The behavioral results showed that the high math anxious group had marginally worse performance (accuracy) overall than the low math anxious children, and showed slower than normal reaction time in the small problems. The neural correlates analyses showed very interesting findings. First, the high math anxious children showed less activity than the low anxious in areas specifically implicated with numerical processing, namely the intraparietal sulcus and superior parietal lobule. Additionally, the high math anxious children showed more activation in the right amygdala than the low math anxious group. In subsequent analysis of current cytoarchitectonic maps, the authors were also able to identify the basolateral nucleus of the amygdala as the prominent site of the activation. Effective connectivity analyses showed that the amygdala activity spread into ventromedial prefrontal cortex regions.

The activation patterns among the low math anxious participants showed adequate preparation to perform in a mathematical task; their activations involved regions known to be involved in mathematical processing, e.g., left parietal structures. In contrast, activations in the high math anxious participants involved circuitry reflecting emotional regulation (ventromedial prefrontal cortex) of learned fear responses (basolateral nucleus of the amygdala). Essentially, during math processing, the high math anxious children recruited neural networks that are activated when participants view emotionally charged faces (McClure et al., 2007) and are engaged in learned fear response regulation, as in classical conditioning paradigms (Phelps, Delgado, Nearing, & LeDoux, 2004). This is in contrast to the low anxious participants, who recruited neural circuits associated with mathematical problem solving (Menon et al., 2000). Thus, in agreement with the Krendl et al. (2008) results on stereotype threat, math anxiety appeared to activate neural circuits related to fear and emotion regulation; among low anxious participants, regular math processing circuits operated (see Mattarella-Micke, Mateo, Kozak, Foster, & Beilock, 2011, for supportive results among high anxious adults, using a cortosol assay).

It is not known at what age we might begin to see the effects of stereotype threat or choking under pressure. One might imagine stereotype effects would appear later in development, since they depend on social identification processes (but see results below on stereotype acceptance in 1st graders). Falling prey to pressure, however, might start appearing fairly early, with standardized testing in schools and other forms of academic pressure. These are areas still to be explored, given their fairly well established effects at this point.[1] But whenever they appear, they are now predicted to yield both established behavioral and neural patterns of results, degraded behavioral performance when working memory is involved, and neural evidence related to emotional and fear processes rather than number and math processes.

As reviewed here, three areas of research have investigated the on-line disruption of math performance due to emotional factors, math anxiety, choking under pressure, and stereotype threat. All three have found convincing evidence that the disruption is due to a disruption in working memory, a deficiency in the operation of the working memory system. According to standard thinking, the emotional reaction involves worry, apprehension, and negative ruminations; the individual attends to those mental worries and ruminations, and thus devotes resources to them rather than to the problem solving task. The consequence is insufficient resources for problem solving, hence degraded performance (e.g., Eysenck & Calvo, 1992).

The newly available fMRI research, however, suggests that high math anxious individuals, or those under stereotype threat, are activating neural regions related to fear and emotion regulation, rather than activating math processing regions. Interestingly, this neurological evidence does not hint at greater activation in language processing regions, i.e., those regions that might be expected to become active if participants were literally engaged in mental "talk" about their worries and fears over math. It is not clear whether activation of emotion regulation regions is equivalent to the process of rumination, or attending to one's ruminations; perhaps the emotional reaction, from one's conscious perspective, is simply one of lack of attentional focus, or inability to screen out interference (e.g., Engle, 2002). These are important questions to be addressed by cognitive science. When trying to solve $43 \equiv 17$ (mod 4), is the math anxious individual's train of thought interrupted by something specific like "I always get confused when I have to borrow," or by something amorphous like "I feel panicky?" Or is it that attention and focus simply cannot be maintained due to sympathetic nervous system activities, including cortical activation of emotion regulation areas? Several hypotheses deserve testing; that working memory is degraded by attention to math-specific worries and ruminations, by interference from non-specific, fear-related processes, or possibly by lack of attentional focus, due to the swirl of competing thoughts and underlying processes.

---

[1] A recent paper, by Delgado and Prieto (2008) suggests that stereotype threat, at least in the domain of math, is mediated by math anxiety; that is, only those high in math anxiety demonstrate the drop in performance attributed to stereotype threat. Given possible cultural differences (the study was conducted in Spain), and the lack of replication, it is difficult to judge how serious a challenge this study poses to the stereotype threat literature.

We close with a few thoughts on causation related to math anxiety. For obvious reasons, including the correlational nature of the evidence, little is currently known about the causes of math anxiety. A recent study provides at least a partial, suggestive answer to the question, however. Beilock, Gunderson, Ramirez, and Levine (2010) investigated the role of the teachers' attitudes and emotions about math in 1st and 2nd grade students' performance. They measured the teachers' math anxiety, and collected measures of math achievement from the students, both at the beginning and the end of the school year. The authors reasoned that children might be acquiring the attitudes and anxieties modeled by their teachers, especially when modeled by a same-gender teacher. Thus, given that some 90% of elementary school teachers in North America are female, Beilock et al. predicted that girls would be especially prone to adopt the negative attitudes and math anxiety modeled by their (female) teachers, and this might influence their math achievement scores (see Hembree, 1990, for evidence of the high incidence of math anxiety among elementary school teachers). Boys were not expected to be as influenced by these attitudes, given the much stronger tendency to model same-gender attitudes (Bussey & Bandura, 1984; Perry & Bussey, 1979).

In short, the results confirmed their suspicions. The post-test scores in these children, at the end of the school year, showed that girls tended to adopt their teacher's negative attitudes and math anxiety; they also endorsed gender stereotyped statements such as "math is for boys, and reading is for girls" (see also Cvencek, Meltzoff, & Greenwald, 2011). Critically, their performance on math achievement tests dropped at the end of the year, compared to their male counterparts. The results of the study seemed to suggest strongly that one likely source of math anxiety is the classroom teacher (see also Turner et al., 2002, for additional teacher effects having to do with social and emotional support of students). The Beilock et al. (2010) paper on teacher modeling effects is a clear demonstration, in our view, and yet is surely not the entire story.

An interesting line of recent research, by Maloney and colleagues, is leading to a different hypothesis concerning the onset of math anxiety (Maloney et al., 2010a; 2010b). These researchers have found that high and low math anxiety groups (adults) perform differently in tasks that have previously been understood to not require substantial working memory capacity to complete. For example, Maloney et al., (2010b) found that high math anxious participants were slower to count the total number of dots on a computer screen, the standard subitizing task, and Maloney et al., (2010a) found this same pattern of math anxiety impairment in a number comparison task (shown two digits, participants must indicate which is larger). The traditional sense of math anxiety has been that the anxiety induced by math consumed working memory processes, leaving little processing capacity for the accurate and efficient completion of the actual task. What Maloney and colleagues suggest, however, is that math anxiety might actually be the product of a low-level deficit in numerical processing, experienced early in childhood. Thus, the individual has always had difficulty dealing with number and mathematics, and this inability to excel across the years developed into an emotional reaction to the domain as a whole. If so, then the connection between math anxiety and working memory would be, as before, a consequence of the anxiety-induced worry and ruminations, but would not be related to the original onset of math anxiety. Instead, onset would be related to a low-level deficit in actual numerical processing, which then triggered difficulties that led to the cascade of emotional consequences and subsequent learning deficiencies. These ideas are intriguing and should be followed up more closely, in developmental samples, to investigate the nature and consequences of these deficits in such basic processing (see also Rubinsten & Tannock, 2010).

Note, in closing, that the Maloney hypothesis suggests an internal cause for math anxiety, a low-level deficit in numerical processing, experienced early in formal education, with cascading, cumulative effects involving emotionality. This is in contrast to external cause explanations like teacher effects (Beilock et al., 2010), or the kind of societal attitudes mentioned here at the outset, e.g., the "Barbie effect" and other such influences. It is vitally important, of course, to come to a better understanding of these causal factors, certainly for math anxiety, but also for situational effects such as choking under pressure and stereotype threat. Only when the mechanisms for these effects are understood can they be addressed either in treatment or prevention.

REFERENCES

Aronson, J., Lustina, M. J., Good, C., Keough, K., Steele, C. M., & Brown, J. (1999). When White men can't do math: Necessary and sufficient factors in stereotype threat. *Journal of Experimental Social Psychology, 35*, 29-46.

Ashcraft, M. H. (1995). Cognitive psychology and simple arithmetic: A review and summary of new directions. *Mathematical Cognition, 1*, 3-34.

Ashcraft, M. H. (2002). Math anxiety: Personal, educational, and cognitive consequences. *Current Directions in Psychological Science, 11*, 181-185.

Ashcraft, M. H., & Faust, M. W. (1994). Mathematics anxiety and mental arithmetic performance: An exploratory investigation. *Cognition and Emotion, 8*, 97-125.

Ashcraft, M. H., & Kirk, E. P. (2001). The relationships among working memory, math anxiety, and performance. *Journal of Experimental Psychology: General, 130*, 224-237.

Ashcraft, M. H., Krause, J. A., & Hopko, D. R. (2007). Is math anxiety a mathematical learning disability? In D. B. Berch & M. M. M. Mazzocco (Eds.), *Why is math so hard for some children? The nature and origins of mathematical learning difficulties and disabilities* (pp. 329-348). Baltimore, MD: Paul H. Brookes.

Ashcraft, M. H., & Moore, A. M. (2009). Mathematics anxiety and the affective drop in performance. *Journal of Psychoeducational Assessment, 27*, 197-205.

Ashcraft, M. H. & Moore, A. M. (2012). Cognitive processes of numerical estimation in children. *Journal of Experimental Child Psychology, 111*, 246-267.

Ashcraft, M. H., & Rudig, N. O. (2012). Higher cognition is altered by noncognitive factors: How affect enhances and disrupts mathematics performance in adolescence and young adulthood. In V. F. Reyna, S. B. Chapman, M. R. Dougherty, & J. Confrey (Eds.), *The Adolescent Brain: Learning, Reasoning, and Decision Making* (pp. 243-263). Washington, D. C.: APA.

Ashcraft, M. H., & Stazyk, E. H. (1981). Mental addition: A test of three verification models. *Memory & Cognition, 9*, 185-196.

Baddeley, A. D. (1996). Exploring the central executive. *Quarterly Journal of Experimental Psychology: Human Experimental Psychology, 49A*, 5-28.

Baddeley, A. D. (2000). The episodic buffer: A new component of working memory? *Trends in Cognitive Sciences, 4*, 417-423.

Baddeley, A. D., & Hitch, G. (1974). Working Memory. In G. H. Bower (Ed.), *The psychology of learning and motivation, Vol 8* (pp. 47-89). New York: Academic Press.

Baddeley, A. D., & Logie, R. H. (1999). Working memory: The multiple-component model. In A. Miyake & P. Shah (Eds.), *Models of working memory: Mechanisms of active maintenance and executive control* (pp. 28-61). Cambridge: Cambridge University Press.

Bandura, A. (1977). Self-efficacy: Toward a unifying theory of behavioral change. *Psychological Review, 84*, 191-215.

Beilock, S. L., & Carr, T. H. (2005). When high-powered people fail: Working memory and choking under pressure in math. *Psychological Science, 16*, 101-105.

Beilock, S. L., & DeCaro, M. S. (2007). From poor performance to success under stress: Working memory, strategy selection, and mathematical problem solving under pressure. *Journal of Experimental Psychology: Learning, Memory, & Cognition, 33*, 983-998.

Beilock, S. L., Gunderson, E. A., Ramirez, G., & Levine, S. C. (2010). Female teachers' math anxiety affects girls' math achievement. *Proceedings of the National Academy of Sciences Early Edition*; www.pnas.org/cgi/doi/10. 1073.pnas.0910967107.

Beilock, S. L., Kulp, C. A., Holt, L. E., & Carr, T. H. (2004). More on the fragility of performance: Choking under pressure in mathematical problem solving. *Journal of Experimental Psychology: General, 133*, 584-600.

Beilock, S. L., & Ramirez, G. (2011). On the interplay of emotion and cognitive control: Implications for enhancing academic achievement. In J. P. Mestre & B. H. Ross (Eds.), *The Psychology of Learning and Motivation: Cognition in Education* (Vol. 55, pp. 137-170). Oxford: Aca- demic Press.

Beilock, S. L., Rydell, R. J., & McConnell, A. R. (2007). Stereotype threat and working memory: Mechanisms, alleviation, and spillover. *Journal of Experimental Psychology: General, 136*, 256-276.

Berger, J. -L., & Karabenick, S. A. (2011). Motivation and students' use of learning strategies: Evidence of unidirectional effects in mathematics classrooms. *Learning and Instruction, 21*, 416-428.

Bush, G., Luu, P. & Posner, M.I. (2000). Cognitive and emotional influences in anterior cingulate cortex. *Trends in Cognitive Sciences, 4*, 215-222.

Bussey, K. & Bandura, A. (1984). Influence of gender constancy and social power on sex-linked modeling. *Journal of Personality and Social Psychology, 47*, 1292-1302.

Bynner, J., & Parsons, S. (1997). Does numeracy matter? Evidence from the national child development study on the impactof poor numeracy on adult life. London: The Basic Skills Agency.

Camos, V., & Barrouillet, P. (2004). Adult counting is resource demanding. *British Journal of Psychology, 95*, 19-30.

Cooper, S. E., & Robinson, D. A. (1991). The relationship of mathematics self-efficacy beliefs to mathematics anxiety and performance. *Measurement and Evaluation in Counseling and Development, 24*, 4-11.

Cvencek, D., Meltzoff, A. N., Greenwald, A. G. (2011). Math-gender stereo- types in elementary school children. *Child Development, 82*, 766-779.

DeCaro, M. S., Rotar, K. E., Kendra, M. S., & Beilock, S. L. (2010). Diagnosing and alleviating the impact of performance pressure on mathe- matical problem solving. *The Quarterly Journal of Experimental Psychology: Human Experimental Psychology, 63*, 1619-1630.

Deldago, A. R. & Prieto, G. (2008). Stereotype threat as validity threat: The anxiety-sex-threat interaction. *Intelligence, 36*, 635-640.

Dehaene, S. (1997). *The number sense*. New York: Oxford University Press.

Dehaene, S., Izard, V., Spelke, E., & Pica, P. (2008) Log or linear? Distinct intuitions of the number scale in western and Amazonian indigene cultures. *Science, 30*, 1217-1220.

Dehaene, S., Spelke, E., Pinel, P., Stanescu, R. and Tsivkin, S. 1999: Sources of mathematical thinking: behavioral and brain–imaging evidence. *Science, 284*, 970–974.

Delazer, M., Domahs, F., Bartha, L., Brenneis, C., Lochy, A., Trieb, T., & Benke, T. (2003). Learning complex arithmetic: an fMRI study. *Cognitive Brain Research, 18*, 76-88.

DeRammelaere, Stuyven, E., & Vandierendonck, A. (1999). The contribution of working memory resources in the verification of simple mental arithmetic sums. *Psychological Research, 62*, 72-77.

DeStefano, D. & LeFevre, J. (2004). The role of working memory in mental arithmetic. *European Journal of Cognitive Psychology, 16*, 353-386.

Engle, R. W. (2002). Working memory capacity as executive attention. *Current Directions in Psychological Science, 11*, 19-23.

Eysenck, M. W., & Calvo, M. G. (1992). Anxiety and performance: The processing efficiency theory. *Cognition and Emotion, 6*, 409-434.

Eysenck, M. W., Derakshan, N., Santos, R., & Calvo, M. G. (2007). Anxiety and cognitive performance: Attentional control theory. *Emotion, 7*, 336-353.

Faust, M. W. (1988). Arithmetic performance as a function of mathematics anxiety: An in-depth analysis of simple and complex addition problems. Unpublished M. A. thesis, Cleveland State University, Cleveland, Ohio.

Faust, M. W., Ashcraft, M. H., & Fleck, D. E. (1996). Mathematics anxiety effects in simple and complex addition. *Mathematical Cognition, 2*, 25-62.

Fürst, A. J., & Hitch, G. J. (2000). Separate roles for executive and phono- logical components of working memory in mental arithmetic. *Memory and Cognition, 28*, 774-782.

Gauss, C. F. (1966). *Disquisitiones arithmeticae*. New Haven, CT: Yale University Press.

Geary, D. C. (1995). Reflections of evolution and culture in children's cogni- tion: implications for mathematical development and instruction. *American Psychologist, 50*, 24-37.

Geary, D. C. (2000). From infancy to adulthood: the development of numerical abilities. *Journal of European Child & Adolescent Psychiatry, 9*, 11-16.

Gelman, R. & Gallistel, C. R. (1978). *The Child's Understanding of Number*. Cambridge, MA: Harvard University Press.

Greenwald, A. G., McGhee, D. E., & Schwartz, J. L. K. (1998). Measuring individual differences in implicit cognition: The implicit association test. *Journal of Personality and Social Psychology, 74*, 1464-1480.

Heathcote, D. (1994). The role of viuso-spatial working memory in the mental addition of multi-digit addends. *Current Psychology of Cognition, 13*, 207-245.

Hecht, S. A. (2002). Counting on working memory in simple arithmetic when counting is used for problem solving. *Memory and Cognition, 30*, 447-455.

Hembree, R. (1990). The nature, effects, and relief of mathematics anxiety. *Journal for Research in Mathematics Education, 21*, 33-46.

Imbo, I., & LeFevre, J. (2010). The role of phonological and visual working memory in complex arithmetic for Chinese- and Canadian-educated adults. *Memory and Cognition, 38,* 176-185.

Imbo, I., & Vandierendonck, A. (2007a). The role of phonological and executive working memory resources in simple arithmetic strategies. *European Journal of Cognitive Psychology, 19,* 910-933.

Imbo, I., & Vandierendonck, A. (2007b). Do multiplication and division strategies rely on executive and phonological working memory resources? *Memory and Cognition, 35,* 1759-1771.

Imbo, I, & Vandierendonck, A. (2008). Effects of problem size, operation, and working-memory span on simple-arithmetic strategies: Differences between children and adults? *Psychological Research, 72,* 331-346.

Imbo, I., Vandierendonck, A., & DeRammelaere, S. (2007). The role of work- ing memory in the carry operation of mental arithmetic: Number and value of the carry. *Quarterly Journal of Experimental Psychology, 60,* 708-731.

Imbo, I., Vandierendonck, A., & Vergauwe, E. (2007). The role of working memory in carrying and borrowing. *Psychological Research, 71,* 467-483.

James, W. (1890/1981). *The Principles of Psychology.* Cambridge, MA: Harvard University Press.

Köller, O., Baumert, J., & Schnabel, K. (2001). Does interest matter? The relationship between academic interest and achievement in mathematics. *Journal for Research in Mathematics Education, 32,* 448-470.

Krause, J. A. (2008). *The effect of math anxiety on learning a novel math task.* Unpublished M.A. thesis, University of Nevada Las Vegas.

Krause, J. A., Rudig, N. O., & Ashcraft, M. H. (2009, November). *Math, Working Memory, and Math Anxiety Effects.* Poster presented at the meetings of the Psychonomic Society, Boston.

Krendl, A. C., Richeson, J. A., Kelley, W. M., & Heatherton, T. F. (2008). A functional magnetic resonance imaging investigation of the neural mechanisms underlying women's underperformance in math. *Psychological Science, 19,* 168-175.

LeDoux, J. E. (2000). Emotion circuits in the brain. *Annual Review of Neuroscience, 23,* 155-184.

Lee, J. (2009). Universals and specifics of math self-concept, math self-efficacy, and math anxiety across 41 PISA 2003 participating countries. *Learning and Individual differences, 19,* 355-365.

Lee, K., & Kang, S. (2002). Arithmetic operation and working memory: Differential suppression in dual tasks. *Cognition, 83,* B63-B68.

Lemaire, P., Abdi, H., & Fayol, M. (1996). The role of working memory resources in simple cognitive arithmetic. *European Journal of Cognitive Psychology, 8,* 73-103.

Leuwerke, W. C., Robbins, S., Sawyer, R., & Hovland, M. (2004). Predicting engineering major status from mathematics achievement and interest congruence. *Journal of Career Assessment, 12,* 135-149.

Logie, R. H., Gilhooly, K. J., & Wynn, V. (1994). Counting on working memory in arithmetic problem solving. *Memory and Cognition, 22,* 395-410.

Lopez, F. G., Lent, R. W., Brown, S. D., & Gore, P. A. (1997). Role of social-cognitive expectations in high school students' mathematics-related interest and performance. *Journal of Counseling Psychology, 44,* 44-52.

Ma, X. (1999) A meta-analysis of the relationship between anxiety toward mathematics and achievement in mathematics. *Journal for Research in Mathematics Education, 30,* 520-541.

Maloney, E. A., Ansari, D., & Fugelsang, J. A. (2010a). The effect of mathematics anxiety on the processing of numerical magnitude. *Quarterly Journal of Experimental Psychology,* iFirst, 1-7: DOI: 10.1080/17470218. 2010.533278.

Maloney, E. A., Risko, E. F., Ansari, D., & Fugelsang, J. (2010b). Mathematics anxiety affects counting but not subitizing during visual enumeration. *Cognition, 114,* 293-297.

Mattarella-Micke, A., Mateo, J., Kozak, M. N., Beilock, S. L. (2011). Choke or thrive? The relation between salivary cortisol and math performance depends on individual differences in working memory and math-anxiety. *Emotion, 11,* 1000-1005.

McClure, E. B., Monk, C. S., Nelson, E. E., Parrish, J. M., Adler, A., Blair, R. J., & Pine, D. S. (2007). Abnormal attention modulation of fear circuit function in pediatric generalized anxiety disorder. *Archives of General Psychiatry, 64,* 97-106.

McKenzie, B., Bull, R., & Gray, C. (2003). The effects of phonological and visual-spatial interference on children's arithmetical performance. *Educational and Child Psychology, 20,* 93-108.

Menon, V., Rivera, S. M., White, C. D., Glover, G. H., & Reiss, A. L. (2000). Dissociating prefrontal and parietal cortex activation during arithmetic processing. *NeuroImage, 12,* 357-365.

Miyake, A., & Shah, P. (1999) *Models of working memory: Mechanisms of active maintenance and executive control.* Cambridge, UK: Cambridge University Press.

Moore, A. M., & Ashcraft, M. H. (2012a). Children's developing mathematical knowledge in grades one through five. Manuscript in preparation.

Moore, A. M. & Ashcraft, M. H. (2012b). Mathematics anxiety. *Encyclopedia of Language and Literacy Development* (pp. 1-8). London, ON: Canadian Language and Literacy Research Network. Retrieved from: http:// www. literacyencyclopedia.ca/pdfs/topic.php? topId=308.

Moore, A. M., Rudig, N. O., Ashcraft, M. H. (2012). Affect, motivation, working memory, and mathematics. To appear in R. Cohen & A. Dowker (Eds.), *The Oxford handbook of numerical cognition.* Submitted.

National Mathematics Advisory Panel. (2008). *Foundations for success. Reports of the Task Groups and Subcommittees.* Washington, D. C.: U. S. Department of Education. Retrieved from: http://edpubs.ed.gov.

Nosek, B. A., Banaji, M. R., & Greenwald, A. G. (2002a). Math = male, me = female, therefore math not = me. *Journal of Personality and Social Psychology, 83,* 44-59.

Nosek, B. A., Banaji, M. R., & Greenwald, A. G. (2002b). Harvesting implicit group attitudes and beliefs from a demonstration website. *Group Dynamics: Theory, Research, and Practice, 6,* 101-115.

Perry, D. G. & Bussey, K. (1979). The social learning theory of sex differences: Imitation is alive and well. *Journal of Personality and Social Psychology, 37,* 1699-1712.

Phelps, E. A., Delgado, M. R., Nearing, K. I., LeDoux (2004). Extinction learning in humans: Role of the amygdala and vmPFC. *Neuron, 43,* 897-905.

Pietsch, J., Walker, R., & Chapman, E. (2003). The relationship among self-concept, self-efficacy, and performance in mathematics during secondary school. *Journal of Educational Psychology, 95,* 589-603.

Raghubar, K. P., Barnes, M. A., & Hecht, S. A. (2010). Working memory and mathematics: A review of developmental, individual difference, and cognitive approaches. *Learning and Individual Differences, 20,* 110-122.

Ramirez, G., Gunderson, E. A., Levine, S. C., & Beilock, S. L. (in press). Math anxiety, working memory, and math achievement in early elementary school. *Journal of Cognition and Development.*

Richardson, F. C. & Suinn, R. M. (1972). The mathematics anxiety rating scale: Psychometric data. *Journal of Counseling Psychology, 19,* 551-554.

Rubinsten, O., & Tannock, R. (2010). Mathematics anxiety in children with developmental dyscalculia. *Behavioral and Brain Functions, 6.*

Ryan, A. M., & Pintrich, P. R. (1997). Should I ask for help? The role of motivation and attitudes in adolescents' help seeking in math class. *Journal of Educational Psychology, 89,* 329-341.

Schmader, T. (2002). Gender identification moderates stereotype threat effects on women's math performance. *Journal of Experimental Social Psychology, 38,* 194-201.

Schmader, T., Johns, M., & Forbes, C. (2008). An integrated process model of stereotype threat effects on performance. *Psychological Review, 115,* 336-356.

Seitz, K., & Schumann-Hengsteler, R. (2000). Mental Multiplication and working memory. *European Journal of Cognitive Psychology, 12,* 552-570.

Seitz, K., & Schumann-Hengsteler, R. (2002). Phonological loop and central executive processes in mental addition and multiplication. *Psychologische Beitrage, 44,* 275-302.

Seyler, D. J., Kirk, E. P., & Ashcraft, M. H. (2003). Elementary subtraction. *Journal of Experimental Psychology. Learning, Memory, and Cognition, 29,* 1339-1352.

Siegler, R. S. (1996). *Emerging minds: The process of change in children's thinking.* New York: Oxford University Press.

Siegler, R. S., & Booth, J. L. (2004). Development of numerical estimation in young children. *Child Development, 75,* 428-444.

Simpkins, S. D., Davis-Kean, P. E., & Eccles, J. S. (2006). Math and science motivation: A longitudinal examination of the links between choices and beliefs. *Developmental Psychology, 42,* 70-83.

Somerville, L. H., Heatherton, T. F., & Kelley, W. M. (2006). Dissociating expenctancy violation from social rejection. *Nature Neuroscience, 9,* 1007-008.

Spencer, S. J., Steele, C. M., & Quinn, D. M. (1999). Stereotype threat and women's math performance. *Journal of Experimental Social Psychology, 35,* 4-28.

Steele, C. M., & Aronson, J. (1995). Stereotype threat and the intellectual test performance of African-Americans. *Journal of Personality and Social Psychology, 69,* 797-811.

Szmalec, A., Vandierendonck, A., & Kemps, E. (2005). Response selection involves executive control: Evidence from the selective interference paradigm. *Memory and Cognition, 33,* 531-541.

Stevenson, H. W., Lee, S., Chen, C., Lummis, M., Stigler, J., Fan, L., & Ge, F. (1990). Mathematics achievement of children in China and the United States. *Child Development, 61,* 1053-1066.

The New York Times (1992, October 21). Mattel says it erred: Teen Talk Barbie turns silent on math. Retrieved from: http:// www.nytimes.com/ 1992/10/21/business/company-news-mattel-says-it-erred-teen-talk-barbie-turns-silent-on-math.html.

Trbovich, P. L., & LeFevre, J. (2003). Phonological and visual working memory in mental addition. *Memory and Cognition, 31*, 738-745.

Turner, J. C., Midgley, C., Meyer, D. K., Gheen, M., Anderman, E. M., Kang, Y., & Patrick, H. (2002). The classroom environment and students' reports of avoidance strategies in mathematics: A multimethod study. *Journal of Educational Psychology, 94*, 88-106.

Wynn, K. (1992). Addition and subtraction by human infants. *Nature, 358*, 749-750.

Wynn, K (1996). Infants' individuation and enumeration of actions. *Psychological Science, 7*, 167-169.

Young, C. B., Wu, S. S., Menon, V. (2012). The neurodevelopmental basis of math anxiety. *Psychological Science, 23*, 492-501.

Zakaria, E., & Nordin, N. M. (2008). The effects of math anxiety on matriculation students as related to motivation and achievement. *Eurasia Journal of Mathematics, Science & Technology Education, 4*, 27-30.

Zebian, S., & Ansari, D. (2012). Differences between literates and illiterates on symbolic but not nonsymbolic numerical magnitude processing. *Psychonomic Bulletin & Review, 19*, 93-100.

In: Handbook of Psychology of Emotions
Editors: C. Mohiyeddini, M. Eysenck and S. Bauer

ISBN: 978-1-62808-053-7
© 2013 Nova Science Publishers, Inc.

Chapter 9

THE SELF-CONSCIOUS EMOTIONS OF GUILT, SHAME AND PRIDE IN EDUCATION

Shaalan Farouk[*]
University of Roehampton
Department of Education, London, UK

ABSTRACT

The experience of self-conscious emotions is associated with a person's evaluations of the self and his or her conduct in a particular situation. In particular an individual is expected to experience guilt, shame and pride when they perceive themselves to have succeeded or failed to abide by internalised values and moral standards. Hence an examination of how and when individuals experience self-conscious emotions can provide considerable psychological insight into their personal values and moral imperatives. Moreover, the different self-conscious emotions a person experiences do not remain inert within the confines of their body. Instead, they have a prevailing influence on an individual's thoughts and their behaviour. With this in mind substantial psychological and some educational research has been conducted on the self-conscious emotions. In this chapter, a brief review of the literature on the development of self-conscious emotions is followed by a detailed examination of guilt, shame and pride as experienced by school children and adolescents. The analysis of each emotion will include an exploration of how it is experienced by learners and its potential influence on their behaviour and their ability to learn. Furthermore, each self-conscious emotion is examined as an achievement emotion, which learners experience in relation to their work, or as a social emotion, which students experience in their social interactions. At the end of the chapter the circumstances under which teachers experience guilt and pride are also described and discussed. The purpose of research in this field has been to study teachers' self-understanding and moral purpose by examining their self-conscious emotions.

---

[*] Shaalan.Farouk@roehampton.ac.uk.

INTRODUCTION

In the last thirty years the field of education has experienced a slow awakening to the fact that it is emotions intertwined with cognition, rather than cold cognition, which determine a student's capacity to learn and a teacher's ability to teach. While there has been interest in the study of negative emotions of students who display social and behavioural difficulties the influence of emotions on learning is a new and developing field of research. Similarly, teachers' varied emotional experiences, stemming from their professional identity and personal relationships, have only recently attracted the attention of educational research.

With the exception of research on test anxiety (see Zeidner 2007 for a review of the literature) educational research has predominantly focussed on the experience of negative and positive affect rather than on specific emotions. In particular there has been research on positive and negative affect associated with students' academic achievement (for instance,Elliot 1999; Elliot and McGregor 2001; Linnenbrink and Pintrich 2002; Pekrun, Goetz et al. 2002; Linnenbrink 2007) and their social relationships and behaviour (Arsenio, Gold et al. 2004; Krettenauer and Eichler 2006; Malti, Gasser et al. 2009). Along similar lines, some studies have explored valence in teachers' emotional experiences rather than the examination of specific emotions (for instance, Nias 1996; Hargreaves 1998; Hargreaves 1999; Kelchtermans 2005). The shortcoming inherent in studying positive and negative affect is that such research ignores the variety of emotions a person experiences and the influence specific emotions may have on their thoughts and behaviour. A measure of negative affect, for instance, does not take into consideration whether a person predominantly feels sad, angry or guilty; separate negative emotions with their own phenomenology, cognitive associations, and behavioural consequences. Only Pekrun and Elliot (2006) and Krettenauer et al (2011) seem to have recognised the significance of this emotional variety by shifting their research focus from children and adolescents' negative and positive affect to examining their emotions.

The specific literature examined in this chapter focuses on the self-conscious emotions of guilt, shame and pride. The rationale for considering these emotions in particular is that they are experienced when an individual reflects back on the self and the actions s/he has taken. When engaged in this process of self-appraisal it is an individual's evaluation of the extent to which they have succeeded or failed to live up to internalised values and moral standards that determine the self-conscious emotions s/he experiences. An examination of self- conscious emotional experiences may therefore reveal what matters most to an individual since these emotions are an expression of internalised values and moral norms. Moreover psychological research on children has begun to chart the evolution and progress of their self -awareness and moral understanding by examining the complexity of their self-conscious emotional experiences at different phases of development (Hart and Matsuba 2007; Lagattuta and Thompson 2007; Lewis 2007; Krettenauer and Johnston 2011).

In their review of research on the development of self-conscious emotions Lagattuta and Thompson (2007) maintain that these emotions are cognitively more complex than basic emotions, such as anger, sadness and fear. In order to experience and differential between self-conscious emotions children require self –awareness and the ability to recognise external standards against which their own characteristics and behaviour can be judged. Moreover, these external standards must be accepted and adopted by the child so that they are of sufficient relevance to them for cognitive appraisal and an emotional response. Research on 2-3 year old children suggests that toddlers are sufficiently self-aware to experience self-conscious affect. By observing their non-verbal responses to situation that elicit a self-conscious emotional response researchers have explored the earliest signs of embarrassment, guilt, and pride (Stipek 1995; Kochanska, Gross et al. 2002). For instance, Stipek (1995) found that toddlers who have completed a task by themselves will show early signs of pride by looking up and smiling at the adult. Therefore research has shown that young children are sufficiently self-aware to display early signs of experiencing different self- conscious emotions. Yet, when children are required to differentiate between these self-conscious emotions consistently and are required to demonstrate an understanding of particular emotions they are not able to do so until they are seven to eight years old. As suggested in a number of studies they do so when they have acquired the capacity to cognitively evaluate themselves and their actions in relation to internalised social values and standards and what they imagine other people think about them and their behaviour (Lagattuta and Thompson 2007; Lewis 2007).

In the above discussion of self-conscious emotions and their development there is the assumption that these emotions depend on cognitive appraisal or evaluation of the self and one's actions. In fact, most psychological research on emotions draws on cognitive appraisal theory, which proposes that an individual's emotional response is predominantly determined by his/her cognitive appraisal (evaluation) of events and situations (Lazarus 1991; Scherer, Schorr et al. 2001). Indeed even when there is no direct reference to cognitive appraisal theory most authors assume that the difference between emotions depends on how particular events are cognitively appraised by the individual either consciously or unconsciously. Most of the studies reviewed in this chapter assume that it is variations in cognitive appraisal which differentiate the self-conscious emotions from each other and also from other emotions.

The literature on the self-conscious emotions of guilt, shame and pride will now be examined in turn. The analysis of each emotion will include an exploration of the cognitive appraisals associated with the causation of each self-conscious emotion and its potential influence on students' behaviour and their ability to learn. For the purpose of this chapter the research on each emotion is separated into two lines of inquiry: the first examines them as achievement emotions (associated with students' academic success or failure) and the second as social emotions that emerge from interactions and personal relationships. The emotions of shame and pride have been studied as both achievement and social emotions while guilt has only been considered as a social emotion. The final part of the chapter reviews research on teachers' self conscious emotions. This review will be limited to experiences of guilt and pride since teachers' shame has not been the subject of substantial educational research. The emphasis will be on what the experiences of guilt and pride reveal about teachers' moral imperatives and teacher/student relationships, rather than on the influence of these emotions on teachers' attitude and behaviour.

LEARNERS' EXPERIENCES OF GUILT

The emotion of guilt is usually associated with the appraisal of having failed to attain a moral outcome that is of personal and in most cases also social significance. Besides being a self-conscious emotion, guilt is also considered to be a moral and interpersonal emotion since feeling guilty is usually engendered by a disregard for the just treatment and welfare of others (Baumeister, Stillwell et al. 1994; Baumeister, Stillwell et al. 1995; Tangney and Dearing 2002; Berndsen, van der Pligt et al. 2004). In their study of guilt in interpersonal relationships Baumeister et al (1995) demonstrated how individuals predominantly experience guilt as a result of the negative impact of one's actions on the other person, rather than the extent to which the person actually perceives him or herself to be culpable. They found that in relationships individuals will often experience guilt when their behaviour has caused another person whom they care about to feel unhappy or upset, even though their actions were not deliberate and the negative outcome was unforeseen. In addition, Tracy and Robins (2004) and Weiner (1985) maintain that individuals experiences guilt outside the social sphere of personal affiliations. They propose that individuals may also feel guilty when they perceive themselves to have transgressed social and personally held moral values. Hence, a student may experience guilt as a result of a failed exam predominantly because social expectations and internalised moral norms have been transgressed.

There is agreement in the psychological literature that guilt motivates a person to take constructive action and to make amends (Barrett 1994; Baumeister, Stillwell et al. 1995; Lewis 2000; Tangney and Dearing 2002; Parkinson, Fischer et al. 2005). The person who feels guilty is inclined to apologise and to try and repair or ameliorate the harm s/he has caused. Baumeister et al (1994) therefore suggest that the purpose of interpersonal guilt is to maintain relationships by motivating the person responsible for upsetting others to take reparative action and to re-establish rapport. According to Tangney and Dearing (2002) the only instance when guilt is not constructive is when individuals are not in a position to take reparative action. Under these circumstances the feelings of guilt may linger and become a persistent form of gnawing guilt that does not fade. In this connection Tangney and Dearing (2002) suggest that individuals who tend to accept responsibility for negative outcomes over which they in fact had limited or no control are particular prone to experiencing this form of persistent guilt.

In the field of education guilt has been approached as a social emotion experienced by students in interpersonal relationships. In particular, guilt has been studied as one of the negative emotions children and adolescent may experience when they have upset or hurt other children, either physically or verbally. Early research with young children identified an apparent dissociation between their ability to engage in moral reasoning and the emotions they experienced; a phenomenon which has became known as the *happy victimiser* (please see Krettenauer, Malti et al. 2008 for a review of the literature). In these studies preschoolers and children starting school were presented with scenarios – where one child victimised another child - and asked to describe what they would think and feel if they were the victimiser. Several studies that have adopted this method in different contexts found that most four to six-year old children would express feeling happy in the role as 'victimiser' while also being able to explain how it is morally wrong to hurt others. What these findings suggest is that in young children there appears to be dissociation between the ability to engage in moral reasoning on the one hand and the experience of moral emotions and moral conduct on the other. Further research conducted by Malti et al (2009) considered the *happy victimiser* scenario by comparing prosocial children and outwardly aggressive children attending a kindergarten. The investigation was structured around an examination of the emotions that the six year old children attributed to themselves when presented with scenarios where they featured as the 'victimizer'. Their findings indicated that the aggressive children attributed fewer negative emotions to themselves in the role as victimisers than the prosocial children. Hence, it seems that it is the potential of experiencing negative affect which prevents children from aggressive behaviour towards their peers.

Keeping the research on the *happy victimizer* in mind Krettenauer and colleagues (Krettenauer and Eichler 2006; Krettenauer and Johnston 2011) proposed that older children and adolescents develop the capacity to experience specific moral emotions – such as guilt and pride – by having internalised moral values and standards into their self-concept. They maintain that by having developed a substantive moral identity, moral issues become personally significant and self-important to the individual. Thus it is the personal relevance (or self-importance) of moral issues which enables older children and adolescents to experience specific self-conscious emotions. In order to examine the relationship between the self-importance of moral values and the experience of moral emotions and behaviour Krettenauer and Johnston (2011) conducted a study involving 155 adolescents and young adults between the age of eleven and nineteen years. Participants were presented with three types of scenarios taking place within a prosocial, antisocial or temptation context. The prosocial context gave the main protagonist the opportunity to help others, the antisocial context presented him/her with the option to stop victimizers from harming others, and the temptation context presented him/her with the choice of breaking a moral rule for their own benefit. Following each scenario participants were asked to indicate the emotions they expected to experience and, in particular, the extent to which they would feel pride or guilt. In addition the participants completed a questionnaire which assessed the self-importance of moral values. The study identified a significant correlation between the self-importance of moral values and the expectation of experiencing guilt. Moreover, the findings indicate that adolescents are more likely to experience guilt when they actively give way to temptation and engage in immoral behaviour than when they remain inactive and refrain from taking morally appropriate action.

In a follow up study Krettenauer et al. (2011) examined the relationship between emotion expectancy and the moral choices of adolescents. Their findings indicated that the expectation of experiencing guilt was a strong predictor of making the moral choice to refrain from engaging in antisocial action, such as stealing from a shop. By contrast, the expectation of guilt did not encourage participation in morally appropriate behaviour, such as donating to a charity. Engaging in such prosocial action was more strongly associated with the expectation of experiencing pride rather than avoiding feelings of guilt. According to Krettenauer et al a possible reason for the lack of association between guilt and prosocial behaviour is that most adolescents consider it to be a personal choice rather than a moral obligation.

To conclude, one of the most important findings to emerge from research on guilt in children and adolescents is that for them to make moral choices and behave accordingly they need to have acquired the capacity to experience guilt alongside other self conscious emotions. The research on the *happy victimiser* phenomenon has yielded important results by demonstrating that the ability to engage in moral reasoning in itself does not result in moral behaviour. What is also required is the internalisation of moral values so that they become an integral part of any self-appraisal and self-conscious emotional response. The ability to experience guilt, alongside other self-conscious emotions, may therefore be an important indicator of moral development and of an ability to engage in morally appropriate behaviour.

LEARNERS' EXPERIENCES OF SHAME

In 1971, Lewis published her seminal work entitled *Shame and Guilt in Neurosis* which continues to have a substantial influence on psychological research today. Drawing on her therapeutic practice as a clinical psychologist she provided an analysis of shame, and how it differs from guilt. Lewis maintained that shame is a painful emotion which individuals experience when they negatively evaluate stable aspects of the self, such as one's innate inabilities or features of one's character. She proposed that shame differs from guilt by being associated with a negative evaluation of the stable global self rather than one's behaviour in a particular context. Therefore while guilt encourages individuals to try and improve the situation shame - by making them focus on aspects of the stable self - makes them want to shrink away and withdraw. This overwhelming desire to retreat then leaves individuals unable to engage in constructive or conciliatory behaviour towards those they may have offended and upset. Recent empirical research has mostly supported Lewis's analysis of shame (for instance, Barrett 1994; Lewis 2000; Tangney and Dearing 2002; Weiner 2006). In addition, Tangney and her colleagues have found that instead of withdrawing from the situation some individuals try and cope with shame by displacing it with righteous anger. By finding fault in others and becoming angry they avoid, at least in the short term, having to blame themselves and endure this painful emotion (Tangney 1995; Tangney, Burggraf et al. 1995; Tangney, Wagner et al. 1996). According to Tangney et al. (1996) this displacement of shame with anger is particularly prevalent amongst individuals who are prone to experiencing shame rather than guilt in situations that promote critical self-appraisal. In fact, their findings suggest that shame-prone children and adults are not only more likely to experience anger but that they are also more likely to engage in unconstructive behaviour than their less shame-prone peers.

In contrast to research indicating that shame is associated with unhelpful and defensive behaviour Gausel and Leach (2011) have recently propose that shame can motivate individuals to engage in constructive action. In their conceptualisation of shame, the experience of shame is associated with the cognitive appraisal of a specific self-defect which is potentially alterable. Hence, the individual who experiences shame may be motivated to improve his/her self image by engaging in behaviour that will improve their perception of an aspect of the self. In support of Gausel and Leach studies by de Hooge et al. (2010) suggest that feelings of shame are more strongly correlated with the motivation to restore self-image than to protect the self by engaging in defensive behaviour. The literature on restorative justice and shame management is also in agreement with this particular understanding of shame (Ahmed, Harris et al. 2001). In fact, research on criminal behaviour and bullying in schools conducted by Braithwaite (1989) and Ahmed (2006) has shown how the acknowledgement and management of shame is a necessary precondition for constructive and conciliatory behaviour on the part of the perpetrator. Therefore while feeling ashamed may bring about defensive behaviour - especially in clinical cases where individuals are prone to feeling ashamed – the acknowledgement of shame is also associated with the motivation to engage in constructive and reconciliatory conduct.

In educational research shame has predominantly been studied as one of the achievement emotions which students experience when evaluating their academic progress or their performance in an exam. Using undergraduate University students in Germany and North

America to study shame alongside other achievement emotions Pekrun and Elliot (2006) concluded that shame is associated with students holding themselves personally responsible for having failed in class or obtaining a lower than expected result in a test or an exam. Most interestingly they also found a significant correlation between shame and the ways in which students approached an activity. Students who were predominantly pre-occupied with avoiding failure were more likely to experience shame than students who either focussed on performing well and experiencing success or were predominantly interested in mastering the activity for its own sake.

Besides examining the possible causes of shame Pekrun et al. (2009) also considered the influence that shame (alongside other achievement emotions) may have on undergraduate students' academic performance. Since earlier research by Pekrun et al. (2002) had suggested that feeling ashamed was associated with critical introspection rather than engagement in learning the expectation was that shame would contribute to poorer academic performance. The research matched this expectation in that its findings showed a significant correlation between shame and poor academic performance. Moreover, the study identified a positive association between a pre-occupation to avoid failure (rather than striving for success) , the experience of shame and poor academic performance.

Besides, Pekrun et al.'s study of achievement emotions Turner and colleagues specifically investigated how university students experience shame after having failed an exam and their subsequent engagement in academic study (Turner and Schallert 2001; Turner, Husman et al. 2002; Turner and Waugh 2007). In contrast to the survey design adopted by Pekrun and colleagues, Turner et al used interviews to gain a better understanding of students' individual experiences of shame. They obtained a contrasting and varied picture of shame depending on individual students' disposition towards taking an exam. They found that some students expected to experience shame in exam situations while for others feeling ashamed was a rare and shocking experience.

In addition Turner and colleagues examined the potential consequences of experiencing shame. They concluded that while shame initially resulted in cognitive confusion in most students the subsequent responses to feeling ashamed varied depending on personal circumstances and the motivational reasons for studying. Students uncertain about the purpose of their studies – such as simply wanting to gain a degree – remained confused and did not change their approach to studying. They seemed to become disorientated and lose focus without regaining the motivation and composure to re-engage in their studies. In contrast, other students who had a well defined and important future goal continued to belief in their academic abilities and seemed to have a wider repertoire of strategies to draw on. They were more likely to re-engage in their studies and adopt new learning methods to improve their performance. The finding that shame may contribute to constructive action supports the proposition put forward by Gausel and Leach (2011) that experiencing this emotion may not involve a negative evaluation of a stable self. Instead, experiences of shame may be based on the cognitive appraisal of a specific self-defect which can potentially be changed. Indeed it may only be shame-prone individuals who in most situations respond to a negative outcome by blaming a persistent and unalterable self.

As was evident in the review of psychological research conducted outside the field of education shame has mostly been studied as a social and interpersonal emotion rather than as an achievement emotion. In such interpersonal circumstances shame may motivate a person to withdraw from further social involvement or provoke defensive anger at the person who has made the individual experience this painful emotion (Tangney 1995; Tangney and Dearing 2002). Feelings of shame may therefore often be at the heart of why some students respond angrily and aggressively to what may appear to the teacher or fellow student to be quite reasonable requests. For instance, a student who perceives him or herself to lack academic ability may respond angrily when asked to complete an activity in a set period of time. S/he would rather blame the other person for making such an unreasonable demand than acknowledge how ashamed s/he would feel at not being able to complete the task.

The one area in educational research where shame has been examined as a social emotion is in studies on bullying at school. In 2001 a study by Ahmed et al placed shame and the way it is managed at the heart of bullying behaviour. Drawing on the work of Braithwaite (1989) and Tangney (1995) they maintained that pupils who engage in bullying do not acknowledge the shame associated with their behaviour but displace this unpleasant emotion by blaming others and experiencing anger instead. In contrast, children not engaged in bullying acknowledge and accept feeling ashamed when they have done something wrong such as upsetting or hurting another child. A substantial body of work has subsequently built on this premise and established the idea that bullies need help to acknowledge and manage their feelings of shame (for instance, Ahmed 2006; Morrison 2006). In particular they have emphasised shame management as an important part of the restorative justice approach to combating bullying in schools.

To conclude, educational research has consistently demonstrated that students experience shame when they blame themselves for having failed in class and or in an exam. Moreover, Pekrun et al. suggested that students who are pre-occupied with avoiding failure are more likely to blame themselves and feel ashamed than other adolescents who take a more positive and constructive approach. As far as the consequences of experiencing shame are concerned the findings are less consistent. On the one hand, research on achievement emotions indicates that shame has a negative impact on academic performance, and on the other, the work by Turner et al on failing an exam suggests that some students respond constructively to experiences of shame. The study of shame in students' social relationships has been confined to bullying in schools. The research suggests that adolescents who bully others are less able to acknowledge and accept feelings of shame than their peers. Hence, it may be the case that students who engage in bullying do so in part to displace the painful emotion of shame with anger directed at someone else.

LEARNERS' EXPERIENCES OF PRIDE

In 2003 Tangney described pride as the "neglected sibling" amongst the self-conscious emotions as it had received the least attention in psychological research. Seemingly, this lack of interest was based on the assumption that feeling proud has limited influence on thoughts and behaviour. More recently, however, psychologists have noted the potential importance of pride to moral development and to maintaining moral behaviour in everyday situations (Hart and Matsuba 2007; Tracy and Robins 2007). Moreover, Tracey and Robins (2007a) have emphasised how pride may have a more complex cognitive antecedence and more varied phenomenological configuration than most other self-conscious emotions.

The psychological literature suggests that pride is experienced by individuals who perceive themselves to have contributed to a positive outcome which is of substantive personal and social significance (Tangney 1999; Tangney, Stuewig et al. 2007; Tracy and Robins 2007). In addition psychological research has identified how individuals may experience two quite different forms of pride. Drawing on the work of Tagney (1999) and Lewis (2000) and their own research, Tracy and Robins (2004) make a distinction between *authentic pride* and *hubristic pride*. According them, individuals experience *authentic pride* when they attribute success to their behaviour and actions, such as the effort they have put in to prepare for an exam. In contrast, individuals are expected to experience *hubristic pride* when they attribute success to a stable aspect of the self, such as their innate ability in being successful at exams. They suggest that the differences in cognitive appraisal between these two forms of pride are similar to those that differentiate guilt and shame. While guilt and *authentic pride* are both associated with reflective evaluations of one's actions, shame and *hubristic pride* are based on evaluations of stable aspects of the self.

Alongside identifying variations in cognitive appraisal Tracy and Robins (2007; 2007) also examined how these two forms of pride may vary in the influence they have on a person's attitudes and behaviours. On the basis of their research findings they concluded that *authentic pride* is the "adaptive, prosocial, achievement oriented facet of the emotion" (Tracy and Robins 2007 p.267) which contributes to the development of a persistent and stable sense of self esteem. In contrast, the hubristic facet of pride is "uniquely related to narcissistic self-aggrandizement" (Tracy and Robins 2007 p.267). Hence the experience of pride can, according to Tracy and Robins, have very different consequences depending on the cognitive appraisal of a successful outcome and whether *authentic pride* or *hubristic pride* is experienced. It is worth noting that so far no study has engaged with the key issue of whether particular individuals are prone to experiencing authentic or hubristic facets of pride or whether there are consistent variations across cultures and social systems.

In the field of education students' experiences of pride have only been studied to a limited extent with no consideration for the two facets of pride identified by psychological research. Pekrun and colleagues (Pekrun and Elliot 2006; Pekrun, Elliot et al. 2009), for instance, have included pride in their examination of achievement emotions. Their research indicates that undergraduate students experience enjoyment and pride as a result of success in class or when taking an exam. In addition, students were more likely to feel proud when they were focused on performing well rather than pre-occupied with avoiding failure. Most interestingly, there was also the finding that students also reported feeling proud when they focused on the intrinsic value of the activity rather than obtaining a successful normative result at the end. This positive correlation between pride and mastering an activity for its own sake was an unexpected finding since experiencing this emotion is usually associated with having completed a task and attained a successful outcome that is of both social and personal significance. In contrast, the findings here suggest that pride is an emotion which students may experience for personal reasons, when they are engaged in an activity and are making good progress. In such circumstances it seems that students experience an intrinsic form of pride by comparing their current progress to their performance on previous occasions. Moreover, when pride is experiences in action it may also motivate students to complete an activity to a higher standard than before.

Besides approaching pride as an achievement emotion, Krettenauer and colleagues examined pride in the context of adolescents' social relationships (Krettenauer, Jia et al.

2011; Krettenauer and Johnston 2011). In particular they explored the extent to which moral behaviour may be influenced by the expectation of experiencing pride or guilt. Their findings indicate that adolescents are more likely to engage in pro-social action when they expect to experience pride as a consequence of their actions rather than guilt for not having taken part. For instance, a young person is more inclined to donate money to a charity or help another person because they expect to feel proud of what they have done than guilty for not having made a contribution. In contrast, the opposite seems to apply when it comes to resisting temptation and not engaging in a moral transgression, such as stealing from a shop. Here the expectation of experiencing guilt seems to prevent adolescents for engaging in antisocial behaviour rather than the emotion of pride at having resisted the temptation to do so. Therefore amongst adolescents the emotion of pride seems to promote pro-social action rather than prevent immoral and antisocial behaviour.

Although the study of pride in children and adolescents is still at a very early stage, it has obtained some intriguing findings which merit further investigation. Pekrun and colleagues have identified a positive correlation between students' experiences of intrinsic pride and a *master approach goal* orientation to learning. This finding suggests that students may experience an intrinsic form of pride which motivates students to perform well while engaged in an activity. In addition, the suggestion that pride encourages prosocial behaviour amongst adolescents is of significance as their ability to experience this specific emotion consistently may be a good indication of their moral development.

TEACHERS' EXPERIENCES OF GUILT AND PRIDE

Although teaching is both a cognitive and an emotional activity research on specific emotions and what they reveal about teachers' professional identities and their social relationships is scarce. Within this limited field of research studies on teachers' frustration and anger have taken centre stage (Liljestrom, Roulston et al. 2007; Sutton 2007; Farouk 2010). Amongst the self-conscious emotions pride and guilt have received some attention while shame has not been considered at all, at least from a psychological perspective. The idea that teachers often experience guilt was first articulated by Nias (1989) in her seminal study on primary school teaching as work. She observed that teachers often experienced anxiety and guilt when unable to maintain the level of care they aspired to. The importance of guilt in teaching has also been validated by Hargreaves and Tucker (1991) who found this emotion prevalent among participants of a research project on teacher culture and educational change in Canada. Drawing on the work of Davis (1989), Hargreaves and Tucker made the distinction between two kinds of guilt in teaching: *persecutory guilt* and *depressive guilt*. They maintain that teachers experience *persecutory guilt* when they have been unable to meet the performance indicators set by the education system and the school. In contrast, *depressive guilt* is linked to the culture of caring normally associated with this profession. In agreement with Nias, Hargreaves emphasised the extent to which teachers may experience *depressive guilt* because of the high expectation they have of themselves to care for and advance the interests of their pupils. Hargreaves goes on to suggest that teachers are particularly susceptible to experiencing this form of guilt because of the open ended nature of their work and the lack of prescribed boundaries as to the appropriate level of care.

More recently, Farouk (2012) has investigated primary school teachers' guilt from the perspective of cognitive appraisal theory. Taking a qualitative approach he interviewed twenty two teachers about recent events in which they predominantly experienced guilt. The findings suggest that primary school teachers most often feel guilty when they blame themselves for having upset or let down a child or a group of children in their class. Moreover, they illustrated how teachers would on occasion experience guilt without blaming themselves. In such cases the main cause of guilt seemed to be a sense of having caused distress to others who are emotionally close rather than blaming oneself. The outcome of this study supports earlier research by Frijda (1993) and Baumeister et al. (1995) who linked guilt to the perception of having upset significant others rather than blaming oneself. On the basis of their research on personal relationships Baumeister et al. (1995) concluded that individuals most often tended to feel guilty when their actions had unintentionally affected the welfare of others who were emotionally close. The extent to which the outcome from Farouk's (2012) investigation coincide with those obtained by Baumeister et al. (1995) suggests that the close relationships associated with the experience of guilt in people's personal life also seem to be present in the context of the professional affiliations that bind teachers to their pupils. It is precisely these affiliations that may cause individuals to experience guilt without necessarily perceiving themselves to be at fault.

In one of the earliest studies on teaching as work Lortie (1975) noted that teachers experience some of their most prideful moments when they were successful in helping individual students to progress. Later research by Nias (1996) and Hargreaves (1999) demonstrated that teachers predominantly experienced positive emotions and job satisfaction as a result of affective relationships with their pupils and their educational progress. In a qualitative study on teachers' experiences of pride Farouk (2008) interviewed fifty-two primary school teachers. The findings demonstrated that while a few teachers remembered situations in which they felt proud of their own accomplishments the majority recalled events that made them proud of their pupils' achievements. Moreover, teachers most often recalled feeling proud when a child or group of children had accomplished a task on their own. For instance, teachers frequently reported feeling proud when a pupil had completed a challenging task independently or when the class performed well while another teacher was teaching them. In psychological literature there is almost no acknowledgement that pride is often based on the identification with the achievements of individuals who are emotionally close. Yet in the field of philosophy (Goldie 2000) there are many examples where feeling proud is associated with the accomplishments of relevant others, such as family members or individuals from the same community. The findings from this study agree with this proposition, suggesting that in the school context feeling proud is usually elicited through the accomplishments of one's pupils. There may indeed be a greater emphasis on feeling proud of one's own achievements in other work settings, but the nature of teaching as a helping profession seems to make it logical to shift the focus towards the accomplishments of the children.

Studies of teachers' guilt and pride offer important insights into their moral concerns and the kind of relationships they develop with their pupils. In particular research has demonstrated how primary school teachers develop close and caring relationships with their students and how the purpose of their professional affiliation is the educational progress of their pupils. As the children's well being and their educational success matters most to teachers, recent research on educational reform has clearly indicated that they experience guilt and other negative emotions when other demands supersede their focus on students (Kelchtermans 2005; van Veen, Sleegers et al. 2005).

CONCLUSION

Although the study of self-conscious emotions in education is still at an early stage the findings demonstrate the insightfulness and potential importance of research in this area. Research on students' experiences of guilt, shame and pride has highlighted the influence these emotions may have on their thoughts and actions. They have also illustrated how these emotions are not internalized sensations that remain inert within the confines of the body but are integral to the ways in which learners relate to one another and approach their studies. In relation to their approach to learning research has demonstrated how shame may have a negative and de-motivating influence on students' academic performance or, in some cases, may prompt learners to re-evaluate their approach and try to improve their grades (Pekrun and Elliot 2006; Turner and Waugh 2007; Pekrun, Elliot et al. 2009). Moreover, on the basis of their examination of pride as an achievement emotion Pekrun and colleagues have suggested that it not only encourage students to engage in further academic study when reflecting on their success but may also maintain their motivation when engaged in an activity (Pekrun and Elliot 2006; Pekrun, Elliot et al. 2009).

Research on social behaviour suggests that adolescents are more likely refrain from antisocial behaviour when they anticipate feelings of guilt. Moreover, they are more likely to engage in prosocial behaviour when they expect to feel proud for having acted appropriately (Krettenauer, Jia et al. 2011). In support of these findings, research on the *happy victimiser* phenomenon has demonstrated how moral reasoning in itself does not result in moral behaviour in children and adolescents (Krettenauer, Malti et al. 2008). To be able to engage in moral behaviour children and young adults require the internalisation of moral values and a capacity to experience the self-conscious emotions of guilt and pride consistently. As such when confronted with a moral situation they are able to anticipate the experiences of guilt, pride or some other moral emotion depending in the choices that they make.

When considering that psychological research has demonstrated the negative influence of shame on social relationships it is surprising how shame has not featured prominently in educational research on students' interpersonal relationships. According to Tangney and Dearing (2002) shame usually motivates people to withdraw from social situations or to displace the experience of shame with righteous anger. In either case the experience of shame has a harmful influence on relationships which is a significant finding that has not yet been studied within the context of students' peer relationships or teacher/student relationships. In fact students' experiences of shame in social situations have only been investigated in relation to bullying at school. The findings from this strand of research suggest that adolescents who engage in bullying are less able to acknowledge and accept feelings of shame than their peers (Ahmed 2006).

This chapter has also reviewed investigations into teachers' experiences of pride and guilt. The purpose of research in this field has been to study teachers' self-understanding and moral purpose by examining their emotional experiences. The research involved a close examination of teachers' experiences of pride and guilt in order to gain insight into aspects of their professional selves which teachers consider to be particularly important. The findings indicate that primary school teachers experience guilt when they perceive themselves not to have been successful in educating or caring for their pupils and they feel proud when their pupils experiences success. In the future it is hoped that research will also include the examination of teachers' self-conscious emotions in other educational contexts, such as secondary schools, and at different phases of their careers. Moreover, future research should also examine teachers' experiences of shame as this emotion in particular may provide considerable insights into stable and substantive believes teachers have about themselves and the purpose of their work.

REFERENCES

Ahmed, E. (2006). "Understanding bullying from a shame management perspective: Findings from a 3 year follow up study." *Educational and Child Psychology 23:* 26 -40.

Ahmed, E., N. Harris, et al. (2001). *Shame management through reintegration.* Melbourne, Cambridge University Press.

Arsenio, W., J. Gold, et al. (2004). "Adolescents' emotion expectancies regarding aggressive and nonagressive events: Connections with behavior problems." *Experimental Child Psychology 89*: 338 - 355.

Barrett, K. C. (1994). A functionalist approach to shame and guilt. *Self conscious emotions: The psychology of shame, guilt, embarrassment and pride.* J. P. Tangney and K. W. Fischer. London, The Guilford Press.

Baumeister, R. F., A. M. Stillwell, et al. (1994). "Guilt: An interpersonal approach." *Psychological Bulletin 115*: 243-267.

Baumeister, R. F., A. M. Stillwell, et al. (1995). "Personal narratives about guilt: Role in action control and interpersonal relationships." *Basic and Applied Social Psychology 17*: 173-198.

Berndsen, M., J. van der Pligt, et al. (2004). "Guilt and Regret: The determining role of interpersonal and intrapersonal harm." *Cognition and Emotion 18*(1): 55-70.

Braithwaite, J. (1989). *Crime, shame and reintegration.* Cambridge,UK, Cambridge University Press.

Davies, A. F. (1989). *The human element: Three essays in political psychology.* Harmondsworth, Penguin.

de Hooge, I. E., M. Zeelenberg, et al. (2010). "Restore and protect motivations following shame." *Cognition and Emotion 24*: 111-127.

Elliot, A. J. (1999). "Approach and Avoidance motivation and achievement goals." *Educational Psychologist 34*: 169 - 189.

Elliot, A. J. and H. H. McGregor (2001). "A 2 x 2 achievement goal framework." *Journal of Personality and Social Psychology 80*: 501 - 519.

Farouk, S. (2008). How school teachers' thoughts differentiate the emotions that they experience: A qualitative study of cognitive appraisal. *School of Management and Organizational Psychology.* London, University of London, Birkbeck College. PhD.

Farouk, S. (2010). "Primary school teachers' restricted and elaborated anger." *Cambridge Journal of Education 40*(4): 353-368.

Farouk, S. (2012). "What can the self-conscious emotion of guilt tell us about primary school teachers' moral purpose and the relationships they have with their pupils?" *Teachers and Teaching: Theory and Practice 18*(4).

Frijda, N. H. (1993). "The place of appraisal in emotion." *Cognition and Emotion 7*: 357-388.

Gausel, N. and C. W. Leach (2011). "Concern for self-image and social image in the management of moral failure." *European Journal of Social Psychology 41*: 468-478.

Goldie, P. (2000). *The emotions: A philosophical exploration.* New York, Oxford University Press.

Hargreaves, A. (1998). "The emotional practice of teaching." *Teaching and Teacher Education 14*(8): 845-54.

Hargreaves, A. (1999). The psychic rewards (and annoyances) of teaching. *Researching school experience: Ethnographic studies of teaching and learning.* M. Hammersley. London and New York, Routledge.

Hargreaves, A. and E. Tucker (1991). "Teaching and guilt: Exploring the feelings of teaching." *Teaching and Teacher Education 7*(5/6): 491-505.

Hart, D. and K. M. Matsuba (2007). The development of pride and moral life. *The self-conscious emotions: Theory and research.* J. L. Tracy, R. W. Robins and J. P. Tangney. London, The Guilford Press: 114-133.

Kelchtermans, G. (2005). "Teachers' emotions in educational reforms: Self-understanding, vulnerable commitment and micropolitical literacy." *Teaching and Teacher Education 21*: 995-1006.

Kochanska, G., J. Gross, et al. (2002). "Guilt in young children: development determinants, and relations with a broader system of standards." *Child Development 73*: 461-482.

Krettenauer, T. and D. Eichler (2006). "Adolescents' self attributed moral emotions following a moral transgression: Relations with delinquency, confidence in moral judgement, and age." *British Journal of Developmental Psychology 24*: 489 - 506.

Krettenauer, T., F. Jia, et al. (2011). "The role of emotion expectancies in adolescent moral decision making." *Journal of Experimental Child Psychology 108*: 358 - 370.

Krettenauer, T. and M. Johnston (2011). "Positively versus negatively charged moral emotion expectancies in adolescence: The role of situational context and the developing moral self." *British Journal of Developmental Psychology.*

Krettenauer, T., T. Malti, et al. (2008). "The development of moral emotion expectancies and the happy victimizer phenomenon: A critical review of theory and application." *European Journal of Developmental Science 2*: 221 - 235.

Lagattuta, K. H. and R. A. Thompson (2007). The development of self conscious emotions; Cognitive processes and social influences. *The self-conscious emotions: Theory and research.* J. L. Tracy, R. W. Robins and J. P. Tangney. London, The Guilford Press: 91-113.

Lazarus, R. S. (1991). *Emotion and adaptation.* New York, Oxford University Press.

Lewis, H. B. (1971). *Shame and guilt in neurosis.* New York, International University Press.

Lewis, M. (2000). Self-conscious emotions: embarrassment, pride, shame and guilt. *Handbook of emotions.* M. Lewis and J. M. Haviland-Jones. New York, Guilford Press.

Lewis, M. (2007). Self-conscious emotional development. *The self-conscious emotions: Theory and research.* J. L. Tracy, R. W. Robins and J. P. Tangney. London, The Guilford Press: 91-113.

Liljestrom, A., K. Roulston, et al. (2007). "There is no place for feeling like this in the workplace": Women teachers' anger in school settings. *Emotion in Education*. P. A. Schutz, D. I. Cross, J. Y. Hong and J. N. Osbon. London, Elsevier.

Linnenbrink, E. A. (2007). The role of affect in student learning: A multi-dimensional approach to considering the interaction of affect, motivation and engagement. *Emotion in Education*. P. A. Schutz and R. Pekrun, Elsevier.

Linnenbrink, E. A. and P. R. Pintrich (2002). "Achievement goal theory and affect: an asymmetrical bidirectional model." *Educational Psychologist* 37(2): 69-78.

Lortie, D. C. (1975). *School teacher: A sociological study*. Chicago, University of Chicago.

Malti, T., L. Gasser, et al. (2009). "Aggressive and prosocial children's emotion attributions and moral reasoning." *Aggressive Behaviour* 35: 90-102.

Morrison, B. (2006). "School bullying and restorative justice: Towards a theoretical understanding of the role of respect, pride and shame." *Journal of Social Issues* 62(2): 371-392.

Nias, J. (1989). *Primary teachers talking: A study of teaching as work*. London, Routledge.

Nias, J. (1996). "Thinking about feeling: The emotions in teaching." *Cambridge Journal of Education* 26(3): 293-306.

Parkinson, B., A. H. Fischer, et al. (2005). *Emotion in social relations*.

Pekrun, R. and A. J. Elliot (2006). "Achievement goals and discrete achievement emotions: A theoretical model and prospective test." *Journal of Educational Psychology* 98(3): 583 - 597.

Pekrun, R., A. J. Elliot, et al. (2009). "Achievement goals and achievement emotions: Testing a model of their joint relations with academic performance." *Journal of Educational Psychology* 101(1): 115 - 135.

Pekrun, R., T. Goetz, et al. (2002). "Academic emotions in students' self-regulated learning and achievement: a programme of qualitative and quantitative research." *Educational Psychologist* 37(2): 91-105.

Scherer, K. R., A. Schorr, et al., Eds. (2001). *Appraisal processes in emotions: Theory, method, research*. New York, Oxford University Press.

Stipek, D. J. (1995). The development of pride and shame in toddlers. *Self-conscious emotions: The psychology of shame, guilt, embarrassment and pride*. J. P. Tangney and K. W. Fischer. New York, Guilford Press.

Sutton, R. E. (2007). teachers' anger, frustration and self-regulation. *Emotion in Education*. P. A. Schutz and P. Reinhard. London, Elsevier.

Tangney, J. P. (1995). Shame and guilt in interpersonal relationships. *Self-conscious emotions: The psychology of shame, guilt,embarrassment and pride*. J. P. Tangney and K. W. Fischer. New York, Guilford Press: 343-267.

Tangney, J. P. (1999). The self conscious emotions: shame, guilt, embarrassment and pride. *Handbook of cognition and emotion*. T. Dalgleish and M. Power. New York, Wiley.

Tangney, J. P. (2003). Self-relevant emotions. *Handbook of self and identity*. M. R. Leary and J. P. Tangney. London, Guilford Press: 384 - 400.

Tangney, J. P., S. A. Burggraf, et al. (1995). Shame-proneness, guilt-proneness and psychological symptoms. *Self-conscious emotions: The psychology of shame, guilt and embarrassment and pride*. J. P. Tangney and K. W. Fischer. New York, Guilford Press: 343-267.

Tangney, J. P. and R. L. Dearing (2002). *Shame and Guilt*. London, The Guilford Press.

Tangney, J. P., J. Stuewig, et al. (2007). "Moral emotions and moral behavior." *Annual Review of Psychology 58*: 346-372.

Tangney, J. P., P. E. Wagner, et al. (1996). "The relation of shame and guilt to constructive vs. destructive responses anger across the lifespan." *Journal of Personality and Social Psychology 70*: 797-809.

Tracy, J. L. and R. W. Robins (2004). "Putting the self into self-conscious emotions: A theoretical model." *Psychological Inquiry 15*(2): 103-125.

Tracy, J. L. and R. W. Robins (2007). The nature of pride. *The self-conscious emotions: Theory and research*. J. L. Tracy, R. W. Robins and J. P. Tangney. London, The Guilford Press*: 263-282.

Tracy, J. L. and R. W. Robins (2007). The self in self-conscious emotions: A cognitive appraisal approach. *The self-conscious emotions: Theory and research*. J. L. Tracy, R. W. Robins and J. P. Tangney. London, The Guilford Press.

Turner, J. E., J. Husman, et al. (2002). "The importance of students' goals in their emotional experience of academic failure: investigating the precursors and consequequences of shame." *Educational Psychologist 3*(2): 79-89.

Turner, J. E. and D. L. Schallert (2001). "Expectancy-value relationship of shame reactions and shame resliency." *Journal of Educational Psychology 98*(2): 320-329.

Turner, J. E. and R. M. Waugh (2007). A dynamical systems perspective regarding students' learning processes: Shame reactions and emergent self-organisations. *Emotion in Education*. P. A. Schutz and R. Pekrun. London, Elsevier.

van Veen, K., P. Sleegers, et al. (2005). "One teacher's identity, emotions, and commitment to change: A case study into the cognitive-affective processes of a secondary school teacher in the context of reforms." *Teaching and Teacher Education 21*: 917-934.

Weiner, B. (1985). "An attribution theory of achievement motivation and emotion." *Psychological Review 92*: 548-573.

Weiner, B. (2006). *Social motivation, justice, and the moral emotions*. Mahwah, New Jersey, Lawrence Erlbaum Associates.

Zeidner, M. (2007). Test anxiety in educational contexts: concepts, findings, and future directions. *Emotion in Education*. P. A. Schutz and R. Pekrun, Elsevier.

PART III: EMOTIONS, PSYCHOPATHOLOGY AND HEALTH

In: Handbook of Psychology of Emotions
Editors: C. Mohiyeddini, M. Eysenck and S. Bauer

ISBN: 978-1-62808-053-7
© 2013 Nova Science Publishers, Inc.

Chapter 10

EMOTION AND PSYCHOPATHOLOGY

Stephanie Bauer[1] and Changiz Mohiyeddini[2]

[1]Center for Psychotherapy Research, University Hospital Heidelberg, Germany
[2]Roehampton University, London, UK

ABSTRACT

Emotions are intrinsically tied to mental health and mental well-being as well as to various forms of psychopathology. In this chapter we give an overview on the role that emotions and emotional processing play in different mental disorders. Specifically we review key approaches and empirical findings related to depression, anxiety disorders, and eating disorders. For each of these conditions there is a considerable evidence base documenting the relevance of emotions, emotion processing and emotion regulation for the development and maintenance of psychopathology. These findings are of immediate relevance to clinical sciences and intervention research as they offer opportunities to develop new interventions or to enhance existing treatment approaches by addressing the relationship between emotions, emotional processing, and emotion regulation on the one side and psychopathological symptoms and impairment on the other side. However, more research is needed in order to better align treatment approaches to evidence from basic research. To that end we outline priorities for such future research related to emotion and psychopathology.

INTRODUCTION

Emotions play a central role in mental health and mental illness. Most psychological and psychiatric disorders are associated with some form of impairment or disturbance in one or several components of emotional processing. Such disturbances may relate to the way individuals with mental illnesses perceive, experience, display, or regulate emotions. For example various forms of anxiety disorders are associated with an excess of experienced emotion, anorexia nervosa is characterized by fear of gaining weight, and schizophrenia is associated with a diminished expression of emotions (Kring & Bachorowski, 1999).

Studying psychopathology and mental illness from an emotion perspective has provided numerous theoretical and empirical impulses to clinical research over the past decades (Kring & Sloan, 2009). Especially the topic of emotion regulation and psychopathology has increasingly gained attention of both researchers and practitioners in the fields of clinical psychology, psychiatry, psychosomatics, and psychotherapy. Deficits in emotion regulation skills are considered a key factor in the development and maintenance of various disorders (Aldao & Nolen-Hoeksema, 2012). The Diagnostic and Statistical Manual of Mental Disorders (DSM-IV; American Psychiatric Association, 1994) reflects this central role that emotions and emotion regulation play in relation to psychopathology. A considerable number of the symptoms that characterize the various diagnoses in DSM-IV are directly or indirectly related to emotions, emotional processing, and emotion (dys)regulation.

As a result of affective theories and research into emotions and emotion regulation also a number of therapeutic concepts and interventions have been developed. Such approaches highlight the importance to educate patients about emotions in general as well as about the perception and regulation of own emotions and the relationship between these processes and psychological and physical well-being. Some of them aim to convey specific skills to patients that should help them to detect and handle their emotions more adequately in order to ultimately reduce their psychological distress. It is of note, however, that these strategies that are assumed to be adaptive (e.g. acceptance, problem solving) have shown a less accentuated relationship to (an improvement of) psychopathology compared to the robust relationship that has been found between maladaptive emotion regulation and psychopathological impairment (Aldao & Nolen-Hoeksema, 2012). Therefore there is a clear need for more research on the relationship between emotion, emotion regulation, and psychopathology in order to conceptualize powerful therapeutic interventions.

In the following we provide an overview on the role that emotions and emotional processing play in three different psychopathologies, i.e. in depression, anxiety, and eating disorders.

DEPRESSION

Depression is one of the most prevalent mental illnesses and accounts for a substantial portion of the global burden and cost caused by mental illness. Developing more effective prevention and treatment approaches are therefore considered public health priorities. Research into emotions and emotional processing related to depression may help to better understand these severe conditions and to ultimately target them more effectively and efficiently.

The key role that emotions and emotion regulation play in the development and maintenance of depression has been emphasized repeatedly in theoretical frameworks as well as in empirical research. Individuals suffering from depressive disorders are assumed to experience difficulties to identify, describe, and interpret emotions as well as to tolerate and modify them through adequate emotion regulation strategies (see Berking & Wupperman, 2012 for an overview).

It has been argued that difficulties to functionally regulate negative emotions exist prior to the onset of clinically relevant depressive symptoms (e.g. Kovacs, Joormann & Gotlib,

2008) and that dysfunctional strategies to regulate emotions predict future levels of depressive impairment. Therefore depression, at least to some extent, may be considered a consequence of inadequate emotion regulation. A number of studies have shown that depression is associated with deficits in regulating negative emotions. Specifically, a relationship between depression and frequent engagement in rumination (e.g. Nolen-Hoeksema, 2000) and suppression (e.g. Gross & John, 2003; Wenzlaff & Luxton, 2003) has been established. In contrast, utilization of strategies such as reappraisal (Campbell-Sills & Barlow, 2007) and problem solving (Hong, 2007) seems to be associated with less depressive impairment.

In order to further investigate the role of emotions and emotional processing in depression it seems promising to study depression in different age groups and to contrast different forms of depressive disorders rather than considering them part of the same broad illness category. For example, a recent study compared patients suffering from episodic versus chronic depression with respect to socio-emotional information processing. The results show that chronically ill patients (who suffered from depression for more than two years) score higher in alexithymia than patients with episodic depression, indicating that chronic depression is associated with more deficits related to the perception of own emotions (van Randenborgh, Hüffmeier, Victor, Klocke, Borlinghaus & Pawelzik, 2012). Systematic research investigating whether subgroups of individuals with different clinical pictures of depression (e.g. chronic versus episodic depression, early versus late onset depression or first episode major depression versus recurrent depression) differ in their emotion regulation skills and deficits could have important implications for understanding and treating these psychopathologies.

ANXIETY DISORDERS

Anxiety disorders are prevalent mental disorders and include a range of different specific diagnoses. They are typically characterized by elevated negative affect and involve- to different extent depending on the specific disorder- emotions such as fear, anxiety, and disgust. A number of theoretical approaches have addressed the relationship between emotion, emotional processing, and anxiety disorders (see Kring & Bacherowski, 1999 for an overview).

The majority of individuals suffering from anxiety disorders experience emotion regulation difficulties and engage in dysfunctional strategies (Cisler, Olantunji, Feldner, & Forsyth, 2010). For example, it is well-known that individuals suffering from specific phobias use strategies to avoid fearful situations, contexts, and objects in an attempt to avoid the occurrence of negative emotions which in turn prevents them from engaging in adaptive strategies when facing such emotional challenging situations (Campbell-Sills & Barlow, 2007). Furthermore, the strategy of suppression seems to be associated with various anxiety disorders such as panic disorders, social phobia, generalized anxiety disorders, and posttraumatic stress disorder (e.g. Campbell-Sills, Barlow, Brown & Hofmann, 2006; Ehlers, Mayou & Bryant, 1998).

In terms of adaptive emotion regulation, there is some empirical evidence that reappraisal may be associated with reduced symptoms of anxiety. However, as in other disorders, the association between maladaptive emotion regulation strategies and psychopathology seem to be more pronounced in anxiety disorders (Aldao & Nolen-Hoeksema, 2012).

EATING DISORDERS

Eating disorders such as anorexia nervosa, bulimia nervosa and binge eating disorder are severe mental illnesses. The relationship between eating disorders and the experience and regulation of emotion has been addressed in a number of empirical studies (see Svaldi, Griepenstroh, Tuschen-Caffier, & Ehring, 2012 for an overview). For example, there is evidence that negative mood precedes behavioral eating disorder symptom s (i.e. binge eating, compensatory behaviours) in both bulimia nervosa (e.g. Crosby, Wonderlich, Engel, Simonich, Smyth & Mitchell, 2009; Smyth, Wonderlich, Heron, Sliwinski, Crosby, Mitchell & Engel, 2007; Smyth, Wonderlich, Sliwinski, Crosby, Engel, Mitchell, & Calogero, 2009) and binge eating disorder (e.g. Hilbert & Tuschen-Caffier, 2007; Stein, Kenardy, Wiseman, Dounchis, Arnow, & Wilfley,. 2007).

It is assumed that individuals suffering from bulimia nervosa or binge eating disorder may engage in such behaviors in order to cope with unpleasant emotions as they experience that these behaviors – at least on the short term- reduce negative affect. This may be concluded from studies that took advantage of innovative assessment methods by using electronic diaries (Wild, Eichler, Feiler, Friederich, Hartmann, Herzog & Zipfel, 2007) and ecological momentary assessment (Smyth et al., 2007) to investigate the course of negative affect in relation to eating disorder symptoms. For example, Smyth et al. (2007) studied a sample of 131 females with bulimia nervosa who recorded their mood, stress level and bulimic behaviors (binge and vomit episodes) for two consecutive weeks with multiple assessments per day. The analysis of the temporal sequencing of the assessed indicators support the assumption that bulimic symptoms may occur as a consequence of negative affect that individuals cannot tolerate or regulate in an adaptive way.

In comparison to non-clinical samples, individuals with eating disorders have been found to experience more deficits in recognizing and labeling emotions correctly (Svaldi, Caffier, & Tuschen-Caffier, 2010) and to express emotions less frequently (Sim & Zeman, 2004). Furthermore, individuals with eating disorders tend to suppress (Aldao et al., 2010) and avoid (Corstorphine, Mountford, Tomlipson, Waller & Meyer, 2007) emotions and to engage in rumination (Aldao et al., 2010).

In a recent study, Svaldi et al. (2012) investigated whether the different eating disorder diagnostic groups show specific emotion regulation profiles and specific deficits in regulating emotions. As in previous research, individuals with eating disorders reported less emotional awareness and more emotion regulation difficulties than healthy controls. However, only very few differences between the diagnostic groups emerged. Overall the findings suggest that difficulties in emotion regulation are a transdiagnostic rather than a disorder-specific factor (Svaldi et al., 2012).

IMPLICATIONS FOR CLINICAL RESEARCH, HEALTH PROMOTION AND PSYCHOTHERAPY

The well-established link between emotion and psychopathology has resulted in numerous research efforts in each of the two specialist fields of emotion research and clinical research. In line with previous versions of the Diagnostic and Statistical Manual of Mental Disorders (DSM), its next version, i.e. DSM-5 which will be published in 2013, continues to acknowledge the major role that difficulties with emotion or emotion regulation play for psychopathology and mental illness. There seems to be increasing agreement to the notion of Werner and Gross (2009) that "emotion regulatory difficulties lie at the heart of many types of psychopathology and may be a key to their treatment " (p. 14).

Similarly one could argue that addressing emotion and emotion regulation as part of health promotion and prevention efforts should help to counteract the development of psychopathologies and illness onset. Given that the majority of mental disorders first develop in adolescence and young adulthood, prevention and early intervention in young age groups have gained increasing attention among both health professionals and health politicians over the last decade. The fact that today emotion regulation is mostly considered a transdiagnostic factor that is associated with various psychopathologies (e.g. Aldao et al., 2010), invites researchers and clinicians to develop and evaluate programs that promote adaptive emotion regulation and equip young people with strategies and skills to manage emotional challenges in youth and adulthood. If emotion regulation deficits precede onset of psychopathology, we might be able to identify such deficits as unspecific risk factor for mental illness. Targeted and indicated prevention programs could then be developed that aim to reduce or eliminate difficulties related to emotion and emotion regulation early on in order to ultimately reduce the number of young people that are affected by psychopathology.

A related topic, that also deserves additional research efforts in the future, concerns the longitudinal course of the emotion-psychopathology-link across the lifespan. To date, most studies in this field are conducted in adult samples. Research in children, adolescents, and elderly people promises relevant additional insights into the relationship between emotion and psychopathology.

Also in clinical samples the relationship between emotion and emotion regulation on the one side and treatment effects and recovery on the other side warrants further research. Questions such as "(How) do emotion regulation strategies and competencies change during treatment?" "To which extent are they related to treatment success and treatment failure?" "Which role do they play in the occurrence of relapse following successful treatment?" need to be addressed in order to further explore the role of emotion and emotion regulation in clinical contexts. Research into moderators and mediators of treatment outcome is still in an early phase. Input from emotion and emotion regulation researchers may make an important contribution to better understand underlying processes and mechanisms and inform us how and for whom psychotherapy works. Such research may also enable psychotherapy researchers to further refine current therapeutic approaches.

Overall, in both clinical and non-clinical contexts there is a clear need for more prospective longitudinal studies on the link between emotion and psychopathology in order to further advance the state of the art. Limitations of current research include that many studies used cross-sectional and/or experimental designs and thus our ability to draw causal, generalizable, and externally valid conclusions has been limited. In addition, in the past, longitudinal studies were only feasible to conduct with quite long durations between assessments due to the cost and effort of data collection at shorter intervals. Recent advances in assessment technology promise new opportunities to study the relationship between emotion and psychopathology.

For example, ecological momentary assessment (EMA; Stone & Shiffman, 1994), i.e. techniques that use "computer-assisted methodology to assess self-reported symptoms, behaviors, or physiological processes while the participant undergoes normal daily activities" (Ebner-Priemer & Trull, 2009; p. 464), offer a number of advantages in this respect. These include that EMA may overcome some of the challenges that are related to retrospective assessments and recall biases as data are not assessed retrospectively but in real time. This advantage of EMA may be of special relevance in research on emotions, affective states, and emotion regulation as it is known that mood and the affective valence of situations and events may have a significant impact on recall. A number of studies confirmed that EMA can reduce retrospective bias and enhance accuracy of collected data (e.g. Ben-Zeev, Young & Madsen, 2009; Ebner-Priemer et al., 2006). Another advantage inherent to EMA is that data may be collected within the specific context of interest rather than in a research environment. It would therefore allow, for example, to further investigate the recent notion of Aldao and Nolen-Hoeksema (2012) that context has a major impact on the implementation of adaptive emotion regulation strategies.

Furthermore, in contrast to traditional research and assessment methods, EMA allows to take into account that symptoms, feelings, and behaviors are dynamic rather than static phenomena. Through flexible and frequent assessments, fluctuations over time can be captured much more accurately than traditional assessment methods (Ebner-Priemer & Trull, 2009). This is of special relevance in psychopathologies that are per se characterized by any form of instability, such as borderline personality disorder, which is characterized by highly instable affect or bulimia nervosa in which key symptoms (binge–purge episodes) ebb and flow substantially over time.

Emotion research would benefit from an increased use of assessment methods such as EMA as this would allow to assess emotions, their intensity as well as processes of emotional processing and emotion regulation in everyday life. Individuals can submit information in real-time at reasonable cost and effort using mobile devices such as mobile phones or smart phones. In parallel to relevant aspects of emotions and emotion processing, psychopathology and symptom distress may be monitored continuously over time. In addition to self-report data, EMA also allows to collect information from other sources, e.g. on the physiological level. Such research efforts promise to advance the field by enhancing our current knowledge on the interplay of psychopathology, emotions and emotional processing and their temporal patterns.

Based on EMA research, a logical next step is to combine the assessment approach with tailored intervention modules in order to deliver information and support to participants which should ultimately attenuate individuals' psychopathological impairment. Heron and Smith (2010) have recently introduced the concept of ecological momentary interventions (EMIs). The basic idea of such interventions is to take advantage of the data that is continuously collected through EMA and to target relevant aspects as they occur in the real world in participants' everyday lives.

In the context of emotion and psychopathology, for example EMIs could remind participants flexibly of adaptive emotion regulation strategies as soon as they report an increase in specific negative emotions. This reminder could even be tailored to the current context which might help to increase the impact that adaptive emotion regulation strategies have on the reduction of psychopathological impairment.

Research into EMIs is still in a very early stage. However, there is increasing evidence that such low-intense interventions are feasible and well-accepted by participants and that they may contribute to improved health outcomes (Heron & Smyth, 2010).

Findings from emotion research have the potential to enhance current EMI approaches that mostly focus on the assessment of symptoms and behaviours but to a much lesser extent take into account the emotional component of psychopathology. For example, a specific form of EMI is the approach of 'supportive monitoring' in which continuously assessed data is used to provide supportive feedback to participants (Bauer & Moessner, 2012). It is assumed that this procedure improves participants' self-management competencies, reduces psychopathology and helps individuals to develop or maintain healthy attitudes and behaviors. The supportive monitoring approach using mobile phones, text messaging or Internet-based methods for data collection and provision of supportive feedback, has been successfully implemented in several conditions (see Bauer & Moessner, 2012 for an overview). In such programs, participants are asked to self-monitor relevant symptoms and behaviors continuously at specific intervals (e.g. daily or weekly) for example by sending in text messages in a standardized format to the provider. Based on their entries, they receive tailored feedback. This is automatically generated by an underlying Internet-based software program that analyzes messages as they come in based on specific algorithms. In a clinical context, these feedback messages for example comment on the level of participants' impairment, as well as on symptom improvement or deterioration. When used in the area of relapse prevention or maintenance treatment, they remind patients of strategies they learned in their previous treatment and encourage them to maintain functional behaviours and to seek more intense support in case that they cannot self-manage the maintenance of treatment gains. Overall, the supportive feedback messages provide small but constant doses of support, they reinforce positive developments in symptoms and behaviours, and provide suggestions for self-help or more intense interventions in case that symptom deterioration becomes evident (Bauer & Moessner, 2012).

So far, most interventions based on supportive monitoring tailor the feedback that they provide to participants exclusively depending on psychopathological symptoms and health behaviors that individuals report. Acknowledging the relationship between emotion and psychopathology it seems promising to enhance current systems by including aspects of emotion and emotion regulation in both the continuous assessments and the supportive feedback messages.

CONCLUSION

There is increasing empirical evidence that emotion and emotion regulation play a key role in the development, onset, and maintenance of mental disorders. Numerous studies in healthy and various clinical samples that have contributed to this evidence base. The implications of their findings for clinical psychology and psychotherapy are obvious. However, a lot more research is needed in order to allow for the development of specific interventions. As outlined above, we argue for an integration of research from various fields and a focus on longitudinal research which will allow to enhance the conceptualization and ultimately the prevention and treatment of psychopathology.

REFERENCES

Aldao. A. & Nolen-Hoeksema, S. (2012). The influence of context on the implementation of adaptive emotion regulation strategies. *Behaviour Research and Therapy,* 50, 493-501.

Aldao, A., Nolen-Hoksema, S. & Schweizer, S. (2010). Emotion regulation strategies across psychopathology: A meta-analysis. *Clinical Psychology Review,* 30, 217-237.

Barnow, S. (2012). Emotionsregulation und Psychopathologie: Ein Überblick [Emotion regulation and psychopathology: An overview]. *Psychologische Rundschau,* 63, 111-124.

Bauer, S. & Moessner, M. (2012). Technology-enhanced Monitoring in Psychotherapy and E-mental Health. *Journal of Mental Health,* 21, 355.363.

Ben-Zeev, D., Young, M.A., & Madsen, J.W. (2009). Retrospective recall of affect in clinically depressed individuals and controls. *Cognition & Emotion,* 23, 1021–1040.

Berking, M. & Wupperman, P. (2012). Emotion regulation and mental health: Recent findings, current challenges, and future directions. *Current Opinion Psychiatry,* 25, 128-134.

Campbell-Sills, L. & Barlow, D. H. (2007). Incorporating emotion regulation into conceptualizations and treatments of anxiety and mood disorders. In J.J. Gross (Ed.), *Handbook of emotion regulation* (pp. 542-559). New York: Guilford Press.

Campbell-Sills, L., Barlow, D. H., Brown, T. A. & Hofmann, S. G. (2006). Acceptability and suppression of negative emotion in anxiety and mood disorders. *Emotion,* 6, 587-595.

Cisler, J., Olatunji, B., Feldner, M., & Forsyth, J. (2010). Emotion regulation and the anxiety disorders: An integrative review. *Journal of Psychopathological Behaviour,* 32, 68-82.

Corstorphine, E., Mountford, V., Tomlinson, S., Waller, G., Meyer, C., 2007. Distress tolerance in the eating disorders. Eating Behavior 8, 91–97.

Crosby, R.D., Wonderlich, S.A., Engel, S.G., Simonich, H., Smyth, J., & Mitchell, J.E. (2009). Daily mood patterns and bulimic behaviors in the natural environment. *Behaviour Research and Therapy,* 47, 181–188.

Ebner-Priemer, U.W., Kuo, J., Welch, S.S., Thielgen, T., Witte, S., Bohus, M., et al. (2006). A valence-dependent group-specific recall bias of retrospective self-reports: A study of borderline personality disorder in everyday life. *Journal of Nervous and Mental Disease,* 196, 774–779.

Ebner-Priemer, U.W. & Trull, T.J. (2009). Ecological momentary assessment of mood disorders and mood dysregulation. *Psychological Assessment,* 21, 463–475.

Ehlers, A., Mayou, R. A., & Bryant, B. (1998). Psychological predictors of chronic posttraumatic stress disorder after motor vehicle accidents. *Journal of abnormal Psychology,* 107, 508-519.

Farach, F. J. & Mennin, D. S. (2007). Emotion-Based Approaches to the Anxiety Disorders. In J. Rottenberg & S. L. Johnson (Eds.). *Emotion and psychopathology: Bridging affective and clinical science*. Washington DC: American Psychological Association.

Gross, J. J. & John, O. P. (2003). Individual differences in two emotion regulation processes: Implications for affect, relationships, and well-being. *Journal of Personality and Social Psychology, 85*, 348-362.

Heron, K. E. & Smyth, J. M. (2010). Ecological Momentary Interventions: Incorporating mobile technology into psychosocial and health behavior treatments. *British Journal of Health Psychology, 15*, 1-39.

Hilbert, A. & Tuschen-Caffier, B. (2007). Maintenance of binge eating through negative mood: a naturalistic comparison of binge eating disorder and bulimia nervosa. *International Journal of Eating Disorders, 40*, 521–530.

Hong, R. Y. (2007). Worry and rumination: Differential associations with anxious and depressive symptoms and coping behavior. *Behavior Research and Therapy, 45*, 277-290.

Kring, A. M. & Bachorowski, J.-A. (1999). Emotions and Psychopathology. *Cognition and Emotion, 13*, 575-599.

Kovacs, M., Joormann, J. & Gotlib, I. (2008). Emotion (dys)regulation and links to depressive disorders. *Child Development Perspectives, 2*, 149-155.

Nolen-Hoeksema, S. (2000). The role of rumination in depressive disorders and mixed anxiety/depressive symptoms. *Journal of Abnormal Psychology, 109*, 504-511.

Rottenberg, J., Johnson, S. L. & Gross, J. J. (2007). Bridges yet to come – Future directions for integrating affective and clinical science. In J. Rottenberg & S. L. Johnson (Eds.). *Emotion and psychopathology: Bridging affective and clinical science* (pp. 305-308). Washington DC: American Psychological Association.

Sim, L., & Zeman, J. (2005). Emotion regulation factors as mediators between body dissatisfaction and bulimic symptoms in early adolescent girls. *The Journal of Early Adolescence, 25*, 478–496.

Smyth, J.M., Wonderlich, S.A., Heron, K.E., Sliwinski, M.J., Crosby, R.D., Mitchell, J.E., Engel, S.G. (2007). Daily and momentary mood and stress are associated with binge eating and vomiting in bulimia nervosa patients in the natural environment. *Journal of Consulting and Clinical Psychology, 75*, 629–638.

Smyth, J.M., Wonderlich, S.A., Sliwinski, M.J., Crosby, R.D., Engel, S.G., Mitchell, J.E., & Calogero, R.M. (2009). Ecological momentary assessment of affect, stress, and binge-purge behaviors: day of week and time of day effects in the natural environment. *International Journal of Eating Disorders 42*, 429–436.

Stein, R.I., Kenardy, J., Wiseman, C.V., Dounchis, J.Z., Arnow, B.A., & Wilfley, D.E. (2007). What's driving the binge in binge eating disorder?: a prospective examination of precursors and consequences. *International Journal of Eating Disorders, 40*, 195–203.

Stone, A.A. & Shiffman, S. (1994). Ecological momentary assessment (EMA) in behavioral medicine. *Annals of Behavioral Medicine, 16*, 199–202.

Svaldi, J., Caffier, D., Tuschen-Caffier, B. (2010). Emotion suppression but not reappraisal increases desire to binge in women with binge eating disorder. *Psychotherapy and Psychosomatics, 79*, 188–190.

Svaldi, J., Griepenstroh, J., Tuschen-Caffier, B. & Ehring, T. (2012). Emotion regulation deficits in eating disorders: A marker of eating pathology or general psychopathology? *Psychiatry Research,* 197, 103-111.

Van Randenborgh, A., Hüffmeier, J., Victor, D., Klocke, K., Borlinghaus, J., & Pawelzik, M. (2012). Contrasting chronic with episodic depression: An analysis of distorted socio-emotional information processing in chronic depression. *Journal of Affective Disoders,* doi:10.1016/j.jad.2012.02.039.

Wenzlaff, R. M. & Luxton, D. D. (2003). The role of thought suppression in depressive rumination. *Cognitive Therapy and Research,* 27, 293-308.

Werner, K. & Gross, J. J. (2009). Emotion regulation and psychopathology: A conceptual framework. In A. M. Kring & D. M. Sloan (Eds.), *Emotion regulation and psychopathology: A transdiagnostic approach to etiology and treatment.* New York: The Guilford Press.

Wild, B., Eichler, M., Feiler, S., Friederich, H.C., Hartmann, M., Herzog, W., Zipfel, S. (2007). Dynamic analysis of electronic diary data of obese patients with and without binge eating disorder. *Psychotherapy and Psychosomatics,* 76, 250–252.

In: Handbook of Psychology of Emotions ISBN: 978-1-62808-053-7
Editors: C. Mohiyeddini, M. Eysenck and S. Bauer © 2013 Nova Science Publishers, Inc.

Chapter 11

EMOTION AND GENETICS

Christian Montag[1,2,3,], Brian W. Haas[4,†] and Martin Reuter[1,2,3,‡]*
[1]Department of Psychology, University of Bonn, Bonn, Germany
[2]Laboratory of Neurogenetics, University of Bonn, Bonn, Germany
[3]Center for Economics and Neuroscience, University of Bonn, Bonn, Germany
[4]Department of Psychology, University of Georgia, Georgia, US

ABSTRACT

This chapter gives a brief overview on the genetics of emotions. After an introduction into historical aspects of the field followed by insights on the topic derived by animal models, two lines of research will be highlighted, which both successfully investigated the genetic aspects of emotions. First, Williams Syndrome will be in the focus of the present review. This neurodevelopmental condition is of great interest in the context of genetics and emotions, because here 26-28 genes on chromosome 7 are missing in humans and this condition is associated with abnormal emotional behavior. Second, a molecular genetic approach to emotionality is presented, in which individual differences in emotion-related-personality dimensions are investigated. This chapter closes with a short outlook on future research leads.

INTRODUCTION: A SHORT HISTORY OF EMOTION RESEARCH

The study of emotion is as old as mankind and has evoked interest in generations of researchers. The earliest reports in the study of emotion go back to the classic Greek philosophers such as Epikur. The first important psychological theories of emotions stem from James-Lange (James, 1884; Lange, 1885) and the follow up critique by Cannon (Cannon, 1927; Cannon, 1931) showing that it took a long time in human history until emotions became the focus of strong scientific inquiry (cited after Dagleish et al., 2009).

---

[*] christian.montag@uni-bonn-diff.de.
[†] bhaas@uga.edu.
[‡] martin.reuter@uni-bonn-diff.de.

After these pioneer works in the study of emotion, it took again several decades until the scientific community came back to this important topic. Given the impact of emotions on the pathogenesis of psychiatric disorders including depression and addictions (Panksepp, 1998), but also on decision-making in economic settings (Knoll, 2010; Tversky & Kahneman, 1981), the investigation of emotion represents a timely and important topic.

Emotions are difficult to define. On one hand every lay person knows and understands what is meant by the word "emotion" ("I feel something"). On the other hand, a consensus among researchers does not currently exist in terms of the correct use of words such as emotions, affects and feelings. Until now, a common ground has not been found. For example, Damasio (1996) argues that feelings represent cognitive readouts of bodily changes while processing information from emotional stimuli. This theory was followed up by the theory proposed by James-Lange. The James-Lange theory put forward that the awareness and interpretation of bodily changes give rise to an emotion. Damasio's view has been challenged by Panksepp (2005, 2011), arguing that affective states and feelings arise from older brain circuits and as a consequence are more than the mentioned cognitive read outs. Such debates reflect a renewed interest in the study of emotions, and have also motivated the development of many new research techniques (in particular when researchers opt to not rely solely on introspective thoughts in the investigation of emotions). New brain imaging techniques such as functional magnetic resonance imaging (fMRI) have revolutionized the research field of emotions, because fMRI helps to elucidate brain activity of phylogenetically old parts of the mammalian brain (including humans), where the majority of emotional activity seems to arise from. fMRI provides a metric of the metabolism of oxygen within the human brain (Bandettini, in press). Researchers believe that more oxygen consumption reflects higher activity and thus is an indirect measure of the function of certain brain areas while performing certain tasks (e. g. emotional tasks). Older techniques to investigate functions of the human brain such as electroencephalography (EEG) have not been very successful in terms of measuring emotional brain activity in the evolutionary old parts of the brain, because EEG is more optimal in terms of measuring cortical activity (Bekkedal et al., 2011). Other approaches to studying emotions in humans include the use of experimental measures such as the recording of reaction times (e. g. Wenar, 1954), and the measurement of physiological measures from the periphery of the body such as skin conductance or heart rate (Lang et al., 2007). Another interesting phenomenon represents the affective modulation of the startle reflex, where the startle of the organism towards a loud burst is modulated by emotional stimuli within the environment (Larson et al., 2005).

Neuroimaging together with knowledge from basic animal research has led to an improved understanding of the neuronal circuits involved in processing emotions (Barrett & Wager, 2006). This combination has made it possible to associate activity of certain brain regions with the processing of emotions. Of particular interest are electrical stimulation studies, where the stimulation of a certain brain area has been found to elicit strong emotional behaviors. For example, the electrical stimulation of the periaqueductal gray area can elicit strong withdrawal behavior reflective of fear/panic (Panksepp, 1998; Panksepp, 2011, Schimitel et al., 2012). According to Panksepp's work seven emotional circuits are distinguishable in phylogenetically old brain areas across several species of the mammalian brain including humans. Although researchers still disagree on the number of distinct observable emotions and also on which distinct emotions can be reliably detected (both on a pure psychological and neuroscientific basis), most of the emotional theories agree that emotions related to joy/happiness and fear/anxiety represent basic emotions (Ortony & Turner, 1990). Nevertheless, this debate is not resolved and at the moment a special focus seems to rely on the emotional theories of Russell (1980) postulating a dimensional approach of emotional behavior (with the two dimensions of pleasantness and arousal) and the categorical approach of distinct emotions postulated by Panksepp (1998) (see also Zacchar & Ellis, in press). As the presentation of all arguments for and against the aforementioned theories of emotions is beyond the scope of the present chapter, we'd like to point towards an important fact: No matter if one follows e. g. Russell's dimensional approach or Panksepp's categorical approach of emotional behavior, modern brain imaging has shown that especially evolutionary old brain areas such as parts of the limbic system are of importance for the genesis of emotions (Barrett & Wager, 2006). This fact represents an important starting point for the investigation of genetics of emotional behavior.

1. ON THE GENETICS OF EMOTIONS IN ANIMAL RESEARCH

In addition to brain imaging, the revolutionary discovery of the structure of the desoxyribonucleinacid (DNA) by Watson & Crick (1953) and the development of techniques such as polymerase chain reaction (PCR) in molecular genetics (Mullis et al., 1986) has made it possible to detect genetic variations associated with individual differences in human behavior. Molecular genetics reflect one of the newest endeavors in the investigation of emotions. Despite this, the investigation of genetics of emotions goes back to the 1960s, where selective breeding studies have demonstrated the heritability of anxiety in rodents. Due to the fact that old brain regions such as the limbic system are highly conserved across the mammalian species (see above Panksepp, 1998), it is apparent that these regions must be strongly influenced by genes. Otherwise they would not be observable in this remarkably similar form in all mammals. A gene describes a region on the DNA coding for a certain bodily product such as a protein. Genetic variation of a gene[1] e. g. can lead to differences in the protein structure. This can have a profound impact on the neurotransmission in the brain and as a consequence be associated with emotional behavior.

Retrospectively, it is no surprise that early experiments using selective breeding techniques have demonstrated that anxious behavior has a genetic component. Pioneer studies in the context of selective breeding have been conducted by Broadhurst (see review by Broadhurst, 1975). He used, among others, the experimental paradigm called 'open field test' to investigate anxiety in rodents. Here, rodents are placed into the middle of an open field. As the animals tend to be averse to staying in the middle of the open space, they search for protection and shelter in the corners of this environment. Dependent variables reflecting anxiety include defecation rates of the rodents and time spent in the middle vs. the peripheral parts of the open field. In his studies, Broadhurst selected the most anxious and the most courageous rodents from his experiments and selectively bred the anxious rats among each other and the courageous rats among each other. He replicated this experiment for several generations, which led to the selective breeding of high and low anxious rats (in the literature called the Maudsley reactive and non-reactive rats). These were the earliest studies indicating

---

[1] (At least resulting in two alleles (genetic variants) at a certain gene locus)

that emotions such as anxiety have a genetic component. There has been criticism on the interpretability of the findings from Broadhurst's experiments. For an excellent review with respect to the boundaries of this experimental approach see Flint (2004). Besides all of the criticism, the evidence derived from these studies indicates that genetics are particularly important factors in terms of understanding the etiology of emotional behavior.

Selective breeding studies have helped to elucidate the association between genetics and emotional behavior, but these studies have not identified which genes specifically are involved in the genesis of emotions. Here, more progress in experimental animal research has occurred to answer this question. Researchers now have the opportunity to knock *in* or knock *out* genes. After such a procedure, researchers can investigate the effects of their intervention on well characterized emotional behaviors such as in the aforementioned open field test paradigm. These types of studies demonstrate that certain behaviors are linked to genetics and can more precisely identify specific genes associated with particular emotional behaviors. By knocking *in* a gene, researchers can investigate the effects of including a certain gene in an animal; by knocking *out* a gene the contradictory effects are investigated. These techniques are from ethical standards not applicable in human beings. In order to learn more about the role of certain genes for emotional behavior in humans two approaches will be introduced answering different questions in the context of genetics and emotions. First, we will describe how studying genetic deletion conditions characterized by specific patterns of social and emotional processing can elucidate the relationship between genetic factors and the processing of emotions. Specifically, we will describe the emotional phenotype associated with the genetic deletion condition Williams Syndrome. Second, evidence from molecular genetic research will be presented showing that individual differences in emotional behavior (characterized by differences in personality traits such as being anxious) are associated with distinct genetic variations (and not only to the more global measure of a certain gene). Limitations of both approaches will be discussed.

2. WILLIAMS SYNDROME AS A MODEL FOR INVESTIGATING THE GENETIC BASIS OF EMOTIONALITY IN HUMANS

Williams syndrome (WS) is a neurodevelopmental condition that effects approximately 1 in every 8-10,000 individuals and is caused by a deletion of ~26-28 genes on chromosome 7q11.23 (Meyer-Lindenberg, Mervis, & Berman, 2006). The genes deleted in WS include *CLIP2, CLYN2, ELN, GTF2I, GTF2IRD1* and *LIMK1*. The WS phenotype is characterized by a distinctive pattern of social behavior and emotion processing. Individuals with WS are often described as being hypersocial, overtly social and socially uninhibited. Studying social and emotional processing in WS provides an opportunity to gain insight as to the association between the WS deleted genes and the development of the social-emotional brain.

Several studies have shown that individuals with WS tend to be more motivated to socially interact with others as compared to typically developing (TD) controls. For example, children with WS tend to be more willing to approach strangers relative to TD controls (Dodd, Porter, Peters, & Rapee, 2010). In addition, parents rate children with WS as displaying higher "intensity" of social approach relative to parents of TD children (Tomc, Williamson, & Pauli, 1990). These parents also rate their child with WS as being less reserved around strangers (Gosch & Pankau, 1994) and more "globally social" (Doyle, Bellugi, Korenberg, & Graham, 2004; Zitzer-Comfort, Doyle, Masataka, Korenberg, & Bellugi, 2007) relative to parents of TD children. Together, these studies indicate that individuals with WS are consistently characterized as being more likely to socially interact with others as compared to those who are typically developing.

People with WS tend to focus an abnormally high amount of attention on faces and socially relevant cues such as eyes compared to controls. As evidenced by eye-tracking, people with WS fixate on faces longer (Riby & Hancock, 2008, 2009) and are slower to disengage their gaze once fixated on eyes (Porter, Shaw, & Marsh, 2010) or a face (Riby. et al., 2011) as compared to controls. Together, these findings suggest that the WS deleted genes may in part be associated with the development of face processing systems within the brain.

In terms of emotion processing specifically, individuals with WS are less able to detect social fear signals and exhibit an increased bias toward processing positive emotional facial expressions as compared to controls. Plesa-Skewer and colleagues (2006) showed that individuals with WS are less able to perceive negative emotions conveyed through facial expressions and voices relative to controls. In terms of positive social signals, individuals with WS tend to focus a greater amount of attention on happy faces (relative to other emotions) as compared to controls (Dodd & Porter, 2010). Together, these finds support the hypothesis that WS deleted genes may be associated with the development of the structure and function of brain regions important for social and emotional processing.

Recently, neuroimaging studies have shown that WS is associated with atypical function of brain regions important for processing emotions. The amygdala is located within the medial temporal lobe and is involved in assessing the emotional salience of stimuli within the environment (Aggleton, 2000). Meyer-Lindenberg and colleagues (2005) used fMRI to show that individuals with WS exhibit a reduced, or blunted, amygdala response to fearful facial expressions as compared to TD controls. We have replicated this finding (Haas, et al., 2009). Interestingly, in contrast to the pattern of amygdala response to fearful facial expressions, individuals with WS exhibit greater amygdala response to happy facial expressions relative to controls (Haas, et al., 2009). Combined, these findings suggest that the WS genetic deletion may influence the functional development of brain regions, such as the amygdala, important to processing emotions.

Recent studies suggest that specific genes may be associated with the development of brain regions important for emotion processing in WS. For example, Feyder and colleagues (2010) utilized a histological approach in knockout mice and showed that CYLN2 expression (a candidate gene for WS) and DLG4 variation are associated with subtle dysmorphology of amygdala dendritic spines. These findings suggest that CLYN2 and DLG4 may interact with one another to influence the development of the social brain. Other studies of humans with partial WS deletions also support the hypothesis that specific genes may influence the development of the social brain. Dai and colleagues (2009) compared social behavior of an individual with a large portion of the WS affected genes deleted, but spared GTF2I, to a group with the full WS deletion. Results indicated that the individual with spared GTF2I gene was more social inhibited than the group with the full WS deletion. Together, these findings support the hypothesis that some of the WS affected genes (including CYLN2 and GTF2I) may influence the development of the social-emotional brain.

Although there is considerable support for a model relating genetic risk in WS to atypical social-emotional brain development, it is also extremely important to consider the influence of environmental factors. Altered social behavior and emotion processing may in part be influenced by environmental factors operating throughout development in WS. In addition, the majority of individuals with WS exhibit IQ scores far below average (Martens, Wilson, & Reutens, 2008). It is therefore difficult to determine the specificity of the WS deletion genes on influencing social and emotional processing independent of observed abnormalities in cognitive functioning in this condition.

3. MOLECULAR GENETICS AND INDIVIDUAL DIFFERENCES IN EMOTIONALITY: THE NEW KID IN TOWN

Before turning to molecular genetics of emotionality, we will shortly refer to the fact that not only selective breeding studies such as those conducted by Broadhurst, but also twin studies in humans have helped to quantify heritability estimates for individual differences in emotional behavior (e. g. Kendler & Myers, 2010). Twin studies often compare emotional behavior of monozygotic twins with emotional behavior of dizygotic twins. As the latter share only 50% of the genetic code (compared to 100% in monozygotic), higher similarities in identical twins compared to dizygotic twins indicate the influence of genetics on individual differences in emotional behavior. These studies show by applying Falconer's formula[2] that approximately .40 - .50 of individual differences in emotional behavior can be accounted for by genetics (Plomin et al., 2007). Summarizing, based on selective breeding studies in animals and twin studies in humans genetics play an important factor associated with emotional behavior. Moreover, based on knock *in / out* studies in animals and from disorders such as Williams Syndrome in humans, certain genes play pivotal roles in terms of influencing emotionality. Now, we will turn to the question of which polymorphisms (genetic variations occurring with more than 1% in the population) may be associated with individual differences in emotional behavior. Given the huge information load of DNA it is extremely challenging to detect those polymorphisms being associated with individual differences in emotional behavior such as being overly happy, sad or anxious. The DNA itself is represented by a sequence of three billion bases. This information is densely packed in the form of chromosomes and can be found in each cell of the human body with the exception of erythrocytes. It is therefore difficult to determine the optimal place to initiate the search for the molecular genetics basis of emotionality.

Currently, there exist two main research strategies. A rather atheoretical research strategy can be found in genome wide association studies (GWAS), where the researcher compares the DNA between groups of humans that vary according to a particular emotional construct. In GWAS up to two million polymorphisms (numbers are changing fast) can be analyzed simultaneously. By applying this approach in the context of the 'Big Five of Personality' Terraciano et al. (2010a) has shown, among others, that a genetic variation on the SNAP25 gene is associated with neuroticism. Neuroticism is a personality construct describing human variation of anxiousness, affinity towards negative mood states and emotional instability (Costa & McCrae, 1992). GWAS provides the opportunity to discover new candidate genes

---

[2] Heritability can be estimated by substracting the correlation of a phenotype for monozygotic twins and dizygotic twins. The resulting number needs to be multiplied by two (as dizygotic twins only share 50% of their genes). The formula is as follows: $h^2 = 2 (r_{mz} - r_{dz})$.

that play an important role for emotionality without any *a priori* hypotheses. One major disadvantage of GWAS is the need to control for multiple testing. As a consequence many polymorphisms of interest do not survive the rigorously applied statistical correction procedures. Moreover, interaction effects between genetic variations on emotional behavior cannot be made visible without complex computational models that have to be developed in the future. In addition, the function in terms of neurotransmission of many candidate polymorphisms introduced by GWAS is not well understood.

Another research strategy in the field sets up hypotheses derived from animal literature and patient cases in humans (e. g. post mortem analysis of the biochemistry of suicidal' brains). For example, the detection of a genetic variant being associated with negative emotionality has been ascribed in part to the findings of Asberg et al. (1976; see review by Asberg, 1997). In one classic study, Asberg et al. examined the brains of people who committed suicide in a very violent manner. Individuals who committed suicide in a very violent manner showed a lack of the serotonin metabolite 5-hydroxyindoleacetic acid (5-HIAA) within their cerebrospinal fluid. This finding is consistent with the hypothesis that depression is associated with a lack of serotonin. In a pioneering study, Lesch et al. (1996) investigated the association between the 5-HTTLPR polymorphism (on the SLC6A4 gene) and neuroticism. The 5-HTTLPR polymorphism codes for the information of the serotonin transporter, the major psychopharmacological target for the selective serotonin reuptake inhibitors (SSRIs). SSRIs are often prescribed to treat depressed patients by blocking the serotonin transporter – a structure in the presynapse of the synpatic cleft. Due to the block of the transporter, less serotonin is re-uptaked by the presynapse, which in turn leads (often after several weeks) to an up regulation of serotonin within the synaptic cleft and often to a reduction in depressive symptoms. Lesch et al. (1996) demonstrated that the s-allele of the 5-HTTLPR is associated with higher neuroticism scores. s stands here for the short version of this polymorphism, whereas the l-allele represents the long version. This polymorphism is not a single nucleotide polymorphism (SNP) leading to an exchange of a single base, but represents an insertion deletion polymorphism. In humans a certain fragment of the DNA on this gene can be missing which leads to the short variant. Besides the association of the s-allele with negative emotionality Lesch et al. (1996) also provided evidence for the functionality of this polymorphism. They demonstrated that the s-allele is associated with a lower number of serotonin transporters in the presynapse and lower functioning.[3] This seminal study by Lesch et al. (1996) led to a large number of follow up studies with heterogeneous findings. A meta-analysis by Sen et al. (2004) showed that the association between the s-allele and higher neuroticism (measured by the NEO-Five Factor model) is robust; findings with other personality inventories measuring anxiety however are less consistent. This inconsistency demonstrates a profound problem: the lack of replicating molecular genetic association studies. In addition to the reported problem associated with the use of different inventories to measure individual differences of personality/emotionality as

---

[3] One might think that a lower number of serotonin transporters could be good, because less serotonin is able to flow back into the presynapse (= more serotonin in the synaptic cleft). This thought on the pharmacological pathways also contradict a bit with the link between neuroticism and the s-allele. But: the serotonergic neurotransmission is regulated by far more elements than by the serotonin transporter alone (e. g. monoaminooxidase plays an important role for catabolizing serotonin). Furthermore higher anxiety has been proposed to be associated with higher levels of serotonin (which stands in contrast with the findings from depression – e. g. see Cloninger et al., 1993).

well the size and ethnic diversity of samples contribute to the heterogeneity of molecular genetic findings in the literature: Given the fact that personality traits such as neuroticism are normally distributed within the population (Montag et al., 2012), not only one genetic variant, but a large number of genetic variants each with small effects may influence the genetic part of individual differences of emotionality.[4] Larger sample sizes are needed to reliably detect the small effects of a polymorphism on individual differences on emotions. In particular, studies with small sample sizes have higher likelihoods for committing errors such as with false positives. But sometimes this needs to be accepted, in particular when dealing with rare patient groups. Moreover, we already referred shortly to ethnicity issues. Genetic variants can be observed in different numbers across different ethnicities. Therefore, certain genetic variants of a polymorphism are only representative of the ethnic population under investigation. This can have a tremendous influence on the statistics involved when analyzing the association between molecular genetics and emotionality. Another important research strategy has been introduced by Caspi et al. (2003). In this intriguing work the authors reported that the s-allele of 5-HTTLPR is only associated with higher risk for depression, when participants have also experienced adverse life events. Therefore, it is of great importance to consider gene by environment effects when dealing with the molecular genetics of emotionality. A new branch of science has begun to investigate the effects of the environment on the genomic level. Specifically, methylation patterns are investigated in the context of epigenetics, in order to search for influences of the environment on the packing structure of the DNA (Meaney & Fergusson-Smith, 2010).

So far, only one polymorphism has been introduced in this chapter that is associated with emotionality. Since the publication by Lesch et al. (1996) much has happened: In the meantime, there are thousands of molecular genetic association studies dealing with emotionality. For example, there has been extensive research on the BDNF gene. This gene codes for the information of the brain derived neurotrophic factor (BDNF), a molecule playing an important role in mediating antidepressive effects (Groves, 2007). Similar to the gene SLC6A4, a functional polymorphism called BDNF Val66Met has been detected on the BDNF gene impacting the activity-dependent secretion of this molecule (Egan et al, 2003). Carriers of the Met allele or the homozygous Met/Met variant have been associated with higher anxiety scores (Jiang et al., 2005; Montag et al., 2010a), but again - findings are heterogeneous (Sen et al., 2003; Lang et al., 2005). Moreover, the Met-allele has been associated with lower hippocampal and amygdala volume (Pezawas et al., 2004; Montag et al., 2009) and higher amygdala reactivity to emotional stimuli (Montag et al., 2008). Mukherjee et al. (2011) showed that Met-allele carriers exhibit higher reactivity to fearful faces within the brainstem, anterior cingulate cortex and the insula. The results of brain imaging studies demonstrate the utility of combining genetic information with fMRI experiments in order to characterize the nature of a SNP in the context of emotionality in more detail. Both serotonin and BDNF are important neurotransmitters within the human brain and are therefore in need to be investigated together. There is evidence that suggests that the administration of the SSNRIs Venlafaxine[5] is associated with rising BDNF levels (ergo antidepressant effects; Aydemir et al., 2005). Following this, one may question how the

---

[4] If it would be just one genetic variant, one would expect to see only high and low anxiousness in the population. In fact the largest numbers of participants report via questionnaire a medium level of anxiety.

[5] SSNRI block besides the serotonin transporters also the norepinephrine transporters.

polymorphisms 5-HTTLPR and BDNF Val66Met may relate to each other when investigating individual differences in emotionality. A recent study indicated a genetic epistasis[6] effect, although not in the expected direction: among others carriers of the homozygous ss-variant of the 5-HTTLPR together with the Val/Val variant showed higher vulnerability to depression after childhood abuse (Grabe et al., 2012). A study by Terraciano et al. (2010b) reported that the configuration LL/ValVal is associated with lower neuroticism scores. Therefore interaction effects are often surprising and far more complex than would be expected based on the reported main effects in the literature.

In addition to studies on the serotonergic and BDNF systems, recent research has focused on dopamine and positive emotionality (e. g. Depue et al., 1994; Depue & Collins, 1999). COMT Val158Met is a functional polymorphism on the COMT gene coding for catechol-o-methyltransferase (COMT; Lachman et al., 1996). The enyzme COMT catabolizes dopamine and its enzyme activity is influenced by the aforementioned SNP. COMT Val158Met has been associated with both positive and negative emotionality (e. g. Hashimoto et al., 2007; Reuter & Hennig, 2005; Montag et al., 2008a). A recent detailed review on COMT and personality/emotionality has been published by our work group (Montag et al., 2012). In addition to the gene coding for COMT, several other dopaminergic genes such as one coding for the dopamine D2 receptor (DRD2) have been studied (e. g. Reuter et al., 2006; Montag et al., 2010; Smillie et al., 2010; Tsuchimine et al., in press). New genetic candidates in the investigation of emotionality include the genes coding for the receptors for the neuropeptides oxytocin (Kawamura et al., 2010; Ebstein et al., 2012) and vasopressin (Meyer-Lindenberg et al., 2009; Meyer-Lindenberg et al., 2011). Both neuropeptides have been shown to have important functions associated with social emotions and social interaction between humans. For example, a prominent study by Kosfeld et al. (2005) demonstrated that nasal administration of oxytocin led to an increase of trust during an economic game. Other studies have shown that oxytocin enhances the detection of emotions such as fear (Fischer-Shofty et al., 2010) and may be a possible new drug in treating autism (Modi & Young, 2012). The growing body of evidence showing the involvement of these neuropeptides in social emotions make both oxytocin and vasopressin highly promising targets for future studies of molecular genetics and social emotions (e. g. Montag et al., 2011; Walter et al., 2012).

CONCLUSION

Although there have been many advancements in the study of molecular genetics of emotionality, it remains a challenge to fully understand the complex molecular genetics underlying emotionality. Research is currently considerably far away from a complete understanding of these mechanisms. In addition to the problems associated with integrating research findings, new statistical tools are needed to deal with the large amounts of information being processed when investigating molecular genetics and emotions.

Applying MRI techniques including structural and functional MRI in order to detect the brain regions associated with genetic variants (so called genetic imaging; DeGeus et al., 2008; Montag et al., 2013) will likely be an invaluable tool. However, another important avenue to be followed is the investigation of the molecular genetics of emotionality targets within more

---

[6] Interaction effect of two genetic variants

ecologically valid scenarios. Genetic variants associated with individual differences in emotionality are currently investigated in the context of personalized medicine. Here, the aim is to prescribe the right amount of drugs / the right drug according to the genotype of a patient (e. g. Porcelli et al., 2012). The detection of genetic variants being involved in emotionality may contribute to the development of more effective treatments for individuals with affective disorders.

REFERENCES

Aggleton, J. P. (2000). *The Amygdala: A Functional Analysis.* New York: Oxford University Press.

Asberg, M. (1997). Neurotransmitters and suicidal behavior. The evidence from cerebrospinal fluid studies. *Annals of the New York Academy of Sciences,* 836 (1), 158-81.

Asberg, M., Träskman, L., Thorén, P. (1976). 5-HIAA in the cerebrospinal fluid. A biochemical suicide predictor? *Archives of General Psychiatry,* 33 (10), 1193-7.

Aydemir, O., Deveci, A., Taneli, F. (2005). The effect of chronic antidepressant treatment on serum brain-derived neurotrophic factor levels in depressed patients: a preliminary study. *Prog Neuropsychopharmacol Biological Psychiatry,* 29 (2), 261-5.

Bandettini, P. A. (in press). Twenty years of functional MRI: The science and the stories. *Neuroimage.*

Barrett, L. F., Wager, T. D. (2006). The structure of emotion: evidence from neuroimaging studies. *Current Directions in Psychological Sciencs,* 15 (2), 79 – 83.

Bekkedal, M. Y., Rossi, J. 3rd, Panksepp, J. (2011). Human brain EEG indices of emotions: delineating responses to affective vocalizations by measuring frontal theta event-related synchronization. *Neuroscience & Biobehavioral Reviews,* 35 (9), 1959-70.

Broadhurst, P. L. (1975). The Maudsley reactive and nonreactive strains of rats: a survey. *Behavior Genetics,* 5 (4), 299-319.

Cannon, W. B. (1927). The James-Lange theory of emotions: A critical examination and an alternative theory. *American Journal of Psychology*, 39 (1/4), 106–124.

Cannon, W. B. (1931). Again the James-Lange and the thalamic theories of emotions. *Psychological Review*, 38 (4), 281–295.

Caspi, A., Sugden, K., Moffitt, T. E., Taylor, A., Craig, I. W., Harrington, H., McClay, J., Mill, J., Martin, J., Braithwaite, A., Poulton, R. (2003). Influence of life stress on depression: moderation by a polymorphism in the 5-HTT gene. *Science,* 301 (5631), 386-9.

Cloninger, C. R., Svrakic, D. M., Przybeck, T. R. (1993). A psychobiological model of temperament and character. *Archives of General Psychiatry,* 50 (12), 975-90.

Costa, P. T., Jr., & McCrae, R. R. (1992). *NEO PI-R professional manual.* Odessa, FL: Psychological Assessment Resources, Inc.

Dai, L., Bellugi, U., Chen, X. N., Pulst-Korenberg, A. M., Jarvinen-Pasley, A., Tirosh-Wagner, T., Eis, P. S., Graham, J., Mills, D., Searcy, Y., & Korenberg, J. R. (2009). Is it Williams syndrome? GTF2IRD1 implicated in visual-spatial construction and GTF2I in sociability revealed by high resolution arrays. *Amercian Journal of Medical Genetics Part A,* 149 (3), 302-314.

Dagleish, T., Dunn, B. D., Mobbs, D. (2009). Affective Neuroscience: Past, Present, and Future. *Emotion Review,* 1 (4), 355-368.

Damasio, A. R. (1996). The somatic marker hypothesis and the possible functions of the prefrontal cortex. *Philosophical Transactions of the Royal Society of London. Series B: Biological Sciences,* 351 (1346), 1413-20.

de Geus, E., Goldberg, T., Boomsma, D. I., Posthuma, D. (2008). Imaging the genetics of brain structure and function. *Biological Psychology,* 79 (1), 1-8.

Depue, R. A., Collins, P. F. (1999). Neurobiology of the structure of personality: dopamine, facilitation of incentive motivation, and extraversion. *Behavioral and Brain Sciences,* 22 (3), 491-517.

Depue, R. A., Luciana, M., Arbisi, P., Collins, P., Leon, A. (1994). Dopamine and the structure of personality: relation of agonist-induced dopamine activity to positive emotionality. *Journal of Personality and Social Psychology,* 67 (3), 485-98.

Dodd, H. F., & Porter, M. A. (2010). I see happy people: Attention bias towards happy but not angry facial expressions in Williams syndrome. *Cognitive Neuropsychiatry,* 15 (6), 549-567..

Dodd, H. F., Porter, M. A., Peters, G. L., & Rapee, R. M. (2010). Social approach in pre-school children with Williams syndrome: the role of the face. *Journal of Intellectual Disability Research,* 54 (3), 194-203.

Doyle, T. F., Bellugi, U., Korenberg, J. R., & Graham, J. (2004). "Everybody in the world is my friend" hypersociability in young children with Williams syndrome. *American Journal of Medical Genetics Part A,* 124 (3), 263-273.

Ebstein, R. P., Knafo, A., Mankuta, D., Chew, S. H., Lai, P. S. (2012). The contributions of oxytocin and vasopressin pathway genes to human behavior. *Hormones and Behavior,* 61 (3), 359-79.

Egan, M. F., Kojima, M., Callicott, J. H., Goldberg, T. E., Kolachana, B. S., Bertolino, A., Zaitsev, E., Gold, B., Goldman, D., Dean, M., Lu, B., Weinberger, D. R. (2003). The BDNF val66met polymorphism affects activity-dependent secretion of BDNF and human memory and hippocampal function. *Cell,* 112 (2), 257-69.

Feyder, M., Karlsson, R. M., Mathur, P., Lyman, M., Bock, R., Momenan, R., Munasinghe, J., Scattoni, M. L., Ihne, J., Camp, M., Graybeal, C., Strathdee, D., Begg, A., Alvarez, V. A., Kirsch, P., Rietschel, M., Cichon, S., Walter, H., Meyer-Lindenberg, A., Grant, S. G., & Holmes, A. (2010). Association of mouse Dlg4 (PSD-95) gene deletion and human DLG4 gene variation with phenotypes relevant to autism spectrum disorders and Williams' syndrome. *The American Journal of Psychiatry,* 167 (12), 1508-1517.

Fischer-Shofty, M., Shamay-Tsoory, S. G., Harari, H., Levkovitz, Y. (2010). The effect of intranasal administration of oxytocin on fear recognition. *Neuropsychologia,* 48 (1), 179-84.

Flint, J. (2004). The genetic basis of neuroticism. *Neuroscience & Biobehavioral Reviews,* 28 (3), 307-16.

Gosch, A., & Pankau, R. (1994). Social-emotional and behavioral adjustment in children with Williams-Beuren syndrome. *American Journal of Medical Genetics,* 53 (4), 335-339.

Grabe, H. J., Schwahn, C., Mahler, J., Appel, K., Schulz, A., Spitzer, C., Fenske, K., Barnow, S., Freyberger, H. J., Teumer, A., Petersmann, A., Biffar, R., Rosskopf, D., John, U., Völzke, H. (2012). Genetic epistasis between the brain-derived neurotrophic factor Val66Met polymorphism and the 5-HTT promoter polymorphism moderates the susceptibility to depressive disorders after childhood abuse. *Progress in Neuro-Psychopharmacology and Biological Psychiatry,* 36 (2), 264-70.

Groves, J. O. (2007). Is it time to reassess the BDNF hypothesis of depression? *Molecular Psychiatry,* 12 (12), 1079-88.

Haas, B. W., Mills, D., Yam, A., Hoeft, F., Bellugi, U., & Reiss, A. (2009). Genetic influences on sociability: heightened amygdala reactivity and event-related responses to positive social stimuli in Williams syndrome. *The Journal of Neuroscience,* 29 (4), 1132-1139.

Hashimoto, R., Noguchi, H., Hori, H., Ohi, K., Yasuda, Y., Takeda, M., Kunugi, H. (2007). A possible association between the Val158Met polymorphism of the catechol-O-methyl transferase gene and the personality trait of harm avoidance in Japanese healthy subjects. *Neuroscience Letters,* 428 (1), 17-20.

James, W. (1884). What is an emotion? *Mind,* 9, 188–205.

Jiang, X., Xu, K., Hoberman, J., Tian, F., Marko, A. J., Waheed, J. F., Harris, C. R., Marini, A. M., Enoch, M. A., Lipsky, R. H. (2005). BDNF variation and mood disorders: a novel functional promoter polymorphism and Val66Met are associated with anxiety but have opposing effects. *Neuropsychopharmacology,* 30 (7), 1353-61.

Kawamura, Y., Liu, X., Akiyama, T., Shimada, T., Otowa, T., Sakai, Y., Kakiuchi, C., Umekage, T., Sasaki, T., Akiskal, H. S. (2010). The association between oxytocin receptor gene (OXTR) polymorphisms and affective temperaments, as measured by TEMPS-A. *Journal of Affective Disorders,* 127 (1-3), 31-7.

Kendler, K. S., Myers, J. (2010). The genetic and environmental relationship between major depression and the five-factor model of personality. *Psychological Medicine,* 40 (5), 801-6.

Knoll, M. A. (2010). The role of behavioral economics and behavioral decision making in Americans' retirement savings decisions. *Social Security Bulletin,* 70 (4), 1-23.

Kosfeld, M., Heinrichs, M., Zak, P. J., Fischbacher, U., Fehr, E. (2005). Oxytocin increases trust in humans. *Nature,* 435 (7042), 673-6.

Lachman, H. M., Papolos, D. F., Saito, T., Yu, Y. M., Szumlanski, C. L., Weinshilboum, R. M. (1996). Human catechol-O-methyltransferase pharmacogenetics: description of a functional polymorphism and its potential application to neuropsychiatric disorders. *Pharmacogenetics,* 6 (3), 243-50.

Lang, P., Greenwald, M. K., Bradley, M. M., Hamm, A. O. (2007). Looking at pictures: affective, facial, visceral, and behavioral reactions. *Psychophysiology,* 30 (3), 261-273.

Lang, U. E., Hellweg, R., Kalus, P., Bajbouj, M., Lenzen, K. P., Sander, T., Kunz, D., Gallinat, J. (2005). Association of a functional BDNF polymorphism and anxiety-related personality traits. *Psychopharmacology (Berl),* 180 (1), 95-9.

Lange, C. (1922). The emotions. In K. Dunlap (Eds.), The emotions (I. A. Haupt, Trans., pp. 33-90). Baltimore, MD: Williams & Wilkins. (Original work published 1885)

Larson, C. L., Ruffalo, D., Nietert, J. Y., Davidson, R. J. (2005). Stability of emotion-modulated startle during short and long picture presentation. *Psychophysiology,* 42 (5), 604-10.

Lesch, K. P., Bengel, D., Heils, A., Sabol, S. Z., Greenberg, B. D., Petri, S., Benjamin, J., Müller, C. R., Hamer, D. H. & Murphy, D. L. (1996). Association of anxiety-related traits with a polymorphism in the serotonin transporter gene regulatory region. *Science,* 274(5292), 1527-1531.

Martens, M. A., Wilson, S. J., & Reutens, D. C. (2008). Research Review: Williams syndrome: a critical review of the cognitive, behavioral, and neuroanatomical phenotype. *Journal of Child Psychology and Psychiatry,* 49 (6), 576-608.

Meaney, M. J., Ferguson-Smith, A. C. (2010). Epigenetic regulation of the neural transcriptome: the meaning of the marks. *Nature Neuroscience,* 13 (11), 1313-8.

Meyer-Lindenberg A, Domes G, Kirsch P, Heinrichs M. (2011). Oxytocin and vasopressin in the human brain: social neuropeptides for translational medicine. *Nature Reviews Neuroscience,* 12 (9), 524-38.

Meyer-Lindenberg, A., Hariri, A. R., Munoz, K. E., Mervis, C. B., Mattay, V. S., Morris, C. A., & Berman, K. F. (2005). Neural correlates of genetically abnormal social cognition in Williams syndrome. *Nature Neuroscience,* 8 (8), 991-993.

Meyer-Lindenberg, A., Kolachana, B., Gold, B., Olsh, A., Nicodemus, K. K., Mattay, V., Dean, M., Weinberger, D. R. (2009). Genetic variants in AVPR1A linked to autism predict amygdala activation and personality traits in healthy humans. *Molecular Psychiatry,* 14 (10), 968-75.

Meyer-Lindenberg, A., Mervis, C. B., & Berman, K. F. (2006). Neural mechanisms in Williams syndrome: a unique window to genetic influences on cognition and behaviour. *Nature Reviews Neuroscience,* 7 (5), 380-393.

Mukherjee, P., Whalley, H. C., McKirdy, J. W., McIntosh, A. M., Johnstone, E. C., Lawrie, S. M., Hall, J. (2011). Effects of the BDNF Val66Met polymorphism on neural responses to facial emotion. *Psychiatry Research,* 191 (3), 182-8.

Mullis, K. B., Faloona, F. A., Scharf, S. J., Saiki, R. K., Horn, G. T., & Erlich, H. (1986, January). Specific enzymatic amplification of DNA in vitro: the polymerase chain reaction. In Cold Spring Harb Symp Quant Biol (Vol. 51, No. Pt 1, pp. 263-273).

Modi, M. E., Young, L. J. (2012). The oxytocin system in drug discovery for autism: animal models and novel therapeutic strategies. *Hormones and Behavior,* 61 (3), 340-50.

Montag, C., Basten, U., Stelzel, C., Fiebach, C. J., Reuter, M. (2010a). The BDNF Val66Met polymorphism and anxiety: support for animal knock-in studies from a genetic association study in humans. *Psychiatry Research,* 179 (1), 86-90.

Montag, C., Buckholtz, J. W., Hartmann, P., Merz, M., Burk, C., Hennig, J., & Reuter, M. (2008a). COMT genetic variation affects fear processing: psychophysiological evidence. *Behavioral Neuroscience*, 122(4), 901-909.

Montag, C., Fiebach, C. J., Kirsch, P., Reuter, M. (2011). Interaction of 5-HTTLPR and a variation on the oxytocin receptor gene influences negative emotionality. *Biological Psychiatry,* 69(6), 601-3.

Montag, C., Jurkiewicz, M. & Reuter, M. (2012). The role of the COMT gene for personality and related psychopathological disorders. *CNS & Neurological Disorders − Drug Targets,* 11 (3), 236-250.

Montag, C., Markett, S., Basten, U., Stelzel, C., Fiebach, C., Canli, T. & Reuter, M. (2010b). Epistasis of the DRD2/ANKK1 Taq Ia and the BDNF Val66Met polymorphism impacts Novelty Seeking and Harm Avoidance. *Neuropsychopharmacology,* 35 (9), 1860-1867.

Montag, C., Reuter, M., Jurkiewicz, M., Markett, S., & Panksepp, J. (2013). Imaging the structure of the human anxious brain: a review of findings from neuroscientific personality psychology. *Reviews in the Neurosciences,* 24(2), 167-190.

Montag, C., Reuter, M., Newport, B., Elger, C. & Weber, B. (2008b). The BDNF Val66Met polymorphism affects amygdala activity in response to emotional stimuli: evidence from a genetic imaging study. *NeuroImage*, 42 (4), 1554-1559.

Montag, C., Weber, B., Fliessbach, K., Elger, C. & Reuter, M. (2009). The BDNF Val66Met polymorphism impacts parahippocampal and amygdala volume in healthy humans: Incremental support for a genetic risk factor for depression. *Psychological Medicine*, 39 (11), 1831-1839.

Ortony, A., Turner, T. T. (1990). What's basic about basic emotions? *Psychological Review*, 97 (3), 315-331.

Panksepp, J. (1998). *Affective Neurosience*. Oxford University Press, USA.

Panksepp, J. (2005). Affective consciousness: Core emotional feelings in animals and humans. *Consciousness and Cognition*, 14 (1), 30-80.

Panksepp, J. (2011). Cross-species affective neuroscience decoding of the primal affective experiences of humans and related animals. *PLoS One*, 6(9), e21236.

Pezawas, L., Verchinski, B. A., Mattay, V. S., Callicott, J. H., Kolachana, B. S., Straub, R. E., Egan M. F., Meyer-Lindenberg, A., Weinberger, D.R. (2004). The brain-derived neurotrophic factor val66met polymorphism and variation in human cortical morphology. *The Journal of Neuroscience*, 24 (45), 10099-102.

Plesa-Skwerer, D., Faja, S., Schofield, C., Verbalis, A., & Tager-Flusberg, H. (2006). Perceiving facial and vocal expressions of emotion in individuals with Williams syndrome. *American Journal on Mental Retardation*, 111 (1), 15-26.

Plomin, R., DeFries, J. C., McClearn, G. E., McGuffin, P. (2007) *Behavioral Genetics*. Worth Publishers: New York.

Porcelli, S., Fabbri, C., Serretti, A. (2012). Meta-analysis of serotonin transporter gene promoter polymorphism (5-HTTLPR) association with antidepressant efficacy. *European Neuropsychopharmacology*, 22 (4), 239-58.

Porter, M. A., Shaw, T. A., & Marsh, P. J. (2010). An unusual attraction to the eyes in Williams-Beuren syndrome: a manipulation of facial affect while measuring face scanpaths. *Cognitive Neuropsychiatry*, 15 (6), 505-530.

Reuter, M. & Hennig, J. (2005). Association of the functional COMT VAL158MET polymorphism with the personality trait of extraversion. *NeuroReport*, 16 (10), 1135-1138.

Reuter, M., Schmitz, A., Corr, P., Hennig, J. (2006). Molecular genetics support Gray's personality theory: The interaction of COMT and DRD2 polymorphisms predicts the behavioral approach system. *International Journal of Neuro-Psychopharmacology*, 9 (2), 155-166.

Riby, D. M., & Hancock, P. J. (2008). Viewing it differently: Social scene perception in Williams syndrome and Autism. *Neuropsychologia*, 46 (11), 2855-2860.

Riby, D. M., & Hancock, P. J. (2009). Looking at movies and cartoons: eye-tracking evidence from Williams syndrome and autism. *Journal of Intellectual Disability Research*, 53 (2), 169-181.

Riby, D. M., Jones, N., Brown, P. H., Robinson, L. J., Langton, S. R., Bruce, V., & Riby, L. M. (2011). Attention to Faces in Williams Syndrome. *Journal of Autism and Development Disorders*, 41 (9), 1228-39.

Russell, J. (1980). A circumplex model of affect. *Journal of Personality and Social Psychology*, 39 (6), 1161-1178.

Schimitel, F. G., de Almeida, G. M., Pitol, D. N., Armini, R. S., Tufik, S., Schenberg, L. C. (2012). Evidence of a suffocation alarm system within the periaqueductal gray matter of the rat. *Neuroscience, 200*, 59-73.

Sen, S., Burmeister, M., Ghosh, D. (2004). Meta-analysis of the association between a serotonin transporter promoter polymorphism (5-HTTLPR) and anxiety-related personality traits. *American Journal of Medical Genetics Part B: Neuropsychiatric Genetics, 127B* (1), 85-9.

Sen, S., Nesse, R. M., Stoltenberg, S. F., Li, S., Gleiberman, L., Chakravarti, A., Weder, A. B., Burmeister, M. (2003). A BDNF coding variant is associated with the NEO personality inventory domain neuroticism, a risk factor for depression. *Neuropsychopharmacology, 28* (2), 397-401.

Smillie, L. D., Cooper, A. J., Proitsi, P., Powell, J. F., Pickering, A. D. (2010). Variation in DRD2 dopamine gene predicts Extraverted personality. *Neuroscience Letters, 468* (3), 234-7.

Terracciano, A., Sanna, S., Uda, M., Deiana, B., Usala, G., Busonero, F., Maschio, A., Scally, M., Patriciu, N., Chen, W. M., Distel, M. A., Slagboom, E. P., Boomsma, D. I., Villafuerte, S., Sliwerska, E., Burmeister, M., Amin, N., Janssens, A. C., van Duijn, C. M., Schlessinger, D., Abecasis, G. R., Costa, P. T. Jr. (2010a). Genome-wide association scan for five major dimensions of personality. *Molecular Psychiatry, 15* (6), 647-56.

Terracciano, A., Tanaka, T., Sutin, A. R., Deiana, B., Balaci, L., Sanna, S., Olla, N., Maschio, A., Uda, M., Ferrucci, L., Schlessinger, D., Costa, P. T. Jr. (2010b). BDNF Val66Met is associated with introversion and interacts with 5-HTTLPR to influence neuroticism. *Neuropsychopharmacology, 35* (5), 1083-9.

Tomc, S. A., Williamson, N. K., & Pauli, R. M. (1990). Temperament in Williams syndrome. *American Journal of Medical Genetics, 36* (3), 345-352.

Tsuchimine, S., Yasui-Furukori, N., Sasaki, K., Kaneda, A., Sugawara, N., Yoshida, S., Kaneko, S. (in press). Association between the dopamine D2 receptor (DRD2) polymorphism and the personality traits of healthy Japanese participants. *Progress in Neuro-Psychopharmacol and Biological Psychiatry.*

Tversky, A., Kahneman, D. (1981). The framing of decisions and the psychology of choice. *Science*, 211 (4481), 453-8.

Walter, N. T., Montag, C., Markett, S., Felten, A., Voigt, G., Reuter, M. (2012). Ignorance is no excuse: moral judgments are influenced by a genetic variation on the oxytocin receptor gene. *Brain and Cognition, 78* (3), 268-73.

Watson, J. D., Crick, F. H. C. (1953). Molecular structure of nucleic acids: A structure for deoxyribose nucleic acid. *Nature, 171*, 737-738.

Wenar, C. (1954). Reaction time as a function of manifest anxiety and stimulus intensity. The *Journal of Abnormal and Social Psychology, 49* (3), 335-340.

Zachar, P., Ellis, R. D. (in press). Categorical versus dimensional models of affect. *A seminar on theories of Panksepp and Russell.* John Benjamins Publishing Company.

Zitzer-Comfort, C., Doyle, T., Masataka, N., Korenberg, J., & Bellugi, U. (2007). Nature and nurture: Williams syndrome across cultures. *Developmental Science, 10* (6), 755-762.

In: Handbook of Psychology of Emotions
Editors: C. Mohiyeddini, M. Eysenck and S. Bauer

ISBN: 978-1-62808-053-7
© 2013 Nova Science Publishers, Inc.

Chapter 12

RUMINATION AND EMOTIONS

Susan Nolen-Hoeksema, Vera Vine*
and Kirsten Gilbert
Yale University

ABSTRACT

Emotions typically have informational value, arising when there are important changes in the environment (Frijda, 1986; Nesse, 2000) and/or changes in progress toward one's goals (Carver and Scheier, 1998; Duval and Wicklund, 1972; Martin and Tesser, 1996; Pyszczynski and Greenberg, 1987). Thus, when emotions arise, particularly negative emotions that may signal threat or loss in the environment or lack of progress toward goals, people tend to reflect on or evaluate the causes, meanings, and consequences of these emotions. Martin and Tesser (1996) referred to such reflection and evaluation as *rumination*. They argued that rumination is functional when it leads people to take action to reduce the discrepancies between their current state and a desired state, or to give up unattainable goals. If rumination does not lead to such outcomes, and instead persists and focuses a person's attention on unattained goals and negative emotions, it can become maladaptive.

For example, if a woman has the goal of a positive relationship with her husband, but has been having frequent arguments with him, she will experience negative emotion, and this may lead her to ruminate on the discrepancy between her goal (a positive relationship) and her current state (hostility between the couple) (Martin and Tesser, 1996). If she ruminates on the discrepancy in an instrumental, problem-solving way, then her ruminations will end when she either takes action to overcome the discrepancies (e.g., she initiates a conversation with her husband in an effort to repair the relationship) or when she relinquishes the desired goal (e.g., she decides her husband is impossible to live with and files for divorce). The consequence of such an instrumental approach is positive or neutral affect. In contrast, if her ruminations simply perseverate on the discrepancies between the current state and a desired state, the discrepancy will remain, and she will continue to experience negative affect.

* Corresponding author: Vera Vine, Department of Psychology, Yale University, P.O. Box 208205, New Haven, CT 06520, Vera.Vine@yale.edu.

Our research has focused on maladaptive forms of rumination, their consequences and mechanisms of action, and sources of individual differences in maladaptive rumination. In the Response Styles Theory, Nolen-Hoeksema (1991) defined maladaptive rumination as a perseverative focus on the causes, meanings and consequences of negative affect in the absence of instrumental behavior to relieve that negative affect. She argued that such a perseverative focus maintains and exacerbates negative mood by (a) enhancing negative mood-congruent thinking, (b) interfering with problem-solving, and (c) inhibiting instrumental behavior. Nolen-Hoeksema and Davis (1999) argued that rumination also damages social relationships, as supportive others grow weary of the ruminator's inability or unwillingness to take action on, or "let go" of, ruminations, and subsequently become hostile and/or withdraw their support. Thus, the ruminator not only fails to solve the problems behind the original negative mood, but also develops new problems that may inspire new negative emotions, such as loss of social support.

Most of the research on maladaptive rumination has focused on rumination in the context of sadness or depression, and that will be reviewed here. We will also review work supporting the mechanisms by which rumination has is deleterious effects. However, in recent years, rumination has been conceptualized as a transdiagnostic process occurring in multiple disorders, and exacerbating any emotional state that is present (Nolen-Hoeksema et al., 2008; Nolen-Hoeksema and Watkins, 2011; Watkins, 2009). Thus, we will review work on rumination in the contexts of anxiety and anger, as well as recent work on rumination in the context of positive emotions. We will conclude with questions for future research.

EFFECTS OF RUMINATION ON SADNESS AND DEPRESSION

Rumination has been studied most frequently in relation to sadness and symptoms of depression (see reviews by Mor and Winquist, 2000; Nolen-Hoeksema, Wisco, and Lyubomirsky, 2008; Watkins, 2008). Much of this work has used the Ruminative Responses Scale (RRS; see Treynor, Nolen-Hoeksema and Gonzalez, 2003), a 22-item measure that asks people what they find themselves doing when they feel sad, blue, or depressed. The rumination items are self-focused, symptom-focused, and self-evaluative (e.g., "I think about my feelings of fatigue," "I think "Why can't I handle things better?"). This scale has high internal consistency, acceptable convergent validity, and high test-retest stability even in individuals who experience significant change in their levels of depression (Bagby, Rector, Bacchiochi, and McBride, 2004; Butler and Nolen-Hoeksema, 1994; Just and Alloy, 1997; Kuehner and Weber, 1999; Nolen-Hoeksema et al., 1993; Nolen-Hoeksema, Parker, and Larson, 1994).

Multiple meta-analyses have shown that adults and youth with high scores on the RRS have significantly higher levels of depressive symptoms and are more likely to be diagnosed with Major Depressive Disorder (APA, 2004), both cross-sectionally and longitudinally, with moderate to large effect sizes (Aldao, Nolen-Hoeksema and Schweizer, 2010; Mor and Winquist, 2000; Rood, Roelofs, Bogels, Nolen-Hoeksema, and Schouten, 2009; Watkins, 2008). Other individual difference measures of rumination (e.g., Trapnell and Campbell, 1999) also show moderate relationships to depression (see meta-analyses just cited).

Concerns have arisen that some portion of the relationship between rumination and depression is due to content overlap in the measures of the two constructs. To address this, Treynor and colleagues (2003) removed items from the Ruminative Responses Scale (RRS) with obvious overlap with depressive symptoms (e.g., "I think about how passive and unmotivated I feel") and submitted the remaining 10 items to factor analysis. Two factors emerged, a "brooding" factor with items indicating abstract self-evaluation (e.g., "I think "Why do I always react this way?""), and a "reflection" factor with items indicating a more problem-solving orientation (e.g., "I write down what I am thinking about and analyze it."). Both the brooding and reflection factors were positively correlated with depressive symptoms in a large cross-sectional community sample of adults, but only the brooding items predicted increases in depression over a year period, while the reflection items predicted decreases over this period (Treynor et al., 2003). Subsequent studies have confirmed that the brooding items of the RRS are consistently associated with more depression cross-sectionally and longitudinally (see Aldao et al., 2010), but the relationships between the reflection items and depression have been mixed (see Nolen-Hoeksema, Wisco and Lyubomirsky, 2008). Thus, the abstract, self-evaluative, and often self-critical thoughts indexed by brooding seem to be the more toxic form of rumination (Watkins, 2008).

We noted above that self-regulation theories argue that rumination will be adaptive if it can focus on problem solving (e.g., Martin and Tesser, 1996). The mixed results for the reflection scale of the RRS, and the fact that reflection and brooding tend to be correlated positively with each other (Treynor et al., 2003), raise the possibility that at least some people have difficult engaging in problem-solving without lapsing into a brooding form of rumination (Nolen-Hoeksema et al., 2008). Recent experimental work by Joormann and colleagues (see Joormann, 2010) suggests that these individuals have difficulty inhibiting negative self-evaluative thoughts when such thoughts arise in working memory. In other words, although these individuals may attempt to focus on instrumental problem-solving thoughts, their brooding thoughts keep intruding.

A large body of experimental work in which participants are induced to ruminate in the laboratory confirms that an evaluative self-focus can exacerbate existing sad or depressed moods (Mor and Winquist, 2000; Watkins, 2008). Much of this work has used the rumination induction developed by Nolen-Hoeksema and Morrow (1993). Participants are asked to focus on the meanings, causes, and consequences of their current feelings for 8 minutes (e.g., "Think about the level of motivation you feel right now," "Think about the long-term goals you have set"). Because these prompts are neutral in valence, they are expected to have no effect on the moods of nondysphoric people. But because dysphoric or depressed people have more negative feelings and cognitions, this ruminative self-focus is expected to lead them to become significantly more dysphoric. The contrasting distraction induction is meant to take participants' minds off themselves and their problems temporarily. In this condition, participants' attention is focused on non-self-relevant images (e.g., "Think about a fan slowly rotating back and forth," "Think about the layout of your local shopping center"). These distracting prompts are expected to have no effect on the moods of nondysphoric people, but to lead dysphoric people to become significantly less depressed for a short time. These predictions have been upheld in dozens of studies (Donaldson and Lam, 2004; Lavender and Watkins, 2004; Lyubomirsky and Nolen-Hoeksema, 1993, 1995; Lyubomirsky, Caldwell, and Nolen-Hoeksema, 1998; Lyubomirsky et al., 1999; Nolen-Hoeksema and Morrow, 1993; Watkins and Baracaia, 2002; Watkins and Moulds, 2005; Watkins and Teasdale, 2001).

Recently, Watkins (2008) isolated the abstract, evaluative prompts in this rumination induction and compared their effects to prompts that focused participants' attention more on the concrete experience of their emotions, which he argues, should better facilitate a problem-solving orientation. In several studies, Watkins and his colleagues have shown that an abstract, evaluative focus on feelings and problems exacerbates sad mood and interferes with problem-solving more than a concrete focus on mood (see review by Watkins, 2008).

Mechanism Linking Rumination and Sadness/Depression

Research on rumination provides converging support for the mechanisms Nolen-Hoeksema (1991) originally proposed linking rumination to sad mood and depression. First, rumination appears to enhance negative mood-congruent thinking. Experimental induction of rumination (versus distraction or concrete focus) has been used to investigate its effects on thinking and problem-solving in the context of sadness and clinical depression. When thinking about the past, dysphoric participants induced to ruminate, compared to dysphoric participants induced to distract or nondysphoric participants, focus more on negative memories and rate negative events as having occurred more frequently in their lives (Lyubomirsky et al., 1998; McFarland and Buehler, 1998; Pyszczynski, Hamilton, Herring, and Greenberg, 1989). When thinking about the present, dysphoric participants induced to ruminate focus more on current problems, such as conflict with others, and are more self-blaming and pessimistic about resolving these problems (Lyubomirsky et al., 1999; Lyubomirsky and Nolen-Hoeksema, 1995; see also Greenberg, Pyszczynski, Burling, and Tibbs, 1992). When thinking about the future, dysphoric participants induced to ruminate are less optimistic, seeing positive events as less likely to happen to them (Lyubomirsky and Nolen-Hoeksema, 1995; see also Pyszczynski, Holt, and Greenberg, 1987). In all of these studies, dysphoric participants (or people meeting criteria for major depressive disorder) instructed to distract for 8 minutes have been no more pessimistic or negative in their thinking than nondysphorics (Lavender and Watkins, 2004; Rimes and Watkins, 2005).

Secondly, rumination appears to interfere with problem solving. Although individuals who tend to ruminate often say they do so in order to solve their problems (Papageorgiou and Wells, 2002), dysphoric individuals induced to ruminate generate less optimal solutions to interpersonal problems than dysphoric individuals distracted from ruminations (Donaldson and Lam, 2004; Lyubomirsky et al., 1999; Lyubomirsky and Nolen-Hoeksema, 1995; Watkins and Baracaia, 2002; Watkins and Moulds, 2005). Even when individuals prone to rumination are able to generate good solutions to problems, they are less confident about these solutions, ask for more time to think about the solution before committing to it, and are less confident in implementing the solution (Ward, Lyubomirsky, Sousa, and Nolen-Hoeksema, 2003).

Thirdly, rumination interferes with instrumental behavior, which perpetuates problems in their lives. Although dysphoric or depressed individuals can gain some relief from ruminations and negative mood through pleasant, distracting activities, they are less willing to engage in such activities, even when they can acknowledge that such activities would be beneficial to them (Lyubomirsky and Nolen-Hoeksema, 1993). Rumination also appears to interfere with critically important instrumental behaviors, such as health behaviors. Lyubomirsky and colleagues (Lyubomirsky, Kasri, Chang, and Chung, 2006) found that women prone to ruminate, upon finding a lump in their breast, experienced higher levels of distress and delayed seeking a diagnosis for 2 months longer than women not prone to ruminate. Other studies of cancer patients confirm that ruminators are less compliant with medical regimes (Aymanns, Filipp, and Klauer, 1995).

If ruminators are excessively focused on their negative feelings and the causes of them, why wouldn't they take action, especially obvious and simple action such as going to a doctor, to potentially relieve their feelings and concerns? Recent theories of rumination suggest that it may be motivated by a desire to avoid certain aspects of emotion and maintain a passive stance toward problems (Jacobson, Martell, and Dimidjian, 2001; Marroquín, Fontes, Scilletta, and Miranda, 2010; Moulds, Kandris, Starr, and Wong, 2007; Nolen-Hoeksema et al., 2008). Although rumination maintains a focus on problems and negative feelings, this may be less aversive than confronting emotions deemed unacceptable or confronting problematic situations or people in one's life.

Some support for this avoidance perspective on rumination has emerged. The tendency to ruminate is associated with self-reported experiential avoidance (Bjornsson et al., 2010; Giorgio et al., 2010; Tull and Gratz, 2008) and the tendency to escape, avoid, or modify unpleasant internal experiences including bodily sensations, thoughts, and emotions (Hayes, Wilson, Gifford, Follette, and Strosahl, 1996). Rumination is also associated with lower acceptance of, and fear of losing control over, emotions (Giorgio et al., 2010; Liverant, Kamholz, Sloan, and Brown, 2011; Tull and Gratz, 2008), self-reported avoidance of unpleasant thoughts and behaviors (Moulds et al., 2007), and suppression of emotions (see review by Nolen-Hoeksema et al., 2008). Rumination is also associated with behavioral disengagement and a passive coping style (Hong, 2007; Marroquin et al., 2010).

Finally, as Nolen-Hoeksema and Davis (1999) suggested, ruminators appear to behave in ways that irritate others, excessively sharing their concerns and feelings, and turning the conversation back to themselves when others try to share their own concerns (Schwartz-Mette and Rose, 2009). Ruminators also score high on measures of dependency and neediness (Spasojevic and Alloy, 2001), and sociotropy (Gorski and Young, 2002). Even though ruminators seek support in stressful times from others more often than do nonruminators, they report receiving lower quality emotional support and having greater friction in their social network (Nolen-Hoeksema and Davis, 1999).

Overall, rumination appears to exacerbate and maintain sad and depressed moods, and increase the probability that a moderate depressed mood will become a major depressive episode (Nolen-Hoeksema, 2000). The most toxic form of rumination appears to be an abstract, evaluative self-focus. Numerous studies of rumination in dysphoric or clinically depressed individuals suggests that it has its effects by enhancing mood-congruent thinking, impeding good problem-solving, reducing instrumental behavior in favor of avoidance, and driving away social support.

EFFECTS OF RUMINATION ON ANXIETY

Rumination has also been studied extensively with respect to anxiety, but this research has virtually exclusively focused on rumination in the context of anxiety disorders rather than anxious emotions or moods. To our knowledge, only two studies have examined the effects of rumination in the context of anxious mood unrelated to psychopathology (Blagden and

Craske, 1996; Wong and Moulds, 2009). We discuss these experimental studies before reviewing the literature on rumination in the anxiety disorders.

RUMINATION AND ANXIOUS MOOD

Blagden and Craske (1996) were the first to extend Nolen-Hoeksema's (1991) response styles theory from sad to anxious mood. Above we described evidence supporting mood-congruent cognitive processing as part of the mechanism maintaining sad mood during rumination. Blagden and Craske reasoned that mood-congruent processing effects should lead rumination to maintain whatever negative mood was present. Given the distinction between adaptive vs. maladaptive forms of rumination (see Martin and Tesser, 1996), they also predicted that a more passive ruminative style should have stronger mood maintenance effects than a more active style. An undergraduate sample underwent an idiographic anxious mood induction followed by one of four response manipulations, to which they were randomly assigned: passive rumination, active rumination, passive distraction, or active distraction. The passive manipulations were modeled closely after the response manipulations used by Nolen-Hoeksema and Morrow (1993). There were no effects of activity vs. passivity, but Blagden and Crakse did find a significant effect of rumination vs. distraction that paralleled previous findings on sad mood. According to multiple indices of anxious mood, participants induced to ruminate maintained their anxiety, while participants who were distracted showed significant reductions in anxiety.

Wong and Moulds (2009) replicated and extended these findings in participants high and low in social anxiety. They induced an anxious mood by having participants perform a speech, for which they were given inadequate time to prepare, in front of a video camera. Participants then underwent a rumination or distraction response manipulation modeled closely after Nolen-Hoeksema's and Morrow's (1993), to which they were randomly assigned. Even among the non-socially anxious group, the rumination manipulation maintained anxious mood while the distraction manipulation alleviated it, consistent with the response styles theory of rumination. Together, these studies provide evidence that ruminating does indeed prolong anxious mood in non-clinical populations.

Rumination and Anxiety Disorders

Several studies have found that rumination as measured by the RRS is positively correlated with symptoms of anxiety (Muris, Roelofs, Rassin, Franken, and Mayer, 2005; Nolen-Hoeksema, 2000; Starr and Davila, 2011). A recent meta-analysis found that after depression ($r = .55$), anxiety symptoms were most strongly related to rumination ($r = .42$). Anxiety and depression symptoms are highly comorbid (Clark and Watson, 1991; Kessler, Merikangas, and Wang, 2007; Mineka, Watson, and Clark, 1998), and this association appears to be mediated in part by rumination (McLaughlin and Nolen-Hoeksema, 2011; Starr and Davila, 2011; Watkins, 2009). Here we review the research examining rumination in the anxiety disorders and discuss the relationship between rumination and other forms of repetitive thinking.

Generalized anxiety disorder and worry. Rumination is reliably correlated with worry (Fresco, Frankel, Mennin, Turk, and Heimberg, 2002; Segerstrom, Tsao, Alden, and Craske, 2000; Watkins, 2004; Watkins, Moulds, and Mackintosh, 2005), a hallmark of generalized anxiety disorder (GAD; APA, 2004). Given the robustness of this association, and the widespread theoretical recognition of ruminative thought processes in the anxiety disorders (e.g., Fresco et al., 2002; Gentes and Ruscio, 2011; Watkins et al., 2005; Wells, 1995), it is surprising that rumination is rarely studied with respect to GAD specifically. One theory of GAD suggests that in this disorder worry itself becomes the topic of rumination, such that individuals ruminate about their problem of worrying too much (Wells, 1995).

The widely accepted definition of worry describes it as a "chain of thoughts and images, negatively affect-laden and relatively uncontrollable, it represents an attempt to engage in mental problem-solving on an issue whose outcome is uncertain but contains the possibility of one or more negative outcomes" (Borkovec, Robinson, Pruzinsky, and DePree, 1983, p. 10). This definition highlights the conceptual overlap between worry and rumination. Recent efforts to distinguish worry from rumination suggest considerable similarities between the two forms of thought, including among other things, their repetitive nature, negative valence, and relationships to uncertainty. Ultimately, it appears that rumination and worry may resemble one another in terms of form or process, but differ significantly in terms of their content and conscious motives.

Both rumination and worry are repetitive, negative, and abstract. Segerstrom and colleagues (2000) found that the shared variance between rumination and worry could be largely explained by a general tendency towards repetitive thought. Furthermore, they found that a latent repetitive thought factor underlying both rumination and worry was associated with both anxiety and depression symptoms longitudinally, suggesting that nonspecific features of repetitive thought process itself may be problematic for mental health (Segerstrom et al., 2000). However, as suggested by the self-regulation theories of repetitive thought discussed above, not all repetitive thought is maladaptive. Rather, it has been suggested that negative valence and abstract (vs. concrete) construal level can make repetitive thought unhealthy. Unfortunately, both rumination and worry share these negative and abstract qualities. Some researchers have found that repetitive thought generally, regardless of type, is associated with negative affect (McEvoy, Mahoney, and Moulds, 2010; Ruscio, Seitchik, Gentes, Jones, and Hallion, 2011; Segerstrom et al., 2000).

Like worry, rumination may occur in response to states of uncertainty. Prominent models of GAD emphasize the relationship between uncertainty or cognitions about the uncontrollability of circumstances and worry (Borkovec, Alcaine, and Behar, 2004; Dugas, Gagnon, Ladouceur, and Freeston, 1998; Wells, 1995; Woody and Rachman, 1994). In the case of worry, this relationship makes intuitive sense – indeed, the very definition of worry provided above highlights its function in coping with discomfort related to uncertain future outcomes. The relationship of rumination to uncertainty is perhaps less obvious, but recent literature suggests that the two are in fact related. People who ruminate (de Jong-Meyer, Beck, and Riede, 2009) and those with anhedonic depression (Berenbaum, Bredemeier, and Thompson, 2008; Miranda, Fontes, and Marroquín, 2008) tend to report considerable difficulty tolerating feelings of uncertainty. Yook and colleagues (2010) extended the notion from the GAD literature that people may use repetitive thinking to quell feelings of uncertainty to suggest that the same process may occur in depression. Accordingly, they found in a clinical sample that while worry mediated the relationship between intolerance of uncertainty and anxiety symptoms, rumination statistically mediated the relationship between intolerance of uncertainty and depressive symptoms. Thus, it appears that distress in the face of uncertainty may be related to repetitive styles of thinking of multiple sorts.

This parallel between worry and rumination suggests that rumination may serve some function associated with reducing uncertainty or increasing the perception of controllability. One possibility is that rumination counteracts uncertainty by increasing certainty in negative future outcomes. Miranda, Fontes, and Marroquin (2008) found that increases in pessimistic certainty over the course of six weeks mediated the influence of intolerance of uncertainty on later depressive symptoms. In other words, depressed individuals may manage uncertainty by increasing their confidence that future events will go poorly. Another possibility is that the tendency to ruminate in response to uncertainty may stem from the need to understand and resolve ambiguity about the meanings and origins of present distress. This possibility is consistent with the finding that ruminators report a greater need to understand situations (Watkins, 2004).

As discussed above, rumination is associated with the tendency to avoid instrumental behavior. The avoidance theory of worry suggests that repetitive thinking may also facilitate not just behavioral avoidance, but cognitive or experiential avoidance as well (see Borkovec et al., 2004). According to this theory, the verbal-linguistic properties of worry make it less emotionally arousing than more image-based thinking, a notion that has recently been borne out empirically (Holmes and Mathews, 2010). This relative difference in arousal leads people to use worry in order to dampen the arousal associated with strong emotional experiences, a strategy that is continually reinforced by the down-regulation of distress. Psychophysiological research supports this theory: worry is associated with significant blunting of physiological reactivity (Castaneda and Segerstrom, 2004) and neural activity (Schienle, Schäfer, Pignanelli, and Vaitl, 2009) during aversive affective tasks.

These avoidance properties of repetitive thought may not be limited to worry, but rather pertain to any form of verbal thinking, including rumination. A recent study examining the trait tendency to engage in negative repetitive thinking of any sort found that trait to be associated with cognitive avoidance, as well as the use of thought suppression strategies (McEvoy et al., 2010). Researchers now speculate that rumination may promote experiential avoidance as well (e.g., Fresco et al., 2002; Goldwin and Behar, 2011; Liverant, Kamholz, Sloan, and Brown, 2011). Preliminary evidence of physiological blunting, which is associated with worry as mentioned previously, is now beginning to emerge in the context of rumination (Giorgio et al., 2010; Liverant et al., 2011).

Rumination and worry thus share considerable similarities, particularly in terms of their process (i.e., both are repetitive, negative, and abstract) and possibly their function (i.e., as a response to uncertainty or to facilitate avoidance). Watkins and colleagues (2005) compared the two and found a number of other process-related similarities. Participants reported no differences between the uncontrollability, frequency, duration, attentional capture, or verbal nature of worry and rumination. What, then, differentiates rumination and worry?

It appears that rumination is characterized by unique content, in terms of both time orientation and themes. Theorists typically observe that rumination concerns past events, whereas worry concerns possible future events (for review see Nolen-Hoeksema et al., 2008). This distinction is not perfectly clear-cut, since it is possible to worry about the future implications of one's past behavior (as we will discuss later with respect to social anxiety), and it is possible to ruminate on the certainty of negative events or feelings in the future (i.e., depressive certainty as discussed above). However, head-to-head comparison appears to confirm a general tendency of worry to be relatively forward-looking and rumination to be relatively backward-looking. Watkins and colleagues (2005) asked participants to select one topic they worried about most frequently and one topic they ruminated about most frequently, and then rate each in terms of a number of domains including time orientation. Consistent with the patterns of time orientation observed in the rumination and worry literatures, participants rated worry thoughts as significantly more about the future and worry thoughts as significantly more about the past.

The broader themes and motives of rumination are distinct from themes and motives of worry in ways consistent with the relative differences in time orientation. Nolen-Hoeksema and colleagues (2008) suggested that rumination is concerned with themes of loss and failure, whereas worry is concerned with danger and anticipated threat. People report that when they worry they tend to experience a greater sense of insecurity than when they ruminate. They also report that when they worry they dwell more on consequences and attempt to problem solve, whereas when they ruminate they dwell on causes and experience a greater need to understand a situation (Watkins, 2004). Meta-cognitive research on the conscious motives of repetitive thought further demonstrate this difference. Worriers report that worrying helps them to anticipate and prepare for threats (Borkovec et al., 2004), whereas ruminators report that ruminating helps them make sense of themselves, their problems, and their symptoms (Papageorgiou and Wells, 2001; Papageorgiou and Wells, 2002; Watkins and Moulds, 2005).

In sum, the comparison of depressive rumination to anxious worry helps sharpen our understanding of the process and content of rumination. Perhaps most interestingly, this comparison sheds light on the functional relationship of repetitive thought to emotion. The literature we have reviewed in this section suggests that repetitive thought is associated with negative affect, and may function as a response to feelings of uncontrollability or uncertainty. Cognitively, repetitive thinking may help alleviate uncertainty, although the mechanisms by which it does so are not well understood. Worry may mitigate uncertainty by appearing to reveal problem solving strategies and solutions to possible threats, whereas rumination may resolve uncertainty by increasing pessimistic or depressive confidence in negative outcomes. Affectively, the deployment of repetitive thinking processes may regulate distress by dampening neural and physiological arousal.

Social anxiety disorder and post-event processing. Social anxiety is excessive fear of negative evaluation in interpersonal contexts that leads to distress and/or avoidance of social situations (APA, 2004), and it is characterized by a particular form of self-focused, perseverative thinking typically called *post-event processing* (PEP; also called *retrospective brooding, post-mortem thinking,* or *post-event rumination,* among other terms) (for reviews see Brozovich and Heimberg, 2008; Spurr and Stopa, 2002). PEP tends to occur following social interactions and consists of a mental reviewing of distressing or embarrassing aspects of the interaction (Rachman, Grüter-Andrew, and Shafran, 2000).

PEP is highly related to rumination—indeed, there is great conceptual overlap. Like rumination, PEP is perseverative, negative, self-focused, and focuses on implications of one's perceived flaws and failures (see Brozovich and Heimberg, 2008; Spurr and Stopa, 2002). Like rumination and worry, PEP has been theorized to occur in response to the ambiguity or uncertainty inherent in social situations (Clark and Wells, 1995). Within the PEP literature, PEP is often described as a form of thinking about recent social interactions that is "ruminative" in nature (e.g., Gaydukevych and Kocovski, 2012). This conceptual overlap makes it unsurprising that rumination and PEP are correlated at the trait level (Gaydukevych and Kocovski, 2012).

There is also some evidence that ruminative thinking promotes unpleasant PEP and negative affect in response to social situations. Those with a ruminative thinking style were significantly less likely to engage in *positive* PEP following social anxiety manipulations in the lab (e.g, Gaydukevytch and Kocovski, 2011). Similarly, the presence of depressive symptoms has been found to moderate the relationship between social anxiety symptoms and negative PEP following social interactions (Kashdan and Roberts, 2007). In their study extending the response styles theory to anxiety, Wong and Moulds (2009) found that the maintaining effect of the rumination induction for anxious mood was particularly pronounced among individuals with social anxiety disorder. Being induced to ruminate also led socially anxiety participants, but not healthy controls, to maintain distorted negative beliefs about the self (e.g., people think badly of me).

As we have shown, study of rumination in the anxiety disorders sheds some light on both negative repetitive thinking broadly, as well as rumination specifically. Broadly, the process of repetitive negative thinking has the potential to magnify and perpetuate negative affect, distorted cognitions, and promote both mood and anxiety psychopathology. What appears to distinguish rumination specifically is largely its theme and content, which are past-focused and concerned with losses and failures. In contrast, worry tends to be future-oriented and concerned with threat, while PEP is largely focused on one's past social experiences or social behaviors. Although rumination appears to perpetuate anxious mood just as it does sad mood, the mechanisms by which rumination perpetuates anxious mood are not yet well understood. Future research could examine whether the same mechanisms linking rumination to sadness and depression – mood-congruent recall and impairment of problem solving and instrumental behavior – operate the same way with respect to anxiety.

EFFECTS OF RUMINATION ON ANGER

Just as ruminating in depressed or anxious states exacerbates those emotions, ruminating in the context of an angry emotional state exacerbates anger (e.g., Bushman, Bonacci, Pedersen, Vasquez, and Miller, 2005; Rusting and Nolen-Hoeksema, 1998). Anger rumination has been defined as on of the "unintentional and recurrent cognitive processes that emerge and continue after an episode of anger experience" (p. 690; Sukhodolsky, Golub, and Cromwell, 2001). Anger rumination has been defined in various ways. *Self-focused anger rumination* is conceptually similar to rumination as it is usually studied in the context of depressed moods. Self-focused anger rumination involves an inward focus of attention on the causes and consequences of the current angry state (Rusting and Nolen-Hoeksema, 1998). For example, when a woman receives a passive-aggressive email from a boss insulting her work, she might ruminate about how angry she feels in the moment, how she always reacts this way to her bosses emails, and what her angry feeling reveals about her character. Self-focused rumination in an angry mood has been found to increase the emotional experience of anger, increase self-critical negative affect, and maintain elevated cortisol levels following a transgression (Denson, Fabiansson, Creswell, and Pedersen, 2008; Pedersen et al., 2011).

Another form of rumination studied in the context of angry moods is *provocation-focused rumination* (Bushman, 2002; Pedersen et al., 2011). Provocation-focused rumination maintains a more external focus of attention on the provoking negative event or other person (Bushman, 2002). In the above mentioned situation, the employee might read the passive-aggressive email and instead ask herself why her boss sends such emails, imagine what the boss might have been thinking while sending the insulting email, and replay mentally what it was like to first open and read the email. Most research on anger rumination studies examines provocation-focused rumination by inducing anger either by having the participant recall and imagine a recent interpersonal provocation or by generating an interpersonal transgression in the lab with a scripted insult or provocation by an experimenter (e.g., Bushman et al., 2005; Ray, Wilhelm, and Gross, 2008). Self-report measures of individual differences in anger rumination assess ruminating in response to specific interpersonal situations (Wade, Vogel, Liao, and Goldman, 2008) and identify factors of anger rumination to be thoughts of revenge, angry memories, understanding the causes, and having angry afterthoughts of the transgression episode (Sukhodolsky et al., 2001). Thus, a majority of work on anger rumination assesses how individuals ruminate on the experience of the transgression or the transgressor, rather than on self-critical thoughts as depressive rumination often does.

Research on rumination following a transgression, interpersonal provocation, or recalled anger episode demonstrates a variety of downstream emotional, physiological, and behavioral consequences. For example, following an experimentally induced anger event, individuals induced to ruminate experience more angry cognitions associated with aggressive actions towards others and more cognitive perseveration about the provoking event than individuals not induced to ruminate (Gerin, 2006; Pedersen et al., 2011; Ray et al., 2008). Individuals induced to ruminate about a provoking insult while punching a punching bag later show increased aggressive behavior towards the person who angered them (Bushman, 2002). Ruminating following a provocation even leads to more displaced aggression towards innocent individuals (Bushman et al., 2005). Moreover, the angry emotional responding elicited by ruminating mediates the relationship between anger rumination and engaging in aggressive behavior (Bushman et al., 2005; Pedersen et al., 2011). Using our previous example, the angrier the disgruntled employee gets by ruminating on the passive-aggressive email, the more likely the she is to retaliate by sending back a terse or insulting email to her boss.

Angry rumination has negative physiological consequences. Ruminating in the context of angry moods, compared to reappraising the situation, elevates physiological responding by increasing sympathetic nervous system activation (Ray et al., 2008). Rumination when recalling angry autobiographical situations also increases cardiovascular reactivity (Ayduk and Kross, 2008). Provocation-focused rumination increases blood pressure compared to self-focused rumination or distraction (Pedersen et al., 2011), and high trait anger rumination is associated with slower blood pressure recovery following an angry recall task compared with low trait anger rumination (Gerin, 2006). In sum, angrily ruminating on a past transgression or provocation (either experimental or autobiographical recalled transgression) leads to increased emotional experiencing of anger and elevated physiological arousal. This heightened emotional reactivity directly results in increased behavioral aggression towards others.

Anger rumination, especially externally focused anger rumination, has strong implications for relationship interactions. For example, anger rumination is associated with the desire for revenge after an interpersonal transgression or slight (e.g., "I want to see her hurt and miserable;" McCullough, Bellah, Kilpatrick, and Johnson, 2001; McCullough et al., 1998). Increased anger rumination is also associated with reductions in forgiveness towards the transgressor (McCullough, Bono, and Root, 2007). In an experience sampling study, when individuals engaged in more anger rumination than was typical for them, elevations in vengefulness towards and avoidance of their transgressors also increased, supporting a causal role between anger rumination and forgiveness in relationships (McCullough et al., 2007). In fact, the more successful individuals are in reducing anger rumination over the course of time following a transgression, the more likely they are able to make progress in forgiving their transgressor (McCullough et al., 2001; McCullough et al., 2007). The emotional experience of anger also appears to mediate the relationship between rumination and revenge or avoidance of the transgressor (McCullough et al., 2007). In other words, the anger that results from ruminating on an interpersonal transgression is an important factor that impedes forgiveness.

In conclusion, anger rumination is most commonly researched as rumination about a personal transgression or provocation and this outwardly focused rumination leads to an exacerbation of anger. This increased anger reactivity appears to be directly implicated in a variety of maladaptive outcomes, including increased aggressive cognitions (i.e., revenge and hurtful thoughts), increased aggressive behaviors, and decreased forgiveness towards their transgressors. Given the consistent findings in anger rumination, it is surprising that this work has not been applied more extensively to clinical populations. Initial findings indicate that anger rumination is associated with bulimic symptoms, anxiety, depression, alcohol use and borderline personality disorder (BPD) symptoms (Selby, Anestis, and Joiner, 2008). Anger rumination even predicts BPD features, above and beyond depressive rumination and trait emotional tendencies (Baer and Sauer, 2011). Clinical research would benefit by examining more closely anger rumination in the context of specific psychopathologies that exhibit dysregulated anger, such as BPD.

EFFECTS OF RUMINATION ON POSITIVE EMOTION

Most work has examined rumination in the context of negative emotional states, but emerging work is examining the effects of ruminating in response to positive or happy moods. This literature arose out of research on rumination in bipolar disorder, a disorder in which individuals ruminate not only in the context of sad and depressed states, but also in the context of happy and manic states. In order to assess rumination in the context of positive mood states, Feldman et al. (2008) developed the Responses to Positive Affect scale (RPA), a self-report measure designed to parallel Nolen-Hoeksema's RRS (Treynor et al., 2003). The RPA measures trait tendencies to engage in positive rumination, which is defined as "the tendency to respond to positive affective states with recurrent thoughts about positive self-qualities, positive affective experience, and one's favorable life circumstances." The RPA consists of three subscales: *emotion focused positive rumination* (e.g., "Thing about how happy you feel"), *self-focused positive rumination* (e.g., "Think about how proud you are of yourself") and *dampening of positive emotion* (e.g., "Think about things that could go wrong") (Feldman et al., 2008). Dampening refers to the down-regulation of positive affect and is defined as "the tendency to respond to positive mood states with mental strategies to reduce the intensity and duration of the positive mood state" (p. 509; Feldman et al., 2008). Emotion- focused and self-focused positive rumination are often correlated with each other and are hypothesized to spiral a positive mood upwards, while dampening, in contrast, diminishes positive moods (Feldman et al., 2008; Johnson, McKenzie, and McMurrich, 2008).

Trait tendency to ruminate in response to positive mood states is associated with manic and depressive symptoms and clinical characteristics in both healthy and clinical populations. For example, positive rumination (emotion- and self-focused positive rumination) is associated with increased vulnerability to mania, greater self-esteem, elevated current manic symptoms, and fewer current depressive symptoms in young adult samples (Feldman et al., 2008). Positive rumination is also associated with higher trait positive affect and lower negative affect in a non-clinical sample (Raes, Daems, Feldman, Johnson, and Van Gucht, 2009). In the context of bipolar disorder, positive rumination is associated with both a history of mania and current manic symptoms as well as higher frequency of past manic and depressive episodes (Gruber, Eidelman, Johnson, Smith, and Harvey, 2011; Johnson et al., 2008). Thus, when feeling happy, that positive emotion may be further exacerbated by engaging in emotion or self-focused positive rumination.

The dampening subscale of the RPA, on the other hand, appears to be associated with trait depressive rumination (brooding and reflection) as well as current depressive symptoms in young adult non-clinical samples (Feldman et al., 2008). Dampening is associated with lower self-esteem, higher negative affect and lower positive affect (Feldman et al., 2008; Raes et al., 2009). Dampening also predicts increased depressive symptoms in non-clinical youth and young adult samples, above and beyond the effects of depressive rumination (Bijttebier, Raes, Vasey, and Feldman, 2011; Raes et al., 2009). Interestingly, dampening is also associated with higher vulnerability towards mania but not with current manic symptoms (Feldman et al., 2008; Johnson and Jones, 2009). In bipolar disorder, dampening is associated with elevated frequency of previous manic symptoms and it also predicts the onset of both manic and depressive symptoms six months later (Gilbert and Gruber, in preparation; Gruber et al., 2011). Although at first glance a subscale on dampening positive emotion may seem out of place on a positive rumination questionnaire, what the subscale really appears to be assessing is a form of negative rumination when in a positive mood state. For instance, having just gained a job promotion, an individual may begin ruminating (i.e., engage in "dampening") about all the ways it could go wrong and reasons for which the promotion is not deserved. In this way, dampening exacerbates negative affect rather than the initial positive affect.

Positive rumination and dampening have also been studied in experimental paradigms. For example, both healthy individuals and those with bipolar disorder show higher positive affect and elevated heart rate when engaging in an immersed and self-focused rumination induction while thinking of a positive memory compared with a distanced reflection of the memory (Gruber, Harvey, and Johnson, 2009). When ruminating about a future goal, individuals with bipolar disorder, major depression, and healthy adults all demonstrate increases in negative and positive emotional arousal and elevated heart rate (Gilbert and Gruber, in preparation), possibly indicating competing influences of positive rumination and dampening. Trait tendencies to engage in positive rumination are also correlated with increased positive affect following a rumination induction in individuals with bipolar disorder

(Gilbert and Gruber, under review), while trait tendencies to engage in dampening are correlated with increased negative affect following a rumination induction (Gilbert and Gruber, under review). Lastly, elevated heart rate during a rumination induction is associated with a history of more depressive episodes in individuals with bipolar disorder (Gruber et al., 2011). In sum, experimental research demonstrates mixed results on the emotions that are exacerbated by ruminating, potentially indicating the different influences of positive rumination and dampening.

Taking stock, it appears that individuals can ruminate in the context of positive mood states, and that doing so exacerbates the current emotional state, as it does in the context of negative emotional states. Moreover, these tendencies to engage in positive rumination appear to be related to increased manic and depressive symptom severity. The construct of dampening of positive emotion is an interesting facet of the trait positive rumination scale, as it appears to capture a form of negative rumination (i.e., brooding) in the context of a positive mood state. Interestingly, although related to negative rumination, this type of regulation of positive emotion uniquely predicts manic and depressive symptoms in both clinical and non-clinical samples. These findings highlight the importance of studying how tendencies to ruminate in various emotional states may differ between individuals. Further investigation of positive rumination is warranted, given the initial associations with manic and depressive clinical characteristics. Future work should focus on understanding why some individuals tend to engage in positive rumination in positive mood states while other individuals tend to engage in dampening of positive mood states.

CONCLUSION

Rumination, defined as perseverative, non-instrumental thinking about an emotion or mood, and its causes, consequences, and meanings, thus appears to be a transdiagnostic risk factor for the maintenance and exacerbation of emotions and moods of a variety of types (see also Nolen-Hoeksema and Watkins, 2011; Watkins, 2009). Given an individual with a strong tendency to ruminate, what then determines what emotion or mood he or she ruminates on, and the likelihood that this rumination leads to clinically significant mood symptoms?

Nolen-Hoeksema and Watkins (2011) argue that the specific mood or symptom outcomes of rumination depend on environmental or biological moderators that (a) raise particular concerns or themes that rumination then amplifies or (b) shape ruminative responses through reinforcements and punishments.

First, environmental events or changes can raise specific concerns or themes that rumination operates on: events that signal threat trigger anxiety, events that signal loss trigger sadness, events that signal provocation trigger anger, and events that signal gain trigger positive affect (Frijda, 1986). For example, McCabe, Antony, Summerfeldt, Liss, and Swinson (2003) reported that 92% of adults with social phobia reported a history of severe teasing in childhood, compared with only 50% and 35% of people with panic disorder or obsessive–compulsive disorder, respectively. Among people who have had socially traumatizing experiences, ruminators will rehearse memories of the experiences, analyzing what they did right and wrong, and how other people reacted to them, potentially leading to social anxiety disorder (Kashdan and Roberts, 2007). In contrast, a long-term study of bereavement found that after the loss of a close loved one, rumination was significantly more strongly related to symptoms of depression than symptoms of anxiety or anger (see Nolen-Hoeksema and Larson, 1999; Nolen-Hoeksema and Watkins, 2011).

Biological factors may also lead individuals to experience more of one emotion or type of concern than another, and in interaction with rumination, may then lead to specific symptom types. For example, a susceptibility to panic attacks due to dysfunction in systems regulating the fight-or-flight response (Roy-Byrne et al., 2006) could interact with ruminative tendencies to lead to panic disorder. On the other hand, dysfunction in the frontal cortex, basal ganglia and thalamus, regions implicated in obsessive thoughts and compulsive behaviors (Rauch et al., 2003; Saxena and Rauch, 2000), could interact with ruminative tendencies and lead to obsessive-compulsive disorder (Salkovskis, 1999).

Second, the environment and biology may also shape ruminative responses through reinforcements and punishments. For example, men and women seem to differ in the types of emotions they ruminate about, and these differences are likely shaped by social conditioning (Nolen-Hoeksema, 2012). Women are more likely than men to ruminate in the context of sadness or anxiety (Butler and Nolen-Hoeksema, 1994), while men are more likely than women to ruminate in the context of anger (Knobloch-Westerwick and Alter, 2006; Rusting and Nolen-Hoeksema, 1998; Sukhodolsky, Golub, and Cromwell, 2001). Sadness and anxiety are more socially acceptable emotions for women than men, whereas anger is a more socially acceptable emotion for men than women (Nolen-Hoeksema and Rusting, 1999). Thus, women with ruminative tendencies may be more likely to develop depressive or anxiety disorders because their ruminations are reinforced, or at least not discouraged, when they are sad or anxious, but men will not be reinforced, and indeed may be punished socially, for ruminating on sadness or anxiety. In contrast, men with ruminative tendencies may not be punished as much for ruminating on anger as women.

Much more research is needed on the moderators that determine what types of outcomes rumination will contribute to in different individuals. Further, research is needed to determine whether the mechanisms linking rumination to persistent symptoms of anxiety, anger, and excessive positive mood are the same as those linking rumination to persistent symptoms of depression. The research to date, however, provides compelling evidence that rumination is an important transdiagnostic factor leading everyday emotions to become clinically significant mood symptoms.

REFERENCES

Aldao, A., Nolen-Hoeksema, S., and Schweizer, S. (2010). Emotion regulation strategies across psychopathology: A meta-analytic review. *Clinical Psychology Review, 30*, 217-237.

American Psychiatric Association. (2004). *Diagnostic and statistical manual of mental disorders* (4th ed., Text Revision). Washington, D C: Author.

Ayduk, Ö., and Kross, E. (2008). Enhancing the pace of recovery: Self-distanced analysis of negative experiences reduces blood pressure reactivity. *Psychological Science, 19*(3), 229-231. doi: 10.1111/j.1467-9280.2008.02073.x.

Aymanns, P., Filipp, S. H., and Klauer, T. (1995). Family support and coping with cancer: Some determinants and adaptive correlates. *British Journal of Social Psychology, 34,* 107-124.

Baer, R. A., and Sauer, S. E. (2011). Relationships between depressive rumination, anger rumination, and borderline personality features. *Personality Disorders: Theory, Research, and Treatment, 2*(2), 142-150. doi: 10.1037/a0019478.

Bagby, R. M., Rector, N. A., Bacchiochi, J. R., and McBride, C. (2004). The stability of the response styles questionnaire rumination scale in a sample of patients with major depression. *Cognitive Therapy and Research, 28,* 527-538.

Bijttebier, P., Raes, F., Vasey, M. W., and Feldman, G. C. (2011). Responses to Positive Affect Predict Mood Symptoms in Children Under Conditions of Stress: A Prospective Study. *Journal of Abnormal Child Psychology, 40*(3), 381-389. doi: 10.1007/s10802-011-9579-2.

Bjornsson, A., Carey, G., Hauser, M., Karris, A., Kaufmann, V., Sheets, E., and Craighead, W. E. (2010). The Effects of Experiential Avoidance and Rumination on Depression among College Students. *International Journal of Cognitive Therapy, 3*(4), 389-401.

Berenbaum, H., Bredemeier, K., and Thompson, R. J. (2008). Intolerance of uncertainty: Exploring its dimensionality and associations with need for cognitive closure, psychopathology, and personality. *Journal of Anxiety Disorders, 22*(1), 117-25. doi:10.1016/j.janxdis.2007.01.004.

Blagden, J. C., and Craske, M. G. (1996). Effects of active and passive rumination and distraction: A pilot replication with anxious mood. *Journal of Anxiety Disorders, 10*(4), 243 - 252. doi:10.1016/0887-6185(96)00009-6.

Borkovec, T. D., Alcaine, O., and Behar, E. (2004). Avoidance theory of worry and generalized anxiety disorder. In D. Mennin, R. Heimberg, and C. L. Turk (Eds.), *Generalized anxiety disorder: Advances in research and practice* (pp. 77-108). New York, NY: Guilford Press.

Borkovec, T. D., Robinson, E., Pruzinsky, T., and DePree, J. A. (1983). Preliminary exploration of worry: Some characteristics and processes. *Behaviour Research and Therapy, 21*(1), 9-16.

Brozovich, F., and Heimberg, R. G. (2008). An analysis of post-event processing in social anxiety disorder. *Clin. Psychol. Rev., 28*(6), 891-903. doi:10.1016/j.cpr.2008.01.002.

Bushman, B. J. (2002). Does Venting Anger Feed or Extinguish the Flame? Catharsis, Rumination, Distraction, Anger, and Aggressive Responding. *Personality and Social Psychology Bulletin, 28*(6), 724-731. doi: 10.1177/0146167202289002

Bushman, B. J., Bonacci, A. M., Pedersen, W. C., Vasquez, E. A., and Miller, N. (2005). Chewing on it can chew you up: Effects of rumination on triggered displaced aggression. *Jounral of Personality and Social Psychology, 88*(6), 969-983.

Butler, L. D., and Nolen-Hoeksema, S. (1994). Gender differences in responses to depressed mood in a college sample. *Sex Roles, 30,* 331-346.

Carver, C. S., and Scheier, M. F. (1998). *On the self-regulation of behavior.* New York, NY: Cambridge University Press.

Castaneda, J. O., and Segerstrom, S. C. (2004). Effect of stimulus type and worry on physiological response to fear. *J Anxiety Disord, 18*(6), 809-23. doi:10.1016/j.janxdis.2003.10.003.

Clark, D. M., and Wells, A. (1995). A cognitive model of social phobia. In R. G. Heimberg, M. R. Liebowitz, D. A. Hope, and F. R. Schneider (Eds.), *Social phobia: Diagnosis, assessment, and treatment* (pp. 69-93). New York, NY: Guilford Press.

Clark, L. A., and Watson, D. (1991). Tripartite model of anxiety and depression: Psychometric evidence and taxonomic implications. *Journal of Abnormal Psychology, 100*(3), 316.

de Jong-Meyer, R., Beck, B., and Riede, K. (2009). Relationships between rumination, worry, intolerance of uncertainty and metacognitive beliefs. *Personality and Individual Differences, 46*(4), 547-551. doi:10.1016/j.paid.2008.12.010.

Denson, T. F., Fabiansson, E. C., Creswell, J. D., and Pedersen, W. C. (2008). Experimental effects of rumination styles on salivary cortisol responses. *Motivation and Emotion, 33*(1), 42-48. doi: 10.1007/s11031-008-9114-0.

Donaldson, C., and Lam, D. (2004). Rumination, mood and social problem-solving in major depression. *Psychological Medicine, 34,* 1309-1318.

Dugas, M. J., Gagnon, F., Ladouceur, R., and Freeston, M. H. (1998). Generalized anxiety disorder: A preliminary test of a conceptual model. *Behaviour Research and Therapy, 36*(2), 215-226.

Duval, S., and Wicklund, R. A. (1972). *A theory of objective self awareness.* Oxford, England: Academic Press.

Feldman, G. C., Joormann, J., and Johnson, S. L. (2008). Responses to positive affect: A self-report measure of rumination and dampening. *Cognitive Therapy and Research, 32*(4), 507-525. doi: 10.1007/s10608-006-9083-0.

Fresco, D. M., Frankel, A. N., Mennin, D. S., Turk, C. L., and Heimberg, R. G. (2002). *Cognitive Therapy and Research, 26*(2), 179-188. doi:10.1023/A:1014517718949.

Frijda, N. H. (1986). *The emotions.* Cambridge: Cambridge University Press.

Gaydukevych, D., and Kocovski, N. L. (2012). Effect of self-focused attention on post-event processing in social anxiety. *Behaviour Research and Therapy, 50*(1), 47-55. doi:10.1016/j.brat.2011.10.010.

Gentes, E. L., and Ruscio, A. M. (2011). A meta-analysis of the relation of intolerance of uncertainty to symptoms of generalized anxiety disorder, major depressive disorder, and obsessive-compulsive disorder. *Clinical Psychology Review, 31*(6), 923-33. doi:10.1016/j.cpr.2011.05.001.

Gerin, W. (2006). The Role of Angry Rumination and Distraction in Blood Pressure Recovery From Emotional Arousal. *Psychosomatic Medicine, 68*(1), 64-72. doi: 10.1097/01.psy.0000195747.12404.aa.

Gilbert, K., and Gruber, J. (in preparation). Are goals really rewarding? Emotion regulation and goal pursuit in bipolar disorder and major depression.

Gilbert, K., Nolen-Hoeksema, S. and Gruber, J. (under review). Positive emotion regulation srategies: Divergent relationships with emotional responding and prospective illness course in mood disorders. Giorgio, J. M., Sanflippo, J., Kleiman, E., Reilly, D., Bender, R. E., Wagner, C. A., . . . Alloy, L. B. (2010). An experiential avoidance conceptualization of depressive rumination: Three tests of the model. *Behaviour Research and Therapy, 48*(10), 1021-31. doi:10.1016/j.brat.2010.07.004.

Goldwin, M., and Behar, E. (2011). Concreteness of idiographic periods of worry and depressive rumination. *Cognitive Therapy and Research.* doi:10.1007/s10608-011-9428-1

Gorski, J., and Young, M. A. (2002). Sociotropy/autonomy, self-construal, response style, and gender in adolescents. *Personality and Individual Differences, 32*, 463-478.

Greenberg, J., Pyszczynski, T., Burling, J., and Tibbs, K. (1992). Depression, self-focused attention, and the self-serving attributional bias. *Personality and Individual Differences, 13*, 959-965.

Gruber, J., Eidelman, P., Johnson, S. L., Smith, B., and Harvey, A. G. (2011). Hooked on a feeling: Rumination about positive and negative emotion in inter-episode bipolar disorder. *Journal of Abnormal Psychology, 120*(4), 956-961. doi: 10.1037/a0023667.

Gruber, J., Harvey, A. G., and Johnson, S. L. (2009). Reflective and ruminative processing of positive emotional memories in bipolar disorder and healthy controls. *Behavior Research and Therapy, 47*(8), 697-704. doi: 10.1016/j.brat.2009.05.005.

Hayes, S. C., Wilson, K. G., Gifford, E. V., Follette, V. M., and Strosahl, K. (1996). Experiential avoidance and behavioral disorders: a functional dimensional approach to diagnosis and treatment. *Journal of consulting and Clinical Psychology, 64*(6), 1152.

Holmes, E. A., and Mathews, A. (2010). Mental imagery in emotion and emotional disorders. *Clinical Psychology Review, 30*(3), 349-62. doi:10.1016/j.cpr.2010.01.001.

Hong, R. Y. (2007). Differential associations with anxious and depressive symptoms and coping behavior. *Behaviour Research and Therapy, 45*, 277-290.

Jacobson, N. S., Martell, C. R., and Dimidjian, S. (2001). Behavioral activation treatment for depression: Returning to contextual roots. *Clinical Psychology: Science and Practice, 8*, 255-270.

Johnson, S. L., and Jones, S. (2009). Cognitive correlates of mania risk: are responses to success, positive moods, and manic symptoms distinct or overlapping? *Journal of Clinical Psychology, 65*(9), 891-905. doi: 10.1002/jclp.20585

Johnson, S. L., McKenzie, G., and McMurrich, S. (2008). Ruminative responses to negative and positive affect among students diagnosed with bipolar disorder and major depressive disorder. *Cognitive Therapy and Research, 32*(5), 702-713. doi: 10.1007/s10608-007-9158-6.

Joormann, J. (2010). Cognitive inhibition and emotion regulation in depression. *Current Directions in Psychological Science, 19*, 161-166.

Just, N., and Alloy, L. B. (1997). The response styles theory of depression: Tests and an extension of the theory. *Journal of Abnormal Psychology, 106*, 221-229.

Kashdan, T. B., and Roberts, J. E. (2007). Social anxiety, depressive symptoms, and post-event rumination: Affective consequences and social contextual influences. *Journal of Anxiety Disorders, 21*(3), 284-301. doi:10.1016/j.janxdis.2006.05.009.

Kessler, R. C., Merikangas, K. R., and Wang, P. S. (2007). Prevalence, comorbidity, and service utilization for mood disorders in the united states at the beginning of the twenty-first century. *Annual Review of Clinical Psychology, 3*, 137-58. doi:10.1146/annurev.clinpsy.3.022806.091444.

Knobloch-Westerwick, S., and Alter, S. (2006). Mood adjustment to social situations through mass media use: How men ruminate and women dissipate angry moods. *Human Communication Research, 32*, 58–73. doi:10.1111/j.1468-2958.2006.00003.x.

Kuehner, C., and Weber, I. (1999). Responses to depression in unipolar depressed patients: An investigation of Nolen-Hoeksema's response styles theory. *Psychological Medicine, 29*, 1323-1333.

Lavender, A., and Watkins, E. (2004). Rumination and future thinking in depression. *British Journal of Clinical Psychology, 43*, 129-142.

Liverant, G. I., Kamholz, B. W., Sloan, D. M., and Brown, T. A. (2011). Rumination in clinical depression: A type of emotional suppression? *Cognitive Therapy and Research, 35*(3), 253-265. doi:10.1007/s10608-010-9304-4.

Lyubomirsky, S., and Nolen-Hoeksema, S. (1993). Self-perpetuating properties of dysphoric rumination. *Journal of Personality and Social Psychology, 65*, 339-349.

Lyubomirsky, S., and Nolen-Hoeksema, S. (1995). Effects of self-focused rumination on negative thinking and interpersonal problem solving. *Journal of Personality and Social Psychology, 69*, 176-190.

Lyubomirsky, S., Caldwell, N. D., and Nolen-Hoeksema, S. (1998). Effects of ruminative and distracting responses to depressed mood on retrieval of autobiographical memories. *Journal of Personality and Social Psychology, 75*, 166-177.

Lyubomirsky, S., Kasri, F., Chang, O., and Chung, I. (2006). Ruminative response styles and delay of seeking diagnosis for breast cancer symptoms. *Journal of Social and Clinical Psychology, 25*, 276-304.

Lyubomirsky, S., Tucker, K. L., Caldwell, N. D., and Berg, K. (1999). Why ruminators are poor problem solvers: Clues from the phenomenology of dysphoric rumination. *Journal of Personality and Social Psychology, 77*, 1041-1060.

McFarland, C., and Buehler, R. (1998). The impact of negative affect on autobiographical memory: The role of self-focused attention to moods. *Journal of Personality and Social Psychology, 75*, 1424-1440.

Marroquín, B. M., Fontes, M., Scilletta, A., and Miranda, R. (2010). Ruminative subtypes and coping responses: Active and passive pathways to depressive symptoms. *Cognition and Emotion, 24*(8), 1446-1455. doi: 10.1080/02699930903510212.

Martin, L. L., and Tesser, A. (1996). Some ruminative thoughts. In R. S. Wyer, Jr. (Ed.), *Ruminative thoughts* (pp. 1-47). Mahwah, NJ: Lawrence Erlbaum.

McCabe, R. E., Antony, M. M., Summerfeldt, L. J., Liss, A., and Swinson, R. P. (2003). Preliminary examination of the relationship between anxiety disorders in adults and self-reported history of teasing or bullying experiences. *Cognitive Behavior Therapy*, 32,187-193.

McCullough, M. E., Bellah, C. G., Kilpatrick, S. D., and Johnson, J. L. (2001). Vengefulness: Relationships with Forgiveness, Rumination, Well-Being, and the Big Five. *Personality and Social Psychology Bulletin, 27*(5), 601-610. doi: 10.1177/0146167201275008.

McCullough, M. E., Bono, G., and Root, L. M. (2007). Rumination, emotion, and forgiveness: Three longitudinal studies. *Journal of Personality and Social Psychology, 92*(3), 490-505. doi: 10.1037/0022-3514.92.3.490.

McCullough, M. E., Rachal, K. C., Sandage, S. J., Worthington Jr., E. L., Brown, S. W., and Hight, T. L. (1998). Interpersonal forgiving in close relationships: II. Theoretical elaboration and measurement. *Journal of Personality and Social Psychology, 75*(6), 1586-1603.

McEvoy, P. M., Mahoney, A. E. J., and Moulds, M. L. (2010). Are worry, rumination, and post-event processing one and the same? Development of the repetitive thinking questionnaire. *J Anxiety Disord, 24*(5), 509-19. doi:10.1016/j.janxdis.2010.03.008.

McLaughlin, K. A., and Nolen-Hoeksema, S. (2011). Rumination as a transdiagnostic factor in depression and anxiety. *Behaviour Research and Therapy*, *49*(3), 186-93. doi:10.1016/j.brat.2010.12.006.

Mineka, S., Watson, D., and Clark, L. A. (1998). Comorbidity of anxiety and unipolar mood disorders. *Annual Review of Psychology*, *49*(1), 377-412.

Miranda, R., Fontes, M., and Marroquín, B. (2008). Cognitive content-specificity in future expectancies: Role of hopelessness and intolerance of uncertainty in depression and GAD symptoms. *Behaviour Research and Therapy*, *46*(10), 1151-9. doi:10.1016/j.brat. 2008.05.009.

Moulds, M.L., Kandris, E., Starr, S., and Wong, A.C.M. (2007). The relationship between rumination, avoidance and depression in a non-clinical sample. *Behaviour Research and Therapy, 45*, 251-261.

Mor, N., and Winquist, J. (2002). Self-focused attention and negative affect: A meta-analysis. *Psychological Bulletin, 128*, 638-662.

Muris, P., Roelofs, J., Rassin, E., Franken, I., and Mayer, B. (2005). Mediating effects of rumination and worry on the links between neuroticism, anxiety and depression. *Personality and Individual Differences*, *39*(6), 1105-1111. doi:10.1016/j.paid. 2005.04.005.

Nesse, R. M. (2000). Is depression an adaptation? *Archives of General Psychiatry, 57,* 14-20.

Nolen-Hoeksema, S. (1991). Responses to depression and their effects on the duration of depressive episodes. *Journal of Abnormal Psychology, 100*, 569-582.

Nolen-Hoeksema, S. (2000). The role of rumination in depressive disorders and mixed anxiety/depressive symptoms. *Journal of Abnormal Psychology*, *109*(3), 504. doi:10.1037/0021-843X.109.3.504.

Nolen-Hoeksema, S. (2012). Emotion regulation and psychopathology: The role of gender. *Annual Review of Clinical Psychology, 8*, 161-87. doi: 10.1146/annurev-clinpsy-032511-143109.

Nolen-Hoeksema, S., and Davis, C. G. (1999). "Thanks for sharing that": Ruminators and their social support networks. *Journal of Personality and Social Psychology, 77*, 801-814.

Nolen-Hoeksema, S., and Larson, J. (1999). *Coping with loss*. Mahwah, NJ: Lawrence Erlbaum.

Nolen-Hoeksema, S., Larson, J., and Grayson, C. (1999). Explaining the gender difference in depressive symptoms. *Journal of Personality and Social Psychology, 77,* 1061-1072.

Nolen-Hoeksema, S., and Morrow, J. (1993). Effects of rumination and distraction on naturally occurring depressed mood. *Cognition and Emotion, 7*, 561-570.

Nolen-Hoeksema, S., Parker, L., and Larson, J. (1994). Ruminative coping with depressed mood following loss. *Journal of Personality and Social Psychology, 67*, 92-104.

Nolen-Hoeksema, S. and Rusting, C. (1999). Gender differences in well-being. In D. Kahneman, E. Diener, and N. Schwarz (Eds.*), Foundations of hedonic psychology: Scientific perspectives on enjoyment and suffering.* (pp. 330-352). New York: Russell Sage Foundation.

Nolen-Hoeksema, S., Wisco, B. E., and Lyubomisky, S. (2008). Rethinking rumination. *Perspectives on Psychological Science, 3*, 400-424.

Nolen-Hoeksema, S., and Watkins, E. R. (2011). A heuristic for developing transdiagnostic models of psychopathology: Explaining multifinality and divergent trajectories.

Perspectives on Psychological Science, 6, 589-609.Papageorgiou, C., and Wells, A. (2001). Metacognitive beliefs about rumination in recurrent major depression. *Cognitive and Behavioral Practice,* 8(2), 160-164.

Papageorgiou, C., and Wells, A. (2002). Positive beliefs about depressive rumination: Development and preliminary validation of a self-report scale. *Behavior Therapy,* 32(1), 13-26.

Pedersen, W. C., Denson, T. F., Goss, R. J., Vasquez, E. A., Kelley, N. J., and Miller, N. (2011). The impact of rumination on aggressive thoughts, feelings, arousal, and behaviour. *British Journal of Social Psychology, 50*(2), 281-301. doi: 10.1348/014466610x515696.

Pyszczynski, T., Hamilton, J. C., Herring, F. H., and Greenberg, J. (1989). Depression, self-focused attention, and the negative memory bias. *Journal of Personality and Social Psychology, 57,* 351-357.

Pyszczynski, T., Holt, K., and Greenberg, J. (1987). Depression, self-focused attention, and expectancies for positive and negative future life events for self and others. *Journal of Personality and Social Psychology, 52,* 994-1001.

Rachman, S., Grüter-Andrew, J., and Shafran, R. (2000). Post-event processing in social anxiety. *Behaviour Research and Therapy,* 38(6), 611-617.

Rauch S.L., Shin L.M., Segal E, Pitman R.K., Carson M.A., Whalen P.J., et al (2003). Selectively reduced regional cortical volumes in posttraumatic stress disorder. *Neuroreport 14*(7), 913–916.

Raes, F., Daems, K., Feldman, G. C., Johnson, S. L., and Van Gucht, D. (2009). A psychometric evaluation of the Dutch version of the responses to positive affect questionnaire. *Psychologica Belgica,* 49(4).

Ray, R. D., Wilhelm, F. H., and Gross, J. J. (2008). All in the mind's eye? Anger rumination and reappraisal. *J. Pers. Soc. Psychol., 94*(1), 133-145. doi: 10.1037/0022-3514.94.1.133.

Rimes, K. A., and Watkins, E. (2005). The effects of self-focused rumination on global negative self-judgments in depression. *Behaviour Research and Therapy, 43,* 1673-1681.

Rood, L. R., J, Bogels, S., Nolen-Hoeksema, S., and Schouten, E. (2009). The influence of emotion-focused rumination and distraction on depressive symptoms in non-clinical youth: A meta-analytic review. Clinical Psychology Review, 29, 607-616.

Roy-Byrne, P.P., Craske, M., and Stein, M.B. (2006). Panic Disorder. *The Lancet,* 369, 1023-1032.

Ruscio, A. M., Seitchik, A. E., Gentes, E. L., Jones, J. D., and Hallion, L. S. (2011). Perseverative thought: A robust predictor of response to emotional challenge in generalized anxiety disorder and major depressive disorder. *Behaviour Research and Therapy, 49*(12), 867-74. doi:10.1016/j.brat.2011.10.001.

Rusting, C. L., and Nolen-Hoeksema, S. (1998). Regulating responses to anger: Effects of rumination and distraction on angry mood. *Journal of Personality and Social Psychology,* 74(3), 790-803. doi: 10.1037/0022-3514.74.3.790.

Salkovskis, P. M. (1999). Understanding and treating obsessive-compulsive disorder. *Behavior Research and Therapy, 37,* S29–S52. doi.org/10.1016/S0005-7967(99)00049-2. Cited by in Scopus (183).

Saxena, S. and Rauch, S. (2000). Functional neuroimaging and the neuroanatomy of obsessive-compulsive disorder. Psychiatric Clinics of North America, 23, 563-586. doi: 10.1016/S0193-953X%2805%2970181-7.

Schienle, A., Schäfer, A., Pignanelli, R., and Vaitl, D. (2009). Worry tendencies predict brain activation during aversive imagery. *Neuroscience Letters*, *461*(3), 289-92. doi:10.1016/j.neulet.2009.06.041

Schwartz-Mette, R. A., and Rose, A. J. (2009). Conversational self-focus in adolescent friendships: Observational assessment of an interpersonal process and relations with internalizing symptoms and friendship quality. *Journal of Social and Clinical Psychology, 28,* 1263-1297.

Segerstrom, S. C., Tsao, J. C. I., Alden, L. E., and Craske, M. G. (2000). Worry and rumination: Repetitive thought as a concomitant and predictor of negative mood. *Cognitive Therapy and Research*, *24*(6), 671-688.

Selby, E. A., Anestis, M. D., and Joiner, T. E. (2008). Understanding the relationship between emotional and behavioral dysregulation: Emotional cascades. *Behavior Research and Therapy, 46*(5), 593-611.

Spasojevic, J., and Alloy, L. B. (2001). Rumination as a common mechanism relating depressive risk to depression. *Emotion, 1,* 25-37.

Spurr, J. M., and Stopa, L. (2002). Self-focused attention in social phobia and social anxiety. *Clinical Psychology Review*, *22*(7), 947-975.

Starr, L. R., and Davila, J. (2011). Responding to anxiety with rumination and hopelessness: Mechanism of anxiety-depression symptom co-occurrence? *Cognitive Therapy and Research.* doi:10.1007/s10608-011-9363-1.

Sukhodolsky, D. G., Golub, A., and Cromwell, E. N. (2001). Development and validation of the anger rumination scale. *Personality and Individual Differences, 31,* 689-700.

Trapnell, P. D., and Campbell, J. D. (1999). Private self-consciousness and the five-factor model of personality: Distinguishing rumination from reflection. *Journal of Personality and Social Psychology, 76,* 284-304.

Treynor, W., Gonzalez, R., and Nolen-Hoeksema, S. (2003). Rumination reconsidered: A psychometric analysis. *Cognitive Therapy and Research, 27,* 247-259.

Tull, M. T., and Gratz, K. L. (2008). Further examination of the relationship between anxiety sensitivity and depression: the mediating role of experiential avoidance and difficulties engaging in goal-directed behavior when distressed. *Journal of Anxiety Disorders, 22*(2), 199-210. doi: 10.1016/j.janxdis.2007.03.005.

Wade, N. G., Vogel, D. L., Liao, K. Y.-H., and Goldman, D. B. (2008). Measuring state-specific rumination: Development of the Rumination About an Interpersonal Offense Scale. *Journal of Counseling Psychology, 55*(3), 419-426. doi: 10.1037/0022-0167.55.3.419.

Ward, A., Lyubomirsky, S., Sousa, L., and Nolen-Hoeksema, S. (2003). Can't quite commit: Rumination and uncertainty. *Personality and Social Psychology Bulletin, 29, 96-107.*

Watkins, E. R. (2008). Constructive and unconstructive repetitive thought. *Psychological Bulletin, 134,* 163-206.

Watkins, E. (2004). Appraisals and strategies associated with rumination and worry. *Personality and Individual Differences*, *37*(4), 679-694. doi:10.1016/j.paid.2003.10.002.

Watkins, E. R. (2009). Depressive rumination and co-morbidity: Evidence for brooding as a transdiagnostic process. *Journal of Rational-Emotive and Cognitive-Behavioral Therapy*, *27*(3), 160-175. doi:10.1007/s10942-009-0098-9.

Watkins, E., and Baracaia, S. (2002). Rumination and social problem-solving in depression. *Behaviour Research and Therapy, 40,* 1179-1189.

Watkins, E., and Moulds, M. (2005). Distinct modes of ruminative self-focus: Impact of abstract versus concrete rumination on problem solving in depression. *Emotion, 5,* 319-328.

Watkins, E., and Moulds, M. (2005). Positive beliefs about rumination in depression--a replication and extension. *Personality and Individual Differences, 39*(1), 73-82.

Watkins, E., Moulds, M., and Mackintosh, B. (2005). Comparisons between rumination and worry in a non-clinical population. *Behaviour Research and Therapy, 43*(12), 1577-85. doi:10.1016/j.brat.2004.11.008.

Watkins, E., and Teasdale, J. D. (2001). Rumination and overgeneral memory in depression: Effects of self-focus and analytic thinking. *Journal of Abnormal Psychology, 110,* 353-357.

Wells, A. (1995). Meta-Cognition and worry: A cognitive model of generalized anxiety disorder. *Behavioural and Cognitive Psychotherapy, 23,* 301-301.

Wong, Q. J. J., and Moulds, M. L. (2009). Impact of rumination versus distraction on anxiety and maladaptive self-beliefs in socially anxious individuals. *Behaviour Research and Therapy, 47*(10), 861-7. doi:10.1016/j.brat.2009.06.014.

Woody, S., and Rachman, S. (1994). Generalized anxiety disorder (GAD) as an unsuccessful search for safety. *Clinical Psychology Review, 14*(8), 743-753.

Yook, K., Kim, K. H., Suh, S. Y., and Lee, K. S. (2010). Intolerance of uncertainty, worry, and rumination in major depressive disorder and generalized anxiety disorder. *Journal of Anxiety Disorders, 24*(6), 623-8. doi:10.1016/j.janxdis.2010.04.003.

In: Handbook of Psychology of Emotions
Editors: C. Mohiyeddini, M. Eysenck and S. Bauer

ISBN: 978-1-62808-053-7
© 2013 Nova Science Publishers, Inc.

Chapter 13

Strengthening Positive Functioning in Children Growing up Amidst Political and Military Violence: The Role of Emotions in Adjusting to Trauma

Guido Veronese and Marco Castiglioni
University of Milano-Bicocca, Italy

Abstract

Mainstream clinical studies on children living and growing-up in war-affected areas appear to emphasize the symptoms and dysfunction that can arise when children are exposed to political and military violence. This focus may reflect Western preconceptions regarding the fragility and vulnerability of children, which also inform diagnostic and intervention programs.

The very construct of resilience is too closely related to pathological frameworks, accounting for the successful adaptation of only a small minority of the population affected by trauma. In fact, resilience does not explain why the greater part of the child population does not develop symptoms in the aftermath of war despite multiple exposures to traumatic events.

To gain a better understanding of functioning factors and positive adjustment in children affected by war, a change of framework is required. Positive emotions, optimism and life satisfaction are pivotal factors that can affect children's well-being, enabling them to overcome traumas and psychological suffering.

In this chapter we present two quantitative cross-sectional studies carried out in the Palestinian Occupied Territories, which show that despite adverse life conditions and the ongoing chronic conflict affecting the area, Palestinian children remain optimistic, satisfied with their lives and able to deal with environmental constraints via positive emotions. The children completed self-reported measures before receiving psycho-educational interventions aimed at reinforcing positive emotions as protective factors in coping with trauma. Ecological dimensions promoting positive emotions and life satisfaction in children are discussed.

INTRODUCTION

The devastating effects of war and military violence on children have been extensively documented in a sizable body of research conducted in different geographical contexts (Thabet *et al.,* 2009; Slone, Lobel, Gilat, 1999). Many studies have indicated that post-traumatic reactions and aggressive behaviors in youth and children are consequences of political and military violence (Espie et *al.*, 2009; Qouta, Punamäki, El Sarraj, 2008).

Considerable attention has also been devoted to the long-term effects of exposure to war and political violence on children as victims, perpetrators or both, as well as to the rehabilitation needs of children growing up in such contexts (Denov, 2010; Dubow *et al.*, 2010; Kohrt *et al.*, 2008). However, some research has found that the resolution of a conflict does not necessarily mitigate negative outcomes for children's mental health if the children continue to live in a sociopolitical context in which the peace solution itself is perceived to threaten the well-being of individuals and the community (Darby, 2006). In addition, many studies on children living in war contexts examine the construct of resilience (Betancourt and Khan, 2008; Massad *et al.*, 2009; Thabet *et al.*, 2009). Resilience is part of a dynamic process characterized by positive development despite significant adversities such as war and military violence (Luthar, Cicchetti, and Becker, 2000; Masten and Obradovic, 2006; Ungar, 2011). Bonanno (2004) defines resilience as a trajectory along which the individual maintains a stable equilibrium following adversity, while Boyden (2005) and Roisman (2005) view it as a process of adaptation following a period of maladaptation. It is widely acknowledged in the literature that the resilience construct is somewhat ambiguous and difficult to identify. In fact, the concept of resilience arises within a predominantly Western perspective that tends to overlook individual resistance to psychological and emotional suffering and the associated biomedical needs, as well as undervaluing the importance of positioning individual resilience within a context of 'social suffering' (Nguyen-Gillham, Giacaman, Naser, and Boyce, 2008; Ungar, 2008). Furthermore, a recent work of Barber and Doty (2013) underlined how in the literature the prevalence of resilience is unclear, and perhaps even inflated, because investigations have not assessed children or youth who live in very high risk contexts (Barber and Doty, 2013). The authors' thesis is that most youths growing up in contexts of violence are resilient despite the theory-driven expectations which are (inappropriately) the reverse; namely, that violence invariably causes trauma and severe stress. Most of the research simply does not support such an expectation. This is not to say that violence has no impact - surely it does - and the extent, depth, and duration of effect vary importantly from past experiences, the meaning of the violence, individual differences, etc. Nevertheless, it appears to be the case that the majority of young people (as well as people of other ages) adjust to this adversity effectively - especially if they are provided opportunities to move forward in accomplishing basic life desires and cultural expectations. The authors concluded that the construct of resilience is unuseful to understanding the functioning of children and youth living in conflict affected areas. In our opinion, the concept of resilience continues to reflect a 'disease' oriented framework rather than the 'ease' driven perspectives that inspire our research (Giacaman *et al.*, 2011). Instead, we elected to focus on children's positive functioning and well-being, which we consider to be more comprehensive and understandable constructs (Barber, 2008; Veronese, Said, and Castiglioni, 2010). In this chapter, the first study aims to explore positive and negative affects as well as self-perceived life satisfaction and happiness in a group of Palestinian children living under occupation and military violence. We hypothesized that the children would display generally satisfactory well-being and functioning in terms of positive affect and overall life satisfaction and happiness despite their negative life context (Veronese *et al.*, 2012). The second study examines adaptive qualities such as optimism, perceived life satisfaction and life orientation in Palestinian school-age children. We hypothesize that despite the inhuman living conditions and the daily violence that crushes the area, the children reported high levels of optimism and life satisfaction because the social context enabled them to make sense of their suffering (Veronese *et al.* 2012). Along these lines, starting from the summer of 2008 until now, a conjoint consortium of international and Palestinian NGOs, under the umbrella of Psychologists for Human Rights, implemented a child/community-oriented plan to respond to the needs of Palestinian children in the Tulkarm region exposed to prolonged military violence (Veronese, Castiglioni, Said, 2010). An intervention program aimed to enforce the well-being of children and their positive emotions was carried out focusing on structured experiential activities (Loughry et al., 2006). In both the two previously mentioned studies we recorded quantitative data through questionnaires before and after the intervention in order to understand the effectiveness and the efficacy of the program in enabling children's natural orientation to optimism, life satisfaction and happiness (study 2), and positive emotions and life satisfaction (study 1). The activities were structured as follows: the children were asked to do some physical exercises designed to facilitate awareness of their bodily emotions and feelings, and also to create a team spirit. Then, they were invited to speak about their personal experiences of stress and fear, using collage and dramatization techniques (theatre, mime, human sculpture, etc.). The combination of verbal and non-verbal techniques allowed the children to express themselves as freely as possible. We did not use these tools for diagnostic purposes, nor to interpret the children's production as in a psychodynamic framework, but simply to assist the children in producing "good" (i.e. coherent, understandable, structured etc.) narratives. The aims of the interventions were to:

(1) Improve the children's well-being or prevent it from deteriorating by using play as a framework;
(2) Support the process of adjustment to stress by actively engaging the children in play;
(3) Encourage community involvement in order to safeguard the children's well-being.

In line with research that empirically demonstrates the efficacy of experiential activities and structured play in relieving stress, relatively low-cost and potentially sustainable actions have both a strong impact on the community and also considerable political significance.

POSITIVE EMOTIONS, LIFE SATISFACTION AND OPTIMISM IN CHILDREN LIVING IN WAR CONTEXTS

Little is known about the well-being, subjective happiness, life satisfaction and optimism of children and youths living in war contexts. All of these constructs equally refer to the way individuals relate to their quality of life (Diener, 1984, 1994).

Psychological well-being consists of three principal components: positive affect, negative affect and general life satisfaction (Diener, 1984; Huebner and Dew, 1996). Positive affect is assessed in terms of frequency of positive emotions such as happiness or tenderness, and negative affect in terms of frequency of negative feelings such as sadness or anxiety, while general life satisfaction is understood as a "...cognitive judgmental evaluation of one's life" (Diener, 1984, p. 550). Seligman (1991) suggested that optimism is learned early in life. It might be possible to inoculate groups to the consequences of trauma by instilling optimism in children and to protect them from feelings of helplessness. Dispositional optimism-pessimism has been described as a generalized inclination to expect favorable or unfavorable life events (Hjelle, Busch, and Warren, 1996).

Scheier and Carver (1985) argued that optimism and pessimism are stable personality characteristics that have important implications for the manner in which people regulate their actions and give sense to the world. Much of the research on optimism-pessimism, which looks at topics such as depression (Seligman, Abramson, Semmel, and Von Baeyer, 1979), anxiety (Seligman *et al.*, 1979), and physical illness (Peterson, Seligman, and Vaillant, 1988), has been clinical in nature. In a study carried out by Riolli and his colleagues (2002) in Kosovo the authors take the position that dispositional optimism functions as a buffer against the adverse effects of intense traumatic stress during a crisis, whereas pessimism exacerbated them. According to Seligman (1991), learned optimism helps children to achieve more and to maintain better health. Learned optimism enables positive adjustment to trauma helping the individuals in overcoming their problems through appraisal and direct coping (Riolli *et al.*, 2002).

Nevertheless, a small number of studies show that a large proportion of children exposed to conflict who do not develop symptoms continue to function well despite extremely negative living conditions (Barber, 2008; Barber and Olsen, 2009; Sack, Clarke, and Seeley, 1996; Veronese, Said, and Castiglioni, 2011). Research on war and political violence has shown how children learn to cope with political violence and how traumatic experiences influence their well-being (Tol, Reis, Susanty, and De Jong, 2010). In addition, some studies indicate that contextual variables shape the relationship between war and psychosocial well-being (Boothby, Strang, and Wessels, 2006; De Jong, 2002; Miller and Rasco, 2004). For example, self-perceived well-being in Israeli children displaying strong ideological commitment appears to be greater than in children without ideological commitment (Punamäki, 1996).

A recent study by Veronese (Veronese *et al.*, 2012; Veronese, Castiglioni, Tombolani, and Said, 2012) found that Palestinian children living in a refugee camp display greater optimism, life satisfaction and perceived quality of life than Palestinian children living in Israel. The study shows how environmental factors such as freedom of movement and safety at home as well as individual factors such as positive emotions and feelings of competence and life satisfaction can help children to cope with trauma.

There is a great deal of individual variability in the capacity of children and adolescents to adapt despite adverse experiences with war and violence (Sagi-Schwartz, 2008). Therefore, one may conclude that despite experiencing extreme traumatic experiences, children and youth living and growing up in war affected zones have been able to maintain an adequate mental health infrastructure based on underestimated strength and coping capacities.

BACKGROUND

The Occupied Palestinian Territories (OPT) are made up of two physically separated regions: the Gaza Strip and the West Bank (the latter of which includes East Jerusalem).The living conditions of the Palestinian population worsen from year to year. From 2000 to date, over 6000 Palestinians have been killed. In January 2009 alone, during the 22-day Gaza War, about 1400 casualties were incurred. Conditions of poverty, owing to the border blockade, the destruction of infrastructure facilities during conflict and ongoing socio-economic decline, make the civil population feel increasingly insecure and under threat (Batniji *et al.*, 2009). At least 55% of children experience cumulative traumatic life events (Khamis, 2000), while approximately 33% of children in Gaza have been diagnosed with acute and posttraumatic stress disorder (Qouta and Odeh, 2004). The childhood of Palestinian children living under Israeli military occupation is compromised by the extreme experiences to which they are exposed: these children are affected by curfews and night raids; they have lost, and witnessed assaults on family members; and they have themselves been injured or detained (Abu Hein, Qouta, Thabet, and El Sarraj, 1993; Nixon, 1990; Quota, Punamäki, andEl-Serraj, 1996).Both studies were carried out in the Tulkarm Region of the West Bank (see Figure 1), a context severely affected by poverty and a permanent lack of security and terror. The city of Tulkarm, including the Tulkarm and the Nur Shams refugee camps is a small, densely populated centre of 60,000 inhabitants, located close to the Israeli border.

Figure 1. Tulkarm Region.

STUDY 1

If we look at the Palestinian context, we see how it is affected by pervasive conditions of suffering. The mental health issue requires a shift in emphasis from narrow Western informed medical indicators, trauma and maladaptation to the lack of human security and human rights violations experienced by Palestinians generally (Veronese, Prati, and Castiglioni, 2011) and by children particularly.

In keeping with the framework provided by this new paradigm, scholars have shifted the focus onto functioning factors and positive adjustment to trauma in Palestinian children (Barber, 2008; Punamäki, Qouta, and El-Sarraj, 2001; Veronese *et al.*, 2010). These studies emphasize that an active response to military violence, creativity, positive affects, and perceived positive parenting can be protective factors for Palestinian children exposed to violence. These individual and family-related factors are termed "functioning factors" for Palestinian children (Barber, 2009a; Veronese *et al.*, 2010). Lastly, in research carried out in Palestine and Bosnia, Barber (2009b) has identified political involvement and activism as functioning factors contributing to the well-being of children living amidst military threat.

Method

Participants and Procedures

Seventy-four Palestinian school-age children (age 10.80; SD 2.06; range of 7–15 years), 43 males (average age 11.23; SD 1.91; range of 7–14 years) and 31 females (average age 10.19; SD 2.15; range of 7–15 years) completed three self-report instruments: the PANAS-C (Laurent *et al.*, 1999), the Multidimensional Students' Life Satisfaction Scale (Huebner and Gilman, 2003, 2006), and the Faces Scale (FS) (Andrews and Withey, 1976; Holder and Klassen, 2010). The questionnaires were administered during a summer camp run by an International NGO (nongovernmental organization) in 2010 in Tulkarm City, West Bank. All the children came from poor areas on the outskirts of Tulkarm, including Tulkarm and Nur Shams refugee camps. Participants were selected following meetings with their families and in line with the recommendations of local institutions that had been in charge of the children during the school year (Veronese *et al.*, 2010). Parental consent was sought verbally. The children themselves were also free to take part in the research or to withdraw from it; similarly they could decline to answer any of the questions they were asked. It must be noted that written informed consent is often refused in Palestinian culture and to request it may be viewed as threatening by heads of family in particular (Krogstad *et al.*, 2010; Schultz, 2004). In addition, it is culturally acceptable, and indeed almost taken for granted, that consent for children to participate in research may be provided by those in charge of summer camps and summer schools in lieu of the parents. While we consider the principle of informed consent to be universal, it is imperative for researchers to adopt methods of applying it that respect the cultural values, traditions and particular health-care systems of the country or region of interest.

Data Analysis

The statistical analyses were carried out using SPSS PASW Statistics 18. To identify differences occurring as a function of age, the sample was divided into two age groups: 7-10 years and 11-15 years.Descriptive statistics were calculated to determine levels of negative and positive affect and life satisfaction in the sample of children divided by age and gender.

We measured the correlations (Pearson's *r*) between age group, gender, emotion (positive and negative affect and their sub-domains), self-perceived happiness (FS) and the dimensions of life satisfaction (MLSS) fifteen days before (T_1) and one month after (T_2) the intervention to verify the relationship between emotional states, self-perceived well-being in terms of personal satisfaction and happiness and to test changes after the experiential activities aimed to enhance positive affects.

PANAS-C, MLSS and FS scores were compared using a *t*-test with gender and age group as independent (grouping) variables in T_1 and T_2, and between T_1 and T_2.Finally we conducted a linear regression analysis to verify which emotions, as independent variables, explain life satisfaction.

Results

In Table 1 we summarize the descriptive statistics for the main variables under study: life satisfaction, perceived happiness and positive and negative emotions in the sample of children selected for study 1.

Satisfactory Cronbach's alpha reliability coefficients were found for all the scales administered. With regard to the subscales of the MSLSS, the following Cronbach's alpha values were obtained: Family $\alpha=.85$; Friends $\alpha=.87$; School $\alpha=.88$; Living Environment $\alpha=.85$; and Self $\alpha =.83$. Cronbach's alpha values for the PANAS-C subcategories were somewhat lower: "pleasantness" $\alpha=.77$; "activation/potency" $\alpha=.80$; "sadness" $\alpha=.77$; "anger" $\alpha=.67$; "anxiety/fear" $\alpha=.75$. However, the overall scales for positive and negative affect showed higher levels of reliability ($\alpha=.91$ and $\alpha=.95$ respectively). Average life satisfaction scores on the MSLSS scale were high, generally falling at around point three (*"often"*). The highest scores for satisfaction were recorded on the School scale (average 3.1; *SD* 0.4), while the greatest variability (0.28) was found for the Self subscale (average 2.9; *SD* 0.5). With regard to PANAS-C, lower scores were obtained for negative affect (average 1.9; *SD* 0.5 – "*a little*") than for positive emotion (average 3.8; *SD* 0.6 – "*quite a bit*"). In terms of positive affect, the "pleasantness" scale yielded the highest scores (average 3.9; *SD* 0.7) but with greater variability (0.48) than the "activation/potency" scale (average 3.7; *SD* 0.6). In terms of negative emotions, the "anxiety and fear" scores were highest, while scores for "anger" displayed the greatest variability (average 3.9; *SD* 0.7; variance 0.6). Very high scores were obtained for happiness as measured by the FS, with 86.5% of the children scoring between 3 and 6 points (the maximum).

Regarding the pre-intervention administration of the self-reported measures (T_1) the *t*-test revealed few statistically significant differences as a function of gender. On the MSLSS, females had higher scores than males for the dimensions "Friends" (*t* (59)=1.641; p<.10) and "General Satisfaction" (t(45)=1.936; p<.10); no other gender differences were found. As a function of age, statistically significant differences were found in the PANAS-C scores for overall negative affect (t(55)= 2.131; p<.05) and for the "anxiety/fear" subscale (t(602.316; p=.024 <.05). Specifically, older children obtained higher scores on both negative emotion and anxiety/fear scales, while younger children obtained significantly higher scores than older children on the FS (t(73)=1.707; p<.10).

Table 1. Descriptive data on life satisfaction, positive and negative affect and perceived happiness

Variables	Mean	sd	Range	Percentile 25	Percentile 50	Percentile 75
Family	3.00	.51	2.14	2.57	3.00	3.43
Friends	3.10	.59	2.50	2.75	3.25	3.50
School	3.08	.57	3.00	2.83	3.17	3.38
Environment	3.01	.49	1.86	2.57	3.00	3.29
Self	2.96	.54	2.29	2.57	2.86	3.43
Total satisfaction	3.04	.43	1.68	2.70	3.00	3.3
Positive emotions	3.80	.60	2.85	3.54	3.85	4.23
Negative emotions	1.79	.56	2.77	1.46	1.69	2.04
Pleasentness	3.93	.75	3.33	3.50	4.00	4.50
Activation /Potency	3.70	.64	2.86	3.18	3.86	4.14
Sadness	1.76	.69	3.67	1.33	1.67	2.00
Anger	1.93	.93	4.00	1.00	1.50	2.50
Anxiety/Fear	1.83	.62	2.50	1.33	1.67	2.21
Happiness	4.81	1.27	5.00	4.00	5.00	6.00

Variables: 1-6 MSLSS; 7-13 PANAS-C; 14 FS.

Table 2 shows the correlations between MSLSS, PANAS-C and FS scores in T_1 (before the structured activities). There was a strong positive correlation between positive self-perception on the one hand and overall positive affect, "pleasantness" and "activation/potency" on the other. There was a negative correlation between overall life satisfaction and "anger".

The happiness scale correlates with several other measures, namely Family, Friends, Self and overall life satisfaction as well as "pleasantness" and overall positive affect.

A negative correlation was found between "happiness" and "anxiety/fear". In addition, a strong negative correlation emerged between overall negative affect and "sadness" on the one hand and positive emotion on the other. Positive affect was positively correlated with its subscales as well as the subscales with one another. Similarly, negative affect was positively correlated with its own sub-dimensions, but negatively correlated with "activation/potency" and "pleasantness"; "sadness" was strongly correlated with "anger" and "anxiety/fear", but negatively with "activation/potency", "pleasantness" and overall positive affect.

Correlations between measures maintain the same trend in T_2 (after the structured activities). There is a large correlation between positive self-perception and overall positive emotions, a negative correlation between positive self perception and negative affect (see Table 3). The *t*-test in the post-intervention phase (T_2) shows statistically significant differences as a function of gender and class of age. Females revealed themselves to be more satisfied with school (t(62)= 2.640; p=.011 <.05),whereas the older children felt emotions such as anger more than the younger ones (t(66)=1.940; p=.057 <.05).

Table 2. Correlation between measures of life satisfaction (MSLSS); positive and negative affect (PANAS-C) and happiness (FS) in T$_1$

Variables[1]	1	2	3	4	5	6	7	8	9	10	11	12	13	14
1. Family	1	.45**	.32*	.51**	.59**	.81**	.23	.08	.22	.22	-.03	-.02	.04	.36**
2. Friends		1	.31*	.43**	.47**	.75**	.17	-.01	.24	.04	-.12	-.07	-.004	.43**
3. School			1	.516**	.48**	.66**	.24	.01	.15	.21	.01	.01	.07	.13
4. Environment				1	.59**	.85**	.14	.13	.15	.09	.06	-.27*	.15	.20
5. Self					1	.81**	.40**	.01	.38**	.30*	-.05	-.10	-.03	.26*
6. Total Satisfaction						1	.30	.18	.27	.19	.06	-.31*	.13	.46**
7. Positive emotions							1	-.44**	.88**	.89**	-.55**	-.19	-.11	.27*
8. Negative emotions								1	-.49**	-.28*	.85**	.56**	.80**	-.21
9. Pleasantness									1	.57**	-.55**	-.23	-.20	.37**
10. Activation/Potency										1	-.43**	-.15	.02	.07
11. Sadness											1	.43**	.45**	-.19
12. Anger												1	.24	.02
13. Anxiety/Fear													1	-.25*
14. Happiness														1

Variables: 1-6 MSLSS; 7-13 PANAS-C; 14 FS. ** p<0.5; * p<0.1

Table 3. Correlation between measures of life satisfaction (MSLSS); positive and negative affect (PANAS-C) and happiness (FS) in T_2

Variables[1]	1	2	3	4	5	6	7	8	9	10	11	12	13	14
1. Family	1													
2. Friends	,56**	1												
3. School	,49**	,42**	1											
4. Environment	,61**	,52**	,56**	1										
5. Self	,47**	,32*	,40**	,39**	1									
6. Total Satisfaction	,81**	,78**	,78**	,82**	,65**	1								
7. Positive emotions	,28*	,19	,18	,24	,39**	,44**	1							
8. Negative emotions	-,18	-,27	-,17	-,34*	-,20	-,33*	-,16	1						
9. Pleasantness	,21	,20	,12	,24	,30*	,38*	,89**	-,21	1					
10. Activation/Potency	,23	,15	,13	,19	,29*	,33*	,93**	-,04	,67**	1				
11. Sadness	-,24	-,14	-,16	-,39**	-,15	-,35*	-,18	,87**	-,19	-,10	1			
12. Anger	-,14	-,18	-,30*	-,36**	-,09	-,24	-,13	,73**	-,15	-,05	,45**	1		
13. Anxiety/Fear	-,13	-,33*	-,09	-,24	-,10	-,23	-,07	,92**	-,13	,02	,666**	,626**	1	
14. Happiness	,24	,20	,04	,27*	,24	,26	,34*	-,20	,28*	,29*	,00	-,16	-,28*	1

Variables[1]: 1-6 MSLSS; 7-13 PANAS-C; 14 FS. ** $p<0.5$; * $p<0.1$.

Table 4. Regression coefficients (Beta) and t values for the Significant Predictors of Life Satisfaction and Happiness calculated via a series of Hierarchical, Multiple, Linear Regression Analyses[1]

Dependent variable	Life Satisfaction		Happiness		Adjusted R^2	F
	β	t	β	t		
Positive Emotions	0.25[*]	3.51	-	-	0.13	12.33[**]
Pleasantness	-	-	0.51[*]	3.68	0.10	13.60[**]
Fear	-0.1[*]	-2.0[*]		-	0.4	3.99[*]

[1]Independent variables entered in the equation: step 1, positive emotions; step 2, activation/potency, pleasantness; step 3, negative emotions; step 4, fear, anger, sadness;
[*]p< .05; [**]p<.01.

In addition, the results showed statistically significant differences between T_1 and T_2 respectively on satisfaction with school (t(130)= 1.648; p=.102), anger (t(138)= 2.013; p=.046 <.05) and on general life satisfaction (t(141)= 4.282; p=.000 <.01). After the intervention both the males and females appeared more satisfied overall with their own life (t(69)= 3.086; p=.003 <.01); (t(73)= 2.824; p=.006 <.05).

However, while the males showed themselves to be more satisfied with school (t(62)= 2.146; p=.036 <.05),the females felt more anger than before the experiential activities, while the older children after the intervention were more satisfied than before (t(82)= -3.986; p=.000 <.01).

The hierarchical linear regression analysis showed a strong influence of positive affect on life satisfaction; however overall negative affect was not found to have a significant effect on life satisfaction, and of its subscales only "anxiety and fear" impacted negatively on life satisfaction (see Table 4). Happiness was only impacted by the positive emotion of pleasantness, with no other dimension appearing to influence it (Table 4).

Discussion

Our hypothesis appears to be partially confirmed by these findings. In general, the children are satisfied with their lives and happy despite a dangerous and uncertain life context. Positive emotions play a key role in ensuring general life satisfaction, enjoying a greater influence than negative affect. School is perceived by children as a satisfying place, likely to be safer than home and outdoor spaces. A positive perception of self and positive emotions such as potency and pleasantness are factors that contribute to positive adjustment and happiness. On the contrary, high levels of anxiety and fear place the children at risk of negative adjustment to their uncertain living conditions. The findings in relation to anger are more difficult to interpret; the considerable variance found may be explained by the children's ambivalence towards anger. On the one hand, anger is socially discouraged as a negative emotion; on the other hand, lack of freedom and daily exposure to internal and external violence inevitably lead these children to experience anger frequently. It can be suggested that increased anger after activities focuses on emotions.

Gender plays a secondary role in differentiating subgroups of well-being. However, females display greater ability than males to exploit both social relationships and personal resources. In fact, girls were found to be significantly more satisfied both with their friends and with their lives overall. This finding is in line with cultural perceptions of gender in the OPT (Veronese et. al., 2011): Girls are generally more protected than boys who are under social pressure both to repress negative emotions such as fear and sadness and to actively participate in the struggle against occupation, displaying bravery despite their fear (Veronese et al., 2010; Barber, 2008; Veronese et al., 2008). As expected, older children are more exposed to fear and to negative affect in general. Growing up in an occupied land is challenging due to the risk of imprisonment, exposure to violence, disillusionment, lack of opportunities and lack of hope. Palestinian youths must unavoidably deal with horrific life events as they grow older. Younger children display higher levels of happiness given that they are more sheltered from environmental dangers by adults and older children.

The findings point to a strong interrelationship between affectivity and the various dimensions of life satisfaction. Positive emotions favor a satisfactory perception of self, which in turn leads to positive levels of self-esteem and competency. Feelings of pleasantness in particular are related to a perception of self as active and competent despite conditions of deep uncertainty. In other words, children strive to actively cope with uncontrollable events as protagonists of their own well-being (Barber, 2009; Gilligan, 2009). The negative correlation between anger and general satisfaction confirms that children perceive this negative emotion to be dangerous and unacceptable, but on another level unavoidable.

Contextual and social factors such as family and friends, as well as personal factors such as self-satisfaction, favor happiness in children. Positive emotions, in particular feelings of pleasantness, are also related to perceptions of happiness. Conversely, anxiety and fear seem to negatively affect perceptions of happiness, while low levels of potency and activation are associated with increased negative emotions in children, specifically sadness, anxiety and fear.

As confirmed by numerous studies (Bordwine and Huebner, 2010; Fredrickson, 2001; Froh, Yurkewicz, and Todd, 2009; Huebner, 2004), positive emotions have a strong influence on life satisfaction. With regard to negative emotion, only anxiety and fear affect life satisfaction. This finding may be explained by the daily exposure to military and political violence affecting Palestinian children. Other negative emotions, such as anger, may at times play a useful role in spurring the children to react actively to the threats of occupation. On the contrary, anxiety and fear undermine children's levels of potency and activation, leading them to feel powerless and unable to manage traumatic events.

Summary

In term of life satisfaction, positive affects and perceived happiness, the children reported high levels of wellbeing. The girls reported to be more satisfied of their life than boys (in particular regarding the friends). The older children appeared to be more aware of the daily risks and have more experience of suffering than the younger children. In addition, social factors (especially relationships with family and friends) are keys to promoting positive adaptation and adequate personal growth.

Summarizing, positive emotions and life satisfactionmay be viewed as protective factors in contexts marked by instability and violence. The key role of contextual and social factors points up the need for clinical interventions (not solely focused on symptoms) aimed at social groups, families and the broader community.Finally, the experiential activities contributed to a greater general life satisfaction, satisfaction with the school, and an unexpected increasing of anger, particularly in the girls.

STUDY 2

Most research carried out in contexts of political violence and war does not view the child as a socially-situated actor with active status and the capacity to attribute sense to her/his own experience; in contrast, he/she is held to be a passive actor, mentally disadvantaged and commonly diagnosed with psychiatric, behavioral and emotional trauma-related disorders. The construct of child vulnerability is strongly and culturally mediated in Westernsociety, where dysfunction and maladaptivity are considered to be part and parcel of the human condition and to become dominant in the context of war (Gilligan, 2009). This study examines adaptive qualities such as optimism, perceived life satisfaction and life orientation in Palestinian school-age children growing up. We consider these qualities to be protective factors and indicators of positive adjustment to adverse life conditions.

Method

Participants and Procedures

A group of 216 children was selected from amongst the children taking part in the intervention (M: 10, 81 Ds: 1,98; range from 9 to 11 years), 119 were male (55%) and 97 female (44,8%). For analytical purposes, the group was divided into three sub-groups that were representative of the different contexts under study: urban (Tulkarm city); rural (the villages of Assalam and Shufia); and refugee camp (Nur Shams) (see Table 5).

It is critical to note that the Nazareth subgroup differed from the others in terms of living conditions; although the Nazareth children came from a poor and disadvantaged district of the city, they did not live in such severely poor conditions as the children from the OPT (Occupied Palestinian Territories), and – importantly – they were not constantly affected by military violence and extreme and cumulative war traumas. On this basis, we took the Nazareth subgroup as a sort of "comparison" group with respect to the other subgroups, and hypothesized that this group would obtain higher optimism and life satisfaction scores than the other groups. Three self-evaluation tools were adapted for the Arab-Palestinian contexts. They were first translated from English to Arabic and then translated back by two Palestinian teachers of English, in order to verify the equivalence of the translations. The accuracy of the translation into Arabic was satisfactory.

The measurements administered were:

The Youth Life Orientation Test (YLOT) (Ey *et al.*, 2005), a 16-item scale assessing optimism and pessimism.

The Subjective Happiness Scale (Lyubomirsky, 1999; Tkach, and Lyubomirsky, 2006), a 4-item measure of subjectively perceived happiness.

The Life Satisfaction Scale, or Face Scale (FS) (Abdel-Khalek, 2006; Harry, 1976) is a single-item measure consisting of 7 faces representing a scale from maximum to minimum perceived satisfaction (Holder *et al.*, 2010). This scale is particularly appropriate for children, given that from 3 years and onward they can recognize and accurately categorize emotions represented via schematic drawings (MacDonald, *et al.*, 1996).

Table 5. Breakdown of the sample and description of subgroups

Place	MA	SD	N
Nazareth (Israel)	10.53	2.32	52
Nur Shams Refugee Camp (CAMP)	9.66	2.58	37
Tulkarm city (URBAN)	11.04	0.81	29
Assalam village	10.10	1.24	32
Shufia village (RURAL)	11.03	2.22	66

The items were individually read and explained to the children by a mother tongue educational social worker. The children completed the questionnaires under adult supervision. This procedure enabled us to avoid excluding children affected by dyslexia and dysgraphia from the research.

The questionnaires were administered one week before the intervention (T_1), of which all the children subsequently participated. The same measures were repeated one week after the experiential activities (T_2).The research was carried out in line with the Ethics Committee Guidelines of the University of Milano-Bicocca and approved by the Ethics Committee of MIUR (Italian Ministry of Education, University and Research).

Data Analysis

In order to compare the subgroups, an analysis of variance was carried out, with areas of residence – namely RURAL (Assalam and Shufia villages), URBAN(Tulkarem city), CAMP (Nur Shams Refugee Camp) and urban-Israeli (Nazareth) – as independent variables and scores on the self-reported measures as dependent variables. A further ANOVA was carried out on the entire sample with gender as independent variable and self-reportedmeasures as dependent variables. Gender differences were not explored for the individual subgroups on account of the small sample size. For the same reason, a correlational analysis (Pearson's *r*) was carried out on the self-report scores for the entire sample only.

The scores of the self-evaluation measures were compared using a *t*-test with gender and age group as independent variables between T_1 (pre-intervention) and T_2 (after the end of the activities).

Results

With regard to the optimism scale of the YLOT, no significant difference was found between urban areas (URB), Nazareth in Israel (ISR), RURAL areas (Shufia and Assalam villages) and refugee camp environments (CAMP). With regard to the pessimism scale, the only statistically significant difference was found between the Palestinian children resident in Israel and the children of rural areas (RUR) (F(3,173)=3.15; p< 0.05).

Table 6. Breakdown of the sample by gender

Age		N	
Boys	Girls	Boys	Girls
10.8 (sd: 1.98)	9.7(1.42)	119 (55.1%)	97 (44.8%)

**Table 7. ANOVA of YLOT (Youths Live Orientation Test),
Shs (Subjective happiness scale), and FS (Faces Scale) scores
between the subgroups**

Variables	RUR	URB	CAMP	ISRA
YLOT*				
Pessimism	2.30[a]	2.22[ab]	2.13[ab]	1.76[b]
Optimism	2.61[a]	2.56[a]	2.63[a]	2.53[a]
SHS*				
Happiness	5.62[a]	5.66[a]	6.22[b]	5.53[a]
Unhappiness	4.77[a]	3.69[ab]	4.54[ab]	3.52[b]
FS**	5.99[a]	5.00[b]	6.06[a]	6.08[a]

*significantly different scores have a p-value of $p < 0.05$.
** significantly different scores have a p-value of $p< 0.01$.

While all the subgroups were found to display a generally optimistic life orientation, youths from the city of Nazareth (ISR) are less pessimistic than others and the children from Nur Shams camp (CAMP) displayed the highest scores in the optimistic life orientation. The children from the refugee camp obtained the highest scores of all (see Table 7).

With regard to perceived happiness,, the Nur Shams (CAMP) refugee camp children obtained significantly higher scores on the Subjective Happiness Scale (SHS) than their counterparts in the other subgroups (F (3,193)=3.36; p< 0.05).

With regard to life satisfaction, the children from the Tulkarm city subgroup had significantly lower FS scores (F(3,196)=4.23; p< 0.01) than the participants in the other subgroups.Though all groups showed very low scores at the self perceived unhappiness scale, a statistically significant difference between rural villages (RUR) and Israeli towns emerged (F=3.57; p< 0.05).

With regard to gender, no significant differences were found for the YLOT optimism and pessimism scales nor for the SHS, while the female group (F = 11.01; p< 0.01) had significantly higher life satisfaction (FS) scores than the males.

A positive correlation was found between perceived happiness (SHS) and life satisfaction (FS) ($r = 0.27$; p<0.5). The subjective happiness scale correlated positively with the optimism scale (YLOT) ($r = 0.24$; p< 0.5). Moreover, age correlated negatively with life satisfaction ($r = -0.23$; p< 0.5).

The only statistically significant difference between T_1 and T_2 emerged at FS scale with class of age as independent variables. In fact, younger children after the intervention perceived themselves more satisfied than before (T (432)=2.817; p < 0.5).No differences were found in optimism/pessimism and perceived happiness.

Discussion

The results are both unexpected and support our initial hypothesis. In general, Palestinian children – whether resident in the Arab-Israeli city of Nazareth, in Tulkarm city, in rural Palestinian villages or the refugee camp – define themselves as happy, optimistic and satisfied with their lives. Although poor, with low socio-economic status, the children from the Arab-Israeli city of Nazareth do not encounter the same level of difficulty in their daily lives as the children of Tulkarm city, which is affected by extreme poverty and is the scene of much internal violence related to the Israeli military occupation. The children in the refugee camp are subject to highly negative socio-economic and sanitary conditions. They are frequently victims of extreme trauma, and direct and indirect violence. The children in the rural villages also are very poor; they are less exposed to military violence, but highly prone to ill-health, malnutrition, and the consequences of poverty in general. The functioning and well-being of Palestinian children is generally very high and does not differ from that of Israeli Arab children living in the city of Nazareth. The children in the refugee camp are more optimistic – along with children from the rural villages – than the children in the other subgroups, and had the highest scores of all the subgroups for perceived subjective happiness. The Tulkarm children - who come from a city devastated by continuous military incursions, curfews, night-time house-to-house searches, imprisonment and targeted murders - rate themselves as less satisfied than the other groups of children. However, the children from the refugee camp, whose living conditions are as bad as or worse than their counterparts in the other groups, consider themselves to be as satisfied as the children from Nazareth and from the rural villages near Tulkarm.

With regard to gender differences, males report lower life satisfaction than females, which may be due to greater pressure stemming from adult cultural expectations with respect to male children. In Palestine, those most impacted by the conflict are adult males; unemployment, imprisonment and targeted killings mainly affect men. This could negatively influence the life satisfaction of male children who are both more at risk and required to live up to greater expectations and pressures from adults. Ultimately, as the children grow older, they appear at risk of becoming disillusioned, although they generally continue to define themselves as optimistic, happy and satisfied with their lives.

Summary

Optimism, life satisfaction and self-perceived happiness are major component of subjective well-beingof Palestinian children living both in Israel and in the rural, urban and refugee camp areas of OPT (Occupied Palestinian Territories). What appears really surprising is that the children living in the refugee camp, despite the terrible living conditions, show high rates of life satisfaction, optimism and self-perceived happiness as well as the children living in OPT and resident in Israel. In some cases, as for example regarding the variationof optimism in the different groups, the children living in the refugee camp obtained the highest scores. Confirming the results of the previous study (study 1)the girls are more satisfied than the boys of their own life.

Finally, confirming the results of study 1, the experiential activities centered on enhancement of positive emotions favored a better perception of life satisfaction in the younger children.

CONCLUSION AND CLINICAL IMPLICATIONS

In conclusion, the two studies strongly confirm the ecological nature of well-being in children in war contexts (Barber, 2009a; Bootby, Strang, andWessels, 2006; Tol, Reis, Sustanty, 2010; Ungar, 2011).

Positive emotions contribute to children's well-being and life satisfaction, acting as protective factors in dealing with daily violence (Johnson and Cronister, 2010; Veronese *et al.*, 2010). The children of Tulkarm display considerable personal resources facilitated above all by the functioning community structure supporting them. Military and political violence systematically undermine resources of well-being such as the family, peer groups, home, and open spaces, constraining the children to draw more on personal than on micro-social resources in coping with trauma; the community on the other hand continues to provide significant protection, enabling the children to attribute sense to uncontrollable events, poverty and lack of facilities (Layne *et al.* 2009; Schmidt, 2007).

Despite the extreme violence to which Palestinian children are daily exposed, the group in our study displayed positive adjustment to traumatic events, defining themselves as optimistic, happy and resistant in the face of adversity, which in turn appears to be due to a relatively high level of life satisfaction. The protective factors promoting positive functioning in such a difficult context are to be sought amongst the contextual and ecological variables of the children's living environment (Barber, 2009a, d; Gilligan, 2009; Veronese, *et al.*, 2012; Veronese, Said, and Castiglioni, 2010). For example, the refugee camp children construct their identity as "resistant" in the context of the camp itself, and the want, poverty and fear which they are obliged to face do not diminish their satisfaction and pride in taking active part in the life of the camp and in "combat" (Veronese, Castiglioni, and Said, 2010; Veronese, Said, and Castiglioni, 2011). In contrast, the Palestinian Arab children living in Israel seem to be frailer in terms of identity, perceiving themselves as half-way between Palestinian "internal refugees" in a hostile country, and second-class Israeli citizens (Giacaman, *et al.*, 2009).

In our opinion, positive functioning in contexts of political and military violence will be promoted if, in the face of adversity, the child is able to remain optimistic and satisfied with themselves and their cultural group (Barber, 2009c; Lewin, 1948; Veronese *et al.*, 2012). Thus, the more the context is able to attribute meaning to adversity and to actively involve children in the struggle to overcome it, the more individual well-being will be protected and the traumatic and posttraumatic effects of war reduced (Veronese *et al.*, 2012; Veronese, Said, Castiglioni, 2011; Barber, 2009; Barber, 2001).

Emphasis should be on promotion of well-being and reinforcement of factors leading to stronger outcomes in terms of posttraumatic and personal growth (Hunt, 2010; Veronese *et al.*, 2010).

It is our belief that enhancement of individual well-being and contextual factors can prepare new generations to adopt more democratic and peaceful forms of struggle and resistance to occupation, overcoming violence, aggressive attitudes and exploitation that all too often prove to be "the solutions that confirm the problem" with a consequent increase of fear, anxiety, guilt and shame.

The small sample size prevents us from generalizing the results of this study. In addition, some methodological issues arose in the data collection phase due to disrupted environmental conditions which may have created some bias in the results. However, field experience and international studies on youth and political violence support our findings (Barber, 2009a) and suggest that it is important to continue to focus on well-being and community-driven interventions (Montoya and Kent, 2011), while developing more sophisticated and culturally sensitive measures (Figley *et al.*, 2009) supported by qualitative data analysis.

To promote positive adjustment to trauma and stress and reinforce protective factors in children, clinical efforts must be directed towards families, groups and more in general towards the entire community. Participative frameworks and action research models can be complementary to, and help clinicians to implement and enhance therapeutic interventions focused on symptoms.

It would be of value to construct future clinical interventions aimed at promoting well-being and health (Brodhagen, Wise, 2008; Ai, *et al.*, 2006) so as to reflect the socio-ecological, anthropological, and cultural factors influencing the functioning and positive adjustment to trauma of children affected by military and political violence (Ai, *et al.*, 2006; Punamäki, 1996). Clinical and community interventions fostering health and well-being need to take into account contextual variables, such as endemic cultural and environmental factors, by using action-research frameworks and procedures and participative interventions (Razer, Friedman, Veronese, 2009).

The use of experiential and expressive methods with children in the Occupied Territories helps them to cope with stressful and traumatic experiences.

The action-research approach encourages us to think that our project may increasingly match the field requirements and increasingly involve a large number of social players who can adapt the instruments used and make them culturally sensitive.

From this point of view, we are convinced that, over the years, the children, the local professionals, the families and the civil society of the Tulkarm region, in partnership with the Western professional teams, will cooperate to completely re-formulate the stages of our work, benefiting, on the one hand, from the advantages of taking an active part in the project and, on the other, helping our working models to evolve and become more effective.

REFERENCES

Abdel-Khalek, A. M. (2006). Measuring happiness with a single-item scale. *Social Behavior and Personality*, 34, 139–150.

Abu Hein, F., Qouta, S., Thabet, A. A., and El Sarraj, E. (1993). Trauma and mental health of children in Gaza. *British Medical Journal*, 306, 1129–1131.

Ai, A.L., Evans-Campbell, T., Santangelo, L. K., Cascio T. (2006). The traumatic impact of the September 11, 2001, terrorist attacks and the potential protection of optimism. *Journal of Interpersonal Violence*, 21, 689–700.

Andrews, F. M., and Withey, S. B. (1976). *Social indicators of well-being*. New York: Plenum Press.

Barber, B. K. (2001). Political violence, social integration, and youth functioning: Palestinian youth from the Intifada. *Journal of Community Psychology*, 29 (3), 259- 280.

Barber, B. K. (2008). Contrasting portraits of war: Youths' varied experiences with political violence in Bosnia and Palestine. *International Journal of Behavioral Development*, 32 (4), 298–309.

Barber, B. K. (2009a). *Adolescents and war: How youth deal with political violence*. Oxford: Oxford University Press.

Barber, B. K. (2009b). Moving forward with research with adolescents and political violence. In B. K. Barber (Ed.), *Adolescents and war: How youth deal with political violence* (pp. 315–322). Oxford: Oxford University Press.

Barber, B., K. (2009c). Glimpsing the complexity of youth and political violence, in B., K., Barber (ed.) *Adolescents and war: How youth deal with political violence*; pp. 3-32. New York: Oxford University Press.

Barber, B. K., & Doty, S. B. (2013). Can a majority be resilient? The questionable utility of the construct of resilience for understanding youth in contexts of political conflict. In C. Fernando and M. Ferrari (Eds.). *The handbook on resilience in children of war*. NY: Springer.

Barber, B. K., and Olsen, J. A. (2009). Positive and negative psychological functioning after political conflict: Examining adolescents of the first Palestinian Intifada. In B. K. Barber (Ed.), *Adolescents and war: How youth deal with political violence* (pp. 207–236). Oxford: Oxford University Press.

Batniji, R., Rabaia Y., Nguyen-Gillham, V., Giacaman, R., Sarraj, E., Punamaki, R.L., Saab, H., Boyce, W. (2009). Health as human security in the occupied Palestinian territory. *Lancet*, 373, 1133–43.

Betancourt, T. S., and Khan, K. T. (2008). The mental health of children affected by armed conflict: Protective processes and pathways to resilience. *International Review of Psychiatry*, 20(3), 317–328.

Bonanno, G. A. (2004). Loss, trauma, and human resilience. *American Psychologist*, 59 (1), 20–28.

Boothby, N., Strang, A., andWessels, M. (2006). *A world turned upside down: Social ecological approaches to children in war zones*. Bloomfield, CT: Kumarian Press.

Boyden, J. (2005). Children's risk, resilience, and coping in extreme situations. In M. Ungar (Ed.), *Handbook for working with children and youth. Pathways to resilience across cultures and contexts* (pp. 3–25). Thousand Oaks, CA: Sage.

Brodhagen, A., Wise, D. (2008). Optimism as a mediator of experience of child abuse, other traumatic events and distress. *Journal of Family Violence*, 23, 408–411.

Darby J. (2006). *Violence and Reconstruction*. Notre Dame, IN: University of Notre Dame Press.

De Jong, J. T. V.M. (2002). Public mental health, traumatic stress, and human rights violations in low-income countries. In J. T. V. M. de Jong (Ed.), *Trauma, war, and violence: Public mental health in socio-cultural context* (pp. 1–91). New York: Kluwer Academic/ Plenum Publishers.

Denov, M. (2010). Coping with the trauma of war: Former child soldiers in post conflict Sierra Leone. *International Social Work*, doi:10.1177/0020872809358400.

Diener, E. (1984). Subjective well-being. *Psychological Bulletin*, *95*, 542-575.

Diener, E. (1994). Assessing subjective well-being: Progress and opportunities. *Social Indicators Research*, 31, 103-157.

Dubow, E. F., Boxer, P., Huesmann, L. R., Shikaki, K., Landau, S., Gvirsman, S. D., et al. (2010). Exposure to conflict and violence across contexts: Relations to adjustment among Palestinian children. *Journal of Clinical Child and Adolescent Psychology*, 39 (1), 103–116.

Espie, E., Gaboulaud, V., Baubet, T., Casas, G., Mouchenik, Y., Yun, O., Grais, R.F., Moro, M.R. (2009) Trauma-related psychological disorders among Palestinian children and adults in Gaza and West Bank, 2005–2008. *International Journal of Mental Health Systems*, 3. doi: 10.1186/1752-4458-3-21.

Ey, S.,. Hadley, W., Nuttbrock Allen, D., Palmer, S., Klosky, J., Deptula, D., Thomas, J., and R Cohen (2005). A new measure of children's optimism and pessimism: the youth life orientation test. *Journal of Child Psychology and Psychiatry*, 46 (5), 548–558.

Giacaman R, Khatib R, Shabaneh L, Ramlawi A, Belgacem S, Sabatinelli G, Khawaja M and T. Laurance (2009). Health status and health services in the occupied Palestinian territory. *The Lancet*, 373 (9666) 837-849.

Gilligan, C. (2009). Highly Vulnerable'? Political Violence and the Social Construction of Traumatized Children. *Journal of Peace Research*, 46 (1), 119-134.

Harry, J. (1976). Evolving sources of happiness for men over the life cycle: A structural analysis. *Journal of Marriage and Family*, 38, 289–296.

Hjelle, L. A., Busch, E. A., and Warren, J. E. (1996). Explanatory style, dispositional optimism, and reported parental behavior. *Journal of Genetic Psychology,* 157, 489-500.

Holder, M. D., Colleman, B., Wallace, J.M. (2010). Spirituality, Religiousness and Happiness in children Aged 8-12 Years. *Journal of Happiness Studies*, 11, 131-150.

Holder, M. K., and Klassen, A. (2010). Temperament and happiness in children. *Journal of happiness studies*, 11(4), 419–439.

Huebner, E. S., and Dew, T. (1996). The interrelationship of positive affect, negative affect, and life satisfaction in an adolescent sample. *Social Indicators Research*, 38(2), 129–137.

Huebner, E. S., and Gilman, R. (2003). Toward a focus on positive psychology in school psychology. *School Psychology Quarterly*, 18(2), 99–102.

Huebner, E. S., and Gilman, R. (2006). Students who like and dislike school. *Applied Research in Quality of Life*, 1(2), 139–150.

Khamis, V. (2000). *Political violence and the Palestinian family: Implications for mental health and wellbeing*. New York: Haworth Press.

Kohrt, B. A., Jordans , M. J. D., Tol,W. A., Speckman, R. A., Maharjan, S.M., Worthman, C.M., et al. (2008). Comparison of mental health between former child soldiers and children never conscripted by armed groups in Nepal. *Journal of the American Medical Association*, 300(6), 691–702.

Krogstad, D. J., Diop, S., Diallo, A., Mzayek, F., Keating, J., Koita, O. A., et al. (2010). Informed consent in international research: The rationale for different approaches. *American Journal of Tropical Medical Hygiene*, 83(4), 743–747.

Laurent, J., Catanzaro, S., Joiner, T., Rudolf, K., Potter, K., and Lambert, S. (1999). A measure of positive and negative affect for children: Scale development and preliminary validation. *Psychological Assessment*, 11(3), 326–338.

Lewin, K. (1948). *Resolving social conflicts*. New York: Harper and Brothers.

Loughry, M., Ager, A., Flouri, A., and Qouta, S. (2006). The impact of structured activities among Palestinian children in a time of conflict. *Journal of Child Psychology and Psychiatry*, 47, 1211–1218.

Luthar, S. S., Cicchetti, D., and Becker, B. E. (2000). The construct of resilience: A critical evaluation and guidelines for future work. *Child Development*, 71(3), 543–562.

Lyubomirsky, S. and Lepper, H. (1999). A Measure of Subjective Happiness: Preliminary Reliability and Construct Validation'. *Social Indicators Research*, 46 (2), 137-155.

MacDonald, P. M., Kirkparick, S. W., and Sullivan, L. A. (1996). Schematic drawings of facial expression for emotion recognition and interpretation by preschool-aged children. *Genetic, Social, and General Psychology Monographs*, 122, 373–388.

Massad, S., Nieto, F. J., Palta, M., Smith, M., Clark, R., and Thabet, A. A. (2009). Mental health of children in Palestinian kindergartens: Resilience and vulnerability. *Child and Adolescent Mental Health, 14(2), 89–96*.

Masten, A. S., and Obradovic, J. (2006). Competence and resilience in development. *Annals of the New York Academy of Sciences*, 1094, 13–27.

Miller, K. E., and Rasco, L. M. (2004). An ecological framework for addressing the mental health needs of refugee communities. In K. E. Miller, and L. M. Rasco (Eds.), *The mental health of refugees: Ecological approaches to healing and adaptation* (pp. 1–64). Mah Wah, NJ: Lawrence Erlbaum Associates, Inc.

Nguyen-Gillham, V., Giacaman, R., Naser, G., and Boyce, W. (2008). Normalising the abnormal: Palestinian youth and the contradictions of resilience in protracted conflict. *Health and Social Care in the Community*, 16(3), 291–298.

Nixon, A. E. (1990). *The status of Palestinian children during the uprising in the occupied territories. Stockholm*, Sweden: Riidda Barnen.

Peterson, C., Seligman, M. E. P., and Vaillant, Ci. E. (1988). Pessimistic explanatory style is a risk factor for physical illness: A thirty-five year longitudinal study. *Journal of Personality and Social Psychology, 55*,23-27.

Punamäki, R. L. (1966). Can ideological commitment protect children's psychosocial well-being in situations of political violence? *Child Development*, 67(1), 55–69.

Punamäki, R. L., Qouta, S., and El-Sarraj, E. (2001). Children resiliency factors predicting psychological adjustment after political violence among Palestinian. *International Journal of Behavioral Development*, 25(3), 256–267.

Qouta, S., and Odeh, M. D. (2004). The impact of conflict on children: The Palestinian experience. *Journal of Ambulance Care Management*, 28(1), 75–79.

Quota, S., Punamäki, R. L., and El-Serraj, E. (1996). The impact of the peace treaty on psychological well-being: A follow-up study of Palestinian Children. *Child Abuse and Neglect*, 19 (10), 1197–1208.

Qouta, S., Punamäki, R.L., El Sarraj, E. (2008). Child development and family mental health in war and military violence: the Palestinian experience. *International Journal of Behavioral Development*, 32 (4), 310–321.

Razer, M., Friedman, V., and Veronese, G. (2009). The educational–psychological approach to overcome social exclusion in Israeli schools. *Ricerche di Psicologia*, 32(3–4), 219–235.

Riolli, L., Savicki, V., Cepani, A. (2002). Resilience in the face of catastrophe: optimism, personality and coping in the Kosovo crisis. *Journal of Applied Social Psychology*, 32 (8), 1604-1627.

Sack, W. H., Clarke, G. N., and Seeley, J. (1996). Multiple forms of stress in Cambodian adolescent refugees. *Child Development*, 67(1), 107–116.

Sagi-Swartz, A. (2008). The well-being of children living in chronic war zones. *International Journal of Behavioral Development*, 32 (4), 322-336.

Scheier, M. F., and Carver, C. S. (1 985). Optimism, coping, and health: Assessment and implications of generalized outcome expectancies. *Health Psychology*, 4, 2 19-247.

Schultz, A. A. (2004). Role of research in reconstructing global healthcare for the 21st century. *Nursing Administration Quarterly*, 28(2), 133–143.

Seligman, M. E. P., Abramson, L. Y., Semmel, A., and Von Baeyer, C. (1979). Depressive attributional style. *Journal of Abnormal Psychology*, 88, 242-247.

Slone, M., Lobel T., Gilat I. (1999). Dimension of the political environment affecting children's mental health. *Journal of Conflict Resolution*, 43(1), 78–91.

Thabet, A. A., Ibraheem, A.N., Shivram, R., Winter, E. A., Vostanis, P. (2009). Parenting support and PTSD in children of a war zone. *International Journal of Social Psychiatry*, 55 (3), 226–237.

Tkach, C., and S. Lyubomirsky (2006). How do people pursue happiness? Relating personality, happinessincreasing strategies and well-being. *Journal of Happiness Studies*, 7, 183–225.

Tol, W. A., Reis, R., Susanty, D., and De Jong, J. T. V. M. (2010). Communal violence and child psychosocial well-being: qualitative findings from Poso Indonesia. *Transcultural Psychiatry*, 47(1), 112–135, doi:10.1177/ 1363461510364573.

Ungar, M. (2008). Resilience across cultures. *British Journal of Social Work*, 38(2), 218–235.

Ungar, M. (2011). The social ecology of resilience: Addressing contextual and cultural ambiguity of a nascent construct. *The American Journal of Orthopsychiatry*, 81(1), 1–17.

Veronese, G., Castiglioni,M., Tombolani,M., and Said, M. (2012). My Happiness is the Refugee Camp, my future Palestine': Optimism, life satisfaction and perceived happiness in a group of Palestinian children. Manuscript submitted for publication. *Scandinavian Journal of Caring Sciences*. doi: 10.1111/j.1471-6712.2011.00951.x.

Veronese, G., Castiglioni, M., Barola, G., Said, M. (2012). Living in the shadow of occupation: Life satisfaction and positive emotion as protective factors in a group of Palestinian school children. *Children and Youth services review*. 34 (2), 225-233.

Veronese, G., Prati, M., and Castiglioni, M. (2011). Postcolonial perspectives on aid systems in multicultural contexts: Uganda and Palestine. *Procedia, Social and Behavioural Sciences*, 15, 545–551.

Veronese, G., Said, M., and Castiglioni, M. (2011). Growing-up amidst military violence: Socio-ecological implications of resilience in Palestine. In G. M. Ruggiero, S. Sassaroli, Y. Latzer,and S. Suchday (Eds.), *Perspectives on immigration and terrorism* (pp. 127–142). Amsterdam: IOS.

Veronese, G., Castiglioni, M., and Said, M. (2010). The use of narrative-experiential instruments in contexts of military violence: The case of Palestinian Children in the West-Bank. *Counselling Psychology Quarterly*, 23(4), 411–423.

Veronese, G., Said, M., and Castiglioni, M. (2010). Narratives from Jenin Refugee Camp: Children as extreme defense against the disintegration of family and community. *International Journal of Human Sciences*, 7(2), 85–104.

In: Handbook of Psychology of Emotions
Editors: C. Mohiyeddini, M. Eysenck and S. Bauer

ISBN: 978-1-62808-053-7
© 2013 Nova Science Publishers, Inc.

Chapter 14

EMOTION AND OBESITY

Allan Jones
Institute of Psychology
University of Southern Denmark

ABSTRACT

Obesity has reached epidemic proportions and is today one of the most costly chronic diseases in terms of morbidity, mortality and healthcare consumption. Obesity carries with it numerous serious health related consequences including type II diabetes, cardiovascular diseases, neuropathy and cancer. It has previously been estimated that over half a million people die each year in the United States alone due to obesity related health problems (Mokdad et al., 2004), with obesity related healthcare costs estimated to be over 100 billion dollars (report published by the U.S. Department of Health and Human Services, 2007). In a study by Kelly et al., (2008) it was estimated that in 2005 9.8% of the world's adult population, approximately 400 million people, were obese. In the same period (2005-2006) the National Health and Nutrition Examination Survey estimated that 34.3% of the adult population in the United States had excess body weight in the obese range (Nguyen and El-Serag, 2009). It is therefore of considerable concern that the prevalence rates in obesity are on the rise. Within the next decade it is estimated that prevalence rates in obesity will be as high as 40% in the United States (Ohsiek and Williams, 2011), while by the year 2030 it is estimated that 573 million to 1.12 billion people worldwide will suffer from obesity (Kelly et al., 2008).

A person is defined as obese if their excess body fat exceeds 30 on the body mass index (BMI = weight in kilograms divided by height in meters squared), and morbidly obese if excess body fat reaches 40 or more on the BMI. In simplistic terms obesity is a result of an energy imbalance. In overweight and obese individuals more energy is consumed than is expended. The aetiologies of energy imbalance are however potentially numerous and multifaceted, as such biological, physiological and psychosocial risk factors need to be considered. The increase in prevalence rates of obesity are unlikely to be explained by changes in our biology (for example genetic), as prevalence rates have increased rapidly over a relatively short period of time. The increase in obesity can most likely be explained by changes in behaviour, lifestyle and nutrition, such as decreases in physical activity, easier access to inexpensive food high in fat and sugar and significantly larger portion sizes compared to 30 years ago (Wadden et al., 2002; French et al., 2003;

Campbell et al., 2007; Young and Nestle 2002), leading to significant increases in consumption of unhealthy food and increases in energy imbalance (for a debate on the respective contribution of physical activity vs. nutrition in explaining the global increase in obesity see Biddle and Dovey, 2009). Specific causal and contributing factors leading to individual differences in weight gain are less clear. Factors that determine increases in unhealthy eating habits and sedentary behaviours are being explored, and it appears that emotions may play an important role in explaining the growing rates of obesity in the global population (de Wit et al., 2010; Luppino et al., 2010). Moreover, obesity may be a risk factor not only in relation to somatic health but also in relation to mental health, for example obese individuals may be more vulnerable to adverse changes in affective state compared to normal weight individuals (Gariepy et al., 2010). The current chapter aims to explore the relationship between emotion and obesity. The associations between emotion and energy imbalance will be examined in an attempt to explain individual differences in weight gain and to identify potential determinants of the obesity epidemic. The chapter will also explore pathways that attempt to explain how emotional distress and obesity are linked, as well as take a critical look at current treatment practices for obese individuals.

All emotions influence eating in one way or another, although negative affect such as anxiety and depression have been the most widely researched, with the majority of research findings showing negative affect to be detrimental to dietary restraint and a contributing factor to the onset and maintenance of obesity. Not all people who are overweight or obese have emotional difficulties, although many it appears are emotionally distressed. Several studies looking at the association between negative affectivity (e.g. depression and anxiety) and obesity have found higher symptom levels among obese compared to non-obese individuals (e.g. Erermis et al. 2004; de Wit et al. 2010). A study by Tuthill et al. (2006) examined 253 obese patients for psychiatric comorbidities, and found that 48% of obese patients had above normal levels of depression and 56% were found to have above normal levels of anxiety. Cross sectional and longitudinal studies have found evidence for an association between depression, anxiety and obesity, with some community based studies suggesting depressed individuals are 18% more likely of becoming obese (de Wit et al., 2010).

In a recent review of the literature (Luppino et al., 2010) the longitudinal association between depression and obesity was examined, with results showing that depression increased significantly the odds for developing obesity (pooled odds ratio = 1.58; pooled adjusted odds ratio 1.40). In another review, this time examining the association between anxiety disorders and obesity, odds ratios ranging from 1.1. to 2.6 (with a pooled odds ratio of 1.40) were found, suggesting an overall moderate positive association between anxiety and obesity (Gariepy et al., 2010). Associations between negative affect and body-weight were also observed in a recent large randomised intervention trial, in which overweight and obese individuals were randomized into a weight reduction/physical activity intervention group or a control group (Ruusunun et al., 2012). While no effects of treatment group were observed, depressive symptoms were found to significantly reduce as a result of participating in the study, with reductions in body weight and energy intake most strongly associated with reductions in depressive symptoms (Ruusunun et al., 2012). The causal relationship between negative affect and obesity is still unclear however, although there is some evidence for a bidirectional association (e.g. Luppino et al., 2010).

How Do Emotions Contribute to the Onset of Obesity?

It is not clear how affective states such as anxiety and depression contribute to the onset and maintenance of obesity, however possible pathways and mechanisms have been explored. In addition to satisfying hunger, eating also elicits an emotional response. We gain pleasure from eating and this reward process can be independent of hunger satisfaction (Zheng and Berthoud, 2007). One potential pathway links consumption of carbohydrates (not protein) with increases in tryptophan/serotonin release by way of insulin secretion (Wurtman, 1993, Wurtman and Wurtman 1996). Serotonin effects mood and individuals under distress may be particularly vulnerable to overconsumption of carbohydrates as a form of self-medication. The desire to feel better through overconsumption of carbohydrates can override feedback mechanisms involved in feelings of satiety (Wurtman and Wurtman 1996). Thus, individuals suffering from distress may use carbohydrate rich food to regulate mood even when there is no physical need to consume. Such food is simultaneously high in fat thus increasing risk of obesity. In such individuals pleasure rather than appetite control is the main drive for consumption, such overconsumption is termed *hedonic hyperphagia* (also termed emotional eating, comfort eating and avoidance eating). A study by Golay et al. (2004), looked at eating habits of dieters 5 years after achieving weight loss. Out of those who regained weight (over half of the dieters) 55% reported depression and 58% reported anxiety as the cause of weight regain as opposed to hunger. Moreover a reduction in the consumption of carbohydrates has been observed in obese individuals in which serotonin levels were pharmacologically increased (Wurtman, 1990; Wurtman, 1993).

Overeating in response to distress has been acknowledged for some time and earlier theories have tried to explain this relationship. For example, Kaplan and Kaplan (1957) proposed that fear/anxiety and eating are not compatible. They stated (in addition to any learned positive associations to eating) that physiologically the process of eating cancels out (temporarily) feelings of distress. Newer theories trying to explain the effects of anxiety/stress on eating have focused on the role of the hypothalamic–pituitary–adrenal (HPA) axis. Torres and Nowson (2007) state that chronic anxiety/stress may lead to increased appetite via *hyper-activation of the HPA axis,* which, via an increase in cortisol levels, promotes secretion of neuropeptide-Y (involved in increased food intake / hyperphagia) and inhibits the role of leptin in appetite regulation. Stress/anxiety induced cortisol release may also be related to increased abdominal fat mass and stimulate cravings for palatable foods high in fat and sugar leading to increased incidences in hedonic hyperphagia and greater risk of developing obesity (Torres and Nowson 2007). Moreover, corticosterone – a hormone secreted under episodes of stress - appears to be associated with food-related drives, with insulin moderating increased consumption of pleasurable foods leading to stress relief, improved mood and ultimately for some to obesity (Dallman et al., 2005).

Seeking pleasure from consumption as a coping strategy to regulate mood is most likely a determinant for obesity. However, according to Mela (2001) eating to regulate mood may only account for part of the behaviour leading to obesity. Mela argues that overeating is also prompted by *situational food cues* and motivation to eat. The increased focus on food as a result of dieting may paradoxically, according to Mela, increase the potency of food cues that affect motivation to eat, leading to overconsumption. Moreover, studies looking at automaticity of behaviour and habit formation have found that situational/environmental cues are important in reinforcing automatic behaviours (behaviours that require little energy, deliberation or awareness), especially if behaviours are intrinsically rewarding (Lally et al, 2010, 2011). Intrinsically rewarding behaviours repeated at regular intervals over a period of time can, when paired with an environmental cue (a consistent context such as watching television in the evening), become automatic, i.e. the environmental cue can trigger the unhealthy behaviour becoming a habit. An automatic behaviour paired with an environmental cue may be sustained as long as the cue is perceived/prevalent (Verplanken and Wood, 2006). Pairing of repeated behaviours with consistent cues thus helps maintain and strengthen further the automaticity of the prescribed unhealthy behaviour, and counteract efforts for potential change, such as changes in lifestyle needed to lose weight. Intrinsically rewarding behaviours are subjective, in other words the pleasure derived from eating high-density foods may be motivation for some, while for others the benefits derived from eating healthily may be more motivating. Environmental factors can influence eating behaviours in a positive or negative direction. According to Stice et al., (2009) an unhealthy food environment defined as an environment in which access to high fat and high sugar food is readily available is associated with increased consumption of such food and increased risk for future weight gain, while food environments in which healthy foods (fruit, nuts, vegetables) are readily available are associated with increased consumption of such food. Moreover, research has shown that parents have a tendency to offer their children food choices that the parents themselves find palatable and seldom offer their children types of food that the parents dislike (Skinner et al., 2002). Findings such as these point toward a degree of *automaticity* in our food choices and suggest that reward systems are not the only factors influencing food choice.

Easy, repeated access to inexpensive foods that are high in sugar and fat may, for some, lead to cravings for such foods, to the extent where the individual becomes addicted. Studies have found a link between sugar consumption and dopamine release that is characteristic of addiction (Liu et al., 2010). There are two main explanatory models of *food addiction* suggesting that neurological pathways involved in satiety and reward systems may be different in obese individuals compared to non-obese individuals. One model proposes that some individuals may have a *hypersensitive reward system* to palatable food (Davis et al., 2004), and that individuals with sensitized food related neural networks could be at greater risk for developing obesity. Indeed, there is some evidence to suggest that brain regions involved in food reward (e.g. oral somatosensory cortex, anterior insula) have higher levels of activation in obese individuals than in non-obese individuals supporting a hypersensitive reward system hypothesis (Stice et al., 2009), however data in this area remains sparse. Conversely, food addiction leading to obesity may stem from a *hyposensitivity* in individuals to the positive affects of palatable food. Blum et al., (2000) terms such individuals as having a hypodopaminergic trait. Repeated consumption of food high in fat and sugar may impede the expression of receptors in the striatum (DAD2 receptors), akin to the processes involved in drug abuse. Down-regulation of DAD2 receptors is associated with addictive behaviours through a dysregulation of feedback from internal reward systems. Individuals on high sugar and fat diets may through DAD2 receptor degradation experience a progressive reduction in the pleasure gained from consumption of palatable foods leading to increased consumption in order to compensate (Stice et al., 2009). According to Stice and colleagues the hyper- and hypo- sensitivity models are not necessarily incompatible. Overconsumption of foods high in fat and sugar as a result of hypersensitive reward systems may through dysregulation of neural reward systems (down regulation of DAD2 receptors) lead to hyposensitivity resulting in progressively increased consumption of palatable foods to attain pleasure, further exacerbating down regulation, hyposensitivity and overconsumption, resulting in a persistent imbalance of energy intake in relation to expenditure and increasing the likelihood of developing obesity.

Negative affect such as depression and anxiety may not only affect energy consumption but may also influence energy imbalance through impacting on *energy expenditure*. For example, stress and anxiety are known to trigger respiratory-conditions such as asthma (Lehrer et al., 2002), which in turn affects energy expenditure through reductions in physical activity. When paired with depressive symptoms anxiety is associated with a reduction in the ability to control asthma (Urrutia et al., 2012). Anxiety is also linked to other conditions affecting energy expenditure through reductions in physical activity including subjective health complaints such as chronic fatigue (Brosschot, 2002). In addition, specific anxiety conditions such as agoraphobia, social phobia and panic disorder may reduce activity in individuals who avoid certain feared situations. It is also well documented that individuals suffering from depression/ depressive symptoms display a lack of motivation to engage in daily activities, especially activities requiring physical exertion, and have generally low energy levels. For example, Lindwell et al. (2011) examined over two years the relationship between depressive symptoms and physical activity in 17,593 adults from 11 countries in Europe, finding a bidirectional association between depressive symptoms and physical activity. Physical activity was associated with fewer depressive symptoms and depressive symptoms appeared to impede physical activity.

Eating to regulate mood, situational and environmental food cues affecting motivation to eat and habit formation, emotion linked appetite dysregulation and emotion related effects on energy expenditure could all contribute to override homeostatic processes that regulate food intake. The effects of emotion on weight-control is further illustrated by studies on weight loss showing that lower levels of depression and avoiding using food to regulate mood were associated with better outcome (Oshiek and Williams, 2011). There is evidence therefore, that emotional distress may be a contributing factor for the development of obesity. What is still not clear however, is the direction of causation between emotion and obesity. Only a few prospective studies have been conducted in this area with evidence for emotional distress as a determinant of obesity and evidence for obesity as a determinant of emotional distress (e.g. Atlantis and Baker 2008; Herva et al., 2006).

HOW CAN OBESITY AFFECT US EMOTIONALLY?

A number of studies have pointed to obesity as a determinant for emotional distress. The longitudinal association between obesity and depression was recently examined (Luppino et al., 2010), with results showing that obesity increased the odds for developing depression (pooled odds ratio = 1.55; pooled adjusted odds ratio 1.57). Obesity as a predictor for anxiety was also examined in two prospective studies, with findings showing that obese individuals are also more at risk for developing anxiety (odds ratio = 1.16, Bjerkeset et al., 2008; odds ratio = 6.27, Kasen et al, 2008). Despite causal evidence for the onset of emotional distress as a function of obesity, it is not exactly clear why obesity leads to emotional distress in some but not in others, although a number of pathways have been suggested.

For some individuals, being overweight has been associated with *discrimination*, not only from others but also self-discrimination derived from the negative stigma associated with being overweight.

In western countries media amplified social and cultural norms associate being slim with beauty, health and success (Derenne and Beresin, 2006). Overweight individuals may therefore experience distress from others reactions and prejudices as well as self-perceptions of what it means to be overweight. Perceived distress as a result of discrimination may in turn affect the individual's feelings of self-esteem, lead to an increase in dissonance, contribute to avoidance of social situations and increase the likelihood of developing anxiety and depression. For example, Puhl and Luedicke (2012) have recently examined the effects of weight-based victimization among adolescents, finding that 40-50% of adolescents exposed to weight-based victimization reported felling depressed, angry and negative about their body. Those who reported distress in relation to weight-based victimization reported using emotional eating and avoidance as a means of coping (Puhl and Luedicke, 2012). Obesity may, via feelings of anxiety and depression, increase the individual's level of *avoidance* resulting in limited social networks and even isolation. Avoidance behaviours can promote physical inactivity, which can exacerbate the energy imbalance leading to increased problems with weight.

The HPA axis, believed involved in the onset of obesity as a function of depression, could also be involved in the onset of depression as a function of obesity. Obese individuals have higher levels of adipose tissue compared to lean individuals and the stress hormone cortisol is generated in greater amounts from inactive cortisone found in adipose tissue (Walker, 2001).

Increased cortisol secretion is associated with *HPA dysregulation*, or more specifically with impaired corticosteroid receptor signalling, and is causally linked to the onset and maintenance of depression (Holsboer, 2000). Thus, another possible pathway linking obesity to depression as a function of HPA dysregulation is suggested. It is further hypothesized that the beneficiary effects of antidepressant medication are achieved in part by regulation of the HPA axis (Holsboer, 2000).

The effect of obesity on health can also be a major source of distress and reduce significantly *quality of life* (Dixon, 2010). Overweight individuals are more prone to experiencing painful conditions, reduced physical function, are at greater risk for developing cardiovascular diseases, diabetes mellitus as well as other weight related chronic conditions. Binge eating and other maladaptive eating behaviours can also be very distressful for overweight and obese individuals, especially after multiple failed attempts to correct this behaviour. Weight related health risks could therefore lead to increases in depressive symptoms and risk for depression (Gariepy et al., 2010).

Studies indicating a *bidirectional association between obesity and emotional distress* have implications for treatments that attempt to help overweight and obese individuals lose weight.

Obese patients with affective problems would require multifaceted interventions that address the affective, physiological and environmental components of obesity in order to break the self-reinforcing cycle of overconsumption and affect regulation. However, while there is evidence for a bidirectional association between obesity and distress, associations are not always observed, third variables may mediate/moderate the association, and causation is difficult to pinpoint due to methodological difficulties.

NOT ALL OBESE INDIVIDUALS ARE DISTRESSED

It is important to reiterate that not all overweight, or obese individuals are distressed and this is mirrored in the scientific literature. Despite evidence for an association between negative affect and obesity, not all studies have found an association, and associations that do exist may partly be mediated/ moderated by other variables. For example, in a longitudinal study (Bjornelv et al., 2011) only weak associations were found between emotional problems or personality traits and weight-problems in adolescents, although an association was found between low self-esteem and problems with overweight, suggesting that self-esteem may moderate/mediate the effect of emotion on obesity for some. Similar findings were reported in an earlier review looking at the impact of obesity on psychological wellbeing in children and adolescents. Wardle and Cooke (2005) found limited evidence for an association between depression and obesity in community based studies, moreover, and in contrast to the findings of Bjornelv et al (2011), self- esteem was seldom found to be abnormal in obese individuals. Wardle and Cooke argue that these findings may be clouded by potential moderators/mediators such as different socio-cultural norms and tolerances for overweight and obese individuals as a function of gender and ethnicity.

In several studies in which associations between obesity and emotional distress were observed, *gender* appeared to be an important moderating factor. The associations observed were significant for females but not for males (e.g. de Wit et al., 2010; Anderson et al., 2006; Richardson et al., 2003; Carpenter et al., 2000). Why associations between obesity and emotional distress are more prevalent for women is not clear. According to Wardle and Cooke (2005), one possible explanation may be that being overweight is feared and stigmatized more amongst girls than boys. Vamosi et al., (2010) argue that women may be more vulnerable than men to the effects of emotional distress on energy imbalance, suggesting that women may experience greater increases in appetite and reduced energy expenditure as a function of depression compared to men; also there appears to be a greater vulnerability for unhealthy eating patterns - including binge eating - as a function of emotional distress in females compared to males. Differences in the association between obesity and distress may also be moderated by *ethnicity*. Different ethnic groups may hold different views regarding weight, which in turn may impact on prevalence rates in weight-related teasing and the distress caused by such teasing. Wardle and Cooke (2005) in their review of the literature point to cultural differences in how obesity is stigmatised, finding that being overweight may be more acceptable among some ethnic groups compared to others, although they stress that more research is needed in this area.

According to Luppino et al. (2010), inconsistencies in associations between obesity and emotional distress across studies may also be due to difficulties in measuring the constructs under investigation. For example, differences in associations between depression and obesity may be more stable when a clinical interview is used to diagnose depression, as opposed to subjective measures of depressive symptoms. Alternatively, associations may be dose-dependent with clinically depressed individuals at more risk of developing obesity than those below the threshold of clinical depression. Gender specific measures also need to be developed to reflect differences in body-image norms and ideals. For example, while being heavier may carry more stigma for girls/women, for boys/men being heavier or more muscular may be the ideal (Wardle and Cooke, 2005).

CLINICAL INTERVENTIONS FOR OBESITY

There exist several types of treatment for overweight and obese individuals, which can be categorized as pharmacological (e.g. appetite reducing drugs), non-pharmacological (e.g. restricted diet and increased physical activity) and surgical (bariatric surgery). Bariatric surgery has become the treatment of choice for obese individuals, as it is the most effective treatment option in terms of achieved weight loss. An example of bariatric surgery is Gastric bypass (GBP) a procedure which restricts energy intake by promoting satiety and by moderately reducing absorption. Bariatric surgery is a forced-behaviour intervention, which means that the individual's consumption is restricted despite the presence of food cravings or unhealthy eating habits (e.g. fast-food consumption).

Despite the general success of GBP surgery in helping obese individuals lose weight, the procedure has not produced satisfactory weight-loss in all patients. It is estimated that 20% of patients fail to achieve satisfactory weight-loss following GBP - satisfactory weight-loss is defined as >50% reduction of excess weight (Livhits et al., 2010; Lutfi er al., 2006; Herpertz et al., 2004). Problems with weight-loss can arise as soon as six months after GBP surgery (van Hout et al., 2005; Green et al., 2004), and can get progressively worse with a significant amount of patients regaining weight around two years post surgery (Hsu et al., 1998). Patients typically feel as though they lose control over eating, begin to revert to unhealthy eating habits, have problems adapting to life without overeating etc. For some patients (both those with and without successful weight-loss), complications resulting in morbidity can arise contributing to a poorer quality of life, and even mortality as a result of GBP treatment (Herpertz et al., 2004). There has been a lot of media focus about the adverse effects of bariatric surgery, and some high profile patients have documented their failure to lose weight following surgery, further fuelling the debate about the efficacy of the physiological changes from bariatric surgery in modifying unhealthy eating behaviours. Bariatric surgery is a forced behaviour intervention that effectively induces satiety, however, in many patients underlying cognitive-affective determinants of disturbed eating patterns remain, exposing the patient to continued risk of weight regain and poor quality of life. For example, patients experiencing loss of control over eating prior to surgery (e.g. binge eaters) may continue to express such loss of control post surgery in the form of grazing (eating small amounts of food at regular intervals). Through behaviours such as grazing coupled with ingestion of liquids high in fat and sugar (Niego et al., 2007), GBP patients may learn to bypass the bypass. Continued loss of control over eating following GBP surgery will over time increase stomach capacity affecting satiety restriction and weight-loss.

One way to address the problem of potential weight-regain following GBP surgery has been to screen patients pre-operatively for eating disorders and other risk factors that may affect post surgery weight-loss. For some patients, screening for psychological risk factors has lead to deferment and even denial of surgery (Ashton et al., 2008). Ashton and colleagues question the premise for denying potentially life saving surgery on the basis of psychological screening, arguing that evidence for an adverse affect of pre-operative psychological risk-factors on post-operative weight loss is limited and until more compelling evidence is found the practice of denying patients surgery on the basis of psychological screening should cease. To further support their argument Ashton et al., point to findings showing that patients who have effectively lost weight following bariatric surgery report fewer psychological problems (for an example see Dymek et al, 2001). While the association between affective disorders, abnormal eating patterns and weight gain is arguably moderate at best, the existing evidence cannot be ignored and should be considered when providing healthcare to overweight and obese individuals. On the other hand, and in line with the comments from Ashton et al., depriving patients of potentially life saving surgery is difficult to justify based on current empirical evidence, especially when acknowledging the *bi-directional association of obesity and emotion*. It can therefore be argued that the practice of screening patients for eating disorders and other psychological problems can only be justified when applied in prescribing supplemental care that addresses such problems pre and/or post surgery, not as a precursor for deferment or denial of bariatric surgery.

SUMMARY AND CONCLUDING REMARKS

Obesity has reached epidemic proportions and is projected to rise significantly in the next decade. Obesity is linked to a number of serious chronic illnesses and is one of the leading causes of mortality. It is therefore important that researchers, health professionals and policy makers attempt to gain a comprehensive understanding of the aetiologies of obesity in an attempt to curb the epidemic. The causes of obesity are complex and any sustainable solutions will require interventions that target the spectrum of contributing factors - from macro such as societal and cultural to micro such as biological. A potentially important piece of the puzzle is the bidirectional association between emotion and obesity. Further research is needed into food related mood regulation, the effects of emotion in overriding homeostatic appetite regulation, situational/environmental food cues affecting motivation to eat and habit formation, emotion related affects on energy expenditure, weight related discrimination and victimization, weight related emotional dysregulation, weight related psychomotor retardation (both avoidance and heath related), weight related health risks on quality of life, as well as the role of ethnicity and gender in the association between obesity and emotion. Findings from such research may contribute towards improving interventions that attempt to break the *self-reinforcing cycle of overconsumption and affect regulation*. More research looking at the long-term effects (over several years) of bariatric surgery on weight loss is also needed with specific focus on the potential additive effect of pre- and post- surgery psychological interventions that focus on removing barriers to weight loss such as emotional distress. Without more research looking at the relative contribution of emotion and other psychological factors on eating behaviour, forced behaviour interventions such as bariatric surgery, whilst effective, will remain controversial.

REFERENCES

Anderson SE, Cohen P, Naumova EN, Must A. Association of depression and anxiety disorders with weight change in a prospective community-based study of children followed up into adulthood. *Arch. Pediatr. Adolesc. Med.* 2006; 160: 285–291.

Ashton D, Favretti F, Segato G. Preoperative Psychological Testing - Another Form of Prejudice. *OBES. SURG.* 2008; 18: 1330–1337.

Atlantis E, Baker M. Obesity effects on depression: systematic review of epidemiological studies. *Int. J. Obes*. 2008; 32: 881–891.

Biddle S, Dovey T. Obesity – is physical activity the key? *The Psychologist*. 2009; 22 (1): 32-35.

Bjerkeset O, Romundstad P, Evans J, Gunnell D. Association of adult body mass index and height with anxiety, depression, and suicide in the general population. *Am. J. Epidemiol*. 2008; 167: 193–202.

Bjornelv S, Nordahl HM, Holmen TL. Psychological factors and weight problems in adolescents. The role of eating problems, emotional problems, and personality traits: the Young-HUNT study. *Soc. Psychiatry Psychiatr. Epidemiol*. 2011; 46: 353–362.

Blum K, Braverman ER, Holder JM, Lubar JF, Monastra VJ, Miller D, Lubar JO, Chen TJ, Comings DE. Reward deficiency syndrome: A biogenic model for the diagnosis and treatment of impulsive, addictive, and compulsive behaviors. *Journal of Psychoactive Drugs*. 2000; 32 (Suppl:i-iv): 1-112.

Brosschot JF. Cognitive-emotional sensitization and somatic health complaints. *Scandinavian Journal of Psychology*. 2002; 43: 113–121.

Campbell K, Crawford D, Salmon J, Carver A, Garnett S, Baur L. Associations between the home food environment and obesity-promoting eating behaviors in adolescence. *Obesity*. 2007; 15: 719–730.

Carpenter KM, Hasin DS, Allison DB, Faith MS. Relationships between obesity and DSM-IV major depressive disorder, suicide ideation, and suicide attempts: results from a general population study. *Am. J. Public Health*. 2000; 90: 251–257.

Dallman MF, Pecoraro NC, la Fleur SE. Chronic stress and comfort foods: self-medication and abdominal obesity. *Brain Behav. Immun*. 2005; 19: 275–280.

Davis C, Strachan S, Berkson M. Sensitivity to reward: Implications for overeating and obesity. *Appetite*. 2004; 42: 131–138.

de Wit L, Luppino F, van Straten A, Penninx B, Zitman F, Cuijpers P. Depression and Obesity: A meta-analysis of community-based studies. *Psychiatry Res*. 2010; 178:230-235.

Derenne JL, Beresin EV. Body image, media, and eating disorders. *Acad. Psychiatry*. 2006; 30(3):257-261.

Dixon JB. The effect of obesity on health outcomes. *Molecular and Cellular Endocrinology*. 2010; 316: 104–108.

Dymek MP, le Grange D, Neven K, Alvergy J. Quality of life and psychosocial adjustment in patients afer Roux-en-Y Gastric Bypass: A brief report. *Obesity Surgery*, 2001;11: 32-39.

Erermis S, Cetin N, Tamar M, Bukusoglu N, Akdeniz F, Goksen D. Is obesity a risk factor for psychopathology among adolescents? *Pediatr. Int*. 2004; 46: 296–301.

French SA, Story M, Fulkerson JA, Gerlach AF. Food environment in secondary schools: A la carte, vending machines, and food policies and practices. *American Journal of Public Health* 2003; 93: 1161–1167.

Gariepy G, Nitka D, Schmitz N. The association between obesity and anxiety disorders in the population: a systematic reviewcand meta-analysis. *International Journal of Obesity*. 2010: 34; 407–419.

Golay A, Buclin S, Ybarra J, Toti F, Pichard C, Picco N, de Tonnac N, Allaz AF. New interdisciplinary cognitive-behavioural-nutritional approach to obesity treatment: A 5-year follow-up study. *Eating and Weight Disorders*. 2004; 9(1): 29–34.

Green AEC, Dynek-Valentine M, Pytluk , le Grange D, Alverdy J. Psychosocial outcome of gastric bypass surgery for patients with and without binge eating. *Obesity Surgery.* 2004; 14: 975-985.

Herpertz S, Kielmann R, Wolf AM, Herbebrand J, Senf W. Do psychosocial variables predict weight loss or mental health after obesity surgery? A systematic review. *Obesity Research.* 2004; 12(10): 1554-1569.

Herva A, Laitinen J, Miettunen J, Veijola J, Karvonen JT, Laksy K, Joukamaa M. Obesity and depression: results from the longitudinal Northern Finland 1966 Birth Cohort Study. *Int. J. Obes.* 2006; 30: 520–527.

Holsboer F. The corticosteroid receptor hypothesis of depression. *Neuropsychopharmacology.* 2000; 23(5): 477-501.

Hsu LK, Benotti PN, Dwyer J, Roberts SB, Saltzman E, Shikora S, Rolls BJ, Rand W. Nonsurgical factors that influence the outcome of bariatric surgery: A review. *Psychosom. Med.* 1998; 60:338–346.

Kaplan HI, Kaplan HS. The psychosomatic concept of obesity. *Journal of Nervous and Mental Disease.* 1957; 125: 181- 201.

Kasen S, Cohen P, Chen H, Must A. Obesity and psychopathology in women: a three decade prospective study. *Int. J. Obes.* 2008; 32: 558–566.

Kelly T, Yang W, Chen CS, Reynolds K, He J. Global burden of obesity in 2005 and projections to 2030. *Int. J. Obes.* 2008; 32: 1431–1437.

Lally P, Van Jaarsveld CHM, Potts HWW, Wardle J. How are habits formed: Modelling habit formation in the real world. *European Journal of Social Psychology.* 2010; 40: 998-1009.

Lally P, Wardle J, Gardner B. Experiences of habit formation: A qualitative study. *Psychology, Health and Medicine.* 2011; 16(4): 484-489.

Lehrer p, Feldman J, Giardino N, Song HS, Schmaling K. Psychological aspects of asthma. *Journal of Consulting and Clinical Psychology.* 2002; 70(3): 691-711.

Lindwell M Larsman P, Hagger MS. The reciprocal relationship between physical activity and depression in older European adults: a prospective cross-lagged panel design using SHARE data. *Health Psychol.* 2011; 30(4): 453-62.

Liu Y, von Deneen KM, Kobeissy FH, Gold MS. Food addiction and obesity: evidence from bench to bedside. *J. Psychoactive Drugs.* 2010; 42 :133–45.

Livhits M, Mercado C, Yermilov I, Prikh JA, Dutsom E, Mehran A, Ko CY, Gibbons MM. Behavioral factors associated with successful weight loss after gastric bypass. *The American Surgeon.* 2010; 76: 1139-1142.

Luppino, FS, de Wit LM, Bouvy PF, Stijnen , Cuijpers, P, Penninx BWJH, Zitman FG. Overweight, Obesity, and Depression. A Systematic Review and Meta-analysis of Longitudinal Studies. *Arch. Gen. Psychiatry.* 2010; 67(3): 220-229.

Lutfi R, Torquati A, Sekhar N, Richards WO. Predictors of success after laparoscopic gastric bypass: a multivariate analysis of socioeconomic factors. *Surg. Endosc.* 2006; 20: 864-7.

Mela DJ. Determinants of food choice: relationships with obesity and weight control. *Obes Res.* 2001; 9(4): 246S – 255S.

Mokdad AH, Marks JS Stroup DF, Gerberding JL. Actual causes of death in the United States. *JAMA.* 2004; 291(10):1238-45.

Nguyen DM, El-Serag HB. The big burden of obesity. *Gastrointestinal Endoscopy* 2009; 70(4): 757-757.

Niego SH, Kofman MD, Weiss JJ, Geliebter A. Binge Eating in the Bariatric Surgery Population: A Review of the Literature. *Int. J. Eat. Disord.* 2007; 40: 349–359.

Ohsiek S, Williams M. Psychological factors influencing weight loss maintenance: An integrative literature review. *Journal of the American Academy of Nurse Practitioners.* 2011; *23:* 592–601.

Puhl RM, Luedicke J. Weight-Based Victimization Among Adolescents in the School Setting: Emotional Reactions and Coping Behaviors. *J. Youth Adolescence.* 2012; 41: 27–40.

Richardson LP, Davis R, Poulton R, McCauley E, Moffitt TE, Caspi A, Connell F. A longitudinal evaluation of adolescent depression and adult obesity. *Arch. Pediatr. Adolesc. Med.* 2003; 157: 739–745.

Ruusunen A, Voutilainen S, Karhunen L, Lehto SM, Tolmunen T, Keinänen-Kiukaanniemi S, Eriksson J, Tuomilehto J, Uusitupa M and Lindström J. How does lifestyle intervention affect depressive symptoms? Results from the Finnish Diabetes Prevention Study. *Diabetic Medicine,* 2012 (in Press).

Skinner JD, Caruth BR, Wendy B, Ziegler PJ. Children's food preferences: a longitudinal analysis. *J. Am. Diet.* Assoc. 2002; 102: 1638–1647.

Stice E, Spoor S, Ng J, Zald DH. Relation of obesity to consummatory and anticipatory food reward. *Physiol.* Behav., 2009; 97 (5): 551-560.

Torres SJ, Nowson CA. Relationship between stress, eating behavior, and obesity. *Nutrition* 2007; 23: 887–894.

Tuthill A, Slawik H, O'Rahilly S, Finer N. Psychiatric comorbidities in patients attending specialist obesity services in the UK. *Q. J. Med.* 2006; 99: 317–325.

U.S. Department of Health and Human Services. (2007). The Surgeon General's call to action to prevent and control overweight and obesity: *Economic consequences* (retrievable from: http://www.surgeongeneral. gov).

Urrutia I, Aguirre U, Pascual S, Esteban C, Ballaz A Arrizubieta I, Larrea I. Impact of anxiety and depression on disease control and quality of life in asthma patients. *J. Asthma.* 2012; 49(2): 201-208.

Vámosi M, Heitmann BL, Kyvik KO. The relation between an adverse psychological and social environment in childhood and the development of adult obesity: a systematic literature review. *obesity reviews.* 2010; 11: 177–184.

van Hout GCM, Vershure SKM, van Heck GL. Psychosocial predictors of success following bariatric surgery. *Obesity Surgery.* 2005; 15: 552-560.

Verplanken B, Wood W. Interventions to break and create consumer habits. *Journal of Public Policy and Marking.* 2006; 25: 90-103.

Wadden TA, Brownell KD, Foster GD. Obesity: Responding to the global epidemic. *Journal of Consulting and Clinical Psychology* 2002; 70: 510–525.

Walker BR. Activation of the hypothalamic-pituitary-adrenal axis in obesity: cause or consequence? *Growth Horm IGF Res.* 2001; 11(suppl A): S91-S95.

Wardle J, Cooke L. The impact of obesity on psychological well-being. *Best Pract. Res. Clin. Endocrinol. Metab.* 2005; 19: 421–440.

Wurtman JJ. Carbohydrate craving. Relationship between carbohydrate intake and disorders of mood. *Drugs.* 1990; 39(Suppl. 3): 49-52.

Wurtman JJ. Depression and weight gain: the serotonin connection. *Journal of Affective Disorders.* 1993; 29: 183-192.

Wurtman RJ, Wurtman JJ. Brain serotonin, carbohydrate-craving, obesity and depression. *Adv. Exp. Med. Biol.* 1996; 398: 35-41.

Young LR, Nestle M. The Contribution of Expanding Portion Sizes to the US Obesity Epidemic. *American Journal of Public Health.* 2002; 92 (2); 246-249.

Zheng H, Berthoud HR. Eating for pleasure or calories. *Curr. Opin. Pharmacol.* 2007; 7: 607–612.

In: Handbook of Psychology of Emotions
Editors: C. Mohiyeddini, M. Eysenck and S. Bauer

ISBN: 978-1-62808-053-7
© 2013 Nova Science Publishers, Inc.

Chapter 15

DIFFERENTIAL EFFECTS OF NEGATIVE METACOGNITIONS AND POSITIVE METACOGNITIONS AND META-EMOTIONS ON ANXIETY AND DEPRESSION

*Nils Beer**
The University of Westminster, London, UK

1. EXECUTIVE SUMMARY

This study attempts to derive and investigate adaptive metacognitive and meta-emotional self-regulatory processes by partially reversing and, moreover, extending Wells and Matthews' (1994, 1996) and Wells' (2000) metacognitive model of psychological and emotional disorders within a positive psychology framework. The assumption of this study is that adaptive metacognitive and meta-emotional self-regulation, specifically in the light of challenge, unpredictability or ambiguity, should contribute to state emotional equilibrium, measured as absence or low levels of state depression and comorbid state anxiety. Investigating the metacognitive and meta-emotional etiology of (state) depression and anxiety appears to be valuable in light of steadily increasing prevalence rates of both disorders in Western societies. Depressive disorders are the predominant mental disorders affecting an estimated 340 million people worldwide with increasing tendency (Lyddy, 2000). The current economic crisis with increased job insecurity necessitates even more pronounced adaptations to challenge and change to maintain psychological stability.

Examining both maladaptive metacognitions and adaptive metacognitions and meta-emotions in terms of their effects on anxiety and depression sheds light on the core question: Is mere absence of maladaptive metacognitions sufficient for buffering potential (state) depression and anxiety and subsequent successful problem-solving in situations of challenge?

---

* Correspondence should be addressed to Dr Nils Beer, Department of Psychology, 309 Regent Street, London W1B 2UW, United Kingdom, e-mail: nilsbeer@gmail.com.

The assumption of the present study is that pure absence of dysfunctional metacognitions is a necessary but not sufficient precondition for successful resolution of challenge. In addition to the absence or low levels of maladaptive metacognitions, psychological stability and success in challenging or unpredictable situations requires high levels of adaptive metacognitions and meta-emotions.

The present study explores the linear relationships between dysfunctional metacognitions, positive metacognitions and meta-emotions as independent variables and anxiety and depression as outcome measures. A mixed sample of 212 worker and student participants was utilized and completed the following battery of questionnaires: the five dimensions comprising Meta-Cognitions Questionnaire 30 (*MCQ-30*, Wells and Cartwright-Hatton, 2004), the three-dimensional Positive Metacognitions and Positive Meta-Emotions Questionnaire (*PMCEQ*, Beer and Moneta, 2010) and the Hospital Anxiety and Depression Scale (*HADS*, Zigmond and Snaith, 1983). A cross-sectional design was employed and data analysis comprised correlation analysis and subsequent structural equation modeling (SEM) analyses. PMCEQ-F1 – Confidence in Extinguishing Perseverative Thoughts and Emotions – was negatively predictive of Anxiety and Depression. PMCEQ-F2 – Confidence in Interpreting Own Emotions, Restraining from Immediate Reaction and Mind-Setting for Problem-Solving – also negatively predicted state Anxiety and state Depression but to a far lesser extent than PMCEQ-F1. This can be explained in the light of what these factors measure: PMCEQ-F1 reflects an inverse construct of Wells and Matthews' (1996) Self-Regulatory Executive Function (S-REF) perseveration and rumination as assessed by the MCQ-30, specifically by the MCQ-F2 subscale "Negative Beliefs about Worry concerning Uncontrollability and Danger". Above and beyond the perseveration-inhibiting PMCEQ-F1, the PMCEQ-F2 factor also incorporates problem-focused or agentic properties. The ability to quickly terminate worry and rumination cycles as assessed by the PMCEQ-F1 items has by nature more pronounced decreasing effects on (state) Anxiety and Depression than the agency-related constructs as measured by some of the PMCEQ-F2 items. This argument was further supported by the finding that the even more agency-related PMCEQ-F3 factor – Confidence in Setting Flexible and Feasible Hierarchies of Goals – was a non-significant predictor of both (state) Anxiety and Depression in the SEM model. As expected and in line with a plethora of previous studies, the MCQ-30 construct, comprising the five MCQ-30 subscales utilized as indicators in this study, was strongly and negatively predictive of state Anxiety and state Depression. Comparing the relative contributions of PMCEQ-F1 and MCQ-30 to (state) Anxiety and Depression in absolute terms revealed that the predictive power of the MCQ-30 was slightly higher than the one of the PMCEQ-F1 subscale.

The study findings suggest that absence of psychological distress, here assessed by (low levels of) anxiety and depression, not only requires the absence of maladaptive metacognitive traits as measured by the MCQ-30 but also the presence of adaptive metacognitions and adaptive meta-emotions as assessed by the PMCEQ. Compared to the MCQ-30, the PMCEQ instrument covers a more encompassing range of psychological dimensions by assessing problem-focus and goal-setting as positive traits, beyond the worry- and rumination-related maladaptive traits measured by the MCQ-30. It is therefore concluded that potential self-empowering coaching applications of the PMCEQ should be wider in scope than the corresponding, however inverse and clinical, ones of the MCQ-30. This has already been reflected in Beer and Moneta's (2011) study with PMCEQ factors having significant negative effects on maladaptive coping and perceived stress and significant positive effects on adaptive coping.

In terms of interventions it is argued that potential clinical and coaching interventions aimed at development and cultivation of PMCEQ-F1 "skills" would reduce anxiety and depression. Cultivation of the agentic psychological constructs measured by PMCEQ-F2 and PMCEQ-F3 is hypothesized to increase problem-solving, self-determination and goal-setting. This in turn should have enhancing impacts on academic and professional performance measures, potentially enhancing happiness and life satisfaction above and beyond merely buffering against anxiety and depressive states. It conclusion, it can be argued that PMCEQ-F1 better informs potential clinical interventions whereas PMCEQ-F2 and PMCEQ-F3 could be at the focus of self-empowering coaching practices.

Keywords: Emotional stability; anxiety disorders; depressive disorders; maladaptive metacognitions; positive metacognitions; positive meta-emotions; psychological well-being

2. INTRODUCTION

Wells and Matthews' (1994, 1996) Self-Regulatory Executive Function (S-REF) model has stimulated clinical and experimental research in terms of different dimensions of metacognitions in generalized anxiety disorder (GAD), major depressive disorder (MDD) and other psychological or mental disorders, e.g. obsessive-compulsive disorder (OCD) and substance-related disorders. GAD and MDD have high life time prevalence rates. With regards to MDD the (2000) prognosis of the American Psychiatric Society estimates that 5 to 12 per cent of males and 10 to 25 per cent of females develop at least one major depressive episode at some point in their lives. In addition, the comorbidity rate between GAD and MDD is high: Watson, Weber, Assenheimer and Clark (2005) report correlation coefficients between anxiety disorders and depressive disorders in the range of 0.45 to 0.75. Both disorders have debilitating effects on quality of life and also imply high costs for mental health settings and as results of decreased work productivity and increased absenteeism. Moreover, prevalence rates for both GAD and MDD have steadily been increasing and according to WHO's (1996) prediction MDD will represent the most prevalent disease cluster by 2020. In light of the current economic crisis, which implies high job insecurity with potentially stress-increasing effects, it can be hypothesized that individuals will become even more vulnerable to anxiety-related disorders, specifically GAD and comorbid depressive disorders, specifically MDD.

From a cognitive perspective metacognitive beliefs have been found to be a crucial etiological agent of both anxiety and depression. Wells' (2000) conceptualizes metacognitive beliefs as being "concerned with the interpretation of one's own cognition" (p. 34). It will be shown that two types of dysfunctional metacognitive beliefs – positive and negative ones – play a fundamental role in the onset and maintenance of anxiety disorders and depressive disorders.

This section will first outline metacognitive models and corresponding research evidence specifically with regards to anxiety disorders and depressive disorders. Such metacognitions of the dysfunctional type are assessed by means of the Meta-Cognitions Questionnaire (*MCQ*, Cartwright-Hatton and Wells, 1997) and by its shorter version used in this study, the Meta-Cognitions Questionnaire 30 (*MCQ-30*, Wells and Cartwright-Hatton, 2004). The subsequent section will then infer the resulting framework for the contribution of the opposite type of metacognitions and meta-emotions, i.e. adaptive ones as measured by the Positive Metacognitions and Positive Meta-Emotions Questionnaire (*PMCEQ*, Beer and Moneta, 2010) as potential protectors or buffers against the state negative emotions of anxiety and depression. The core aim is to investigate the differential effects of MCQ-30 factors and PMCEQ factors on the same outcome measures of state Anxiety and state Depression.

2.1. Characterization, Metacognitive Theory and Research of Anxiety Disorders

There is a plethora of disorders grouped under the umbrella term anxiety disorders, e.g. generalized anxiety disorder (GAD), obsessive compulsive disorder (OCD), post-traumatic stress disorder (PTSD) and phobias. Since research evidence suggests that phobias are predominantly learned by means of classical or operant conditioning and since PTSD is the result of severe and highly traumatic events, the focus here will be on GAD which also has the highest prevalence rate. The predominant characteristic of GAD, the most frequently diagnosed anxiety disorder, is unspecified or free-floating anxiety with persistent levels of anxiety or worry in many life domains and over many life circumstances. The chronic disorder implies severe social and functional impairments with pronounced risks of deteriorations in social and occupational respects. Due to the predominantly unspecified nature of GAD sufferers are often unable to identify the genuine source of their disproportionate fear, resulting in maintenance of high anxiety levels and, frequently, in the experience of even more acute anxious episodes. It is estimated that there is comorbidity with MDD in over two-thirds of GAD cases (Sue, Sue and Sue, 2006).[1]

From an encompassing and holistic biopsychosocial perspective the etiology of GAD is threefold and comprises biological vulnerability (diathesis), psychological factors and social factors. Psychological factors can be further broken down, e.g. into cognitive, behavioral and even psychodynamic ones. The focus within this study lies in the cognitive domain; the specific mechanisms within the S-REF model (Wells and Matthews, 1994, 1996) can be summarized as follows. Both positive and negative beliefs about worry, as measured by corresponding MCQ-F1 and MCQ-F2 subscale items, contribute to excessive and perseverative S-REF activity which then predominantly operates in the disadvantageous object mode characterized by dysfunctional and negatively biased attention, threat monitoring and maladaptive and inflexible coping. Cartwright-Hatton and Wells (1997) and Wells and Carter (2001) provided empirical evidence that GAD-diagnosed patients hold significantly stronger negative beliefs about worry (measured by MCQ-F2) than non-patient controls. MCQ-30 items for such negative metacognitive beliefs about worry concerning uncontrollability and danger, measured by the MCQ-F2 subscale, are "When I start worrying,

---

[1] DSM-IV criteria for GAD are: Excessive anxiety and apprehensions over a number of life circumstances for a period of at least six months, difficulty in controlling the worry, and general anxiety symptoms, e.g. restlessness, vigilance and difficulty concentrating.

I cannot stop" and "My worrying could make me go mad". More recent clinical evidence has been provided by Sica, Steketee, Ghisi, Chiri and Franceschini's (2007) study which found that such negative metacognitive beliefs about worry strongly predict GAD and OCD.

In addition, empirical evidence has shown that positive beliefs about worry (measured by MCQ-F1), i.e. beliefs that involve positive attributions to worry, contribute to the onset and maintenance of GAD and other anxiety-related disorders. Example items that tap such positive metacognitive beliefs are "Worrying helps me to avoid problems in the future" and "Worrying helps me to cope" and are measured by the MCQ-F1 subscale.[2]

In his (1995) metacognitive theory Wells proposed that positive metacognitive beliefs about worry (MCQ-F1) and negative beliefs about worry (MCQ-F2) significantly contribute to the maintenance of intermittent episodes of worry cycles which are the pronounced manifestations of GAD. With regards to both GAD and MDD Wells' (2000, 2009) metacognitive theory of emotional disorders conceptualizes maladaptive metacognitive beliefs as antecedent factors in the initiation of maladaptive coping and as being central to maladaptive coping strategy selection. The theory states that emotional disorders and potential psychological dysfunctions are maintained by (a) perseverative thinking, (b) maladaptive use of attention and (c) maladaptive coping, which conjointly constitute a cognitive-attentional syndrome (*CAS*; Wells, 2000)

2.2. Characterization, Metacognitive Theory and Research of Depressive Disorders

Depressive disorders are the predominant mental disorders affecting an estimated 340 million people worldwide with increasing tendency (Lyddy, 2000). In Britain, in 1998, approximately nine million people sought help from their GPs for depression-related symptoms (British Psychological Society, 2000). In addition to the high prevalence rates of depressive disorders, two recent developments within Western societies are of particular concern. There is not only a trend of decreasing age of onset (Hammen, 1997) but depressive disorders also incorporate high risks of recurrence. Severely depressed individuals suffer from an average of four depressive episodes, each lasting typically for three to five months (Judd, 1997). While the debilitating effects of MDD are readily apparent[3], several studies have provided evidence that even relatively mild forms of depression (e.g. dysthymic disorders) often induce impairing consequences in terms of professional performance, economic status and quality of interpersonal relationships. Hence, even mildly, not clinically, depressed individuals may display impaired functioning (Hammen, 1997). An estimated 12 per cent of these milder types of depression display chronic patterns with a duration of more than two years (Davison, Neale and Kring, 2003).

Depressive disorders are subsumed under mood or affective disorders. With regard to unipolar depression there is a distinction between major depressive disorders (MDD) and dysthymic disorders. The formal DSM-IV diagnosis of MDD requires either depressed mood

---

[2] The five subscales of the MCQ-30 instrument utilized in this study (i.e. the brief version of the MCQ) are referred to as MCQ-1, MCQ-2, through MCQ-5.

[3] The most severe effect of MDD and other mood disorders is suicide; Culbertson (1997) estimates that about 10% of those suffering from affective disorder commit suicide.

or significant loss of interest and pleasure for a period of at least two weeks and four additional symptoms such as sleep and appetite disturbances, loss of energy, feeling of worthlessness, difficulty in concentrating and even suicidal thoughts (American Psychiatric Association, 2000). Dysthymic disorder encompasses chronically depressed mood lasting most of the time for at least two years (Gotlib and Hammen, 1992) requiring only three of the mentioned symptoms but excluding suicidality (Davison et al., 2003).

The diagnostic criteria imply a distinction between somatic and mood symptoms of depression. Whereas somatic symptoms of depression (e.g. weakness, fatigue and gastrointestinal problems) are predominant in non-Western cultures, mood symptoms (e.g. feelings of extreme sadness and worthlessness with the common consequence of withdrawal) seem to be predominant in Western cultures (Gleitman, Fridlund and Reisberg, 2004).

Within a holistic biopsychosocial approach the etiology of MDD is threefold and comprises biological vulnerability (diathesis) and psychological and social factors. The focus within this study lies in the cognitive domain; the specific mechanisms within the S-REF model can be summarized as follows. Whereas positive and negative beliefs about worry play a crucial role in GAD, positive beliefs about rumination have been found to be positively associated with MDD. With reference to Just and Alloy (1997) Sue, Sue and Sue (2006) put it: "In particular, ruminative responses – in which one dwells on how bad one feels, considers the possible consequences of one's symptoms, and expresses to others how bad one feels – are believed to prolong and intensify depressive moods and possibly bring about the onset of depressive episodes" (p. 370). In Wells and Matthews' terminology rumination is the explicit manifestation of prolonged, excessive and perseverative S-REF activity with its previously outlined dysfunctional impacts not only on mood but also on attention, coping and even the formulation of inappropriate goals.

Positive metacognitive beliefs about rumination are depicted in Papageorgiou and Wells' (2001) Positive Beliefs about Rumination Scale (PBRS), e.g. "I ruminate to try to find an answer to my problems" or "I need to ruminate about this problem to prevent future mistakes". In their (2001) study Papageorgiou and Wells administered the PBRS and found a significant positive correlation between intensity of rumination and severity of MDD. Using a much larger sample size, Watkins and Moulds (2005) replicated and extended Papageorgiou and Wells' (2001) study approach and also found that rumination results in significantly elevated symptoms of MDD.

In their (2008) review article *Metacognition in Depressive and Anxiety Disorders: Current Directions* Corcoran and Segal emphasize the recent interest in investigating whether the process of relating thoughts or metacognitive awareness is linked to, or even predictive of, depressive disorders. They conceptualize metacognitive awareness (psychological acceptance or mindfulness) as the "degree to which individuals adopt a 'decentered set' with respect to their thoughts and feelings" (p. 37). It is argued here that this conceptualization reflects, in Wells and Matthew's (1996, 1994) taxonomy, the functional and adaptive metacognitive mode. As opposed to the object mode, only being adaptive in genuinely threatening situations, the metacognitive mode captures the interpretation of thoughts not as facts but just as mental "events" or cues necessitating subsequent evaluations. Interestingly and in contrast to depressive disorders, metacognitive awareness appears to play a less pronounced role in anxiety disorders.

Somewhat surprisingly, both depression and anxiety (subsequently referred to as negative emotions) have been explained predominantly by MCQ-30 factors, i.e. without taking depressive rumination and lack of metacognitive awareness into account in terms of depression. A (2007) study by Spada, Nikčević, Moneta and Wells showed that positive and negative metacognitive beliefs about worry (MCQ-F1 and MCQ-F2), low cognitive confidence in memory (MCQ-F3) and beliefs about the need to control thoughts (MCQ-F4) significantly contributed to the relationship between perceived stress and negative emotions.[4] The potential mechanisms underlying the findings were explained by inferring that negative beliefs about worry (MCQ-F2) and beliefs about the need to control thoughts (MCQ-F4) are likely to foster persistent and negative interpretations of experience such that perceived stress results in more pronounced negative emotional outcomes. Similarly, low cognitive confidence (MCQ-F3) is also likely to contribute to an increased transmission of perceived stress by potentially reducing the awareness and choice of effective coping strategies.

Concluding from the research findings for a metacognitive etiology of anxiety and depressive disorders, in recent years there has been increasing empirical evidence for the detrimental effects of positive and negative metacognitive beliefs, which significantly contribute to onset and maintenance of anxiety and depressive disorders. In terms of anxiety disorders, chronic worry represents the most relevant dysfunctional coping strategy resulting in perseverative object mode S-REF activity. With regards to depressive disorders depressive rumination and lack of metacognitive awareness or mindfulness exert analogous prolonged S-REF hyperactivity. Yet, some studies have provided evidence that depression can be accounted for purely by the dysfunctional MCQ-30 constructs. The latter can be explained by means of the comorbidity between depression and anxiety. It appears, however, that holistic metacognitive models of unipolar depression (MDD) would take worry-related MCQ-30 factors, depressive rumination and lack of or low levels of metacognitive awareness (mindfulness) simultaneously into account. Most likely, this view also holds for less severe but more chronic dysthymic disorders.

The next section will employ the inverse perspective by deriving hypothesized relationships and mechanisms between metacognitions and meta-emotions of a functional and adaptive nature (assessed by the PMCEQ) on state anxiety and depression. In order to compare and contrast the contributions of dysfunctional and functional metacognitions within the following analysis, the same outcome measures will be utilized. This means that emotional equilibrium and psychological well-being will be conceptualized as absence or extremely low levels of the state negative emotions of anxiety and depression.

2.3. Hypothesized Effects of Positive Metacognitions and Meta-Emotions on State Negative Emotions

Positive or functional metacognitions and meta-emotions, i.e. those of an adaptive and self-empowering nature, are at the heart of this study. Beer and Moneta's (2010) kernel theory of adaptive metacognition and meta-emotion proposes that absence of maladaptive metacognition is not sufficient for an individual to succeed when tackling problematic situations or challenging encounters. Hence, the study draws on the commonly utilized

---

[4] In addition to the direct effects they found that the MCQ-30 factors partially mediated the relationship between perceived stress and negative emotion; furthermore the maladaptive MCQ-30 factors moderated the relationship between perceived stress and negative emotions.

positive psychology paradigm that psychological adaptation is not merely attributable to the absence or low prevalence of maladaptive dispositions, but also requires being fostered by adaptive dispositions (e.g. Vaillant, 2000; Wright and Lopez, 2002). In particular, successful resolution of challenging and difficult situations necessitates (a) metacognitive beliefs that facilitate to switch S-REF activity on and off based on the strategic demands of the situation, (b) meta-emotions of interest and curiosity (Mitmansgruber et al., 2009) in one's own primary responses to challenges, and (c) metacognitive beliefs of an agentic type that support identification of alternative pathways and flexible goal restructuring.

Beer and Moneta's measurement instrument of adaptive metacognitions and meta-emotions, the Positive Metacognitions and Positive Meta-Emotions Questionnaire (PMCEQ), was derived within a qualitative study (Beer and Moneta, 2012) and psychometrically validated (Beer and Moneta, 2010).

The PMCEQ measures three related albeit distinct dimensions of adaptive metacognitive and meta-emotional beliefs people hold about their own cognitive and emotional processes when facing challenging situations or encounters in the form of traits: (1) PMCEQ-F1: Confidence in Extinguishing Perseverative Thoughts and Emotions, (2) PMCEQ-F2: Confidence in Interpreting Own Emotions as Cues, Restraining from Immediate Reaction and Mind-Setting for Problem-Solving and (3) PMCEQ-F3: Confidence in Setting Flexible and Attainable Hierarchies of Goals. All three factors (traits) are hypothesized to foster what Hudlicka (2005) describes as a "feeling of confidence" (p. 57).

Since their effects on state negative emotions have not been investigated before, potential effects of these positive constructs can only be (inversely) inferred from the outlined existing theory and research of dysfunctional metacognitions. The three confidence constructs assessed by the PMCEQ are hypothesized to be negatively correlated with both state negative emotions of Anxiety and Depression. It is hypothesized that the negative relationship specifically holds for PMCEQ-F1 – Confidence in Extinguishing Perseverative Thoughts and Emotions – since this subscale taps the reverse (or at least a capability to quickly terminate processes) of perseverative worry and rumination in the sense of Wells and Matthews' (1994, 1996) S-REF model.

It is predicted that individuals with stable and positive metacognitive and meta-emotional traits would score low on the (negatively worded) PMCEQ-F1 items, e.g. "If things go really badly I tend to brood and dwell on my negative thoughts" which explicitly addresses depressive rumination and "I tend to think that worrying thoughts might reflect the reality" which depicts the disadvantageous object mode as opposed to the functional metacognitive mode. Based on these arguments it is hypothesized that:

(H1) Confidence in Extinguishing Perseverative Thoughts and Emotions (PMCEQ-F1) will be negatively correlated with both Anxiety and Depression.

PMCEQ-F2 – Confidence in Interpreting Own Emotions as Cues, Restraining from Immediate Reaction and Mind-Setting for Problem-Solving – taps the core ability to make sense of one's own emotions in a non-judgmental way and thus captures a mindfulness-related capability. PMCEQ-F2 also depicts confidence in not getting into chronic or perseverative rumination cycles as reflected by the item "I can stop any negative thinking cycles and focus on what I can do in the situation". In so far PMCEQ-F2 depicts confidence constructs which resemble those assessed by the PMCEQ-1 factor. Above and beyond this domain PMCEQ-F2 measures more agentic and problem-focused confidence domains as assessed by the item "When I experience taxing demands I try to act as in the motto: 'There are no problems, only solutions'". In analogy to hypothesis 1 is it predicted: that:

(H2) Confidence in Interpreting Own Emotions as Cues, Restraining from Immediate Reaction and Mind-Setting for Problem-Solving (PMCEQ-F2) will be negatively correlated with both Anxiety and Depression.

The third positive metacognitive and meta-emotional factor PMCEQ-F3 – Confidence in Setting Flexible and Feasible Hierarchies of Goals – differs from PMCEQ-F1 and PMCEQ-F2 by virtue of the fact that it captures attainable and flexible goal setting. Therefore, PMCEQ-F3 is even more problem-focused and agentic than PMCEQ-F2. Attainable or economic goal setting is assessed by items such as "When I were overwhelmed by a big task I would stop and take smaller steps"; flexible goal setting is measured by items such as "I can prioritise my needs and formulate a hierarchy of goals". The resulting prediction is:

(H3) Confidence in Setting Flexible and Feasible Hierarchies of Goals (PMCEQ-F3) will be negative correlated with both Anxiety and Depression.

2.4. Hypothesized Effects of Maladaptive Metacognitions on State Negative Emotions

The core aim is to take Wells and Matthews' (1994, 1996) dysfunctional metacognitions, measured by the MCQ-30, and Beer and Moneta's (2010) adaptive metacognitions and meta-emotions, assessed by the PMCEQ, simultaneously into account. The rationale is based on the underpinning aim to differentially assess effects of both maladaptive metacognitions (measured by the MCQ-30) and adaptive metacognitions and adaptive meta-emotions (measured by the PMCEQ) on state Negative Emotions conceptualized as state Anxiety and state Depression.

The five subscales of the MCQ-30, i.e. MCQ-F1 to MCQ-F5, were defined as latent variables of the overall construct MCQ-30 measuring dysfunctional or maladaptive metacognitive constructs. The resulting research hypothesis, which has been supported by a plethora of aforementioned empirical studies, is:

(H4) The MCQ-30 construct, consisting of the five maladaptive metacognitive factors as indicators, will be positively correlated with both Anxiety and Depression.

3. METHOD

3.1. Participants

A convenience sample of 212 worker and student participants was utilized comprising 108 (50.9%) students from metropolitan universities in Greater London, and 104 (49.1%) workers from various occupations. The age range was 18 to 70 years ($M = 30.2$, $SD = 11.27$); 61 (28.8%) were males, 151 (71.2%) were females. The ethnic background of the sample comprised 120 (56.6%) White, 36 (17.0%) Asian, and 28 (13.2%) Black participants; 28 (13.2%) were of other ethnicity.

3.2. Materials

Meta-Cognitions Questionnaire 30 (MCQ-30, Wells and Cartwright-Hatton, 2004)

The MCQ-30 consists of the five following replicable factors with six items for each factor: (1) MCQ-F1: Positive Beliefs about Worry (e.g. "Worrying helps me to avoid problems in the future") , (2) MCQ-F2: Negative Beliefs about Worry concerning Uncontrollability and Danger (e.g. "I could myself sick with worrying"), (3) MCQ-F3: Lack of Cognitive Confidence (e.g. "I have little confidence in my memory for words and names"), (4) MCQ-F4: Beliefs about the Need to Control Thoughts (e.g. "I should be in control of my thoughts all the time "), and (5) MCQ-F5 Cognitive Self-Consciousness (e.g. "I pay close attention to the way my mind works").[5] Using a four-point scale, respondents are asked to what extent they "generally agree" with the statements presented. The MCQ-30 possesses good psychometric properties of internal consistency and both construct and convergent validity (Wells and Cartwright-Hatton, 2004). The complete MCQ-30 instrument is shown in Appendix 1.

Positive Metacognitions and Positive Meta-Emotions Questionnaire (PMCEQ; Beer and Moneta, 2010)

The instrument consists of three replicable factors assessed by 18 items in total (with six items for each factor). The three factors measure the following three dimensions of positive metacognitions and positive meta-emotions: (1) PMCEQ-F1: Confidence in Extinguishing Perseverative Thoughts and Emotions (e.g. "If things go really badly I tend to brood and dwell on my negative thoughts"), (2) PMCEQ-F2: Confidence in Interpreting Own Emotions as Cues, Restraining from Immediate Reaction, and Mind-Setting for Problem-Solving (e.g. "I tend to rationally evaluate unpredictable situations rather than getting anxious"), and (3) PMCEQ-F3: Confidence in Setting Flexible and Feasible Hierarchies of Goals (e.g. "I can easily divide important long-term goals into achievable and short-term sub-goals"). Using a four-point scale, respondents are asked to what extent they "generally agree" with the statements presented.

The PMCEQ possesses good internal consistency with Cronbach's alpha coefficients of 0.85 for PMCEQ-F1, 0.76 for PMCEQ-F2, and 0.85 for PMCEQ-F3; in addition the PMCEQ shows good construct and concurrent validity (Beer and Moneta, 2010). The single items of the PMCEQ (including the key how these are assigned to the factors) are shown in Appendix 2.

Hospital Anxiety and Depression Scale (HADS, Zigmond and Snaith, 1983)

Both subscales of the HADS consist of seven items measuring anxiety and depression, respectively. The 7 items comprising the anxiety subscale include items such as "I get a sort of frightened feeling as if something awful is about to happen" and "I get sudden feelings of panic".

The 7 items comprising depression subscale contains items such as "I still enjoy the things I used to enjoy" and "I have lost interest in my appearance". Respondents are asked to measure their emotional state over the course of the previous week with each item being

---

[5] The single five subscales of the MCQ-30 are referred to as MCQ-F1, MCQ-F2, … , MCQ-F5.

measured on a 4-point scale (0 to 3); thus the range for both subscales is 0-21 with higher scores indicating the potential presence of emotional problems. Various cut-offs have been applied by different researchers – Bowling (2005) suggests the following interpretation of subscale scores: < 7: non-cases; sores in the range from 8-10: doubtful cases; and scores > 11: likely cases. For this study the timeframe was increased, asking participants to rate their emotional state over the course of the last month (rather than the last week); thus potential effects of possible short-term events on emotions were counterbalanced, still measuring state rather than trait anxiety and depression.

The HADS scale has been applied to a variety of both clinical and non-clinical samples. The majority of validation studies confirmed the two-factor structure with expected loadings of the anxiety and the depression items on the constructs anxiety and depressive symptoms respectively; this held again for both clinical and non-clinical samples (Mykletun, Stordal and Dahl, 2001). Even in non-clinical samples there appears to be comorbidity between anxiety and depression as reflected by reported intercorrelations between the subscales in the range from 0.49 to 0.63 (Mykletun, Stordal and Dahl, 2001). Overall the HADS has sound psychometric properties reflected by good reliability and validity (Zigmond and Snaith, 1983; Mykletun, Stordal and Dahl, 2001).

It should be emphasized that in spite of its possibly misleading name the HADS is suitable for administration to non-clinical samples. Moreover, compared to other alternative instruments, e.g. Beck Depression Inventory (BDI), the HADS items are "not intimidating". The absence of potentially distressing statements as used in the BDI, e.g. "I feel that the future is hopeless and that things cannot improve" or even items to assess suicidal thinking was the main (ethical) selection criterion for the HADS rather than the BDI within this research. The complete HADS instrument is shown in Appendix 3.

3.2. Statistical Analysis

The hypothesized relationships were tested using structural equation modeling (SEM) techniques (e.g., Kline, 1998) as implemented in LISREL 8.8 (Jöreskog and Sörbom, 1996).

The tested model comprised the following measurement model: the study constructs (PMCEQ-F1, PMCEQ-F2, PMCEQ-F3, MCQ-30, Anxiety and Depression) were defined as latent variables. The five maladaptive metacognitive traits, measured by the MCQ-30 subscales MCQ-F1 through MCQ-F5, were defined as indicators of the aggregated dysfunctional metacognition construct MCQ-30. The six subscale items of each of the three PMCEQ factors were defined as indicators of the three constructs PMCEQ-F1, PMCEQ-F2 and PMCEQ-F3.

The seven anxiety measuring items of the HADS were defined as latent variable of the outcome variable Anxiety and the seven depression-related HADS items as indicators of the second outcome variable Depression.

For the structural model the following paths were specified: (a) paths from PMCEQ-F1 to Anxiety and Depression, (b) paths from PMCEQ-F2 to Anxiety and Depression, (c) paths from PMCEQ-F3 to Anxiety and Depression, and (d) paths from MCQ-30 to Anxiety and Depression.

4. RESULTS

4.1. Data Description

Descriptive statistics and Pearson product-moment correlation coefficients for all questionnaire variables are presented in Table 1. Whereas the sample scored extremely low on HADS Depression (M = 4.2), the average HADS Anxiety score was high (M = 8.5) indicating potentially doubtful cases with reference to Bowling's (2005) suggested cut-off classification. In line with expectations all five MCQ-30 factors were positively correlated with both Anxiety and Depression; the Pearson bivariate correlation coefficients were moderate to strong, ranging from 0.35 to 0.60 (all of them significant at the .001 level). Also in line with expectations all three PMCEQ dimensions were negatively correlated with both Anxiety and Depression; the Pearson bivariate correlation coefficients were moderate to strong, ranging from 0.28 to 0.60 (all of them significant at the .001 level). Anxiety and Depression was strongly intercorrelated (r = .64, p < .001) indicating high comorbidity.

The correlation analyses furthermore showed that PMCEQ-F1 (Confidence in Extinguishing Perseverative Thoughts and Emotions) represents the PMCEQ factor which is most strongly and negatively related with the MCQ-30 – more specifically with the MCQ-F1 (r = -.52, p < .001) and MCQ-F2 subscales (r = -.53, p < .001), i.e. Positive Beliefs about Worry and Negative Beliefs about Worry concerning Uncontrollability and Danger, respectively. This was in line with expectations since, in conceptual and item content respects; PMCEQ-F1 represents the PMCEQ subscale which is most closely, yet inversely, related to MCQ-30 subscales.

Above and beyond bivariate correlations, the hypothesized relationships between the study variables were tested simultaneously using SEM. Results reflecting the possible underlying processes are subsequently outlined.

4.2. Test of the fitted Structural Equation Model

The relative effects of the PMCEQ factors and the MCQ-30 construct on both outcome measures state Anxiety and state Depression were simultaneously examined using SEM (e.g. Kline, 1998). The overall fit of the SEM model was assessed on the basis of four goodness-of-fit indices: (1) Chi-Square assessing the overall fit of the model by estimating the discrepancies between the observed covariance matrices and those implied by the model, (2) Goodness of Fit Index (GFI) as an overall fit index ranging from 0 to 1 and indicating good fit by values close to 1, (3) Comparative Fit Index (CFI) as an absolute fit index with values close to 1 indicating good fit and (4) Root Mean Square Error of Approximation (RMSEA) with values below .05 indicating good fit and values in the range of 0.05 to 0.08 representing acceptable fit (Hu and Bentler, 1999).

The SEM model did not fit in a strict statistical sense based merely upon the Chi-Square fit index (Chi-Square = 706.50, df = 421, p < .0001) but the three non-Chi-Square-based statistics indicated adequate to good fit with GFI = .82, CFI = .97 and RMSEA = .057.

Table 1. Means, standard deviations, Cronbach's alpha coefficients and intercorrelations of Study variables

*p<0.05[N=212; *p<0.05 **p<0.01.]	M	SD	Scale Range	Range Scores	Alpha	2.	3.	4.	5.	6.	7.	8.	9.	10.
1. PMCEQ-F1 – Confidence in Extinguishing Perseverative Thoughts and Emotions	16.8	4.3	6-24	6-24	.84	.43**	.42**	-.52**	-.53**	-.36**	-.39**	-.45**	-.60**	-.48**
2.PMCEQ-F2 – Confidence in Interpreting Own Emotions, Restraining from Immediate Reaction and Mind-Setting for Problem-Solving	14.9	3.8	6-24	6-24	.76	-	.69**	-.12*	-.23**	.01	-.01	-.21**	-.37**	-.29**
3. PMCEQ-F3 – Confidence in Setting Flexible and Feasible Hierarchies of Goals	16.9	4.0	6-24	7-24	.86	-	-	-.18**	-.26**	.01	-.07	-.23**	-.35**	-.28**
4. MCQ-F1 – Positive Beliefs about Worry	10.9	4.3	6-24	6-23	.69	-	-	-	.76**	.71**	.75**	.71**	.56**	46**
5. MCQ-F2 – Negative Beliefs about Worry concerning Uncontrollability and Danger	12.1	4.9	6-24	6-24	.67	-	-	-	-	.69**	.72**	.79**	.60**	.49**
6. MCQ-F3 – Low Cognitive Self Confidence	10.1	3.9	6-24	6-24	.57	-	-	-	-	-	.73**	.65**	.43**	.36**
7. MCQ-F4 – Beliefs about the Need to Control Thoughts	11.6	4.4	6-24	6-24	.62	-	-	-	-	-	-	.71**	.47**	.35**
8. MCQ-F5 – Cognitive Self-Consciousness	15.5	4.4	6-24	6-24	.68	-	-	-	-	-	-	-	.56**	.49**
9. ANXIET – HADS Anxiety	8.49	4.6	0-21	0-21	.86	-	-	-	-	-	-	-	-	.64**
10. DEPRESS – HADS Depression	4.23	8.4	0-21	0-15	.76	-	-	-	-	-	-	-	-	-

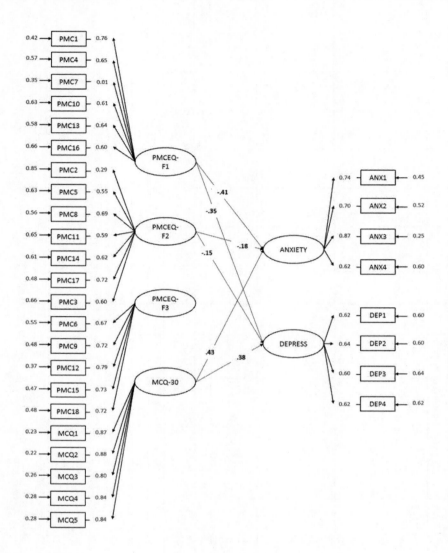

Figure 1. SEM relationships of PMCEQ factors and MCQ-30 with Anxiety and Depression.

The model is depicted in Figure 1. The hypothesized relationships among the latent variables are shown in the structural part of the model; the standardized path coefficients supported three out of the four hypotheses: (1) PMCEQ-F1 negatively and strongly predicted Anxiety (β = -.406) and Depression (β = -.348), (2) PMCEQ-F2 negatively, yet weakly, predicted Anxiety (β = -.177) and Depression (β = -.145) and (3) MCQ-30 positively and strongly predicted Anxiety (β = .429) and Depression (β =.383).

Only hypothesis 3, stating that PMCEQ-3 should be predictive of (state) Anxiety and Depression, was not supported, neither in terms of state Anxiety nor in terms of state Depression.

Figure 1 depicts the SEM of the relationships between maladaptive metacognitions (MCQ-30) and adaptive metacognitions and meta-emotions (PMCEQ-F1, PMCEQ-F2 and PMCEQ-F3) as independent variables and state Anxiety (ANXIETY) and state Depression

(DEPRESS) as outcome variables (standardized coefficients). The individual items of the PMCEQ are abbriviated as PMC. The single items of the PMCEQ measure and their assigments to the three PMCEQ-factors F1, F2 and F3 are shown in Appendix 2.

5. DISCUSSION

Data supported the first two hypotheses with PMCEQ-F1 strongly predicting decreased state Anxiety and state Depression and PMCEQ-F2 also negatively predicting the state negative emotions of Anxiety and Depression, yet to a lesser extent. The hypothesized state Anxiety- and state Depression-reducing effects of the more agentic PMCEQ-F3 were not supported. In line with previous empirical evidence the aggregated MCQ-30 was strongly and positively predictive of both state Anxiety and state Depression.

Comparing the absolute values of the standardized β-coefficients reveals that PMCEQ-F1's (negative) correlation with state Anxiety and state Depression was only marginally weaker than the (positive) correlation of the MCQ-30 with both state negative emotions. This is in line with the prediction and based on the argument that PMCEQ-F1 – Confidence in Extinguishing Perseverative Thoughts and Emotions – taps an inverse construct of the perseverative and ruminative S-REF activity as assessed by the MCQ-30. Moreover, PMCEQ-1 does this in an efficient way since the construct (subscale) is made up of only six items. Hence, in terms of their "predictive power" both instruments PMCEQ-1 and MCQ-30 show fair equality with regards to both state negative emotions of Anxiety and Depression.

Importantly, the findings of the present study can be interpreted in the sense that absence or low levels of (state) Anxiety and/or Depression not only require the absence of dysfunctional metacognitive constructs (as measured by the MCQ-30) but also the presence of functional metacognitions and functional meta-emotions as measured by the PMCEQ dimensions, specifically PMCEQ-F1. It can be argued that PMCEQ-F1 taps (inverse) metacognitive constructs which partially overlap with those measured by the MCQ-30, specifically the MCQ-F1 and MCQ-F2 subscales. Above and beyond MCQ-30 factors the PMCEQ instrument, however, also includes meta-emotional confidence domains: Inclusion of rumination-related items in the PMCEQ-1 subscale (e.g. the items "When confronted with ongoing troublesome circumstances I often start brooding and find it difficult to stop" and "If things go really badly I tend to 'brood' and dwell on my negative thoughts") was based upon two grounds: (1) the general necessity of investigating meta-emotions in addition to metacognitions, and (2) research evidence that beliefs about rumination play a core role in MDD as opposed to the predominant relevance of beliefs about worry in GAD. Hence, the PMCEQ-F1 dimension extends the MCQ-30 constructs by explicitly including (functional) meta-emotions in addition to (functional) metacognitions.

The finding that the PMCEQ-F2 factor predicted both state negative emotions of Anxiety and Depression to a much lesser extent than the PMCEQ-F1 factor can be explained in light of the confidence components the former factor attempts to measure. PMCEQ-F2 is of somewhat hybrid nature assessing mindfulness-related confidence constructs (Confidence in Interpreting Own Emotions as Cues and Restraining from Immediate Reaction) as well as problem-focused and agentic properties (Mind-Setting for Problem-Solving). The results underpinned this two-fold nature by virtue of the fact that PMCEQ-F2 emerged as a negative but only weak predictor of state Anxiety and state Depression. Interestingly, Beer and Moneta's (2010) validation study provided evidence that PMCEQ-F2 is also a positive and moderately strong predictor of Intrinsic Motivation, which can be explained in light of the agency-related and problem-focussed items.

With regard to PMCEQ-F3 – the most agentic PMCEQ dimension - the study results imply the interesting question on what potential grounds there was no effect of PMCEQ-F3 – Confidence in Setting Flexible and Feasible Hierarchies of Goals – on the state negative emotions of Anxiety and Depression. The direct effects of PMCEQ-F1 and to a lesser extent of PMCEQ-F2 on (state) Anxiety and Depression on one hand and the lack of effects of the goal-setting-related PMCEQ-F3 on (state) Anxiety and Depression on the other hand are potentially linked to distinct psychological well-being concepts.[1]

PMCEQ-F1 and PMCEQ-F2 appear to measure "feeling good states" in the sense of hedonic well-being, i.e. absence of emotional distress (anxiety and depression). PMCEQ-F3, tapping flexible and attainable goal-setting and self-determination, however, refers to flourishing and self-actualization. Flourishing and self-actualization are expressions of eudemonic well-being which is less focused on pleasure or the absence of emotional distress but more concerned with curiosity and engagement. Empirical evidence for these arguments was again provided by Beer and Moneta's (2010) validation study of the PMCEQ with evidence for a strong positive correlation between PMCEQ-F3 and Intrinsic Motivation as opposed to only moderate positive correlation between PMCEQ-F2 and Intrinsic Motivation and merely weak positive correlation between PMCEQ-F1 and Intrinsic Motivation.

In conclusion, it can be argued that the PMCEQ extends the scope of the (inverse) MCQ-30 constructs in two ways: (1) The PMCEQ implies meta-emotional constructs which are not assessed by the MCQ-30, and (2) within the dimensions PMCEQ-2 and PMCEQ-3 the PMCEQ instrument takes psychological constructs into account which are related to eudemonic well-being, above and beyond the hedonic well-being focus of the PMCEQ-F1 and its (inverse) pendant MCQ-30.

Prior to discussing core strengths of this study – with regards to potential applications and implications – inherent limitations shall be outlined. Firstly, due to the questionnaire-based survey design, potential self-report bias and social desirability bias might have occurred. Secondly, the employed cross-sectional design imposes limitations for inferring cause-and-effect relationships. Hence, future research could be improved by utilizing a longitudinal design which will allow a rigorous test of stability over time and inference of potential cause-and-effect relationships. Thirdly, the somewhat small sample size of 212 participants required certain compromises for the SEM techniques: All three subscales of the PMCEQ were conceptualized as single latent variables, whereas this was no longer possible for the five MCQ-30 subscales in light of the sample size restriction. Hence, the whole MCQ-30 scale was defined as compound latent variable using its five factors or subscales as indicators. Future research should address this limitation by using larger samples and defining all MCQ-30 subscales – equivalent to the PMCEQ subscales – as single latent exogenous variables.

The current study can inform applications in terms of potential interventions. In (inverse) analogy to metacognitive therapy for psychological disorders (Wells, 2009) the PMCEQ confidence factors might be amenable to some cultivation via therapeutic or coaching

---

[1] Although absence/low levels of anxiety and/or depression do not necessarily equate with "psychological well-being" the approximation appears legitimate for the following discussion.

interventions. Such interventions should specifically be tailored to build individuals' confidence in quickly extinguishing perseveration and depressive rumination as a reliable means to prevent or at least buffer the state negative emotions of Anxiety and Depression.

Beer and Moneta's (2012) study revealed further adaptive synergy effects in light of the core findings that PMCEQ-F1 not only reduces stress perception but also prevents maladaptive coping strategies and, moreover, fosters adaptive coping strategies. It can be concluded, that the PMCEQ-F1 informs potential interventions beyond buffering against negative state emotions by virtue of the finding that the constructs enhance adaptive coping strategies.

Interventions tailored to PMCEQ-F2 and PMCEQ-F3 constructs should have even more pronounced beneficial effects in terms of desensitizing long-term stress perception and, moreover, fostering adaptive coping strategies and also intrinsic motivation. The hypothesized effects should be of special interest with regards to efficiency-increasing coaching in academic and professional settings.

In conclusion, it can be tentatively inferred that PMCEQ-derived psychological interventions should extend the scope of MCQ-30-related ones by not just preventing or buffering against state negative emotions of depression and comorbid anxiety but potentially enhancing self-empowering and agentic problem-focus and increasing the likelihood of agentic problem solutions. The goal-setting focus on of the most agentic PMCEQ dimension, PMCEQ-F3, increases the likelihood of goal-attainment and, hence, potentially contributes to "self-actualization" – at least to eudemonic well-being.

APPENDIX 1. META-COGNITIONS QUESTIONNAIRE 30 (MCQ-30)

This questionnaire is concerned with beliefs people have about their thinking. Listed below are a number of beliefs that people have expressed. Please read each item and indicate how much you generally agree with it. *For each question please tick <u>one</u> response (box) which appears to be the most appropriate one for you:* *1 Do not agree* *2 Agree Slightly* *3 Agree moderately* *4 Agree very much*	1	2	3	4
1. Worrying helps me to avoid problems in the future.				
2. My worrying is dangerous for me.				
3. I think a lot about my thoughts.				
4. I could make myself sick with worrying.				
5. I am aware of the way my mind works when I am thinking through a problem.				
6. If I did not control a worrying thought, and then it happened, it would be my fault.				
7. I need to worry in order to remain organised.				
8. I have little confidence in my memory for words and names.				
9. My worrying thoughts persist, no matter how I try to stop them.				
10. Worrying helps me to get things sorted out in my mind.				
11. I cannot ignore my worrying thoughts.				
12. I monitor my thoughts.				

Appendix 1. (Continued)

This questionnaire is concerned with beliefs people have about their thinking. Listed below are a number of beliefs that people have expressed. Please read each item and indicate how much you generally agree with it. For each question please tick one response (box) which appears to be the most appropriate one for you: 1 Do not agree 2 Agree Slightly 3 Agree moderately 4 Agree very much	1	2	3	4
13. I should be in control of my thoughts all the time.				
14. My memory can mislead me at times.				
15. My worrying could make me go mad.				
16. I am constantly aware of my thinking.				
17. I have a poor memory.				
18. I pay close attention to the way my mind works.				
19. Worrying helps me to cope.				
20. Not being able to control my thoughts is a sign of weakness.				
21. When I start worrying, I cannot stop.				
22. I will be punished for not controlling certain thoughts.				
23. Worrying helps me to solve problems.				
24. I have little confidence in my memory for places.				
25. I think it's bad to think certain thoughts.				
26. I do not trust my memory.				
27. If I could not control my thoughts I would not be able to function.				
28. I need to worry in order to work well.				
29. I have little confidence in my memory for actions.				
30. I constantly examine my thoughts.				

APPENDIX 2. THE POSITIVE METACOGNITIONS AND POSITIVE META-EMOTIONS QUESTIONNAIRE (PMCEQ)

This questionnaire is concerned with beliefs people have about their thinking and emotions in difficult situations. Listed below are a number of such beliefs that people have expressed. Please read each item and indicate how much you generally agree with it. *For each question please tick one response (box) which appears to be the most appropriate one for you: 1 Do not agree 2 Agree Slightly 3 Agree moderately 4 Agree very much*	1	2	3	4
1.In times of "feeling in the dumps" it's hard for me to regulate my low mood.				
2.In difficult situations I quickly "rationalise" my fear by assessing costs and benefits of "confronting versus escaping".				
3.I can easily divide important long-term goals into achievable and short-term sub-goals.				
4.If things go really badly I tend to brood and dwell on my negative thoughts.				

	1	2	3	4
This questionnaire is concerned with beliefs people have about their thinking and emotions in difficult situations. Listed below are a number of such beliefs that people have expressed. Please read each item and indicate how much you generally agree with it. *For each question please tick one response (box) which appears to be the most appropriate one for you:* *1 Do not agree* *2 Agree Slightly* *3 Agree moderately* *4 Agree very much*				
5.I feel that negative or anxious thoughts do not depict the reality – I regard them just as "events" which I have to evaluate				
6 I can prioritise my needs and formulate a hierarchy of goals.				
7 When the "blues" overcomes me I tend to struggle with controlling my low mood.				
8 I can stop any "negative thinking spirals" and focus on what I can do in the situation				
9 When I find it difficult to cope with a huge task I tend to tackle it in smaller steps.				
10 I tend to overreact when things are really going wrong.				
11 I tend to rationally evaluate unpredictable situations rather than getting anxious.				
12 When progress becomes slow and difficult I can readily adopt a step-by-step approach to remove obstacles.				
13 When confronted with ongoing troublesome circumstances I often start "brooding" and find it difficult to stop.				
14 I can make a volitional (free) decision to keep on top of things and remain confident even when I have to face some troublesome events.				
15 When a problem appears to be insurmountable I know that it's just a matter of breaking it down into smaller problems				
16 I tend to think that my worrying thoughts might reflect the reality.				
17 When I experience taxing demands I try to act as in the motto: "There are no problems, only solutions".				
18 If I were overwhelmed by a big task I would stop and take smaller steps.				

PMCEQ-items: 1+4+7+10+13+16 = PMCEQ-F1; PMCEQ-items: 2+5+8+11+14+17 = PMCEQ-F2; PMCEQ-items: 3+6+9+12+15+18 = PMCEQ-F3

APPENDIX 3. HOSPITAL ANXIETY AND DEPRESSION SCALE (HADS)

Instructions

This questionnaire is designed to assess how you feel. Please ignore the numbers printed on the left of the questionnaire. Read each item and underline the reply which comes closest to how you have been feeling in the past month. Don't take too long over your replies; your immediate reaction to each item will probably be more accurate than a long thought-out response.

A *I feel tense or 'wound-up':*

3   Most of the time

2   A lot of the time

1   From time to time, occasionally

0   Not at all

D *I still enjoy the things I used to enjoy:*
0   Definitely as much
1   Not quite so much
2   Only a little
3   Hardly at all

A *I get a sort of frightened feeling as if something awful is about to happen:*
3   Very definitely and quite badly
2   Yes, but not too badly
1   A little, but it doesn't worry me
0   Not at all

D *I can laugh and see the funny side of things:*
0   As much as I always could
1   Not quite so much now
2   Definitely not so much now
3   Not at all

A *Worrying thoughts go through my mind:*
3   A great deal of the time
2   A lot of the time
1   From time to time but not too often
0   Only occasionally

D *I feel cheerful:*
3   Not at all
2   Not often
1   Sometimes
0   Most of the time

A *I can sit at ease and feel relaxed:*
0   Definitely
1   Usually
2   Not often
3   Not at all

D *I feel as if I am slowed down:*
3   Nearly all the time
2   Very often
1   Sometimes
0   Not at all

A *I get a sort of frightened feeling like 'butterflies' in the stomach:*
0   Not at all
1   Occasionally
2   Quite often
3   Very often

D   *I have lost interest in my appearance:*
3   Definitely
2   I don't take as much care as I should
1   I may not take quite as much care
0   I take just as much care as ever

A   *I feel restless as I have to be on the move:*
3   Very much indeed
2   Quite a lot
1   Not very much
0   Not at all

D   *I look forward with enjoyment to things:*
0   As much as I ever did
1   Rather less than I used to
2   Definitely less than I used to
3   Hardly at all

A   *I get sudden feelings of panic:*
3   Very often indeed
2   Quite often
1   Not very much
0   Not at all

D   *I can enjoy a good book or radio or TV programme:*
0   Often
1   Sometimes
2   Not often
3   Seldom

REFERENCES

American Psychiatric Association (2000). Diagnostic and Statistical Manual of Mental Disorders, 4th Ed. Washington DC: Author.

Beer, N., and Moneta, G.B. (2012). Adaptive metacognitive self-regulation and resilience-related assets in the midst of challenge: A qualitative analysis. In: V. Barkoukis, [Ed.] *Psychology of Self-Regulation*, (pp. 1-37), Hauppage, NY: NOVA Science Publishers.

Beer, N., and Moneta, G.B (2012). Coping and perceived stress as a function of positive metacognitions and positive meta-emotions. *Individual Differences Research, 10*, 105-112.

Beer, N., and Moneta, G.B (2010). Construct and Concurrent Validity of the Positive Metacognitions and Positive Meta-Emotions Questionnaire. *Personality and Individual Differences, 49*, 977-982.

Bowling, A. (2005). *Measuring Health – A review of quality of life measurement scales.* London: Open University Press.

British Psychological Society – Division of Clinical Psychology (2000). *Understanding mental illness and psychotic experiences: A report by the British Psychological Society Division of Clinical Psychology.* Leicester: British Psychological Society.

Cartwright-Hatton, S., and Wells, A. (1997). Beliefs about worry and intrusions: the meta-cognitions questionnaire and its correlates. *Journal of Anxiety Disorders, 11*, 279-315.

Corcoran, K. and Segal, Z. (2008). Metacognition in depressive and anxiety disorders: Current Directions. *International Journal of Cognitive Therapy, 1*, 33-44.

Culbertson, F.M. (1997). Depression and gender, *American Psychologist, 52*, 25-31.

Davison, G.C., Neale, J.M., and Kring, A.M (2003). *Abnormal Psychology* (9th Ed.). USA: Wiley.

Fredrickson, B., and Joiner, T. (2002). Positive emotions trigger upward spirals toward emotional wellbeing. *Psychological Science, 13*, 172-175.

Gleitman, H., Fridlund, A.J., and Reisberg, D. (2004). *Psychology*, 6th Ed., New York: Norton.

Gotlib, I.H. and Hammen, C.L. (1992). *Psychological aspects of depression: Towards a cognitive-interpersonal integration.* Chichester: Wiley.

Hammen, C. (1997). *Depression.* Hove: Psychology Press.

Hu, L., and Bentler, P. M. (1999). Cut-off criteria for fit indices in covariance structure analysis: Conventional versus new alternatives. *Structural Equation Modeling, 6*, 1-55.

Hudlicka, E. (2005). Modeling Interaction between Metacognition and Emotion in a Cognitive Architecture. *Proceedings of the AAAI Spring Symposium on Metacognition in Computation.* AAAI Technical Report, 55-61.

Jöreskog, K. G., and Sörbom, D. (1996). *LISREL 8: User's reference guide.* Chicago, IL: Scientific Software International, Inc.

Judd, L.L. (1997). The clinical course of unipolar depressive disorders. *Archives of General Psychiatry, 54*, 989-993.

Just, N., and Alloy, L.B. (1997). The response styles of depression: Tests and extension of the theory. *Journal of Abnormal Psychology, 106*, 221-229.

Kline, R. B. (1998). *Principles and practice of structural equation modeling.* New York: Guilford Press.

Lyddy, F. (2000). Depression: The state of the disorder. *The Psychologist, 13(8)*, 414-415.

Mitmansgruber, H., Beck, T. N., Höfer, S, and Schüßler, G. (2009). When you don't like what you feel: Experiential avoidance, mindfulness and meta-emotion in emotion regulation. *Personality and Individual Differences, 46*, 448-453.

Mykletun, A., Stordal, E. and Dahl, A.A. (2001). Hospital Anxiety and Depression (HADS) Scale: Factor structure, item analysis and internal consistency in a large population. *British Journal of Psychiatry Research, 104*, 247-257.

Papageorgiou, C., and Wells, A. (2001). Positive beliefs about depressive rumination: Development and preliminary validation of a self-report scale. *Behavior Therapy, 32*, 13-26.

Sica, C., Steketee, G., Ghisi, M. Chiri, L. and Franceschini, S., (2007). Metacognitive beliefs and strategies predict worry, obsessive–compulsive symptoms and coping styles: A preliminary prospective study on an Italian non-clinical sample. *Clinical Psychology and Psychotherapy, 14*, 4, 258-268.

Spada, M., Nikčević, A., Moneta, G.B., and Wells, A. (2007). Metacognitions as a mediator between emotion and smoking dependence. *Addictive Behaviours, 32*, 2120-2129.

Sue, D., Sue, D.W., and Sue, S. (2006). *Understanding Abnormal Behavior*, 8th Ed. Houhgthon Miffin Company, Boston.

Vaillant, G.E. (2000). Adaptive Mental Mechanisms: Their Role in a Positive Psychology, *American Psychologist, 55*, 89-98.

Watkins, E., and Moulds, M. (2005). Positive beliefs about rumination in depression – a replication and extension. *Personality and Individual Differences, 39*, 73-82.

Watson, D., Weber, K. Assenheimer, J., and Clark, L. (2005). Testing a tripartite model: Evaluating the convergent and discriminating validity of anxiety and depression symptom scales. *Journal of Abnormal Psychology, 104*, 3-14.

Wells, A. (2009). *Metacognitive Therapy for Anxiety and Depression.* New York: The Guilford Press.

Wells, A. (2000). *Emotional Disorders and Metacognition: Innovative Cognitive Therapy.* Chichester, UK: Wiley.

Wells, A. (1995). Metacognition and Worry: A cognitive model of generalised anxiety disorder. *Behavioural and Cognitive Psychotherapy, 32*, 301-320.

Wells, A. and Carter (2001). Further tests of a cognitive model of GAD: Worry and metacognitions in patients with GAD, panic disorder, social phobia, and depression. *Behavior Therapy, 32 (1)*, 85-102.

Wells, A., and Cartwright-Hatton, S. (2004). A short form of the metacognitions questionnaire: properties of the MCQ-30. *Behavior Therapy, 42*, 385-396.

Wells, A., and Matthews, G. (1996). Modelling cognition in emotional disorder: The S-REF model. *Behaviour Research and Therapy, 34*, 881-888.

Wells, A., and Matthews, G. (1994). *Attention and Emotion. A Clinical Perspective.* Hove: Erlbaum.

World Health Organisation (1996). The global burden of disease: A comprehensive assessment of mortality and disability from diseases, injuries and risk factors in 1990 projected to 2020. (C.J.L. Murray and A.D. Lopez, Eds.). Cambridge, MA: Harvard University Press.

Wright, B. A., and Lopez, S. J. (2002). Widening the diagnostic focus: A case for including human strengths and environmental resources. In C. R. Snyder and S. J. Lopez (Eds.), *Handbook of Positive Psychology* (pp. 26-45). Oxford: Oxford University Press.

Zigmond, A.S., and Snaith, R.P. (1983). The Hospital Anxiety and Depression Scale. *Acta Psychiatrica Scandinavica, 67*, 361-370.

In: Handbook of Psychology of Emotions   ISBN: 978-1-62808-053-7
Editors: C. Mohiyeddini, M. Eysenck and S. Bauer   © 2013 Nova Science Publishers, Inc.

Chapter 16

SENSATION SEEKING AND EMOTION

Nico Liebe and Marcus Roth*
Department of Psychology, University of Duisburg-Essen, Germany

ABSTRACT

The following chapter addresses the concept of *sensation seeking* and its wide-reaching connections to emotions. The first part introduces the conceptualization and measurement of sensation seeking and presents a chronological overview of its development. For a better understanding of the construct of sensation seeking, different conceptual perspectives and their implications are considered and discussed. The second subchapter follows and elaborates on a number of links that connect sensation seeking to a wide range of emotions (e.g., excitement, curiosity, depression, anger, fear, disgust, and frustration) and tries to embed the reported results into a neurophysiological framework. The third part presents our own study in which we investigated the moderating effect of sensation seeking on affect caused by stress to prove the stress-buffering effects of sensation seeking and to look for differences between high vs. low sensation seekers in the strategies they use and in their abilities to self-regulate emotion.

INTRODUCTION: THE CONCEPTUALIZATION AND MEASUREMENT OF SENSATION SEEKING

The concept of sensation seeking can be traced back to the works of Zuckerman (1971; Zuckerman, Kolin, Price, & Zoob, 1964). Initially, Zuckerman (1979) defined sensation seeking as a "trait defined by the need for varied, novel and complex sensations and experiences and the willingness to take physical and social risks for the sake of such experience" (p. 10). In later years, he rejected his own definition, which identified sensation seeking as a need, by trying to define it as a trait involving the "seeking of varied, novel, complex and intense sensations and experiences" (1994, p. 27). This was done because Zuckerman tried to avoid confusing the term "need" with "compulsion" (ibid., p. 26). It is,

* Corresponding authors: nico.liebe@uni-due.de, marcus.roth@uni-due.de.

however, virtually impossible to avoid conceiving of sensation seeking as a need: An exclusively behavioral definition without a motivational component would lead to a completely descriptive conceptualization without explicative function. Even Zuckerman himself sometimes spoke of a "need" for sensations (ibid., p. 374).

The most widely used instrument for assessing sensation seeking is the *Sensation Seeking Scale - Form V* (SSS-V) developed by Zuckerman (1994). The SSS-V is a self-report inventory with four factorially derived subscales as well as a total score. The *Thrill and Adventure Seeking* (TAS) subscale reflects a desire to engage in thrill-seeking, risky, and adventurous recreational pursuits. The *Experience Seeking* (ES) subscale presents the need to seek new experiences through, for example, travel, drugs, music, art, and an unconventional style of life. The *Disinhibition* (Dis) subscale reflects a desire for social release through drinking, partying, and a variety of sexual experiences, whereas items on the *Boredom Susceptibility* (BS) subscale tap into an aversion for repetitive experiences.

There has been much critique of the conceptualization as well as of the assessment of sensation seeking via the SSS-V using highly specific behavior (Arnett, 1994; Beauducel & Roth, 2003; Hammelstein, 2004; Hammelstein & Roth, 2003). Major critical points include the low internal consistency of the subscale BS (Ferrando & Chico, 2001), the lack of theoretical foundation of the chosen items on the SSS-V (Jackson & Maraun, 1996), the lack of a conceptual differentiation between sensation seeking and impulsivity (Möller & Huber, 2003), the use of items that are age dependent (e.g., "skiing," "mountaineering"; cf. Arnett, 1996; Roth, 2003), and the inclusion of items describing dysfunctional behavior itself (e.g., the use of marijuana), and therefore possibly creating a confounding of predictor (sensation seeking) and criterion (substance abuse; ibid.). An inspection of the items included in the SSS-V leads us to conclude that a *specific* behavioral style is being assessed. This style can be described as physically strenuous, socially uninhibited, and tendencially antisocial. Moreover, this pattern of behavior seems to be typical of adolescents and young adults so that it can be summarized as a "youthful behavior style" (Roth, Hammelstein, & Brähler, 2007, 2009). Although such a behavioral style could potentially represent a form of sensation seeking, it would seem necessary to bear in mind that it is surely only *one* expressive form.

In order to avoid the limitations inherent in the SSS-V, an alternative measure of sensation seeking was developed by Arnett (1994). The *Arnett Inventory of Sensation Seeking* (AISS) consists of 20 items, none of which are age-related or concerned with physical strength or antisocial or norm-breaking behavior, ensuring the absence of criterion contamination when the scale is used to predict behavior such as alcohol or drug use. Arnett (1994) views this concept in a more general light as a quality that reflects the search for intensity and novelty in sensory experiences (Arnett, 1994, 1996; Beauducel & Roth, 2003). These conceptual differences are reflected in the wording of the items. Zuckerman's SSS-V contains highly specific descriptions of behavior, whereas Arnett, being more interested in the underlying needs, had formulated the items in a more general fashion and had thus minimized the – surely inevitable – involvement of concrete behavioral description. With this, Arnett (1994) also wanted to reconceptualize sensation seeking: Whereas in Zuckerman's (1979) first conception, sensation seeking is viewed as a need for novelty and complexity of stimulation, Arnett's conception of sensation seeking is characterized by the need for novelty and intensity of stimulation. According to the theoretical issues, the AISS is composed of two 10-item subscales and a total score. The *Intensity* scale assesses the intensity of stimulation of the senses (e.g., "When I listen to music, I like it to be very loud"), whereas the items of the

Novelty scale refer to openness to experience (e.g., "I can see how it would be interesting to marry someone from a foreign country").

However, although Arnett (1994), in contrast to the SSS-V, did not include delinquent or effusive and socially conspicuous behavior, his neutrally evaluated items continue to seem more typical of young people (e.g., "I like a movie where there are a lot of explosions and car chases"), even if they show no bias toward social deviance.

More consequently, based on the conception of sensation seeking as a need rather than a behavioral style, Roth and Hammelstein (2012) developed a new assessment tool called the *Need Inventory of Sensation Seeking* (NISS). This instrument aims to measure sensation seeking as a global need for stimulation without describing specific behaviors in which the need could potentially be expressed. Explicitly, sensation seeking is to be assessed only by its aim (namely, stimulation) and not by possible behaviors meant to satisfy this need. To this end, the 17 items included in the NISS address the pleasure of the target state (stimulation) or its opposite (rest, calmness) and not concrete behaviors (e.g., "I like the feeling of excitement in my body," "I like to find myself in situations which make my heart beat faster"). Subjects are required to rate how often they have felt this way in the past six months on a five-point Likert scale. In addition to a total score, the NISS comprises two factor-analytically determined subscales: *need for stimulation* (NS) and *avoidance of rest* (AR). The two-dimensional structure, which was cross-validated by Roth and Hammelstein (2012) using an English version of the NISS in British students, is in line with the theoretical considerations of Grawe (2002) concerning fundamental needs. In his view, schemes of approach as well as avoidance emerge for each and every fundamental need: The first factor assesses the aim of approach (which corresponds to the *need for stimulation* subscale of the NISS); the second one measures the aim of avoidance (which corresponds to *the avoidance of rest* subscale of the NISS).

As shown by Roth and Hammelstein (2012), there were moderate correlations between the NISS and the SSS-V (correlations with the SSS-V total score: NISS-total: $r = .37$; NS: $r = .54$; AR: $r = .02$). Hammelstein and Roth (2012) found that the scales of both instruments significantly predicted a willingness toward occupational change in a sample of employees between the ages of 19 and 65 years. However, when age was entered as a covariate, the effects of the SSS-V disappeared, whereas the effects of the NISS scales remained stable. Therefore, as argued by the authors, "we cannot be sure whether the SSS-V actually measures sensation seeking or merely an age-related activity status" (p. 21).

However, although we have to be concerned with different measurement approaches based on different conceptions, we found similar results with these measurements; for example with respect to age and sex differences in sensation seeking. Zuckerman (1979) postulated early on that sensation seeking is related to developmental phases and is generally "lower in children, reaches a peak in adolescence and declines thereafter" (p. 92). To date, three studies have used the SSS-V to examine age and sex differences in sensation seeking in samples with a broad age range. The first comprehensive data on age differences were analyzed by Zuckerman, Eysenck, and Eysenck (1978). Total scores decreased from the youngest age group (16–19 years) to the oldest group (60 and older) in both sexes. Furthermore, sex differences were significant in all age groups with males scoring higher than females. These results were supported by Ball, Farnill, and Wangeman (1984) in an Australian sample as well as by Beauducel, Strobel, and Brocke (2003) in a German sample with nearly the same age range. Interestingly, the decline in sensation seeking with age as well as the sex differences could also be demonstrated in studies using the AISS (Roth, Schumacher, & Brähler, 2005) and the NISS (Roth, Hammelstein, & Brähler, 2007).

SENSATION SEEKING AND ITS LINKS TO EMOTIONS

As may be obvious from reading the first part of the text, none of the before-mentioned conceptions of sensation seeking explicitly took emotional aspects into account. But a closer look at this lack assessment of emotions in the theories of sensation seeking unveils that there are indeed a lot of indirect links that we want to discuss next. Thereby the previously described characterizations of low and high sensation seekers will be expanded in stages. First, we will outline some emotional aspects of sensation seeking when characterized as a need and the intented emotions that accompany sensation-seeking behavior. After that, we will focus on *curiosity* and *interest* as two important emotional facets with a notable physiological link to sensation seeking, followed by an overview of studies concerning the neural bases of sensation seeking and their link to *depression* and *anxiety*. Another important link leads to *impulsiveness* and *emotional responsiveness* together with *anger* and *aggression* but also *enjoyment of emotional expression*. A look at related constructs such as *emotional instability* and *neuroticism* leads on to *fear* and *disgust* and their relation to the risk-behavior aspects of sensation seeking and possible connections to psychopathy. Finally, the last paragraph addresses *stress* and *frustration*.

Emotional Aspects of Sensation Seeking as a Need

First, sensation seeking at its core is understandable only in a motivational framework because the definition itself points to a need for at least new and intense sensations (see above), and therefore the satisfaction of this need should lead to an emotional state that is suggested to be more comfortable and pleasant than the current one (Deci & Ryan, 2000). But besides the relief that is expected to emerge as a result of the successful satisfaction of the need, it is mainly the sought for (pleasurable) emotions that are bound to the very sensation-seeking behaviors that define the sensation seeker.

Zuckerman (1979, 1994) used the term "sensation" instead of "stimulation", because he wanted to emphasize that the inner sensations, understood as consequences of stimulation, work as reinforcers (and not the stimulation itself), and therefore, the resulting sensations do not depend only on the intensity of a stimulation but also on characteristics such as novelty and complexity. As a result of this definition and the research that followed it, the high sensation seeker must be thought of as somebody who typically prefers the experience of high levels of physiological, emotional, and/or cognitive arousal (Arnett, 1994; Roth & Hammelstein, 2012). Because these sensations feel pleasant to them, high sensation seekers show a variety of (more or less typical) behaviors that create situations in which they can experience such strong sensations, and therefore, they tend to evoke emotions and feelings that especially involve high levels of such phenomenal aspects such as excitement, euphoria, disinhibition, surprise, suspense, sexual lust, or even fear and horror.

To satisfy their need for stimulation and to experience strong emotions, some high sensation seekers engage in (dangerous) extreme sports such as bungee jumping, parachuting or diving, whereas others prefer wild parties with alcohol and illegal drugs, and others watch horror movies or travel to far and exotic countries or use other strategies to broaden their horizons because they get bored easily (Zuckerman, 1994).

Based on factor analytical studies, Zuckerman (1994, 2005) tried to define stable subcategories and divided sensation seeking in his wide-spread *Sensation Seeking Scale – Form V* into four subscales (see above) that reflect different types of sensation seeking behavior and involve different emotional aspects, which must be considered separately.

The *Thrill and Adventure Seeking* subscale (TAS) points to physically risky activities like extreme sports that provide the feeling of being thrilled. However, there is no consensus with regard to the degree to which persons high on this scale like the feeling of being thrilled and experience it as pleasant excitement or whether they are less frightened by risky situations in general, perhaps because of a weaker emotional response or because of underestimating an objective danger (Rheinberg, 2006). *Experience Seeking* (ES) as the search for mainly new sensations and experiences is also bound to the search for novel emotional experiences or a broad variety of emotions, for example through reaching altered states of mind by meditation or using drugs (Maio & Esses, 2001; Mastandrea, Bartoli, & Bove, 2009). Regarding the *Disinhibition* (Dis) subscale, its name already points to the impulsive character of the subsumed behaviors in a social context. This link from sensation seeking to impulsiveness reveals a relation to a higher emotional responsiveness and an enjoyment of expressing emotions but also to emotional instability and aggression (Zuckerman, 1994). The implications of this link to impulsiveness are discussed in detail later on. Finally the *Boredom Susceptibility* (BS) factor describes an intolerance for repetitive experiences in general, which, in other words means that high sensation seekers get bored more easily and experience states of boredom as more unpleasant than low sensation seekers do (Zuckerman, 1994).

Due to these differently characterized subscales, a lot of studies have found very complex results and interactions concerning emotional aspects even in studies with straightforward designs. For example, Zaleski (1984) investigated the impact of sensation seeking on the preference for emotional visual stimuli. In addition to a main effect of the total SSS-V-score, he found different effects for each single subscale. Whereas high sensation seekers tended to prefer pictures that had been rated emotionally negative, and low sensation seekers showed a stronger preference for the positive stimuli, these findings did not hold for the BS subscale and for TAS and Dis scores of women. But besides the interesting preference of some high sensation seekers (specifically men) for emotionally negative stimuli, which may be perceived as more excitable in the end, it seems to be impossible to understand in detail the interactions that were found with regard to the behavioral characteristics of the four subscales. This problem of giving a systematic and consistent interpretation of the findings seems to be a consequence of the already mentioned methodological problems of the SSS-V and the weak theoretical foundation of the content of the subscales.

The alternative characterization of sensation seeking by a more basal and thereby more common feature that is shared by all high sensation seekers as presented by the NISS concept (Roth & Hammelstein, 2012; see above) avoids this overly complex differentiation on the level of concrete behavior. The items focus on the pleasure of the target state of stimulation beyond the limitation of specific examples of "typical" sensation-seeking behavior and refer to explicit phenomenal aspects of arousal such as the feeling of excitement in the body or feeling totally charged and whether these sensations are liked or disliked.

As a result of the different conceptual approaches that have been used to define and operationalize sensation seeking, the emotional implications for sensation seeking depend on the very concept of it and which scale is used. Due to its prevalence most of the following findings refer to the SSS-V despite its methodological weaknesses.

Curiosity and Interest and Their Link to the Physiological Bases of Sensation Seeking

Another emotion, which seems to be typical if not essential for sensation seeking, and which is also bound to the context of a preference for excitement and arousal – and which therefore is also linked to a susceptibility to boredom – is curiosity. A lot of studies indicate that there is a significant difference between high and low sensation seekers concerning curiosity and connected constructs such as interest and exploratory activity (for a detailed overview, see Roth & Hammelstein, 2003; Zuckerman, 1994). This difference is not only obvious on the level of concrete behavior, but it is also evident on physiological and neural levels.

Depending on the intensity of a new stimulus and its interaction with personal factors, there are different categories of reactions that are accompanied by typical changes in heart rate and specific patterns in the phasic skin conductance response (Brocke, Strobel, & Müller, 2003). For example, new stimuli with a low intensity cause a decline in the heart rates of most people, and this can be interpreted as an orienting reflex that represents a sensitivity to or focused attention on a specific stimulus enabled by reduced arousal. By contrast, new stimuli with a high intensity cause an increase in the heart rates of most people, which can be seen as a defensive reflex or a startle reflex and which indicates either a preparation for physical action or a disruption of action and a focusing on the threatening stimulus (Zuckerman, 1994).

Of special interest are the differences found between high and low sensation seekers exposed to stimuli with a mid-level intensity. In this condition, high sensation seekers (especially those high on Dis) still typically show an orienting reflex, whereas low sensation seekers respond with a defensive reflex (Zuckerman, 1994). These results depend on the personal relevance of the new stimuli and have been found for changes in heart rate and for changes in the patterns of skin conductance response as well (Brocke, Strobel, & Müller, 2003; Neary & Zuckerman, 1976; Orlebeke & Feji, 1979; Smith, Perlstein, Davidson, & Micheal, 1986).

In contrast to skin conductance and heart rate, which can represent the effects of novelty and the intensity of a stimulus only in a combined way, analyses of cortical evoked potentials on an EEG allow for discrimination between novelty and intensity because of the different patterns displayed by these characteristics (Zuckerman, 1994). Normally the presentation of stimuli with increasing intensities leads to higher amplitudes for early components like P100 (positive peak at about 80 – 130 ms after stimulus onset) and N100 (negative peak at about 80 – 120 ms after the stimulus) (*Mangun, 1995*). This increase is called *augmenting* (Buchsbaum & Silverman, 1968). At higher levels of intensity, some people still show growing amplitudes, whereas other people's amplitudes stay the same or even decrease, which is called *reducing* (Buchsbaum & Silverman, 1968). These response patterns reflect stable differences in cortical activities processing stimuli, which can be related to different types of sensation seeking. Although the results have not been consistent across different studies and for all types of stimuli, it seems that regarding mid to high intensity conditions, high sensation seekers (especially those high on Dis, TAS or ES) tend to augmenting response patterns, whereas low sensation seekers more often show reducing response patterns (Brocke, Strobel, & Möller, 2003). These findings are coherent with the characterization of high sensation seekers as being more curious and interested and showing more exploratory activity than low sensation seekers (Zuckerman, 1994).

The Neural Bases of Sensation Seeking and Their Link to Depression and Anxiety

As shown in the previous paragraph, there are hints indicating that fundamental differences exist in the correlation between neural information processes and the extent to which a person engages in sensation seeking. The following studies show how these differences are also connected to emotional subsystems on a neural level.

According to Gray's (1994) theory, there are two basic systems of human behavior. These describe behavioral approach (or activation) and behavioral inhibition in an emotional-motivational framework and which are associated with distinct neurobiological structures.

The *behavioral approach system* (BAS) – also known as the behavioral activation system or behavioral facilitation system (Revelle, 1995) – realizes approach behavior via positive emotions in the context of anticipated and experienced reward. Behavioral inhibition or the avoidance behavior of the *behavioral inhibition system* (BIS) – also known as the aversive or avoidance motivational system – is a result of cues of uncertainty or danger and is accompanied by or – depending on the model – regulated by negative emotions (e.g., fear) (Carver, 2005). On the neurochemical level, the BAS is typically associated with dopamine and the BIS with serotonin (Depue & Collins 1999; Revelle, 1995; Suhara et al., 2001).

Joseph, Liu, Jiang, Lynam, and Kelly (2009) demonstrated that high sensation seekers exposed to high-arousal stimuli show stronger functional magnetic resonance imaging (fMRI) responses in brain areas that are associated with reinforcement and arousal than low sensation seekers. This result suggests that the high sensation seekers have a stronger appetitive-approach system, which is more sensible and active compared to low sensation seekers.

Besides this overactive BAS in high sensation seekers, there are some studies that emphasize the role of the aversive BIS for understanding the behavioral patterns of low sensation seekers (Lissek et al., 2005; Zheng et al., 2011). Low sensation seekers confronted with high-arousal stimuli showed a higher activation and earlier onset of fMRI responses in brain regions that are typically involved in emotional regulation. Furthermore, low sensation seekers showed a greater sensitivity to the valence of the stimulus compared to the reactions of high sensation seekers (Joseph et al., 2009).

Finally, the differences that were found in the preferences and concrete behaviors of high and low sensation seekers can be understood by the interaction of differently weighted BAS and BIS in the groups (Joseph et al., 2009; Lang, Shin, & Lee, 2005; Netter & Roed, 1996).

As already mentioned, there are also some implications for differences concerning emotional aspects that result from these profiles: A lot of studies have indicated that low sensitivity of the BAS is associated with depression, and that high sensitivity of the BIS predicts anxiety and depression (Bowins, 2012; Hundt, Nelson-Gray, Kimbrel, Mitchell, & Kwapil, 2007; Revelle, 1995). These findings are in agreement with sometimes reported negative correlations between sensation-seeking scores and anxiety and depression (Carton, Jouvent, Bungener, & Widlöcher, 1992; Carton, Morand, Bungenera, & Jouvent, 1995; Farmer et al., 2001; Zuckerman, 1994) and lead to the suggestion that high sensation seekers are less vulnerable to these disorders because the neural bases of high sensation seekers are incongruent with the neural correlates of depression and anxiety.

In our own study, we analyzed the relation between depression symptoms and sensation seeking in a sample of older adults between the ages of 65 and 95 years (N=325). Sensation seeking was measured by the Need Inventory of Sensation Seeking (NISS; Roth & Hammelstein, 2012). Depressive symptoms were measured via a German short form from the Center for Epidemiologic Studies-Depression Scale (CES-D; Radloff, 1979) by Hautzinger and Bailer (1993). The correlation between the two instruments was $r = -.23$ ($p < .001$). To determine differences between high, medium, and low sensation seekers the total sample was grouped by percentile split. The results of an ANOVA showed significant differences ($F = 5.00$, $p < 0.05$). As indicated by a post-hoc test, only low sensation seekers differed from medium and high sensation seekers with respect to having a higher level of depressive symptoms. No differences were found between the medium and high groups. A potential explanation may be found in the role of social support between sensation seeking and psychological adjustment in older adults. Path analyses of the named data set by Roth (2009), demonstrated that sensation seeking in old age in case of social support may be seen as a protective factor with respect to psychological adjustment.

But the whole picture remains somewhat unclear. Whereas another study found low but significant correlations between SSS-V and the Positive Emotions subscale of Extraversion from the NEO (Costa & McCrae, 1985), people with a bipolar disorder were also found to score higher than normal controls on the Dis and BS scales regardless of whether they were in a manic or in a depressed state (Zuckerman, 1994).

A way out of these inconsistent results may be realized through a more precise differentiation of the constructs involved. For example, Pierson, Le Houezec, Fossaert, Dubal, and Jouvent (1999) hypothesized that high sensation seeking behavior (in this study, it was skydiving) is used as a compensation strategy for anhedonia, which is thought to result from a basal arousal deficit. Compared to the control group, the high sensation seekers (skydivers) showed more negative symptoms (anhedonia and blunted affect) without the presence of a depressive episode. Event-related potential results showed that the skydivers had larger amplitudes of the frontal P300 than the control group. Interestingly, a previous study had shown the opposite in depressed patients with similar emotional deficits. So it could be assumed that a large frontal P300 amplitude reflects a capacity to use high sensation seeking behavior, which improves automatic attentional processes to experience arousing stimulation to counterbalance the emotional deficit (Pierson et al., 1999). Although the study focused on a very special subpopulation of high sensation seekers and the authors presented a daring interpretation, the result itself points to very complex problems in the research that seeks to find the neural correlates of sensation seeking and their connections to emotional processes.

Although there is evidence that high and low sensation seekers differ with regard to neural levels and that these differences are also bound to symptoms of depression and anxiety such that high sensation seekers seem to be less vulnerable to these disorders, there are also findings that point to much more complex associations and interactions.

Nevertheless, an overactive BAS – which is associated with higher sensation seeking scores (see above) – is also linked to impulsive behavior (Leone, Maricchiolo, & Presaghi, 2011; Revelle, 1995). The following paragraph addresses this relation and discusses some relevant implications for emotions.

Links to Impulsiveness and Emotional Responsiveness

As reported above high sensation seekers can be characterized by an overactive BAS which is also linked to impulsive behavior (Leone et al., 2011; Revelle, 1995), and this connection is compatible with the results of Carton et al. (1992), whose findings suggest that high sensation seekers are emotionally hyperexpressive, impulsive, and irritable. Even genetic correlations were investigated with the aim of gaining a better understanding of the relation between these two traits, and the findings point to common biological mechanisms that underlie the associations between impulsiveness and sensation seeking (Hur & Bouchard, 1997).

However, as shown above for the connection between sensation seeking and depressive symptoms, when taking several studies into account, the reported correlations between sensation seeking and impulsiveness have been very inconsistent (Beauducel & Brocke, 2003).

Actually, the two constructs are clearly distinguishable on a theoretical level when sensation seeking is understood as a need and impulsiveness as a lack of control dealing with needs and impulses (Hammelstein, 2004). One problem, however, is the broad meaning of "impulsive," which has led to some conceptions of impulsiveness that even include aspects of sensation seeking (Evenden, 1999). On the other hand, the two constructs are closely entangled with each other on the level of concrete behavior, and so some SSS-V items (esp. those from the Dis, e.g., "I like wild parties") by Zuckerman, who conceptualized sensation seeking as a trait, also refer to impulsive aspects (Zuckerman, 1994). This strong relation and the correlations he found in his own research led Zuckerman to even broaden his sensation seeking conception by including impulsive aspects more directly. The result of this development was the concept of *impulsive sensation seeking* (ImpSS), which became one factor of the *Zuckerman-Kuhlman Personality Questionaire* (ZKPQ; Zuckerman, Kuhlman, Joireman, Teta, & Kraft, 1993).

By putting sensation seeking close to impulsiveness it also gets closer to the construct of aggression as an often impulsive expression of anger and frustration (Barratt, 1994). Thus, it is not surprising that some sensation-seeking subscales have shown significant correlations with aggression and anger, especially in males. Due to its conception, the relation to the Dis subscale (see above) was the highest (Zuckerman, 1994).

In addition, the close relation between sensation seeking and impulsiveness suggests a higher emotional responsiveness in general for high sensation seekers, which would also lead to stronger affect. But in considering such emotional high sensation seekers, it seems contradictory that they simultaneously show a stronger preference for risky behavior and horror movies than low sensation seekers do. To make these aspects more plausible, we have to remember that high sensation seekers show a stronger BAS and a weaker BIS than low sensation seekers (see above), so they tend to act more impulsively and tend to prefer intense stimuli, whereas they also show a reduced sensitivity to stressors (Joseph et al., 2009; Lang,

Shin, & Lee, 2005). In other words, high sensation seekers often show a higher emotional responsiveness combined with a preference for arousal (due to a stronger BAS), but at the same time, they are less affected by fear and worry (due to a weaker BIS). Low sensation seekers, on the other hand, often show a lower emotional responsiveness in general (due to a weaker BAS), but at the same time, they are more strongly affected by stressors, and they experience arousal as uncomfortable (due to a stronger BIS).

This combination may be one good reason for why there are typically no significant correlations between sensation seeking and most neuroticism scales (Andresen, 2003; Zuckerman, 1994). These scales often feature aspects of impulsiveness as well as aspects of emotional instability connected with fear and worry, and occasionally include harm avoidance (Andresen, 2003).

In accordance with the assumption of a stronger emotional responsiveness in high sensation seekers Zuckerman (1994) presented some results indicating that high sensation seekers (esp. males) can be characterized by an enjoyment of expressing emotions combined with the capacity to express them freely and intensively.

All in all, the neural link from sensation seeking to impulsiveness extends the characterization of high and low sensation seekers. Compared to low sensation seekers, high sensation seekers can be described as more impulsive, which also affects a broad range of emotional aspects. They show higher levels of emotional responsiveness in general, which ranges from a higher capacity and an enjoyment of emotional expression to emotional instability (e.g., higher levels of aggression).

Fear and Disgust

As already discussed, high sensation seekers are less affected by fear and worry due to having only minor activity of the BIS (see above). These assumptions are supported by significant negative correlations between fear and sensation seeking found by the majority of studies regarding this relation (Hammelstein & Pietrowsky, 2003; Möller & Huber, 2003; Zuckerman, 1994).

Lissek et al. (2005) investigated the role of the BIS for low sensation seekers, and more precisely their greater anxious reactivity to dangerous activities by comparing levels of fear and anxiety in relation to predictable and unpredictable aversive stimuli (acoustic and airpuff startle stimuli) across high and low sensation seekers. They found that low sensation seekers showed greater fear-potentiated startle responses (via eyeblink electromyography) to predictable aversive stimuli than high sensation seekers. During the experiments with unpredictable aversive stimuli, only low sensation seekers displayed fear-potentiated startle and skin conductance response effects (Lissek et al., 2005).

In addition, as already reported, Zaleski (1984) found that high sensation seekers (esp. men) had a stronger preference for pictures that were rated emotionally negative than low sensation seekers, and in turn, low sensation seekers displayed a greater preference for visual stimuli rated emotionally positive compared to high sensation seekers. From this point, it seems quite understandable that high sensation seekers would prefer horror and violence in movies because they get aroused without feeling unpleasant (Burst, 2003; Goldstein, 1999; Johnston, 1995; Sparks & Sparks, 2000). In contrast to frightened and shocked low sensation seekers, the reception of such movies leads to the feeling of a pleasant thrill in high sensation seekers.

That is why some authors (e.g., Schmidt, 2003; Lissek & Powers, 2003) suggest an association between high sensation seekers and psychopaths, who show similar physiological response patterns when confronted with aversive stimuli (Herpertz et al., 2001; Patrick, 1994) and who have also been found to score high on sensation seeking (Blackburn, 1987; Dåderman, 1999; Lissek & Powers, 2003; Zuckerman, 1994). Although a preference for horror and violent movies does not cross the line of real danger or physical risk, many studies have found that high sensation seekers engage more often in dangerous sports or other high risk activities than low sensation seekers (Arnett, 1996; Greene, Kremar, Walters, Rubin, & Hale, 2000; Zuckerman, 1994). But these findings cannot answer whether high sensation seekers know about the risks at all.

Rosenbloom (2003) investigated the influence of mortality salience on risky driving on high and low sensation seekers. Not surprisingly, in the control group (who watched a nature video film without mortality salience), the high sensation seekers reported more risk taking when driving than low sensation seekers. In the experimental condition, the subjects were exposed to a terrifying film clip that dealt with the consequences of risky driving. Low sensation seekers' reports of speeding were lower in this mortality salience group than in the non-mortality salience group. By contrast, the reports of speeding from high sensation seekers were even higher in mortality salience than in the control group (Rosenbloom, 2003). But against the background of the weaker activity of the BIS in high sensation seekers, the extent to which the high sensation seekers of the experimental group could respond to the cues of mortality in the movie remains unclear.

Finally, the reported findings are consistent with regard to the definition of sensation seeking put forth by Zuckerman (1994) who emphasized the high sensation seekers' "willingness to take physical, social, legal, and financial risks for the sake of such experience" (p. 27).

Another emotion that is related to the aversive motivational system is disgust. Based on the finding of a weaker sensitivity of the BIS in high sensation seekers, one must expect a weaker disgust response in high sensation seekers compared to low sensation seekers. Dvorak, Simons, and Wray (2010) addressed this hypothesis and investigated whether there is an impact of sensation seeking on the feeling of disgust moderated by poor control, which was used as an indicator of the automatic and associative processing of the "impulsive system" from the Reflective-impulsive-model by Strack and Deutsch (2004). The stimulus used to evoke the feeling of disgust was a video that showed two persons vomiting on each other and then consuming each other's vomit. The authors found that lower levels of sensation seeking combined with higher levels of poor control led to stronger disgust reactions and increased the likelihood of experiencing an emesis perception (Dvorak et al., 2010).

Although high sensation seekers can be characterized by higher emotional responsiveness in general than low sensation seekers (due to a stronger BAS), they experience lower levels of fear and disgust and are less affected by these emotions (due to a weaker BIS). All in all, the reported findings suggest that high sensation seekers tend to be better protected from potential stressors and stress in general than low sensation seekers. This hypothesis will be discussed more precisely in the next paragraph.

Stress and Frustration

With regard to the findings that were outlined above, one can suggest that high sensation seekers show hypersensitivity to intense stimuli, but a lower sensitivity to stressors in general (Joseph et al., 2009). It seems plausible that high sensation seekers – who prefer situations associated with emotional cognitive arousal – are at the same time able to tolerate the higher arousal that is bound to stress and workload better than low sensation seekers and are therefore also better at coping in situations with stressful demands (e.g., Smith, Ptacek, & Smoll, 1992).

In line with this stress-buffering hypothesis, de Brabander, Hellemans, Boone, and Gerits (1996) found that students with high scores on the TAS reported significantly less experienced stress than those with lower ones.

Other studies have focused on life events (esp. those regarded as negative) as seldom but very stressful events (e.g., Siegel, Johnson & Sarason, 1979; Cohen 1982). Jorgensen and Johnson (1990) showed that low sensation seekers tend to rate more imagined life events as stressful and to expect a longer time in recovery compared to high sensation seekers. Cohen (1982) found that negative and stressful life events of high sensation seekers were mainly a consequence of their own activities, like being jailed for breaking the law or trouble at work. In contrast, Farmer et al. (2001) found more life events for low sensation seekers. Clarke and Innes (1983) even found that in a population of Australian firemen, it was the high sensation seekers who showed a greater response to stress.

Solomon, Ginzburg, Neria, and Ohry (1995) investigated consequences of war imprisonment by comparing Israeli soldiers who were imprisoned during the Yom Kippur War in 1973 with their comrades who also fought in this war without being captured (who served as a control group) and found notable interaction effects between group and sensation seeking: Whereas in the control group, no differences between high and low sensation seekers' mental states occurred, low sensation seekers in the imprisonment group reported more PTSD symptoms and more severe psychiatric symptoms than high sensation seekers (Solomon et al., 1995).

Additional evidence for a stress moderating role of high levels of sensation seeking was found by comparing (retrospectively reported) experiences during the imprisonment: Low sensation seekers reported more feelings of hopelessness, loss of control, and *hostility against the enemy* (Neria, Solomon, Ginzburg, & Ohry, *1996).

The altogether inconsistent results suggest that there are some mediating and moderating variables that need to be investigated more intensively, probably especially those typically bound to stress; for instance, *locus of control* and *social support* (Zuckerman, 1994). Additionally, another fundamental problem is grounded in the method of mainly using retrospective self-reports on seldom-experienced life events instead of concrete behavioral and physiological measurements in controlled experimental settings (Roth, 2004).[1]

In contrast to the stress-buffering hypothesis, some authors (Hammelstein & Pietrowsky, 2003; Zuckerman, 1994) argue that high levels of sensation seeking could also be a vulnerability factor for stress and point to the consequences of high sensation seeking

---

[1] The last subchapter presents our own study in which we investigated the moderating effect of sensation seeking on affect caused by stress in a controlled experimental setting.

behavior as a source of more psychosocial stressors, which is in line with the findings of Cohen (1982) reported above.

Another surprising finding that points to more complex unknown interactions was reported by Holmes (2001). She investigated whether sensation seeking had an impact on film preference after anxiety arousal (which was induced by a speech-preparation task). Her hypothesis was that after anxiety arousal, high sensation seekers would prefer a high arousal film, whereas low sensation seekers would rather watch a low arousal film to recover from the induced stress. But almost half of the high sensation seekers decided to watch the low arousal film, and half of the low sensation seekers chose the high arousal film. In other words, sensation seeking had no effect on film preference after the anxiety arousal (Holmes, 2001).

These unexpected results are congruent with a study by Liebe (2006) in which he investigated the impact of the sensation-seeking trait score on the sensation-seeking state score (both measured by the NISS, see above) in relation to feelings of frustration among students. The frustration in the experimental group was induced by manipulated intelligence test tasks, which were very difficult to solve and even partly unsolvable. The control group was confronted with very easy intelligence test tasks and should therefore not have felt frustrated and perhaps even felt proud. Mood indicators showed that this manipulation worked in the expected way. Nevertheless, he found that the sensation-seeking state scores of high sensation seekers tended to decrease in both groups, whereas those of low sensation seekers tended to increase and finally reached the same mean level as high sensation seekers.

Although some findings support a stress-buffering effect for sensation seeking, there are also theories and studies that have pleaded for high levels of sensation seeking as a vulnerability factor to stress. Altogether, the extent to which these contradictions can be explained by methodological weaknesses or unaccounted-for interactions with further moderators remains unclear.

THE MODERATING EFFECT OF SENSATION SEEKING ON AFFECT CAUSED BY STRESS: FIRST RESULTS

One main problem in analyzing the stress-buffering effect of sensation seeking lies in the fact that in most studies, both the existence and the extension of the stressors as well as the stress reactions were measured by self-reports. Thus, we cannot exclude the possibility that correlations between stress exposition and reactions can be traced back to response sets and styles. Therefore, our aim was to use an experimental design to implement stressors that were objective and identical for all individuals. Thus, we operationalized the stressor for the participants by a task in which the participants had to present a specialized text in front of a video camera under performance pressure. We analyzed the use of the coping strategies "supression" and "reappraisal" (Gross & John, 2003) during the task and the change in affective mood caused by the stress.

With regard to the findings presented in the subchapter before, there are two reasons why we assumed that high sensation seekers would experience the speech as less stressful and less unpleasant than low sensation seekers. First, in line with a less sensitive and less active behavioral inhibition system (BIS, see above) in high sensation seekers compared to low sensation seekers, we supposed that high sensation seekers would show a weaker responsiveness to the stressors and therefore would feel less worry or fear than low sensation seekers. Second, because of their preference for situations associated with emotional cognitive arousal, high sensation seekers were expected to be able to tolerate the higher arousal bound to the speech task and were expected to feel less unpleasantness than low sensation seekers.

Therefore, we assumed that high sensation seekers would show lower levels of negative affect and higher levels of positive affect both before and after the speech compared to low sensation seekers, who were expected to feel less comfortable when anticipating the speech task and the stress that would be experienced during it.

In addition, we expected that low sensation seekers would need to use more conscious coping strategies to handle the stressful task than high sensation seekers, who are better protected by their psychological constitution and would need fewer extra coping strategies. Considering the characterization of high sensation seekers as more impulsive, less anxious, and tending to express emotions more freely than low sensation seekers (see above), we expected a stronger difference between the groups for the supression scale.

The realization of the study was completed in March of 2012. In this subchapter we want to present the first results of the study. [2]

Sample

The sample was recruited from high schools in Leipzig (Germany). Pupils in grades 11 and 12 were invited to take part in a "study dealing with stress and coping." The participants were promised a reward (24 Euros) for their participation, and they were assured of the confidentiality and anonymity of the data. 112 pupils took part in the study. Participants who had more than 10 missing data points were excluded. The final sample consisted of 107 participants (54.2% female, 45.8% male) between the ages of 15 and 19 years (M = 16.8; SD = 0.8).

Measures

As described above, the *Need Inventory of Sensation Seeking* (NISS) by Roth and Hammelstein (2012) was used to measure sensation seeking based on need theory. As recommended by Roth, Hammelstein, and Brähler (2007), only the 11-item subscale *need for stimulation* (NS) was used for the analyses as an indicator of global sensation seeking (e.g., "I like to find myself in situations which make my heart beat faster"). Respondents were required to rate how often they felt this way in the past 6 months on a five-point Likert scale ranging from 1 = "almost never" to 5 = "almost always." Additionally, the "classic" instrument form for measuring sensation seeking was implemented: The *Sensation Seeking Scale – Form V* (Zuckerman et al., 1978). The SSS-V is a 40-item, forced-choice questionnaire. In the present context, only the total score was used for analysis.

---

[2] This research was supported by a Grant from the German Research Foundation (Deutsche Forschungsgemeinschaft, DFG), RO 3059/3-1.

The *Emotion Regulation Questionnaire* (ERQ) by Gross and John (2003) was designed to assess individual differences in the habitual use of two emotion regulation strategies: cognitive reappraisal and expressive suppression. The strategies were measured with 10 items (e.g., cognitive reappraisal: "When I want to feel less negative emotion (such as sadness or anger), I change what I'm thinking about"; expressive suppression: "When I am feeling positive emotions, I am careful not to express them"). Because we were not interested in the habitual use, but rather in the concrete use of the coping strategies in the speech condition, pupils were asked to answer the questionnaire with respect to the speech, and accordingly, the items were rephrased in the past tense (e.g., "When I was feeling positive emotions, I was careful not to express them"). For each item, respondents had to indicate the extent of their agreement with ratings in a seven-point Likert format. The instrument was administered after the speech.

The 20-item *Positive and Negative Affect Schedule* (PANAS) by Watson, Clark, and Tellegen (1988) comprises two mood scales, one measuring positive affect and the other measuring negative affect on the basis of presented adjectives (e.g., "angry," "happy"). Each item is rated on a five-point scale ranging from 1 = "very slightly or not at all" to 5 = "extremely" to indicate the extent to which the respondent felt this way in the indicated time frame. We used a German adaptation of the scales by Krohne, Egloff, Kohlmann, and Tausch (1996) to measure affect at the current moment. The PANAS was administered at baseline and directly after the speech.

Procedure

Participants were investigated twice at intervals of about one month. During the first session, participants answered the sensation-seeking questionnaires (NISS, SSS-V) in groups. The second session was arranged individually. On arrival, pupils indicated their emotion (baseline measurement via the PANAS). Afterwards, participants were given the following introductions for their speech:

> "This experiment analyzes how well you are able to comprehend and present a specialized text under time pressure. This ability is an important prerequisite for successful academic studies at a university. The experiment will proceed as follows: You will first read and prepare the text for 10 minutes. Then you will orally present the contents of this text for 3 minutes. Your speech will be videotaped and later analyzed by experts. Please try to deliver a comprehensive and well-structured speech, speaking for the full 3 minutes. Note that you are not allowed to use the text or the notes you made during the speech."

The text was concerned with the history of health effects caused by coal mining. The task was very difficult because the text to be presented included a lot of details (total length: 1,570 words). To maximize the evaluative nature of the task, the video camera was positioned in front of the participants who had to give the speech in the standing position.

After delivering their speech, participants indicated their emotions during the speech (PANAS). Then they indicated the extent to which they had used reappraisal and/or suppression as emotion regulation strategies during the speech (ERQ). At the end, participants were informed about the purpose of the study, especially about the fact that the study was not concerned with analyzing their ability to study at a university. The experimenter then asked the participants not to discuss the study with classmates.

Results

Means, standard deviations, minimum-maximum scores, and Cronbach's alphas of the measures are given in Table 1. As shown, with the exception of the scale *Supression* (ERQ), the reliability coefficients were adequate, ranging from $\alpha=.72$ to $\alpha=.90$. The two sensation-seeking instruments, the NISS and the SSS-V, showed a moderate correlation of $r=.49$ ($p<.001$). The correlation between the emotion regulation strategies was lower ($r=.33$, $p<.001$). We found low correlations between the positive and negative emotion scores at the baseline ($r=.22$, $p<.05$). After the speech, the two affect scores varied independently ($r=-.04$, n.s.).

Table 1. Descriptive Statistics of the Variables

Variable	M	SD	MIN	MAX	α
Sensation Seeking score (NISS, NS)	34.81	7.56	12.00	55.00	.85
Sensation Seeking score (SSS-V, Total)	61.17	5.35	47.00	71.00	.72
Emotion regulation strategy (ERQ)					
Suppression	3.67	1.04	1.25	6.00	.58
Reappraisal	3.15	1.11	1.00	6.00	.73
Positive Affect (PANAS)					
Baseline	2.71	0.60	1.00	4.10	.82
After speech	2.90	0.77	1.10	4.50	.89
Negative Affect (PANAS)					
Baseline	1.48	0.49	1.00	3.40	.85
After speech	1.65	0.68	1.00	4.30	.90

Note. N = 107. NISS: Need Inventory of Sensation Seeking; NS: Need for Stimulation-Subscale; SSS-V: Sensation Seeking Scale; ERQ: Emotion Regulation Questionnaire; PANAS: Positive and Negative Affect Schedule

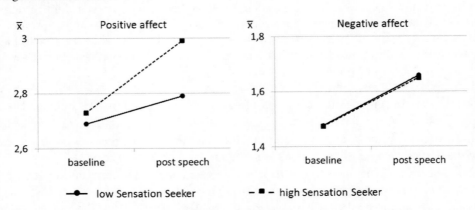

Figure 1. Changes in positive and negative affect (PANAS) by low (n=52) and high sensation seekers (n=55).

Using a median-split procedure, subjects were divided post hoc into two groups ("high sensation seekers" (HSS) vs. "low sensation seekers" (LSS)) based on their NS-NISS scores. To test our assumption that high sensation seekers were less affected by the stress condition than low sensation seekers, a MANOVA was calculated with time (baseline vs. post speech) and group (high vs. low sensation seeker) as independent factors and positive and negative affect (PANAS subscales) as dependent variables. As can be seen in Figure 1, positive (F=9.97, p<.05) as well as negative affect (F=11.63, p<.001) ascends from baseline to the period directly after the speech, indicating that participants were subjectively affected by the speech (as we intended). However, no time x group interaction effects were found (positive affect: F=2.02, p=n.s.; negative affect: F<0.1, p=n.s.), indicating that the affect caused by the speech did not differ between high and low sensation seekers. Further, no main effects for sensation-seeking groups were found (positive affect: F=0.92, p=n.s.; negative affect: F<.01, p=n.s.). Both high and low sensation seekers showed comparable amounts of positive and negative affect. Almost the same result pattern emerged when the total score of the SSS-V was used as the criterion to dichotomize high vs. low sensation seekers. Here, we also found a significant increase from baseline to speech in positive (F=9.88, p=0.002) as well as in negative affect (F=11.59, p=0.001) for the total sample. Again, no interaction effects between the measurement time (baseline vs. post speech) and sensation seeking (high vs. low) were identified (positive: F=0.18, p=n.s.; negative: F=0.02, p=n.s.) indicating that the increase in positive and negative affect resulting from the speech performance did not differ between high and low sensation seekers.

To test differences between high and low levels of sensation seeking, one-way MANOVAS were conducted with SS-group (high vs. low sensation seekers based on the NISS) as the factor and the two coping strategies as dependent variables. Here, no differences in the use of the coping strategies as reported by the participants after the speech were found for "Suppression" (M_{LSS}=3.67, SD_{LSS}=0.99, M_{HSS}=3.65, SD_{HSS}=1.10; F=0.01, p=n.s.) or for "Reappraisal" (M_{LSS}=3.17, SD_{LSS}=1.02, M_{HSS}=3.13, SD_{HSS}=1.20; F=0.02, p=n.s). Again, when the SSS-V was used as the criterion for a median split in high and low sensation seekers, the same pattern of results emerged.

Conclusion

Surprisingly none of the expected stress-buffering effects or any other effect of sensation seeking was found. Regarding our experimental design, there are two main reasons for why our results must be considered to be more valid than the data from previous studies that referred to life events (see above): First, we controlled the conditions of the stress situation, and second, our data were collected within a small time frame and were not collected retrospectively except for the ERQ. Additionally, we used two different scales for sensation seeking to compensate for blind spots due to narrow conceptual perspectives and differences in the operationalization of sensation seeking.

But nonetheless, the conclusion that there is no stress-buffering effect of sensation seeking beyond situations comparable to our experimental setting remains a bit unconvincing against the background of the numerous findings reported in the second subchapter regarding fear, worry, and stress. Aside from that, there are still some methodological weaknesses in our design, which we would like to discuss.

First, we still used self-report measures to gather emotional data, which require a valid conscious access to one's emotions, which itself again is supposed to be affected by current emotional states. Second, both positive and negative affect were rated only before and after the speech, so we obviously do not know what happened emotionally during the 3 minutes of the task. Third, regarding the answers concerning the coping strategies, which were given retrospectively, distortions in self-reports become more likely with the distance of time and situational differences between the time of interest and the moment of responding. Although the items were presented very close to the speech situation, this approach remains problematic. As is obvious, the level of the second measure of positive affect was significantly greater than the level from before the speech, which does not reflect an increase in positive mood during the task itself, but which is plausible as a sudden relief after leaving the stressful situation. But because the results of the ERQ were based on retrospectively answered items, the problem is that such a sudden shift in mood worsens the recall of experiences during the task situation, which may be experienced in a completely different mood profile, and which is additionally characterized by extraordinary mental demands that affect conscious awareness and therefore decrease the likelihood of accurate recall afterwards.

To conclude, based on these problems, it seems too soon to reject the stress-buffering hypothesis of sensation seeking at this point in time. For further research, it will be necessary to involve more objective measurements, such as physiological parameters (e.g., skin conductance, heart rate) and behavioral parameters (e.g., video ratings of typical stress reactions) to collect more valid data to further examine the hypothesis.

REFERENCES

Andresen, B. (2003). Integration von Sensation Seeking in umfassende und geschlossene Modelle der Persönlichkeit. In M. Roth, & P. Hammelstein (Eds.), *Sensation Seeking – Konzeption, Diagnostik, Anwendung* (52-76). Göttingen: Hogrefe.

Arnett, J. J. (1994). Sensation seeking: A new conceptualization and a new scale. *Personality and Individual Differences, 16*, 289-296.

Arnett, J. J. (1996). Sensation seeking, aggressiveness, and adolescent reckless behaviour. *Personality and Individual Differences, 20*, 693-702.

Ball, I. L., Farnill, D. & Wangeman, J. F. (1984). Sex and age differences in sensation seeking: Some national comparisons. *British Journal of Psychology, 75*, 257-265.

Barratt, E. S. (1994). Impulsiveness and aggression. In J. Monahan, & H. Stedman (Eds.), *Violence and mental disorder: developments in risk assessment* (61-80). Chicago: University of Chicago Press.

Beauducel, A. & Brocke, B. (2003). Sensation Seeking Scale-Form V: Merkmale des Verfahrens und Bemerkungen zur deutschsprachigen Adaptation. In M. Roth, & P. Hammelstein (Eds.), *Sensation Seeking - Konzeption, Diagnostik und Anwendung* (77-99). Göttingen: Hogrefe.

Beauducel, A. & Roth, M. (2003). Methoden zur Erfassung von Sensation Seeking - Versuch einer Systematik. In M. Roth, & P. Hammelstein (Eds.), *Sensation Seeking - Konzeption, Diagnostik, Anwendung* (122-137). Göttingen: Hogrefe.

Beauducel, A., Strobel, A. & Brocke, B. (2003). Psychometrische Eigenschaften und Normen einer deutschsprachigen Fassung der Sensation Seeking-Skalen, Form V. *Diagnostica, 49*, 61-72.

Blackburn, R. (1987). Two scales for the assessment of personality disorder in antisocial populations. *Personality and Individual Differences, 8,* 81-93.

Bowins, B. E. (2012). Augmentation behavioural activation treatment with the behavioural activation and inhibition scales. *Behavioural And Cognitive Psychotherapy, 40*, 233-237.

Brocke, B., Strobel, A. & Möller, J. (2003). Sensation Seeking: Eine biopsychologische Mehr-Ebenen-Theorie. In M. Roth, & P. Hammelstein (Eds.), *Sensation Seeking - Konzeption, Diagnostik und Anwendung* (29-52). Göttingen: Hogrefe.

Buchsbaum, M. S. & Silverman, J. (1968). Stimulus intensity control and the cortical evoked response. *Psychosomatic Medicine, 30,* 12-22.

Burst, M. (2003). Sensation Seeking in der Medienpsychologie. In M. Roth, & P. Hammelstein (Eds.), *Sensation Seeking - Konzeption, Diagnostik und Anwendung* (235-252). Göttingen: Hogrefe.

Carton, S., Jouvent, R., Bungener, C. & Widlöcher, D. (1992). Sensation seeking and depressive mood. *Personality and Individual Differences, 13,* 843-849.

Carton, S., Morand, P., Bungenera, C. & Jouvent, R. (1995). Sensation-seeking and emotional disturbances in depression: relationships and evolution. *Journal of Affective Disorders, 34,* 219-225.

Carver, C. S. (2005). Impulse and constraint: Perspectives from personality psychology, convergence with theory in other areas, and potential for integration. *Personality and Social Psychology Review, 9,* 312-333.

Clarke, A. & Innes, J. M. (1983). Sensation-seeking motivation and social-support moderators of the life stress/illness relationship: some contradictory and confirmatory evidence. *Personality and Individual Differences, 4,* 547-550.

Cohen, L. H. (1982). Life change and the sensation seeking motive. *Personality and Individual Differences, 3,* 221-222.

Costa, P. T., Jr. & McCrae, R. R. (1985). *The NEO Personality Inventory manual.* Odessa, FL: Psychological Assessment Resources.

Dåderman, A. M. (1999). Differences between severely conduct-disordered juvenile males and normal juvenile males: the study of personality traits. *Personality and Individual Differences, 26,* 827-845.

De Brabander, B., Hellemans, J., Boone, C. & Gerits, P. (1996). Locus of control, sensation seeking, and stress. *Psychological Reports, 79,* 1307-1212.

Deci, E. L. & Ryan, R. M. (2000). The" what" and" why" of goal pursuits: Human needs and the self-determination of behaviour. *Psychological Inquiry, 11,* 227-268.

Depue, R. A. & Collins, P. F. (1999). Neurobiology of the structure of personality: Dopamine, facilitation of incentive motivation, and extraversion. *Behavioral and Brain Sciences,* 22, 491–569. 22, 491-517.

Dvorak, R. D., Simons, J. S. & Wray, T. B. (2010). Poor Control Strengthens the Association Between Sensation Seeking and Disgust Reactions. *Journal of Individual Differences, 32,* 219-224.

Evenden, J. L. (1999). Varieties of impulsivity. *Psychopharmacology, 146,* 348–361.

Farmer, A., Redman, K., Harris, T., Mahmood, A., Sadler, S. & McGuffin, P. (2001). Sensation-seeking, life events and depression - The Cardiff Depression Study. *British Journal of Psychiatry, 178,* 549-552.

Ferrando, P. J. & Chico, E. (2001). The construct of sensation seeking as measured by Zuckerman's SSS-V and Arnett's AISS: a structural equation model. *Personality and Individual Differences, 31,* 1121-1133.

Goldstein, J. (1999). The attractions of violent entertainment. *Media Psychology, 1,* 271-282.

Grawe, K. (2002). *Psychological therapy.* Cambridge: Hogrefe.

Gray, J. A. (1994). Personality dimensions and emotion systems. In P. Ekman, & R. J. Davidson (Eds.), *The nature of emotion: Fundamental questions* (329-331). New York: Oxford University Press.

Greene, K., Kremar, M., Walters, L. H., Rubin, D. L. & Hale, L. (2000). Targeting adolescent risk-taking behaviors: the contributions of egocentrism and sensation-seeking. *Journal of Adolescence, 23,* 439-461.

Gross, J. J. & John, O. P. (2003). Individual differences in two emotion regulation processes: implications for affect, relationships, and well-being. *Journal of Personality and Social Psychology, 85,* 348-362.

Hammelstein, P. (2004). Faites vos jeux! Another look at sensation seeking and pathological gambling. *Personality and Individual Differences, 37,* 917-931.

Hammelstein, P. & Pietrowsky, R. (2003). Sensation Seeking in der Klinischen Psychologie und Psychotherapie. In M. Roth, & P. Hammelstein (Eds.), *Sensation Seeking - Konzeption, Diagnostik und Anwendung* (253-285). Göttingen: Hogrefe.

Hammelstein, P. & Roth, M. (2003). Sensation Seeking: Herausforderung zu einer Dynamischen Perspektive in der Persönlichkeitspsychologie. In M. Roth, & P. Hammelstein (Eds.), *Sensation Seeking - Konzeption, Diagnostik und Anwendung* (286-292). Göttingen: Hogrefe.

Hautzinger, M. & Bailer, M. (1993). *Allgemeine Depressions Skala: ADS.* Manual. Göttingen: Beltz Test GmbH.

Herpertz, S. C., Werth, U., Lukas, G., Qunaibi, M., Schuerkens, A., Kunert, H. J., Freese, R., Flesch, M., Mueller-Isberner, R. & Osterheider, M. (2001). Emotion in criminal offenders with psychopathy and borderline personality disorder. *Archives of General Psychiatry, 58,* 737-745.

Holmes, S. D. (2001). Sensation seeking and negative emotion recovery: differential speeds of emotional recovery and preferences for personality-congruent positive emotions among high and low sensation seekers. *Dissertation Abstracts International, 61,* 10B.

Hundt, N. E., Nelson-Gray, R. O., Kimbrel, N. A., Mitchell, J. T. & Kwapil, T. R. (2007). The interaction of reinforcement sensitivity and life events in the prediction of anhedonic depression and mixed anxiety-depression symptoms. *Personality and Individual Differences, 43,* 1001-1012.

Hur, Y. M. & Bouchard, T. J. (1997). The genetic correlation between impulsivity and sensation seeking traits. *Behavior Genetics, 27,* 455-463.

Jackson, J. S. H. & Maraun, M. (1996). The conceptual validity of empirical scale construction: The case of the sensation seeking scale. *Personality and Individual Differences, 21,* 103-110.

Johnston, D. D. (1995). Adolescents' motivations for viewing graphic horror. *Human Communication Research, 21,* 522-552.

Jorgensen, R. S. & Johnson, J. H. (1990). Contributors to the appraisal of major life changes: Gender, perceived controllability, sensation seeking, strain, and social support. *Journal of Applied Psychology, 20,* 1123-1138.

Joseph, J. E., Liu, X., Jiang, Y., Lynam, D. & Kelly, T. H. (2009). Neural correlates of emotional reactivity in sensation seeking. *Psychological Science, 20,* 215-223.

Krohne, H. W., Egloff, B., Kohlmann, C. W. & Tausch, A. (1996). Untersuchungen mit einer deutschen Version der "Positive and Negative Affect Schedule" (PANAS). *Diagnostica, 42,* 139-156.

Lang, A., Shin, M. & Lee, S. (2005). Sensation seeking, motivation, and substance use: A dual system approach. *Media Psychology, 7,* 1-29.

Leone, L., Maricchiolo, F. & Presaghi, F. (2011). Appetitive and impulsive components in the Appetitive Motivation Scale. *Journal of Research in Personality, 45,* 655-661.

Liebe, N. (2006). *Mit dem Frust kommt die Lust? – Veränderung des Stimulationsbedürfnisses nach Frustrierung.* Unpublished master's thesis, University of Leipzig.

Lissek, S., Baas, J. M. P., Pine, D. S., Orme, K., Dvir, S., Rosenberger, E. & Grillon, C. (2005). Sensation seeking and the aversive motivational system. *American Psychological Association, 5,* 396-407.

Lissek, S. & Powers, A. S. (2003). Sensation seeking and startle modulation by physically threatening images. *Biological Psychology, 63,* 179-197.

Maio, G. R. & Esses, V. M. (2001). The need for affect: Individual differences in the motivation to approach or avoid emotions. *Journal of Personality, 69,* 583-614.

Mangun, G. R. (1995). Neural mechanisms of visual selective attention. *Psychophysiology, 32,* 4-18.

Mastandrea, S., Bartoli, G. & Bove, G. (2009). Preferences for ancient and modern art museums: Visitor experiences and personality characteristics. *Psychology of Aesthetics, Creativity, and the Arts, 3,* 164-173.

Möller, A. & Huber, M. (2003). Sensation Seeking - Konzeptbildung und -entwicklung. In M. Roth, & P. Hammelstein (Eds.), *Sensation Seeking - Konzeption, Diagnostik und Anwendung* (pp. 5-28). Göttingen: Hogrefe.

Neary, R. S. & Zuckerman, M. (1976). Sensation seeking, trait and state anxiety, and the electrodermal orienting response. *Psychophysiology, 13,* 205-211.

Neria, Y., Solomon, Z., Ginzburg, K. & Ohry, A. (1996). The experience of war captivity: The role of sensation-seeking. *Israel Journal of Psychology, 5,* 188-198.

Netter, P., Hennig, J. & Roed, I. S. (1996). Serotonin and dopamine as mediators of sensation seeking behaviour. *Neuropsychobiology, 34,* 155-165.

Orlebeke, J. F. & Feij, J. A. (1979). The orienting reflex as a personality correlate. In E. H. van Olst, & J. F. Orlebeke (Eds.), *The orienting reflex in humans* (567-585). Hillsdale, NJ: Erlbaum.

Patrick, C. J. (1994). Emotion and psychopathy: Startling new insights. *Psychophysiology, 31,* 319-330.

Pierson, A., Le Houezec, J., Fossaert, A., Dubal, S. & Jouvent, R. (1999). Frontal reactivity and sensation seeking an ERP study in skydivers. *Progress in Neuro-Psychopharmacology and Biological Psychiatry, 23,* 447-463.

Radloff, L. S. (1979). The CES-D Scale: A self-report depression scale for research in the general population. *Applied Psychological Measurement, 1,* 385–401.

Revelle, W. (1995). Personality processes. *Annual Reviews for Psychology, 46*, 295-328.

Rheinberg, F. (2006). *Motivation* (6th ed.). Stuttgart: Kohlhammer.

Rosenbloom, T. (2003). Sensation seeking and risk taking in mortality salience. *Personality and Individual Differences, 35*, 1809-1819.

Roth, M. (2003). Validation of the Arnett Inventory of Sensation Seeking (AISS): efficiency to predict the willingness towards occupational chance, and affection by social desirability. *Personality and Individual Differences, 35*, 1307-1314.

Roth, M. (2004). *Sensation Seeking und Drogenkonsum im Jugendalter.* Unpublished Habilitation thesis. University of Leipzig.

Roth, M. (2009). Social support as a mediator in the relation between sensation seeking (need for stimulation) and psychological adjustment in older adults. *Personality and Individual Differences, 47*, 798-801

Roth, M. & Hammelstein, P. (2012). The Need Inventory of Sensation Seeking (NISS). *European Journal of Psychological Assessment, 28*, 11-18.

Roth, M., Hammelstein, P. & Brähler, E. (2007). Beyond a youthful behavior style - Age and sex differences in sensation seeking based on need theory. *Personality and Individual Differences, 43*, 1839-1850.

Roth, M., Hammelstein, P. & Brähler, E. (2009). Towards a multi-methodological approach in the assessment of sensation seeking. *Personality and Individual Differences, 46*, 247-249.

Roth, M., Schumacher, J. & Brähler, E. (2005). Sensation seeking in the community: Sex, age and sociodemographic comparisons on a representative German population sample. *Personality and Individual Differences, 39*, 1261-1271.

Schmidt, A. (2003). Sensation Seeking und delinquentes Verhalten. In M. Roth, & P. Hammelstein (Eds.), *Sensation Seeking - Konzeption, Diagnostik und Anwendung* (214-234). Göttingen: Hogrefe.

Siegel , J. M., *Johnson*, J. H. & *Sarason*, I. G. (1979). *Mood states* and the reporting of life changes. *Journal of Psychosomatic Research, 23*, 103-108.

Smith, B. D., Perlstein, W. M., Davidson, R. A. & Michael, K. (1986). Sensation seeking: Differential effects of relevant, novel stimulation on electrodermal activity and memory task performance. *Personality and Individual Differences, 7*, 445-452.

Smith, R. E., Ptacek, J. T. & Smoll, F. L. (1992). Sensation seeking, stress, and adolescent injuries: A test of stress-buffering, risk-taking, and coping skills hypotheses. *Journal of Personality and Social Psychology, 62*, 1016-1024.

Solomon, Z., Ginzburg, K., Neria, Y. & Ohry, A. (1995). Coping with war captivity: The role of sensation seeking. *European Journal of Personality, 9*, 57-70.

Sparks, G. G. & Sparks, C. W. (2000). Violence, mayhem, and horror. In D. Zillmann, & P. Vorderer (Eds.), *Media Entertainment* (73-91). Mahawa: Lawrence Erlbaum.

Strack, F. & Deutsch, R. (2004). Reflective and impulsive determinants of social behaviour. *Personality and Social Psychology Review, 8*, 220-247.

Suhara, T., Yasuno, F., Sudo, Y., Yamamoto, M., Inoue, M., Okubo, Y. & Suzuki, K. (2001). Dopamine D2 receptors in the insular cortex and the personality trait of novelty seeking. *NeuroImage, 13*, 891-895.

Watson, D., Clark, L. A. & Tellegen, A. (1988). Development and validation of brief measures of positive and negative affect: the PANAS scales. *Journal of Personality and Social Psychology, 54*, 1063-1070.

Zaleski, Z. (1984). Sensation-seeking and preference for emotional visual stimuli. *Personality and Individual Differences, 5,* 609-611.

Zheng, Y., Xu, J., Jia, H., Tan, F., Chang, Y., Zhou, L., Shen, H. & Qu, B. (2011) Electrophysiological correlates of emotional processing in sensation seeking. *Biological Psychology, 88,* 41-50.

Zuckerman, M. (1971). Dimensions of sensation seeking. *Journal of Consulting and Clinical Psychology, 36,* 45-52.

Zuckerman, M. (1979). *Sensation seeking: Beyond the optimal level of arousal.* Hillsdale: Erlbaum.

Zuckerman, M. (1994). *Behavioral expressions and biosocial bases of sensation seeking.* Cambridge: Cambridge University Press.

Zuckerman, M. (2005). *Psychobiology of personality.* Cambridge: Cambridge University Press.

Zuckerman, M., Eysenck, S. B. & Eysenck, H. J. (1978). Sensation seeking in England and America: Cross-cultural, age, and sex comparisons. *Journal of Consulting and Clinical Psychology, 46,* 139-149.

Zuckerman, M., Kolin, E. A., Price, L. & Zoob, I. (1964). Development of a sensation seeking scale. *Journal of Consulting Psychology, 28,* 477-482.

Zuckerman, M., Kuhlman, D. M., Joireman, J., Teta, P. & Kraft, M. (1993). A comparison of three structural models for personality: The Big Three, the Big Five, and the Alternative Five. *Journal of Personality and Social Psychology, 65,* 757-768.

In: Handbook of Psychology of Emotions   ISBN: 978-1-62808-053-7
Editors: C. Mohiyeddini, M. Eysenck and S. Bauer   © 2013 Nova Science Publishers, Inc.

Chapter 17

THE INFLUENCE OF LIGHT ON MOOD AND EMOTION

*Elisabeth M. Weiss[1], * and Markus Canazei[2], *
[1]Department of Psychology
Karl-Franzens University, Graz, Austria
[2]BARTENBACH LICHTLABOR GMBH
Forschung und Entwicklung

ABSTRACT

In the 7 th century William Shakespeare wrote „A sad tale's best for winter". However, he was not the first who understood the power of light on our psyche. 2000 years ago Hippocrates, the father of modern medicine, already acknowledged that the absence of light, particularly in winter, can produce diseases. Since then, the impact of light on mood and the use of bright light as a treatment-option for affective disorders have been studied extensively by scientists (for a review see Terman & Terman 2005). Light is the major zeitgeber for human circadian rhythms, much more powerful than social zeitgebers eg. work or school schedules (Challet 2007). Non-visual effects of light include hormone regulation, the synchronization of the circadian system, the regulation of body temperature, but also the regulation of cognition and alertness (Brainard et al. 2005; Lockley et al. 2006; Vandewalle et al. 2009; Dijket al. 2009; Cajochen et al. 2007). Bright light treatments are dating back to Lewy et al. (1987) who could demonstrate that exposure to bright white light (a mixed spectrum of wavelengths similar to day light) can adjust circadian rhythms and suppress melatonin. The most extensive clinical trials on bright light therapy have focused on seasonal affective disorders suggesting that light can modulate mood in the long term (Wirz-Justice et al. 2004). Today light therapy is used to treat different disorders like sleep disorders, affective disorders, dementia etc. (for a review see Shirani et al. 2009). This chapter will give an overview about the neurobiological basis for light therapy and discuss different mood disorders responsive to light therapy. Additionally, the influence of light on normal brain emotional processing will be discussed.

*Corresponding authors: e.weiss@uni-graz.at, Markus.Canazei@bartenbach.com, www.bartenbach.com.

LIGHT AND CIRCADIAN RHYTHMS

Light is transduced into neural impulses by the activation of ocular photoreceptors, which are responding to light independently of the classic photoreceptors the rods and cones (Berson et al. 2002). These retinal ganglion cells are containing the light-sensitive photopigment melanopsin and are maximally sensitive to blue light ($\approx$480 nm), whereas the classical photopic luminance visual pathways are maximally sensitive to green light ($\approx$550 nm) (Hankins et al. 2008). Retinal ganglion cells project via the retinohypothalamic tract directly to the circadian clock in the suprachiasmatic nucleus (SCN), then to the superior cervical ganglion and finally continues to the pineal gland, where Melatonin is produced (Sparks et al. 1998; Teclemariam-Mesbah et al. 1999). This neural system can be suppressed by light and promoted by darkness (Brzezinski et al. 1997). The endogenous circadian period is generated by neurons in the SCN exhibiting a near 24-hour circadian rhythm which tend to move into phase synchrony with the environmental rhythms (zeitgebers), mainly the timing of exposure to light and darkness (Czeisler et al. 1999; Roenneberg et al. 1997). This process is called entrainment. Circadian rhythms are essential for many body functions including body temperature, hormone levels but also the sleep-wake cycle. Furthermore light also modulates mood and cognition such as attention, alertness, and working memory performance (Vandewalle et al. 2006; 2007a; 2007b; 2009; Perrin et al. 2004).

BRIGHT LIGHT THERAPY

There are four important variables influencing the efficacy of bright light therapy:

1) the light intensity,
2) the time of exposure,
3) the duration of exposure and
4) the spectral composition of light.

Depending on the biologic clock time at which light is administered SCN phase shifts can be obtained. However, the SCN activity phase cannot be directly measured. Therefore the biologic clock time must be inferred from indirect markers such as body temperature, plasma corticosteroids or plasma/salivary concentration of melatonin (Lewy & Sack1989; Voultsios et al. 1997; Deacon & Arendt 1995). An approximation of the dim light melatonin onset (DLMO) can be made from the Horne-Östberg Morningness-Eveningness Questionnaire (MEQ) score to determine the initial timing of light exposure (Horne et al. 1976). Since the circadian system is most sensitive to light during the biological night, the most phase delay (negative shift) of the biologic clock is achieved by light administration in the first half of the subjective night, when the melatonin concentration is high. Phase advancement (positive shift) of the biologic clock can be induced by light administration in the second half of the subjective night, when the melatonin concentration is falling. Therefore light therapy is administered shortly after awakening or shortly before bedtime in clinical trials (Czeisler et al. 1999; Minors et al. 1991).

Recent studies indicate that short wavelength blue light (≈460nm) is more effective in phase shifting and suppressing night-time melatonin than the rest of the visible light spectrum (Lockley et al. 2003; Warman et al. 2003; Wright et al. 2004; Cajochen et al. 2005). The efficacy of light treatment to reset the human biologic clock is also dependent on the intensity of the light stimulus (which is measured in lux). For example, the intensity of ordinary room light is about 180 lux, whereas the intensity of sunlight at midday is over 100.000 lux. The intensity of bright light therapy typically ranges from 2.500-10.000 lux with a duration between 30 minutes and 2 hours. Most clinical studies used 10.000 lux for 30 minutes for treating SAD patients (for a review see Golden et al. 2005).

SEASONAL AFFECTIVE DISORDERS

Affective disorders are highly prevalent and typically associated with disturbances of the circadian rhythm. One subtype of affective disorders with prominent disturbances in the biological clock function is the seasonal affective disorder (SAD) (Magnusson & Boivin 2003). SAD - also known as winter-depression - is a type of depression with serious mood changes during fall and winter time and with full remission in spring and summer time. Atypical signs of depression like increased sleepiness and fatigue during the day, increased appetite and carbohydrate craving leading to weight gain as well as higher irritability are predominate in SAD. 4 to 18% percent of the general population experience SAD (Magnusson & Stefansson 1993; Kasper et al. 1989) with women outnumbering men four to one (Magnusson & Boivin 2003; Kasper & Pjerk 2004).

The first controlled trial of bright light treatment dates back to the report by Rosenthal and colleagues, showing an antidepressant effect of bright light in 11 patients with SAD (Rosenthal et al. 1984). Today, light therapy is the treatment of choice for SAD with remission rates of up to 80% (Terman et al. 2001) and an effect size equivalent or better to those in most pharmacotherapy trials (Golden et al. 2005).

Although bright light therapy is effective for winter depressive episodes, its mechanism of neurobiological actions has not been established. Postulated mechanism for the antidepressant effect of light are the reversing of the increased melatonin, decreased 5-hydroxytryptamine and decreased dopamine neurotransmission (Lam et al. 1996; Neumeister et al. 1997). Another controversial hypothesis is the circadian phase shift hypothesis, postulating that the later dawn during the winter season leads to a phase delay in the circadian rhythm. Early morning bright light therapy should produce the desired shift in rhythms (Wirz-Justice et al.1993; Terman et al. 2001).

Bright light therapy is also effective in sub-syndromal SAD, which has a far higher prevalence in the general population than SAD itself (10 to 20 percent) (Terman 1988; Levitt et al. 2002). In sub-syndromal SAD patients display primarily neurovegetative symptoms like hypersomnia and hyperphagia, but a lower severity of depressed mood.

Bright-Light Therapy in Non-Seasonal Affective Disorders and Other Psychiatric and Neurological Indications

In the last years several clinical trials were conducted to prove the therapeutic efficacy of light for different neurological and psychiatric disorders (for a review see Terman & Terman 2005; Pail et al. 2011). Several studies could show that the combination of antidepressant medication and bright light therapy is an efficacious treatment of non-seasonal depressions and has the ability to shorten the latency respond (Niederhofer & vonKlitzing 2012; Thalen et al. 1995). Additionally light therapy could also improve depressive symptoms in patients with chronic depressions. Other indications for light therapy in non-seasonal affective disorders are premenstrual dysphoric disorder (Parry et al. 1993; Lam et al. 1999), antepartum depression (Epperson et al. 2004; Oren et al. 2002) and geriatric depression (for a review see Shirani et al. 2009). Since abnormal circadian rhythms in neuroendocrine functions, physiology and behavior such as sleep disturbances are prevalent in many psychiatric disorders light therapy was studied in a variety of psychiatric disorders like bulimia nervosa, attention deficit/hyperactivity disorders, Alzheimer and Parkinson dementia (for a review see Shirani et al. 2009; Terman & Terman 2005). Until now, most studies in these promising new indications for light therapy used only small samples sizes with various protocols and applications, therefore yielding mixed results. Large randomized, controlled clinical trials as well as controlled long-term studies are necessary to establish the therapeutic effect of light therapy in these indications.

Bright Light Therapy in Healthy Individuals

Previous research could show, that bright light therapy during winter time can also improve mood, vitality, alleviates distress (Partonen et al. 2000) and lead to more positive social interactions (aan het Rot et al. 2008) in non-depressed healthy persons without history of seasonal difficulties. Combining bright light exposure with physical exercise during winter time (Leppämäki et al. 2002; Partonen et al. 1998) or a short nap in the afternoon was also improving mood, vitality, and general well-being in non-depressed, healthy individuals.

Furthermore, several studies could demonstrate that during the night light has an alerting effect on people and can positively improve the mental state of shift working nurses, due to the suppression of melatonin (Campbell et al. 1990; Daurat et al. 2000; Iwata et al. 1997), with high lighting levels turning out to be more effective in the suppression of melatonin than low levels (e.g. Cajochen et al. 2000).

The Impact of Workplace Illumination on Mood

Most people spend a lot of time inside buildings and especially during winter time the exposure to daylight is limited. Therefore workplace illumination could become an important preventive factor by influencing indirectly the productivity and well-being of employee's. In the last years a large amount of research was done to develop recommendations and standards for lighting criteria in the work environment to assure high quality light and improve alertness and productivity. However, the European lighting standards list requirements for office-lighting are based on visual needs. As mentioned above indoor lighting levels are much lower than the lighting levels used for bright light therapy, varying between 100 and 2000 lux depending on geographical orientation of the office, daylight availability and season (Nabil & Mardaljevic 2005). The knowledge on the effects of environmental lighting conditions on non-visual processes are limited and the question remain, whether current lighting standards are sufficient for non-visual processes on mood and cognition. Only a few studies have investigated the impact of daytime artificial light on mood and cognition in indoor working or school environments and the results are mixed, with some studies showing that lighting levels during daytime can directly influence alertness and mood, while others failed to find any influence (Gornicka 2006; Phipps-Nelson et al. 2003; Knez 1995; Mishima et al. 2001; Takasu et al. 2006; Tanner 2008; Viola et al. 2008). These inconsistencies in study results are mainly due to methodological differences in study designs, such as different lighting levels at eye level, differences in the subjects sleep history and experimental measurement of work routine as well as differences in which season the study was performed. Preliminary evidence pointing in the direction that variable lighting intensities during daytime exerts a potential advantage in indoor office accommodations with respect to subjective mood and cognitive performance (Hoffmann et al. 2008; Gornicka 2006).

Another important line of research is investigating the influence of the spectral quality of ambient light on body functions such as blood pressure, pulse or respiration rate, but also on brain activity and circadian rhythms. A large amount of research was done on the effect of colors on cognitive tasks and mood. Previous results suggest that red color is often associated with hazard, danger and high levels of compliance and therefore performance on detail-oriented visual tasks can be enhanced by red color (Mehta & Zhu 2009; Elliot et al. 2007; Braun & Silver 1995). In contrast blue color increases creativity and innovation (Mehta & Zhu 2009). Vandewalle et al. (2010) could show that the spectral composition of ambient light influences the processing of emotional stimuli, via a network, including the amygdala and the hypothalamus. Blue light, relative to green light, not only increased responses to emotional stimuli in cortex regions that are necessary for memory processing such as the temporal cortex and the hippocampus, but also enhanced the functional coupling with areas that are important for emotion regulation like the amygdala and brain regions essential for biological rhythms regulation such as the hypothalamus. As mentioned above the human circadian system is maximally sensitive to short-wavelength radiation (blue light) (Brainard et al. 2001; Thappan et al. 2001; Rea et al. 2005). In the treatment of SAD, blue enriched light was found to be more effective than red light (Glickman et al. 2006; Strong et al. 2009; Gordijn et al. 2006) however, recent data about the superiority of blue-enriched light over standard bright light yielded mixed results (Gordijn et al. 2012; Meesters et al. 2011; Anderson et al. 2009). Only a few studies have investigated the influence of color temperature on mood and performance in healthy subjects and the results are heterogeneous. Color temperature (measured in Kelvin) refers to the quality of white light and runs from "cool" (bluish-white) to "warm" (warm-white) along the radiation spectrum of light. Baron et al. (1992) reported that cool white fluorescent lighting was associated with an increased reading speed and accuracy, whereas warm white lighting was improving social skills like working together and minimizing conflicts. On the other hand Knez (2001) could show that subjects performed better in the 'warm' than in the 'cool' and artificial 'daylight' white lighting.

There is the need for more studies, especially with larger sample sizes, to specify the optimum intensity, spectral quality, duration and timing of ambient daytime light exposure.

Therefore, the accumulation of lighting knowledge may contribute to architectural lighting designs and new lighting solutions in our homes and work environments.

REFERENCES

aan het Rot, M., Moskowitz, D. S. & Young, S. N. (2008). Exposure to bright light is associated with positive social interaction and good mood over short time periods: A naturalistic study in mildly seasonal people. *J Psychiatr Res.* Mar,42 (4), 311-9.

Anderson, J.L., Glod, C.A., Dai, J. & Lockley, S.W. (2009). Lux vs. wavelength in light treatment of Seasonal Affective Disorder. *Acta Psychiatrica Scandinavica, 120*, 203-212.

Baron, R.A., Rea, M. S. & Daniels, S. G. (1992). Effects of indoor lighting (illuminance and spectral distribution) on the performance of cognitive tasks and interpersonal behaviors: The potential mediating role of positive affect. *Motivation and Emotion, 16*, 1-33.

Berson, D.M., Dunn, F.A. & Takao, M. (2002). Phototransduction by retinal ganglion cells that set the circadian clock. *Science, 295*, 1070–1073.

Brainard, G., Hanifin, J., Greeson, J., Byrne, B., Glickman, G., Gerner, E. & Rollag, M. (2001). Action spectrum for melatonin regulation in humans: Evidence for a novel circadian photoreceptor. *J Neurosci, 21*, 6405-6412.

Brainard, G.C. & Hanifin, J.P. (2005). Photons, clocks, and consciousness. *J Biol Rhythms, 20*, 314–325.

Braun, C. C. & Silver, N.C. (1995). Interaction of signal word and colour on warning labels: differences in perceived hazard and behavioural compliance. *Ergonomics*, Nov, *38*(11), 2207-20.

Brzezinski, A. (1997). Melatonin in humans. *N Engl J Med., 336*, 186–95

Cajochen, C., Zeitzer, J., Czeisler, C. & Dijk, D. (2000). Dose-response relationship for light intensity and ocular and electroencephalographic correlates of human alertness. *Behav Brain Res, 115*, 75-83.

Cajochen, C., Munch, M., Kobialka, S., Kräuchi, K., Steiner, R., Oelhafen, P., Orgül, S. & Wirz-Justice, A. (2005). High sensitivity of human melatonin, alertness, thermoregulation, and heart rate to short wavelength light. *J Clin Endocrinol Metab., 90*, 1311–1316.

Cajochen, C. (2007). Alerting effects of light. *Sleep Med Rev, 11*, 453–464.

Campbell, S.S. & Dawson, D. (1990). Enhancement of nighttime alertness and performance with bright ambient light. *Physiol Behav, 48* (2), 317-320.

Challet, E. (2007). Entrainment of the suprachiasmatic clockwork in diurnal and nocturnal mammals. *Endocrinology, 148*, 5648-5655

Czeisler, C.A., Duffy, J.F., Shanahan, T.L., Brown, E.N., Mitchell, J.F., Rimmer, D.W., Ronda, J.M., Silva, E.J., Allan, J.S., Emens, J.S., Dijk, D.J. & Kronauer, R.E. (1999). Stability, precision, and near-24-hour period of the human circadian pacemaker. *Science, 284*, 2177–2181

Daurat, A., Foret, J., Benoit, O. & Mauco, G. (2000). Bright light during nighttime: effects on the circadian regulation of alertness and performance. *Biol Signals Recept, 9* (6), 309-318.

Deacon, S. & Arendt, J. (1995). Melatonin-induced temperature suppression and its acute phase-shifting effects correlate in a dose-dependent manner in humans. *Brain Res., 688*,77–85

Dijk, D. J. & Archer, S.N. (2009). Light, sleep, and circadian rhythms: Together again. *PLoS Biol, 7,* 6.

Elliot, A.J., Maier, M.A., Moller, A.C., Friedman, R. & Meinhardt, J. (2007). Color and psychological functioning: the effect of red on performance attainment. *J Exp Psychol Gen.,* Feb *136* (1),154-68.

Glickman, G., Byrne, B., Pineda, C., Hauck, W. & Brainard, G.C. (2006). Light therapy for seasonal affective disorder with blue narrow-band light-emitting diodes (LEDs). *Biological Psychiatry, 59,* 502-507.

Golden, R.N., Gaynes, B.N., Ekstrom, R.D., Hamer, R.M., Jacobsen, F.M., Suppes, T., Wisner, K.L. & Nemeroff, C.B. (2005). The efficacy of light therapy in the treatment of mood disorders: a review and meta-analysis of the evidence. *AM J Psych., 162,* 656-662.

Gordijn, M.C.M., 't Manneje, D. & Meesters, Y. (2006).The effects of blue-enriched light treatment compared to standard light treatment in SAD. *SLTBR abstracts, 18,* 6.

Gordijn, M.C., 't Mannetje, D. & Meesters, Y. (2012). The effects of blue-enriched light treatment compared to standard light treatment in Seasonal Affective Disorder. *J Affect Disord,* Jan; *136* (1-2),72-80

Gornicka, G.B. (2006). Effect of lighting level and colour temperature on alertness and vigilance during the day. *Sleep-Wake Research in The Netherlands, 17,* 59 - 63.

Hankins, M.W., Peirson, S.N. & Foster, R.G. (2008). Melanopsin: an exciting photopigment. *Trend Neursci, 31,* 27-26

Hoffmann, G., Gufler, V., Griesmacher, A., Bartenbach, C., Canazei, M., Staggl, S. & Schobersberger, W. (2008). Effects of variable lighting intensities and colour temperatures on sulphatoxymelatonin and subjective mood in an experimental office workplace.Applied Ergonomics, 39, 719 – 728.

Horne, J.A. & Ostberg, O. (1976). A self- assessment questionnaire to determine morningness-eveningness I humn circadian rhythms. *In J Chronobiol, 4,* 97-110

Iwata, N., Ichii, S. & Egashira, K. (1997). Effects of bright artificial light on subjective mood of shift work nurses. *Ind Health, 35*(1), 41-7.

Kasper, S., Wehr, T.A., Bartko, J.J., Gaist, P.A. & Rosenthal, N.E. (1989). Epidemiological findings of seasonal changes in mood and behavior. *Arch Gen Psychiatry, 46,* 823–33.

Kasper, S. & Pjrek, E. (2004). Diagnose Behandlung der subsyndromalen SAD. In Kasper, S. Möller, H.J. (Hrsg.), *Herbst-/Winterdepression und Lichttherapie.* Wien, New York: Springer.

Knez, I. *(1995).* Effects of indoor lighting on mood and cognition. *Journal of Environmental Psychology, 15, 39-51.*

Knez, I. (2001). Effects of colour of light on nonvisual psychological processes. *Joural of Environmental Psychology. 21* (2), 201–208

Lam, R.W., Zis, A.P., Grewal, A., Delgado, P.L., Charney, D.S. & Krystal, J.H. (1996). Effects of rapid tryptophan depletion in patients with seasonal affective disorder in remission after light therapy. *Arch Gen Psychiatry.* Jan; *53* (1), 41-44.

Leppämäki, S., Partonen, T. & Lönnqvist, J. (2002). Bright-light exposure combined with physical exercise elevates mood. *J Affect Disord,* Nov; *72* (2), 139-44.

Levitt, A.J., Lam, R. W. & Levitan, R.D. (2002). A comparison of open treatment seasonal major and minor depression with light therapy. *J Affect Disorder ,71,* 243-248

Lewy, A.J., Sack, R.L., Miller, L.S. & Hoban, T.M. (1987). Antidepressant and circadian phase-shifting effect of light. *Science, 235,* 352-354

Lewy, A.J. & Sack, R.L. (1989). The dim light melatonin onset as a marker for circadian phase position. *Chronobiol Int., 6,* 93–102

Lockley, S.W., Brainard, G.C. & Czeisler, C.A. (2003). High sensitivity of the human circadian melatonin rhythm to resetting by short wave length light. *J Clin Endocrinol Metab., 88,* 4502–5

Lockley, S. W. & Gooley, J.J. (2006). Circadian photoreception: Spotlight on the brain. *CurrBio, l16,* 795–797.

Magnússon, A. & Stefánsson, J. G. (1993). Prevalence of Seasonal Affective Disorder in Iceland. *Archives of General Psychiatry, 50,* (12), 941-946.

Magnusson, A. & Boivin, D. (2003). Seasonal affective disorder: an overview. *Chronobiol Int.,* Mar; *20* (2), 189-207.

Meesters, Y., Dekker, V., Schlangen, L.J., Bos, E. H. & Ruiter, M.J. (2011). Low-intensity blue-enriched white light (750 lux) and standard brightlight (10,000 lux) are equally effective in treating SAD. A randomized controlled study. *BMC Psychiatry,* Jan 28, *11,* 17.

Mehta, R. & Zhu, R.J. (2009). Blue or red? Exploring the effect of color on cognitive task performances. *Science,* Feb 27, *323* (5918), 1226 - 1229

Minors, D.S., Waterhouse, J.M. & Wirz-Justice, A. (1991). A human phase-response curve to light. *Neurosci Lett., 133,* 36–40

Mishima,K., Okawa,M., Shimizu,T. & Hishikawa,Y. *(2001).* Diminished melatonin secretion in the elderly caused by insufficient environmental illumination. *Journal of Clinical Endocrinology & Metabolism, 86, 129-134.*

Nabil, A. & Mardaljevic, J. (2005). Useful daylight illuminance: A new paradigm for assessing daylight in buildings. *Lighting Research and Technology, 37* (1), 41- 59.

Neumeister, A., Praschak-Rieder, N., Besselmann, B., Rao, M.L., Glück, J. & Kasper, S. (1997). Effects of tryptophan depletion on drug-free patients with seasonal affective disorder during a stable response to bright light therapy. *Arch Gen Psychiatry,* Feb, *54* (2), 133-8.

Niederhofer, H. & von Klitzing, K. (2012). Brightlight treatment as mono-therapy of non-seasonal depression for 28 adolescents. *Int J Psychiatry Clin Pract.* Sep, *16* (3), 233-7.

Pail, G., Huf, W., Pjrek, E., Winkler, D., Willeit, M., Praschak-Rieder, N. & Kasper, S. (2011). Bright-light therapy in the treatment of mood disorders. *Neuropsychobiology, 64* (3), 152-62.

Partonen, T., Leppämäki, S., Hurme, J. & Lönnqvist, J. (1998). Randomized trial of physical exercise alone or combined with brightlight on mood and health-related quality of life. *Psychol Med.,* Nov, *28* (6), 1359-64.

Partonen, T. & Lönnqvist, J. (2000) Brightlight improves vitality and alleviates distress in healthy people. *J Affect Disord,* Jan-Mar, *57* (1-3), 55-61.

Perrin, F., Peigneux, P., Fuchs, S., Verhaeghe, S., Laureys, S., Middleton, B., Degueldre, C., Del Fiore, G., Vandewalle, G., Balteau, E., Poirrier, R., Moreau, V., Luxen, A.,

Maquet,P. & Dijk, D.J. (2004). Nonvisual responses to light exposure in the human brain during the circadian night. *Curr Biol, 14*, 1842–1846.

Phipps-Nelson, J., Redman, J.R., Dijk, D.J. & Rajaratnam, S.M.W. (2003). Daytime exposure to bright light, as compared to dim light, decreases sleepiness and improves psychomotor vigilance performance. *Sleep, 26* (6), 695-700.

Rea, M., Figueiro, M., Bullough, J. & Bierman, A. (2005). A model of phototransductionby the human circadian system. *Brain Res Rev, 50* (2), 213-228.

Roenneberg, T.& Foster, R.G. (1997). Twilight times: light and the circadian system. *PhotochemPhotobiol., 66*, 549–61

Rosenthal, N.E., Sack, D.E., Gillin, J.C., Lewy, A.J., Goodwin, F.K., Davenport, Y., Mueller, P.S., Newsome, D.A. & Wehr, T.A. (1984). Seasonal affective disorder; a description ofthe syndrome and preliminary findings with light therapy. *Arch Gen Psychiatry, 41*, 72-80

Shirani, A. & St. Louis, E.K. (2009). Illuminating Rationale and Uses for Light Therapy. *Journal of Sleep Medicine*, Vol. 5, No. 2., 155-163

Sparks, D.L. (1998). Anatomy of a new paired tract of the pineal gland in humans. *Neuroscience Lett., 248*, 179–82.

Strong, R.E., Marchant, B.K., Reimherr, F.W., Williams, E., Soni, P. & Mestas, R. (2009). Narrowband blue-light treatment of seasonal affective disorder in adults and the influence of additional nonseasonal symptoms. *Depression and Anxiety, 26*, 273-278 .

Takasu, N. N., Hashimoto,S., Yamanaka,Y., Tanahashi,Y., Yamazaki,A., Honma,S. & Honma,K. *(2006).* Repeated exposures to daytime bright light increase nocturnal melatonin rise and maintain circadian phase in young subjects under fixed sleep schedule. *American Journal of Physiology—Regulatory, Integrative and Comparative Physiology, 291*, 1799-1807.

Tanner, K. C.*(2008).* Explaining relationships among student outcomes and the school's physical environment. *Journal of Advanced Academics, 19*, 444-471.

Teclemariam-Mesbah, R., Ter Horst, G.J., Postema, F., Wortel, J. & Buijs, R.M. (1999). Anatomical demonstration of the suprachiasmatic nucleus-pineal pathway. *J Comp Neurol., 406*, 171–82.

Terman, M. (1988). On the question of mechanism in phototherapy for seasonal affective disorder: considerations of clinical efficacy and epidemiology. *J Biol Rhythms, 3*, 155-172.

Terman, J.S., Terman, M., Lo, E.S. & Cooper, T.B. (2001). Circadian time of morning light administration and therapeutic response in winter depression. *Arch Gen Psychiatry, 58*, 69–75.

Terman, M. & Terman, J.S. (2005). Light therapy for seasonal and nonseasonal depression: Efficacy, protocol, safety, and side effects. *CNS Spectrums, 10* (8), 647-663.

Thalén, B. E., Kjellman, B. F., Mørkrid, L. & Wetterberg, L. (1995). Melatonin in light treatment of patients with seasonaland nonseasonaldepression. *Acta Psychiatr Scand.* Oct; *92* (4), 274-84.

Thapan, K., Arendt, J. & Skene, D.J. (2001). An action spectrum for melatonin suppression: evidence for a novel non-rod, non-cone photoreceptor system in humans. *J Physiol, 535* (Pt 1), 261-267.

Vandewalle, G., Balteau, E., Phillips, C., Degueldre, C., Moreau, V., Sterpenich, V., Albouy, G., Darsaud, A., Desseilles, M., Dang-Vu, T.T., Peigneux, P., Luxen, A., Dijk, D.J. &

Maquet, P. (2006). Daytime light exposure dynamically enhances brain responses. *CurrBiol*, *16*, 1616–1621.

Vandewalle, G., Gais, S., Schabus, M., Balteau, E., Carrier, J., Darsaud, A., Sterpenich, V., Albouy, G., Dijk, D. J. & Maquet, P. (2007a). Wavelength-dependent modulation of brain responses to a working memory task by daytime light exposure. *Cereb Cortex*, *17*, 2788–2795.

Vandewalle, G., Schmidt, C., Albouy, G., Sterpenich, V., Darsaud, A., Rauchs, G., Berken, P.Y., Balteau, E., Degueldre, C., Luxen, A., Maquet, P. & Dijk, D.J. (2007b). Brain responses to violet, blue, and green monochromatic light exposures in humans: Prominent role of blue light and the brainstem. *PLoS ONE*, Nov 28; *2* (11), e1247.

Vandewalle, G., Maquet, P. & Dijk, D.J. (2009). Light as a modulator of cognitive brain function. *Trends CognSci*, *13*, 429–438.

Vandewalle, G., Schwartz, S., Grandjean, D., Wuillaume, C., Balteau, E., Degueldre, C., Schabus, M., Phillips, C., Luxen, A., Dijk, D.J. & Maquet, P. (2010). Spectral quality of light modulates emotional brain responses in humans. *Proc Natl Acad Sci U S A.*, Nov 9, *107* (45), 19549-54.

Viola, A. U., James, L. M., Schlangen, L. J. & Dijk, D. J. (2008). Blue-enriched white light in the workplace improves self-reported alertness, performance and sleep quality. *Scandinavian Journal of Work, Environment & Health, 34, 297-306.*

Voultsios, A., Kennaway, D. J. & Dawson, D. (1997). Salivary melatonin as a circadian phase marker: validation and comparison to plasma melatonin. *J Biol Rhythms, 12,* 457–65.

Warman, V.L., Dijk, D.J., Warman, G.R., Arendt, J. & Skene, D.J. (2003). Phase advancing human circadian rhythms with short wave length light. *Neurosci Lett., 342,* 37–40

Wirz-Justice, A., Graw, P. & Bucheli, C. (1984). Seasonal affective disorder in Switzerland: a clinical perspective. In: Thompson C, Silverstone T eds. Seasonal Affective Disorder. *London, England: Clinical Neuroscience Publisher*; 69-76

Wirz-Justice, A., Graw, P., Kräuchi, K., Gisin, B., Jochum, A., Arendt, J., Fisch, H.U., Buddeberg, C. & Pöldinger, W. (1993). Light therapy in seasonal affective disorder is independent of time of day or circadian phase. *Arch Gen Psychiatry*, Dec, *50* (12), 929-37.

Wirz-Justice, A., Terman, M., Oren, D.A., Goodwin, F.K., Kripke, D.F., Whybrow, P.C., Wisner, K.L., Wu, J.C., Lam, R.W., Berger, M., Danilenko, K.V., Kasper, S., Smeraldi, E., Takahashi, K., Thompson, C. & van den Hoofdakker, R.H. (2004). Brightening depression. *Science*, *303*, 467–469.

Wright, H., Lack, L.C. & Kennaway, D.J. (2004). Differential effects of light wavelength in phase advancing melatonin rhythm. *J Pineal Res.*, *36*, 140–4

In: Handbook of Psychology of Emotions   ISBN: 978-1-62808-053-7
Editors: C. Mohiyeddini, M. Eysenck and S. Bauer   © 2013 Nova Science Publishers, Inc.

Chapter 18

AFFECTIVE REACTIONS TO PHYSICAL ACTIVITY, EXERCISE AND THE ACTIVITIES OF DAILY LIVING: A REVIEW

Wolfgang Schlicht, Annelie Reicherz and Martina Kanning
University of Stuttgart
Department of Sport and Exercise Science, Stuttgart, Germany

ABSTRACT

This narrative review deals with the association between physical activity or exercise and affective reactions. It outlines what is known about affective reactions, accompanying or following increasing exercise intensities. It also summarizes the results of ambulatory assessment studies. Those studies monitor the individuals' activity levels in daily routine and their reactions to it.

INTRODUCTION

Most people avoid behaviours that cause a bad mood or reduce wellbeing. Instead, they strive to maintain and enhance wellbeing and to gain a sense of positive feeling. Williams (2008) explained behaviour as a function of affective reactions or the anticipated reactions associated with this behaviour. He named this theory the *hedonic theory*. Empirical results by Schneider, Dunn and Cooper (2009), for example, have supported this assumption. This theory is contrary to the suggestion of Parrot (1993) that people do not always behave to avoid unpleasant feelings and to maximise pleasant feelings. Maintaining positive wellbeing is obviously a fundamental psychological need, as shown by several scientists (cf. Grawe, 1998; Deci & Ryan, 1985).

The behaviour we focus on in this review is physical activity, which will later be defined in more detail. Diurnal active living, especially moderate intense physical activity, reduces the risk of non-communicable diseases. Physical activity is also associated with affective reactions. We argue that these reactions vary and can be either positive or negative. The outcome depends on the quality of these reactions and whether a person will stick to a given behaviour such as physical activity or whether the person will cease this behaviour and, for example, return to an inactive and sedentary lifestyle. It has been shown that the affect experienced after exercising is predictive of the amount of time spent on future exercise (Williams, Dunsiger, Ciccolo, Lewis, Albrecht & Marcus, 2008).

Affective reactions in this view function as a type of reward, and they are an essential motivating entity. The scientific literature has delivered a great amount of ostensibly consistent results indicating that a bout of physical activity is usually associated with positive mood after finishing the activity. Meta-analyses showed moderate weighted effect sizes between physical activity and mood (e.g., Schlicht, 1993; Biddle & Mutrie 2008). However, there are several methodological deficiencies with the studies integrated in the analyses:

1. The term "physical activity" is ambiguously defined.
   Sometimes, it is termed "exercise," and it is sometimes called "sport". Sometimes, there is only a single bout of physical activity, and sometimes, there are longer time periods of physical activity on one or several days a week.
2. "Mood" is often measured only by uni-dimensional scales or is ambiguous in the underlying construct.
   Uni-dimensional scales ignore the multi-dimensionality of the construct. Furthermore, there is no clear differentiation between emotions, mood, affective reactions, wellbeing, and feelings.
3. The measurement designs most often have discrete, at least two (pre and post) or, in rare cases, more measurement points (at several post times), but there is no continuous data collection during the activity.
   Measuring only post-exercise data points gives no information about what happens during the exercise. Depending on the intensity of the exercise, it is possible that there is a detrimental effect during exercise recovery that subsequently becomes positive after the exercise has been completed.

In the first section of this chapter, the two constructs addressed in this review will be defined: (1) physical activity and (2) affective reaction. Secondly, the current knowledge obtained from study results will be reported, and we will describe the hypotheses regarding the association between these two constructs. Our review then addresses a special type of physical activity: active diurnal living.

The chapter at hand is a narrative literature review. We searched articles in common databases such as PubMed, Google Scholar, and Science Direct. We used the following search terms: physical activity, exercise, sport, activities of daily living, free time physical activity and affective reactions, emotions, wellbeing in combination.

WHAT DOES PHYSICAL ACTIVITY MEAN?

In sport and exercise science, health psychology and public health research, physical activity (PA) is an expression with two meanings. First, it is an umbrella term and as this a meta-construct. In this sense, it comprises different types of planned, intentional and even unintentional bodily movement requiring an amount of energy expenditure higher than that of the resting metabolic rate. Ranked on an intensity scale one can identify and start with Non-Exercise Activity Thermogenesis (NEAT), Activities of Daily Living (ADLs), exercise or sport. These behaviours differ not only in their intensities, but also in the objectives pursued. Sport, for example, is of higher intensity than NEAT. ADLs are used to fulfil daily requirements, and exercise is performed to improve fitness.

Secondly, PA is a categorical construct. In this sense, PA is characterised by bodily movements with larger muscle groups that require a significant increase in energy expenditure. The energy expenditure (EE) is defined as sufficient if a person's EE in PA is equivalent to an additional amount (additional to the metabolic resting and thermic EE) of approximately 1.000 kcal/week (US DHHS, 1996). With this scale, the risk reduction for non-communicable diseases becomes evident.

NEAT was first defined by Levine et al. (2005) as energy expended for all types of ambulation that provoke a higher amount of energy expenditure than lying down or sitting (which is termed *sedentariness* when these behaviours are habitual). NEAT has a significant impact on metabolism and could be a critical component in reducing overweight and obesity and, consequently, reducing the risk of type 2 diabetes.

ADLs have three different forms: 1) *Basic ADLs* are self-care activities such as personal hygiene, dressing, and so on; 2) *Instrumental ADLs* are activities that fulfil an intended work task such as preparing a meal and doing chores; 3) *Advanced ADLs* are activities performed to take part in social interaction (e.g., meeting with others, partaking in hobbies, attending concerts). ADLs are a category often used in gerontology or geriatrics to evaluate an elderly individual's degree of autonomy.

Exercise is a regular type of PA that enhances a person's cardiovascular or muscular "fitness" and is often measured as vital capacity (VO_2-max) or muscular power. Typical types of exercise include walking, jogging, biking, power training, and callisthenics.

Sports are PAs that are rule-based, competitive, and take place in standardised environments (e.g., soccer, track and field, tennis). The Council of Europe Committee of Ministers (1995) defined sport as "... all forms of PA, which through casual or organised participation, aim at expressing or improving physical fitness and mental well-being, forming social relationships or obtaining results in competition at all levels." In this chapter, we focus on PA as a meta-construct and have excluded sports.

Some years ago, Ainsworth and colleagues (e.g., Ainsworth et al., 1995) reported the metabolic intensity associated with several different activities. The common intensity unit is the *multiple of the resting metabolic rate* or MET. One MET unit stands for an EE of approximately $1 \text{ kcal} \times \text{kg}^{-1} \times \text{h}^{-1}$ or $4.2 \text{ kJ} \times \text{kg}^{-1} \times \text{h}^{-1}$ or an oxygen uptake of $3.5 \text{ ml O}_2 \times \text{kg}^{-1} \times \text{min}^{-1}$. One MET unit represents the EE of sitting.

In order to assess the impact of PA on affective responses, it is important to calculate the intensity of the PA because some studies with single bouts of PA have shown that affective reactions vary with the intensity of the PA. We will focus on this finding later in this review.

WHAT DO THE TERMS AFFECTIVE REACTIONS, MOOD, EMOTIONS, FEELINGS AND WELLBEING MEAN?

With regard to the categories of PA (used as a meta-construct here), there is also a need to differentiate between the affective constructs. The terms *affective reactions, emotions, feelings, mood,* and *wellbeing* are often used indeterminately in this context. All of these constructs are multi-dimensional. Let us start with *wellbeing* (see, e.g., Diener, 1984), which is defined as a state and a trait and is labelled as subjective wellbeing (SWB) in psychology. SWB can be broken down into a cognitive and an affective dimension. The cognitive dimension embraces life satisfaction as a cognitive balance of one's life. The affective dimension gives wellbeing an emotional hue or a feeling such as anger, anxiety, pleasantness, and so on. There is a great amount of scientific work that shows that people usually feel well (see, e.g., Staudinger, 2000). To feel and to keep feeling well is one of a person's fundamental needs (e.g., Grawe, 1998). As Diener, Sandvik and Pavot (1991) and other authors note, it is the frequency of positive affective reactions and not the intensity that makes us feel well. Positive and negative affective feelings are not only the contrary or inversely correlated poles of one dimension. Therefore, it is obvious that any behaviour, including PA, will cause an impact on both feelings. Ideally, PA enhances positive feelings and hinders negative feelings. This fact is often ignored, especially in (sport) psychology.

To define feelings such as anger, anxiety or pleasantness as affective or emotional, these terms must first be clarified. Damasio (2003) and other authors such as Davidson, Scherer and Goldsmith (2003) have noted that *emotions* are states that individuals feel in situations relevant for the individual. Persons attribute such situations as meaningful, and they are affected by the situation. Most scientists in affective science assume the existence of a limited number of primary emotions: fear, anxiety, anger, disgust, astonishment, grief, shame, pride, jealousy, envy, abhorrence and others. These emotions are all considered necessary entities with evolutionary functions in promoting the survival and reproduction of the species. Emotions are bound to a bundle of different reaction modalities: motivational (appetence versus avoidance), cognitive (e.g., to appraise a situation as harmful or challenging), arousal (e.g., increased or lowered pulse or breathing frequency), expressive (e.g., facial expression) and a qualitative attribution of feelings that give the emotional feeling its special definition. All of these reaction modalities last only a short time. They persist as long as the situation and its interpretation exist or as long as they are remembered. *Feelings,* as defined by Damasio (2003), are perceptions of bodily states. These perceptions are combined with a special type of thoughts dealing with special themes. Feelings in this sense are somatic reactions combined with typical thoughts belonging to this emotion (e.g., danger and anxiety; possession and love; loss and grief). Therefore, feelings are more than emotional appraisals alone.

If emotions persist and lose their link to a situation, they transfer to moods. *Moods* are unfocused, global phenomena that give everyday life a "colour". Moods are diffuse states. People are often unable to report a cause for a given mood. Moods are linked with emotional feelings. People feel, for example, anxious, angry, nervous, worried, sad, jocular, or calm.

Feeling calm or aroused, powerful or weak, good or bad, points to another facet of emotional reactions, named *affective reactions*. People feel comfortable or uncomfortable, well or uneasy, awake or tired, powerful or weak. Affective reactions are the basic, subjective qualities of all emotions or moods.

These states are the focus of this review, and these are the reactions that have dominated recent research in exercise psychology. For research dealing with wellbeing and focussing on older persons, see, for example, Lehnert, Sudeck and Conzelmann (2012), and for research dealing with mood, see, for example, McAuley and Rudolph (1995). As an example of the meta-analyses dealing with emotions, see Petruzzello, Landers, Hatfield, Kubitz and Salazar (1991), North, McCullagh and Tran (1990) or Schlicht (1994a) for the effects of exercise on anxiety.

HOW ARE AFFECTIVE REACTIONS STRUCTURED?

Affective reactions are multi-dimensional constructs (Schimmack, 1998). This fact has often been ignored in previous research investigating the impact of PA. In a first approach, the German psychologist Wilhelm Wundt (1905) identified three independent dimensions when he asked subjects how they felt. These dimensions were pleasantness (pleasant versus unpleasant), calmness (calm versus aroused) and alertness (alert versus relaxed). Affective science after Wundt differentiated three dimensions that were named the Pleasure dimension (pleasure versus displeasure), the Arousal dimension (calm versus aroused) and the Power dimension (powerful versus weak). Thayer (1989) reduced these three dimensions to two arousal dimensions (energetic arousal and tense arousal) measured with the Activation-Deactivation Checklist. Tellegen, Watson and Clark (1999) also suggested measuring two dimensions. These authors labelled them positive and negative activation (in a former approach from Watson and Tellegen (1985), the dimension was named "positive versus negative affect"), and the instrument developed here is the Positive-and-Negative Affect Scale (PANAS; Watson, Clark & Tellegen, 1988). To account for the multi-dimensionality of the affective constructs, other authors attempted to measure different feelings (e.g., good or bad mood, angry, anxious or depressive mood). One prominent questionnaire here is the Profile of Mood States (POMS) constructed by McNair, Lorr and Droppleman (1971). The POMS assesses six mood states (tension, depression, anger, vigour, fatigue, confusion). The questionnaire has often been used in the context of (competitive) sports. Other inventories measuring discrete moods (but not affective reactions) are the Exercise Feeling Inventory (EFI: Gauvin & Rejeski, 1993), the Subjective Exercise Experience Scale (SEES: McAuley & Courneya, 1994) and the Physical Activity Affect Scale (PAAS: Lox, Jackson, Tuhilsky & Treasure, 2000). Therefore, there are sufficiently valid and reliable instruments to assess the different forms of affective states. The objectives the authors followed defined which construct and which instrument was suitable.

In recent studies, the *circumplex model* defines the state of the art to measure affective reactions in the context of PA. Ekkekakis (2008) suggested a model with two dimensions: valence (pleasantness versus unpleasantness) and activation (high versus low activation). Figure 1 shows a circumplex model (for more details, see Hall, Ekkekakis & Petruzzello, 2002, p. 50).

These or similar dimensions are often reproduced in studies using the semantic differential technique (Osgood, Succi & Tannenbaum, 1957). With this technique, adjectives are arranged in a bipolar manner (e.g., good versus bad; alert versus tired; powerful versus weak) representing the three dimensions of valence, activation and power. Depending on the question asked at the beginning of the questionnaires or lists, subjects may assess how often or how intense they feel, how they feel at the moment or how they feel in general (habitual).

Russel (1980) introduced the circumplex model into the scientific literature and removed the power dimension. His model measures only intensity but not the frequency of affective reactions. This model is a two-dimensional model arranged as an orthogonal axis spanning a space in which mixed affective reactions can be assessed instead of just individual parameters, for example, *"pleasure and high activation"*, *"displeasure and high activation"*, *"pleasure and low activation"*, *"displeasure and low activation"*.

We conclude our methodological discussion of the different affective or emotional constructs and measurement models here. For additional details, see Ekkekakis and Petruzzello (2000, 2002).

In total, the circumplex model is a usable and parsimonious model to assess the affective reactions linked with PA, especially in the context of PA in everyday life, which is the focus of this review.

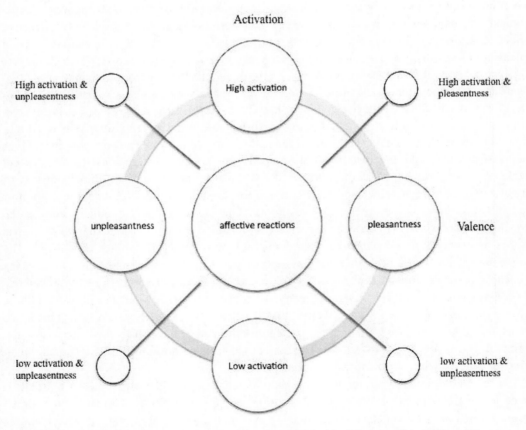

Figure 1. *Circumplex model of affective reactions* (Hall, Ekkekakis & Petruzzello, 2002, p. 50).

WHAT IS KNOWN ABOUT AFFECTIVE REACTIONS LINKED WITH PA?

Early studies dealing with the effect of PA on affective reactions, mood, emotions, and subjective wellbeing examined the general impact of PA on these psychological states. The starting points for these studies were anecdotal materials reporting a "feel-better effect" or the so-called "runner's high" after completing an endurance exercise or sport. In most of these studies, the subjects are invited to answer questionnaires on the intensity of their mood (often with unclear construct validity) before and after participating in a sporting event. Meta-analyses of these studies have delivered weak to moderate effect sizes (e.g., Schlicht, 1994b; Biddle & Mutrie, 2008).

One problem of pre- and post-measurement studies could be that post-measurement data do not indicate what happens during the PA. In this type of study, it is possible that the "runner's high" could be ascribed to the subject feeling relieved that the bout of exercise or sport is finished (rebound effect).

To address this problem, recent studies have followed a repeated measurement design (pre-exercise data point, several measurement points during the activity, and post-exercise data points). These studies (1) described the process of affective reactions during a single bout of exercise and (2) assessed, among other things, whether the intensity of the load moderates the affective responses and (3) clarified which mechanisms explain these responses.

As we will describe in more detail later in this review, activity intensity moderates the affective responses. But it is not the entire time of a single exercise bout, which moderates the process. Furthermore, not everyone experiences a "feel-better-effect" after exercise. Among the different hypotheses for the positive affect changes (e.g., thermogenic, endorphin, distraction; for more detail see Lehnert et al., 2012), two coherent theories are prominent to explain the affective reactions. It is the Opponent-Process Theory (Solomon & Corbit, 1974; Solomon, 1980) and the Dual-Mode Model *(Ekkekakis, 2003, 2005)*.

The Opponent-Process Theory (OPT), which explains habituation, is well known in learning experiments. The OPT postulates in its core assumptions that a person who is confronted with a positive (or negative) stimulus will first respond with a positive (or negative) reaction. After repeated confrontations with the stimulus or when the highest intensity of the response has been reached, the response begins to weaken or the opposite reaction begins to occur (positive turns to negative and negative turns to positive). If the stimulus is not present for a period of time, the opposite affective reaction becomes evident.

The *Dual-Mode Model* (DMM) postulates an evolutionary mechanism to prevent the organism from becoming exhausted. Exercises lasting a long period of time and requiring energy delivered by aerobic metabolic processes are accompanied by positive affective reactions. However, if these exercises require energy delivered by anaerobic processes, organismic homeostasis is threatened. The resulting reaction is a negative affective feeling, signalling that it would be better to stop the load before the organism takes damage.

Experimental studies testing the theories mentioned above consider that different intensity levels during exercise require different types of energy consumption. At the beginning of an exercise bout, aerobic processes are dominant (aerobic means that there is enough oxygen offered to fulfil the requirements of a given load). Energy is mainly gained by the uptake of oxygen. Ascending intensity is accompanied by an increasing oxygen demand that cannot be compensated for by increased breathing. This increased demand leads to an oxygen deficit. Therefore, anaerobic processes (anaerobic = without oxygen) dominate further energy generation, and energy is gained from lactate. Lactate delivers energy but also provokes muscle fatigue and pain and causes the abandonment of activity. If the intensity ascends too high, the organism is not able to sustain the load and ceases exercising.

Sports medicine differentiates three phases during a single bout of exercise with increasing intensity. In the first phase, oxygen requirements and the oxygen supply are balanced (below the ventilatory-threshold). With ascending intensity, the subject reaches the so-called aerobic or ventilatory threshold. Here the second phase begins in which "lactate-" and "oxygen-equivalent" accelerate, and reach the anaerobic (or lactate) threshold. In the third phase, the lactate steady-state is imbalanced. Lactate then accumulates in the muscle cells, and the carbon dioxide concentration reaches a maximum. Corresponding with these three phases, the affective reactions during the first phase are postulated to be positive (high valence and high activation) for almost all subjects (inter-individual homogeneity). This phenomenon is due to pleasant interoceptive sensations (e.g., a thermo-effect). In the second phase, some of the subjects shift to negative affective reactions (low valence and low activation), but for others, the reactions are still positive (inter-individual heterogeneity). The direction of the affective reaction here depends on cognitive processes, meaning that some subjects worry about the consequences of the physiological strain (negative outcome expectancies). During the third phase, the affective reactions are negative for almost all of the subjects (inter-individual homogeneity). This phenomenon could be due to an increase in negative interoceptive sensations such as pain. After finishing the exercise bout, the affective reactions return back to positive reactions that are higher in intensity than before starting the bout (inter-individual homogeneity; rebound effect). Markowitz and Arent (2010) showed in an experiment with 14 active and 14 inactive subjects who performed 20 minutes of treadmill exercise with ascending intensity that affective responses above the lactate threshold are negative. After the task, the subjects felt a mood improvement with a 30-minute delay when the intensity was above the lactate threshold (see also Markowitz, 2009).

WHAT IS STATE OF THE ART WITH RESPECT TO SINGLE BOUTS OF EXERCISE?

Two collaborating groups at the University of Illinois have delivered most of the results for the OPT and DMM theoretical models and the abovementioned hypotheses (see Ekkekakis & Backhouse, 2009; Ekkekakis, Hall & Petruzzello, 2005). Their experimental results are in line with the hypotheses, as are the results of other authors, including Rose and Parfitt (2007), who found that affective reactions were the most positive below the ventilatory threshold and least positive above the lactate threshold. Differences between the subjects were the greatest below and at the lactate threshold. Reed and Buck (2009), in their study on the positive quadrant of the circumplex model, found that the process was moderated by the baseline affective state at the pre-test time point. If a subject was in a low positive state prior to the exercise bout, the increased positive affect was higher than the increase experienced by those who began with a high level of positive affect. In an ambulatory assessment study, our own group (Kanning & Schlicht, 2010) found the same facts, as did Reed and Ones (2006). Parfitt and Hughes (2009) discussed another moderating condition. They found that the inter-individual heterogeneous processes in the second phase of a single bout with increasing load depended on the fitness levels of the subjects. Fitter subjects reacted with positive affective changes, whereas unfit subjects experienced negative changes. In the third phase, both reacted with a decrease in positive affective reactions. However, the decrease was faster in subjects with a low fitness level.

In addition to metabolic and cognitive processes, some authors have suggested examining brain activity and explaining the different processes during the different phases of a single bout of exercise (Petruzzello, Ekkekakis & Hall, 2006; Ekkekakis, 2009). The frontal brain lobes process affective stimuli. In the left hemisphere, brain activity is associated with positive, and in the right hemisphere, it is associated with negative affective reactions. The hypothesis is that there is a shift from left to right hemispheric processing during the ascending intensity of an exercise bout. This hypothesis needs further clarification. In their review, Harmon-Jones, Gable and Peterson (2010) also showed that motivational states are hemispheric processes. They found that appetence is linked to the left hemisphere and aversive motivation is linked to the right hemisphere. This finding corresponds with the hypothesized hemispheric processing of affective states. However, affective valence and motivational tendencies are not linked in a clear manner. Positive valence does not mean appetence, and negative valence does not mean retreat per se. This has been shown for anger (e.g., Peterson, Gravens & Harmon-Jones, 2011). Anger is an affective reaction with negative valence, but it is processed in the left hemisphere. This finding could be explained by the fact that anger has an offensive motivational tendency.

WHAT HAPPENS OUTSIDE THE LAB IN EVERYDAY LIFE?

As we know from studies describing the activity levels of adults living in modern societies, most people lack a sufficient amount of PA during their leisure time. In addition to this inactivity, their everyday life is characterised by extended periods of sitting either at the working desk or while watching TV during leisure time. This latter behaviour is named *sedentariness*. Inactivity and sedentariness cause a high prevalence of non-communicable diseases such as cardiovascular disease, stroke, type 2 diabetes and some types of cancer. Consequently, from a public health view, the objective must be to motivate people to be as active as possible in their everyday lives and to have as many breaks from sitting as possible. It is obvious that people will only persist with the desired behaviour if the affective reactions associated with the active behaviour are positive. Studies in the lab are useful in suggesting which amounts of PA provoke which response and which are suitable for preventing excessive activity for beginners. However, they lack external ecological validity. Real day-to-day life is much more complex than an experiment arranged in a lab, and behaviour is often forced by environmental or social constraints, affordances and incentives, and it is seldom possible to control for an exact intensity.

First, field studies were conducted to investigate the affective reactions provoked by activities in which the subjects selected their own intensities for walking. Armstrong and

Edwards (2004) and Rhodes et al. (1999) postulated that self-selected (moderate intense) walking bouts were associated with positive affective reactions. Ekkekakis, Backhouse, Gray and Lind (2008) preserved doubts that self-selection provokes positive reactions. They hypothesised that self-selected walking intensities often missed a threshold where positive reactions could arise. Other authors contradicted these findings and assumed that, especially for beginners, a low walking intensity was suitable for avoiding an exercise overload and a feeling of discomfort.

In a study by Ekkekakis et al. (2008), one group of subjects read a text, whilst a second group of subjects walked 15 minutes at a self-selected speed. The experimenters instructed subjects to walk as fast as they would in real life if he or she knew that they had to reach the post office before it closed in the near future. The design followed a measurement plan with pre-, during and post-measurement points. In a second arrangement of this study, a group of subjects walked 15 minutes at a self-selected intensity on a treadmill and then rested for 15 minutes. A second group of subjects rested first and then walked 15 minutes.

In both experimental arrangements, the subjects of the walking condition reported an increased feeling of energy (energetic arousal). In the first arrangement, the walking group reported an additional feeling of increased pleasantness. Both changes were volatile, thus contradicting the assumption that exercises provoke long-lasting affective reactions (Raglin, Wilson & Galper, 2007; Thayer, 1989). Stytch and Parfitt (2011) delivered further arguments for choosing intensities below the ventilatory threshold or a self-selected intensity. In their study with adolescents, those intensities both provoked positive feelings.

Again, as in the study by Ekkekakis et al. (2008), walking was a structured, planned activity even when the intensity was self-selected and not standardised as in a laboratory setting. As noted at the beginning of this chapter, walking is included in the category of exercise.

In another approach, the ADLs, NEATS, or everyday life activities have been the focus of several studies (Schlicht, 2010; Schott & Schlicht, 2012). Everyday life activities are unstructured and are often automatically processed and habitual (linked to typical situations). There is less known about the affective reactions associated with those actual activities than for exercise or sports. One focus of those studies was on the within-subject effect of actual PA during everyday life. The question addressed in these studies was if a subject experienced changes in affect when performing PA on days or parts of days to those when the subject was less active or even inactive or sedentary. Analysing within-subject effects allows researchers to assess the dynamics of the association between affective states and actual PA. Assessing variables repeatedly over time in real life requires the use of another methodological approach. Ecological or ambulatory assessment (Fahrenberg, Myrtek, Pawlik & Perrez, 2007; Shiffman, Stone & Hufford, 2008) refers to a category of methods that involves the collection of real-time data about current states (e.g., affective states, PA) in the natural environment repeatedly over the course of a day. Gauvin, Rejeski and Norris (1996) labelled those studies *naturalistic* or *ecological*.

Most studies assessing affective states and PA during everyday life used pagers to remind the subjects to assess their states and small booklets to collect data. In such studies, a pager sounded off several times during a day mostly due to a stratified random schedule. Subjects were requested to assess their momentary affective states and to describe their momentary activity (e.g., Carels, Coit, Young & Berger, 2007; Dunton, Atienza, Castro & King, 2009; Kanning & Schlicht, 2010, LePage & Crowther, 2009). In a study with older adults (older than 50 years old) conducted by Kanning and Schlicht (2010), subjects felt energised and relaxed after each active episode in their everyday life but not after inactive episodes.

Carels et al. (2007) specifically examined the mutual effects of actual physical activities and affective states. Obese subjects (N = 36; M$_{age}$ = 49, BMI = 41.5) completed an exercise and mood diary following a behavioural weight loss program. Subjects felt better after PA, and if they felt better, they were more active. In particular, beginning the day in a positive mood increased the likelihood of exercising during the day.

In some studies, actual PA was assessed only with a single item indicating how active a subject had been since the last "beep" of the pager (e.g., Bohnert, Richards, Kohl & Randall, 2009; Vendrig & Lousberg, 1997; Wichers, et al., 2011). For example, in the study recently published by Wichers et al. (2011), 504 female twins were asked over the course of five consecutive days to rate their affects related to actual PA during the day. A pager beeped between 7:30 a.m. and 10:30 p.m. in each of ten 90-minute-blocks. The authors used twins for the cross-validation of their findings. Subjects felt better (a significant increase in positive affect using the PANAS as a measurement instrument) following an increase in actual PA. Negative affect (PANAS) was not associated with increased actual PA. The positive impact on positive affect was maintained for up to 180 minutes following the increase in activity. However, due to the self-report of actual PA by one single item, it was not clear what an increase of actual PA actually meant. As a consequence, these results should be interpreted carefully. During day-to-day activities, individuals are not often able to remember every moment of their activities because they are most often performed automatically and habitually. For those activities, it is very difficult to provide reliable memory retrieval (Fahrenberg et al., 2007; Ebner-Priemer & Trull, 2009).

To assess the amount of actual PA, devices such as pedometers or accelerometers are more reliable and valid. Affective reactions can be assessed with handheld computers using short but reliable scales. With electronic diaries, researchers are able to control at which point in time affective states are being assessed. Recall bias is minimised, and compliance can be controlled (for detailed insight into this methodological discussion, see Kanning, Ebner-Priemer & Schlicht, 2013).

To provide an overall impression of this type of study and their main results, we have selected a few to describe here. Some of these studies analysed the data of healthy people, children or patients. These data are all highly reliable and assessed actual PA with accelerometers. Affective states were assessed in time using handhelds, for example. Schwerdtfeger, Eberhardt and Chmitorz (2008) showed that actual PA during everyday life produced positive but not negative affect. The age of the subjects here ranged between 18 and 73 years with a mean age of 32 years. In a second analysis using the same data set, the authors (Schwerdtfeger, Eberhard, Chmitorz, & Schaller, 2010) analysed the mutual influence of affective states and actual PA. The affective states influenced if a person became physically active, and actual PA influenced the affective states. A further study reported by Powell and colleagues (2009) indicated that individuals with higher ratings of negative affect were more active. This finding was contrary to the results of Carels et al. (2007) mentioned above. In that study, negative affect was associated with less PA during the day. Specifically, the association between PA and negative affect shows inconsistent findings and, therefore, needs further investigation. Some studies (e.g., Schwerdtfeger et al., 2008; Powell et al., 2009, Vansteeland, Rijmen, Pieters, Probs & Vanderlinden, 2007; Wichers et al., 2011) could not identify any significant association between PA and negative affect. Other studies (e.g.,

Dunton, Liao, Intille, Wolch & Pentz, 2011; LePage et al., 2010) found that their subjects experienced less negative affect after being physically active.

The search for moderating conditions is another focus of research. Dunton and colleagues (2011) asked if PA performed in different locations (e.g., at school, in recreation centres) and with different social arrangements (e.g., joining others or being active alone) might moderate the association between actual PA and momentary affective states. These authors assessed data of 121 children between 9 and 13 years at a random time within seven pre-established intervals over a period of four days. The results confirmed the hypothesised moderator effect. The children felt better if they were physically active outdoors compared to indoor activities. They felt worse if they were physically active alone compared to activities with others. Positive affect in this study was assessed with two items (happy and joyful), and negative affect was assessed with four items (sad, angry, stressed, and nervous). A further study (Kanning, Ebner-Priemer & Brand, 2012) investigated the interaction of autonomous regulation (self-determination theory, e.g., Ryan & Deci, 2000) and actual PA with affective states in 44 university students. Participants digitally rated their affective states and regulation mode approximately every 45 minutes during a defined 14-hour daytime period. The findings supported the moderator effect of autonomous regulation. That is, the higher the volume of actual PA and, thereby, the more autonomously regulated the preceding bout of that activity was, the higher was the effect on affective states.

Other studies analysed actual PA and affective states in selected groups of subjects. The relationship of psychological states (momentary mood and fatigue) and physiological functioning (actual PA, respiration, cardiac functioning) were analysed in post-treatment breast cancer patients (Grossmann, Deuring, Garland, Campbell & Carlson, 2008). These authors compared post-treatment breast cancer patients with healthy females (33 subjects in each group). The focus here was on physiological and psychological recovery. Subjects digitally rated mood and fatigue every 50 minutes over a single day. Actual PA and physiological functioning were assessed continuously during the day using a multi-channel ambulatory monitor. The patients and the healthy females did not differ in activity. The patients were less happy over the course of the day than the healthy controls. For both groups, the authors found significant associations between momentary mood states and actual PA. The study also provided some additional information. The authors asked for momentary mood states and used retrospective measures (POMS) to assess each individual's habitual mood. A significant association between actual PA and mood state was only found for the ambulatory measures of mood. Habitual mood was unrelated to actual PA. If researchers are interested in the effects of an actual daily behaviour on psychological states, it is important to assess the behaviour and the psychological state at the same time in real-life settings.

CONCLUSION

It is often claimed, especially in popular magazines, that exercise and sports are associated with positive affective reactions, positive mood states and positive emotions. This general claim requires differentiation by beginning the sentence with, "Under conditions of...".

This generalisation is the result of a control group design that measures the affective reactions, moods or emotions pre- and post-exercise. Following such a design, the dynamic affective responses accompanying exercise and sports are not represented. The states measured after participation in exercise or sports could be caused by the fact that an exhaustive load is stopped and recovery is perceived as comfortable or pleasant (rebound effect).

Indeed, experiments that varied the intensity of a single bout of exercise and looked for a dose-response interaction showed a complex process of affective reactions during the load. Both dimensions of affective reactions (valence and activation) ascended during an intensity that required aerobic energy consumption relative to the pre-exercise baseline (positive valence and high activation) for almost all subjects. This effect was higher for those subjects who started with a lower level of positive affective states. With higher intensity, those that outreached the oxygen steady-state, affective states worsened. The inter-individual responses of affective reactions were different. For better-trained subjects, the decline in positive affect was less steep, or the reactions remained stable. For less-trained subjects (not able to tolerate the oxygen debt and the rising amount of lactate), positive affective states showed a steep decline. Increasing the intensity so that the anaerobic threshold was surpassed all subjects responded in the same way. There was a shift to negative affective reactions. After ceasing the activity subjects responded with affective states. Especially during the first minutes after an exercise bout the positive reactions overreached the affective states found at baseline (*rebound effect*).

According to the results of field studies or naturalistic studies, it is essential to differentiate the generalised statement that exercise causes positive mood and emotions. Self-selected low to moderate intensity exercise bouts "caused" positive shifts in energy arousal but not implicitly positive shifts in valence.

We recommend future research to investigate the following:

- Provide a clear definition of the different affective-emotional constructs that are the focus of the study (*feelings, subjective wellbeing, emotions, moods or (basic) affective reactions*);
- Conduct multi-dimensional and continuous, or at least multiple, assessments of the defined and focused construct using a valid and reliable instrument;
- If possible, accompany the assessment by measurements of metabolic or cardiac reactions to assess the strain caused by a given load of activity;
- Focus either on single-bout exercises with varying intensities, habitual exercises or everyday life activities; these foci require different methodological approaches;
- Use theory-based approaches (e.g., the opponent-process theory and/or the dual-mode-model).

REFERENCES

Ainsworth, B.E., Haskell, W.L., Leon, A.S., Jacobs, D.R., Montoye, H.J., Sallis, J.F. & Paffenbarger, R.S. (1993). Compendium of Physical Activities: Classification of energy costs of human physical activities. *Medicine & Science in Sports & Exercise*, *25*(1), 71–80.

Armstrong, K. & Edwards, H. (2004). The effectivness of a pram walking exercise programe in reducing depressive symptomatology for postnatal women. *International Journal of Nursing Practice*, *10*, 177-194.

Biddle, S.J.H. & Mutrie, N. (2008). *Psychology of physical activity: Determinants, well-being and interventions* (2nd ed.). London: Routledge.

Bohnert, A.M., Richards, M., Kohl, K. & Randall, E. (2009). Relationships between discretionary time activities, emotional experience, delinquency and depressive symptoms among urban africanamerican adolescents. *Journal of Youth and Adolescence*, *38*, 587-601.

Carels, R.A., Coit, C., Young, K. & Berger, B. (2007). Exercise makes you feel good, but does feeling good make you exercise?: An examination of obese dieters. *Journal of Sport & Exercise Psychology*, *29*, 706-722.

Council of Europe Committee of Ministers (1995). *Recommendation No. R. (95) 16*. The committee of ministers to member states on young people and sport.

Damasio, A.R. (2003). *Der Spinoza-Effekt. Wie Gefühle unser Leben bestimmen*. Berlin: List.

Davidson, R.J., Scherer, K.R. & Goldsmith, H.H. (Eds.) (2003). *Handbook of Affective Sciences*. Oxford: University Press.

Deci, E.L. & Ryan, R.M. (1985). *Intrinsic motivation and self-determination in human behavior*. New York: Plenum.

Diener, E. (1984). Subjective well-being. *Psychological Bulletin*, *95*, 542-575.

Diener, E., Sandvik, E. & Pavot, W. (1991). Happiness is the frequency, not the intensity, of positive versus negative affect. In F. Strack, M. Argyle & N. Schwarz (Eds.), *Subjective well-being: An interdisciplinary perspective* (p.119-140). Oxford: Pergamon Press.

Dunton, G.F., Atienza, A.A., Castro, C.M. & King, A.C. (2009). Using ecological momentary assessment to examine antecedents and correlates of physical activity bouts in adults age 50+years: A pilot study. *Annals of Behavioral Medicine, 38*, 249-255.

Dunton, G.F., Liao, Y., Intille, S., Wolch, J. & Pentz, M.A. (2011). Physical and social contextual influences on children's leisure-time physical activity: An ecological momentary asessment study. *Journal of Physical Activity and Health, 8*(Suppl1), S103-S108).

Ebner-Priemer, U.W. & Trull, T.J. (2009). Ambulatory Assessment. *European Psychologist, 14,* 109-119.

Ekkekakis, P. (2003). Pleasure and displeasure from the body: Perspectives from exercise. *Cognition and Emotion*, *17*(2), 213-239.

Ekkekakis, P. (2005). The study of affective responses to acute exercise: The dual mode model. In R. Stelter & K.K. Roessler (Eds.), *New approaches to exercise and sport psychology* (p.119-146). Oxford: University Press.

Ekkekakis, P. (2008). Affect circumplexredux: The discussion on its utility as a measurement framework in exercise psychology continues. *International Review of Sport and Exercise Science, 1*(2), 139-159.

Ekkekakis, P. (2009). Illuminating the black box: Investigating prefrontal cortical hemodynamics during exercise with near-infrared spectroscopy. *Journal of Sport & Exercise Psychology, 31*(4), 505-553.

Ekkekakis, P. & Backhouse, S.H. (2009). Exercise and psychological well-being. In R. J. Maughan (Ed.), *The olympic textbook of science in sport* (p.251-271). Oxford: Wiley-Blackwell.

Ekkekakis, P., Backhouse, S.H., Gray, C. & Lind, E. (2008). Walking is popular among adults but is it pleasant? A framework for clarifying the link between walking and affect as illustrated in two studies. *Psychology of Sport and Exercise*, 9(3), 246-264.

Ekkekakis, P., Hall, E.E. & Petruzzello, S.J. (2005). Variation and homogeneity in affective responses to physical activity of varying intensities: An alternative perpective on dose-response based on evolutionary considerations. *Journal of Sport Sciences, 23*(5), 477-500.

Ekkekakis, P. & Petruzzello, S.J. (2000). Analysis of the affect measurement conundrum in exercise psychology: I. Fundamental issues. *Psychology of Sport and Exercise, 1*, 71-88.

Ekkekakis, P. & Petruzzello, S.J. (2002). Analysis of the affect measurement conundrum in erxercise psychology: IV. A conceptual case for the affect circumplex. *Psychology of Sport and Exercise, 3*, 35-63.

Fahrenberg, J., Myrtek, M., Pawlik, K. & Perrez, M. (2007). Ambulatory Assessment – Monitoring behavior in daily life settings. *European Journal of Psychological Assessment, 23*(4), 206-213.

Gauvin, L. & Rejeski, W.J. (1993). The exercise-induced feeling inventory: Development and initial validation. *Journal of Sport & Exercise Psychology, 15*(4), 403-423.

Gauvin, L., Rejeski, W.J. & Norris, J. (1996). A naturalistic study of the impact of acute physical activity on feeling states and affect in women. *Health Psychology, 15*(5), 391-397.

Grawe, K. (1998). *Psychologische Therapie*. Göttingen: Hogrefe.

Grossmann, P., Deuring, G., Garland, S.N., Campbell, T.S. & Carlson, L.E. (2008). Patterns of objective physical functioning and perception of mood and fatigue in postreatment breast cancer patients and healthy controls: an ambulatory psychophysiological investigation. *Psychosomatic Medicine, 70*, 819-828.

Hall, E.E., Ekkekakis, P. & Petruzzello, S.J. (2002). The affective beneficence of vigorous exercise revisited. *British Journal of Health Psychology, 7*, 47-66.

Harmon-Jones, E., Gable, P.A. & Peterson, C.K. (2010). The role of asymmetric frontal cortical activity in emotion-related phenomena: A review and update. *Biological Psychology, 84*(3), 451-462.

Kanning, M., Ebner-Priemer, U. & Brand, R. (2012). Autonomous regulation mode moderates the effect of physical activity on mood: An ambulant assessment approach to the role of self-determination. *Journal of Sport & Exercise Psychology, 34*(2), 260-269

Kanning, M., Ebner-Priemer, U. & Schlicht, W. (2013). How to investigate within-subject associations between physical activity and momentary affective states in everyday life: A position statement based on a literature overview. *Frontiers in Psychology, 4*(187), doi: 10.3389/fpsyg.2013.00187.

Kanning, M. & Schlicht, W. (2010). Be active and become happy: An ecological momentary assessment of physical activity and mood. *Journal of Sport & Exercise Psychology, 32*, 253-261.

Lehnert, K., Sudeck, G. & Conzelmann, A. (2012). Subjective well-being and exercise in the second half of life: a critical review of theoretical approaches. *European Review of Aging and Physical Activity, 7*(1).

LePage, M.L. & Crowther, J.H. (2010). The effects of exercise on body satisfaction and affect. *Body Image, 7*, 124-130.

Levine, J.A., Laningham-Foster, L.M., McCrady, S.K., Krizan, A.C., Olson, L.R., Kane, P.H., Jensen, M.D. & Clark, M.M. (2005). Interindividual variation in posture allocation: Possible role in human obesity. *Science, 307*, 584-586.

Lox, C.L., Jackson, S., Tuholsky, S.W., Wasley, D. & Treasure, D.C. (2000). Revisting the measurement of exercise-induced feeling states: The Physical Activity Affect Scale (PAAS). *Measurement in Physical Education and Exercise Science, 4*(2), 79-95.

Markowitz, S. (2009). *The exercise mood relation: Testing the dual-mode model and self - selected speeds.* Dissertation, Graduate School of New Brunswick Rutgers, Psychology.

Markowitz, S.M. & Arent, S.M. (2010). The exercise affect relationship: evidence for the dual-mode model and a modified opponent process theory. *Journal of Sport & Exercise Psychology, 32(5)*, 711-730.

McAuley, E. & Courneya, K.S. (1994). The Subjecive Exercise Experiences Scale (SEES): Development and preliminary validation. *Journal of Sport & Exercise Psychology, 16*, 163-177.

McAuley, E. & Rudolph, D.L. (1995). Physical activity, aging, and psychological well-being. *Journal of Aging and Physical Activity, 3*(1), 67-96.

McNair, D., Lorr, M. & Droppleman, L. F. (1971). *Profile of mood states.* San Diego: Educational and Industrial Testing Service.

North, T.C., McCullagh, P. & Tran, Z.V. (1990). Effects of exercise on depression. *Exercise and Sport Science Reviews, 18*, 379-415.

Osgood, C.E., Suci, G.J. & Tannenbaum, P.H. (1957). *The measurement of meaning.* Urbana: University of Illinois Press.

Parfitt, G. & Hughes, S. (2009). The exercise-intensity-affect relationship: Evidence and implications for exercise behavior. *Journal of Exercise Science and Fitness, 7* (Suppl. 2), S34-41.

Peterson, C.K., Gravens, L.C. & Harmon-Jones, E. (2011). Asymmetric frontal cortical activity and negative affective responses to ostracism. *Social Cognitive and Affective Neuroscience, 6*, 1-9.

Petruzzello, S., Ekkekakis, P. & Hall, E.E. (2006). Physical activity, affect, and electroencephalogram studies. In E. O. Acevedo & P. Ekkekakis (Eds.), *Psychobiology of physical activity* (p.111-128). Champaign, IL: Human Kineteics.

Petruzzello, S.J., Landers, D.M., Hatfield, B.D., Kubitz, K.A. & Salazar, W. (1991). A meta-analysis on the anxiety reducing effects of acute and chronic exercise. *Sports Medicine, 11*(3), 143-182.

Powell, R., Allan, J.L., Johnston, D.W., Pollard, B., Kenardy, J. & Rowely, D.I. (2009). Activity and affect: repeated within-participant assessment in people after joint replacement surgery. *Rehabilitation Psychology, 54*(1), 83-90.

Raglin, J.S., Wilson, G.S. & Galper, D. (2007). Exercise and its effect on mental health. In C. Bouchard, S.N. Blair & W.L. Haskell (Eds.), *Physical activity and health* (p.247-257). Champaign, IL: Human Kinetics.

Reed, J. & Buck, S. (2009). The effect of regular exercise on positive-activated affect: A meta-analysis. *Psychology of Sport and Exercise, 10*(6), 581-594.

Reed, J. & Ones, D. S. (2006). The effect of acute aerobic exercise on positive activated affect: A meta-analysis. *Psychology of Sport and Exercise, 7*(5), 477-514.

Rhodes, R.E., Martin, A.D., Taunton, J.E., Rhodes, E.C., Donelly, M. & Elliot, J. (1999). Factors associated with exercise adherence among older adults: An individual perspective. *Sports Medicine, 28*(6), 397-411.

Rose, E.A. & Parfitt, G. (2007). A quantitative analysis and qualitative explanation of the indiuidal differences in affective responses to prescribed and self-selected exercise intensities. *Journal of Sport & Exerxcise Psychology, 29*(3), 281-309.

Russel, J. (1980). A circumplex model of affect. *Journal of Personality and Social Psychology, 39*(6), 1161-1178.

Ryan, R. M. & Deci, E. L. (2000). Self-determination theory and the facilitation of intrinsic motivation, social development and well-being. *American Psychologist, 55*(1), 68-78.

Schimmack, U. (1998). Strukturmodelle der Stimmungen: Rückschau, Rundschau und Ausschau. *Psychologische Rundschau, 50*(2), 90-97.

Schlicht, W. (1994a). Does physical exercise reduce anxious emotions? A Meta-analysis. *Anxiety, Stress, and Coping, 6*, 275-288.

Schlicht, W. (1994b). *Sport und Primärprävention.*Göttingen: Hogrefe.

Schlicht, W. (1993). Mental health as a consequence of physical exercise: A meta-analysis. [Psychische Gesundheit durch Sport – Realität oder Wunsch: Eine Meta-Analyse]. *Zeitschrift für Gesundheitspsychologie, 1*, 65-81.

Schlicht, W. (2010). Mit körperlicher Aktivität das Altern gestalten. In H. Häfner, K. Beyreuther & W. Schlicht (Hrsg.), *Altern gestalten. Medizin – Technik – Umwelt* (S. 25-40). Heidelberg: Springer.

Schneider, M., Dunn, A. & Cooper, D. (2009). Affect, exercise, and physical activity among healthy adolscents. *Medicine & Science in Sports & Exercise, 41*(4), 947-955.

Schott, N. & Schlicht, W. (2012). Körperlich-sportliche Aktivität und gelingendes Altern. In R. Fuchs & W. Schlicht (Hrsg.), S*eelische Gesundheit und sportliche Aktivität* (S. 315-336). Göttingen: Hogrefe.

Schwerdtfeger, A., Eberhardt, R. & Chmitorz, A. (2008). Gibt es einen Zusammenhang zwischen Bewegungsaktivität und psychischem Befinden im Alltag? *Zeitschrift für Gesundheitspsychologie, 16*, 2-11.

Schwerdtfeger, A., Eberhard, R., Chmitorz, A. & Schaller, E. (2010). Momentary affect predicts bodily movement in daily life: An ambulatory momentary study. *Journal of Sport & Exercise Psychology, 32*(5), 674-693.

Shiffman, S., Stone, A. A.& Hufford, M. R. (2008). Ecological momentary assessment. *Annual Review of Clinical Psychology, 4*, 1-32.

Solomon, R.L. (1980). The opponent-process theory of acquired emotion: The costs of pleasure and the benefits of pain. *American Psychologist, 35*(8), 691-712.

Solomon, R.L. & Corbit, J.D. (1974). An opponent-process theory of motivation: I. The Temporal dynamics of affect. *Psychological Review, 81*(2), 119-145.

Staudinger, U. (2000). Viele Gründe sprechen dagegen, und trotzdem geht es vielen Menschen gut: Das Paradox des subjektiven Wohlbefindens. *Psychologische Rundschau, 51*(4), 185-197.

Stytch, K. & Parfitt, G. (2011). Exploring affective responses to different exercise intensities in low-active young adolescents. *Journal of Sport & Exercise Psychology, 33*, 548-568.

Tellegen, A., Watson, D. & Clark, L.A. (1999). On the dimensional and hierarchical structure of affect. *Psychological Science, 10*, 297-303.

Thayer, R. (1989). *The biopsychology of mood.* New York: Oxford University Press.

US Department of Health and Human Services (USDHHS) (1996). *Physical Activity and Health*. Washington, D.C.: CDC.

Vansteelandt, K., Rijmen, F., Pieters, G., Probst, M. & Vanderlinden, J. (2007). Drive for thinness, affect regulation and physical activity in eating disorders: a daily life study. *Behaviour Research and Therapy, 45,* 1717-1734.

Vendrig, A.A. & Lousberg, R. (1997). Within-person relationships among pain intensity, mood and physical activity in chronic pain: a naturalistic approach. *Pain, 73,* 71-76.

Watson, D., Clark, L.A. & Tellegen, A. (1988). Development and validation of a brief measure of positive and negative affect: The PANAS Scales. *Journal of Personality and Social Psychology, 54*(6), 1063-1070.

Watson, D. & Tellegen, A. (1985). Toward a consensual structure of mood. *Psychological Bulletin, 98*(2), 219-235.

Wichers, M., Peeters, F., Rutten, B.P.F., Derom, C., Delespaul, P., Jacobs, N., Thiery, E. & van Os, J. (2011). A time-lagged momentary assessment study on daily life physical activity and affect. *Health Psychology, 31*(2), 135-144.

Williams, D.M. (2008). Exercise, affect, and adherence: an integrated model and a case for self-paced exercise. *Journal of Sport & Exercise Psychology, 30*(5), 471-496.

Williams, D.M., Dunsiger, S., Ciccolo, J.T., Lewis, B.A., Albrecht, A.E. & Marcus, B.H. (2008). Acute affective response to a moderate-intensity exercise stimulus predicts physical activity participation 6 and 12 months later. *Psychology of Sport and Exercise, 9*(3), 231-245.

Wundt, W. (1905). *Grundzüge der physiologischen Psychologie* (5. Auflage). Leipzig: Engelmann.

In: Handbook of Psychology of Emotions
Editors: C. Mohiyeddini, M. Eysenck and S. Bauer

ISBN: 978-1-62808-053-7
© 2013 Nova Science Publishers, Inc.

Chapter 19

EMOTIONS AND PERFORMANCE: VALUABLE INSIGHTS FROM THE SPORTS DOMAIN

Sylvain Laborde, [1,2] *Markus Raab*[1] *and Fabrice Dosseville*[2]
[1]German Sport University, Cologne, Germany
[2]UFR STAPS, EA 4260, University of Caen, France

1. INTRODUCTION

Emotions not only color our lives and give meaning to them (S. Scott, 2009) but also have a strong impact on human performance (Eccles, et al., 2011). Why is it so important to consider the relationship between emotions and performance? From an evolutionary perspective, emotions have been at the core of our struggle to survive and, more prominently in today's world, to perform. We chose to study this relationship in sports, a high-pressure domain that reflects, to some degree, survival fights and contests (Lazarus, 2000). In addition, sports is an applied field that is concerned with enhancing performance (Eccles, et al., 2011).

In this chapter, we will use sports examples to illustrate (a) a select set of theories that have been developed to explain the emotion–performance relationship, (b) the methodologies used to study this relationship, and finally (c) the applied interventions that can be derived from previous theoretical considerations. Our hope is that the chapter will improve comprehension of the role of emotions in performance.

At the theoretical level, we will draw on two foundational works of the early 2000s: the work of Hanin (2000) and Lazarus (2000), as well as on the more recent work of Jones and colleagues (Jones, Meijen, McCarthy, & Sheffield, 2009), to see how the field has evolved over the last decade. At the methodological level, we provide a guide to eliciting and assessing emotions. We stress the fact that sports researchers are increasingly considering the mind–body interaction (Laborde & Raab, in press). In the last section, we discuss practical interventions that have been inspired by the theories reviewed. For example, following Lazarus's theory, (e.g., Jones, 2003) recognized that it is possible to change cognitions to change the emotional state, and following Hanin's theory, others recognized that changing emotions alters choices in risky tasks (Robazza & Bortoli, 2005; Robazza, Bortoli, Carraro, & Bertollo, 2006).

2. EMOTIONS AND PERFORMANCE—THEORY

2.1. Definition of Emotion

Affects, moods, emotions, feelings, preferences, affective states, and attitudes are often used as synonyms, but they are not (for a review, see Gray & Watson, 2007; Scherer, 2005). Affect is generally an umbrella term covering the different phenomena that can be categorized as either good or bad in valence (Gross, 1998). In sports science research, affective states have been studied mainly under two broad terms: mood (e.g., Beedie, Terry, & Lane, 2000) and emotions (e.g., Hanin, 2000). Emotions and moods are similar in that they both refer to feeling states that can be characterized as pleasant or unpleasant (i.e., positive or negative); however, mood reflects more the overall affective state of the individual (Gray & Watson, 2007), whereas emotions can be linked to a specific event or moment that causes the response (Davidson, et al., 1994). In this chapter we focus on the concept of emotions.

Two approaches have been adopted to study emotions: the discrete approach and the dimensional approach. Within the **discrete** approach, emotions are categorized based on their qualitative content, with the notion of appraisal being central (Scherer, 2005). They can be identified according to their core relational themes (Lazarus, 1999). Lazarus (1999) established a list of 15 emotions classified as positively toned (i.e., compassion, gratitude, happiness, hope, love, pride, relief) or negatively toned (i.e., anger, anxiety, envy, fright, guilt, jealousy, sadness, shame). The **dimensional** approach sees emotions on a continuum varying from negative to positive, where intensity differentiates the emotions (Feldman Barrett, 1998).

2.2. Theories of Emotions and Performance in Sports

We introduce here three main theories explaining the emotion–performance relationship in sports: Lazarus's (2000) cognitive-motivational-relational theory (CMRT), Hanin's (2000) individual zone of optimal functioning (IZOF), and (Jones, et al., 2009) theory of challenge and threat states in athletes (TCTSA).

2.2.1. The Cognitive-Motivational-Relational Theory

The CMRT (Lazarus, 2000) postulates that individuals continuously appraise their ongoing relationship with the environment. The appraisal will depend on the integration of a set a six separate appraisal judgments: goal relevance, goal congruence, type of ego involvement, options for coping, coping potential, and future expectations. There is a core relational theme for each emotion, and when the appraisal corresponds to a core relational theme an emotion will arise. The core relational theme for each emotion is linked to a specific action tendency. According to Lazarus (2000), the function of emotion is to facilitate adaptation and, by extension, performance.

According to the CMRT, how will emotions influence performance?

"One main mechanism whereby performance is affected negatively is the self-statements and ruminations produced by emotional struggles that interfere with attention and concentration, without which a top performance is not possible" (Lazarus, 2000, p. 249). Another influence is lessening motivation, which increases the tendency to give up. This will depend on the core relational theme of each emotion. Also, the way an emotion is expressed will change its influence on performance (Lazarus, 2000).

The CMRT postulates that the influence of emotion on performance will depend on the match between the action tendencies derived from the core relational theme and the task demands (Lazarus, 2000). This prediction was empirically supported with the emotion anger (H. Davis, et al., 2008; Woodman, et al., 2009), that is, "a demeaning offense against me and mine" (Lazarus, 2000, p. 234). One action tendency derived from the emotion anger is "a powerful impulse to counterattack in order to gain revenge for an affront or repair a wounded self-esteem" (Lazarus, 2000, p. 243). Two studies (P. A. Davis, Woodman, & Callow, 2010; Woodman, et al., 2009) showed that on a maximal force task, anger has a positive influence on performance.

Regarding the perspectives offered by this theory, research examining the relationship between Lazarus's action tendency predictions and performance is warranted. A promising recent research direction is also the extension of CMRT to moderators such as individual differences. For example, P. A. Davis et al. (2010) studied the influence of trait anger on the anger–performance relationship, and Woodman et al. (2009) showed the influence of extraversion on the anger–performance relationship. P.A. Davis et al. showed that trait anger was positively associated with performance on a peak-force task when associated with anger-out, while an association with anger-in decreased the performance on the same task. Woodman et al. (Woodman, et al., 2009) showed that extroversion moderated the anger–performance relationship: when angry, extroverts' peak force increased more than introverts' with a small effect size. Finally, applications can be derived from the CMRT, such as the different emotion regulation strategies aimed to modify cognition proposed by Jones (2003), which we detail in Section 4.1.

The CMRT can be considered a nomothetic approach, as the core relational theme of each discrete emotion does not change according to the person. Taking the example of anger, different people can be angry about different things and can also express anger differently, but anger still corresponds to a situation appraised as "a demeaning offense against me and mine." Note, however, that Lazarus's (2000) discrete emotions approach was not designed specifically for the sports context. Another perspective was taken by Hanin (2000), who stressed the idiosyncratic nature of emotion in a sports-specific theory, the IZOF.

2.2.2. Individual Zone of Optimal Functioning

The IZOF theory (Hanin, 2000) postulates that precompetitive emotional states will influence performance during competition. It adopts a multidimensional approach to describe emotional experiences in athletic performance: form (e.g., cognitive, bodily-somatic, behavioral), intensity, content, time (e.g., duration, frequency), and context (Hanin, 2007). This theory also assumes that the influence of emotions on performance involves not only hedonic tone but also emotion functionality. A traditional methodology of the IZOF theory is to establish individualized performance profiles for each athlete from retrospective recall about good and bad performance.

According to the IZOF theory, how will emotions influence performance?

According to Hanin (2000, p. 84), "two constructs related to energizing and organizing aspects of emotion may account for the impact of emotions upon performance process: energy mobilization (demobilization) and energy utilization (misuse)." As a general rule, the interaction of specific emotional content (anxiety, anger, etc.) with specific emotional intensity (high, moderate, or low) will produce specific optimal or dysfunctional effects on athletic performance (Hanin, 2007, p. 48). In addition, the functionality of emotion is expected to be determined according to a resource-matching hypothesis, that is, an evaluation of the individual resources at hand in association with the demands of the task (Hanin, 2007). The influence of emotions on performance in terms of energy mobilization and utilization has been detailed by Martinent and Ferrand (2009). In a descriptive qualitative study in table tennis, Martinent and Ferrand suggested five main categories: confidence, sensations, motivation, concentration, and adaptation of the behavior of individuals to the constraints and characteristics of the situation. For example, optimizing emotions are expected to be linked with increased concentration, increased motivation, increased confidence, positive sensations, and adaptive behaviors. A promising direction for IZOF could be to use it together with objective measures, such as physiological variables (Bertollo, et al., 2012).

What are the differences between CMRT and IZOF?

IZOF and CMRT share some basics: "any disagreement between us seems to be more a matter of emphasis than one of basic substance," said Lazarus about Hanin's work (Lazarus, 2000, p. 238). The main difference is Lazarus's emphasis on relational meaning and the coping process. These topics are not absent from Hanin's work: First, with the IZOF the relational meaning is seen as more implicit, in the sense that any emotion can be seen as facilitative of or debilitating to performance. Second, with IZOF, coping is not central but is referred to as emotion regulation (Lazarus, 2000). There are also discrepancies in the lists of emotions. Lazarus identified 15 discrete emotions with their core relational themes; the IZOF list (Hanin, 2000) contains not only emotions but also words reflecting motives and attitudes (e.g., slack, lazy).

In the CMRT and the IZOF, emphasis is placed on appraisal, of the emotion core relational themes for Lazarus (2000) and of emotion functionality with the resource-matching hypothesis for Hanin (2007). Another theory, the TCTSA (TCTSA; Jones, et al., 2009), puts the emphasis on different appraisals components, the challenge and threat appraisals.

2.2.3. The Theory of Challenge and Threat States in Athletes

The TCTSA (Jones, et al., 2009) is concerned not with emotions directly but with the appraisal of challenge and threat in a situation, which will have different motivational, emotional, and physiological consequences for performance. The challenge or threat state in response to competition is determined by self-efficacy, control perception, and achievement goals (Jones, et al., 2009). The TCTSA assumes that positive and negative emotions can occur in a challenge state, while only negative emotions are supposed to occur in a threat state

(Jones, et al., 2009). In challenge states, emotions (positive or negative in valence) are perceived as functional, and in threat states, emotions (negative in valence) are perceived as dysfunctional.

According to the TCTSA, how will emotions influence performance?

As indicated earlier, the TCTSA does not deal primarily with emotions but relates challenge and threat states to performance. A challenge state can be accompanied by either positive (e.g., hope) or negative emotions (e.g., anxiety) and is expected to be helpful to performance. A threat state is accompanied by only negative emotions and is thought to harm performance. This is different from the IZOF, where positive (in terms of hedonic valence) emotions are thought to have the potential to harm performance, as well. In addition, challenge and threat states are thought to influence effort, attention, decision making, and physical functionality, and hence athletic performance. Finally, the dichotomy of challenge and threat is important to take into consideration but alone cannot describe the richness of the emotion–performance relationship.

2.2.4. Critique and Integration of the Theories Presented

There seems to be a consensus to consider not only the hedonic valence but also the functional impact of emotions on performance. However, what mechanisms are involved in the influence of emotions on performance have yet to be clarified. Most studies have been focused on the descriptive level, using retrospective reports (Martinent, Campo, & Ferrand, 2012; Martinent & Ferrand, 2009) or correlating pregame emotional reports with performance (Hanin, 2000). Such studies can claim some ecological value, but they are of little help in understanding the mechanisms at hand, because conditions are generally not manipulated. Therefore causal empirical evidence to support such descriptive findings should still be encouraged, because causality cannot be assumed from former studies. Testing for correlation with either subjective or objective performance (Pensgaard & Duda, 2003) is not sufficient either, because the processes involved in performance are still unknown. Some interesting empirical work in this direction examined the influence of emotions on specific components of performance, such as visual attention (Janelle, 2002; M. Wilson, 2008), maximal peak force (P. A. Davis, et al., 2010; Woodman, et al., 2009), and decision making (Laborde & Raab, in press; Laborde, Dosseville & Raab, in press). Such research endeavors should be encouraged to improve our understanding of the influence of emotions on performance. Finally, the influence of individual moderators in the emotion–performance relationship should be examined further (P. A. Davis, et al., 2010; Woodman, et al., 2009).

One focus has been the focus on the emotional state of the athlete before competition, at the psychophysiological level. If precompetitive emotional states are repeatedly found to have an influence on athletic performance (Cerin, 2003; Hanin, 2000), emotions are more likely to change during competition (Cerin, Szabo, Hunt, & Williams, 2000). In fact, emotions are expected to be constantly modified through cognitive appraisal (Lazarus, 2000; Martinent & Ferrand, 2009). In addition, it has been argued that various positive and negative emotions can occur at the same time, with different hedonic valences, especially if they are of mild intensity (Cerin, 2004). Consequently, the frequency, intensity, and direction of emotions are expected to be transient (Martinent, et al., 2012), and rather than acting alone, emotions are expected to act together with other transitory subcomponents of performance, such as motivation, self-efficacy, and perceived control (Jones, et al., 2009).

This previous focus raised some methodological problems. While it is relatively easy to assess the psychophysiological response before a competition, with self-report questionnaires and physiological variables, it is harder to do so during a competition. This is why some researchers used a retrospective qualitative methodology to explore how emotions evolve during competition (Martinent, et al., 2012). McCarthy (2011, p. 53) indicated that "measures with sufficient temporal resolution and proximity are necessary for each specific emotion" and that self-report, observer ratings, and facial, autonomic, brain-based, and vocal measures should be used in combination (Larsen & Fredrickson, 1999). Research on the emotion–performance link will benefit from a combination of different methodologies within the same research project (Cooke, Kavussanu, McIntyre, & Ring, 2010), such as collecting qualitative and quantitative data (e.g., Laborde, Dosseville, Wolf, Martin, & You, submitted); (McCarthy, 2011).

A fourth theory (beyond CMRT, IZOF, and TCTSA) was recently proposed to explain the emotion–performance relationship (McCarthy, 2011): the broaden-and-build theory of positive emotions in sports (Fredrickson, 2001). This theory assumes that positive emotions "broaden people's momentary thought-action repertoires and build enduring personal resources" (Fredrickson, 2001, p. 218). Empirical evidence in sports for this theory is still needed. Building enduring personal resources might make sense for an athlete from a long-term perspective, but it is difficult to predict how emotions might alter movements. In addition, a recent study (Laborde & Raab, in press) showed that the influence of emotions on cognitive performance in sports was not about hedonic tone but about physiological activation. In a decision-making task the decision time and decision quality were similar under positive and negative emotion (i.e., hedonic valence) conditions, whereas the physiological state allowed discriminating them.

The theories presented thus far deal with emotions in general; what do we learn from theories addressing the relationship with performance of one emotion in particular, such as anxiety (M. Wilson, 2008)? The processing efficiency theory (Eysenck & Calvo, 1992) assumes that anxiety has two functions: emptying working memory, and providing motivation to allocate additional effort to maintain task performance. This theory motivated the more recently developed attentional control theory (Eysenck, Derakshan, Santos, & Calvo, 2007), which assumes that "anxiety reduces attentional control by increasing the influence of the stimulus-driven attentional system at the cost of goal directed control." (M. Wilson, 2008, p. 184). Both theories have received support in sports settings (Oudejans & Pijpers, 2010; M. Wilson, 2008), and such theoretical considerations should be encouraged for other emotions, as well.

Finally, the theories presented here focus on the influence on performance of current emotions, neglecting the role of anticipated emotions. The influence of anticipated emotions on performance has been demonstrated at the neurological level (Watanabe, 2007). When a reward is expected, the activity of working memory is enhanced, inducing changes in attention, and this state is therefore able to modify behavioral performance. In cognitive psychology anticipated emotions have also been shown to influence decision making (Mellers, 2001). In sports, anticipated emotions are strongly linked with motivation; studying them would help us understand what drive athletes to be involved in strenuous and painful training (Bagozzi, Dholakia, & Basuroy, 2003). Anticipated emotions are also linked with goal setting; when people work on accomplishing their goals they anticipate feeling good about themselves in the future (Brown & McConnell, 2011; Perugini & Bagozzi, 2001). Anticipated emotions still need to be considered in sports research. Research has examined anticipated emotions and physical activity intention (Wang, 2011) but not the role they play in athletic performance.

In this section, we introduced a general definition and several theories of emotion and highlighted open questions that could be addressed in further research in the field. We are now ready to give a definition of emotions that is specific to the domain of sports.

2.3. Operational Definition of Emotions in Sport

To **measure a construct**, there is a need for an operational definition specific to the domain being studied. In competitive sports, performance is the main objective, and Hanin (2000) showed that beyond hedonic tone (i.e., positive and negative), the functionality (i.e., optimizing or dysfunctional) of emotions has to be considered. This is in line with (Lazarus, 1999) evolutionary perspective that emotions played a beneficial role in the adaptational struggle to survive and flourish but could also be counterproductive in such struggles.

We propose here an **operational definition of emotions in sports** that is based on the work of(based on Hanin, 2000; Lazarus, 2000):

> An **emotion** is a phenomenon that is an organized psychophysiological reaction to the **appraisal** of ongoing relationships with the environment. This reaction consists of responses at three levels of analysis: subjective, behavioral, and neurophysiological: (a) Introspective reports are generated at the **subjective level**; (b) at the **behavioral level** are overt actions or impulses to act; and (c) at the **neurophysiological level** bodily symptoms and physiological changes make the emotion organismic. Each emotion can be characterized by a **hedonic tone** (i.e., positive and negative) and by its **functional impact** on performance (optimizing or dysfunctional).

As does any definition, this one has its limits, but it can provide a starting point for discussions of emotions in sports. As emotion is assumed to be part of a single conceptual unit together with stress and coping (Lazarus, 2000; Nicholls, Polman, & Levy, 2012), we now define these two closely related concepts.

2.4. Stress and Coping

When athletes are asked how they feel before a competition, in most cases the answer will be "stressed." When an athlete says stress, it often means anxiety (based on Lazarus, 2000), which has been the focus of most of the research in the sports literature to date (Hanin, 2000). However, the emotional landscape is much wider, and looking only for anxiety may not be the optimal way to predict performance (Cerin, 2003). Athletes sometimes talk about "good" and "bad" stress; they might be referring to (a) the influence of stress on performance, as in the IZOF theory (Hanin, 2000), (b) the extent to which emotions' action tendencies match the task at hand, as in the CMRT (Lazarus, 2000), (c) the appraisal of the competition as a challenge or a threat, as with the TCTSA (Jones, et al., 2009), or (d) more likely a combination of the above. Inevitably when discussing stress the topic of coping is raised. Coping refers to the way athletes handle stress, as discussed below.

Stress represents both the degree of pressure faced by an organism and the reaction/adaptation of the organism to this pressure (Lazarus, 2000; Selye, 1951). Stress has remained a unidimensional concept, and all its interesting characteristics are encompassed by the concept of emotion. Studying emotion provides a broader and richer way to understand the role of affective experiences in human adaptation and performance, particularly with the concept of discrete emotions and (Lazarus, 2000) core relational themes. Moreover, stress is not only linked with negative emotions; it represents the psychological basis of certain positive emotions, such as relief and hope (Lazarus, 2000). **Coping** is how we manage or regulate emotions; it is not a separate process (Lazarus, 2000). It will influence which emotions occur according to one's particularities, and how emotions change. "The competitor must learn how to cope with strong and counterproductive action tendencies that are part of any emotion. Coping is a crucial component of the solution" (Lazarus, 2000, p. 241). Finally, Lazarus pointed out that the emotion–performance relationship represents a dynamic process, because "appraisal, coping, and the emotions they result in are influenced by continual feedback from our performance" (2000, p. 237).

Now that we have defined stress and coping, we will review emotions at two levels, trait and state. Individuals can be driven by emotional dispositions (i.e., trait level), and these dispositions will have an influence on the current emotions experienced (i.e., state level).

2.5. Emotions: Trait and State

Lazarus (2000, p. 236) differentiated the psychological structure of emotion, which is stable over time, from the process, which is about how things change. When we think about the influence of emotions on performance, we "should focus on process as much or more than structure" (p. 236). Two notions that are similar to structure and process are trait and state, respectively.

We first consider emotions at the **state level**, relying mostly on the CMRT of Lazarus (2000). For example, according to Lazarus, at first glance we might think that there is overlap between anxiety and fright, but they actually differ in what causes them and in their subjective feel, as well as in their behavioral and physiological implications. The questionnaire developed by Jones and colleagues (Jones, Lane, Bray, Uphill, & Catlin, 2005) pointed out the five main emotions experienced in sports settings: anger, excitement, anxiety, dejection, and happiness. The prevalence of such emotions might vary according to the sport and the level considered; for example, with high-level table tennis players, anger, joy, and anxiety accounted for more than 80% of the emotional experience during games (Martinent, et al., 2012). Although for methodological and ethical reasons (Tenenbaum, Lloyd, Pretty, & Hanin, 2002) emotions have been studied mostly before competitions, they are by nature subject to vary during the activity (Cerin, et al., 2000). It also seems possible that various emotions are experienced at the same time, a phenomenon that is referred to as emotional blend (Martinent, et al., 2012). In contrast, the experience of such emotions cannot be simultaneous and they are assumed to be processed sequentially (Brehm & Miron, 2006). Martinent and colleagues (2012) found some evidence of this in high-level table tennis players, using retrospective reports. The most common pairs of emotions were joy/relief, joy/pride, self-oriented anger/anxiety, and self-related anger/discouragement. **State emotions have been found to influence different parameters of performance,** such as attention and concentration (Vast, Young, & Thomas, 2010), sensorimotor skills (Vast, Young, & Thomas, 2011), perception (Cañal-Bruland, Pijpers, & Oudejans, 2010), visual attention (Nieuwenhuys, Pijpers, Oudejans, & Bakker, 2008), and movement (Pijpers, Oudejans, & Bakker, 2005).

The state level of emotions can be influenced by many contextual factors, such as "ambient mood (e.g., depressed, irritable), recent life events (e.g., bereavement), emotion-related personality-traits (e.g., pessimistic), [and] diurnal and circadian influences on mood" (McCarthy, 2011, p. 53). Among these factors, the so-called emotion-related personality traits are of particular importance. **We consider them either as trait emotions (e.g., trait anger, trait anxiety) or as individual differences that influence the emotional state (e.g., personality, trait emotional intelligence).** They might influence the emotion–performance relationship at different phases of behavior, such as during the appraisal or emotion expression phase.

Trait anger predicts the tendency of an individual to experience anger (Spielberger, Jacobs, Russell, & Crane, 1983). Trait anger also has two components that determine its influence on performance, according to how anger is regulated, anger-in and anger-out (P. A. Davis, et al., 2010). A sports-specific conceptualization of anger has been realized with competitive aggressiveness and anger (Maxwell & Moores, 2007), that is, a propensity to engage in acts of aggression during athletic competitions (Maxwell & Moores, 2008). **Trait anxiety** represents the tendency of an individual to experience anxiety (Spielberger, 1983). Again, we find a specific conceptualization in sports: Competitive trait anxiety is defined as an athlete's "tendency to perceive competitive situations as threatening and to respond to these situations with (increased state)-anxiety" (Martens, Vealey, & Burton, 1990, p. 11). Trait anger and trait anxiety are defined as the tendency of individuals to experience on a regular basis the corresponding state emotions.

Personality is most often assessed according to the Big Five personality dimensions (extroversion, agreeableness, conscientiousness, neuroticism, and openness; (McCrae & John, 1992). Each of the dimensions is related to the stress and coping appraisal (Allen, Greenlees, & Jones, 2011; Kaiseler, Polman, & Nicholls, 2012). Neuroticism, for instance, seems to negatively affect the direction of precompetitive anxiety (Cerin, 2004); and extroversion has been found to moderate the anger–performance relationship: Woodman et al. (2009) found that when extroverts were angry, their peak force increased more than introverts'. **Trait emotional intelligence** (trait EI) is a constellation of emotional self-perceptions situated at the lower levels of personality hierarchies (Petrides, Pita, & Kokkinaki, 2007). Trait EI has been found to promote positive emotions and reduce negative emotions in athletes with high stress before a performance (Laborde, Dosseville, & Scelles, 2010). During the event, trait EI might continue to influence emotions through a greater use of adaptive coping strategies

(Laborde, You, Dosseville, & Salinas, 2012), moderating the physiological parameters linked with emotions (Laborde, Brüll, Weber, & Anders, 2011). In summary, these effects at the trait level should be taken into account because they may influence the frequency, intensity, and duration of state emotions (Verduyn & Brans, 2012).

3. EMOTIONS AND PERFORMANCE—METHODOLOGY

In this methodological section, we provide the reader with an overview of how to elicit and assess emotions in order to study their influence on performance.

3.1. Emotion Elicitation

In sports research, elicitation of positive emotions has been realized mainly in real-competition settings and elicitation of negative emotions in experiments. A look at the research about affective state manipulation in sports shows that there have been many more studies focusing on the elicitation of negative states than on the elicitation of positive states. The studies focusing on negative states have been aimed mostly at understanding the impact of anxiety on performance (e.g., Oudejans & Pijpers, 2010), while the studies about positive states have been more application oriented, aimed at understanding how to make athletes feel better before competition (e.g., Bishop, Karageorghis, & Loizou, 2007).

3.1.1. Positive Emotion Elicitation in Sports

Two approaches have been used to help athletes cope with stress in precompetitive settings. One uses a technique to decrease negative emotions and the other focuses on provoking positive emotions. Techniques for the latter have been suggested by Jones (2003) and are presented in Section 4.1. It should be noted that by positive or negative most of the studies do not refer to the hedonic tone alone but to the functional effect of emotions on performance, as well. Therefore, a great deal of work has also been done to change the interpretation of emotional symptoms seen first as debilitative in optimizing emotions (e.g., Thomas, Hanton, & Maynard, 2007). We summarize these techniques in Table 1.

3.1.2. Negative Emotions Elicitation in Sports

In sports psychology research, elicitation of negative emotions is often synonymous with elicitation of anxiety. To the best of our knowledge, only a few studies have sought to elicit other negative discrete emotions (P. A. Davis, et al., 2010; Woodman, et al., 2009). Originally, the elicitation of negative emotions in the laboratory was aimed at understanding the processes underlying choking under pressure (e.g., Baumeister & Showers, 1986). More recently researchers have explored the cognitive functioning associated with anxiety with the processing efficiency theory and the attentional control theory (for a review, see M. Wilson, 2008). Negative emotions have been elicited in sports research with the stressors presented in Table 2.

In the sports literature techniques for eliciting negative states seem to outnumber those for eliciting positive states. Moreover, in laboratory experiments, the purpose has almost always been to compare functioning under a negative state to functioning under a "neutral" state. A notable exception can be found in Woodman et al. (2009), where the authors elicited three discrete emotions, two positively and one negatively toned (i.e., happiness, hope, anger). A systematic consideration of emotions of different hedonic valence (i.e., positive, neutral, negative) would allow a greater understanding of the influence of emotions on athletic performance.

Table 1. Methods for Inducing Positive Emotions in Sports

Method	Selected References
Emotional words	(Vast, et al., 2011)
Imagery	(Page, Sime, & Nordell, 1999; Woodman, et al., 2009)
Music	(Bishop, Karageorghis, & Kinrade, 2009; Bishop, et al., 2007)
Perfume	(Raudenbush, Corley, & Eppich, 2001)
Psychological skills training intervention	With a focus on three emotional dimensions, arousal, pleasantness, and functionality: (Hanin, Syrja, Cohen, Tenenbaum, & English, 1995), and using metaphors: (Lindsay, Thomas, & Douglas, 2010)
Success and failure manipulation	(G. V. Wilson & Kerr, 1999)
Team-building meeting	(Dunn & Holt, 2004)

Table 2. Methods for Inducing Negatives Emotions in Sports

Method	Selected References
Audience-induced pressure	(Baumeister, 1984; Oudejans & Pijpers, 2009)
Being judged by experts	(Oudejans & Pijpers, 2009)
Being videotaped	(Beilock & Carr, 2001; Lewis & Linder, 1997; Oudejans & Pijpers, 2009), in order to increase self-awareness and therefore self-evaluation: (Maxwell, Masters, & Poolton, 2006)
Cognitive load	Arithmetic task: (Acevedo, et al., 2006; Lewis & Linder, 1997) or Stroop color-word task: (Acevedo, et al., 2006)
Competition	(Williams & Elliott, 1999)
Crowd noise	(Balmer, et al., 2007; Laborde, et al., 2011; Laborde & Raab, in press)
Deception	"The trials that you did to warm up before the task will be integrated in your performance" (Williams & Elliott, 1999)
Ego-threatening stressor	"The [performance on the] task reflects your ability in real life": (Behan & Wilson, 2008; Murray & Janelle, 2003)
Emphasis on time	(Masters, Polman, & Hammond, 1993)
Imagery	(P. A. Davis, et al., 2010; Oudejans & Pijpers, 2009; Woodman, et al., 2009; Woolfolk, Parrish, & Murphy, 1985)
Manipulating task's perceived risk	Climbing a wall to various heights: (Cañal-Bruland, et al., 2010; L. Hardy & Hutchinson, 2007; Nieuwenhuys, et al., 2008; Oudejans & Pijpers, 2009, 2010)
Negative sound	Loud beep if participants failed: (Masters, et al., 1993)
Noncontingent feedback (success and failure manipulation)	Critical feedback is given regardless of actual performance: (Williams & Elliott, 1999; G. V. Wilson & Kerr, 1999; M. R. Wilson, Vine, & Wood, 2009)

Table 2. (Continued)

Method	Selected References
Performance-contingent reward	Financial incentive: (Baumeister, 1984; Behan & Wilson, 2008; Beilock & Carr, 2001; Masters, et al., 1993; Williams & Elliott, 1999; M. R. Wilson, Wood, & Vine, 2009)
Preparation shortened before performing the task	(Masters, et al., 1993)
Results shown to others	(Behan & Wilson, 2008; M. R. Wilson, Wood, et al., 2009)
Scenarios	(Behan & Wilson, 2008; M. R. Wilson, Wood, et al., 2009)
Social stressor	With group inclusion or exclusion: (Boyes & French, 2009)
Trier Social Stress Task	(Lautenbach & Laborde, submitted)

3.1.3. Use of a Cover Story

To ensure that participants do not try to respond with what they think the experimenter expects, researchers do not want participants to be aware that they are trying to manipulate their emotional state. Therefore, using a cover story that reinforces the purported main aim of the experiment (main aim for the participant, that is, not for the researcher) allows the true object of investigation, emotional states, to be kept hidden. In a study about anger, P.A. Davis et al. (2010) told their participants that they were involved in an experiment aimed at assessing their peak-force performance under different conditions. Laborde and Raab (in press), when assessing the influence of emotions on decision making performance, told their participants that they were involved in an experiment about concentration and that they had to remain as focused as possible for all the tasks. To reinforce this cover story, they used a concentration grid (Harris & Harris, 1984). In future, researchers should include a manipulation check, to check whether their participants were motivated to uncover the true nature of the experiment, and an open question, to check whether the participants believed the cover story (e.g., Laborde & Raab, in press). They should ensure that participants leave the laboratory in a good mood, for example, by telling them jokes. Finally, debriefing participants after emotional manipulation studies is also important for ethical reasons.

3.2. Assessment

3.2.1. Subjective

3.2.1.1. Potential stressors

Understanding the antecedents of emotions is crucial to being able to act on emotions (Laborde, et al., submitted). Existing research has focused mainly on potential stressors as antecedents and on one emotion in particular, namely, anxiety (e.g., J. Hammermeister & Burton, 2001). Stressors are often investigated through qualitative methodologies that assess both competitive and noncompetitive stress (Hanton, Fletcher, & Coughlan, 2005) and elite and nonelite athletes (Mellalieu, Neil, Hanton, & Fletcher, 2009). By examining stressors, it is also possible to explore the coping strategies used (Holt & Hogg, 2002) and how emotions developed (Neil, Hanton, Mellalieu, & Fletcher, 2011). If identifying stressors is important per se, understanding how athletes can appraise these stressors is perhaps even more important.

3.2.1.2. Appraisal

To date, there is no psychometrically validated inventory that measures appraisal in sports. The Stress Appraisal Measure (Peacock & Wong, 1990) was used in a recent study (Nicholls, et al., 2012). It contains 28 items and assesses six dimensions of appraisal including both primary and secondary appraisal and relational meaning with challenge and threat. Due to the lack of complete instruments, research in sports has used single items to assess separately different dimensions of appraisal, such as challenge and threat with two items (Cerin, 2003), and stressor intensity and controllability with two items (Nicholls, Levy, Grice, & Polman, 2009).

3.2.1.3. Discrete

For self-report measures of emotions, two approaches exist: individualized (i.e., idiosyncratic) and group oriented (i.e., nomothetic).

3.2.1.3.1. Ideographic

The **individualized approach** was initiated by the work of Hanin and colleagues, with the IZOF (Hanin, 2000; Jokela & Hanin, 1999), which we introduced above in Section 2.2.2. An individualized approach allows the researcher to get closer to the real emotional experiences of athletes, capturing their idiosyncratic nature by generating content relevant to each athlete. The IZOF was further developed to use probabilistic methods and has been coupled with physiological measures (Bertollo, et al., 2012). Since theory testing and the synthesis of data across different studies is difficult using this ideographic approach (Jones, et al., 2005), researchers often adopt more group-oriented approaches.

3.2.1.3.2. Nomothetic

For the **group-oriented approach**, several standardized sport-specific measures exist that focus on a specific emotion, namely, anxiety. These include the Competitive State Anxiety Inventory-2 (Martens, Vealey, Burton, Bump, & Smith, 1990), which has been recently revised (Martinent, Ferrand, Guillet, & Gautheur, 2010), and the Sport Anxiety Scale-2 (Smith, Smoll, Cumming, & Grossbard, 2006).

To assess a broader range of affective states, two non-sport-specific scales were used: the Profile of Mood States (McNair, Lorr, & Droppleman, 1971), with a derivative used in sports, the Brunel Mood Scale (Terry, Lane, & Fogarty, 2003); and the Positive and Negative Affect Schedule (Watson, Clark, & Tellegen, 1988). Although the POMS and the PANAS were used in sports contexts, they were not designed to assess emotions in sports (Jones, et al., 2005). A sport-specific questionnaire has therefore been developed, the Sport Emotion Questionnaire (Jones, et al., 2005), containing 22 emotional adjectives representing five dimensions (i.e., anxiety, dejection, excitement, anger, and happiness). This questionnaire was validated for use in precompetition settings. A self-rating measure to assess emotions during and after the competition is still needed, especially because specific emotions are elicited at these times (Jones, et al., 2005; Woodman, et al., 2009).

3.2.1.4. Dimensions

Several instruments exist to assess emotions as dimensions. They usually take into account the hedonic valence (i.e., positive vs. negative) and sometimes the intensity, as well. The Affect Grid (Russell, Weiss, & Mendelsohn, 1989) assesses hedonic tone and intensity. The Sport Affect Grid is based on the same principle (Woodman, et al., 2009). It assesses two independent dimensions of affect: intensity and pleasantness. It is presented as a 9 × 9 grid, the vertical axis assessing intensity (from extremely low to extremely high) and the horizontal axis assessing hedonic tone (from unpleasant feeling to pleasant feeling). "Participants are asked to mark an X on the part of the grid that best represents how he/she feels right now. Scores for the intensity and hedonic tone of the emotions (were) are calculated separately by converting the location of the X on each axis to a value from 1 to 9" (Woodman, et al., 2009, p. 177). The Feeling Scale (C. J. Hardy & Rejeski, 1989) is a bipolar rating scale commonly used for the assessment of affective responses during exercise. And finally the Visual Analogic Scale is a two-axis orthogonal grid (200-mm axes each anchored by *not at all* and *very much so*) that measures the dimensions of arousal and hedonic tone. It has been used in particular as a quick and effective measure to control for emotional manipulation (P. A. Davis, et al., 2010). In summary, these instruments convey less information than the inventory with discrete emotions, but nevertheless they can be helpful for within-competition designs.

3.2.1.5. Conclusion

Combining ideographic and nomothetic measures seems very interesting for research and sports applications (e.g., Robazza, Bortoli, Nocini, Moser, & Arslan, 2000). In addition, to predict performance better (like in P. A. Davis, et al., 2010), it seems important to consider emotions in general rather than focusing on only one emotion (e.g., anxiety, (J Hammermeister & Burton, 1995; J. Hammermeister & Burton, 2001). Self-rating measures are easy to use, cost effective, and can capture the subjective nature of the emotional experience of the individual, but they are subject to social desirability bias (Pedregon, Farley, Davis, Wood, & Clark, 2012). This is why the assessment of emotions needs to be combined with the study of other components, such as physiology and behavior. In addition, the development of implicit assessment of emotions is warranted, as with the Implicit Positive and Negative Affect Test (Quirin, Kazen, & Kuhl, 2009). The question of using a sports-specific instrument versus a general one is also worth addressing. Perhaps different instruments could be used within the same research design to see how performance can be best predicted.

Finally, when manipulating emotions in the laboratory it is important to have a **manipulation check.** A combination of discrete and dimensional subjective instruments (like in P. A. Davis, et al., 2010) allows the collection of additional discriminant information about the success of the emotional manipulation. The manipulation check is also an indication that it is possible to draw valid conclusions from the emotion manipulation. Subjective measures are easy to implement both in the laboratory and in the field because they require nothing other than a paper and a pencil to be filled out. However, they are somehow limited to the subjective experience of the emotion, and to understand emotions better it is necessary to go to the neurophysiological level, which "makes emotions organismic" (Lazarus, 2000).

3.2.2. Neurophysiological measures

Subjective experiences of emotions, appropriately assessed by self-report measures, provide an incomplete view of the emotional experience of the individual. One must also look at the neurophysiological manifestations of emotions.

3.2.2.1. Electrodermal activity

By measuring electrodermal activity we can provide a tonic–phasic distinction. The tonic level of skin resistance or conductance is the absolute level of resistance or conductance at a given moment in the absence of a measurable phasic response, and it is referred to as SRL (skin resistance level) or SCL (skin conductance level). Superimposed on the tonic level are phasic decreases in resistance (increases in conductance; (Dawson, Schell, & Filion, 2000).

Electrodermal activity is an indication of arousal, but not of the valence. The skin conductance response (SCR) is thought to be linked solely with the sympathetic nervous system, whose output results in a broad state of activation (Venables & Christie, 1980). Indeed, the sympathetic innervations of sweat glands induce changes in skin conductance (Gutrecht, 1994), which is associated with emotional arousal in a wide range of psychological states and processes (Dawson, et al., 2000). Self-reports on the emotional valence and arousal dimensions are correlated with autonomic and somatic responses to emotional stimuli, while SCR positively correlates with the emotional arousal independently of valence (Bradley & Lang, 2000). In sports, SCR has rarely been used as a measure of emotions because of potential confounding induced by movement activity (e.g., Collet, Guillot, Bolliet, Delhomme, & Dittmar, 2003; Rada, et al., 1995).

3.2.2.2. Heart rate

Heart rate can indicate emotional valence and intensity. Bradley and Lang (2000) reported a study about the response to emotional pictures, where a classic tri-phasic pattern of heart rate was obtained: an initial deceleration, an acceleratory component, and a secondary deceleration. **Affective valence** contributes to the amount of initial deceleration and acceleratory activity, with unpleasant stimuli producing more initial deceleration, and pleasant stimuli producing greater peak acceleration. However, heart rate is just one of the many interacting variables in the cardiovascular system, which include posture, respiratory anomalies, and individual physical differences. Any of these variables can contribute to hiding the affective covariation (Bradley & Lang, 2000). Nevertheless, when the processing context is controlled and the subject is passive and oriented, it is possible to observe the effect of affective valence. This explains why it is difficult to use this measure as an emotional indicator in moving individuals, such as in the sports context in the field. However, some studies in sports have related an increase in heart rate to **anxiety,** for example, in climbing (Oudejans & Pijpers, 2010) and in gymnastics (Tremayne & Barry, 1988).

From heart rate beat-to-beat data the heart rate variability (HRV) can be calculated. This is an interesting variable that can describe parasympathetic and sympathetic influences of the autonomic nervous system on the heart, and thus it serves as an indirect indicator of emotions.

3.2.2.3. Heart rate variability

The heart rate is never constant but varies from beat to beat. HRV corresponds to the variability of RR intervals (i.e., intervals between consecutive R-R peaks; Niskanen, Tarvainen, Ranta-Aho, & Karjalainen, 2004). HRV identifies the branch of the autonomic nervous system that actually mediates the heart rate. Measuring HRV allows us to assess the sympathetic–vagal balance of an organism (Camm, et al., 1996). The sympathetic and parasympathetic branches of the autonomous nervous system are involved in emotions (Levenson, 2003). Therefore, HRV can be considered an objective measure of emotional responding (Appelhans & Luecken, 2006).

The analysis of HRV can be divided into time-domain, frequency-domain, and nonlinear methods. The first two have been the most commonly used to reflect emotional states (Appelhans & Luecken, 2006). It should be noted that it is inappropriate to compare time-domain measures obtained from recordings of different durations (Camm, et al., 1996, p. 357). Frequency data are generally extracted through fast Fourier transform (Appelhans & Luecken, 2006), which can usually provide easily interpretable results in terms of physiological regulation (Camm, et al., 1996, p. 364). These methods are detailed in Table 3, together with their expected links with the autonomous system and their supposed evolution under stress during stressful events. According to the physiological stress model, stress often comes with an increase of sympathetic tone caused by an increased catecholamine level (Axelrod, 1984) and a reduction of the vagal tone (Watkins, Grossman, Krishnan, & Sherwood, 1998). Overall, a decrease in HRV, indicating a disturbed autonomic nervous system function, has been associated with mental stress and is a sign of an inability to respond to physiological variability and complexity (Horsten, et al., 1999).

In sports, HRV has been used successfully as an indicator of precompetitive anxiety (Murray & Raedeke, 2008) and of the response to a stressful event (Laborde, et al., 2011). Further research is warranted to investigate the links between HRV and specific emotional responses in the sports context, using, for example, different calculations, such as the traditional fast Fourier transform (Costa, Galati, & Rognoni, 2009).

Table 3. Heart Rate Variability (HRV) Parameters and Their Evolution during Stressful Events

HRV parameters		Link with autonomous system	Evolution during stressful event (with examples from the literature)
Time domain	PNN50 (percentage of successive normal sinus RR intervals more than 50 ms)	Parasympathetic activity (Camm, et al., 1996)	Decrease (e.g., Filaire, Portier, Massart, Ramat, & Teixeira, 2010)
	RMSSD (root mean square of the successive normal sinus RR interval difference)		Decrease (e.g., Filaire, et al., 2010)
	SDNN (standard deviation of all normal sinus RR intervals)	Sympathetic activity (Camm, et al., 1996) or a mix between sympathetic and parasympathetic activity (Kleiger, Stein, Bosner, & Rottman, 1992)	Increase of SDNN (e.g., Lehrer, et al., 2010)

HRV parameters		Link with autonomous system	Evolution during stressful event (with examples from the literature)
Frequency domain (involves the distribution of oscillations in at least two frequency bands and the determination of the power in each of these bands)	**VLF** (very low frequency)	The physiological correlate of VLF is still unknown, and this parameter is not considered a reliable measure (Camm, et al., 1996)	-
	LF (low frequency)	A complex interplay between sympathetic and parasympathetic influences (Camm, et al., 1996)	Increase (e.g., Dishman, et al., 2000)
	HF (high frequency)	Parasympathetic activity (Camm, et al., 1996)	Decrease (e.g., Sloan, et al., 1994)
	LF/HF ratio	Balance between sympathetic and parasympathetic systems (Camm, et al., 1996)	Increase (e.g., Kristal-Boneh, Raifel, Froom, & Ribak, 1995; Laborde, et al., 2011). Due to the likely contamination of LF by parasympathetic influence, the LF/HF ratio has been shown to be a more consistent characteristic of individuals than LF and HF (Sloan, et al., 1995)

3.2.2.4. Hormonal measures

Measuring hormones can help detect stress, and especially measures of **cortisol** (Denson, Spanovic, & Miller, 2009a, 2009b). Salivary cortisol measurement is noninvasive, pain-free, and thus ethically acceptable. It can be performed without medical expertise (Kirschbaum & Hellhammer, 2000). A rise in the cortisol level reflects that the individual is experiencing stress, as has been found during athletic competitions (Filaire, Duché, Lac, & Robert, 1996; Filaire, Le Scanff, Duche, & Lac, 1999; Filaire, Maso, Sagnol, Ferrand, & Lac, 2001). The closer to the competition, the higher the cortisol level has been found to be (Strahler, Ehrlenspiel, Heene, & Brand, 2010). The cortisol rise is less important in elite than in nonelite athletes (Moya-Albiol, et al., 2001). Although cortisol is a well-known marker in stress research (Hellhammer, Wüst, & Kudielka, 2009), research integrating its measurement in studies of the emotion–performance relationship is still lacking (e.g., Lautenbach & Laborde, submitted).

3.2.2.5. Brain measurements

Brain studies are a recent and promising advance in the field of emotion and performance research. In sports, functional magnetic resonance imagery (fMRI) studies have been used to show the effects of cognitive interventions at the neurological level, when helping athletes to cope with failure (H. Davis, et al., 2008). This first study was followed with a study that combined fMRI with measures of neuroendocrine responses, to explore the correlates of neural activation with cortisol and testosterone (H. Davis, et al., 2012). This combination of different measures was advocated by Daamen and Raab (2012) in their review of how to assess affect in the context of exercise, where they underlined that implicit and explicit measurements of affective responses should both be used. Such a combined approach addresses the fact that reflecting consciously about an emotional experience to fill out subjective reports can influence brain activation (Taylor, Phan, Decker, & Liberzon, 2003).

One challenge faced by researchers willing to use brain measurements in their research is the adaptation of their emotional tasks to the specificities of fMRI (Daamen & Raab, 2012), given that a large number of observations is required to derive reliable brain activation patterns. Researchers must grapple with how to assess emotions, which are by definition of short duration, and which are expected never to be identical. Despite the methodological challenges, brain research in this domain is warranted to further our understanding of the emotion–performance relationship.

3.2.3. Behavioral component

According to Bradley and Lang (2000), behavioral events can be assessed either by **direct actions** (e.g., approach, avoidance, escape, attack, defensive reflexes) or **by task enhancement and deficits analyses** (e.g., response latency, amplitude).

Effects of emotions on motor behavior and movement patterns - The effects of emotions can be estimated in controlled observations of changes in movement patterns and muscular tension and under different emotion intensity levels (e.g., Pijpers, et al., 2005; Pijpers, Oudejans, Holsheimer, & Bakker, 2003). These studies showed that it was possible to use electromyography data to check for qualitative differences in motor behavior and movement patterns. Taking the behavioral component into account allows researchers to focus more on the quality of the movement, rather than on the outcome, that is, the performance. Finally, a recent study showed that muscle activity and kinematic parameters mediated the pressure–performance relationship in a golf putting task (Cooke, et al., 2010).

Emotions can influence the tendency to engage in certain risk-taking activities, through emotion regulation. Engaging in specific activities, for example, mountaineering, was found to have an emotion regulation purpose (Castanier, Le Scanff, & Woodman, 2010, 2011; Woodman, Cazenave, & Le Scanff, 2008). Here the influence of emotions on performance is not direct but might influence certain types of risk-taking behaviors.

Finally, some research examined **emotion behavior at the trait level**. Anger, for example, may be related to aggressive behaviors, and research using the Competitive Aggressiveness and Anger Scale (Maxwell & Moores, 2007) showed that scores on this scale correlated with illegal aggressive behavior in rugby (Maxwell & Visek, 2009). It should also be noted that the emotional disposition to take part in motor activity can be assessed with a questionnaire, the Motor Activity Anxiety Test (Bortoli & Robazza, 1994), which has been used in sports to assess the tendency to participate in adventurous sports (Robazza, et al., 2006).

In this section, we reviewed ways to elicit and assess emotions, providing researchers in the field with guidelines to design their studies. Some of the ideas presented can also be used in the applied field by sports psychology consultants willing to develop interventions based on emotions, providing them with instruments for evaluating the efficacy of such interventions. In the next section, we show how to transfer knowledge from theories to effective, practical interventions, answering the question, "How do I deal with athletes' emotions?" We also elaborate on the possible extension of theories presented in domains other than sports.

4. EMOTIONS AND PERFORMANCE—APPLICATIONS

4.1. Application in the Sports Domain

"If I am right about the way emotion and coping influence performance in competitive sports, it would help if athletes understood which emotions are aroused in competition, their individual vulnerability to them, and how best to cope" (Lazarus, 2000, p. 241). What seems so important to Lazarus is that people become aware of their emotions and of the influence they might have on their performance.

The three main theories that we reviewed above (i.e., CMRT, IZOF, TCTSA) can inform this applied perspective. Lazarus's (2000) **CMRT** indicates that cognitive interventions might influence the way we deal with our emotions. In an applied paper, "Controlling Emotions in Sport", Jones (2003) presented strategies aimed at changing cognitions, with the goal of either eliciting a more adapted emotional response or suppressing emotional expression and any maladaptive behavioral consequences. He proposed a number of different techniques, including self-statement modification, imagery, Socratic dialogue, storytelling metaphors and poetry, reframing, and the use of problem-solving skills. The **IZOF** (Hanin, 2000) can provide good insight into emotion regulation that fits the individual's needs (Woodcock, Cumming, Duda, & Sharp, 2011), allowing to act at the physiological and subjective levels (Cohen, Tenenbaum, & English, 2006). The **TCTSA** (Jones, et al., 2009) also stresses the importance of appraisal. To create a "challenge state" that benefits performance (Nicholls, et al., 2012), athletes should be encouraged to enhance self-efficacy and focus on the aspects of the situation under their control, and on approach goals (Jones, et al., 2009).

To design applied interventions that address emotions and performance, practitioners are encouraged to go beyond coping, which focuses particularly on negative emotions, and direct their interest toward emotion regulation, which is concerned with both positive and negative emotions (Gross, 1998). Emotion regulation can be seen not only from a hedonic point of view (positive and negative) but also from an instrumental point of view. This means, for example, that people can actually try to regulate their emotions not to experience positive ones but to experience those that can be helpful for performance, even if they are negative in hedonic tone, such as anger and anxiety (Lane, Beedie, Devonport, & Stanley, 2011).

Different methods can be implemented to make the best use of one's emotions in competition. Some researchers advise **experiencing the emotion beforehand** in training, so as to deal with it better at competition. For example, training with mild anxiety may prevent choking under higher levels of anxiety (Oudejans & Pijpers, 2009, 2010). This principle is similar to the theory of stress inoculation (Mace & Carroll, 1985, 1986; Stetz, Wildzunas, Wiederhold, Stetz, & Hunt, 2006). Recent applications with *biofeedback* appear very promising in optimizing relaxation methods (Beauchamp, Harvey, & Beauchamp, 2012; Shaw & Zaichkowsky, 2012; Zaichkowsky, 2012). In particular, biofeedback aiming to modify the vagal tone should be encouraged, because vagal tone has been recognized as an index of emotion regulation (Morgan, Aikins, Steffian, Coric, & Southwick, 2007). Another method is the *development of emotional competencies*. We talked earlier about trait EI as a potential moderator of the emotion–performance relationship. Research has shown that interventions aimed at modifying abilities linked with trait EI were successful in modifying trait EI (Nelis, et al., 2011; Nelis, Quoidbach, Mikolajczak, & Hansenne, 2009).

4.2. Extension to Other Domains

In this chapter, we focused on sports as a showcase for studying the relationship of emotions and performance. Yet this relationship is pertinent to many other domains, as well.

In **organizational contexts**, both emotional dispositions (e.g., O'Boyle, Humphrey, Pollack, Hawver, & Story, 2011; B. A. Scott, Colquitt, Paddock, & Judge, 2010) and state emotions (Wiltermuth & Tiedens, 2011) have been found to play a role in performance. In particular, the role of EI in managing teams has been emphasized (Mikolajczak, Balon, Ruosi, & Kotsou, 2012; O'Boyle, et al., 2011). Thus, particular care should be taken in the development of such competencies. State emotions should be taken into account as well, for example, during negotiations, because of their role in manipulation (Andrade & Ariely, 2009; Filipowicz, Barsade, & Melwani, 2011). This role is reinforced by displays of emotion, which can reflect an ability to influence others (Cote & Hideg, 2011).

In the **military domain**, the need to keep the mind sharp under pressure is an indispensable survival tool. Soldiers with better emotion regulation measured at the physiological level reach a higher performance (Morgan, et al., 2007). Such emotion regulation competencies are also required for the police (van Gelderen, Bakker, Konijn, & Demerouti, 2011). Recent research showed that the gaze pattern when firing a weapon is crucial when performing under pressure and can differentiate elite and rookie police officers (Vickers & Lewinski, 2012).

In the **medical domain**, EI has been shown to play an important role in dealing efficiently with patients (Zijlmans, Embregts, Gerits, Bosman, & Derksen, 2011). People working in the healthcare system should receive more training regarding emotional competencies, because they will be facing daily strong emotional issues, such as pain experienced by patients and their families (Hilliard & O'Neill, 2010). Moreover, in addition to managing their own emotional issues, people working in healthcare should be able to provide emotional support to patients and their families.

In **school/academia**, emotions have a strong influence on learning performance and academic achievement, and emotions of both learners and teachers are important. Concerning teachers, evidence has shown that students learn better when they are in a good mood, when their teachers make them laugh (Roth, Ritchie, Hudson, & Mergard, 2011). At the dispositional level, academic success is not only about cognitive abilities but also about emotional competencies. In fact, trait EI has been found to influence positively academic performance during one exam (Laborde, et al., 2010) and during the whole academic year (Parker, et al., 2004). At the state level, students have better grades when they experience more positive affect before an exam and when they learn, as was shown in a study manipulating students' affect with classical music in the background during lectures (Dosseville, Laborde, & Scelles, 2012). The way emotions influence students' learning and performance has been studied with the Achievement Emotions Questionnaire (Pekrun, Goetz, Frenzel, Barchfeld, & Perry, 2011), and interesting intervention ideas can be found in a chapter by Beilock and Ramirez (2011).

In the **artistic domain**, emotions are also important. In music, the emotional display is important for those seeing a performance (Nakahara, Furuya, Masuko, Francis, & Kinoshita, 2011), and the role of the performer in making listeners experience emotions is fundamental (Juslin & Timmers, 2010). Finally, in any tasks where **creativity** is required, people should know how to deal with their emotions in order to optimize their creativity according to the task (Baas, De Dreu, & Nijstad, 2008; M. A. Davis, 2009).

CONCLUSION

Athletes, referees, coaches, and managers daily face situations of high pressure, making the sports domain an appropriate showcase for our examination of the emotion–performance relationship. After reviewing and comparing the three main theories in the field, we provided researchers with an up-to-date review of how to elicit and assess emotions. Finally, we examined the potential practical implications of the theories mentioned.

The scope of this chapter did not include other variables that can be interesting to take into account to understand the emotion–performance link, such as motivation. According to the self-determination theory, when basic psychological needs (autonomy, competence, relatedness) are satisfied, this state allows for a better response to stress (Quested, et al., 2011). In addition, we did not study the influence of group emotions on group performance. Finally, we focused here on the influence of emotions on athletic performance, but we did not address their influence on sports participation, which can have a long-term significant effect on performance (Mohiyeddini, Pauli, & Bauer, 2009).

Future research could be carried out on several levels. At the theoretical level, an integration of the different theories proposed could lead to a clearer and more global understanding of the emotion–performance relationship. Empirical research on this topic often relies on the combination of different theories, such as the CMRT and the IZOF (Martinent, et al., 2012; Pensgaard & Duda, 2003). Providing such integration more systematically would ensure the emergence of an integrated theory aimed at a better understanding of both the antecedents and consequences of emotions, as well as their relationship with performance. At the methodological level, we encourage researchers to combine different emotion components in their research and to explore the possibilities offered by the promising field of neurosciences. At the applied level, the findings about emotions and performance in sports seem likely to inform other fields, such as organizational development and education, integrating methodologies that help guide people to higher efficacy in emotion regulation, such as biofeedback.

To conclude, emotions are a very important parameter to take into account for anyone trying to reach peak performance, whatever the domain considered. Following Lazarus's recommendation (2000), taking the first step—becoming aware of our emotions and their impact on our performance—opens the door to a more exciting and accomplished life.

REFERENCES

Acevedo, E. O., Webb, H. E., Weldy, M. L., Fabianke, E. C., Orndorff, G. R., & Starks, M. A. (2006). Cardiorespiratory responses of hi fit and low fit subjects to mental challenge during exercise. *International journal of sports medicine, 27*, 1013. doi: 10.1055/s-2006-923902.

Allen, M. S., Greenlees, I. & Jones, M. V. (2011). An investigation of the five-factor model of personality and coping behaviour in sport. *Journal of sports sciences, 29*, 841-850. doi: 10.1080/02640414.2011.565064.

Andrade, E. B. & Ariely, D. (2009). The enduring impact of transient emotions on decision making. *Organizational Behavior and Human Decision Processes, 109*, 1-8. doi: 10.1016/j.obhdp.2009.02.003.

Appelhans, B. M. & Luecken, L. J. (2006). Heart rate variability as an index of regulated emotional responding. *Review of General Psychology, 10*, 229-240. doi: 10.1037/1089-2680.10.3.229.

Axelrod, J. (1984). The relationship between the stress hormones, catecholamines, ACTH and glucocorticoids. In E. Usdin, R. Kvetnansky & R. Axelrod (Eds.), *Stress: the Role of Catecholamines and other Neurotransmitters* (Vol. *1*, 3 - 13). New York, NY: Gordon and Breach.

Baas, M., De Dreu, C. K. W. & Nijstad, B. A. (2008). A Meta-Analysis of 25 Years of Mood-Creativity Research: Hedonic Tone, Activation, or Regulatory Focus? *Psychological Bulletin, 134*, 779-806. doi: 10.1037/a0012815.

Bagozzi, R. P., Dholakia, U. M. & Basuroy, S. (2003). How Effortful Decisions Get Enacted: The Motivating Role of Decision Processes, Desires, and Anticipated Emotions. *Journal of Behavioral Decision Making, 16*(4), 273-295. doi: 10.1002/bdm.446.

Balmer, N. J., Nevill, A. M., Lane, A. M., Ward, P., Williams, A. M. & Fairclough, S. (2007). Influence of crowd noise on soccer refereeing consistency in soccer. *Journal of Sport Behavior, 30*, 130-145.

Baumeister, R. F. (1984). Choking under pressure: Self-consciousness and paradoxical effects of incentives on skillful performance. *Journal of Personality and Social Psychology, 46*, 610-620.

Baumeister, R. F. & Showers, C. J. (1986). A review of paradoxical performance effects: Choking under pressure in sports and mental tests. *European Journal of Social Psychology, 16*, 361-383.

Beauchamp, M. K., Harvey, R. H. & Beauchamp, P. H. (2012). An Integrated Biofeedback and Psychological Skills Training Program for Canada ' s Olympic Short-Track Speedskating Team. *Journal of Clinical Sport Psychology, 6*, 67-84.

Beedie, C., Terry, P. & Lane, A. (2000). The profile of mood states and athletic performance: Two meta-analyses. *Journal of Applied Sport Psychology, 12*, 93-109. doi: 10.1080/10413200008404213.

Behan, M. & Wilson, M. R. (2008). State anxiety and visual attention: the role of the quiet eye period in aiming to a far target. *Journal of Sports Sciences, 26*, 207-215. doi: 10.1080/02640410701446919.

Beilock, S. L. & Carr, T. H. (2001). On the Fragility of Skilled Performance: What Governs Choking Under Pressure? *Journal of Experimental Psychology: General, 130*, 701-725.

Beilock, S. L. & Ramirez, G. (2011). On the Interplay of Emotion and Cognitive Control: Implications for Enhancing Academic Achievement. In P. M. Jose & H. R. Brian (Eds.), *Psychology of Learning and Motivation* (Vol. 55, 137-169). Oxford: Academic Press.

Bertollo, M., Robazza, C., Falasca, W. N., Stocchi, M., Babiloni, C. & Del Percio, C. et al. (2012). Temporal pattern of pre-shooting psycho-physiological states in elite athletes: A probabilistic approach. *Psychology of Sport and Exercise, 13*, 91-98. doi: 10.1016/j.psychsport.2011.09.005.

Bishop, D. T., Karageorghis, C. I. & Kinrade, N. P. (2009). Effects of Musically-Induced Emotions on Choice Reaction Time Performance. *Sport Psychologist, 23*, 59-76.

Bishop, D. T., Karageorghis, C. I. & Loizou, G. (2007). A Grounded Theory of Young Tennis Players' Use of Music to Manipulate Emotional State. *Journal of Sport & Exercise Psychology, 29*, 584-607.

Bortoli, L. & Robazza, C. (1994). The Motor Activity Anxiety Test. *Perceptual & Motor Skills, 79*(1 Part 1), 299-305.

Boyes, M. E. & French, D. J. (2009). Having a Cyberball: Using a ball-throwing game as an experimental social stressor to examine the relationship between neuroticism and coping. *Personality and Individual Differences, 47*, 396-401.

Bradley, M. M. & Lang, P. J. (2000). Measuring emotion: behavior, feeling and physiology. In R. Lane & L. Nadel (Eds.), *Cognitive neuroscience of emotion* (pp. 242-276). Oxford, England: Oxford University Press.

Brehm, J. W. & Miron, A. M. (2006). Can the Simultaneous Experience of Opposing Emotions Really Occur? *Motivation and Emotion, 30*, 13-30. doi: 10.1007/s11031-006-9007-z.

Brown, C. M. & McConnell, A. R. (2011). Discrepancy-based and anticipated emotions in behavioral self-regulation. *Emotion, 11*, 1091-1095.

Camm, A. J., Malik, M., Bigger, J. T., Breithardt, G., Cerutti, S. & Cohen, R. J. et al. (1996). Heart rate variability. Standards of measurement, physiological interpretation, and clinical use. *European Heart Journal, 17*, 354-381.

Cañal-Bruland, R., Pijpers, J. R. & Oudejans, R. R. (2010). The influence of anxiety on action-specific perception. *Anxiety, stress, and coping, 23*, 353-361. doi: 10.1080/10615800903447588.

Castanier, C., Le Scanff, C. & Woodman, T. (2010). Beyond sensation seeking: affect regulation as a framework for predicting risk-taking behaviors in high-risk sport. *Journal of sport & exercise psychology, 32*, 731-738.

Castanier, C., Le Scanff, C. & Woodman, T. (2011). Mountaineering as affect regulation: the moderating role of self-regulation strategies. *Anxiety, stress, and coping, 24*, 75-89. doi: 10.1080/10615801003774210.

Cerin, E. (2003). Anxiety versus fundamental emotions as predictors of perceived functionality of pre-competitive emotional states, threat, and challenge in individual sports. *Journal of Applied Sport Psychology, 15*, 223-238. doi: 10.1080/10413 200390213344.

Cerin, E. (2004). Predictors of competitive anxiety direction in male Tae Kwon Do practitioners: a multilevel mixed idiographic/nomothetic interactional approach. *Psychology of Sport and Exercise, 5*, 497-516. doi: 10.1016/S1469-0292(03)00041-4.

Cerin, E., Szabo, A., Hunt, N. & Williams, C. (2000). Temporal patterning of competitive emotions: a critical review. *Journal of Sports Sciences, 18*, 605-626.

Cohen, A. B., Tenenbaum, G. & English, R. W. (2006). Emotions and golf performance: An IZOF-based applied sport psychology case study. *Behavior modification, 30*, 259-280. doi: 10.1177/0145445503261174.

Collet, C., Guillot, A., Bolliet, O., Delhomme, G. & Dittmar, A. (2003). Correlats neurophysiologiques des processus mentaux enregistres en situation reelle par micro-capteurs non invasifs [Neurophysiological correlates of mental processes through non invasive micro-sensors recording in the field]. *Science & Sports, 18*, 74-85. doi: 10.1016/S0765-1597(03)00081-9.

Cooke, A., Kavussanu, M., McIntyre, D. & Ring, C. (2010). Psychological, muscular and kinematic factors mediate performance under pressure. *Psychophysiology, 47*, 1109-1118. doi: 10.1111/j.1469-8986.2010.01021.x.

Costa, T., Galati, D. & Rognoni, E. (2009). The Hurst exponent of cardiac response to positive and negative emotional film stimuli using wavelet. *Autonomic neuroscience: basic & clinical, 151*, 183-185. doi: 10.1016/j.autneu.2009.08.011.

Cote, S. & Hideg, I. (2011). The ability to influence others via emotion displays: A new dimension of emotional intelligence. *Organizational Psychology Review, 1*, 53-71. doi: 10.1177/2041386610379257.

Daamen, M. & Raab, M. (2012). Psychological Assessments in Physical Exercise *Functional Neuroimaging in Exercise and Sport Sciences*.

Davidson, R. J., Ekman, P., Frijda, N. H., Goldsmith, H. H., Kagan, J. & Lazarus, R. et al. (1994). How are emotions distinguished from moods, temperament, and other related affective constructs? In P. Ekman & R. J. Davidson (Eds.), *The nature of emotion: Fundamental questions* (49-96). New York, NY: Oxford University Press.

Davis, H., Liotti, M., Ngan, E. T., Woodward, T. S., Snellenberg, J. X. & Anders, S. M. et al. (2008). fMRI BOLD Signal Changes in Elite Swimmers While Viewing Videos of Personal Failure. *Brain Imaging and Behavior, 2*, 84-93. doi: 10.1007/s11682-007-9016-x.

Davis, H., van Anders, S., Ngan, E., Woodward, T. S., Snellenberg, J. X. V. & Mayberg, H. S. et al. (2012). Neural, Mood, and Endocrine Responses in Elite Athletes Relative to Successful and Failed Performance Videos. *Journal of Clinical Sport Psychology, 6*, 6-21.

Davis, M. A. (2009). Understanding the relationship between mood and creativity: A meta-analysis. *Organizational Behavior and Human Decision Processes, 108*, 25-38. doi: 10.1016/j.obhdp.2008.04.001.

Davis, P. A., Woodman, T. & Callow, N. (2010). Better out than in: The influence of anger regulation on physical performance. *Personality and Individual Differences, 49*, 457-460. doi: 10.1016/j.paid.2010.04.017.

Dawson, M. E., Schell, A. M. & Filion, D. L. (2000). The electrodermal system. In J. T. Cacioppo, L. G. Tassinary & G. G. Berntson (Eds.), *Handbook of psychophysiology* (2nd ed., 200-223). Cambridge, England: Cambridge University Press.

Denson, T. F., Spanovic, M. & Miller, N. (2009a). Cognitive Appraisals and Emotions Predict Cortisol and Immune Responses: A Meta-Analysis of Acute Laboratory Social Stressors and Emotion Inductions. *Psychological Bulletin, 135*, 823-853.

Denson, T. F., Spanovic, M. & Miller, N. (2009b). Stress and Specificity: Reply to Miller (2009). *Psychological Bulletin, 135*, 857-858.

Dishman, R. K., Nakamura, Y., Garcia, M. E., Thompson, R. W., Dunn, A. L. & Blair, S. N. (2000). Heart rate variability, trait anxiety, and perceived stress among physically fit men and women. *International Journal of Psychophysiology, 37*, 121-133. doi: 10.1016/S0167-8760(00)00085-4.

Dosseville, F., Laborde, S. & Scelles, N. (2012). Music during lectures: Will students learn better? *Learning and Individual Differences, 22*, 258-262.

Dunn, J. G. H. & Holt, N. L. (2004). A Qualitative Investigation of a Personal-Disclosure Mutual-Sharing Team Building Activity. *Sport Psychologist, 18*, 363-380.

Eccles, D. W., Ward, P., Woodman, T., Janelle, C. M., Le Scanff, C. & Ehrlinger, J. et al. (2011). Where's the Emotion? How Sport Psychology Can Inform Research on Emotion in Human Factors. *Human Factors, 53*, 180-202. doi: 10.1177/0018720811403731.

Eysenck, M. W. & Calvo, M. G. (1992). Anxiety and performance: The processing efficiency theory. *Cognition & Emotion, 6*, 409-434. doi: 10.1080/02699939208409696.

Eysenck, M. W., Derakshan, N., Santos, R. & Calvo, M. G. (2007). Anxiety and cognitive performance: Attentional control theory. *Emotion, 7*, 336-353.

Feldman Barrett, L. (1998). Discrete Emotions or Dimensions? The Role of Valence Focus and Arousal Focus. *Cognition & Emotion, 12*, 579-599. doi: 10.1080/026999398379574.

Filaire, E., Duché, P., Lac, G. & Robert, A. (1996). Saliva cortisol, physical exercise and training: influences of swimming and handball on cortisol concentrations in women. *European journal of applied physiology and occupational physiology, 74*, 274-278.

Filaire, E., Le Scanff, C., Duche, F. & Lac, G. (1999). The relationship between salivary adrenocortical hormones changes and personality in elite female athletes during handball and volleyball competition. *Research quarterly for exercise and sport, 70*, 297-302.

Filaire, E., Maso, F., Sagnol, M., Ferrand, C. & Lac, G. (2001). Anxiety, hormonal responses, and coping during a judo competition. *Aggressive Behavior, 27*, 55-63.

Filaire, E., Portier, H., Massart, A., Ramat, L. & Teixeira, A. (2010). Effect of lecturing to 200 students on heart rate variability and alpha-amylase activity. *European Journal of Applied Physiology, 108*, 1035-1043. doi: 10.1007/s00421-009-1310-4.

Filipowicz, A., Barsade, S. & Melwani, S. (2011). Understanding Emotional Transitions: The Interpersonal Consequences of Changing Emotions in Negotiations. *Journal of Personality and Social Psychology, 101*, 541-556.

Fredrickson, B. L. (2001). The role of positive emotions in positive psychology: The broaden-and-build theory of positive emotions. *American psychologist, 56*, 218-226.

Gray, E. K. & Watson, D. (2007). Assessing positive and negative affect via self-report. In J. A. Coan & J. J. B. Allen (Eds.), *Handbook of emotion elicitation and assessment* (pp. 171-183). New York, NY: Oxford University Press.

Gross, J. J. (1998). The Emerging Field of Emotion Regulation: An Integrative Review. *Review of General Psychology, 2*, 271-299.

Gutrecht, J. A. (1994). Sympathetic skin response. *Journal of Clinical Neurophysioly, 11*, 519-524.

Hammermeister, J. & Burton, D. (1995). Anxiety and the Ironman : Investigating the Antecedents and Consequences of Endurance Athletes ' State Anxiety Precompetitive Anxiety Patterns of Endurance Athletes. *The Sport Psychologist, 9*, 29-40.

Hammermeister, J. & Burton, D. (2001). Stress, Appraisal, and Coping revisited: examining the antecedents of competitive state anxiety with endurance athletes. *Sport Psychologist, 15*, 66-90.

Hanin, Y. (2000). *Emotions in sport*. Champaign, IL: Human Kinetics.

Hanin, Y. (2007). Emotions in Sport: Current Issues and Perspectives In G. Tenenbaum & R. Eklund (Eds.), *Handbook of Sport Psychology* (3rd ed., 31-58). New York, NY: Wiley.

Hanin, Y., Syrja, P., Cohen, A., Tenenbaum, G. & English, R. W. (1995). Performance Affect in Junior Ice Hockey Players: An Application of the Individual Zones of Optimal Functioning Model. *The Sport Psychologist, 9*, 169-187.

Hanton, S., Fletcher, D. & Coughlan, G. (2005). Stress in elite sport performers: A comparative study of competitive and organizational stressors. *Journal of Sports Sciences, 23*, 1129-1141. doi: 10.1080/02640410500131480.

Hardy, C. J. & Rejeski, W. J. (1989). Not what, but how one feels: the measurement of affect during exercise. *Journal of Sport & Exercise Psychology, 11*, 304-317.

Hardy, L. & Hutchinson, A. (2007). Effects of performance anxiety on effort and performance in rock climbing: a test of processing efficiency theory. *Anxiety, stress, and coping, 20*, 147-161. doi: 10.1080/ 10615800701217035

Harris, D. V. & Harris, B. L. (1984). *The athlete's guide to sport psychology: Mental skills for physical people*. New York, NY: Leisure Press.

Hellhammer, D. H., Wüst, S. & Kudielka, B. M. (2009). Salivary cortisol as a biomarker in stress research. *Psychoneuroendocrinology, 34*, 163-171. doi: 10.1016/j.psyneuen. 2008. 10.026.

Hilliard, C. & O'Neill, M. (2010). Nurses' emotional experience of caring for children with burns. *Journal of Clinical Nursing, 19*, 2907-2915. doi: 10.1111/j.1365-2702.2009.03177.x.

Holt, N. L. & Hogg, J. M. (2002). Perceptions of stress and coping during preparations for the 1999 women's soccer world cup finals. *Sport Psychologist, 16*, 251-271.

Horsten, M., Ericson, M., Perski, A., Wamala, S. P., Schenck-Gustafsson, K. & Orth-Gomér, K. (1999). Psychosocial Factors and Heart Rate Variability in Healthy Women. *Psychosomatic Medicine, 57*, 49-57.

Janelle, C. M. (2002). Anxiety, arousal and visual attention: a mechanistic account of performance variability. *Journal of sports sciences, 20*, 237-251. doi: 10.1080/026404102317284790.

Jokela, M. & Hanin, Y. (1999). Does the individual zones of optimal functioning model discriminate between successful and less successful athletes? A meta-analysis. *Journal of sports sciences, 17*, 873-887. doi: 10.1080/026404199365434.

Jones, M. V. (2003). Controlling emotions in sport. *Sport Psychologist, 17*, 471-486.

Jones, M. V., Lane, M., Bray, S., Uphill, M. & Catlin, J. (2005). Development and Validation of the Sport Emotion Questionnaire. *Journal of Sport & Exercise Psychology, 27*, 407-431.

Jones, M. V., Meijen, C., McCarthy, P. J. & Sheffield, D. (2009). A Theory of Challenge and Threat States in Athletes. *International Review of Sport and Exercise Psychology, 2*, 161-180. doi: 10.1080/17509840902829331.

Juslin, P. N. & Timmers, R. (2010). Expression and communication of emotion in music performance. In P. N. Juslin, J. A. Sloboda, P. N. E. Juslin & J. A. E. Sloboda (Eds.), *Handbook of music and emotion: Theory, research, applications* (453-489). New York, NY: Oxford University Press.

Kaiseler, M., Polman, R. C. J. & Nicholls, A. R. (2012). Effects of the Big Five personality dimensions on appraisal coping, and coping effectiveness in sport. *European Journal of Sport Science, 12*, 62-72. doi: 10.1080/17461391.2010.551410.

Kirschbaum, C. & Hellhammer, D. H. (2000). Salivary cortisol. In G. Fink (Ed.), *Encyclopedia of stress* (379-383). San Diego, CA: Academic Press.

Kleiger, R. E., Stein, P. K., Bosner, M. S. & Rottman, J. N. (1992). Time domain measurements of heart rate variability. *Cardiology Clinics, 10*, 487-498.

Kristal-Boneh, E., Raifel, M., Froom, P. & Ribak, J. (1995). Heart rate variability in health and disease. *Scandinavian Journal of Work, Environment & Health, 21*, 85-95.

Laborde, S., Brüll, A., Weber, J. & Anders, L. S. (2011). Trait emotional intelligence in sports: A protective role against stress through heart rate variability? *Personality and Individual Differences, 51*, 23-27. doi: 10.1016/j.paid.2011.03.003.

Laborde, S., Dosseville, F. & Scelles, N. (2010). Trait emotional intelligence and preference for intuition and deliberation: Respective influence on academic performance. *Personality and Individual Differences, 49*, 784-788. doi: 10.1016/j.paid.2010.06.031.

Laborde, S., Dosseville, F., & Raab, M. (in press). Special issue "Emotions and decision making in sports": Introduction, comprehensive approach, and vision for the future. *International Journal of Sport & Exercise Psychology.*

Laborde, S., Dosseville, F., Wolf, S., Martin, T. & You, M. (submitted). Consequences and antecedents of debilitative pregame emotions.

Laborde, S. & Raab, M. (in press). The Tale of Hearts and Reason: The Influence of Moods on Decision Making. *Journal of Sport & Exercise Psychology*

Laborde, S., You, M., Dosseville, F. & Salinas, A. (2012). Culture, individual differences, and situation: Influence on coping in French and Chinese table tennis players. *European Journal of Sport Science, 12*, 265-261. doi: 10.1080/17461391.2011.566367.

Lane, A. M., Beedie, C. J., Devonport, T. J. & Stanley, D. M. (2011). Instrumental emotion regulation in sport: relationships between beliefs about emotion and emotion regulation strategies used by athletes. *Scandinavian journal of medicine & science in sports, 21*, 445-451. doi: 10.1111/j.1600-0838.2011.01364.x.

Larsen, R. J. & Fredrickson, B. L. (1999). Measurement issues in emotion research. In D. Kahneman, E. Diener & N. Schwarz (Eds.), *Well-being: Foundations of hedonic psychology* (40-60). New York, NY: Russell Sage.

Lautenbach, F. & Laborde, S. (submitted). Cortisol and sport performance.

Lazarus, R. S. (1999). *Stress and emotion: A new synthesis.* New York, NY: Springer.

Lazarus, R. S. (2000). How emotions influence performance in competitive sports. *The Sport Psychologist, 14*, 229-252.

Lehrer, P., Karavidas, M., Lu, S. E., Vaschillo, E., Vaschillo, B. & Cheng, A. (2010). Cardiac data increase association between self-report and both expert ratings of task load and task performance in flight simulator tasks: An exploratory study. *International Journal of Psychophysiology, 76*, 80-87. doi: 10.1016/j.ijpsycho.2010.02.006.

Levenson, R. W. (2003). Blood, sweat, and fears - The autonomic architecture of emotion. *Annals of the New York Academy of Sciences, 1000*, 348-366. doi: 10.1196/annals.1280.016.

Lewis, B. P. & Linder, D. E. (1997). Thinking about choking? Attentional processes and paradoxical performance. *Personality and Social Psychology Bulletin, 23*, 937-944.

Lindsay, P., Thomas, O. & Douglas, G. (2010). A Framework to Explore and Transform Client-Generated Metaphors in Applied Sport Psychology. *Sport Psychologist, 24*, 97-112.

Mace, R. & Carroll, D. (1985). The control of anxiety in sport: stress inoculation training prior to abseiling. *International Journal of Sport Psychology, 16*, 165-175.

Mace, R. & Carroll, D. (1986). Stress inoculation training to control anxiety in sport: two case studies in squash. *British Journal of Sports Medicine, 20*, 115-117.

Martens, R., Vealey, R. S. & Burton, D. (1990). *Competitive anxiety in sport*. Champaign, IL: Human Kinetics.

Martens, R., Vealey, R. S., Burton, D., Bump, L. & Smith, D. E. (1990). Development and validation of the Competitive Sports Anxiety Inventory-2. In R. Martens, R. S. Vealey & D. Burton (Eds.), *Competitive anxiety in sport* (pp. 127-173). Champaign, IL: Human Kinetics.

Martinent, G., Campo, M. & Ferrand, C. (2012). A descriptive study of emotional process during competition: Nature, frequency, direction, duration and co-occurrence of discrete emotions. *Psychology of Sport and Exercise, 13*, 142-151. doi: 10.1016/j.psychsport.2011.10.006.

Martinent, G. & Ferrand, C. (2009). A Naturalistic Study of the Directional Interpretation Process of Discrete Emotions During High-Stakes Table Tennis Matches. *Journal of Sport & Exercise Psychology, 31*, 318-336.

Martinent, G., Ferrand, C., Guillet, E. & Gautheur, S. (2010). Validation of the French version of the Competitive State Anxiety Inventory-2 Revised (CSAI-2R) including frequency and direction scales. *Psychology of Sport and Exercise, 11*, 51-57.

Masters, R. S., Polman, R. C. J. & Hammond, N. V. (1993). Reinvestment: A dimension of personality implicated in skill breakdown under pressure. *Personality and Individual Differences, 14*, 655-666.

Maxwell, J. P., Masters, R. & Poolton, J. (2006). Performance breakdown in sport: the roles of reinvestment and verbal knowledge. *Research Quarterly for Exercise & Sport, 77*, 271-276.

Maxwell, J. P. & Moores, E. (2007). The development of a short scale measuring aggressiveness and anger in competitive athletes. *Psychology of Sport and Exercise, 8*, 179-193. doi: 10.1016/j.psychsport.2006.03.002.

Maxwell, J. P. & Moores, E. (2008). Measuring aggressiveness and anger, but not aggression? A response to the CAAS critique. *Psychology of Sport and Exercise, 9*, 729-733. doi: 10.1016/j.psychsport.2008.01.002.

Maxwell, J. P. & Visek, A. (2009). Unsanctioned aggression in rugby union: Relationships among aggressiveness, anger, athletic identity, and professionalization. *Aggressive Behavior, 35*(3), 237-243. doi: 10.1002/ab.20302.

McCarthy, P. J. (2011). Positive emotion in sport performance: current status and future directions. *International Review of Sport and Exercise Psychology, 4*, 50-69. doi: 10.1080/1750984X.2011.560955.

McCrae, R. R. & John, O. P. (1992). An Introduction to the Five-Factor Model and Its Applications. *Journal of Personality, 60*, 175-215. doi: 10.1111/j.1467-6494.1992.tb00970.x.

McNair, D. M., Lorr, M. & Droppleman, L. F. (1971). *Profile of Mood State manual*. San Diego, CA: Educational and Industrial Testing Service.

Mellalieu, S. D., Neil, R., Hanton, S. & Fletcher, D. (2009). Competition stress in sport performers: Stressors experienced in the competition environment. *Journal of Sports Sciences, 27*, 729-744. doi: 10.1080/02640410902889834.

Mellers, B. A. (2001). Anticipated Emotions as Guides to Choice. *Current Directions in Psychological Science, 10*, 210-214. doi: 10.1111/1467-8721.00151.

Mikolajczak, M., Balon, N., Ruosi, M. & Kotsou, I. (2012). Sensitive but not sentimental: Emotionally intelligent people can put their emotions aside when necessary. *Personality and Individual Differences, 52*, 537-540.

Mohiyeddini, C., Pauli, R. & Bauer, S. (2009). The role of emotion in bridging the intention-behaviour gap: The case of sports participation. *Psychology of Sport and Exercise, 10*, 226-234. doi: 10.1016/ j.psychsport. 2008.08.005.

Morgan, C. A., III, Aikins, D. E., Steffian, G., Coric, V. & Southwick, S. (2007). Relation between cardiac vagal tone and performance in male military personnel exposed to high stress: Three prospective studies. *Psychophysiology, 44*, 120-127.

Moya-Albiol, L., Salvador, A., Costa, R., Martínez-Sanchis, S., González-Bono, E. & Ricarte, J. et al. (2001). Psychophysiological responses to the Stroop Task after a maximal cycle ergometry in elite sportsmen and physically active subjects. *International Journal of Psychophysiology, 40*, 47-59.

Murray, N. P. & Janelle, C. M. (2003). Anxiety and performance: a visual search examination of the Processing Efficiency Theory. *Journal of Sport & Exercise Psychology, 25*, 171-187.

Murray, N. P. & Raedeke, T. D. (2008). Heart Rate Variability as an indicator of pre-competitive arousal. *International Journal of Sport Psychology, 39*, 346-355.

Nakahara, H., Furuya, S., Masuko, T., Francis, P. R. & Kinoshita, H. (2011). Performing music can induce greater modulation of emotion-related psychophysiological responses than listening to music. *International Journal of Psychophysiology, 81*, 152-158.

Neil, R., Hanton, S., Mellalieu, S. D. & Fletcher, D. (2011). Competition stress and emotions in sport performers: The role of further appraisals. *Psychology of Sport and Exercise, 12*, 470-460. doi: 10.1016/j.psychsport. 2011.02.001.

Nelis, D., Kotsou, I., Quoidbach, J., Hansenne, M., Weytens, F. & Dupuis, P. et al. (2011). Increasing Emotional Competence Improves Psychological and Physical Well-Being, Social Relationships, and Employability. *Emotion, 11*, 354-366. doi: 10.1037/a0021554.

Nelis, D., Quoidbach, J., Mikolajczak, M. & Hansenne, M. (2009). Increasing emotional intelligence: (How) is it possible? *Personality and Individual Differences, 47*, 36-41. doi: 10.1016/j.paid.2009.01.046.

Nicholls, A. R., Levy, A. R., Grice, A. & Polman, R. C. J. (2009). Stress appraisals, coping, and coping effectiveness among international cross-country runners during training and competition. *European Journal of Sport Science, 9*, 285-293. doi: 10.1080/17461390902836049.

Nicholls, A. R., Polman, R. C. & Levy, A. R. (2012). A path analysis of stress appraisals, emotions, coping, and performance satisfaction among athletes. *Psychology of Sport and Exercise, 13*, 263-270. doi: 10.1016/j.psychsport.2011.12.003.

Nieuwenhuys, A., Pijpers, J. R., Oudejans, R. R. & Bakker, F. C. (2008). The Influence of Anxiety on Visual Attention in Climbing. *Journal of Sport & Exercise Psychology, 30*, 171-185.

Niskanen, J. P., Tarvainen, M. P., Ranta-Aho, P. O. & Karjalainen, P. A. (2004). Software for advanced HRV analysis. *Computer Methods and Programs in Biomedicine, 76*, 73-81. doi: 10.1016/j.cmpb.2004.03.004.

O'Boyle, E. H., Humphrey, R. H., Pollack, J. M., Hawver, T. H. & Story, P. A. (2011). The relation between emotional intelligence and job performance: A meta-analysis. *Journal of Organizational Behavior, 32*, 788-818. doi: 10.1002/job.714.

Oudejans, R. R. & Pijpers, J. R. (2009). Training with anxiety has a positive effect on expert perceptual–motor performance under pressure. *The Quarterly Journal of Experimental Psychology, 62*, 1631-1647. doi: 10.1080/17470210802557702.

Oudejans, R. R. & Pijpers, J. R. (2010). Training with mild anxiety may prevent choking under higher levels of anxiety. *Psychology of Sport and Exercise, 11*, 44-50. doi: 10.1016/j.psychsport.2009.05.002.

Page, S. J. S. Sime, W. & Nordell, K. (1999). The effects of imagery on female college swimmer's perceptions of anxiety. *Sport Psychologist, 13*, 458-469.

Parker, J. D. A., Creque, R. E., Barnhart, D. L., Harris, J. I., Majeski, S. A. & Wood, L. M. et al. (2004). Academic achievement in high school: does emotional intelligence matter? *Personality and Individual Differences, 37*, 1321-1330. doi: 10.1016/j.paid.2004.01.002.

Peacock, E. J. & Wong, P. T. P. (1990). The stress appraisal measure (SAM): A multidimensional approach to cognitive appraisal. *Stress Medicine, 6*, 227-236. doi: 10.1002/smi.2460060308.

Pedregon, C. A., Farley, R. L., Davis, A., Wood, J. M. & Clark, R. D. (2012). Social desirability, personality questionnaires, and the "better than average" effect. *Personality and Individual Differences, 52*, 213-217.

Pekrun, R., Goetz, T., Frenzel, A. C., Barchfeld, P. & Perry, R. P. (2011). Measuring emotions in students' learning and performance: The Achievement Emotions Questionnaire (AEQ). *Contemporary Educational Psychology, 36*, 36-48.

Pensgaard, A. M. & Duda, J. L. (2003). Sydney 2000: The Interplay Between emotions, coping, and the performance of olympic-level athletes. *Sport Psychologist, 17*, 253-267.

Perugini, M. & Bagozzi, R. P. (2001). The role of desires and anticipated emotions in goal-directed behaviours: Broadening and deepening the theory of planned behaviour. *British Journal of Social Psychology, 40*, 79-98.

Petrides, K. V., Pita, R. & Kokkinaki, F. (2007). The location of trait emotional intelligence in personality factor space. *British Journal of Psychology, 98*, 273-289. doi: 10.1348/000712606X120618.

Pijpers, J. R., Oudejans, R. R. & Bakker, F. C. (2005). Anxiety-induced changes in movement behaviour during the execution of a complex whole-body task. *The Quarterly journal of experimental psychology. A, Human experimental psychology, 58*, 421-445. doi: 10.1080/02724980343000945.

Pijpers, J. R., Oudejans, R. R., Holsheimer, F. & Bakker, F. C. (2003). Anxiety-performance relationships in climbing: a process-oriented approach. *Psychology of Sport and Exercise, 4*, 283-304.

Quested, E., Bosch, J. A., Burns, V. E., Cumming, J., Ntoumanis, N. & Duda, J. L. (2011). Basic psychological need satisfaction, stress-related appraisals, and dancers' cortisol and anxiety responses. *Journal of sport & exercise psychology, 33*, 828-846.

Quirin, M., Kazen, M. & Kuhl, J. (2009). When Nonsense Sounds Happy or Helpless: The Implicit Positive and Negative Affect Test (IPANAT). *Journal of Personality and Social Psychology, 97*, 500-516. doi: 10.1037/a0016063.

Rada, H., Dittmar, A., Delhomme, G., Collet, C., Roure, R. & Vernet-Maury, E. et al. (1995). Bioelectric and microcirculaiton cutaneous sensors for the study of vigilance and emotional response during tasks and tests. *Biosensors and Bioelectronics, 10*, 7-15.

Raudenbush, B., Corley, N. & Eppich, W. (2001). Enhancing athletic performance through the administration of peppermint odor. *Journal of Sport & Exercise Psychology, 23*, 156-160.

Robazza, C. & Bortoli, L. (2005). Changing students's attitudes towards risky motor tasks: An application of the IZOF model. *Journal of Sports Sciences, 23*, 1075-1088.

Robazza, C., Bortoli, L., Carraro, A. & Bertollo, M. (2006). "I wouldn't do it; it looks dangerous": Changing students' attitudes and emotions in physical education. *Personality and Individual Differences, 41*, 767-777. doi: 10.1016/j.paid.2006.03.020.

Robazza, C., Bortoli, L., Nocini, F., Moser, G. & Arslan, C. (2000). Normative and idiosyncratic measures of positive and negative affect in sport. *Psychology of Sport and Exercise, 1*, 103-116.

Roth, W.-M., Ritchie, S. M., Hudson, P. & Mergard, V. (2011). A study of laughter in science lessons. *Journal of Research in Science Teaching, 48*, 437-458. doi: 10.1002/tea.20412.

Russell, J. A., Weiss, A. & Mendelsohn, G. A. (1989). Affect grid: a single-item scale of pleasure and arousal. *Journal of Personality and Social Psychology, 57*, 493-502.

Scherer, K. R. (2005). What are emotions? And how can they be measured? *Social Science Information, 44*, 695-729. doi: 10.1177/ 0539018405058216.

Scott, B. A., Colquitt, J. A., Paddock, E. L. & Judge, T. A. (2010). A daily investigation of the role of manager empathy on employee well-being. *Organizational Behavior and Human Decision Processes, 113*, 127-140. doi: 10.1016/j.obhdp.2010.08.001.

Scott, S. (2009). *Making Sense of Everyday Life*. Cambridge, England: Polity.

Selye, H. (1951). The general adaptation syndrome and the diseases of adaptation. *The American Journal of Medicine, 10*, 549-555. doi: 10.1016/0002-9343(51)90327-0.

Shaw, L. & Zaichkowsky, L. (2012). Setting the Balance : Using Biofeedback and Neurofeedback With Gymnasts. *Journal of Clinical Sport Psychology, 6*, 47-66.

Sloan, R. P., Shapiro, P. A., Bagiella, E., Boni, S. M., Paik, M. & Bigger, J. T. et al. (1994). Effect of mental stress throughout the day on cardiac autonomic control. *Biological Psychology, 37*, 89-99.

Sloan, R. P., Shapiro, P. A., Bagiella, E., Fishkin, P. E., Gorman, J. M. & Myers, M. M. (1995). Consistency of heart rate and sympathovagal reactivity across different autonomic contexts. *Psychophysiology, 32*, 452-459.

Smith, R. E., Smoll, F. L., Cumming, S. P. & Grossbard, J. R. (2006). Measurement of Multidimensional Sport Performance Anxiety in Children and Adults: The Sport Anxiety Scale-2. *Journal of Sport and Exercise Psychology, 28*, 479-501.

Spielberger, C. D. (1983). *Manual for the State Trait Anxiety Inventory (revised)*. Palo Alto, CA: Consulting Psychologists Press.

Spielberger, C. D., Jacobs, G., Russell, J. S. & Crane, R. S. (1983). Assessment of anger: The State-Trait Anger Scale. In J. N. Butcher & C. D. Spielberger (Eds.), *Advances in Personality Assessment* (161-187). London: Wiley.

Stetz, M. C., Wildzunas, R. M., Wiederhold, B. K., Stetz, T. A. & Hunt, M. P. (2006). The usefulness of virtual reality stress inoculation training for military medical females: A pilot study. *Annual Review of CyberTherapy and Telemedicine, 4*, 51-58.

Strahler, K., Ehrlenspiel, F., Heene, M. & Brand, R. (2010). Competitive anxiety and cortisol awakening response in the week leading up to a competition. *Psychology of Sport and Exercise, 11*, 148-154. doi: 10.1016/j.psychsport.2009.10.003.

Taylor, S. F., Phan, K. L., Decker, L. R. & Liberzon, I. (2003). Subjective rating of emotionally salient stimuli modulates neural activity. *NeuroImage, 18*, 650-659.

Tenenbaum, G., Lloyd, M., Pretty, G. & Hanin, Y. (2002). Congruence of Actual and Retrospective Reports of Precompetition Emotions in Equestrians. *Journal of Sport & Exercise Psychology, 24*, 271-288.

Terry, P. C., Lane, A. M. & Fogarty, G. J. (2003). Construct validity of the Profile of Mood States - Adolescents for use with adults. *Psychology of Sport and Exercise, 4*, 125-139.

Thomas, O., Hanton, S. & Maynard, I. (2007). Intervening with Athletes During the Time Leading up to Competition: Theory to Practice II. *Journal of Applied Sport Psychology, 19*, 398-418. doi: 10.1080/ 10413200701599140.

Tremayne, P. & Barry, R. J. (1988). An application of psychophysiology in sports psychology: heart rate responses to relevant and irrelevant stimuli as a function of anxiety and defensiveness in elite gymnasts. *International Journal of Psychophysioly, 6*(1), 1-8.

van Gelderen, B. R., Bakker, A. B., Konijn, E. A. & Demerouti, E. (2011). Daily suppression of discrete emotions during the work of police service workers and criminal investigation officers. *Anxiety, stress, and coping, 24*, 515-537. doi: 10.1080/10615806.2011.560665.

Vast, R., Young, R. & Thomas, P. R. (2011). Emotion and automaticity: Impact of positive and negative emotions on novice and experienced performance of a sensorimotor skill. *International Journal of Sport and Exercise Psychology, 9*, 227-237. doi: 10.1080/1612197X.2011.614848.

Vast, R., Young, R. L. & Thomas, P. R. (2010). Emotions in sport: Perceived effects on attention, concentration, and performance. *Australian Psychologist, 45*, 132-140. doi: 10.1080/00050060903261538.

Venables, P. H. & Christie, M. J. (1980). Electrodermal activity. In I. Martin & P. H. Venables (Eds.), *Techniques in psychophysiology* (pp. 3-67). Chichester, England: Wiley.

Verduyn, P. & Brans, K. (2012). The relationship between extraversion, neuroticism and aspects of trait affect. *Personality and Individual Differences, 52*, 664-669.

Vickers, J. N. & Lewinski, W. (2012). Performing under pressure: gaze control, decision making and shooting performance of elite and rookie police officers. *Human movement science, 31*, 101-117. doi: 10.1016/j.humov.2011.04.004.

Wang, X. (2011). The role of anticipated negative emotions and past behavior in individuals' physical activity intentions and behaviors. *Psychology of Sport and Exercise, 12*, 300-305. doi: doi: 10.1016/j.psychsport. 2010.09.007.

Watanabe, M. (2007). Role of anticipated reward in cognitive behavioral control. *Current Opinion in Neurobiology, 17*, 213-219. doi: 10.1016/j.conb.2007.02.007.

Watkins, L. L., Grossman, P., Krishnan, R. & Sherwood, A. (1998). Anxiety and vagal control of heart rate. *Psychosomatic medicine, 60*, 498.

Watson, D., Clark, L. A. A. & Tellegen, A. (1988). Development and Validation of Brief measures of positive and negative affect: the PANAS scales. *Journal of personality and social psychology, 54*, 1063. doi: 10.1037/0022-3514.54.6.1063.

Williams, A. M. M. & Elliott, D. (1999). Anxiety, expertise, and visual search strategy in karate. *Journal of Sport & Exercise Psychology, 21*, 362-375.

Wilson, G. V. & Kerr, J. H. (1999). Affective responses to success and failure: a study of winning and losing in competitive rugby. *Personality and Individual Differences, 27*, 85-99. doi: 10.1016/S0191-8869(98)00226-8.

Wilson, M. (2008). From processing efficiency to attentional control: a mechanistic account of the anxiety–performance relationship. *International Review of Sport and Exercise Psychology, 1*, 184-201. doi: 10.1080/17509840802400787.

Wilson, M. R., Vine, S. J. & Wood, G. (2009). The Influence of Anxiety on Visual Attentional Control in Basketball Free Throw Shooting. *Journal of Sport & Exercise Psychology, 31*, 152-168.

Wilson, M. R., Wood, G. & Vine, S. J. (2009). Anxiety, Attentional Control, and Performance Impairment in Penalty Kicks. *Journal of Sport & Exercise Psychology, 31*, 761-775.

Wiltermuth, S. S. & Tiedens, L. Z. (2011). Incidental anger and the desire to evaluate. *Organizational Behavior and Human Decision Processes, 116*, 55-65.

Woodcock, C., Cumming, J., Duda, J. L. & Sharp, L.-A. (2011). Working within an Individual Zone of Optimal Functioning (IZOF) Framework: Consultant Practice and Athlete Reflections on Refining Emotion Regulation Skills. *Psychology of Sport and Exercise, 13*, 291-302. doi: 10.1016/j.psychsport.2011.11.011.

Woodman, T., Cazenave, N. & Le Scanff, C. (2008). Skydiving as Emotion Regulation: The Rise and Fall of Anxiety Is Moderated by Alexithymia. *Journal of Sport & Exercise Psychology, 30*, 424-433.

Woodman, T., Davis, P. A., Hardy, L., Callow, N., Glasscock, I. & Yuill-Proctor, J. (2009). Emotions and Sport Performance: An Exploration of Happiness, Hope, and Anger. *Journal of Sport & Exercise Psychology, 31*, 169-188.

Woolfolk, R. L., Parrish, M. W. & Murphy, S. M. (1985). The effects of positive and negative imagery on motor skill performance. *Cognitive Therapy and Research, 9*, 335-341.

Zaichkowsky, L. (2012). Psychophysiology and Neuroscience in Sport: Introduction to the Special Issue. *Journal of Clinical Sport Psychology, 6*, 1-5.

Zijlmans, L. J. M., Embregts, P. J. C. M., Gerits, L., Bosman, A. M. T. & Derksen, J. J. L. (2011). Training emotional intelligence related to treatment skills of staff working with clients with intellectual disabilities and challenging behaviour. *Journal of intellectual disability research, 55*, 219-230. doi: 10.1111/j.1365-2788.2010.01367.x.

In: Handbook of Psychology of Emotions   ISBN: 978-1-62808-053-7
Editors: C. Mohiyeddini, M. Eysenck and S. Bauer   © 2013 Nova Science Publishers, Inc.

Chapter 20

MINDFULNESS AND EMOTIONS

Sara LeBlanc and Changiz Mohiyeddini*
University of Roehampton

ABSTRACT

Mindfulness is a technique that evolved from Budhism that is now making a positive impact on western psychotheraputic practices (Kabat-Zinn, 2003). Mindfulness is a type of self control that involves paying attention to the current moment without judgment or further cognitive processing (Brown, Ryan & Creswell, 2007). A meta-analysis by Baer Smith, Hopkins, Krietemeyer, and Toney (2006) determined that mindfulness is a multifaceted construct that consists of the following factors, describing, non-judging, acting with awareness, non-reacting and observing. From an emotional standpoint, the objective of mindfulness is to increase a person's awareness of their emotions without avoidance or judgment (Hayes, Wilson, Gifford, Follette, &Strosahl, 1996). This promotes a healthy interaction with both thoughts and emotions, enabling people to cultivate a new perspective whereby they interpret serious life events as challenges, rather than overwhelming threats (Hayes & Feldman, 2004). Mindfulness has been shown to have a positive impact on numerous health issues from physical health complaints such as chronic pain (Kabat-Zinn, 1982) to mental health problems such as depression (Teasdale Williams, Soulsby, Zindel, Segal, Ridgeway and Lau, 2000). Over the past thirty years there has been a growing interest in the mindfulness construct and it's utility for treating a multitude of mental and physical health problems (Weinstein, Brown, Ryan, 2009). To date, a wide variety of training programs have now incorporated mindfulness as an integral part of their treatment due to the pronounced impact it has been shown to have on health and well-being (Allen, Chambers & Knight, 2006).

*Corresponding author: Professor of Personality Psychology and Research Methods DEPARTMENT OF PSYCHOLOGY University of Roehampton Whitelands College Holybourne Avenue LONDON SW15 4JDTel. +44 (0)20 8392 3616c.mohiyeddini@roehampton.ac.uk.

INTRODUCTION

Mindfulness involves paying sustained attention to present moment experience (both internal and external) with heightened awareness in the absence of judgment (Kabatt-Zinn, 1990). Germer (2005) succinctly defines mindfulness as "(1) awareness, (2) of present experience, (3) with acceptance" (p. 7) while avoiding secondary processing. In a related vein, Epstein defines (1995) mindfulness as 'bare attention' (p.110).

According to Brown, et al., (2007) the concept of present-moment experience is crucial, in that what is undergone is simply registered, not necessarily processed. Accordingly, in order to reap the benefits of mindfulness one must 'de-center' from both thoughts and emotions (Segal, Teasdale, & Williams 2002). This allows these sensations to ebb and flow, without any specific truth or significance being attached to them by the observer. Mindfulness involves learning to constantly bring oneself back to the internal and external happenings of the present moment. Information is then processed in an unbiased, undistorted way (Brown & Ryan 2004). This enables a person to adaptively respond to situations, rather than to automatically react to situations when they arise (Bishop, Lau, Shapiro, Carlson, & Anderson, 2004). In this way mindfulness cultivates flexible awareness (Baer, 2003).

Mindfulness promotes present-moment responsiveness, preventing the mind from dwelling on the past or worrying about the future (Begley, 2007). It aims to change the relationship a person has with their thought patterns, teaching them to 'de-center' from both their thoughts and emotions (Segal, et al., 2002). This allows them to see all thoughts and emotions (both positive and negative) float through their mind without attaching any significant truth or meaning to them (Siegel, 2007). Mindfulness encourages participants to acknowledge thoughts and outlooks directly, even if they are perceived as negative. This actively prevents the processes of avoidance and repression, which can be highly destructive to an individual's psyche (Weinstein, et al., 2009). In choosing this direct approach, behavioral choices can be made that promote the accomplishment of long-term goals. This takes the focus away from proximal goals, which only aspire to diminish or even eradicate existing distress. Mindfulness allows for the awareness that the majority of sensations and emotions are not permanent but rather fleeting in nature, passing by 'like waves in the sea' (Linehan, 1993, p. 87). Daydreaming for instance, instead of being viewed as 'a waste of time,' can simply be labeled as 'thinking,' or a time of reflection. With this mindset people can view their actions as a tool to direct attention to the present, while focusing on their surroundings. This effectively removes the judgment attached to this action allowing for it to take place free of bias and regret.

Furthermore, mindfulness aids in the self-regulation of attention (Chatzisarantis & Hagger, 2005). It involves focusing for prolonged periods of time, switching attention to different aspects of the immediate environment and the avoidance of detailed processing or analysis of what is occurring (Kabat-Zinn, 1990). The goal of mindfulness is to improve the ability to observe all aspects of the present moment, while noting their impermanence (Brown, et al., 2007). These can include thoughts, physical sensations, sounds and memories. Mindfulness can create openness to new experiences, enhanced awareness and a greater sensitivity to the environment (Arch, Craske, 2006). It involves a detachment from needs and desires, enabling the mind to stay focused on goal-oriented tasks (Weinstein, et al., 2009). Mindfulness allows one to 'step back' from feelings, thoughts, conversations and other life events. This promotes liberation from automatic or reflexive reactions that occur due to ego involvement (Linehan, 1993).

THE ORIGIN OF MINDFULNESS: HOW DID MINDFULNESS COME INTO MAINSTREAM PSYCHOLOGY?

Mindfulness was derived from Buddhist meditative practices (Kabat-Zinn, 2003). Buddhist teachings suggest that people are often characterized by a 'mindless' mode of functioning, involving inattention and the habitual use of routines (Langer, 1989). This mode of processing can have dangerous consequences. For example, there are more fatalities in the American army due to human error than there are due to actual combat (Snook, 1996). Mindfulness aims to change this way of thinking by refocusing attention to present moment awareness at all times. Thus, mindfulness can be viewed as a type of self-awareness training (Brown, *et al.*, 2007). Initially, in western psychotherapy, mindfulness was developed to help people who suffered from chronic pain that was untreatable in many cases (Kabat-Zinn, 1990), yet in recent years it has been tailored for use in the prevention of recurrent depression (Segal, *et al.*, 2002). Mindfulness has been a central tenant of many contemplative and philosophical traditions for centuries, but it has only been conceptualized within a scientific framework within recent years (Lakey, Campbell, Brown & Goodie, 2007). As early as the 20th century, American psychologist William James predicted that Buddhism would have a powerful impact on Western psychological ideologies (Lau & McMain, 2005). His prediction has come to fruition over the past two decades, as mindfulness has become a popular component of several third wave therapies such as dialectical behavior therapy (DBT) (Linehan, 1993) and Mindfulness Based Stress Reduction (MBSR) (Kabatt-Zinn, 1982).

The first mindfulness intervention program to be introduced and clinically tested in Western psychotherapy was Mindfulness-Based Stress Reduction (MBSR; Kabat-Zinn, 1982). It has proven to be effective in treating incurable chronic pain, with long-term health improvements lasting for more than 15 months (Kabat-Zinn, Lipworth, & Burney, 1985). When MBSR was used to treat patients suffering from General Anxiety Disorder and panic disorder, substantial health improvements were shown in both anxiety and depressive symptomology (Kabat-Zinn Massion, Kristeller, Peterson, Fletcher, Pbert, Linderking, Santorelli, 1992). These effects were long lasting, being maintained at a three- year follow-up (Miller Fletcher & Kabat-Zinn 1995). In addition, MBSR has been shown to have efficacy reducing stress symptomology (Chiesa & Serretti, 2009). It has also been successful in increasing immune system functioning and decreasing mood disturbance in cancer patients (Speca, Carlson, Goodey, & Angen, 2000). Over the past 25 years, MBSR has been proven to have widespread health benefits for both mental and physical health across diverse populations (Chiesa & Serretti, 2009).

An additional therapy developed at approximately the same time as MBSR was Acceptance and Commitment Therapy (Hayes & Wilson, 1994). This therapy differs from MBSR in several ways. It does not have a formal meditation component and it includes a 'wise mind' component that decreases the amount of reactive responding a person does to their thoughts and emotions. In later years, it was combined with cognitive-behavioral therapy, creating mindfulness-based cognitive therapy (Segal *et al.*, 2002). The past thirty years has seen a growing interest into the utility of mindfulness for treating a myriad of both mental and physical illnesses. Hundreds of papers have been written on the topic and a plethora of therapeutic training programs now contain a mindfulness component as a core aspect of their treatment (Allen, *et al.*, 2006).

THE COMPONENTS OF THE MINDFULNESS

In the literature, there is no current consensus on the core components of the mindfulness construct. Various academics have put forth competing ideas regarding this topic (Baer, Smith, & Allen 2004; Dimidjian & Linehan, 2003).

As a precursor to mindfulness, or rather a successful attitude from which to cultivate a deeper perspective into mindfulness, Kabbat-Zin, (1990) describes seven key attitudinal components from which to approach mindfulness which include, letting go, non-judging, beginner's mind, patience, trust, non-striving and acceptance. Non-judging involves becoming a neutral observer of your own life experience, noticing the ongoing stream of thoughts one has, without trying to stop or control them (Kabbat-Zin, 1990). The patience element entails letting things unfold as they happen, without trying to rush through life. The idea of the beginner's mind is that too often people go through life with blinkers on letting past experiences and beliefs stop them from seeing the true reality of a situation (Kabbat-Zin, 1990). Developing a beginners mind, leads one to experience everything as if it were for the first time, free of any preconceived notions or biases. Trust involves cultivating a basic faith in ones emotions and intuitions, even if they are not always completely accurate. Non-striving often requires meditation and paying attention to the way one is right now, without attempting to achieve goals, but rather accepting things the way they are. It is believed that this will eventually lead a person in the direction of their goals (Kabbat-Zin, 1990). The acceptance aspect encourages a person to strive to see the reality of a situation without trying to reappraise it, suppress it or avoid it (Hayes, 1994). It should instead be accepted it in its entirety, even if it is negative. The letting go portion is tied to the acceptance component. It involves accepting things for what they are and then letting go of control (Kabbat-Zin, 1990). For example, if ruminating, it involves letting go of worrisome thoughts. Instead the person labels these thoughts in a non-judgmental way, referring to them as 'thinking' and waits for them to pass.

MEASURING MINDFULNESS AS A MULTIFACETED CONSTRUCT

Dimidjian and Linehan (2003) state that accurate measures of mindfulness are needed to fully understand this construct and its distinctive components. Only then will it be possible to understand the underlying mechanism through which it exerts its salutary effects.

A recently developed psychometric tool known as the Kentucky Mindfulness Questionnaire (Baer, Smith, & Allen 2004) is utilized to measure four aspects of mindfulness. These consist of the ability to observe emotions, thoughts and feelings, the ability to describe current events with words, the ability to stay in the current moment, and the ability to accept the present moment without critically evaluating it. The KIMS has been shown to have sound psychometric properties and to provide an accurate factor structure of mindfulness (Baer et al., 2004). Similar to the four constructs measured via the KIMS, Linehan (1993) has posited that there are six core mindfulness skills that can be divided into two groups of three: the first three 'what' skills are describing (applying accurate labels to situations, behaviors and emotions), observing (attending to the present moment) and participating (engaging in current activities). The second three are 'how' skills, which include taking an unbiased stance, staying in the moment and being efficient. In contrast to these multifaceted models of mindfulness, Brown and Ryan (2004) contend that the entire mindfulness construct is encapsulated in a single dimension, which is paying attention to current moment experience.

A recent meta-analysis by Baer Smith, Hopkins, Krietemeyer, and Toney (2006) set out to unify the divergent hypotheses regarding the factor structure of the mindfulness construct. This meta-analysis combined all the facets from the 5 most frequently (which are: Mindful Attention Awareness Scale (MAAS; Brown & Ryan, 2003; The Freiburg Mindfulness Inventory (FMI; Buchheld, Grossman, & Walach, 2001; The Kentucky Inventory of Mindfulness Skills (KIMS; Baer, Smith, & Allen, 2004; The Cognitive and Affective Mindfulness Scale (CAMS; Feldman, Hayes, Kumar, & Greeson, 2004; S. C. Hayes & Feldman, 2004; The Mindfulness Questionnaire (MQ; Chadwick, Hember, Mead, Lilley, & Dagnan, 2005) used mindfulness scales. It combined all questionnaires into a single data set that was given out to 613 students. This analysis determined that four of the five factors were identical to those found in the KIMS questionnaire: non-judging, acting with awareness, describing and observing. An additional factor was revealed which was a non-reactive stance towards one's internal experience. This meta-analysis supported the fact that mindfulness is a multifaceted construct. It is interesting to note that in this exploratory factor analysis of mindfulness, 4 of the five factors (describe, non-judging act with awareness, and non-reacting) were correlated with expected variables such as thought suppression, anxiety and depression. However, the observe factor did not correlate in the expected direction with certain variables and did not fit the full hierarchical model but instead fit a reduced model consisting of a smaller sample of participants who practiced meditation frequently.

MINDFULNESS - EMOTIONS LINK

Cultivating a mindfulness perspective leads to enhanced acceptance and present moment awareness. It brings a person closer to reality by avoiding memory biases, ego involvement and secondary appraisals (Ryan, et al., 2007). Accordingly, mindfulness leads to a heightened awareness of behavior, emotions and the surrounding environment and is associated positively with high levels of emotional intelligence (Brown & Ryan, 2003). Developing the ability to observe thoughts and emotions without habitually reacting to them allows for greater self-control (Chatzisarantis & Hagger, 2005; Lakey, et al., 2007). Thoughts and emotions that are deemed to be beneficial are chosen and consciously identified with, while negative, self-defeating thought patterns are disregarded. The person chooses not to identify with them, instead waits for them to pass by as if they were clouds travelling over in the sky (Wells & Sembi, 2004).

Mindfulness aims to increase a person's awareness of their emotions, in a nonjudgmental way (Kabat-Zinn, 2003). This promotes an adaptive engagement with one's emotions and thoughts (Hayes & Feldman, 2004). People experience genuine emotion, without over-engaging, e.g. ruminating (Nolen- Hoeksema, 1998,) or under-engaging, e.g. suppressing (Wegner, 1994) with emotions when they arise. Often, people are fearful of negative emotions because they assume negative outcomes are impending. Mindfulness is a pragmatic tool for dealing with this phenomenon because it enables a person to experience negative affect without assuming negative outcomes are forthcoming (Weinstein, et al., 2009). This can stop the exacerbation of negative effect by ceasing the generation of further negative emotions (Chambers, Gullone& Allen, 2009).Consequently, a person can return to their natural emotional baseline quickly, without further emotional disturbance (Lutz, 2008). This fact is supported by the work of Segal and colleagues (2002) who determined that the acceptance of difficult emotions stops the maladaptive chain of automatic responses a person habitually expresses when they experience a negative emotion.

Mindfulness training teaches that thoughts and emotions are passing mental occurrences that do not need to be acted upon each time they arise (Kabat-Zinn, 2003). Facing distressing thoughts and emotions directly is a major aspect of mindfulness training (Lau & McMain, 2005). It is paramount to adopt and acknowledge viewpoints that foster a de-centered perspective of both thoughts and feelings (Safran & Segal, 1990). In mindfulness, cognitions and behaviors that are thought to lead to helpful outcomes are identified with while destructive thought patterns are disregarded. Thus, mindfulness empowers the individual by giving them the right to choose which thoughts to act upon and which thoughts to dismiss (Chambers, et al., 2009).

Mindfulness training differs from cognitive-behavioral therapy (CBT) in a variety of ways (Lau & McMain, 2005). Primarily, mindfulness training eliminates the evaluation of thoughts as either irrational or logical (Hofmann & Asmundson, 2008). It also removes the process of judging or restructuring thoughts in an attempt to increase their validity. In contrast to CBT, individuals are encouraged to observe their cognitions, be aware of their transience, and abstain from assessing them (Brown, et al., 2007). When employing the tools of mindfulness, reality is interacted with directly; it is not biased by distorted memories or reappraised in any way (Brown, et al., 2007). Hence, training in mindfulness involves a dualism of the self, as a person is taught to differentiate themselves from their thoughts and emotions. For example instead of saying "I am unlovable," a person would say "I'm feeling unloved" (Kohlenberg, Hayes, & Tsai, 1993, p. 588). Observing and labeling one's thoughts and feelings descriptively fosters the realization that they are not necessarily accurate depictions of reality (Linehan 1993). For example, the thought "everyone hates me," does not mean you are actually unpopular. Thinking "Everyone's whispering about at me" does not mean everyone is actually having side conversations about you. It could simply signify that you are feeling self-conscious at that very moment (Kristeller & Hallett, 1999). When using mindfulness, one objectively notes that moments in pain and sadness happen as often as all other moments in life. The choice is made to not give these moments more credence or attention than times in life that consist of less intense emotions.

Through mindfulness training participants learn to avoid engaging with troubling emotions, or those that encourage a distorted perception of reality (Bishop, et al., 2004). The emphasis is placed on directly experiencing feelings without having any judgments towards them (Safran & Segal, 1990). Simultaneously, partakers continuously avoid re-structuring or repressing their emotions (Baer, 2003). Waiting is recommended as it allows for both the difficult emotion to elapse, and for the arrival of a more enjoyable emotion. While attempts to appraise or escape emotions may be inevitable in some situations, these impulses are not acted upon; instead they are simply acknowledged (Kabbat-Zinn, 1990). In order to decrease emotional reactivity, participants in mindfulness training are directed to implement a number of strategies throughout this process. First, members are taught to recognize thought-controlling strategies, before subsequently abandoning them (Gardner & Moore, 2004). It then becomes vital to enter into active awareness, a practice that allows participants to experience hostile and negative emotions while merely noticing them instead of reacting to them (Chambers, et al., 2009). They learn not to avoid, dispute or struggle with their feelings, but rather to accept them without prejudice (Hayes, Wilson, Gifford, Follette & Strosahl, 1996). Mindfulness practitioners are taught to distinguish thoughts and emotions from the individual who is experiencing them. For example, a person trained in mindfulness will say to themselves: 'I'm thinking that I'm a bad person', not 'I'm a bad person' (Kohlenberg, Hayes, & Tsai, 1993, p. 588). Mindfulness may be advantageous in decreasing anger reactivity because it establishes a 'mental space' between stimulus and response (Robins Schmidt, & Linehan 2004). Consequently, mindfulness may promote proactive behavioral reactions that are reflective and self-controlled, rather than those that are habitual and impulsively reactive (Lakey, et al., 2007).

In a related vein, meta-cognitive insight can be achieved through mindfulness, as it transforms the way in which thoughts are perceived. Rather than viewing them as exact representations of reality, they are identified as temporary mental occurrences (Bishop, et al., 2004; Mason & Hargreaves, 2001; Teasdale, 1999; Teasdale, Segal, & Williams, 1995). The de-centered view that is characteristic of mindfulness can be extremely beneficial when dealing with depressed individuals (Nolen-Hoeksema, 1991), as it aids in interrupting the ruminative cycle that is a common trait of this illness. This disruption is critical as it allows for the recognition of maladaptive thinking. Individuals can then shift their focus to alternative aspects of the immediate situation (Teasdale et al., 1999; 1995). Ultimately mindfulness allows individuals to adaptively engage with their emotions on an authentic level (Hayes & Feldman, 2004).

HOW MINDFULNESS TRAINING WORKS

The process through which mindfulness facilitates cognitive change is not yet elucidated, however various hypotheses have been proposed.

According to the 'exposure' hypothesis, mindfulness training enhances a person's capacity to handle pain without experiencing a strong, adverse emotional reaction (Baer, 2003). This occurs because mindfulness sets in motion a desensitization process, whereby repeated exposure to pain does not necessarily lead to unbearable outcomes (Goleman, 1971). Thus, even though the actual amount of pain may not be lessened, the amount of distress suffered by the individual is decreased through the procedure.

The 'acceptance' hypothesis states that adaptive emotion regulation can be achieved if an event is experienced in totality, devoid of resistance or secondary appraisals (Brown & Ryan, 2004). Consequently, acceptance strategies typical of mindfulness may transform damaging response-focused regulatory strategies, such as suppression or avoidance (Brown et al., 2007). In contrast cognitive behavioral therapy encourages the transformation of negative thoughts into those that are more pleasing. This practice puts participants at risk of developing avoidant behaviors, which ultimately are more harmful (Chambers, et al., 2009). However, mindfulness as a state characteristic involves paying complete attention to the present moment (Kabat-Zinn, 2003). During stressful times, this level of concentration is thought to decrease the amount of cognitive distortion and improve adaptive emotion regulation (Larsen, 2000). This is evidenced by a greater use of approach and a lower use of avoidant emotion regulatory coping strategies (Hayes et al., 1996) and reduced levels of thought suppression, rumination, and other maladaptive thinking styles (Weinstein, et al., 2009).

When viewing mindfulness-training cognitively, participants are urged to observe their thoughts from a descriptive rather than judgmental standpoint (Bishop et al., 2004). Employing this method allows people to realize that their emotions are not always accurate interpretations of reality and that their thoughts are simply thoughts (Linehan, 1993). Taking this approach, someone who thinks 'no one loves me,' will take note of the thought while at the same time, recognizing that it is simply an insignificant thought. By not accepting thoughts as fundamental truths, the emotional impact of the notion will diminish (Arch &Craske, 2006). This modification of thought processing will accordingly impact subsequent behaviors. Mindfulness at its core concentrates on altering the function of thoughts, not their actual content (Siegel, 2007). It advocates the detachment from damaging cognitions and emotions (Safran& Segal, 1990). As a result it may be described as a form of cognitive reappraisal, occurring on a process rather than content level (Chambers, et al., 2009).

MINDFULNESS AS AN EMOTION REGULATION STRATEGY: A PROCESS LEVEL TYPE OF RE-APPRAISAL

Mindfulness may operate as an emotion regulation strategy by training people to stop connecting with disturbing emotions when they appear (Hayes, 2003). This gives people an enhanced capability to approach stressful or serious life events as challenges, rather than threats (Kabat-Zinn, 1993). From an emotion regulation standpoint, mindfulness epitomizes the ability to stay engaged in the present moment at all times, regardless of what emotion one may be experiencing. While cognitive reappraisal changes the way one thinks about an emotional event, mindfulness changes the way a person relates to their thoughts and emotional perceptions (Siegel, 2007). Mindfulness does not involve restructuring stressful situations, nor does it involve suppressing them. Instead, mindfulness entails a deliberate retraining of attention, to constantly stay focused in the present moment, while maintaining a stance of non-reactivity and non-judgment (Kabatt-Zinn, 1990). This leads to a natural, cognitive diffusion from both thoughts and emotions, allowing the individual to be more objective and consciously choose the thoughts and emotions they will identify with (Safran & Segal, 1990). Mindfulness is characterized by methodical retraining of attention and awareness towards a state of non-reactivity (Weinstein, et al., 2009). It gives the individual more freedom to consciously choose the thoughts and emotions they engage with rather then to automatically react to all experiences (Lakey, et al., 2007). This results in an erosion of the automatic appraisal processes that cultivate damaging emotions.

Hofmann and Asmundson (2008) believe that mindfulness changes the relation one has with the present moment they are experiencing, making it a response-focused emotion-regulation strategy. This is due to the fact that it involves learning to accept emotions, thoughts and feelings as they arise, rather than adopting a reactive stance (Brown, et al., 2007). From this, it could be hypothesized that mindfulness involves altering one's relationship to current life events by learning to accept, rather than reflexively react to every thought and emotion. This is in stark contrast to interventions such as cognitive behavioral therapy, which attempt to restructure the content of both emotional and cognitive events framing them in a more positive light. In essence, mindfulness may be viewed as process level cognitive reappraisal because it does not involve changing the content of thoughts or emotions (Chambers, et al., 2009). Instead, mindfulness changes the overall relationship a person has with their thoughts and emotions (i.e. their appraisals) in a general sense (Siegel et al., 2007). By cultivating non-elaborative awareness, the very act of remodeling, ascribing and predicting (traditional appraisal) which has been implicated to play a key role in the emotion-generative process, may be terminated (Campos, Ehmann, Altman, Lucas, Birmaher, Lorenzo, Ivengar, & Brent, 2004). From a mindfulness perspective, a thought such as "I am unlovable" would first be noticed as an event that was occurring in the mind and labeled something in a non-judgmental way, such as 'thinking'. This thought would be viewed as merely this, not an accurate depiction of reality that defines the self (Kohlenberg, Hayes, & Tsai, 1993). This example illustrates how mindfulness can changes ones attitude and relationship towards their thoughts and feelings, giving them much less power. The person chooses not to except this thought at face value by avoiding the use of emotional reasoning i.e. 'I feel it, therefore it must be true' (Burns, 1989).

Converse to Hofmann and Asmundson (2008)'s perspective that mindfulness is a response focused emotion regulation strategy, Brown and colleagues (2007) view mindfulness as an antecedent-focused emotion regulation strategy. This is due to the fact that it utilizes attentional deployment, as people learn to focus their attention in a particular way and to detach themselves from distressing cognitions and feelings (Lutz, 2008). Accordingly, specific facets of mindfulness such as meditation, improve attentional focus (an antecedent-emotion-regulation strategy), (Slagter, Lutz, Greischar, Nieuwenhuis, & Davidson, 2009), decrease the amount of rumination (RamelGoldin, Carmona, & McQuaid, 2004), improve orientation to a spatial cue (Jha, Krompinger, & Baime, 2007) and improve self-focused attention (Goldin, Wiveka, & Gross, 2009). Thus, from an emotion regulation standpoint mindfulness can be viewed as both an antecedent and a response focused emotion regulation strategy.

Mindfulness involves a greater propensity towards being receptive of both internal and external cues from the environment (Brown & Ryan, 2004). Participants choose to experience each moment rather than filtering it through past memories, previously held beliefs or any other forms of cognitive distortions (Brown et al., 2007). Because mindfulness promotes a more objective way of responding to information, even stressful situations can be viewed in more neutral terms (Weinstein, et al., 2009). Mindfulness fosters a desensitization, which leads to a reduction in emotional responsiveness to stimuli perceived to be threatening (Arch & Craske, 2006). As such, mindfulness may lead to cognitive change by attenuating the negative appraisals of stressful events (Broderick, 2005). Consequently, mindfulness may promote adaptive mental health by decreasing the natural tendency one has to perceive a situation as threatening which elicits a stress response (Weinstein, et al., 2009).

MINDFULNESS INTERVENTION STUDIES AND THEIR RELATIVE IMPACT ON WELL-BEING

Mindfulness is generally taught to people in a didactic, stepwise process that involves "a) learning to pay attention to current moment experience with an accepting attitude b) identifying when attention has turned to maladaptive thought patterns (such as rumination about work problems) c) remembering to reorient to the present moment without placing judgment on the last distraction and d) ceasing to practice when these skills become integrated into daily life" (Bishop et al., 2004, p. 231).

Mindfulness has been shown to have a salutary impact on a variety of health issues. It has been proven to be effective in treating body-image problems (Stewart, 2004), improving mood and wellbeing in individuals with cancer, psychological distress (Brown & Ryan, 2003), psychosis (Gaudiano & Herbert, 2006), anxiety (Evans et al., 2008; Kabat-Zinn, 1990), trauma (Ogden, Minton, & Pain, 2006), nicotine dependence (Gifford Hayes, & Strosahl, 2004), neuroticism (Brown & Ryan, 2003), eating disorders (Fairburn, Cooper, & Shafran, 2003), and treating depression (Ma & Teasdale, 2004) residual depressive symptoms (Kingston, Dooley, Bates, Lawlor, & Malone, 2007). Mindfulness interventions have also had success treating physical ailments such as chronic pain (Kabat-Zinn, 1982), fibromyalgia (Kaplan, Goldenberg, & Galvin-Nadeau, 1993) and psoriasis (Kabat-Zinn, Wheeler, Skillings, Scharf, Cropley, Hosmer, Bernhard,1998). Recent research has also indicated the potential use of mindfulness in treating chronic physical health problems in youth populations (Thompson & Gauntlett-Gilbert, 2008).

In nonclinical populations, mindfulness interventions have been linked to decreased anxiety (Shapiro, Schwartz, & Bonner, 1998), enhanced romantic relationships (Cordova & Jacobson, 1993), increased immune system functioning (Davidson et al., 2003), increased working memory (Chambers et al., 2008), increased melatonin levels (Massion, Teas, Hebert, Wertheimer, & Kabat-Zinn, 1995), decreased negative self-focused attention (Murphy, 1995) and decreased ego-defensive responsively under threat (Brown, Ryan, Creswell, & Niemiec, 2008). In addition, mindfulness may be an important factor in the reduction of rumination (Kumar, Feltman, & Hayes, 2008) and may also be linked to a secure attachment style (Shaver, Lavy, Saron, & Mikulincer, 2007). Mindfulness has also been shown to decrease mood disturbance, anxiety and other indicators of psychological dysfunction (Shapiro, et al., 2007). These findings were supported by the work of Brown and Ryan (2003) who determined that both state and trait mindfulness was predictive of negative emotions over a 2 week and 3 time period in a divergent sample of both students and adult community members. In line with these findings, a more recent study by Shapiro and colleagues (2007) determined that mindfulness training lead to a reduction in worry, anxiety, and stress. This study had a sample of 54 participants who completed an intensive 8-week MBSR intervention. A strength of this study was the fact that these students did not receive extra credit for their participation, thus their motives were impartial. A recent study by Weinstein and colleagues (2009) determined that individuals who rated high in mindfulness used avoidant coping strategies less frequently, as they chose approach coping as a more frequent strategy. A strength of this study was the fact that it employed a longitudinal design and also the fact that it involved keeping a daily diary rather than being retrospective. Adding to the credibility of the study was the fact that it utilized a naturalistic setting to establish the link between mindfulness, well-being and stress processes. A weakness of this study was the fact that is utilized a homogenous sample made up exclusively of undergraduates. A further flaw was the fact that it did not employ a control group; therefore causality could not be inferred.

In clinical populations, numerous studies have shown the effectiveness of psychological interventions that have incorporated mindfulness as an integral part of their treatment. For example, mindfulness training has been successful in treating highly resistant depression (people suffering from more than 3 bouts of clinical depression) (Segal, et al.,, 2002; Teasdale et al., 2000). In a study by Teasdale and colleagues (2000), the risk of relapse for people with resistant depression was reduced by nearly half. The authors of this study speculate that the reason that mindfulness is successful in treating chronic depression is because it may alter the over-general autobiographical memory characterized by this debilitating mental illness (Kuyken & Brewin, 1995).

MINDFULNESS AS A TREATMENT: A CRITICAL REVIEW

A robust meta-analysis of 22 mindfulness studies employing either MBCT or MBSR by Baer (2003) looked at a diverse sample of studies that targeted various issues. These issues included psychological and physical problems such as depression, psoriasis, binge eating, fibromyalgia, anxiety, chronic pain, cancer related stress and psychological and medical functioning among non-depressed populations. The results of this review determined that mindfulness treatment programs have been linked to substantial improvements in psychological wellbeing. Although Baer (2003) found a significant treatment effect, she was critical of the fact that most of the mindfulness studies she reviewed were poorly designed (i.e. small sample sizes, homogenous samples, no control groups). The following year, Grossman, Niemann, Schmidt, & Walach, (2004) introduced a meta-analysis of 20 mindfulness-based stress-reduction studies that were both observational and controlled. This meta-analysis was exhaustive, covering a wide variety of both non-clinical and clinical populations that suffered from both psychological and physical issues. This meta-analysis, determined that both uncontrolled and controlled studies are effective, with comparable effect sizes of 0.5 (medium effect-size) according to Cohen's (1988) guidelines. The authors of this study concluded that mindfulness improves psychological wellbeing and may help to facilitate in recovery from mental health issues.

Although the aforesaid meta-analysis (Baer, 2003; Grossman, et al., 2004) determined that mindfulness treatment programs had a salutary impact on wellbeing, a more recent review of mindfulness by Toneatto and Nguyen (2007), found otherwise. This review had a stringent inclusion criteria, only including controlled studies of MBSR, investigating the following variables: the relative impact on depression and anxiety following the treatment program, length of follow-up, measurement of compliance with MBSR instructions, type of clinical population studied and type of control group utilized. Researchers concluded that mindfulness has an ambiguous effect on both anxiety and depression and that it cannot be used reliably to treat either depression or anxiety. This finding garnered support from Bishop (2002) who also investigated the existing literature on MBSR. Bishop's (2002) comprehensive review concurred with the latter studies, determining that there was a shortage of studies that employed a sound methodology. Therefore, he would not give his endorsement of mindfulness training as a therapy. He did however note that it needed to be investigated further with more adept studies, as it showed some potential. Resultantly, more conclusive research is required to resolve these contrary findings.

CONCLUSION

In conclusion, although preliminary findings are promising, mindfulness research has been plagued by many problems. Small sample sizes, a lack of controlled studies, high drop out rates and the lack of long-term follow-ups which have been detrimental to achieving conclusive answers. Consequently, a more rigorous scientific approach is needed when investigating this construct in the future in order to unlock the true salutary potential of the mindfulness construct, which in practice, seems to exert a strong positive influence on both health and well-being (Kabat-Zinn 1982; Kabat-Zinn et al., 1992; Miller Fletcher &Kabat-Zinn 1995).

REFERENCES

Arch, J. J. &Craske, M. G. (2006). Mechanisms of mindfulness: Emotion regulation following a focused breathing induction. *Behaviour Research and Therapy*, *44*, 1849-1858.

Baer, R.A. (2003). Mindfulness training as a clinical intervention: A conceptual and empirical review. *Clinical Psychology: Science and Practice*, *10*, 125-143.

Baer, R.A., Smith, G.T. & Allen, K.B. (2004). Assessment of mindfulness by report. The Kentucky Inventory of Mindfulness Skills. *Assessment*, *11*, 191-206.

Baer, R. A., Hopkins, J., Krietemeyer, J., Smith, G. T. & Toney, L. (2006). Using self-Report assessment methods to explore facets of mindfulness. *Assessment*, *13*, 27-45.

Begley, S. (2007). *Train your mind, change your brain: How a new science reveals our extraordinary potential to transform ourselves.* New York: Random House

Bishop, S.R., Lau, M., Shapiro, S., Carlson, L., Anderson, N.D. & Carmody J. (2004). Mindfulness: A proposed operational definition. *Clinical Psychology: Science and Practice*, *11*, 230-241.

Bishop, S. R. (2002). What do we really know about mindfulness-based stress reduction? *Psychosomatic Medicine*, *64*, 71–84.

Broderick, K.L. (2005). Mindfulness and coping with dysphoric mood: Contrasts with rumination and distraction. *Cognitive Therapy and Research*, *29*, 501-510.

Brown, K.W., Ryan, R.M., Creswell, J. D. & Niemiec, C.P. (2008). Beyond me: mindful responses to social threat. In. H.A. Wayment & J.J. Bauer (Eds.), *Transcending self-interest: Psychological explorations of the quiet ego.* (75-84). Washington, DC: American Psychological Association.

Brown. K. W. & Ryan, R. M. (2003). The benefits of being present: Mindfulness and its role in psychological well-being. *Journal of Personality and Social Psychology*, *84*, 822-848.

Brown, K. W. & Ryan, R. M. (2004). Perils and promise in defining and measuring mindfulness: Observations from experience. *Clinical Psychology: Science and Practice, 11*, 242-248.

Brown, K. W., Ryan, R. M. & Creswell, J. D. (2007). Mindfulness: Theoretical foundations and evidence for its salutary effects. *Psychological Inquiry, 18*, 211-237.

Buchheld, N., Grossman, P. & Walach, H. (2001). Measuring mindfulness in insight meditation (Vipassana) and meditation-based psycho- therapy: The development of the Freiburg Mindfulness Inventory (FMI). *Journal for Meditation and Meditation Research, 1*, 11-34.

Burns, D. (1989). *The Feeling Good Handbook.* New York: William Morrow and Company, Inc.

Campo, J. V., Bridge, J., Ehmann, M., Altman, S., Lucas, A., Birmaher, B., Di Lorenzo, C., Ivengar, S. & Brent, D. A. (2004). Recurrent abdominal pain, anxiety, and depression in primary care. *Pediatrics, 113*, 817-824.

Carlson, L.E., Speca, M., Kamala, D.P. &Goodey, E. (2004). Mindfulness-based stress reduction in relation to quality of life, mood, symptoms of stress and levels of cortisol, dehydroepiandrosterone sulfate (DHEAS) and melatonin in breast and prostate cancer outpatients. *Psychoneuroendocrinology, 29*, 448-474.

Chadwick, P., Hember, M., Mead, S., Lilley, B. & Dagnan, D. (2005). Responding mindfully to unpleasant thoughts and images: Reliability and validity of the Mindfulness Questionnaire. Unpublished manuscript.

Chambers, R., Lo, B. C. Y. & Allen, N. B. (2008). The impact of intensive mindfulness training on attentional control, cognitive style, and affect. *Cognitive Therapy and Research, 32*, 303-322.

Chambers, R., Gullone, E. & Allen, N.B. (2009). Mindful emotion regulation: An integrative review. *Clinical Psychology Review, 29*, 560-572.

Chiesa, A. & Serrettia A. (2009). Mindfulness-based stress reduction for stress management in healthy people: A review and meta-analysis. *Journal of Alternative Complementary Medicine, 15*, 593-600.

Cohen, J. (1988). *Statistical power analysis for the behavioral sciences.* (2nd ed.). Hillsdale, New Jersey: Erlbaum.

Cordova, J.V. & Jacobson, N.S. (1993). Couples distress. In D.H. Barlow (Ed.), *Clinical Handbook of Psychological Disorders: A step-by-step treatment manual* (2nd ed., 481-512). New York: Plenum.

Davidson, R.J., Kabat-Zinn, J., Schumacher, J., Rosenkranz, M., Muller D. & Santorelli, S.F. (2003). Alterations in brain and immune function produced by mindfulness meditation, *Psychosomatic Medicine, 65*, 564-570.

Dimidjian, S. & Linehan, M. M. (2003a). Defining an agenda for future research on the clinical application of mindfulness practice. *Clinical Psychology: Science and Practice, 10*, 166-171.

Deyo M., Wilson K.A., Ong J. & Koopman C. (2009). Mindfulness and rumination: Does mindfulness training lead to reductions in the ruminative thinking associated with depression? *Explore, 5*, 265-71.

Epstein, M. (1995). *Thoughts without a thinker: Psychotherapy from a Buddhist perspective.* New York: Basic Books.

Fairburn, C.G., Cooper Z. & Shafran, R. (2003). Cognitive behaviour therapy for eating disorders: A "transdiagnostic" theory and treatment. *Behaviour Research and Therapy*, *41*, 509-528.

Feldman, G. C., Hayes, A. M., Kumar, S. M. &Greeson, J. M. (2004). Development, factor structure, and initial validation of the Cognitive and Affective Mindfulness Scale. Unpublished manuscript.

Feltman, R., Robinson, M. D. & Ode, S. (2009). Mindfulness as a moderator of neuroticism–outcome relations: A self-regulation perspective. *Journal of Research in Personality*, *43*, 953–961.

Follette, V., Palm, K.M. & Pearson, A.N. (2006). Mindfulness and trauma: Implications for treatment. *Journal of Rational-Emotive & Cognitive-Behavior Therapy*, *24*(1), 45-61.

Germer, C. K. (2005). Mindfulness: What is it: What does it matter? In C. K. Germer, R. D. Siegel, & P. R. Fulton (Eds.), *Mindfulness and psychotherapy*. New York: Guilford Press.

Gifford, E.V., Kohlenberg, B.S., Hayes, S.C., Antonuccio, D.O., Piasecki M.M. & Rasmussen-Hall, M.L. (2004). Acceptance-based treatment for smoking cessation. *Behavior Therapy*, *35*, 689-705.

Goleman, D. (1971). Meditation as meta-therapy: Hypothesis toward a proposed fifth state of consciousness', *Biofeedback and Self Control* (453-508). Chicago: Atdine Publishing Company.

Goldin, P., Wiveka, R. & Gross, J. (2009). Mindfulness meditation training and self-referential processing in social anxiety disorder: Behavioral and neural effects. *Journal of Cognitive Psychotherapy*, *23*, 242-257.

Grossman, P., Niemann, L., Schmidt, S. & Walach, H. (2004). Mindfulness-based stress reduction and health benefits. A meta-analysis. *Journal of Psychosomatic Research*, *57*, 35-43.

Hayes, S. C. & Wilson, K. G. (1994). Acceptance and commitment therapy: Altering the verbal support for experiential avoidance. *The Behavior Analyst*, *17*, 289-303.

Hayes, S. C., Wilson, K. W., Gifford, E. V., Follette, V. M. & Strosahl, K. (1996). Experiential avoidance and behavioral disorders: A functional dimensional approach to diagnosis and treatment. *Journal of Consulting and Clinical Psychology*, *64*, 1152-1168.

Hayes, S. (2003). Mindfulness: Method and process. *Clinical Psychology: Science and Practice*, *10*, 161-165.

Hayes, A.M. & Feldman, G. (2004). Clarifying the construct of mindfulness in the context of emotion regulation and the process of change in therapy. *Clinical Psychology Science Practice*, *11*, 255-262.

Jha, A.P., Krompinger, J.& Baime, M.J. (2007). Mindfulness training modifies subsystems of attention. *Cognitive, Affective, & Behavioral Neuroscience*, *7*, 109-119.

Kabat-Zinn, J. (1982). An outpatient program in behavioral medicine for chronic pain patients based on the practice of mindfulness meditation: Theoretical considerations and preliminary results. *General Hospital Psychiatry*, *4*, 33-47.

Kabat-Zinn, J., Lipworth, L.& Burney, R. (1985). The clinical use of mindfulness meditation for the self-regulation of chronic pain. *Journal of Behavioural Medicine*, *8*,163-190.

Kabat-Zinn, J. (1990). Full catastrophe living: Using the wisdom of your body and mind to face stress, pain, and illness. NewYork: Delacorte.

Kabat-Zinn, J., Massion, A.O., Kristeller, J., Peterson, L.G., Fletcher, K., Pbert, L., Linderking, W. & Santorelli, S.F. (1992). Effectiveness of a meditation-based stress reduction program in the treatment of anxiety disorders. *American Journal of Psychiatry, 149,* 936-943.

Kabat-Zinn, J. (1993). Mindfulness meditation: Health benefits of an ancient Buddhist practice. In Goleman D. and Gurin J. (Eds.), *Mind/Body Medicine.* Yonkers, New York: Consumer Reports Books.

Kabat-Zinn, J. (2003). Mindfulness-based interventions in context: Past, present, and future. *Clinical Psychology: Science and Practice, 10,* 144-156.

Kabat-Zinn, J. Wheeler, E., Light, T., Skillings, A., Scharf, M.J., Cropley, T.G., Hosmer, D. & Bernhard, J.D. (1998). Influence of a mindfulness meditation-based stress reduction intervention on rates of skin clearing in patients with moderate to severe psoriasis undergoing phototherapy (UVB) and photochemotherapy (PUVA). *Psychosomatic Medicine, 60,* 625-632.

Kaplan, K.H., Goldenberg, D.L. & Galvin-Nadeau, M. (1993). The impact of a meditation-based stress reduction program on fibromyalgia. *General Hospital Psychiatry, 5,* 284-289.

Kingston, T., Dooley, B., Bates, A., Lawlor, E. & Malone, K. (2007). Mindfulness-based cognitive therapy for residual depressive symptoms. *Psychology & Psychotherapy, 80,* 193-203.

Kohlenberg, R.J., Hayes, S. C.& Tsai, M. (1993). Radical behavioral psychotherapy: Two contemporary examples. *Clinical Psychology Review, 13,* 579-592.

Kristeller, J. L. & Hallett, B. (1999). Effects of a meditation-based intervention in the treatment of binge eating. *Journal of Health Psychology,4,* 357-363.

Kumar, S.M., Feldman, G. C.& Hayes, A.M. (2008). Changes in mindfulness and emotion regulation in an exposure-based cognitive therapy for depression. *Cognitive Therapy and Research, 6,* 734-744.

Kuyken, W. &Brewin, C.R. (1995). Autobiographical memory functioning in depression and reports of early abuse. *Journal of Abnormal Psychology, 104,* 585-591.

Kumar, S.M., Feldman, G. C.& Hayes, A.M. (2008). Changes in Mindfulness and Emotion Regulation in an Exposure-Based Cognitive Therapy for Depression. *Cognitive Therapy and Resear*ch, *6,* 734-744.

Kuyken, W. & Brewin, C.R. (1995). Autobiographical memory functioning in depression and reports of early abuse. *Journal of Abnormal Psychology, 104,* 585-591.

Lakey, C.E., Campbell, W.K., Brown, K.W. & Goodie, A.S. (2007). Dispositional mindfulness as a predictor of the severity of gambling outcomes. *Personality and Individual Differences, 43,* 1698-1710.

Langer, E. J. (1989). *Mindfulness. Reading.* MA: Addison-Wesley.

Larsen, R.J. (2000). Towards a Science of Mood Regulation. *Psychological Enquiry, 11,* 129-141.

Lau, M.A.& McMain, S.F. (2005). Integrating mindfulness meditation with cognitive and behavioural therapies: the challenge of combining acceptance- and change-based strategies. *Canadian Journal of Psychiatry, 50,* 863-9.

Linehan, M. M. (1993). *Skills Training Manual For Treatment of Borderline Personality Disorder.* New York: Guilford Press.

Lutz, A., Slagter, H.A., Dunne, J.& Davidson, R.J. (2008). Attention regulation and monitoring in meditation. *Trends in Cognitive Sciences*, *12*, 163-169.

Ma, S.H. & Teasdale, J.D. (2004). Mindfulness-based cognitive therapy for depression: Replication and exploration of differential relapse prevention effects, *Journal of Clinical and Consulting Psychology*, *72*, 31-40.

Massion, A. O., Teas, J., Hebert, J. R., Wertheimer, M. D. & Kabat-Zinn, J. (1995). Meditation, melatonin and breast/prostate cancer: hypothesis and preliminary data. *Medical Hypotheses*, *44*, 39-46.

Mason, O. & Hargreaves, I. (2010). A qualitative study of mindfulness-based cognitive therapy for depression. *British Journal of Medical Psychology*, *74*, 197-212.

Miller, J., Fletcher, K. & Kabat-Zinn, J. (195). Three-year follow-up and clinical implications of a mindfulness-based stress reduction intervention in the treatment of anxiety disorders. *Gen. Hosp. Psychiatry*, *17*, 192-200.

Murphy, R. (1995). The effects of mindfulness meditation vs progressive relaxation training on stress egocentrism anger and impulsiveness among inmates. Dissertation Abstracts International: Section B. *The Sciences & Engineering*, *8*, 3596.

Nolen-Hoeksema, S. (1991). Responses to depression and their effects on the duration of depressive episodes. *Journal of Abnormal Psychology*, *100*, 569-583.

Nolen-Hoeksema, S. (1998). *Abnormal Psychology* (1st Ed). Boston: McGraw-Hill.

Ogden, P., Minton, K. & Pain, C. (2006). Trauma and the body: A sensorimotor approach to psychotherapy. *Clinical Social Work Journal*, *36*(2), 221-223.

Ramel, W., Goldin, P.R., Carmona, P.E. & McQuaid, J.R. (2004). The effects of mindfulness meditation on cognitive processes and affect in patients with past depression. *Cognitive Therapy and Research*, *28*, 433-455.

Robins, C. J., Schmidt, H., III & Linehan, M. M. (2004). Dialectical behavior therapy: Synthesizing radical acceptance with skillful means. In S. C. Hayes, V. M. Follette, & M. M. Linehan (Eds.), *Mindfulness and acceptance: Expanding the cognitive-behavioral tradition* (30–44). New York: Guilford Press.

Safran, J.D. & Segal, Z.V. (1990). *Interpersonal process in cognitive therapy*. New York: Basic Books.

Siegel, D.J. (2007). The mindful brain: *Reflection and attunement in the cultivation of well-being*. New York: W.W. Norton.

Segal, Z., Teasdale, J.& Williams, M. (2002). *Mindfulness-based cognitive therapy for depression*. New York: Guilford Press.

Shapiro, S.L., Schwartz, G.E. & Bonner, G. (1998). Effects of mindfulness-based stress reduction on medical and premedical students. *Journal of Behavioral Medicine*, *21*, 581-599.

Shapiro, S.L., Brown, K.W. & Biegel, G.M. (2007). Teaching self-care to caregivers: Effects of mindfulness-based stress reduction on the mental health of therapists in training. *Training and Education in Professional Psychology*, *1*, 105-115.

Shaver, P., Lavy, S., Saron, C. & Mikulincer, M. (2007). Social foundations of the capacity for mindfulness: An attachment perspective. *Psychological Inquiry*, *18*, 264-271.

Snook, S. (1996). *The friendly fire shootdown over Northern Iraq*. Unpublished doctoral dissertation, Harvard University, Cambridge, MA.

Slagter, H.A., Lutz, A., Greisschar, L.L., Nieuwenhuis, S. & Davidson, R.J. (2009). Theta phase synchrony and conscious target perception: Impact of intensive mental training. *Journal of Cognitive Neuroscience*, *21*, 1536-1549.

Stewart, T. M. (2004). Light on body image treatment: Acceptance through mindfulness. *Behavior Modification*, *28*, 783-811.

Teasdale, J.D., Segal, Z.V., Williams, J.M.G., Ridgeway, V., Soulsby, J. & Lau, M. (2000). Prevention of relapse/recurrence in major depression by mindfulness-based cognitive therapy. *Journal of Consulting and Clinical Psychology*, *68*, 615-623.

Teasdale, J.D., Segal, Z. & Williams, M.G. (1995). How does cognitive therapy prevent depressive relapse and why should attentional control (mindfulness) training help? *Behaviour Research and Therapy*, *33*, 25-39.

Teasdale, J.D. (1999). Metacognition, mindfulness and the modification of mood disorders. *Clinical Psychology & Psychotherapy*, *6*, 146-155.

Thompson, M. & Gauntlett-Gilbert, J. (2008). Mindfulness with children and adolescents: Effective clinical application. *Clinical Child Psychology and Psychiatry*, *13*, 395-407.

Toneatto, T. & Nguyen, L. (2007). Does mindfulness meditation improve anxiety and mood symptoms? A review of the controlled research. *Canadian Journal of Psychiatry*, *52*, 260-266.

Weinstein, N., Brown, K. W.& Ryan, R. M. (2009). A multi-method examination of the effects of mindfulness on stress attribution, coping, and emotional well-being. *Journal of Research in Personality*, *43*, 374-385.

Wells, A. &Sembi, S. (2004). Metacognitive therapy for PTSD: A preliminary investigation of a new brief treatment. *Journal of Behavior Therapy and Experimental Psychiatry*, *35*, 307-318.

Wegner, D.M. (1994). Ironic processes of mental control.*Psychological Review*, *101*, 34-52.

Vøllestad, J., Sivertsen, B. & Nielsen, G.H. (2011). Mindfulness-based stress reduction for patients with anxiety disorders: Evaluation in a randomized controlled trial. *Behaviour Research Therapy*,*49*, 281-288.

In: Handbook of Psychology of Emotions
Editors: C. Mohiyeddini, M. Eysenck and S. Bauer

ISBN: 978-1-62808-053-7
© 2013 Nova Science Publishers, Inc.

Chapter 21

EMOTIONS AND CREATIVITY[*]

Jessica D. Hoffmann
Case Western Reserve University

ABSTRACT

Emotions and moods are inextricably linked to creative potential and creative production. This chapter begins by outlining the psychological definitions of creativity and detailing common ways of measuring creativity. The differential impacts of positive and negative moods on creativity are reviewed. The majority of empirical studies to date suggest that positive feelings can enhance creativity; theoretical models such as the broaden-and-build model and the dopaminergic theory of positive affect support the empirical findings by suggesting that positive mood leads to greater cognitive flexibility and access to more ideas. A smaller, but significant group of studies have suggested that negative moods can also enhance creativity in some circumstances. Theories have also been put forth to explain these findings, including the mood-as-input model and the feelings-as-information theory which both suggest in part that people in a negative mood may persist longer at a task and reach more original solutions to problems. The chapter also discusses other factors that might impact the creativity-mood relationship: the duration and intensity of the affective state, the level of emotional activation, and the type of creative task are all explored. The relationships between affective disorders and creativity are reviewed, most notably the enhancing effects of mania on creative production. It is noted that while the quantity of ideas produced during mania may be high, the quality of the ideas may be low. Finally, a limited number of studies have explored the effects of creative production of subsequent mood states, suggesting both benefits and risks of a creative lifestyle. Artists are often reinforced for their emotionality and most aspiring artists experience much frustration, which can lead to substance abuse or affect regulation problems. Alternatively, true creative achievement may lead to pride or elation, and intrinsic motivation to embark of other creative endeavors, making the creative process itself enjoyable.

---

[*] Corresponding author: Jad86@case.edu.

INTRODUCTION

Creativity and emotion are inextricably linked. Creative activity is typically an affectively charged event in which cognitive processes and emotional experiences co-occur (Amabile, Barsade, Mueller & Staw, 2005). Anecdotes about mental illnesses, particularly mania and depression, among our most eminent rock stars, painters and authors abound in our pop culture. Additionally, creative problem-solving and innovation are highly valued skills in many industries beyond the arts, including engineering, advertising, and medicine. Consequently, much creativity research explores the factors impacting creativity and ways of enhancing people's creative production. Mood stands out as one of the least disputed predictors of creativity (Mumford, 2003) and therefore a great deal of research has been devoted to examining the impact of various affective states on people's creative production.

Overall, there is general agreement that tasks of creative thinking are mood sensitive; however, how specific emotions effect creativity is an ongoing debate (Davis, 2009). Additionally, a wide range of mediators and moderators between emotion and creativity have been proposed, including motivation, the type of creative task, the length and intensity of one's emotional state and other contextual variables. Furthermore, the mood-creativity relationship is bidirectional, and therefore other theorists have chosen to explore the impact of creativity on subsequent emotional states, for example the satisfaction of completing a masterpiece. Observation of the most creative people in society suggest both possible emotional benefits and dangers of creative thought, creative problem-solving and living a creative lifestyle (Feist, 1999).

The purpose of the current chapter is to provide a review of the literature examining the many links between emotions and creativity. Theories addressing why and how emotions can affect creativity are discussed, as well as the ways in which creative processes can consequently affect one's emotions. Empirical research linking creativity and emotions is a relatively young field and though little consensus has been achieved so far, findings to date and their implications are discussed. Mixed findings, contradictory results and recent alternative theories are also presented. A brief review of how affective disorders and creativity are related is included to shed additional light on the mood-creativity relationship at the extreme ends of the emotional continuum. Implications for enhancing creativity and directions for future research in this area are also discussed.

CREATIVITY DEFINED

Creativity is generally defined as the production of novel and useful ideas or solutions to problems (Amabile et al., 2005), or the creation of something new and unusual meant to improve one's effective functioning (Amabile, 1983; Eysenck, 1993; Runco, 2004). Amabile (1983) discusses the social psychology of creativity, pointing out that for something to be deemed new and useful, a social context is required in which the creative product can be judged. Amabile (1983) further notes, that while this process is subjective, creativity is typically something that people can recognize and often agree on.

Creativity research distinguishes between the creative process and the creative product, though the term 'creativity' can refer to both the process and the outcome (Amabile, 1983;

Sternberg, 1988a; Weisberg, 1988). Amabile (1983) identifies a componential framework for creativity with three major components. For creative performance one must have (1) domain relevant skills including knowledge, technical skill and talent, (2) creativity-relevant skills including appropriate cognitive style, knowledge for generating novel ideas, and a conducive work style, and (3) task motivation which includes attitude toward the task and motivation, depending on initial intrinsic motivation toward the task, the presence or absence of extrinsic constraints, and the cognitive ability to minimize any extrinsic constraints (see Figure 1). Through an examination of this model, one can begin to see the many avenues by which particular emotions or mood states may be able to impact one's creativity.

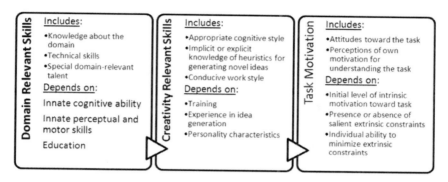

Figure 1. Amabile (1983) Components of creative performance.

Creative performance can take many forms and therefore creativity has been operationalized in a variety of ways. Creativity tasks are often divided into three types: (1) divergent thinking and idea generation tasks, (2) insight tasks, and (3) creative performance tasks. Divergent thinking tasks are open-ended and designed to measure one's ability to generate multiple solutions to a problem (Mumford, 2001). For example, one item on an Alternate Uses Test (Wallach & Kogan, 1965) requires participants to name as many uses as they can think of for a newspaper. Possible answers might include: to read, for paper maché, to protect the table while painting, or to make a paper airplane. Performance on such divergent thinking tasks is typically measured in up to four ways: fluency, flexibility, originality and elaboration. Fluency refers to the number of non-redundant ideas generated, while flexibility refers to the number of distinct categories, approaches or sets that were used. For example, a person who uses a key to lock a house and to lock a car would be considered less flexible than someone who said to lock a house and to start the engine of the car. Originality refers to the uncommonness or infrequency of an idea, and elaboration refers to the detail included in the response.

Distinct from divergent thinking tasks which are open-ended and have many possible solutions, insight tasks, also called eureka tasks, only have a single correct solution (Simonton, 2003). Two well-known insight tasks are Duncker's (1945) candle problem and Mednick's (1962) Remote Associates Test (RAT). The candle problem gives participants a candle, a book of matches and a box of tacks and asks the participant to attach the candle to the wall so that wax will not drip on the table or floor. The correct solution requires people to realize that the tack box can be attached to the wall as a candle holder thus requiring a moment of insight in which one item can be used as something else. The RAT (Mednick, 1962) asks individuals to generate a fourth word that relates to three given words, requiring flexible thinking about each words' potential meanings. For example, given the words, "credit", "playing", and "report", one would generate the correct answer "card". Mednick emphasized the importance that the links be strictly associative such that a subject must use creative thinking rather than logic, concept-formation or problem-solving to reach the correct solution.

The third broad category of measurable creative production is for problems where performance on a particular task is then judged by others' evaluations and impressions. Artwork, poetry, storytelling and architecture, among many other forms of creativity fall within this category. Research in this area has spanned a wide range of topics. Amabile (1985) had independent judges rate a sample of Haikus on a scale of creativity relative to each other. Creativity within the workplace has examined supervisor and peer ratings of worker's creative performance (George & Zhou, 2002). Again, while such ratings are subjective, it appears that people are quite good at recognizing creativity. Several studies examining children's storytelling ability as a measure of creativity found high degrees of inter-rater reliability despite minimal scoring guidelines (Hennessey & Amabile, 1988; Hoffmann & Russ, 2012a). Distinguishing between the types of creativity is important for the study of the emotion-creativity link. It may be that the processes involved in the various types of creative performance are differentially affected by emotional states. Further discussion of task differences is presented below.

When thinking about how people will perform on creativity tasks, it is important to remember that a good portion of creativity measures allow for a range of scores. While it is a common assumption that a person or product is either creative or not, psychological inquiry does not view creativity as a dichotomous variable. Instead, creativity is assumed to be continuous and dimensional (Amabile, 1983). Thus individual differences in creativity should be thought of across a spectrum. Furthermore, Eysenck (1993) distinguishes between the trait of creativity which is supposed to be normally distributed, with a mean value characteristic of the "average person", and creativity as a unique achievement which may be distributed more like a Poissonian curve. In addition, individual differences in creativity are often found to be independent of intelligence (e.g. Russ, 2004; Hoffmann & Russ, 2012b).

When examining creativity as an individual trait, it is helpful to consider associative theory and the associative hierarchy (Mednick, 1962). Associative theory is an approach to creative thinking that emphasizes the process of bringing together disparate elements into new combinations for a useful purpose. Associative theory often refers to an individual's associative hierarchy (see Figure 2), which depicts the ways in which different individuals go about producing associations for a problem. For example, if asked to produce associations to the word "table" a person with a flatter hierarchy will first give the common associations, such as "dinner" or "chair", but would then continue on to less common associations like "ping pong". In contrast, a person with a steeper associative hierarchy will also give "dinner" but will then show a steeper decline in responses resulting in fewer uncommon associations. The person with the flatter hierarchy is said to be more creative, producing not only more total solutions but more original ones. Two implications result from this theory. First, that most people will give the common answers first, and thus more creative ideas tend to come later in the thinking process. Second, that the more creative individual's mind has more ideas connected to each other but with weaker associations allowing for broader thinking. Both theory and research support the notion that affect and mood are robust variables for influencing the range of associations, the gradient of the associative hierarchy, and consequently one's creative potential.

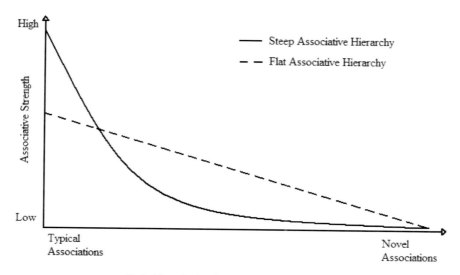

Figure 2. Possible associative hierarchies according to Mednick's associative theory.

CREATIVITY AND EMOTION

The relationship between affect and creativity has received a lot of attention in recent research. Mumford (2003) singled out mood-creativity research as one of particular importance within the field of creativity. Historically creativity research has taken an information-processing perspective, focusing mostly on strategies and heuristics. More contemporary research has shown an increased examination of the impact of affective states on cognition and therefore on creative thinking (Kaufmann, 2003). This research has looked at both the stimulating and inhibiting effects of different emotional states on creativity. In fact, some research suggests that different emotions may trigger differences in information processing style yielding different performances even on the same creative task (Forgas, 2000; Schwarz, 2000). Understanding the impact of emotional states on creativity is not only important for the psychological understanding of creativity, but can also be of practical importance to the success of many workers and organizations within which creativity and innovation are vital (Amabile, 1996; George & Zhou, 2002). A few of the prominent theories addressing the impact of emotions on creativity are discussed below.

Simonton (1999) proposes an evolutionary theory of creative thinking that is particularly useful when considering the relationship between affect and creative thought. Simonton suggests two relevant processes: variation and selection. The process of variation contributes to idea novelty, while selection ensures the usefulness of the ideas. Simonton emphasized that variation is not random but rather guided by one's existing knowledge which can be recombined in new ways. Furthermore, the probability of creating novel ideas is directly linked to how many cognitive elements one has available. This means that the more relevant knowledge one has about a problem, the more possibilities there are for idea generation. Similar to Mednick's associative theory, Simonton's theory implies that the sheer number of ideas one can create is related to the likelihood that some of those ideas will be novel. Simonton maintains that anything that increases variability is therefore likely to increase the probability of creativity, and that affect is one such source of variation.

Idea generation is not the only step of the creative process that emotions can influence. Typically within the creative process, one must first identify or recognize a problem that they feel compelled to address or resolve. Radford (2004) describes how tension, a form of emotional discomfort, arises when one identifies a problem or dissonance. For some people this emotional state of tension may lead to action, possibly taking the form of creative problem solving or innovation. Tension can therefore serve as the impetus to creative development, both in terms of scientific theory or invention, as well as artistic production. Some artists in fact seek to deliberately manufacture dissonances in order to challenge their thinking and produce something both novel and useful (Radford, 2004).

As summarized by Russ and Dillon (2010) psychoanalytic theory also links affect and creativity. Primary process thinking is drive-laden oral, aggressive and libidinal content. This mode of thinking, which is heavily affect-laden and not subject to logic, allows for ideas to be easily interchangeable, and for attention to be widely and flexibly distributed. Thus individuals who are more comfortable with primary process ideation, should be able to conduct broader searches for associations, resulting in flatter associative hierarchies. Murray and Russ (1981) administered the RAT and Rorschach to college students. Using Holt's (1970) primary process measure to score the Rorschach, the authors found that the Adaptive Regression score which measures both primary process content and the control of that content significantly positively related to the RAT. It seems therefore that the type of creativity required for the RAT was a two-step process: the first being the generative stage in which access to affect-laden thoughts was crucial, and the second being an evaluative stage in which the best answer was chosen. This observation is a parallel conclusion to that drawn by Simonton (1999) regarding variation and selection, as discussed previously.

Mood-creativity theory also addresses the impact of creativity on subsequent emotional states. Most commonly research has explored how one's emotions impact one's creativity; however, creative performance and success is also capable of affecting one's mood as a consequence. Radford (2004) states that the subsequent reconciliation of a tension state through creative production is typically emotionally charged as well, as one feels satisfaction during the creative process and in completion of a creative product. The study of the temporal dynamics between creativity and emotion continues to become more nuanced, including examination of the duration of a mood state, the duration of the creative process, or any lag time between a mood-induction and the creative task. Additionally, affect and creativity may occur simultaneously, discussed in more detail below.

POSITIVE AFFECT AND CREATIVITY

While the general link between creativity and emotion is largely accepted, theorists have further suggested that creativity may be particularly susceptible to changes in affect compared to other variables (Clore, Schwarz & Conway, 1994), and especially positive affect. Isen

(1999a; 1999b) suggests a cognitive priming explanation. When one is in a positive mood, more positive material is activated from memory. Given that positive material is more abundant, people in a positive mood should have access to a wider range of information and therefore be able to make more diverse connections. Positive affect also leads to less focused thought and more complex thinking, thus increasing the breadth of cognitive elements considered relevant to a problem. Furthermore, positive affect increases cognitive flexibility, meaning that more disparate ideas become more likely to be associated. The more ideas and associations one can make, the more likely that some will be creative (Mednick, 1962; Simonton, 1999)

Isen and colleagues have conducted a series of studies in which positive affect induction has resulted in changes in information processing associated with creativity, supporting the cognitive priming theory. Isen and Daubman (1984) performed a series of mood induction studies in which mild states of happiness were induced using either a free gift or a comedic film, while controls watched a neutral film, and one group watched a negative film to induce negative affect. Participants were then asked to complete a category inclusion task rating how prototypical items are to a particular category. For example, how prototypical are the words "bus" and "camel" to the category "vehicle"? In this task, higher ratings for the weak exemplar (camel) would indicate a person is using broader cognitive categories which would lead to greater cognitive flexibility. Another sample was asked to place a set of 14 color chips into categories, making as many categories as they wanted. Isen and Daubman (1984) showed that participants in the mild positive mood induction groups gave higher prototypicality ratings, and placed the color chips into more inclusive categories, meaning they used broader and more inclusive thinking compared to controls. While categorization is not a direct measure of creativity, the authors suggest that these findings lend support for the hypothesis that when people are experiencing positive affect they tend to see things are more related, relevant and interconnected which should enhance creativity as well.

Additional studies conducted by Isen and colleagues (Isen, Daubman & Nowicki, 1987; Isen, Labroo & Durlach, 2004; Isen, Johnson, Mertz & Robinson, 1985) have resulted in empirical support for the creativity enhancing effects of positive affect. Isen, Daubman & Nowicki (1987) have shown that positive mood can facilitate performance on creative problem-solving ability. In a series of studies, the authors found that positive affect induction resulted in people giving more unusual first-associates to neutral words than people in control conditions. In an additional study, when word type was varied (positive, neutral or negative), the associates given to the positive words were found to be more unusual and diverse than the associates given for the neutral or negative words. These results are interesting because contrary to associative theory in which novel ideas typically come later in the process, positive affect induction resulted in unusual first associations. Four additional experiments (Isen, Daubman & Nowicki, 1987), showed that positive affect induction improved performance on both Duncker's (1945) candle task and the Remote Associates Test. The negative affect condition did not produce the same improvements, and a physical exercise condition meant to mimic arousal level without affect also did not lead to improvements in creative performance. A more recent study by Isen, Labroo and Durlach (2004) confirmed that performance on the RAT, and the uncommonness of associates to neutral stimuli were influenced by positive affect.

Other laboratory studies involving mood induction have resulted in similar findings regarding the influence of positive affect on cognitive organization. Abele (1992) induced positive, negative and neutral moods through autobiographical recall and found that participants in the positive mood group showed better performance on an ideational fluency task, suggesting that positive mood increases fluency in divergent thinking. Murray, Sujan, Hirt and Sujan (1990) conducted a series of studies using a sorting task to show that positive mood subjects formed broader categories when identifying similarities among exemplars, and narrower categories when identifying differences. Subjects in the positive mood condition also perceived a greater number of similarities and differences between items, identified more distinct types of similarities and differences, and listed more novel similarities and differences. These effects were found for both positive and neutral stimuli. To explain these results, Hirt, Devers & McCrea (2008) suggest a hedonic contingency theory in which individuals in happy moods are interested in sustaining their mood while sad individuals are interested in mood repair. Thus, happy individuals choose their actions carefully to maintain or improve their mood, while people in sad or neutral moods do not scrutinize tasks in the same way. The authors therefore maintain that happy individuals might deliberately set out to generate more creative responses as a means of making a task more interesting or fun since they are invested in maintaining their positive mood.

The effects of positive affect on broadening one's cognitive organization and therefore augmenting creativity is supported by a variety of theoretical models. Fredrickson's (1998; 2001) broaden-and-build model states that positive emotions broaden one's scope of attention which then increases the number of cognitive elements available, and broaden one's scope of cognition, again increasing the number of cognitive elements considered relevant. Additionally, Bowden (1994) reviewed psychometric studies of cognitive characteristics associated with positive mood, and concluded that a positive state of mind was associated with a tendency toward over-inclusion and loose conceptual boundaries. The dopaminergic theory of positive affect supports the notion that positive mood will facilitate creative problem solving as well (Ashby, Isen & Turken, 1999; Ashby, Valentin & Turken, 2002). This theory states that dopamine levels in the brain mediate many of the effects of positive affect. Dopamine release in the anterior cingulate cortex improves selection of and switching among cognitive sets, and therefore improves creative problem solving.

The effects of positive affect on creativity have also been explored with children. Following Isen et al. (1987), Greene & Noice (1988) induced positive affect in a sample of eighth grade students using compliments and gifts. Participants were asked to complete Duncker's (1945) candle task and were presented with a category and asked to generate as many exemplars as possible. The authors reported that subjects in the positive affect condition generated more exemplars for the categories and more unusual exemplars compared to the neutral affect controls. The positive affect subjects also were more likely to correctly solve the candle problem than neutral controls, suggesting that positive affect promotes creative thinking and problem solving in children similarly to the adult samples reported earlier. In a study examining children's pretend play and creativity, Hoffmann and Russ (2012a) found that the children who expressed more positive affect during unstructured play time also told stories rated to be more likeable, imaginative and creative.

The large body of literature addressing positive affect and creativity makes a strong case for the effects of positive mood on creativity (Benjafield, 1996; Forgas, 2000; Hirt, 1999; Hirt et al., 1996; Isen, 1993, 1999; Isen & Baron, 1991; Shapiro & Weisberg, 1999).The many empirical studies suggest that the effect is quite robust, and can be shown using a wide range of mood induction procedures implemented on a variety of creativity tasks. Ashby et al.

(1999) even concluded, "It is now well recognized that positive affect leads to greater cognitive flexibility and facilitates creative problem solving across a broad range of settings" (p. 530). However, recent inquiry into the effects of negative affect have led to many mixed results prompting researchers to propose additional theoretical models to explain the findings.

NEGATIVE AFFECT AND CREATIVITY

While the major focus of mood induction-creativity research has been on positive emotions, there are also studies suggesting the contributions of negative affect to creativity. Kaufman (2003) has written that the generalization regarding positive mood promoting creativity is premature and Mumford (2003) maintains that the field of creativity and mood research is still new and developing. Empirical evidence is not clear enough to support a broad conclusion regarding positive affect and creativity. Work by Kaufmann and colleagues suggests that the effect of mood on creativity is anything but linear, and contains many paradoxes. Kaufmann and colleagues maintain that the area is more nuanced than once thought (Kaufmann, 2003; Kaufmann & Vosburg, 1997), writing "the research findings...are highly discrepant and do not seem to lead to any kind of straightforward link between mood and creativity" (p.32, Vosburg & Kaufmann, 1999).

For example, on a mental synthesis task, a task in which participants are presented with randomly generated letters to combine into possible configurations, Anderson, Arlett and Tarrant (1995) found that positive mood had a significantly negative effect on performance compared to the neutral mood condition. Isen and Daubman (1984) found borderline significant results for negative affect's influence on the categorization process in the same way as the positive affect induction for two of the four studies in that series. Given this unexpected finding, the authors proposed an early theory for why negative affect might sometimes also enhance creativity. The authors suggested that perhaps a process of affect repair occurs following negative affect induction and that the effort required would result in people using simpler strategies and heuristics just as they would have in a positive affect state. Alternatively, people in a negative mood due to mood induction might choose to focus on positive material to make themselves feel better, again gaining access to the broad associations available from positive affect-laden thought.

Martin, Ward, Achee and Wyer (1993) propose a "mood-as-input" model to describe how negative affect might enhance creativity in normal populations. The model suggests that people use negative mood as a cue suggesting that something is wrong with their situation. This implies that people feeling positive regarding their creative product are likely to stop working, while people experiencing negative affect would be motivated to continue working. Therefore, for some tasks in some situations, the experiencing of negative affect could influence a person's persistence or effort during the creative process (George & Zhou, 2002) while positive affect could indicate that the person had achieved their goal. Further discussion of this theory is presented below exploring how task differences may change optimal affective experiences for producing creative products. With regard to associative theory, the people in negative moods who persist longer on a task might be expected to generate the more novel ideas.

Similarly, Schwarz (1990) proposes a "feelings-as-information" theory where positive and negative moods act as signals that elicit different processing strategies when approaching creative tasks. Positive mood may signal a state of well-being and evoke relaxation, or a more playful approach to creative tasks. Negative mood, in contrast, may signal danger or distress and evoke increased effort and systematic thinking. This theory suggests that both positive and negative emotions might help creativity, but for different types of tasks. Positive feelings that evoke a more playful processing approach would likely be beneficial for creative performance, or divergent thinking. Alternatively, negative mood evoking a more systematic processing approach would likely be beneficial for identifying optimal solutions required by more insight-oriented tasks.

Other researchers have addressed the ways in which negative mood might affect one's motivation and the seriousness with which one approaches the creative task (George & Zhou, 2002; Verhaeghen, Joorman & Khan, 2005). Negative moods can cause individuals to become more discerning which may drive them to provide quality ideas that are both novel and useful. Verhaeghen, Joorman and Khan (2005) argue that the self-reflective rumination that often accompanies negative mood or depression, can encourage seriousness about creative endeavours which then affects the level of effort exerted. Russ (1993) distinguishes between induced negative mood which may reduce one's motivation or productivity and other forms of negative affect, such as negative affect in primary process or fantasy play, which could have the potential to positively impact creative production through the broadening of associations. This suggests that perhaps a distinction needs to be made between one's ability to access negative affect for the purposes of broadening associations versus one's actual experience of negative affect which might lead to depression and decreased motivation.

Empirically, the evidence to support negative affect facilitating creativity is more limited and mixed than that for positive affect. The majority of experimental studies whose focus has been on positive affect but have included negative affect groups have not found an impact of negative mood on creativity. However, there is some evidence to support the link between negative affect and creativity and given that less research has been completed in this area, it is not surprising that there are less empirical findings to date. Schuldberg (1995) reports negative correlations between scores on the MMPI-2 depression scale and creativity tests, suggesting that negative mood facilitated better problem-solving in this sample. George and Zhou (2002) were also able to determine workplace conditions under which negative moods were positively related to creative performance. Evidence is also reported by Kaufmann and Vosburg (1997) who used two experiments to demonstrate that positive mood did not facilitate problem-solving on insight tasks, while neutral and negative mood participants performed better. In a two study series Kaufmann and Vosburg (1997) examined the influence of various affective states on creative problem-solving using two insight problems. In the first study, 91 high school students had their natural mood state assessed and then were asked to complete the creative problem-solving tasks. Here, positive mood led to significantly poorer creative problem-solving performance. The second study in the series included an experimentally induced mood state using 10-minute segments of positive, negative and neutral videotape. Negative mood significantly facilitated creative problem solving performance compared to neutral mood and to the control group in whom no mood induction was performed. Subjects in the positive mood condition showed the poorest performance on the creativity tasks.

BEYOND AFFECTIVE TONE

The mixed and seemingly contradictory results that have emerged in the literature have led researchers to move beyond examination of the direct effects of positive and negative affect to more complex models. In a review of workplace affect and workplace creativity, James, Brodersen & Eisenberg (2004) propose a preliminary model designed to integrate the many divergent findings present in the current literature. Their theoretical model outlines the many possible factors that might influence creative production in the workplace, and speaks to the complexity of the mood-creativity relationship in general (see Figure 3). The authors use their model to generate hypotheses about the mood-creativity relationship and to make recommendations about directions for future research. A number of the mediators and moderators of the relationship between affective state and subsequent creative performance are discussed in more detail below.

Effects of Time

The majority of studies assessing mood effects on creativity have been laboratory-based and thus the question of ecological validity remains. It may be that the relationship between mood and creativity is different across settings, such as when creativity is required for work versus for pleasure (Amabile et al., 2005). After a review of the literature, George and Zhou (2002) concluded that the seemingly contradictory results found among mood induction studies may have to do with the nature of the laboratory. Participants in laboratory studies are often asked to work on a fixed task within a certain time limit while employees are often left to their own discretion regarding what is creative enough, when to take initiative and when enough effort has been put forth (Shaw, 1999). While positive mood might lead to more creative production during a finite laboratory task, positive mood in the workplace may actually lead to less creative production as employees are confident and happy with early attempts and do not persist at a task long enough to reach the more unique ideas.

This theory is consistent with meta-analytic findings (Baas, De Dreu & Nijstad, 2008) that the effect of positive mood on creativity is diminished as the time to complete the task becomes longer. Kaufmann and Vosburg (2002) experimentally induced positive and negative mood using film clips and asked participants to complete four different idea production tasks, allowing four minutes per task. The authors reported a significant interaction between mood and production time, such that positive mood led to the highest number of scores in early idea production and the lowest number in late production. Both the control group and negative mood group showed stronger performance in late production, suggesting greater persistence. Positive affect may enhance cognitive flexibility but it does so by facilitating fast and global processing (Ashby et al., 1999; De Dreu, Baas & Nijstad, 2008; Hirt et al., 2008). This may mean that given more time to exert additional effort and persistence, a person in a neutral mood would be able to achieve the same creative product.

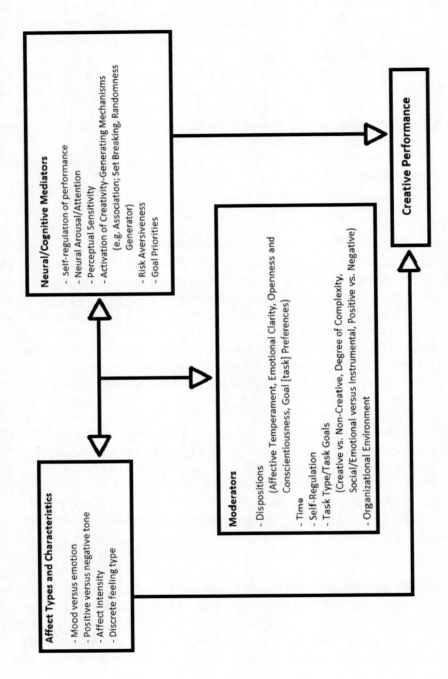

Figure 3. James et al. (2004) Mechanisms of influence of affect on workplace creativity.

Affect Duration

The length of time for which an emotion is experienced may also impact creative performance. James et al. (2004) suggest that "the effects of a given type of affect on creative performance is likely to change depending on the length of time the affect is experienced." (pp. 176). This may be another limitation of laboratory studies using mood induction techniques that cannot examine the effects of a chronic or extended mood state. For example, James et al. (2004) raise the point that while some research links frustration and conflict with improved creativity as people abandon standard problem-solving approaches in favor of more novel ones, chronic frustration can also lead to stress which may inhibit a person's ability to perform well on the creative task. Such changes over time may be true for other mood states as well. For example, induced negative affect from watching a saddening movie clip may enhance creative problem-solving temporarily; however, chronic sadness or depression over time could limit one's problem solving ability as thinking becomes narrowed and motivation decreases.

James et al. (2004) also distinguish between emotion and mood, defining emotion as a type of affect that is more likely to enter conscious awareness while mood is a more background feeling that may influence conscious awareness but is less likely to be a focus of attention. The authors theorize that self-regulatory processes may be more directly related to emotion rather than mood, and therefore emotions are more likely to affect the volitional aspects of creative performance. Mood meanwhile may impact the unconscious elements of creativity such as randomness generation or mechanisms related to attention.

Emotional Intensity

In a recent review of the literature, Amabile et al. (2005) assert that the majority of research seems to assume a linear relationship between mood and creativity, such that higher levels of affect would relate to higher levels of creativity. However, it is possible that a more curvilinear relationship better represents the relationship between affective state and creative performance. Amabile et al. (2005) review neuropsychological research suggesting that stronger emotional experiences lead to enhanced memory (e.g. Canli, Zhao, Brewer, Gabrieli & Cahill, 2000) and therefore suggests that the mood-creativity relationship might follow a U-shaped curve. This would imply that both intense positive and intense negative affect would lead to creativity while moderate levels of affect, either positive or negative, and flat affect would be insufficient to stimulate the cognitive resources needed for enhanced creativity.

Alternatively, the affect-creativity relationship could follow an inverted-U shape (James et al., 2004) where low and moderate levels of affect allow for access to one's cognitive resources, with moderate levels of affect being the optimum, regardless of whether those feelings are positive or negative. Meanwhile, intense emotions, either positive or negative, consume one's attention and may distract from task performance. This perspective is congruent with the Yerkes and Dodson (1908) theory of physiological arousal. Both intense positive and intense negative emotions can generate disordered thinking that can preclude the kind of thinking required for generation, analysis and elaboration of ideas (Eysenck, 1995; Isen, Daubman & Nowicki, 1987). Additionally, very low levels of emotional intensity may not have enough arousal to promote creative thinking at all. Martindale (1999) proposed a neural network model of creativity in which lower than average arousal allows the mind to attend to the associative connections necessary for novel ideas, while higher levels of arousal requires one's attention, making innovative thinking less likely. In other words, low arousal should promote creativity by making it more likely that novel ideas can reach conscious attention. James et al. (2004) point out that this neural network model may explain some of the study findings linking positive affect with creativity. Happiness may be associated with low neural arousal while negative feelings like anger may trigger high neural arousal. Affective tone and arousal level are often linked and may be part of why positive emotions can enhance creativity due to their ability to reduce neural arousal.

It is important to note that the proposals of U-shaped and inverted U-shaped curves are not necessarily contradictory. Amabile et al. (2005) are describing a graph in which the x-axis spans from highly negative to highly positive affect with presumably neutral affect in the middle, Conversely, James et al. (2004) describe a graph in which the x-axis is describing arousal level, regardless of affective tone, thus the two concepts are not mutually exclusive. It may be possible to combine the two curves to form a bi-modal curve in which the U-shaped curve describing positive and negative emotions represents the middle of the graph, while the extreme arousal levels discussed by James et al. (2004) or Yerkes-Dodson (1909), in which creativity would again decrease, may exist further out toward the extremes of the x-axis (see Figure 4).

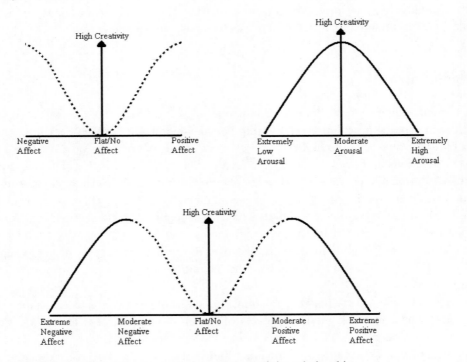

Figure 4. Merging of arousal theories to depict mood-creativity relationship.

Emotional Activation

De Dreu et al. (2008) differentiate between moods that are activating such as anger, fear and happiness, and moods that are deactivating, such as calmness, relaxation, or depression. Their "dual pathway" model of creativity suggests that activating moods, positive or negative, will enhance creative fluency and originality. De Dreu et al. (2008) maintain that if the activating mood is negative, creativity is enhanced through greater perseverance. If the activating mood is positive, creativity is enhanced through greater cognitive flexibility. Therefore, the hedonic tone of the mood is not the only relevant factor but also whether the mood is activating or deactivating. To support this model, De Dreu et al. (2008) conducted a series of four studies with different mood manipulations and different measures of creative performance including a brainstorming task, a measure of cognitive inclusiveness and broadness of categories, and an insight problem. In support of the dual pathway model, activating mood states related to a larger number of unique ideas overall and positive, activating mood states also related to higher levels of originality. The authors conclude that negative activating moods effect creative fluency by enhancing within-category persistence, while positive activating moods effect originality by enhancing cognitive flexibility.

Additional research and theory examining emotional activation supports the dual pathway model. Research examining the neurotransmitters dopamine and noradrenalin support this activation hypothesis through these neurotransmitters' effects on working memory, selective attention, and planning. Activating mood states combined with enhanced working memory capacity should lead to greater cognitive flexibility, abstract reasoning, processing speed and access to long-term memory (e.g. Dietrich, 2004). Activation can also vary as a function of physical exertion rather than a change in mood, and studies examining these effects on creativity have been inconclusive. Some studies have found no differences in creativity between baseline and exercise conditions (Isen et al., 1987; Vosburg, 1998) while others have found that physical exercise can lead to more divergent thinking (Blanchette, Ramocki, O'Del & Casey, 2005; Steinberg, Sykes, Moss, Lowrey, LeBoutillier & Dewey, 1997). De Dreu et al. (2008) argue that further research in this area is needed, as both Isen et al. (1987) and Vosburg (1998) used creativity tasks that measure cognitive flexibility, which may explain why their subjects who experienced a happiness mood induction showed more creativity than the subjects activated by exercise.

Task Differences

The wide variety of tasks used to operationalize creativity across studies may be an essential factor in untangling the seemingly contradictory results currently available. As more becomes understood about the different ways in which positive and negative affect influence a person's problem-solving strategies, it is possible to generate hypotheses regarding how various moods might impact different creative tasks. For example, Schwarz's (1990) feelings-as-information theory addresses how positive affect might enhance divergent thinking while negative affect might enhance insight tasks that require more attention to detail and critical thinking. Russ (1993) supports that argument, suggesting that positive mood may facilitate performance on measures of divergent thinking because individuals relax their category boundaries and are disposed toward accepting that divergent concepts could be connected.

Additionally, critical assessment fostered by negative mood would be detrimental to this flexibility. The opposite pattern emerges however when one must solve an insight problem, therefore generating many ideas but only picking the optimal solution. If positive mood produces contentment with current ideas, an individual may not persist until the optimal solution has been reached. In these cases, negative affect might produce the additional motivation needed to persevere until the optimal solution has been reached. In other words, negative mood may result in enhanced solution frequency on tasks that require concentration, precise execution, and divergent thinking when followed by top-down evaluation of each idea's value (Abele, 1992; Kaufmann & Vosburg, 1997).

Consensus regarding task differences has not been achieved and other possibilities have been put forth. Positive mood may produce more optimal creative performance when tasks require rapid judgment heuristic strategies (Fiedler, 2000; Isen, Daubman & Nowicki, 1987). Yet, Vosburg's (1998) study found the opposite result. Using a quasi-experimental design, the mood states of 188 art and psychology students was measured prior to a divergent thinking task. Vosburg reported that the students' natural positive mood facilitated task performance while negative mood inhibited performance. She suggested that perhaps people in negative moods choose optimizing strategies and are more concerned with the quality of their ideas, which would result in fewer answers and therefore worse performance on this type of task. These results suggest it is the negative affect condition that chooses the optimizing strategy not the positive mood condition. James et al. (2004) propose that perhaps positive affect promotes better performance on well-defined creative problems or tasks, while negative affect promotes better performance on ill-defined creative problems or tasks.

Baas et al. (2008) also review how affective states may influence the three different types of creativity: divergent thinking, insight tasks and performance. Empirical data suggests that perseverance and achievement motivation will influence fluency but not flexibility of divergent thinking (Fodor & Carver, 2000; Rietzschel, De Dreu & Nijstad, 2007). Increased fluency may lead to greater originality and more creative ideas, but not always. Weisberg (1994) discusses how the composer Robert Schumann produced a higher quantity of work during manic episodes, but that this work was not of a higher quality. Similarly, Schuldberg (1999) suggests that there may be optimal matches between affective states and particular creative tasks. More specifically one's cognitions and affect might need to correspond with the type of creativity include the mediums, domains and environment. Furthermore, the creative product is produced within a particular context, and is judged by a particular culture set at a particular time in history or the present. For example, high fluency without regard for quality may be appropriate during the a brainstorming session at a advertising agency, in which case high positive affect, leading to broad thinking and the confidence to take risks may be beneficial. Those same qualities however would not be advantageous for an insight task such as medical diagnosis, where efficiency and overconfidence are not valued traits, but instead detail-oriented, systematic thinking produced by mild negative affect may be more optimal.

George & Zhou (2002) maintain that the impact of positive or negative mood on creative performance is context dependent. For example, Martin and Stoner (1996) described a laboratory study in which participants were given an initial word associations task for three seconds in which there were no differences in the unusualness of responses for those in positive and negative moods. Next, some participants were given the chance to come up with more associations if they wanted to, if they thought they could generate a more creative response. Other participants were asked to decide whether to come up with more associations by deciding if they thought their initial response was creative. In the first condition, people in positive moods were confident that they could generate more creative answers and so chose to do so more often than those in negative moods. In the second condition, people in positive moods were confident their first answer was creative and thus chose not to generate more associations while people in negative moods chose to persevere and ended up generating more creative associations. A simple change in instruction and end goal led to opposite results regarding the type of mood that was optimal for reaching the most creative associations. Baas et al. (2008) confirm this concept in their meta-analysis of mood-creativity research, concluding that when a creativity task is framed in terms of fun and enjoyment, the participants in a positive mood are more creative than those in a negative mood; however, when the task is framed as serious or performance-related, the negative mood participants are the more creative.

Friedman and Förster (2001) suggest that regulatory focus is related to creative performance, specifically whether a task is set up with a promotion focus (reward) or a prevention focus (avoidance of a punishment). Theoretically, a promotion state should cause people to think broadly, facilitating access to more associations, while a prevention focus should cause more narrowed attention, and therefore less access to associations. In one study, participants were given paper with a cartoon mouse trapped in a maze. The task was to find a way out of the maze, either to reach a piece of cheese (promotion focus) or to avoid an owl hovering above the maze (prevention focus). Participants then completed several creativity tasks. Participants in the promotion focus group showed greater creative insight and divergent thinking (Friedman & Förster, 2001). Friedman and Förster (2000, 2002) were also able to achieve a difference in processing style by asking participants to press their hands downward against the top of the table (arm extension, associated with avoidance behavior) or push their hand upward against the bottom of the table (arm flexion, associated with approach behavior). This subtle body feedback was enough to produce results showing that relative to controls, the approach condition provided more inclusive categorizations than the avoidance condition. These results have some implications for workplaces seeking to enhance the creativity of their employees: given employees in a positive mood, tasks that challenge people, are presented as fun and enjoyable, and are presented with a promotion-focus should produce the greatest creative products.

SPECIFIC EMOTIONAL STATES

It is generally assumed that specific emotions such as happiness, sadness or fear are likely to have different effects on creative performance. Beyond tone and activation, different emotions may differentially affect creativity because each emotion activates distinct associational networks. After a review of the literature, James et al. (2004) theorized that specific emotions might differ in their implications for creativity due to activation of distinct cognitive networks that would provide different raw material on which one could base their creative responses. In other words, each specific emotional state unlocks its own set of emotional memories, knowledge and associations. One critique of many workplace studies is that while they discuss positive and negative affect broadly, it is more likely that specific emotional subtypes were present (James et al., 2004). The wide focus on positive versus negative rather than a closer examination of particular emotions may be contributing to the current mixed findings in the literature. Weiss and colleagues (Brief & Weiss, 2002; Weiss & Cropanzano, 1996) have argued for a greater focus on the impact of specific emotions on creative performance rather than the broad focus on positive versus negative affect states.

Baas et al. (2008) review the impact of regulatory focus (Friedman & Forster, 2000; 2001; 2002) on creative problem solving to make predictions about specific emotions. The studies suggest that approach motivation promotes creative insight and divergent thinking while avoidance motivation does not. Using only regulatory focus one could predict that anger, sadness, happiness and joy are all mood states associated with a promotion focus, and thus theoretically would facilitate creative performance. Conversely, fear, relaxation and calmness are all mood states associated with a prevention focus, and therefore should constrict the scope of attention and impede creativity (Baas et al., 2008). However, Friedman and Förster proposed that the interaction between activation level and regulatory focus could provide a more accurate model of the mood-creativity relationship. Hypotheses based simply on regulatory focus are too simplistic. For example, people in a sad mood are promotion focused, but they lack approach motivation (Henriques, Glowacki, & Davidson, 1994). Baas et al., therefore hypothesize that people experiencing sadness should not produce higher levels of creativity. Conversely, people in a relaxed state are prevention focused but because their engagement and avoidance tendencies are reduced they do not show lower levels of creativity (Fredrickson, Mancuso, Branigan & Tugade, 2000). Alternatively, anxiety is both activating and prevention-focused, leading to decreased creative performance due to the narrowed focus of attention. This is in contrast to happiness with is activating and promotion focused, leading to a more global focus, increased access to mental representations and therefore enhanced creativity.

Other aspects of particular emotions may also be related to creativity, such as certainty, expectedness, importance and controllability (Roseman, Weist & Swartz, 1994; Smith & Ellsworth, 1985) and lend some insight into which specific emotions are creativity enhancing. For example, mood states that have higher levels of certainty, such as anger or joy, may be associated with higher levels of creativity than mood states that have lower levels of certainty, such as fear (Baas et al., 2008). George & Zhou (2002) maintain that the clarity of feelings is relevant to understanding how positive and negative moods will relate to creativity. The mood-as-input model requires that people be clear about how they are feeling during the creative process. For those people who are confused about their feelings or have low clarity of feelings, mood will not serve as an indicator. Among a sample of workers whose job involved developing creative designs and manufacturing techniques, negative moods were positively related to creative performance when perceived recognition and reward was high and when clarity of feelings was high. On the other hand, positive moods were negatively correlated with creative performance under the same conditions (high perception of reward, and high clarity of feelings). When these variables were low, mood appeared to have little impact on creativity for the sample.

Alternatively, a person's level of risk tolerance, which can be affected by mood, may also be related to creative performance, but the direction of the effect is unknown. For example, some suggest that an emotion such as anger, which increases one's risk tolerance level, might then trigger more original responding on a creativity task than an emotion, such as fear, that would reduce risk tolerance and promote risk aversion instead (Lerner & Keltner, 2001).

Contrarily, Schwarz (1990) theorized that negative emotions would lead to more cautious problem-solving strategies due to feelings of uncertainty, while positive emotions would lead to more risky problem-solving approaches due to feelings of confidence. Subsequently, those willing to take more risks in their thinking would have increased creativity, thus explaining the common finding relating positive affect to enhanced creativity.

The limited number of studies examining specific emotions may be due to several factors. First, a number of studies reviewed do in fact trigger specific emotional states such as happiness or sadness through their mood induction procedures. Unfortunately, these emotions are not specifically measured or reported but instead are described as dichotomous categories of positive or negative valence. If specific emotions in past studies could be inferred, a meta-analysis of mood induction-creativity studies might reveal more detailed information about the effects of specific emotions. Second, the study of specific emotions will require consensus on what the major, basic emotions are. Ekman (1992) proposes four basic negative emotions (anger, disgust, fear, and sadness), one positive emotion (enjoyment) and one neutral emotion (surprise). Shaver, Schwartz, Kirson and O'Connor (1987) propose 24 emotional subcategories with 6 primary types including 2 positive (love and joy), three negative (anger, sadness and fear) and surprise. The complexity of understanding how each of these emotions effects creativity differentially, particularly when interactions with intensity, regulatory focus, and activation level are incorporated may explain why little consensus has been reached for this line of research given the relative infancy of creativity research altogether.

AFFECTIVE DISORDERS AND CREATIVITY

A thorough discussion of creativity and emotion should include the effects of dysregulated or abnormal emotional experiences on creativity. While a full review of the research on the relationships among creativity, bipolar disorder, schizoaffective disorders and depression is beyond the scope of this chapter, a limited review is presented below. Historical and empirical data often link artistic creativity to depression and other affective disorders (e.g. Akinola & Mendes, 2008). The rates of incidence of affective disorders, particularly bipolar disorder and hypomania appear to be higher in the creative population than in the general population (Andreasan, 1987; 2008). Jamison (1993) maintains that mood disorders are 8 to 10 times more prevalent in writers and artists than the general population.

Several studies examining the individual characteristics of creative people shed light on why creative individuals may have a higher tendency toward mental illness. Creative people tend to be overly sensitive to stimulation, have a broader attentional focus, habituate more slowly, show greater variability in arousal, withdraw to reduce stimulation and seek out controlled task-focused stimulation to compensate for this withdrawal (Martindale, 1999). Feist (1999) completed a review of the past 30 years and maintains that there is a reliable relationship between affective illness and high levels of creative accomplishment. Reviewing the dispositional characteristics of creative scientists and artists, Feist (1999) found that artists showed higher levels of autonomy, independence, introversion, energy, achievement, drive, self-confidence, openness, flexibility, imagination, tolerance for ambiguity, arrogance, hostility and power needs. These findings bring to light not only the interconnections between access to affective experiences and creativity but also the benefits and risks of possessing these personal qualities. Hypersensitivity, hostility, and arrogance are linked with creativity among our eminent stars, however these characteristics are also detrimental to adjustment and functioning within typical social institutions.

Empirical evidence also supports the observed relationship between hypomanic or manic traits and creativity. Schuldberg (1990) reports that unusual perceptual experiences and beliefs, hypomanic traits and impulsive nonconformity are all associated with more creative attitudes and activities. Furthermore, deficits in experiencing pleasure are negatively correlated with creativity scores. This research is consistent with studies reported by Jamison (1993) suggesting that mild hypomanic states are conducive to high levels of ideational fluency, speed of association, thinking that allows for combination of incongruent materials, and looser processing that allows for otherwise irrelevant thoughts to be considered. This data fits with other findings indicating that nonclinical ranges of positive affect enhance creative functioning (Isen, Daubman & Nowicki, 1987; Russ, 1993). The findings also support the hypothesized curvilinear relationship between affect and creativity in which moderate amounts of affect are most effective at enhancing the creative process (Akiskal & Akiskal, 1988; Russ, 1993). In particular, the inverted-U hypothesis in which low levels of affective symptoms may facilitate creativity but higher levels may be destructive seems to fit. In fact, Richards et al. (1988) proposed a modified inverted-U hypothesis in which overall peak creativity is enhanced by milder and subclinical expression of potential bipolar liability (cyclothymes and first-degree relatives of bipolar patients) compared to controls subjects with no bipolar traits and actual bipolar individuals.

The link between creativity and affective disorders does not merely apply to unusually high positive mood. Regarding negative affect, Mraz and Runco (1994) found that an indicator of strongly negative mood, the frequency of suicidal thoughts, was positively related to problem-finding ability, defined as the ability to imagine new and interesting problems, an important beginning step of the creative process (e.g. Runco, 2004). Akinola & Mendes (2008) conducted a study in which positive, neutral or negative moods were induced using social approval or social rejection or a nonsocial situation. Participants then completed artistic collages that were evaluated by artists. Authors reported a person-by-situation interaction, such that social rejection was associated with greater artistic creativity. Additionally, a measure of vulnerability to negative affect measured by taking participants' baseline level of an adrenal steroid (DHEAS), showed that greater vulnerability (lower baseline DHEAS) in the condition where negative affect was induced showed the most creative products. This study in particular emphasizes the multifaceted nature of the relationship between emotions and creativity, included both biological and social components that affect mood and consequently creative production.

Just as there is no consensus in the literature regarding adaptive levels of positive and negative affect, there are no straightforward conclusions regarding mania and depression's effects on creativity either. Despite this, several important conclusions can be drawn from the research. Firstly, it appears that manic or depressive symptoms must be subclinical in order to optimally improve creative functioning. Secondly, clinical levels of mania and depression as well as flat affect are likely to hinder creative performance. This goes against the romanticized, anecdotal view of the tortured artist. Wiesberg (1994) found for one famous artist, manic periods were associated with increased productivity but not heightened quality, fitting with the previously discussed mood-as-input model, suggesting manic individuals may feel more creative but may not be realistically assessing their work. Schuldberg (2001) suggests that eminence studies are flawed in that psychopathology is observed from a distance and diagnostic criteria are often loose. Furthermore, creativity may often be confounded with fame (Kinney et al., 2000-2001; Sass, 2000-2001). Thus, broad conclusions about affective disorders and creativity taken from eminence studies must be viewed critically.

In a special issue of Creativity Research Journal addressing creativity and the schizophrenia spectrum, Sass (2000-2001) argues for the connection between schizophrenic traits and creative potential. In the same issue, Schuldberg (2001) reports the findings from a study exploring connections between creativity and six symptom-like traits: positive symptom thought disorder, negative symptom thought disorder, flat affect, hypomania, depression and impulsivity. Positive symptom thought disorder, hypomania and impulsivity were all positively correlated with creativity. Negative symptom thought disorder, flat affect, and depression were negatively correlated with creativity test scores. Kinney et al. (2000-2001) examined 36 adult adoptees whose biological parents had schizophrenia and 36 matched controls, hypothesizing that people with genetic liability for schizophrenia but not a diagnosis of schizophrenia itself would be the most creative. The results supported this hypothesis, showing that the people with schizotypal and schizoid personality disorder and those with multiple schizotypal signs had significantly higher creativity. Further psychological inquiry in this area is warranted, given the potential to uncover pathways to creative production that involve broad associations and incorporation of irrelevant facts without the strong emotional experiences present in bipolar disorder.

CREATIVITY'S EFFECT ON MOOD

The creativity-mood relationship is bi-directional, such that creative outcomes also have the ability to change the artist's affect. Most empirical research has examined emotion as an antecedent of creativity, yet the affective consequences of creative insight are also important to explore (Feist, 1999). Knowledge regarding the short-term impact of creativity on mood may have important implications for workplaces in which employees are asked to think creatively repeatedly. More long-term consequences of chronic creativity may help psychologists to understand the rates of mood disorders among our eminent artists, as well as how creativity in childhood may impact later adjustment and emotion regulation.

In the short term, creative achievement or insight is often followed by elation (Gruber, 1995; Feist, 1999; Shaw, 1999). Feist (1999) uses Lazarus' (1991) cognitive theory of emotion to explain how creativity might impact emotion. People experience an emotion when they appraise an event to be relevant to their well-being. Moreover, the emotion will be positive if the event was congruent with their goals, and negative if the event was incongruent with their goals. Feist (1999) applies this concept to creative insight, stating that after problem identification, a person experiences a tension state, or anxiety. Upon producing a creative insight, the person should feel a positive emotion, such as happiness, relief or pride, given that the relevant problem was resolved and in a way congruent with the person's goals.

Amabile (1983) discusses how the outcome of a creative attempt (success, partial success, or failure) could impact one's task motivation, thereby setting up a cycle that could increase or decrease later creative performances. Success on a creative task leads to intrinsic gratification, feelings of efficacy and increases in intrinsic motivation, which should then lead to more attempts at creativity in the future. More successful attempts will not only continue to bolster one's intrinsic motivation but would also begin to increase one's domain-relevant skills and creativity-relevant skills through increased motivation to learn about the relevant task, as well as habitual set-breaking and cognitive risk-taking.

One difference between the effects of mood or creativity versus creativity on mood is the duration of the effect. The affective consequences of creativity are likely to be more immediate and relatively fleeting. Amabile et al. (2005) explored the affective consequence of creativity by using multilevel regressions to predict each day's mood from the previous three day's creative thought for a sample of 222 workers and found no evidence that creative thought predicted mood on subsequent days. This suggests that creative thinking does not have affective consequences beyond the day on which the creative thought occurred. Amabile et al. (2005) then examined same day affective consequences by analyzing diary narratives written on the same day as the creative thinking. While 80% of the diary entries did not mention a direct emotional reaction at all, the 20% that did mention an affective consequence mostly described positive emotions including joy, pride, satisfaction and relief, with only 10 entries out of the original 364 describing anger, sadness or fear, typically due to a co-workers poor response to the writer's insight.

The pleasure derived from behaving creatively may even mostly take place during creative production. Amabile et al. (2005) also found diary entries in which the emotion reported was intertwined with the creative process. Workers described feeling pleasure or enjoyment in the creative activity, or expressed a passion for their work and excitement about increasing competence or being challenged. Overwhelmingly, these expressions of emotion were positive. Csikszentmihalyi (1996) suggests that creative behavior can be characterized by a "flow state", in which a person temporarily merges with the creative activity, which inherently involves positive feelings such as enjoyment and enthusiasm. This can also be thought of as intrinsic motivation where a person is enjoying the work as the product is unfolding (Deci & Ryan, 1985).

Not all creativity leads to positive outcomes. There may be some ways in which a creative lifestyle impacts one's mood in a negative way (Murray & Johnson, 2010). For example, emotional sensitivity may promote creativity within the arts, but then artists often receive praise or reward for their valued ability to express emotion (Sass, 2001). This praise for emotional expression may have a reinforcing effect that could then lead to greater emotionality over time. This may be positive for those seeking to be more creative, or a danger for those with existing mood dysregulation vulnerabilities. Murray and Johnson (2010) also cite the life stress associated with being an artist, a lifestyle infamous for being unpredictable, financially unstable, chaotic or frustrating. Such a lifestyle can be considered a risk factor for greater symptoms of anxiety and depression among artists, something that might be especially difficult for those with susceptibility to bipolar traits. Similarly, the intensity associated with creative work may lead to a shallow family life (Policastro & Gardner, 1999), and the frustration and ambiguity associated with creativity could lead some to alcohol abuse (Murray & Johnson, 2010). Again it appears that moderation of creative thinking is optimal.

CONCLUSION

Research and theory both support that creativity and emotion are linked. While the majority of research supports the enhancing effects of positive emotions on creative performance, more recent reviews of the literature maintain that this conclusion is premature. Kaufmann (2003) concludes instead that creativity is a multifaceted construct and therefore different moods are most likely differentially related to the many facets of creative thinking. It is known that positive mood induction can lead to enhanced creative thinking. This may be due to broader access to associations in memory, the activating effects of some positive emotions, increased confidence leading to use of heuristics and risk-taking, or a host of other possibilities. Other findings suggest that negative emotions can also enhance creativity through detailed-oriented thinking, perseverance in generating novel ideas, and in problem identification.

Given these findings, studies have begun to explore beyond affective tone. For example, activating emotions should enhance creativity while deactivating emotions should not. Additionally, the intensity of the emotional experience might function according to the Yerkes-Dodson curve where moderate emotions enhance creative functioning but extreme emotions, positive or negative, are paralyzing. The same pattern is theorized to hold true for affective disorders in which subclinical symptoms of bipolarity or schizotypal thinking increase creativity, while clinical and maladaptive levels do not. Moreover, the ways in which creative problem-solving tasks are presented to people may interact with the effects of mood. Findings suggest that positive mood may lead to less creativity in open-ended tasks where happy people are confident with their first performance, while negative mood might enhance creativity as people persevere to generate more creative solutions. Similarly, presenting tasks such that people take an approach or promotion-focused stance may lead to more creative solutions than avoidance or prevention-focused tasks.

This more modern understanding of the multifaceted relationship between emotions and creativity is evident in two recent meta-analyses reporting substantial variance in effects between mood and creativity across studies (Baas et al., 2008; Davis, 2009). Both of these meta-analyses suggest that the relationship between emotions and creativity is far from understood and maintain that the next direction in mood-creativity research should be to devise more nuanced models and theories capable of explaining the mixed results. Several such models have been proposed, including that by James et al. (2004), however, little research exists to empirically test the many mediators and moderators that have been proposed.

It does appear that further work examining the relationships between mood and creativity is warranted. Baas et al. (2008) conclude that mood-creativity research should continue despite the small effect sizes found so far. The authors assert that even small effect sizes can be impressive when they are produced using minimal experimental designs. In other words, studies with only mild mood induction effects that still find an effect of mood on creativity can be considered a rigorous test, actually emphasizing the impact and importance of the effect. Thus, continuing down the path of studying moods effect on creativity is certainly viable.

In the recent summary of creativity research to-date and the direction of the field, Mumford (2003) points out that beyond merely gaining an understanding of the mood-creativity link, much of the current creativity-mood research seeks to answers questions about assessing creative potential, and developing interventions to improve creative performance. A nuanced understanding of how mood induction and access to affect-laden thoughts can impact one's creativity would have large beneficial not only for artists but also for innovation in the workplace and the development of creativity in children. Russ and colleagues in particular have begun exploring how play interventions for children, in which the children are encouraged to express a range of emotional themes, can also lead to enhancements in these children's divergent thinking and storytelling abilities (Christian, Fehr & Russ, 2011; Hoffmann & Russ, 2012; Moore & Russ, 2008). At both the individual and group levels, an understanding of the potential benefits of allowing oneself to experience a range of emotions, both positive and negative, for the enhancement of creative thinking, problem-solving and insight continues to be worthy of psychological study.

REFERENCES

Abele, A. (1992). Positive versus negative mood influences on creativity: Evidence of asymmetrical effects. *Polish Psychological Bulletin, 23,* 203-221.

Akinola, M. & Mendes, W. B. (2008). The dark side of creativity. Biological vulnerability and negative emotions lead to greater artistic creativity. *Personality and Social Psychology Bulletin, 34,* 1677-1686.

Amabile, T. M. (1983). The Social Psychology of Creativity. New York: Springer-Verlag.

Amabile, T. M. (1996). *Creativity in context.* New York: Westview.

Amabile, T. M., Barsade, S. G., Mueller, J. S. & Staw, B. M. (2005). Affect and creativity at work. *Administrative Science Quarterly, 50,* 367-403.

Anderson, R. E., Arlett, C. & Tarrant, L. (1995). Effects of instructions and mood on creative mental synthesis. In G. Kaufman, T. Helstrup, & K. H. Teigen (Eds.), *Problem solving and cognitive processes* (183-195). Bergen, Norway: Fagbokforlaget.

Andreason, N. C. (1987). Creativity and mental illness: Prevalence rates in writers and their first-degree relatives. *American Journal of Psychiatry, 144,* 1288-1292.

Andreason, N. C. (2008). The relationship between creativity and mood disorders. *Dialogues in Clinical Neuroscience, 10,* 251-255.

Ashby, F. G., Isen, A. M. & Turken, A. U. (1999). A neuropsychological theory of positive affect and its influence on cognition. *Psychological Review, 106,* 529-550.

Ashby, F. G., Valentin, V. V. & Turken, A. U. (2002). The effects of positive affect and arousal and working memory and executive attention: Neurobiology and computational models. In S. C. Moore & M. Oaksford (Eds.), *Emotional cognition: From brain to behaviour* (245-287). Amsterdam: John Benjamins.

Baas, M., De Dreu, C. K. W. & Nijstad, B. A. (2008). A meta-analysis of 25 years of mood-creativity research: Hedonic tone, activation, or regulatory focus? *Psychological Bulletin, 134,* 779-806.

Benjafield, J. G. (1996). *Cognition.* Englewood Cliffs, NJ: Prentice Hall.

Blanchette, D. M., Ramocki, S. P., O'Del, J. N. & Casey, M. S. (2005). Aerobic exercise and creative potential: Immediate and residual effects. *Creativity Research Journal, 17,* 257-264.

Bowden, C. L. (1994). Bipolar disorder and creativity. In M. P. Shaw & M. A. Runco (Eds.), *Creativity and affect* (73-86). Norwood, NJ: Ablex.

Brief, A, P. & Weiss, H. M. (2002). Organizational behavior: Affect in the workplace. *Annual Review of Psychology, 53,* 279-307.

Canli, T., Zhao, Z., Brewer, J., Gabrieli, J. & Cahill, L. (2000). Event-related activation in the human amygdala associates with later memory for individual emotional response. *Journal of Neuroscience, 20,* 1-5.

Christian, K., Fehr, K. & Russ, S. (2011, August). *Effects of a play intervention on play skills in preschool children: A pilot study.* Poster presented at the annual meeting of the American Psychological Association, Washington, DC.

Clore, G. L., Schwarz, N. & Conway, M. (1994). Cognitive causes and consequences of emotion. In R. S. Wyer and Tk K. Srull (Eds.), Handbook of Social Cognition (323-417). Hillsdale, NJ: Lawrence Erlbaum.

Csikszentmihalyi, M. (1996). Creativity: Flow and the psychology of discovery and invention. New York: Harper-Collins.

Davis, M. A. (2009). Understanding the relationship between mood and creativity: A meta-analysis. *Organizational Behavior and Human Decision Process, 108,* 25-38.

Deci, E. L. & Ryan, R. M. (1985*). Intrinsic motivation and self-determination in human behavior.* New York: Plenum Press.

De Dreu, C. K. W., Baas, M. & Nijstad, B. A. (2008). Hedonic tone and activation in the mood-creativity link: Towards a dual pathway to creativity model. *Journal of Personality and Social Psychology, 94,* 739-756.

Dietrich, A. (2004). The cognitive neuroscience of creativity. *Psychonomic Bulletin and Review, 11,* 1011-1026.

Duncker, K. (1945). On problem solving. *Psychological Monographs, 58(5).*

Ekman, P. (1992). An argument for basic emotions. *Cognition and Emotion, 6,* 169-200.

Eysenck, H. J. (1993). Creativity and personality: Suggestions for a theory. *Psychological Inquiry, 4,* 147-178.

Eysenck, H. J. (1995). *Genius: The natural history of creativity.* Cambridge, England: Cambridge University Press.

Feidler, K. (2000). Toward an account of affect and cognition phenomena using the BIAS computer algorithm. In J. P. Forgas (Ed.), *Feeling and thinking: The role of affect in social cognition* (223-252). Paris: Cambridge University Press.

Feist, G. J. (1999). Affect in artistic and scientific creativity. In S. W. Russ (Ed.), Affect, Creative Experience, and Psychological Adjustment (93-109). Philadelphia: Brunner/Mazel.

Fredrickson, B. L. (1998). What good are positive emotions? *Review of General Psychology, 2,* 300-319.

Fredrickson, B. L. (2001). The role of positive emotions in positive psychology. *American Psychologist, 56,* 218-226.

Fredrickson, B. L., Mancuso, R. A., Branigan, C. & Tugade, M. (2000). The undoing effect of positive emotions. *Motivation and Emotion, 24, 237-258.*

Friedman, R. S. & Forster, J. (2000). The effects of approach and avoidance motor actions on the elements of creative insight. *Journal of Personality and Social Psychology, 79,* 477-492.

Friedman, R. S. & Forster, J. (2001). The effects of promotion and prevention cues on creativity. *Journal of Personality and Social Psychology, 81,* 1001-1013.

Friedman, R. S. & Forster, J. (2002). The influence of approach and avoidance motor actions on creative cognition. *Journal of Experimental Social Psychology, 38,* 41-55.

Friedman, R. S. & Forster, J. (2008). Activation and measurement of motivation states. In A. J. Elliot (Ed.), *Handbook of approach and avoidance motivation* (pp. 235-248). New York: Psychology Press.

Fodor, E. M. & Carver, R. A. (2000). Achievement and power motives, performance feedback and creativity. *Journal of Research in Personality, 34,* 380-396.

Forgas, J. P. (2000). *Feeling and thinking: The role of affect in social cognition.* Paris: Cambridge University Press.

George, J. M. & Zhou, J. (2002). Understanding when bad moods foster creativity and good ones don't: The role of context and clarity of feelings. *Journal of Applied Psychology, 87,* 687-697.

Greene, T. R. & Noice, H. (1988). Influence of positive affect upon creative thinking and problem-solving in children. *Psychological Reports, 63,* 895-898.

Gruber, H. E. (1995). Insight and affect in the history of science. In R. J. Sternber and J. E. Davidson (Eds.), *The nature of insight* (397-431). Cambridge, MA: MIT Press.

Hennessey, B. A. & Amabile, T. M. (1988). Storytelling: A method for assessing children's creativity. *Journal of Creative Behavior, 22,* 235-246.

Henriques, J. B., Glowacki, J. M. & Davidson, R. J. (1994). Reward fails to alter response bias in depression. *Journal of Abnormal Psychology, 103,* 460-466.

Hirt, E. R. (1999). Mood. In M. A. Runco & S. R. Pritzker (Eds.), *Encyclopedia of creativity* (Vol. 2, 241-250). New York: Academic Press.

Hirt, E. R., Devers, E. E. & McCrea, S. M. (2008). A want to be creative: Exploring the role of mood in quantitative theory in the positive mood-flexibility link. *Journal of Personality and Social Psychology, 94,* 214-230.

Hirt, E. R., McDonald, H. E. & Melton, R. J. (1996). Processing goals and the affect-performance link: Mood as main effect or mood as input? In L. L. Martin & A. Tesser (Eds.), *Striving and feeling: Interactions among goals, affect, and self-regulation* (303-328). Mahwah, NJ: Lawrence Erlbaum Associates, Inc.

Hoffmann, J. D. & Russ, S. W. (2012a). Pretend play, creativity and emotion regulation in children. *Psychology of Aesthetics, Creativity and the Arts, 6,* 175-184.

Hoffmann, J. D. & Russ, S. W. (2012b). [A pretend play group intervention for elementary school girls]. Unpublished raw data.

Holt, R. R. (1970). Manual for the scoring of primary process manifestations in Rorschach responses. Unpublished manuscript.

Isen, A. M. (1993). Positive affect and decision making. In M. Lewis & J. Haviland (Eds.), *Handbook of emotions* (261-277). New York: Guilford.

Isen, A. M. (1999a). On the relationship between affect and creative problem-solving. In S.W. Russ (Ed.), Affect, Creative Experience and Psychological Adjustment (3-18). Philadelphia: Brunner/Mazel.

Isen, A. M. (1999b). Positive Affect. In T. Dangleish and M .Power (Eds.), Handbook of Cognition and Emotion (521-539). New York: Wiley.

Isen, A. M. & Baron, R. A. (1991). Positive affect as a factor in organizational behavior. *Research in Organizational Behavior, 13,* 1-53.

Isen, A. M. & Daubman, K. A. (1984). The influence of affect on categorization. *Journal of Personality and Social Psychology, 47*, 1206-1217.

Isen, A. M., Daubman, K. A. & Nowicki, G. P. (1987). Positive affect facilitates creative problem solving. *Journal of Personality and Social Psychology, 52*, 1122-1131.

Isen, A. M., Johnson, M. M., Mertz, E. & Robinson, G. F. (1985). The influence of positive affect on the unusualness of word associates. *Journal of Personality and Social Psychology, 48*, 1413-1426.

Isen, A. M., Labroo, A. A. & Durlach, P. (2004). An influence of product and brand name on positive affect: Implicit and explicit measures. *Motivation and Emotion, 28*, 43-63.

James, K. M., Broderson, M. & Eisenberg, J. (2004). Workplace affect and workplace creativity: A review and preliminary model. *Human Performance, 17*, 169-194.

Jamison, K. R. (1993). Touched with fire: Manic-depressive illness and the artistic temperament. New York: Free Press.

Kaufmann, G. (2003). Expanding the mood-creativity equation. *Creativity Research Journal, 15*, 131-135.

Kaufmann, G. & Vosburg, S. K. (1997). "Paradoxical" mood effects on creative problem solving. *Cognition and Emotion, 11*, 151-170.

Kaufmann, G. & Vosburg, S. K. (2002). Mood effects in early and late idea production. *Creativity Research Journal, 3*, 317-330.

Kinney, D. K., Richards, R., Lowing, P. A., LeBlanc, D., Zimbalist, M. E. & Harlan, P. (2000-2001). Creativity in offspring of schizophrenic and control parents: An adoption study. *Creativity Research Journal, 13*, 17-25.

Langley, P. & Jones, R. (1988). A computational model of scientific thought. In R.J. Sternberg (Ed.), *The Nature of Creativity: Contemporary Psychological Perspectives*. (pp. 171-201). Cambridge: Cambridge University Press.

Lazarus, R. S. (1991). *Emotion and adaptation*. New York: Oxford University Press.

Lerner, J. S. & Keltner, D. (2001). Fear, anger, and risk. *Journal of Personality and Social Psychology, 81*, 146-159.

Maier, N. R. F. (1970). *Problem solving and creativity in individuals and groups*. Belmont, CA: Brooks/Cole.

Martin, L. L., Ward, D. W., Achee, J. W. & Wyer, R. S. (1993). Mood as input: People have to interpret the motivational implications of their moods. *Journal of Personality and Social Psychology, 64*, 317-326.

Martindale, C. (1999). Biological basis of creativity. In R.J. Sternberg (Ed.), The Nature of Creativity: Contemporary Psychological Perspectives. (137-152). Cambridge: Cambridge University Press.

Mednick, S. A. (1962). The associative basis of the creative process. *Psychological Review, 69*, 220-232.

Moore, M. & Russ, S. (2008). Follow-up of a pretend play intervention: Effects on play, creativity and emotional processes in children. *Creativity Research Journal, 20*, 427-436.

Mraz, W. & Runco, M. A. (1994). Suicide ideation and creative problem solving. *Suicide and Life-Threatening Behavior, 24*, 38-47.

Mumford, M. A. (2001). Something old, something new: Revisiting Guilford's conception of creative problem solving. *Creativity Research Journal, 13*, 267-276.

Mumford, M. A. (2003). Where have we been, where are we going? Taking stock in creativity research. *Creativity Research Journal, 15*, 107-120.

Murray, G. & Johnson, S. L. (2010). The clinical significance of creativity in bipolar disorder. *Clinical Psychology Review, 30,* 721-732.

Murray, J. & Russ, S. (1981). Adaptive regression and types of cognitive flexibility. *Journal of Personality Assessment, 45,* 59-65.

Murray, N., Sujan, H., Hirt, E. R. & Sujan, M. (1990). The influence of mood on categorization: A cognitive flexibility interpretation. *Journal of Personality and Social Psychology.*

Policastro, E. & Garnder, H. (1995). Naive judgement and expert assessment: A critique of the attributional perspective. *Creativity Research Journal, 8,* 391-395.

Post, F. (1996). Verbal creativity, depression and alcoholism: An investigation of one hundred American and British writers. *British Journal of Psychiatry, 168,* 545-555.

Radford, M. (2004). Emotion and creativity. *Journal of Aesthetic Education, 38,* 53-64.

Richards, R., Kinney, D. K., Lunde, I., Benet, M. & Merzel, A. P. C. (1988). Creativity in manic-depressives, cyclothymes, their normal relatives and control subjects. *Journal of Abnormal Psychology, 97,* 281-288.

Rietzschel, E. F., De Dreu, C. K. W. & Nijstad, B. A. (2007). The effects of knowledge activation on the quantity and quality of ideas. *Journal of Experimental Social Psychology, 43,* 933-946.

Roseman, I. J., Wiest, C. & Swartz, T. S. (1994). Phenomenology, behaviors, and goals differentiate discrete emotions. *Journal of Personality and Social Psychology, 67,* 206-221.

Runco, M. A. (2004). Creativity. *Annual Review of Psychology, 55,* 657-687.

Russ, S. W. (1993). *Affect and creativity: The role of affect and play in the creative process.* Hillsdale, NJ: Lawrence Erlbaum.

Russ, S. W. (2004). *Play in child development and psychotherapy: Toward empirically supported practice.* Mahwah, NJ: Lawrence Erlbaum Associates.

Russ, S. W. & Dillon, J. A. (2011). Associative Theory. In Encyclopedia of Creativity. Runco, M. A., & Pritzker, S. R. (Eds.), Encyclopedia of Creativity (66-71). New York: Academic Press.

Sass, L. A. (2000-2001). Schizophrenia, modernism, and the creative imagination: On creativity and psychopathology. *Creativity Research Journal, 13,* 55-74.

Schuldberg, D. (1990). Schizotypal and hypomanic traits, creativity and psychological health. *Creativity Research Journal, 3,* 218-230.

Schuldberg, D. (1999). Creativity, bipolarity, and the dynamics of style. In S. W. Russ (Ed.), *Affect, creative experience, and psychological adjustment* (221-237). Philadelphia, PA: Brunner/Mazel.

Schuldberg, D. (2000-2001). Six subclinical spectrum traits in normal creativity. *Creativity Research Journal, 13,* 5-16.

Schwarz, N. (1990). Feelings as information: Informational and motivational functions of affective states. In E. T. Huggins & R. M. Sorrentino (Eds.), *Handbook of motivation and cognition* (Vol. 2, pp. 527-561). New York: Guilford Press.

Schwarz, N. (2000). Emotion, cognition and decision making. *Cognition and Emotion, 14,* 433-440.

Shapiro, P. J. & Weisberg, R. W. (1999). Creativity and bipolar diathesis: Common behavioral and cognitive components. *Cognition and Emotion, 13,* 741-762.

Shaver, P., Schwartz, J., Kirson, D. & O'Connor, C. (1987). Emotion knowledge: Further exploration of a prototype approach. *Journal of Personality and Social Psychology, 52,* 1061-1086.

Shaw, M. P. (1999). On the role of affect in scientific discovery. In S. W. Russ (Ed.), *Affect, creative experience and psychological adjustment* (pp. 19-39). Philadelphia, PA: Brunner/Mazel.

Simonton, D. K. (1999). Origins of genius: Darwinian perspectives on creativity. New York: Oxford University Press.

Simonton, D. K. (2003). Scientific creativity as constrained stochastic behavior: The integration of product, person, and process perspectives. *Psychological Bulletin, 129,* 475-494.

Smith, C. A. & Ellsworth, P. C. (1985). Patterns of cognitive appraisal in emotion. *Journal of Personality and Social Psychology, 48,* 813-838.

Steinberg, H., Sykes, E. A., Moss, T., Lowrey S., LeBoutillier, N. & Dewey, A. (1997). Exercise enhances creativity independently of mood. *British Journal of Sports Medicine, 31,* 240-245.

Sternberg, R. J. (1988a). The nature of creativity: Contemporary psychological perspectives. Cambridge: Cambridge University Press.

Sternberg, R. J. (1988b). A three-facet model of creativity. In R.J. In R.J. Sternberg (Ed.), The Nature of Creativity: Contemporary Psychological Perspectives. (pp. 125-147). Cambridge: Cambridge University Press.

Verhaeghen, P., Joorman, J. & Khan, R. (2005). Why we sing the blues: The relation between self-reflective rumination, mood and creativity. *Emotion, 5,* 226-232.

Vosburg, S. K. (1998). The effects of positive and negative mood on divergent thinking performance. *Creativity Research Journal, 11,* 165-172.

Vosburg, S. K. & Kaufman, G. (1999). Mood and creativity research: The view from a conceptual organizing perspective. In S. W. Russ (Ed.), *Affect, creative experience and psychological adjustment* (19-39). Philadelphia, PA: Brunner/Mazel.

Wallach, M. A. & Kogan, N. (1965) *Modes of thinking in young children: A study of the creativity-intelligence distinction.* New York: Holt, Rinehart and Winston.

Weisberg, R. W. (1988). Problem-solving and creativity. In R.J. Sternberg (Ed.), *The Nature of Creativity: Contemporary Psychological Perspectives* (148-176). Cambridge: Cambridge University Press.

Weisberg, R. W. (1994). Genius or madness? A quasi-experimental test of the hypothesis that manic-depression increases creativity. *Psychological Science, 5,* 361-367.

Weiss, H. M. & Cropanzano, R. (1996). Affective events theory: A theoretical discussion of the structure, causes and consequences of affective experiences at work. In B. M. Staw and L. L. Cummings (Eds.), *Research in Organizational Behavior* (1-74). Greenwich, CT: JAI Press.

Yerkes, R. M. & Dodson, J. D. (1908). The relation of strength of stimulus to rapidity of habit-formation. *Journal of Comparative Neurology and Psychology, 18,* 459-482.

In: Handbook of Psychology of Emotions
Editors: C. Mohiyeddini, M. Eysenck and S. Bauer

ISBN: 978-1-62808-053-7
© 2013 Nova Science Publishers, Inc.

Chapter 22

THE PSYCHOBIOLOGY OF DISGUST

Sonja Rohrman[1], and Anne Schienle[2]*

[1]Department of Psychology, Goethe University, Frankfurt, Germany,
[2]Department of Psychology, Karl Franzens University, Graz, Austria

ABSTRACT

This chapter on disgust provides a concise overview about central aspects of this basic emotion. According to bio-evolutionary approaches, disgust evolved from a distaste response, and acquired multi-faceted functions such as disease prevention, and transmission of socio-moral standards over time. The disgust response is a brief state of loathing which is accompanied by changes in three loosely coupled response systems of overt behavior, verbal report, and somatic activation, including characteristic neuro-immunological reactions. Individuals greatly differ in the degree they experience disgust. Disgust proneness constitutes a temporally stable personality feature that is already present in childhood, and can be considered a vulnerability factor of specific mental disorders, such as specific phobias of the animal and blood type, obsessive-compulsive disorders, and hypochondriasis. Several questionnaires have been developed for the assessment of overall as well as domain-specific disgust proneness.

1. INTRODUCTION

Basic emotions are essential components of every human life. Due to their genetic foundation, they are universal. This implies that they are expressed in similar ways by different individuals across the world (Ekman, 1971; 1972). Affective information conveyed by faces is processed automatically and in a prioritized way because this can have survival value in terms of rapidly recognizing potential threat. Emotional signals presented by faces are however not merely reflexive, but also have another purpose, and that is to communicate. The exchange of this type of nonverbal information is of fundamental importance for the social behavior of individuals (Rolls, 1999).

---

* Corresponding author: rohrmann@psych.uni-frankfurt.de.

It is generally accepted that disgust along with surprise, happiness, fear, anger, and sadness make up the group of primary emotions (Ekman, 1982). When an individual expresses disgust his facial mimicry is comparable across different cultural groupings and is clearly recognizable as just that: something disgusting (Ekman, 1984; Ekman et al., 1987; Izard, 1971; Haidt & Keltner, 1998). Disgust as a defensive emotion is widely believed to have the function of protecting the organism against contact with contaminated substances (Ekman & Friesen, 1975; Rozin, Haidt & McCauley, 2008; Woody & Teachman, 2000, Curtis, 2011). Although a multitude of different disgust triggers are described throughout scientific literature, the majority of these relates to food ingestion and excretion. As early as 1872 Darwin referred to disgust as a reaction to something repellent for the taste sense: *"... something revolting, primarily in relation to the sense of taste, as actually perceived or vividly imagined; and secondarily to anything which causes a similar feeling, through the sense of smell, touch and even of eyesight* (p. 231)." From this point on disgust has been conceptualized as a defense/avoidance reaction which should prevent the oral incorporation of pathogenic substances (e.g., Hennig & Netter, 2000).

In the classical work of Angyal (1941), however, the disgust reaction to body secretions is viewed from a psychoanalytic perspective: *"... a specific reaction towards the waste products of the human and animal body* (p. 395)." Angyal extends and modifies the viewpoint by Freud (1953), who understands disgust as an original reaction to the smell of excrements. According to Angyal (1941) disgust is directed against waste products of the body, because of the *"fear of becoming soiled"* (p.1). Following Tomkins (1963; 1987), disgust is an innate defensive reaction which serves to reduce the magnitude of specific biological drives, such as hunger and thirst.

On a phenomenological level, the basic emotion disgust is a brief state of loathing which is accompanied by changes in three loosely coupled response systems of overt behavior, verbal report, and physiological activation.

2. RESPONSES OF DISGUST

Disgust responses can be elicited in the laboratory reliably and realistically without ethical concerns (Rozin, Lowery & Ebert, 1994). The most commonly applied method for experimental disgust induction consists of the presentation of disgust-relevant scenes. These are usually taken from the validated International Affective Picture System (IAPS; Lang, Bradley & Cuthbert, 1995; Lang, Öhman, & Vaitl, 1988), or have been developed for a specific investigation (Buske-Kirschbaum et al. 2001; Schienle et al., 2001; Schienle, Stark et al., 2002; Curtis et al., 2004; Rohrmann et al., 2008; Stevenson, Oaten, Case, Repacholi & Wagland, 2010). In some studies, film clips were shown (Hennig et al., 1996; Gross & Levenson, 1993, 1995; Gross, 1998; Rohrmann et al., 2008). Moreover, the Behavioral Approach Task (BAT) has been applied in many investigations (Adams Jr., Willems & Bridges, 2011; Buske-Kirschbaum et al., 2001; Deacon & Olatunji, 2007; Fluitman et al., 2010; Olatunji, Lohr, Sawchuk & Tolin, 2007; Tsao & McKay, 2004). This is an in-vivo exposition task where certain objects have to be viewed or touched in a controlled setting. Often, artificially made or modified disgust stimuli are presented to the subjects. Examples might include a bedpan with apple juice designed to resemble urine; an urn which supposedly contains the ashes of a person; or a syringe with artificial blood. The distance (measured in meters) that a person keeps from a specific disgust elicitor is considered a state measure of disgust propensity.

As shown in different experimental studies disgust is characterized by a specific psychophysiological reaction pattern. Emotion-relevant responses manifest themselves in different dimensions: subjective, behavioral, and somatic responses.

Subjective Responses

The subjective component of the disgust response ('qualia') consists of feelings of revulsion and loathing (Rozin et al., 2008). Relevant elicitors are always experienced as aversive and arousing (Buske-Kirschbaum, Geiben, Wermke, Pirke & Hellhammer, 2001; Stark et al., 2003; Rohrmann, Hopp & Quirin, 2008). 'Pure disgust', a reaction where the emotion disgust is not mediated, or found in conjunction with other emotions, is rare. The affective response to nauseating stimuli is often a mixture of different negative emotions, such as disgust, fear, anger, and sadness (Stark et al., 2003).

Behavioral Responses

Disgust has a motivating function to initiate specific motor response programs. At the behavioral level, disgust manifests itself by the avoidance of the nauseating object or the rejection of the disgust-inducing stimulus by spitting or cleaning, by physical distancing or closing of the eyes (Davey, 1994; Rozin et al., 2008). The prototypical facial expression (Ekman, 1971, Ekman, 1999) has a communicative function and consists of the raising of the upper lip - a possible vestige of the gag reflex. When a disgust feeling becomes overwhelming the tongue is protruded –in order to expel substances out of the mouth. This response is often accompanied by typical vocalizations such as 'eww' or 'yuck' which arise when food is expelled from the mouth (Davey, 1994; Scherer, 1986). Additionally, the facial disgust expression is characterized by wrinkling the nose, which leads to a closing of the nostrils - a defense mechanism against aversive smells (Davey, 1994; Rozin & Fallon, 1987, Rozin et al., 2008). The combination of these two facial gestures led scientists to propose that disgust has food-related origins. Disgust is believed to have evolved from an oral and visceral defense reaction (Darwin 1872/ 1965).

Somatic Responses

The somatic reaction element of disgust is connected with feelings of nausea and increased salivation which are valid as well as specific disgust indicators (Angyl, 1941; Davey, 1994; Rozin & Fallon, 1987; Rozin et al., 2008). These reactions also support the interpretation of disgust as a food-related emotion. An especially strong disgust stimulus may even lead to vomiting. Disgust is a parasympathetic response. The majority of studies have documented heart rate deceleration during disgust elicitation (Johnson et al., in 1995; Gross, 1998; Gross & Levenson, 1993; Rohrmann et al., 2008; Rozin, Lowery, Imada & Haidt,

1999). Despite this, there have been a few examples where a stable or even an increase in heart rate have been recorded (Ekman, Levenson & Friesen, 1983; Lang, Greenwald, Bradley & Hamm, 1993; Levenson, Ekman & Friesen, 1990; Vrana, 1993). This presumably is a consequence of the method chosen for disgust induction (Rohrmann & Hopp, 2008; Stark et al., 2005). Experimental disgust stimuli only provoked insignificant changes in systolic and diastolic blood pressure (Schienle et al., in 2001; Rohrmann & Hopp, in 2008). In contrast, studies have regularly shown an increase in electrodermal activity (Johnson, Thayer & Hughdahl, 1995; Gross, 1998; Gross & Levensohn, in 1993; Lang, Greenwald, Bradley & Hamm, in 1993; Levenson, Ekman & Friesen, 1990, Rohrmann et al., 2004) clearly illustrating the arousing qualities of disgusting stimuli.

Several studies have looked at neural substrates of disgust by electroencephalogram (EEG). Here, it was shown that the experience of disgust is associated with a relative increase in right-hemispheric frontal activation (decrease of EEG alpha power), and thus with withdrawal tendencies (Davidson, Ekman, Saron, Senulis, & Friesen, 1990; Davidson, 1992). Other EEG studies that investigated event-related potentials (ERPs) demonstrated that the viewing of disgust evoking pictures relative to neutral ones is associated with an enhanced late positivity (approximately 300 – 1000 ms after picture onset) across the parietal cortex (e.g. Leutgeb et al., 2011). This enhanced ERP component indicates increased visual system activation reflecting 'motivated attention'. Repulsive stimuli elicit an automatic attention focusing response within the individual which in turn facilitates perceptual processing to assist adaptive behavior.

There is an increasing number of studies that applied brain imaging methods for the study of disgust within the last years. The research group around Phillips et al. (1997) conducted a classical functional magnetic resonance imaging (fMRI) experiment and was able to demonstrate that the viewing of facial disgust expressions selectively activated the anterior insula. The insula is considered as gustatory cortex and is involved in the detection of chemical stimuli (smell, taste). This fits with the view of disgust as a food-related protection mechanism. There are however other researchers who failed to identify the insula as a specific disgust processor (e.g. Chapman & Anderson, 2012; Schienle et al., 2002). They showed that not only the insula, but also several other brain regions, such as the amygdala and the orbitofrontal cortex were active during the experience of disgust (and also during other basic emotions). This would imply that the process, like so many neurobiological processes, is not handled by one isolated brain region but involves a complex and coordinated interaction from many different neural areas. This extended neural network is involved in the representation of internal body states and valence decoding. Thus, the insula is involved in disgust processing, however not exclusively.

Although a great deal of research has been done on the brain structures involved in the disgust response, comparatively little is known about accompanying biochemical patterns. Over the years it has become apparent that salivary cortisol levels are not affected by an exposure to disgust stimuli (Buske-Kirschbaum et al., 2001; Hennig, Pössel & Netter, 1996; Stevenson et al., 2010), but studies involving secretory immunoglobulin A (sIgA) seem to show it to be a relevant factor (Hennig et al., 1996; Rohrmann et al., 2008; Stevenson et al., 2010). All the aforementioned authors observed a disgust-related reduction of sIgA levels. SIgA is an antibody found in mucous secretions, such as tears, saliva, and in secretions of the respiratory and gastrointestinal tract. It functions as a *first line of defense* against microbes and helps to limit their otherwise uncontrolled reproduction in body secretions (Tomasi,

1972). Stevenson et al. (2010) proposed that a disgust-induced reduction of sIgA may help to conserve proteins of health-threatening food that would otherwise have been incorporated. The first stage of digestion is delayed and with the help of increased salivary flow and gagging the substances can be expelled from the mouth. Finally, subsequent to a disgust elicitation, an increase in the tumor necrosis factor - alpha (TNF-α) concentration has been measured in saliva samples (Stevenson et al., 2010) as well as in the serum (Buske-Kirschbaum et al., 2001). TNF-α belongs to the proinflammatory cytokines and is able to induce fever and inflammation. This in turn inhibits bacterial/viral replication. Thus, disgust can influence our immune functions and by doing so acts as a protection mechanism against contamination and infection.

However, the specific psychophysiological response pattern of disgust can not only be triggered by stimuli that connote disease but by a multitude of different elicitors that have evolved in the cultural development of mankind.

3. DOMAINS OF DISGUST

Disgust is a heterogeneous emotion, elicited in response to very different stimuli. Theoretical approaches suggest that this variety of disgust elicitors can be reduced and grouped together in a limited number of classes or domains. These categories seem to be specifically related to food ingestion/excretion, sexuality/mating, socio-moral interactions, and death. When viewed in this manner the resulting factors seem almost limited, and pertain to a limited number of functions (e.g., Rozin et al., 2000).

Let us take a closer look at these functions: According to bio-evolutionary models the precursor of disgust is **distaste**, which is an innate reaction towards bad taste. Even in newborns the typical facial disgust expression can be elicited when bitter or sour substances are administered to the tongue (Davey, 1994; Peiper, 1963; Rozin, Lowery, Imada & Haid, 1999; Steiner, 1974). As these taste qualities are often characteristic for poisonous, non-nutritious or otherwise unhealthy substances, it seems plausible that the distaste response serves as a protection mechanism of the body against such food threats (Shallenberger & Acree, 1971).

There is wide agreement among disgust researchers that disgust has directly evolved from the distaste response, sometimes labeled **basic or core disgust** (Rozin et al., 2000). Core disgust acts as a safeguard for the mouth and, hence, for the body. The mouth has the last opportunity to monitor and control ingested materials before they finally reach the body (Rozin & Fallon, 1981; Rozin, Nemeroff, Horowitz, Gordon & Voet, 1995). Miller (2004) has referred to disgust as the 'gatekeeper emotion'.

Body products such as excrements, urine, blood, and sweat are further fundamental disgust triggers. Feces belong to the first disgust elicitors in the ontogenesis, and they are considered one of the strongest disgust stimuli as well (Angyl, 1941; Rozin & Fallon, 1987; Davey, 1994). Some animals elicit disgust because they resemble body products (e.g., snails - mucus; snakes - excrements) or because they are potential transmitters of disease since they are viewed as having had contact with decaying animal meat, excrements, or garbage. Examples would be maggots, flies, cockroaches, and rats. Interestingly, our own body secretions have a peculiar disgust status (Rozin & Fallon, 1987). For example, Allport (1955) found that we are not disgusted by saliva in our own mouth. However, saliva becomes an object of disgust when it has left the body. Many of us would not drink a glass of water after having spit into it. Allport (1955) used the term 'ego alien' for this type of response. On the other hand, in intimate relationships the disgust threshold is lowered. The loved one becomes a social extension of the biological self, so that the contact with body secretions is not considered repulsive anymore. This overcoming of disgust secures mating and breeding (cf. also Davey, 1994).

Altogether, core disgust can be understood as an adaptive system that evolved to motivate disease-avoidance behavior. It facilitates the recognition of contaminated objects and promotes hygienic behavior. Curtis (2011) argues that disgust supports personal, food and water hygiene in humans and thus helps to prevent the fecal-oral transmission of diarrheal disease and parasite infection. As a fundamental bioevolutionary mechanism similar behaviors aiming to decrease the risk of infection are also present in animals (e.g. fecal avoidance, grooming, avoidance behavior connected with food intake; Tybur et al., 2009).

Another disgust domain, **'animal-reminder disgust'**, was introduced by Rozin et al. (2000). They propose that humans like to deny their animal nature reflected by their sexuality, somatic vulnerability, and ultimately their own death and decay. In doing so, they try to draw an explicit border between themselves and the animal kingdom. Animal nature disgust serves the protection of the body and soul (Rozin et al., 2000). This type of disgust is elicited by certain sexual activities (e.g., with animals, siblings), and poor hygiene (e.g., body secretions, also see Frijda, 1986; Plutchik, 1984). Interestingly, there is only one body secretion which is not considered disgusting per se. This secretion is specifically human: tears. Due to the fact that this fluid is outside of the animal realm, there is no need for rejection and denial (Ortner, 1973). Further elicitors of animal-reminder disgust include injuries of the body envelope (e.g., open wounds), and death (e.g., contact with dead bodies). Especially the contact with dying and dead organisms is a potent disgust stimulus and serves as a defense mechanism against the universal fear of death (Rozin et al., 2000).

The presence of the disgust category 'animal-reminder disgust' has been viewed critically by different authors. They point out that the conceptual distinctiveness of the domains 'core disgust' and 'animal-reminder disgust' is not clear because of the great overlap in disgust functions which mainly concern disease prevention (Tybur, Lieberman & Griskevicius, 2009). Also, there seems to be no direct bioevolutionary benefit resulting from a disgust of mortality. Nevertheless, in many empirical studies a disgust domain directed towards injured and dead organisms has been identified (e.g., Olatunji et al., 2009, Schienle & Rohrmann, 2011), and this type of disgust could be clearly differentiated from contamination-based revulsion (see paragraph 4: The assessment of disgust proneness).

Another theoretical disgust concept, **interpersonal disgust**, results from contact with foreign and rejected people with the goal to protect the body and soul as well as to stabilize social hierarchies (Rozin et al., 2000; 2008). The function of interpersonal disgust is distancing, withdrawal, and disassociation which go beyond concerns with contracting disease. Accordingly, this type of disgust serves a more general function of protecting and maintaining not only the individual, but also social systems (e.g., Miller, 2004).

Interpersonal disgust becomes apparent when we do not want to wear clean used clothes from others, or avoid sitting on a warm seat vacated by a stranger (Rozin, Nemeroff, Wane & Sherrod, 1989; Rozin, Markwith & McCauley, 1994). The disgust response becomes even more intense when we are asked to wear Adolf Hiltler's sweater despite the fact that it had been previously disinfected (Rozin et al., 1984). Interpersonal disgust obviously protects social norms and orders, and becomes relevant when such norms are violated. It impacts on many aspects of our social life, such as religion, politics, and justice. Unfortunately, there also seems to be a link between this type of disgust and prejudice. Hodson and Costello (2007) showed that interpersonal-disgust sensitivity predicted negative attitudes toward immigrants, foreigners, and socially deviant groups, even after controlling for fear of contamination. This effect of interpersonal-disgust sensitivity on group attitudes was indirect, mediated by ideological orientations (e.g. right-wing authoritarianism).

Moral disgust is provoked by deviations from ethical standards and aims at the protection of social orders. The link between morality and disgust responses becomes obvious by statements on moral offenses such as 'that makes me feel sick' or 'that left a bad taste in my mouth", and perhaps most telling of all, "you disgust me." Whereas some authors consider the association between disgust and morality a metaphorical one, there is empirical evidence for a relationship between core disgust related to contamination and disease, and moral disgust. Chapman et al. (2009) evoked gustatory distaste (elicited by unpleasant tastes), core disgust (elicited by photographs of contaminants), and moral disgust (elicited by unfair treatment in an economic game) in their participants. They revealed that all three types of disgust evoked activation of the levator labii muscle region of the face, characteristic of an oral-nasal rejection response. The authors conclude that immorality is able to elicit the same disgust as disease vectors and bad tastes.

Consequently, disgust combines biological and cultural functions (Davey, 1994). One might say that the basic emotion disgust had the original function to avoid harmful food in order to protect the body (e.g., Oaten, Stevenson & Case, 2009). During the course of evolution disgust acquired a sociomoral dimension with the function to mediate norms and values of a society (Izard, 1977; Rozin, 1982; Rozin et al., 2000). The diversity of disgust triggers from very concrete (e.g. bad tastes) to very abstract (e.g. moral transgressions) reflects the expansion of the role of disgust across evolution (Chapman & Anderson, 2012).

4. THE ASSESSMENT OF DISGUST PRONENESS

State disgust, the brief affective state, can be differentiated from dispositional disgust, which is defined as the temporally stable tendency of a person to experience disgust across different situations (e.g. those involving unusual food or poor hygiene; Schienle et al., 2002). Disgust-prone individuals experience disgust more frequently and more intensely than individuals with low disgust proneness (Haidt et al., 1994; Rozin et al., 2000; Schienle et al., 2002).

For the assessment of disgust proneness different self-report measures have been developed. Some of them focus on specific disgust domains, such as body products (Templer et al.,1984) or food (Rozin et al.,1984), others can be considered measures of overall disgust propensity (e.g., Wronska, 1990; Haidt et al., 1994). The Disgust Scale (DS) by Haidt et al. (1994) is currently the most widely used disgust questionnaire and consists of eight subscales: (1) food (e.g., eating monkey meat), (2) animals (e.g., cockroaches), (3) body products (e.g., vomit), (4) body envelope violations (e.g., injuries), (5) death (e.g., touching a dead body), (6) sex (e.g., homosexuality), (7) poor hygiene (e.g. not changing underwear), and (8) sympathetic magic. The last scale describes stimuli that either resemble contaminants (e.g., feces-shaped candy) or were once in contact with pathogens (e.g., a sweater worn by an ill person). Although the total DS has high reliability and validity, the Cronbach's alpha coefficients of the subscales are not acceptable because they only span from von .34 to .69. Consequently domain-specific disgust sensitivity cannot be identified by means of the DS.

Other authors (e.g., Schienle et al., 2002) performed a variety of analyses on the factor structure of the DS. They suggested that some of the items do not belong in the questionnaire at all (e.g., the sexual disgust items), and that the number of subscales needs to be reduced from eight to five (oral rejection, poor hygiene, mutilation/death, spoilage/decay, and body products). This has been done in the questionnaire for the assessment of disgust sensitivity (QADS, Schienle et al., 2002) that has been validated in different studies. Rohrmann, Schienle, Hodapp & Netter (2004) divided 170 students into groups consisting of individuals with high vs. low disgust proneness with respect to the different QADS subscales. The entire sample group was exposed to a disgust provoking film clip (showing mutilation) and a neutral video. Based on the subscale 'death' it was possible to distinguish high from low scorers by using their facial disgust expression, their heart rate response and their experienced revulsion during disgust elicitation. Thus, the QADS subscales had predictive utility for disgust responses on different dimensions. This was also supported by another investigation by Rohrmann and Hopp (2008), who observed a heart rate deceleration primarily for disease-related disgust, whereas this response was absent during food-associated disgust elicitation. In an fMRI experiment it was possible to predict brain activation in the insula and the orbitofrontal cortex based on the scores participants had obtained on the QADS (Schäfer et al., 2009).

As two of the QADS factors (poor hygiene and body products) show a substantial inter-correlation, the questionnaire might even be reduced to three subscales, which is currently the most consistently reported factor solution for disgust questionnaires (e.g. Olatunji et al., 2009; van Overveld et al., 2011). This structure includes two factors 'core disgust' and 'animal-reminder disgust' (repulsion of our own animalistic nature and mortality) with sufficient internal consistencies (Cronbach's α >.70). The third factor has been labeled contamination-based disgust (risk of infection), with a considerably lower reliability (Cronbach's α <.70).

The three-factor-structure is in accordance with theoretical disgust models (e.g. by Rozin et al., 2000) with the restriction that animal-reminder disgust in newly developed inventories most often exclusively relates to injury and death, but not to the other elicitors subsumed under this heading by Rozin et al. (2000), specifically sexuality. There is evidence of equivalence of the three-factor model in multiple countries, such as Australia, Brazil, Germany, Italy, Japan, the Netherlands, Sweden, and the United States (Olatunji et al., 2009). This supports the view of a universal, cross-cultural structure of disgust.

Two of the identified fundamental disgust domains in adult samples (core disgust and animal-reminder) have also been observed in children. Schienle and Rohrmann (2011) developed a children's version of the QADS with individuals aged between 8 and 13. The extracted factor 'core disgust' combines items describing aversion against spoiled food and poor hygiene, whereas 'animal-reminder disgust' focuses on the disgust elicited by mortality (imagined contact with dead and dying organisms).

It can be stated that there is empirical evidence for the existence of at least two universal disgust domains that are present across the lifespan and across different countries. These two domains are associated with the transmission of pathogens and mortality. Despite this universality, people differ in the intensity of evoked disgust responses. There are marked individual differences in disgust proneness.

5. INDIVIDUAL DIFFERENCES IN DISGUST PRONENESS

In the majority of investigations the disgust construct has not been studied experimentally but by using statistical correlation approaches. Although the available questionnaires for the assessment of disgust proneness are heterogeneous in both their item content and factor structure, the findings on correlations for overall disgust proneness with other personality traits are quite homogeneous: there are positive relationships with trait anxiety, neuroticism, and compulsiveness (Druschel & Sherman, 1999; Haidt et al., 1994; Rozin, Haidt & McCauley, 2000; Schienle et al., 2010; Templer, King, Brooner & Corgiat, 1984; Wronska, 1990), and especially with fear of death (Fear of Death Scale by Boyar, 1964, also see the review article by Rozin, Haidt and McCauley, 1993).

Positive correlations can also be found between disgust proneness and disgust sensitivity. The latter concept describes the tendency of a person to appraise one's own disgust feelings as aversive and uncontrollable (e.g., Schienle et al., 2010; van Overweld et al., 2006). Both components of disgust sensitivity; the shame response to disgust, and the perceived lack of control of such negative emotions, can be assessed by disgust sensitivity scales developed by Schienle et al. (2010) and Overweld et al. (2006). Disgust proneness and disgust sensitivity are clearly distinguishable from one another and are moderately correlated (ranging between r = .29 and .37).

Disgust proneness shows negative associations with sensation seeking, openness for new experiences, and psychoticism (Druschel & Sherman, 1999; Haidt et al., 1994, Rozin, Haidt & McCauley, 1993). Furthermore, disgust prone individuals are characterized by a vigilant, non-repressive coping style, and thus by a deficient avoidance and rejection behavior (Rohrmann et al., 2004; 2009).

One of the most replicated findings on individual differences in disgust proneness relates to sex differences (Arrindell, Mulkens, Kok & Vollenbroek, 1999; Caseras et al., 2007; Haidt et al., 1994; Gross & Levenson, 1995; Schienle et al., 2005; Rohrmann, Hopp & Quirin, 2008, Templer et al., 1984). Women report more intense disgust feeling for several disgust domains, and especially for sexually-related aspects (Tybur, Bryan, Lieberman, Hooper & Merriman, 2011). Despite the fact that women describe themselves as more disgust-prone than men, both gender groups show similar physiological disgust responses (e.g., heart rate response during disgust elicitation, Rohrmann et al., 2008). Additionally, male and female participants of an fMRI experiment did not differ in their activation of the insula and other disgust-related brain regions during visual disgust induction (Schienle et al., 2005), despite the fact that women had indicated higher state and trait disgust. Such findings challenge the bioevolutionary concept of disgust suggesting that women need to be more disgust sensitive than men because they are more important for the survival of the offspring by protecting them from contamination. Nevertheless, it is possible that a heightened sensitivity for disgust is restricted to certain critical life periods in women. According to Power and Dagleish (1997) the disgust proneness of women changes during pregnancy. They show heightened sensitivity in the first trimester (especially for food), a period with the highest maternal as well as fetal vulnerability to pathogens (Fessler, Eng & Navarrete, 2005). Later on, women are typically more involved in the upbringing of their children. By means of facial displays of disgust, they teach their children what is disgusting and should be avoided (Tomkins, 1963). Thus, gender plays a role in the social transmission of disgust. It is of interest, that social stereotypes consider facial disgust expressions more typical and more appropriate for women compared to men (Hess et al., 2000). This underlines, that personal experiences are important for the individual development of one's own disgust proneness.

6. The Development of Disgust Proneness

Empirical data on the development of disgust proneness across the life span are rare. For the acquisition of disgust responses several factors such as developmental, individual, familiar, and cultural influences are relevant and interact with each other. The acquisition of disgust constitutes a special type of acquisition of cultural values and can be understood as a prototypical example for the interplay between affect and cognition (Rozin & Fallon, 1987). The cognitive development of a contamination concept is of vital importance for the disgust response. Hence, disgust is not present at birth, but develops in early and middle childhood (Rozin & Fallon, 1987). For a more nuanced understanding of disgust, children need to have a cognitive representation of their person as an entity as well as of contamination, which is able to threaten the integrity of this entity.

At the age of two, children do not show the typical disgust response displayed by adults when confronted with core elicitors, such as feces (Davey, 1994). For them excrements even have a certain appeal as argued by Freud (1957). Children begin to reject specific disgusting objects, such as feces, as foods by about the age of three (Petó, 1936; Schmidt & Beauchamp, 1988; Stein, Ottenberg & Roulet, 1958). An important experience within this period of time is the toilet training, which helps the child to develop a more elaborate disgust scheme. From this point in time the disgust response generalizes to similarly looking objects, such as dirt, mud, and slimy substance, which all remind us of feces (Rozin et al., 1987). Rozin and Fallon (1987) refer to this process as secondary disgust.

The acquisition of disgust is mediated by the imitation of disgust expressions of other people (Tomkins, 1963). This is a sort of empathic conditioning. Parents show the prototypical facial disgust expression, when they are confronted with certain stimuli. This expression is imitated, and by that elicits a similar emotion in their children (Tomkins, in 1963). For the acquisition of primary disgust social transmission is of central importance. Disgust is taught by caregivers by means of mimic and verbal cues which initiate behavioral conditioning. This is able to explain the observation that measures of disgust proneness show a positive correlation between parents and their children (r = .52; Rozin et al., 1984). A similar association has been reported by Davey, Forster and Mayhew (1993), who also showed that the disgust sensitivity of both parents was able to predict the propensity for disgust in their offspring.

Secondary disgust arises from the coupling of previously neutral with disgusting objects as well as from processes of generalization. The basis for such conditioning processes is the development of a cognitive concept of contamination which starts around the age of 7 years

(Rozin & Fallon, 1987; Piaget, 1971; 1974). Rozin et al. (2000) were able to demonstrate that only after the age of 7, children refused to drink a glass of juice, when a cockroach had been dipped in. Obviously, they had developed a concept that traces of the cockroach were still in the juice and thus contamination sensitivity.

The work by Stevenson et al. (2010) suggests, that the development of disgust proneness is at least partly associated with socialization experiences in childhood. They investigated different disgust elicitors in childhood as well as the time of their acquisition by studying children aged 1 to 18 years. The authors identified three disgust categories labeled 'core disgust', 'animal disgust', and 'socio-moral disgust'. Food-related core disgust emerged first around the age of three years, where the kids showed appropriate verbal and behavioral disgust responses (facial disgust expression, avoidance). This finding is in line with several previous studies demonstrating that the 'distaste response' with its typical facial disgust expression is already present very early in life, even in newborns (e.g. Davidson & Fox, 1982; Rosenstein & Oster, 1988). It can be considered a 'proto-emotion' of disgust (Rozin et al., 2000). The following developmental disgust steps were 'animal disgust' (4 years) and 'socio-moral' disgust (7 years). Also in favor of an early acquisition of disgust responses during development is the study by Widen and Russell (2008). They found evidence that already 3- and 4-year-old children were able to understand the meaning, the elicitors, and the behavioral consequences of disgust; however they had problems to correctly label facial expressions of this emotion. Further, Rozin et al. (1986) observed that children begin to reject certain disgusting non-edible objects (e.g. feces) at the age of three (Rozin, Hammer, Oster, & Marmora, 1986). In another study, Rozin et al. (1985) studied children ranging in age from 3 to 12 years. The participants underwent different behavioral tasks, where a previously appetizing food or beverage was contaminated (e.g. 'Would you drink a glass of juice stirred with (a) a new comb, (b) a used and cleaned comb, and (c) a used and dirty comb?'). Results indicated that contamination sensitivity did not appear in most children before the age of 6 years.

It can be emphasized that developmental processes and learning experiences in the form of classical and instrumental conditioning together with social and cultural factors play a fundamental role for disgust acquisition. Most people learn to adequately deal with the multitude of different disgust elicitors. A minority however is characterized by dysfunctional disgust learning. This might lead to elevated disgust proneness which in turn constitutes a vulnerability factor for certain mental disorders.

7. SYNDROMES OF DISGUST

The potential role of disgust propensity in psychopathology has attracted growing research interest within the last years. The general concept of affective reactivity predicts that individuals with heightened disgust proneness are characterized by intense disgust responses of long duration, which can easily be elicited (Schienle et al., 2002). Therefore, it seems reasonable to assume that increased trait disgust functions as a vulnerability factor for the origin and maintenance of certain psychiatric conditions (Davey, 2011; Phillips, Senior, Fahy & David, 1998).

Intense or even excessive disgust experiences are crucial components of those mental disorders which are associated with concerns of contamination, injury and illness, specifically obsessive-compulsive disorder (OCD) with the key symptom washing compulsions, spider phobia, blood phobia, and hypochondriasis.

Obesessive Compulsive Disorder (OCD)

There is clear evidence that obsessive-compulsive tendencies and disgust proneness are associated with each other (e.g., Davey, 1994; Schienle et al., 2002; 2003). For a nonclinical sample, Schienle et al. (2002) observed a positive correlation between the scores participants' had obtained on the QADS and the Maudsley Obsessive Compulsive Inventory (MOCI; Hodgson & Rachman, 1997). The MOCI assesses the degree of checking and washing compulsions. Checking behaviors were correlated most closely with the disgust domain 'death', whereas repetitive washing correlated with the domain 'poor hygiene' (Schienle et al., 2002). In patients with clinically relevant OCD, symptoms of cleaning and washing are often accompanied by intense disgust feelings and activation of such brain regions which are recruited during disgust elicitation, specifically the insula, the orbitofrontal cortex, and the striatum (Phillips et al., 1997; 1998; Schienle et al., 2005). Moreover, OCD patients have difficulties in correctly identifying facial expressions of disgust (Sprengelmeyer, Young, Pundt et al., 1997). Such a deficit might be linked with their elevated internal experience of disgust, which makes them less sensitive for the disgust of others.

Specific Phobia

Disgust is also involved in specific phobias (spider phobia and blood-injection-injury phobia; BII). For example, Schienle et al. (2002) demonstrated that all subscales of the QADS were significantly correlated with the Mutilation Questionnaire (MQ, Klormann, Weerts, Hastimgs, Melamed & Lang, 1974), which assesses fear of blood and injury. Also, blood phobics display a physiological response pattern which is atypical for fear. When confronted with their phobic object, they react with heart rate deceleration, blood pressure reduction, and nausea (Power & Dalgleish, 1997). This response is similar to the somatic disgust response (Page, 1994).

Several research groups showed that individuals afflicted with spider phobia experience more disgust than fear when confronted with their phobic object, and are characterized by heightened disgust proneness, at least for selective disgust domains (e.g., Davey, 1993; de Jong et al., 1997; Matchett & Davey, 1991; Mulkens et al., 1996; Oßwald & Reinecker, 2004; Page, 1994; Ware et al., 1994; Webb & Davey, 1993). Data from children samples are still limited but also point to an association between disgust and spider fear. De Jong, Andrea and Muris (1997) found elevated disgust proneness in 9 to 14-year old spider-phobic girls. Another questionnaire study observed positive correlations between trait disgust and spider-phobic tendencies in a non-clinical sample of 9 to 13-year old children (Muris, van der Heiden & Rassin, 2008). In a study by Leutgeb et al. (2012) children suffering from spider phobia not only showed elevated disgust responses to spiders, but also to disorder-irrelevant areas (e.g, poor hygiene, spoiled food). Subsequent to a successful exposure therapy the children showed a reduction in self-reported syndrome severity (reduction in spider fear), in overall disgust proneness, and in levator labii activation to spider pictures as well to disorder-irrelevant disgust pictures. Such a broad effect on overall disgust reactivity by means of psychotherapy has not been observed in adult spider phobics, indicating that childhood might be a more sensitive period for such interventions than adulthood (Leutgeb et al., 2009).

Hypochondriasis

Disgust is also implicated in hypochondriasis. Individuals afflicted with this disorder present with the preoccupation about having a serious illness based on a misinterpretation of bodily sensations (Abramowitz, Deacon & Valentiner, 2007; Davey & Bond, 2006; Thorpe, Patel & Simonds, 2003; Warwick, 1998). Ille et al. (2010) compared patients with a tentative diagnosis of hypochondriasis and healthy controls by means of a discriminant analysis. Disgust propensity for selected domains (e.g., poor hygiene) differentiated between the two groups. Further, correlational studies have shown a strong association between disgust proneness and health anxiety, which was independent from trait anxiety (Davey & Bond, 2006, Olatunji, 2009). Moreover, deficient disgust regulation strategies (disgust sensitivity), were correlated with hypochondriasis (Ille et al., 2010, Olatunji, 2009; Schienle, Dietmaier, Ille & Leutgeb, 2010).

It could be shown that a hypersensitive disease avoidance mechanism mediated by increased disgust proneness is crucial for certain anxious psychopathologies, specifically contamination-based OCD, specific phobia of the animal type and the BII type as well as hypochondriasis. For BII phobia, blood, injury and mutilation are assumed to be the medium of pathogen transmission. This association is intuitively apparent, especially when one assumes that the wounded organism has been ill. In the case of spider phobia, this animal might transmit pathogens by means of bites or even by pure contact as it is assumed to live in dirty contaminated environments. There has been a long tradition to connect spiders with the spread of disease as outlined by Davey (2011). This tradition started in the Middle Ages, where spiders were conceptualized as transmitters of epidemics, such as the Great Plagues, and continued into modern times. OCD patients and those individuals afflicted with hypochondriasis seem to be characterized by the lowest disgust threshold. They worry not only about visible disgust elicitors, but also about germs, bacteria, and diffuse pathogens that might be vehicles of disease. For both disorder groups the disgust domain 'poor hygiene' has been proven specific relevance.

Eating Disorders

Although the majority of definitions consider disgust a food-related emotion, the results on the association between disgust proneness and eating disorder have been very mixed. Some authors reported positive correlations between the proneness for selected disgust domains (e.g. food, body products) and the proneness for eating disorders in non-clinical samples (Davey, Buckland, Tantow & Dallos, 1998; 2004; Quigley et al., 1996). Similar findings have been reported for diagnosed patients suffering from anorexia and bulimia nervosa (Cooper et al., 1988). Clinical experience also points to the meaning of disgust for eating disorders: patients afflicted with anorexia nervosa often report disgust of certain types of food (e.g. high-caloric food). Also they experience disgust when confronted with their body weight and figure (Davey et al., 1998; Mitchell & Fensome, 1992; Phillips, Senior, Fahy & David, 1998). Critically, it has to be noted that eating disorder inventories and domain-based questionnaires of disgust enquire about similar stimuli (e.g., food), which leads to inflated correlations.

There are also several questionnaire studies as well as neuroimaging studies that found no elevated disgust proneness in patients suffering from bulimia nervosa and binge-eating disorder (Schienle et al. 2003; 2009). In both fMRI experiments there was no indication of an increased neural sensitivity for visual disgust elicitors in the eating-disordered groups. Finally, there are studies suggesting that the modest correlation between eating disorder symptoms and disgust proneness is substantially mediated by trait measures of anxiety (Davey & Chapman, 2009).

Disgust makes appearance in several mental disorders. Women are over-represented in many of these conditions (e.g., spider phobia, blood phobia, washing compulsions) where the disorder vulnerability is mediated by increased trait disgust. Interestingly, there are also psychophathologies that have no obvious association with a hypersensitive disease-avoidance mechanism, but are nonetheless characterized by heightened disgust proneness. Repeatedly, increased disgust reactivity has been reported for patients suffering from schizophrenia, social phobia, and height phobia (for a summary see Davey, 2011). The function of disgust within these disorders still needs to be unraveled. Also, future research needs to focus on additional trait measures of disgust, such as disgust sensitivity and self-disgust. Problems in efficiently regulating one's own disgust feelings seem to be crucial for many mental disorders and explain variance which cannot be explained by disgust proneness or other affective traits. Moreover, sometimes disgust is not directed towards the outside, but towards oneself. This kind of disgust response has been labeled self-disgust or self-loathing (Power & Dalgleish, 1997). Interestingly, self-disgust has hardly been investigated so far, although it may play a crucial role in specific psychopathologies, specifically depression and borderline personality disorder (e.g. Phillips et al., 1998; Overton et al., 2008).

CONCLUSION

Accumulating evidence from psychobiological studies suggests that disgust constitutes a protection mechanism that helps an individual to avoid contamination and disease. Typical elicitors of this emotion include body secretions such as excrements, urine, blood, sweat, and saliva, as well as contact with dying and dead organisms, which are all potential pathogen transmitters. The bodily reaction with specific neuronal, psychophysiological, and immunological changes further supports the disease-avoidance functionality of disgust. Interestingly, patients suffering from specific mental disorder characterized by contamination fears, display elevated disgust proneness.

However, disgust can not only be triggered by stimuli that connote disease but by a multitude of different elicitors that have evolved in the development of mankind. During the course of evolution disgust acquired a sociomoral dimension with the function to mediate norms and values of a society. Accordingly, disgust combines biological and cultural functions. These functions are context-specific and consequently dynamic. Thus, the psychobiology of disgust will continue to be a promising research area in the future.

REFERENCES

Abramowitz, J. S., Deacon, B. J. & Valentiner, D. P. (2007). The short health anxiety inventory: Psychometric properties and construct validity in a non-clinical sample. *Cognitive Therapy and Research, 31*, 6, 871-883.

Adams Jr., T. G., Willems, J. L. & Bridges, A. J. (2011). Contamination aversion and repeated exposure to disgusting stimuli. *Anxiety, Stress & Coping, 24*(2), 157-65.

Allport, G. W. (1955) *Becoming. Basic considerations for a psychology of personality.* New Haven, CT: Yale University Press.

Angyal, A. (1941). Disgust and related aversions. *Journal of Abnormal and Social Psychology, 36*, 393-412.

Arrindell, W. A., Mulkens, S., Kok, J. & Vollenbroek, J. (1999). Disgust sensitivity and the sex difference in fears to common indigenous animals. *Behaviour Research and Therapy, 37* (3), 273-280.

Becker, E. (1973). *The denial of death.* New York: Free Press.

Boyar, J. I. (1964). The construction and partial validation of a scale for the measurement of the fear of death. *Dissertation Abstracts, 25*(3), 2041.

Buske-Kirschbaum, A., Geiben, A., Wermke, C., Pirke, K. M. & Hellhammer, D. (2001). Preliminary evidence for herpes labialis recurrence following experimentally induced disgust. *Psychotherapy and Psychosomatics, 70*, 86–91.

Caseras, X., Mataix-Cols, D., An, S. K., Lawrence, N. S., Speckens, A., Giampietro, V., Brammer, M. J. & Phillips, M. L. (2007). Sex differences in neural responses to disgusting visual stimuli: implications for disgust-related psychiatric disorders. *Biological Psychiatry, 62* (5), 464-471.

Chapman, H. A. & Anderson, A. K. (2012). Understanding disgust. *Annals of the New York Academy of Sciences*, 62-76.

Chapman, H. A., Kim, D. A., Susskind, J. M. & Anderson, A. K. (2009). In bad taste: Evidence for the oral origins of moral disgust. *Science, 323*, 1222-1226.

Cooper, J. L., Morrison, T. L., Bigman, O. L., Abramowitz, S. I., Levin, S. & Krener, P. (1988). Mood changes and affective disorder in the bulimic binge — Purge cycle. *International Journal of Eating Disorders, 7 (4)*, 469-474.

Curtis, V. (2011). Why disgust matters. *Philosophical Transactions of the Royal Society Biological Sciences, 366*, 3478-3490.

Curtis, V., Aunger, R. & Rabie, T. (2004). Evidence that disgust evolved to protect from risk of disease. *Biological Sciences, 271 (4)*, 131-133.

Darwin, C. R. (1965). *The expression of the emotions in man and animals.* London: Penguin. (Original work published in 1872).

Davey, G. C. L. (2004). Psychopathology of specific phobias. *Psychiatry, 3 (6)*, 83-86.

Davey, G. C. L. (2011). Disgust: The disease-avoidance emotion and its dysfunctions. *Philosophical Transactions of the Royal Society Biological Sciences, 366*, 3453-3465.

Davey, G. C. L. (1994). Disgust. In V. S. Ramachandran (Ed.), *Encyclopedia of human behavior*. San Diego: Academic Press.

Davey, G. C. L. & Bond, N. (2006). Using controlled comparisons in disgust psychopathology research: The case of disgust, hypochondriasis and health anxiety. *Journal of Behavior Therapy and Experimental Psychiatry*, *37* (1), 4-15.

Davey,G. C. L., Buckland, G., Tantow, B. & Dallos, R. (1998). *Disgust and eating disorders. 6 (3)*, 201-211.

Davey, G. C. L. & Chapman, L. (2009) Disgust and eating disorder symptomatology in a non-clinical population: The role of trait anxiety and anxiety sensitivity. *Clinical Psychology & Psychotherapy. Special Issue: Eating disorders and emotions, 16* (4), 268–275.

Davey, G. C. L., Forster, L. & Mayhew, G. (1993). Familial resemblances in disgust sensitivity and animal phobias. *Behavior Research and Therapy, 31*, 41-50.

Davidson, R. J. (1992). Emotion and Affective Style: Hemispheric Substrates. *Psychological Sience, 3* (1), 39-43.

Davidson, R. J., Ekman, P., Saron, C. D., Senulis, J. A. & Friesen, W. V. (1990). Approach, withdrawal and cerebral asymmetry. Emotional expression and brain physiology. *Journal of Personality and Social Psychology*, *58*, 230-341.

Deacon, B. & Olatunji, B. O. (2007). Specificity of disgust sensitivity in the prediction of behavioral avoidance in contamination fear. *Behaviour Research and Therapy, 45* (9), 2110-2120.

De Jong, P. J., Andrea H. & Muris, P. (1997). Spider phobia in children: Disgust and fear before and after treatment. *Behaviour Research and Therapy*, *35* (6), 559-562.

Druschel, B. A. & Sherman, M. F. (1999). Disgust sensitivity as a function of the big five and gender. *Personality and Individual Differences, 26* (4), 739-748.

Ekman, P. (1972). Universals and cultural differences in facial expressions of emotion. In J. Cole (Ed.), *Nebraska Symposium on Motivation* (Vol. *19*, 207-282). University of Nebraska Press.

Ekman, P. (1982). *Emotion in the human face*. New York: Cambridge University Press.

Ekman, P. (1984). Expression and the nature of emotion, In K. Scherer & P. Ekman (Eds.), *Approaches to Emotion* (319-344). Hillsdale, NJ: Erlbaum.

Ekman, P. (1999). Facial Expressions. In T. Dalgleish & M. J. Power (Eds.), *Handbook of Cognition and Emotion* (235-263). Chichester, UK: John Wiley & Sons.

Ekman, P. & Friesen, W. V. (1975). *Unmasking the face*. Englewood Cliffs, NJ: Prentice-Hall.

Ekman, P., Friesen, W. V., O'Sullivan, M., Chan, A., Diacoyanni-Tarlatzis, I., Heider, K., Krause, R., LeCompte, W. A., Pitcairn, T., Ricci-Bitti, P. E., Scherer, K., Tomita, M. & Tzavaras, A. (1987). Universals and cultural differences in the judgments of facial expressions of emotion. *Journal of Personality and Social Psychology, 53* (4), 712-717.

Ekman, P., Levenson, R. W. & Friesen, W. F. (1983). Autonomic nervous system activity distinguishes among emotions. *Science, 221*, 1208-1210.

Fessler, D. M. T., Eng, S. J. & Navarrete, C. D. (2005). Elevated disgust sensitivity in the first trimester of pregnancy: Evidence supporting the compensatory prophylaxis hypothesis. *Evolution and Human Behavior*, *26* (4), 344-351.

Fluitman, S. B. A. H. A., Denys, D. A. J. P., Heijnen, C. J. & Westenberg, H. G. M. (2010). Disgust affects TNF-α, IL-6 and noradrenalin levels in patients with obsessive–compulsive disorder. *Psychoneuroendocrinology, 35* (6), 906-911.

Davidson, R. J. & Fox, N. A. (1982). Asymmetrical brain activity discriminates between positive and negative affective stimuli in human infants. *Science, 218,* 1235-1237

Freud, S. (1953). Three essays on the theory of sexuality. In J. Strachey (Ed. and Trans.), *The standard edition ot the complete psychological works of Sigmund Freud* (Vol. 7, 123-231). London: Hogarth Press. (Original work published 1905).

Freud, S. (1957). Five lectures on psycho-analysis. In J. Strachey (Ed. and Trans.), *The standard edition ot the complete psychological works of Sigmund Freud* (Vol. 11, pp. 3-56). London: Hogarth Press. (Original work published 1910).

Frijda, N. H. (1986). *The emotions.* Cambridge: Cambridge University Press.

Gross, J. J. (1998). Antecedent- and response-focused emotion regulation: Divergent consequences for experience, expression, and physiology. *Journal of Personality and Social Psychology, 74* (1), 224-237.

Gross, J. J. & Levenson, R. W. (1993). Emotional suppression: Physiology, self-report, and expressive behavior. *Journal of Personality and Social Psychology, 64,* 970-986.

Gross, J. J. & Levenson, R. W. (1995). Emotion elicitation using films. *Cognition & Emotion, 9* (1), 87-108.

Haidt, J. & Keltner, D. (1999). *Culture and facial expression: Open ended methods find more expression and a gradient of recognition. Cognition and Emotion, 13,* 225-266.

Haidt, J., McCauley, C. R. & Rozin, P. (1994). Individual differences in sensitivity to disgust: A scale sampling seven domains of disgust elicitors. *Personality and Individual Differences, 16,* 701-713.

Haidt, J., Rozin, P., McCauley, C. R. & Imada, S. (1997). Body, psyche, and culture: The relationship between disgust and morality. *Psychology and Developing Societies, 9,* 107–131.

Hennig, J. & Netter, P. (2000). Ekel und Verachtung. In: J. H. Otto, H.A. Euler & H. Mandl (Hrsg). *Handbuch der Emotionspsychologie,* S.284-296, Weinheim, Beltz.

Hennig, J., Pössel, P. & Netter, P. (1996). Sensitivity to disgust as an indicator of neuroticism: A psychobiological approach. *Personality and Individual Differences, 20,* 589-596.

Hess, U. (2000). Emotional expressivity in men and women: Stereotypes and self-perceptions, *Cognition and Emotion, 14,* 609– 642.

Hodgson, R. & Rachman, S. (1997). Obsessional compulsive complaints. *Behavior Research and Therapy, 15,* 389-395.

Hodson, G. & Costello (2007). Interpersonal disgust, ideological orientations, and dehumanization as predictors of intergroup attitudes. *Psychological Sciences, 18,* 691-698. Ille, R., Dietmaier, G., Müller, S. & Schienle, A. (2010). Die Bedeutung von Ekel- und Angstsensitivität bei Personen mit der Verdachtsdiagnose einer Hypochondrie. *Zeitschrift für Psychiatrie, Psychologie und Psychotherapie, 58* (3), 219-226.

Izard, C. E. (1971). *The face of emotion.* New York: Appleton-Century-Crofts.

Izard, C. E. (1977). *Human emotions.* New York: Plenum Press.

Johnson, B., Thayer, J. F. & Hughdahl, K. (1995). Affective judgment of Ekman faces: A dimensional approach. *Journal of Psychophysiology, 9,* 193-202.

Klorman, R., Weerts, T., Hastings, J., Melamed, B. & Lang, P. (1974). Psychometric description of some fear-specific questionnaires. *Behaviour Therapy, 5,* 401-409.

Lang, P. J., Bradley, M. M. & Cuthbert, B. (1995). *International affective picture system (IAPS).* Gainesville, FL: The Center for Research in Psychophysiology, University of Florida.

Lang, P., Greenwald, M. K., Bradley, M. M. & Hamm, A. (1993). Looking at pictures: affective, facial, visceral, and behavioral reactions. *Psychophysiology, 30,* 261-273.

Lang, P., Öhman, A. & Vaitl, D. (1998). *The International Affective Picture System (photographic slides).* Gainesville, FL: The Center for Research in Psychophysiology, University of Florida.

Leutgeb, V., Schäfer, A. & Schienle, A. (2011). Late cerebral positivity and cardiac responsivity in female dental phobics when exposed to phobia-relevant pictures. *International Journal of Psychophysiology, 79,* 410-416.

Leutgeb, V., Köchel, A., Schäfer, A. & Schienle, A. (in press). Successful exposure therapy leads to enhanced late frontal positivity in 8- to 13-year-old spider phobic girls. *Biological Psychology.*

Leutgeb, V., Schäfer, A. & Schienle, A. (2009). An event-related potential study on exposure therapy for patients suffering from spider phobia. *Biological Psychology, 82,* 293–300.

Leutgeb, V. & Schienle, A. (2012). Therapy effect on facial electromyographic activity in 8- to 14-year-old spider-phobic girls. *Journal of Psychiatric Research, 46*(6), 805–810.

Levenson, R. W., Ekman, P. & Friesen, W. V. (1990). Voluntary facial action generates emotion-specific autonomic nervous system activity. *Psychophysiology, 27,* 363-384.

Matchett, G. & Davey, G. C. L. (1991). A test of a disease-avoidance model of animal phobias. *Behaviour Research & Therapy, 29,* 91-94.

Miller, S. B. (2004). Disgust: The Gatekeeper Emotion, London: The Analytical Press.

Mitchell, J. & Fensome, H. (1992). Eating disorders. In L.A. Champion & M.J. Power (Eds.), Adult psychological problems: an introduction. London: Falmer Press.

Mulkens, S. A. N., de Jong, P. J. & Merckelbach, H. (1996). Disgust and spider phobia. *Journal of Abnormal Psychology, 105* (3), 464-468.

Muris, P., van der Heiden, S. & Rassin, E. (2008). Disgust sensitivity and psychopathological symptoms in non-clinical children. *Journal of Behavior Therapy and Experimental Psychiatry, 39* (2), 133-146.

Oaten, M., Stevenson, R. J. & Case, T. I. (2009). Disgust as a disease-avoidance mechanism. *Psychological Bulletin, 135* (2), 303-321.

Oatley, K. & Johnson-Laird, P. N. (1987). Towards a cognitive theory of emotions. *Cognition and Emotion, 1,* 29-50.

Olatunji, B. O., Moretz, M., McKay, D., Bjorklund, F., de Jong, P., Haidt, J., Hursti, T., Koller, S., Mancini, F., Page, A. & Schienle, A. (2009). Confirming the three-factor structure of the Disgust Scale-Revised in eight countries. *Journal of Cross-Cultural Psychology, 40,* 234-255.

Olatunji, B. O., Williams, N. L., Tolin, D. F., Sawchuck, C. N., Abramowitz, J. S., Lohr, J. M. & Elwood, L. S. (2007). The disgust scale: Item analysis, factor structure, and suggestions for refinement. *Psychological Assessment, 19,* 281-297.

Ortner, S. B. (1973). Sherps purity. *American Psychologist, 75,* 49-63.

Oßwald, S. & Reinecker, H. (2004) Der Zusammenhang von Ekel und Ekelempfindlichkeit mit Spinnen- und Blut-Spritzen-Verletzungsängsten, *Verhaltenstherapie, 14,* 23-33.

Overton, P. G., Markland, F. E., Taggart, H. S., Bagshaw, G. L. & Simpson, J. (2008). Self-disgust mediates the relationship between dysfunctional cognitions and depressive symptomatology. *Emotion, 8*, 379-385.

Overveld, W. J. M. van, de Jong, P. J., Peters, M. L., Cavanagh, L. & Davey, G. C. L. (2006). Disgust propensity and disgust sensitivity: Separate constructs that are differentially related to specific fears. *Personality and Individual Differences, 41*, 1241-1252.

Overveld, W. J. M. van, de Jong, P. J., Peters, M. L. & Schouten, E. (2011). The Disgust Scale-R: A valid and reliable index to investigate separate disgust domains? *Personality and Individual Differences, 51 (3)*, 325-330.

Page, A. C. (1994). Blood-injury phobia. *Clinical Psychology Review, 14*, 443-461.

Peiper, A. (1963). *Celebral function in infancy and childhood.* New York: Consultant's Bureau.

Petó. E. (1936). Contribution to the development of smell feeling. *British Journal of Medical Psychology, 15*, 314-320.

Phillips, M. L., Senior, C., Fahy, T. & David, A. S. (1998). Disgust – the forgotten emotion of psychiatry. *British Journal of Psychiatry, 172*, 373-375.

Phillips, M. L., Young, A. W., Senior, C., Brammer, M., Andrew, C., Calder, A. J., Bullmore, E. T., Perrett, D. I., Rowland, D., Williams, S. C. R., Gray, J. A. & David, A. S. (1997). A specific neural substrate for perceiving facial expressions of disgust. *Letters to Nature, 389*, 495-498.

Piaget, J. (1974). *Understanding causality (J. Piaget, Trans.).* New York: W.W. Norton. (Original work published 1971).

Plutchik, R. (1984). Emotion: a general psychoevolutionary theory. In K. Scherer & P. Ekman (Eds.), Approaches to emotion (216). Hilldale, N.J.: Lawrence Erlbaum Associates, Publishers.

Power, M. & Dagleish, T. (1997). Cognition and Emotion: From *Order to Disorder.* Hove: Psychology Press.

Rohrmann, S. & Hopp, H. (2008). Cardiovascular indicators of disgust. *International Journal of Pschophysiology, 68* (3), 201-208.

Rohrmann, S., Hopp, H. & Quirin, M. (2008). Gender differences in psychophysiological responses to disgust. *Journal of Psychophysiology, 22* (2), 65-75.

Rohrmann, S., Schienle, A., Hodapp, V. & Netter P. (2004). Experimentelle Überprüfung des Fragebogens zur Erfassung der Ekelempfindlichkeit (FEE). *Zeitschrift für Klinische Psychologie und Psychotherapie, 33* (2), 91-100.

Rohrmann, S., Hopp, H., Schienle, A. & Hodapp, V. (2009). Emotion regulation, disgust sensitivity, and psychophysiological responses to a disgust-inducing film. *Anxiety, Stress, and Coping, 22 (2)*, 215-236.

Rolls, E. T. (1999). *The Brain and Emotion.* Oxford University Press, Oxford.

Rosenstein, D. & Oster, H. (1988). Differential facial responses to four basic tastes in newborns. *Child Development, 59*, 1555–1568.

Rozin, P., Fallon, A. & Mandell, R. (1984). Family resemblance in attitudes to foods. *Developmental Psychology, 2*, 309-314.

Rozin, P. (1982). Human food selection: The interaction of biology, culture and individual experience. In L.M. Barker (Ed.), *The psychobiology of human food selection* (pp. 225-254). Bridgeport, CT: AVI.

Rozin, P. & Fallon, A. E. (1980). The psychological categorization of foods and non-foods. A preliminary taxonomy of food rejections. *Appetite, 1*, 193-201.

Rozin, P. & Fallon, A. E. (1981). The acquisition of likes and dislikes for foods. In J. Solms & R.L. Hall (Eds.), *Criteria of food acceptance: How man chooses what he eats. A symposium* (35-48). Zürich: Forster.

Rozin, P. & Fallon, A. (1987). A perspective on disgust. *Psychological Review, 94*, 23-41.

Rozin, P., Fallon, A. & Augustoni-Ziskind, M. L. (1985). The child's conception of food: The development of contamination sensitivity to "disgusting" substances. *Developmental Psychology, 21* (6), 1075-1079.

Rozin, P., Haidt, J. & McCauley, C. R. (1993). Disgust. In M. Lewis & J. Haviland (Eds.), *Handbook of Emotions* (575-594). New York: Guilford.

Rozin, P., Haidt, J. & McCauley, C. R. (2008). Disgust. In M. Lewis & J. Haviland & L.F. Barrett (Eds.), *Handbook of Emotions* (757-776). New York: Guilford Press.

Rozin, P., Haidt, J. & McCauley, C. R. (2000). Disgust. In M. Lewis & J.M. Haviland-Jones (Eds.), *Handbook of emotions*, 2nd Edition (637-653). New York: Guilford Press.

Rozin, P., Haidt, J. & McCauley, C. R. (1999). Disgust. In M. Lewis & JM Haviland (Eds.), *Handbook of emotions* (575–594). New York: Guilford Press.

Rozin, P., Hammer, L., Oster, H., Horowitz, T. & Marmora, V. (1986). The child's conception of food: Differentiation of categories of rejected substances in the 1.4 to 5 year range. *Appetite, 7*, 141-151.

Rozin, P., Lowery, L. & Ebert, R. (1994). Varities of disgust faces and the structure of disgust. *Journal of Personality and Social Psychology, 66*, 870–881.

Rozin, P., Lowery, L., Imada, S. & Haidt, J. (1999). The CAD triad hypothesis: A mapping between three moral emotions (contempt, anger, disgust) and three moral codes (community, autonomy, divinity). *Journal of Personality and Social Psychology, 76* (4), 574-586.

Rozin, P., Markwith, M. & McCauley, C. (1994). Sensitivity to indirect contacts with other persons: AIDS aversion as a composite of aversion to strangers, infection, moral taint, and misfortune. *Journal of Abnormal Psychology, 103*, 495-505.

Rozin, P., Millman, L. & Nemeroff, C. (1986). Operation of the laws of sympathetic magic in disgust and other domains. *Journal of Personality and Social Psychology, 50*, 703-712.

Rozin, P., Nemeroff, C., Horowitz, M., Gordon, B. & Voet, W. (1995). The Borders of the Self: Contamination Sensitivity and Potency of the Body Apertures and Other Body Parts. *Journal of Research in Personality, 29* (3), 318-340.

Rozin, P., Nemeroff, C., Wane, M. & Sherrod, A. (1989). Operation of the sympathetic magical law of contagion in interpersonal attitudes among Americans. *Bulletin of the Psychonomic Society, 27*, 367-370.

Schäfer, A., Leutgeb, V., Reishofer, G., Ebner, F. & Schienle, A. (2009). Propensity and sensitivity measures of fear and disgust are differentially related to emotion-specific brain activation. *Neuroscience Letters, 465*, 262-266.

Scherer, K. R. (1986). Vocal affect expression: A review and a model for future research. *Psychological Bulletin, 99* (2), 143-165.

Scherer, K. R. (1997). Profiles of emotion-antecedent appraisal: Testing theoretical predictions across cultures. *Cognition and Emotion, 11*, 113-150.

Schienle, A., Dietmaier, G., Ille, R. & Lautgeb, V. (2010). Eine Skala zur Erfassung der Ekelsensitivität (SEE). *Zeitschrift für Klinische Psychologie und Psychotherapie, 39* (2), 80-86.

Schienle, A. & Rohrmann, S. (2011) Ein Fragebogen zur Erfassung der Ekelempfindlichkeit bei Kindern (FEEK). *Klinische Diagnostik und Evaluation, 4*, 379-392..

Schienle, A., Stark, R. & Vaitl, D. (2001). Evaluative conditioning: A possible explanation for the acquisition of disgust responses? *Learning and Motivation, 32*, 65-83.

Schienle, A., Stark, R., Walter, B., Blecker, C., Ott, U., Kirsch P., Sammer G. & Vaitl, D. (2002). The insula is not specifically involved in disgust processing: An fMRI study. *Neuroreport, 13*, 2023-2026.

Schienle, A., Walter, B. & Vaitl, D. (2002). Ein Fragebogen zur Erfassung der Ekelempfindlichkeit (FEE). *Zeitschrift für Klinische Psychologie und Psychotherapie, 31*, 110-120

Schienle, A, Walter, B., Schäfer, A., Stark, R. & Vaitl, D. (2003). Ekelempfindlichkeit: Ein Vulnerabilitätsfaktor für essgestörtes Verhalten. *Zeitschrift für Klinische Psychologie und Psychotherapie, 32* (4), 295-302.

Schienle, A., Walter, B., Schaefer, A., Stark, R. & Vaitl, D. (2005). Neural responses of OCD patients towards disorder-relevant, generally disgust-inducing and fear-inducing pictures. *International Journal of Psychophysiology, 57*, 69-77

Schienle, A., Schäfer, A., Hermann, A. & Vailt, D. (2009). Binge-eating disorder: reward sensitivity and brain activation to images of food. *Biological Psychiatry. 65*, 654-61.

Schmidt, H. J. & Beauchamp, G. K. (1988). Adult-like odor preferences and aversions in three-year-old children. *Child Development, 59* (4), 1136-1143.

Shallenberger, R. S. & Acree, T. E. (1971) Chemical structure of compounds and their sweet and bitter taste. *Handbook of sensory physiology, 4*, (Pt. 2, taste), 221-277.

Sprengelmeyer, R., Young, A. W., Pundt, I., Sprengelmeyer, A., Calder, A. J., Berrios, G., Winkel, R., Vollmoeller, W., Kuhn, W., Sartory, G. & Przuntek, H. (1997). Disgust implicated in obsessive- compulsive disorder. *Biological Science, 264*, 1767–1773.

Stark, R., Schienle, A., Walter, B., Kirsch, P., Sammer, G., Ott, U., Blecker, C. & Vaitl, D. (2003). Hemodynamic responses to fear and disgust-inducing pictures: an fMRI study. *International Journal of Psychophysiology, 50*, 2258-234.

Stark, R., Walter, B., Schienle, A. & Vaitl, D. (2005). Psychophysiological Correlates of Disgust and Disgust Sensitivity. *Journal of Psychophysiology, 19* (1), 50-60.

Stein, M., Ottenberg, P. & Roulet, N. (1958). A study of the development of olfactory preferences. *Archives of Neurology and Psychiatry, 80*, 264-266.

Steiner, J. E. (1974). Facial expressions of the neonate infant indicating the hedonics of food-related chemical stimuli. In J.M. Weiffenbach (Ed.), *Taste and development: The genesis of sweet preference* (DHEW Publication No. NIH 77-1068; 173-188). Washington DC: U.S. Government Printing Office.

Stevenson, R. J., Oaten, M. J., Case, T. I., Repacholi, B. M. & Wagland, P. (2010). Children's response to adult disgust elicitors: Development and acquisition. *Developmental Psychology, 46* (1), 165-177.

Templer, D. I., King, F. L., Brooner, R. K. & Corgiat, M. (1984). Assessment of body elimination attitude. *Journal of Clinical Psychology, 3*, 754-759.

Thorpe, S. J., Patel, S. P. & Simonds, L. M. (2003). The relationship between disgust sensitivity, anxiety, and obsessions. *Behaviour Research and Therapy, 41*, 1397–1409.

Tomasi, T. B. (1972). Secretory Immunoglobulins. *New England Journal of Medicine, 7*, 50-56.

Tomkins, S. (1963). *Affect, imagery, consciousness.* New York: Springer.

Tomkins, S. (1987). Shame. In D.L. Nathanson (Ed.), *The many faces of shame.* New York: Guilford Press.

Tsao, S. D. & McKay, D. (2004). Behavioral avoidance tests and disgust in contamination fears: distinctions from trait anxiety. *Behaviour Research and Therapy, 42* (2), 207-216.

Tybur, J. M., Bryan, A. D., Lieberman, D., Hooper, A. E. C. & Merriman, L. A. (2011). Sex differences and sex similarities in disgust sensitivity. *Personality and Individual Differences, 51* (3), 343-348.

Tybur, J. M., Lieberman, D. & Griskevicius, V. (2009). Microbes, mating, and morality: Individual differences in three functional domains of disgust. *Journal of Personality and Social Psychology, 97* (1), 103-122.

Vrana, S. R. (1993). The psychophysiology of disgust: Differentiating negative emotional contexts with facial EMG. *Psychophysiology, 30* (3), 279–286.

Ware, J., Jain, K., Burgess, I. & Davey, G. C. L. (1994). Disease-avoidance model: Factor analysis of common animal fears. *Behaviour Research and Therapy, 32* (1), 57-63.

Warwick, H. M. C. (1998). Cognitive therapy in the treatment of hypochondriasis. *Advances in Psychiatric Treatment, 4*, 285-295.

Widen, S. C. & Russell, J. A. (2008). In building a script for an emotion, Do preschoolers add its cause before its behavior consequence? *Social Development, 20* (3), 471-485.

Woody, S. R. & Teachman, B. A. (2000). Intersection of disgust and fear: Normative and pathological views. *Clinical Psychology: Science and Practice, 7* (3), 291–311.

Wronska, J. (1990). Disgust in relation to emotionality, extraversion, psychoticism and imagery ability. In P.J. D. Drenth, J. A. Sergeant & R. J. Takens (Eds.), European Perspectives in Psychology, Volume *1* (125-138). Chicester: John Wiley & Sons.

PART IV: EMOTIONS AND EMOTIONAL COMPETENCES

In: Handbook of Psychology of Emotions
Editors: C. Mohiyeddini, M. Eysenck and S. Bauer

ISBN: 978-1-62808-053-7
© 2013 Nova Science Publishers, Inc.

Chapter 23

SELF-LEADERSHIP, SELF-REGULATION AND EMOTION REGULATION: IS THERE A COMMON REGULATORY CORE?

Marco R. Furtner and Laura N. Hiller*
Leopold-Franzens University of Innsbruck, Austria

ABSTRACT

Though, self-leadership, self-regulation, and emotion regulation are all related to regulatory processes, they have not yet been related to each other on a conceptual level. Self-leadership is about regulatory processes in order to influence one's own thoughts and behavior. Self-regulation aims to change one's own behavior and emotion regulation to influence one's own emotions. In this chapter, the central question will be whether the different regulatory systems have a common and unifying core. Therefore, the central differences and similarities between self-leadership, self-regulation and emotion regulation are highlighted. The different regulatory systems have in common that they all refer to self-influencing processes. The conceptual analysis shows that goals and (self-) observation are central keys in all self-influencing, self-regulatory, and emotion regulatory processes.

INTRODUCTION

Regulation comes from the Latin word regulare („to direct, govern, rule"). From a psychological perspective, regulation means to guide, direct, and control one's thoughts, emotions, and behaviors. Self-leadership, self-regulation, and emotion regulation have in common that they all relate to regulatory processes. Self-leadership is based on self-regulatory strategies to influence one's own thoughts and behaviors (Furtner & Rauthmann, 2010), self-regulation aims to change one's own behavior (Carver & Scheier, 1998), and

---

* Corresponding author: Marco R. Furtner, Ph.D., Department of Psychology, University of Innsbruck, Innrain 52, 6020 Innsbruck, Austria, E-mail: Marco.Furtner@uibk.ac.at.

emotion regulation to influence one's own emotions (Gross, 1998a). On the one hand, self-leadership, self-regulation and emotion regulation are related to various regulatory processes (e.g., Gross & John, 2003; Tice & Bratlavski, 2000) and on the other hand, they all comprise a different regulatory focus (cognitive-behavioral versus behavioral versus affective-emotional). Thus, the question arises: *Is there a common regulatory core of different regulatory systems and which key functions and features are included in that core?* To answer that question, the theoretical basis of self-leadership, self-regulation, and emotion regulation are presented in this chapter. Subsequently, the main differences and similarities between the different regulatory systems are identified in order to answer the question above.

SELF-LEADERSHIP, SELF-REGULATION AND EMOTION REGULATION

Self-Leadership

Self-leadership is defined as "the process of influencing oneself" (Neck & Manz, 2010, p. 4). It refers to the self-influencing and goal-orientated direction of one's own thoughts and behaviors. Self-leadership consists of three main dimensions: (1) *behavior-focused strategies*, (2) *natural reward strategies*, and (3) *constructive thought pattern strategies*. In contrast to self-management, which relates purely to behavioral regulatory aspects, self-leadership involves a broader spectrum of self-influencing strategies. It refers to higher levels of self-influence, in which it integrates the intrinsic motivation and generally includes a wider range of self-control (Manz, 1986). Self-leadership represents an ongoing self-reinforcing and self-influencing cybernetic system. In general, according to Manz (1986), there are three possible levels of self-influence: (1) *self-regulation*, (2) *self-management*, and (3) *self-leadership*.

Level 1: Self-regulation: Self-regulation often refers to an automatic and unconscious process. In an ongoing cybernetic control process, the goal of self-regulatory activities is a reduction of discrepancies between a current state and a desired standard (= goal).

Level 2: Self-management: By using behavior-focused self-management strategies, behavior should be adapted to a particular standard (= goal). Based on higher-level control loops, discrepancies from a certain standard should be reduced. Self-management refers generally to what should be done (e.g., "X units should be sold by the end of the month").

Level 3: Self-leadership. In contrast to self-regulation and self-management the degree of conscious influence is considerably higher. Self-leadership uses both behavioral-focused strategies (self-observation, self-goal setting, self-reward, self-punishment, self-cueing), natural reward strategies (with particular focus on intrinsic motivation), and constructive thought pattern strategies (visualizing successful performance, self-talk, evaluating beliefs and assumptions). The self-influencing and self-regulatory focus is on *what* persons want to do, *why* they want to do this and *how* they should do it. Beyond self-management strategies, it is also assessed how suitable or desirable standards (= goals) are.

Behavior-Focused Strategies

Behavior-focused strategies include the central self-regulatory mechanisms of *self-goal setting* and *self-observation*. *Self-cueing* supports the self-regulatory process, *self-reward* and *self-punishment* can be used to reinforce one's own behavior as an extrinsic motivation. First, ineffective and unproductive behaviors can be consciously eliminated and replaced with constructive behaviors by using self-observation. Self-observation and self-awareness also support self-goal setting and the self-regulatory process to achieve these goals. By means of self-observation, the current state regarding thoughts and behaviors can be perceived. Thus, persons have self-knowledge about their thoughts and behaviors. By using self-goal setting, thoughts and behaviors can be influenced and changed. It serves to manage and control one's own thoughts and behaviors. Self-reward and self-punishment are systematically used during the process of goal achievement and still after these goals are successfully achieved. According to behavioral learning theories, self-reward serves to (extrinsically) reinforce a desired behavior and self-punishment (in the form of negative reinforcement) is used to weaken an undesirable behavior (Bandura, 1986; Goldiamond, 1965). During the process of goal achievement self-cueing is systematically used as a reminder (e.g., memos, notes, post-its) (Houghton & Neck, 2002).

Natural Reward Strategies

Natural reward strategies put their self-regulatory focus on pleasant, interesting and enjoyable features of a task or activity. Their aim is to increase the intrinsic motivation. For this, two main strategies are used: (1) on a cognitive level, persons remove from unpleasant features of a task or activity and focus more on the pleasant, interesting and enjoyable aspects, (2) persons build pleasant, interesting and enjoyable features into a task or activity so that it becomes "natural" rewarding (Neck & Houghton, 2006). Conscious self-reflection and self-awareness take a key role here. Persons must first become aware, which aspects of their daily tasks or activities are pleasant and enjoyable. Subsequently, these pleasant and enjoyable features can be connected to tasks or activities. Both strategies have an effect on the primary mechanisms of intrinsic motivation. Intrinsic motivation occurs when a person can be captivated by a particular task or activity. Then, these tasks or activities are performed for their own sake, they are funny and joyful, and therefore naturally rewarding. This gives rise to feelings of competence and self-determination of the appropriateness of one's own actions (Deci & Ryan, 1987, 2008; Manz, 1986). These feelings serve to ensure that tasks or activities are carried out for their own sake, and that they are natural rewarding. The perceived competence and self-regulation are taking an important role of intrinsically motivated behavior (Bandura, 1986, 1991).

Constructive thought Pattern Strategies

Constructive thought pattern strategies relate to the specific self-regulatory influence and control of habitual thought patterns. By means of *visualizing successful performance* effective future behavior is anticipated and realized in mind. Individuals who imagine themselves mentally that they are already successful in a task or activity are actually more successful and show a higher performance when they really do these task or activity (Driskell, Copper, & Moran, 1994; Neck & Manz, 2010). By using a carful and reflexive analysis, pessimistic self-talk can be eliminated and finally replaced by *positive self-talk* (Neck & Houghton, 2006;

Seligman, 1991). For an effective *evaluation of beliefs and assumptions*, individuals must first perceive their (dysfunctional) own beliefs and assumptions and consciously deal with them. In a second step, irrational beliefs, assumptions and perceptions can be replaced by constructive thought patterns (Ellis, 1977; Houghton & Neck, 2002).

Self-Regulation

A central aspect of the self-regulatory system is the goal. Once persons set a goal, a discrepancy between a current and desired state is perceived. Persons try to reduce this perceived discrepancy through their behavior. Typical for cybernetic control systems is that the reduction takes place through the mechanism of *negative feedback loops* (Miller, Galanter, & Pribram, 1960). The self-regulation and control theory of Carver and Scheier (1981, 1998) draws its principles from cybernetics and shows close relations to the control theory of Powers (1978). Cybernetics can be described as the science of feedback processes and includes control and regulation of various values of a system (Ashby, 1961; Wiener, 1948). Following Carver and Scheier, a general model of self-regulation is described by Lord, Diefendorff, Schmidt, and Hall (2010). As can be seen in Figure 1, it consists of four main mechanisms: (1) *Input function*. Based on the individual perception, information is passing through a sensory input into the system. (2) *Reference value* (= standard, goal). The reference value is a source of information, to which the sensory input is compared. They may differ from each other. (3) *Comparator*. In a top-down process the sensory input is compared to the reference value (= standard, goal). This comparison has two possible outcomes. First, the information of the reference value is consistent with the sensory input, and second, the information of both differs. (4) *Output function*. Beyond the comparison, there is a result function, which can be equated with behavior. If the comparison between sensory input and reference value (= standard, goal) shows no difference, the result function and therefore the behavior remains the same. If there is a discrepancy, the result function and the behavior will change (= negative feedback loop).

The operation of the negative feedback loop has been described as TOTE unit (*Test-Operate-Test-Exit*) by Miller et al. (1960). *Test* is the comparison of information between a current sensory input and a reference value (= standard, goal). If persons perceive a discrepancy because of this comparison, a specific behavior will be shown to reduce it (= *Operate*). This is followed by an evaluation (= *Test*) whether the perceived discrepancy could be successfully reduced. If there are no discrepancies anymore, other activities will be focused by means of *Exit*. In a negative feedback system, the change in the result function (= behavior) is achieved by a reduction of the discrepancy between input and reference value. It is always crucial that individuals really *perceive* a discrepancy between input and reference value. Besides goal setting, self-monitoring and self-awareness take a key function in the self-regulatory process (cf. Bandura, 1986, 1991; Baumeister & Vohs, 2007). Both the accurate perception of the input function and the behavioral changes are based on negative feedback loops and thus, influenced positively.

Hierarchical Structure of the Self-Regulatory System

The self-regulatory system is arranged hierarchically. It consists of several major and minor goals and feedback loops. The higher a goal is positioned in the hierarchy, the more abstract is the level. The more abstract the level is the longer are the cycle times of the feedback loops. For example, at the highest level of abstraction is the idealized self (Carver & Scheier, 1998; Johnson, Chang, & Lord, 2006). The idealized self refers to how persons see themselves and ideally wants to be. At the highest level of abstraction, a feedback loop may take many years. At the middle and lower level of abstraction are specific goals and specific behavioral sequences. These are used to achieve the higher-level and more abstract goals. On the middle level of abstraction a feedback loop takes from a few minutes to several days. At a very low level of abstraction the feedback loop may take just a second (Lord et al., 2010). For example, persons receive a written word, and immediately get feedback on their actions. Often, parts or even the entire cycle run without conscious awareness and control. According to Carver and Scheier (1998) a top-down regulation of actions runs at the different levels of abstraction. In other words, the goal at the highest level of abstraction (e.g., idealized self) determines which specific sub-goals are set and which specific behavioral sequences are shown by a person. At the same time, a bottom-up control is performed by the lower level of abstraction (e.g., the specific sub-goal has been reached). The self-regulatory system is highly automatic and unconscious. In the literature it is critically discussed, if the often unconscious self-regulatory processes work flawlessly and effectively. According to Latham and Locke (1991) persons have natural self-regulatory mechanisms, whether they actually use self-regulation effectively remains unclear.

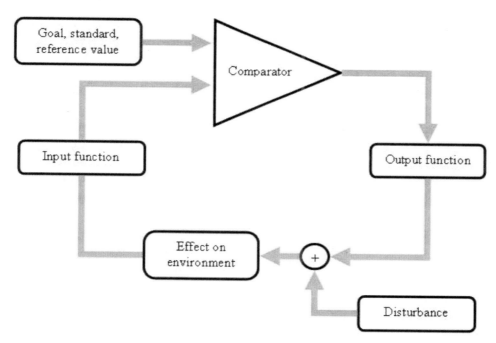

Figure 1. Model of the negative feedback loop (according to Carver & Scheier, 1998).

Regulatory Mode Theory

In the regulatory mode theory Kruglanski et al. (2000) consider that self-regulation consists of two basic functions: (1) *assessment* and (2) *locomotion* (cf. Kruglanski et al, 2010). Assessment includes the comparative aspect of self-regulation. Specific conditions are evaluated critically regarding to particular alternative options as well as strengths and weaknesses according to their quality ("just doing the right thing"). Locomotion refers to the direct action ("just doing it"). Altogether, locomotion and assessment determine any specific self-regulatory activity. Assessment includes the function of perceiving discrepancy between sensory input and a reference value (= standard, goal). Assessment refers to the importance, value and meaning of an activity. However, locomotion includes the aspect of self-regulation, which deals with the movement from one state to another. The motivation lies in the movement from a current state to a desired reference value. For a person with high locomotion the movement itself is the intrinsically motivating element.

Promotion and Prevention Focus

According to Higgins (1997) persons have two basic self-regulatory systems: (1) *promotion* and (2) *prevention*. For promotion goals the attainment of rewards and positive consequences (e.g., the promotion of positive emotions) is important. They include goals, desires, and hopes of persons and represent how they would like to see themselves (= idealized self). Promotion goals aim to develop and change. For prevention goals the avoidance of punishments and negative consequences is regulated (e.g., avoidance of negative emotions). They represent how persons should be like. Prevention goals include duties, obligations, and responsibilities. The purpose of prevention goals is the preservation of security and stability. Elliot (2006) describes a self-regulatory model of approach-avoidance motivation. According to that model an approach goal activates a behavior by focusing on a positive goal stimulus. Compared to approach behavior, avoidance behavior is marked by putting a negative goal in the center of the self-regulatory activity. Elliot (2006) compares a continuous avoidance behavior with the work of an air traffic controller. Through constant monitoring of potential hazards, air traffic controller fatigue in the long run. This profession has one of the highest turnover rates at all (Hopkin, 1995). According to Elliot and Church (1997) approach and avoidance are the central bases for self-regulation and motivation. They are key features of the adaptation of the organisms to changing environmental conditions (Tooby & Cosmides, 1990). Individuals often perform an unconscious assessment of whether a stimulus is perceived as positive or negative (Bargh, 1997). These assessments lead to the immediate approach or avoidance behavior (Lewin, 1935). Core of the self-regulatory activity is the goal. A goal is defined as a cognitive representation of a future object, which takes place within an approach or avoidance (Elliot & Fryer, 2008). Regarding to self-regulation, goals are the central component of the motivational process.

Self-regulation in Social-Cognitive Theory

Bandura and Locke (2003) criticize classical control and self-regulation theories (Carver & Scheier, 1981, 1998; Powers, 1978) as too mechanistic and reductionistic. According to those theories, motivation and behavior are purely determined by the negative feedback system. For Bandura and Locke (2003) the human cognitive activity is highly regulated. The main criticism is directed at the lack of focus on internal processing and the ability to act pro-active. According to Bandura (1986) persons set suitable and appropriate goals. First, a self-assessment is made to determine the viability of different goals and challenges. Subsequently, a strategic plan is carried out. Available resources and personal efforts are judged. The output quality is not only cognitively but also affectively evaluated. Metacognitive self-reflexive strategies are used and assessed. According to Bandura (1991) behavior is motivated by a strong self-affecting process: "In social cognitive theory human behavior is motivated and extensively regulated by the ongoing exercise of self-influence" (p. 248). The central self-regulatory mechanism includes three sub-functions: (1) self-monitoring/self-observation of one's own behavior, (2) assessment of processes based on personal standards (= goals), and (3) emotional self-reaction. Regarding to emotion self-regulation, the self-regulatory control system creates incentives and anticipates emotional reactions to one's own actions. Individuals strive to bring about actions, which trigger positive emotional self-reactions. Both, the anticipated satisfaction with the desired outcome (approach motivation) and the anticipated dissatisfaction with an adverse outcome (avoidance motivation) increase the probability to achieve these goals. Despite the differences between the two self-regulatory theories of Bandura (1986, 1991) and Carver and Scheier (1981, 1998) both emphasize the importance of goals, self-observation, and self-attention (Phillips, Hollenbeck, & Ilgen, 1996; Vancouver, 2008). For Bandura (1986, 1991) the pro-activity of human actions is emphasized. Persons can consciously set themselves goals and can perceive how the discrepancies between actual and desired state have already been successfully reduced by self-observation. Additionally to the reduction of discrepancy, Bandura (1986, 1991) describes a deliberate generation of discrepancy. By using self-goal setting persons consciously and pro-actively set higher goals. Thereby, a discrepancy within the self-regulatory system is generated, which is reduced subsequently (= negative feedback loop). From the mechanistic perspective of Carver and Scheier (1981, 1998) and Powers (1978) self-regulation is a mostly automatic and unconscious process. According to Bandura (1986), persons can consciously influence the self-regulatory system by using self-influencing strategies (e.g., self-goal setting, self-observation).

Emotion Regulation

Why Emotion and Emotion Regulation Are Necessary?
Reeve (2009) defines emotions as a "short-lived [...] phenomena that help us adapt to the opportunities and challenges we face during important life events" (p. 301), which consists of four components. These are *feelings, bodily arousal, sense of purpose* and *social-expressive component*. But the phenomena of emotion alone are not enough to adapt to and challenge life events.

The different components need to be controlled and regulated, so that they perfectly interact with each other and to be really adaptive (cf. Gross, 1998a, 1998b; Koole, 2009; Thompson, 1994; Gross & Thompson, 2007). For example, persons that are scared can show different expressions of fear like freezing or running away. When it is necessary to run away because of a predator (= threat), it would be a major problem, if persons freeze.

To explain the importance of an emotion regulatory system, the changed meaning of emotion and the interaction between emotion and cognition is mentioned hereafter. Subsequently, James' *emotional response theory* is explained, which is the root of several models of emotion regulation.

What is meant by an emotion has changed over time. While emotions were previously seen as non-specific activation states, more recent research accuse that emotions are specific and help to address different adaptive problems (cf. Gross, 1998a). Nevertheless, emotion regulation is necessary to help emotional responses to adapt cognitive processes (Barchard, 2003; Brackett, Rivers, & Salovey, 2011; Mayer, Salovey, & Caruso, 2004; Neubauer &

Freudenthaler, 2006), to prepare rapid motor responses (Frijda, 1986), and to inform about social settings (Labordes, Brüll, Weber, & Anders, 2011; Porter, ten Brinke, Baker, & Wallace, 2011).

Another important aspect of emotion is the understanding of the interplay of emotion and cognition, which has strongly altered. The consideration of cognitive processes and emotional states can be observed already in ancient Greece. There, it was assumed that mind is superior to feeling (cf. Mayer et al., 2004). While various historical movements such as European Sentimentalist Movement or Romantic Movement put emotion on cognition, the scientific debate shows how close and equal cognition and emotion are (cf. Mayer et al., 2004; Mayer, Roberts, & Barsade, 2008). Today's findings clearly show that emotions make cognitive processes adaptive and that individuals can rationally think about their emotions (cf. Brackett et al., 2011).

Emotion Response Theory

According to James (1884, 1894) emotions are adaptive behavioral and physiological response tendencies, which evolutionary developed out of substantial situations. This point of view allows both, a general occurrence or lack of emotion response tendencies as well as a modulation within their expression. Thus, individuals can express these emotion response tendencies, but they must not show them and a particular emotion can be expressed in different ways (cf. Gross, 1998a). For example, individuals that are scared can show different expressions of fear like whistle or running away, but they can also show not any expression of fear at all. The emotion generation process is shown in Figure 2.

Emotion Regulation

According to Gross (1998a) emotion regulation is a self-influencing process by which individuals can regulate the perception and expression of their emotions. Furthermore, emotion regulation includes how individuals assess the experiences they have made with different emotional cues in several situations. Additionally, emotion regulation can be divided into two different kinds of regulatory processes: (1) regulatory processes that are explicit, conscious, determined, controlled, and attentive (2) and those that are implicit, unconscious, automatic, and distracted (cf. Barnow, 2012; Gross, 1998a, 1998b; Gross & Thompson, 2007; Koole, 2009; Koole & Rothermund, 2011; Thompson, 1994).

Emotion regulation is "responsible for monitoring, evaluating, and modify emotion reactions, especially their intense and temporal features, to accomplish one's goals" (Thompson, 1994, pp. 27–28). Other important functions of emotion regulation are preventing, reducing or enhancing one's own emotional responses and those of others (Brackett et al., 2011), satisfying hedonic needs and optimizing personality functioning (Koole, 2009), facilitating performance and goal achievement (Koole, 2009; Thompson, 1994), improving social communication with peers and managing stressful experiences at home (Thompson, 1994), and ego defenses like avoiding certain situations or changing cognitions about certain situations (Gross, 1998a).

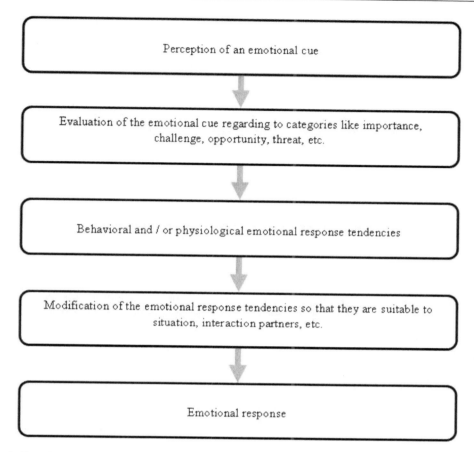

Figure 2. Emotion generation process according to James (1884).

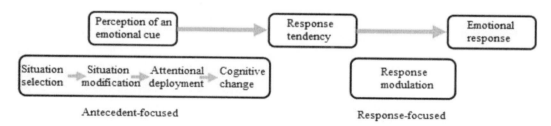

Figure 3. Emotion regulation within the emotion generation process [(based on James (1884) & Gross (1998a)].

Gross' Model of Emotion Regulation

The model of emotion regulation consists of five subcategories, which can be classified into two central strategies. The *antecedent-focused strategy* regulates emotion response tendencies even before they have been activated (Gross, 1998b). It consists of subcategories situation selection, situation modification, attentional deployment and cognitive change. The *response-focused strategy* regulates emotion response tendencies after they have been generated (Gross & John, 2003). It consists of the subcategory response modulation.

According to Gross (2002) emotional regulatory processes take place at several times within the development from perceiving an emotional cue until the full emotional response (cf. Figure 3). Though, even before an emotional cue is perceived emotional regulatory processes can take place. Emotion regulation starts with a situation selection, which can take place before, while and after an emotional cue is perceived. The situation selection includes approaching or avoiding of a certain situation, person, place, etc. that generates a particular emotion (Barnow, 2012). For example, a person with acrophobia tries to avoid heights or a person that wants an adrenalin rush will see a horrifying film. After a situation is selected and an emotional cue is perceived its evaluation starts with a situation modification. Modifying the emotional impact of a certain situation is the core of the situation modification (Gross, 1998b). For Gross (1998a), it depends on a situations possibility, how much it can be modified, because some situations have a high and some a low possibility of modification. For example, persons can change a harmful topic of a conversation, while they are talking to their friends (= high possibility), they cannot change a harmful question within an exam (= low possibility). When the modification is finished, the attentional deployment starts. Attentional deployment means that the focus of attention is set on a specific aspect of the situation (Gross, 1998a; Gross & John, 2003). For instance, individuals can direct a conversation to a loved topic, but they can also start to focus on the pattern of their tie, when they are bored or upset. After the attention is set on a specific aspect, the meaning of this aspect and the whole situation is selected. According to Barnow (2012) and Gross and Thompson (2007) this selection of meaning is called cognitive change. One and the same situation can be described as a threat ("This exam is the biggest thing in the world to me and if I fail, I will always fail.") or an opportunity ("This exam is the biggest thing in the world to me. I am well prepared and I will succeed."), they only differ in the way of its sett meaning. The antecedent-focused strategies lead to the activation of emotional response tendencies (Barnow, 2012; Gross & John, 2003). Then the last step of emotion regulation takes place. For Gross (2002) response modulation consists of the selection of possible responses like certain facial expression or physiological reactions suitable to the situation, the interaction partners, etc. which finally represent the emotional response.

Emotion regulation plays a major role within another popular emotional construct: emotional intelligence. One of the most popular models of emotional intelligence is the Mayer and Salovey revised model of emotional intelligence. The role of emotion regulation within that model is explained hereafter.

Emotion Regulation within Mayer and Salovey's Revised Model of Emotional Intelligence

The revised model of emotional intelligence consists of four hierarchical branches including *perception of emotions*, *use of emotions to facilitate thinking*, *understanding and analyzing emotions* and *reflective regulation of emotions*. According to Mayer and Salovey (1997) the reflective regulation of emotions is the top of the ability model of emotional intelligence. Thus, emotion regulation represents an advanced mental or psychological process, which has four main functions and two kinds of components. The four main functions are to prevent, enhance, reduce and modify an emotional response in oneself and others (cf. Brackett, Rivers, & Salovey, 2011). The components divide into basic and advanced components. To attend and stay open to pleasant and unpleasant feelings, as long as they do not harm the self, constitute the basic component. While more advanced components involve to monitor and reflect on one's own emotions and those of others as well as to permit or inhibit an emotion depending on its perceived utility in a situation (cf. Brackett et al., 2011; Neubauer & Freudenthaler, 2006).

Emotional intelligence and its core component emotion regulation have several positive effects on mental health, social relationships, and work place and academic success. According to Brackett et al. (2011) emotional intelligence helps to faces anxiety-inducing situations. Therefore, some studies could show negative relations between emotional intelligence and emotional disturbed psychopathologies like anxiety, depressions or schizophrenia (David, 2005; Kee et al., 2009; O'Connor & Little, 2003). Furthermore, persons with high emotional intelligence "tend to be more socially competent, to have better quality relationships, and to be viewed as more interpersonally sensitive" (Bracket et al., 2011; p. 96). All in all persons with high emotional intelligence show more supportive behaviors and less negative communication styles within interactions. Studies about work place and academic success also showed positive effects of emotional intelligence. Correlations between emotional, fluid and crystalized intelligence show high relations between emotional and crystalized intelligence (Brackett et al., 2011; MacCann, 2010). Brackett et al. (2011) showed that persons with high emotional intelligence have less learning problems and better attentional skills. Barchard (2003) and Brackett and Mayer (2003) could show positive associations between academic performance and emotional intelligence. Furthermore, emotional intelligence is linked to higher work place performance and stress-tolerance, as well as to better communication patterns between leader and followers (Ashkanasy & Daus, 2005; Lopes, Côté, & Salovey, 2006).

DIFFERENCES BETWEEN SELF-LEADERSHIP, SELF-REGULATION AND EMOTION REGULATION

Self-leadership focuses more on cognitive aspects than self-regulation, while it only marginally influences emotions (cf. Boss & Sims, 2008). In contrast to self-regulation self-leadership is a learnable skill, which describes a wide range of self-influencing strategies (Furtner, Baldegger, & Rauthmann, 2012; Furtner, Sachse, & Exenberger, 2012). According to Manz (1986) self-leadership is a consciously controlled process, while self-regulation and the majority of self-regulated behaviors are unconscious and automatic (Bargh, Chen, & Burrows, 1996). For Latham and Locke (1991) self-regulation may be a natural process. However, it is unclear whether self-regulatory processes actually work so perfectly, and if persons effectively use self-regulation. According to Baumeister, Heatherton, and Tice (1994) self-regulation is often inadequate and even erroneous (cf. Vohs & Heatherton, 2000). This can be lead back to a limited resource of individuals to control certain thoughts and behaviors (Baumeister & Vohs, 2007; Baumeister, Vohs, & Tice, 2007). The largely automated and unconscious self-regulation is closely related to conscious self-control (Carver & Scheier, 1998; Tangney et al., 2004). According to Baumeister et al. (2007) self-control refers to the ability to change one's own thoughts, emotions, and behaviors and can be defined as the conscious control over the self by the self (cf. Muraven & Baumeister, 2000). In contrast to self-regulation and self-control, self-leadership describes a wider range of consciously controlled self-influencing strategies. Furtner (2012) and Furtner, Rauthmann and Sachse (under revision) could show that self-leadership, self-regulation, and self-control differ empirically from each other. The self-influencing strategies of self-leadership impact positively on the effectiveness of self-regulatory processes (cf. Furtner, 2012; Neck & Houghton, 2006). In particular, locomotion is positively influenced by self-leadership, which in turn has positive effects on intrinsic motivation, flow, and performance (Furtner et al., under revision).

Self-leadership refers to a consciously controlled self-influencing process to control and regulate one's own thoughts and behaviors (Furtner, Rauthmann, & Sachse, 2010, 2011; Neck & Manz, 2010). Self-regulation is largely automated and focuses on controlling and regulating one's own behavior. It emphasizes the important role of negative feedback loops. Both self-leadership and self-regulation are behaviorally grounded. In contrast, emotion regulation refers to the self-influencing control and regulation of emotions. It is therefore anchored affective-emotional. Though, self-leadership as well as emotion regulation refer to self-influencing processes, self-leadership focuses on the effective influence of thoughts and behaviors, while emotion regulation align its focus on the self-regulation of emotions. Both Boss and Sims (2008) and Neck and Manz (2010) assume on a theoretical level that self-leadership and emotion regulation have only a small conceptual overlap. Because cognition and emotion reciprocally influence each other and emotions and cognition can regulate behavior (LeDoux, 1995; Lord et al., 2010), Neck and Manz (2010) assume that self-leadership and emotion regulation can complement each other positively. Persons, who can regulate and control their emotions, should have a more effective self-leadership (Stewart, Courthright, & Manz, 2011). Conversely, self-leadership skills influence emotion regulation positively (Furtner et al, 2010; D'Intino, Goldsby, Houghton, & Neck, 2007; Neck & Manz, 2010). In an empirical study, Furtner et al. (2010) examined the relationship between self-leadership, socio-emotional intelligence, and emotion regulation (Riggio & Carney, 2003). The results show that self-leadership is related to socio-emotional intelligence in general. Particularly, positive relations are evident between socio-emotional expressivity and emotional sensitivity. Socio-emotional expressivity refers to the ability of expressing oneself verbally as well as nonverbally and thus positively influencing others. Emotional sensitivity refers to the ability to accurately perceive and interpret verbal and nonverbal emotional cues (Riggio & Reichard, 2008). However, self-leadership shows only weak positive relations to emotion regulation. Hiller (2011) examined the relationship between self-leadership and trait emotional intelligence (Wong & Law, 2002). According to Wong and Law (2002) emotional intelligence includes *self-emotions appraisal*, *others-emotions appraisal*, *use of emotion*, and *regulation of emotions*. As in the study of Furtner et al. (2010) the results show that self-leadership is indeed positively related to emotional intelligence, but has only weak positive associations with emotion regulation. Relations between self-leadership and emotional intelligence can be explained particularly by the subcategories *self-emotions appraisal* and *use of emotion*. In various mediation analyzes Hiller (2011) also examined the mediating role of emotional intelligence between self-leadership and different performance criteria (individual and group performance). The use of one's own emotions to facilitate thought (= *use of emotion*) mediates the relationship between both self-leadership and individual performance and between self-leadership and group performance. Emotion regulation does not show any significant mediation effect. Thus, control and regulation of emotions is only marginally related to self-leadership, the control and regulation of thoughts and behaviors. Self-regulation refers to the control and regulation of one's own behavior (Carver & Scheier,

1998) and emphasizes the important function of goals and negative feedback loops. According to Lord et al. (2010) emotions can support the self-regulatory process. With regard to goal adjustment, the affective system works quickly and automatically. It interrupts and leads to a realignment of conscious processing. This leads to a (micro-)regulation of cognition and behavior. Lord et al. (2010) assume that self-regulation supports and strengthens emotion regulation and vice versa. The relationship of self-regulatory basis functions (assessment and locomotion) on the affective-emotional system show a differentiated pattern of results. Unlike to locomotion, assessment leads to higher emotional instability, larger negative affect, and less optimism (Higgins et al., 2002; Hong, Tan, & Chang, 2004). Contrary to assessment, locomotion is related to a higher intrinsic motivation and flow experience. Thus, the two different self-regulatory basis functions show a different effect on the emotional state and the affective-emotional system (Kruglanski et al., 2000; Kruglanski, Orehek, Higgins, Pierro, & Shalev, 2010).

IS THERE A COMMON REGULATORY CORE?

Despite the differences between self-leadership, self-regulation, and emotion regulation, the question arises: Is there a common regulatory core, so to speak, an underlying or a "meta-regulatory" core? Self-leadership, self-regulation, and emotion regulation have in common that they are related to self-influencing processes. Self-leadership refers to a self-influencing process to control and regulate one's own thoughts and behaviors (Neck & Manz, 2010, Furtner et al., 2011). Self-regulation to control and regulate one's own behavior, in which it is urging the important function of negative feedback loops (Carver & Scheier, 1998). Emotion regulation refers to the self-influencing control and regulation of one's own emotions (Gross, 1998a).

Cognition and emotion influence each other. Cognitive-behavioral strategies of self-leadership and behavioral strategies of self-regulation have a positive influence on the affective-emotional system and emotion regulation and vice versa emotion regulation positively influences cognitive-behavioral processes. According to Bandura (1986, 1991) the self-regulatory control system creates incentives and anticipates emotional reactions regarding to one's own actions. Therefore, the self-regulatory system is influenced by the anticipated emotional reactions. Individuals strive for actions that cause positive emotional reactions (e.g., proud on one's own performance, satisfaction and well-being). Both the anticipation of satisfaction with a desired result as well as dissatisfaction with an adverse outcome motivates for goal achievement. In this context, Bandura (1991) speaks of emotional self-assessment. Besides being influenced by anticipated positive emotional reactions, the self-regulatory system is also influenced by positive emotions. For Bandura (1986) self-efficacy plays a key role in human self-regulatory system. It refers to the belief in one's own abilities to really cope with things. A high self-efficacy immediately triggers positive emotions, which in turn impacts positively the self-regulatory system.

A self-regulatory approach, which aims to change thoughts, emotions, and behaviors is the concept of self-control. Without self-control, persons would always show their habitual, typical or desired behavior. Using self-control can inhibit a person's wishes, intentions or behaviors (Shallice & Burgess, 1993). It refers to controlling conscious aspects, which require a certain effort, and is also linked to the operate phase of self-regulation (cf. Carver & Scheier, 1981, 1998). That is the phase in which the discrepancies between the self and a standard or goal can be reduced. The self has the characteristics of thoughts, feelings, and behaviors. Therefore, a change of the self presupposes that already existing patterns of thoughts, emotions, and behaviors will be "overwritten" (Muraven & Baumeister, 2000). According to Tangney et al. (2004) self-control is a significant predictor of adaptability, better performance, and interpersonal success. Individuals with higher self-control show better performance during problem solving and have a greater impulse control. Thus, it describes a construct that takes self-regulatory effects on the cognitive-behavioral *and* the affective-emotional system. For Hoyle (2006) self-control is therefore a self-regulatory process by which individuals control their own thoughts, emotions, and behaviors. Accordingly, it can be assumed that self-control influences both the self-regulatory and emotion regulatory system. Self-leadership in turn has a positive impact on the effectiveness of self-control (cf. Furtner, 2012, Neck & Houghton, 2006).

What are the most common and basic mechanisms of self-leadership, self-control, self-regulation, and emotion regulation? Both self- and emotion regulatory approaches have in common that goals are needed to change one's own thoughts, feelings, and behaviors. To effectively influence these thoughts, feelings, and behaviors, the controlling aspect of self-observation, self-awareness, and monitoring are required. Thus, goals and (self-)observation (monitoring) take a key role in all self-regulatory and emotion regulatory processes and could be seen as the common regulatory core (Tice & Bratslavsky, 2000):

(1) **Goals.** In order to influence, regulate and control thoughts, emotions, and behaviors, personal goals are needed. So that regulation and change can actually take place, goals, a certain standard or reference value are necessary (Baumeister & Vohs, 2007; Bandura, 1991; Carver & Scheier, 1998; Manz, 1986), which need to be specified and well-defined (Baumeister & Vohs, 2007; Higgins, 1987; Locke & Latham, 1990; Thompson, 1994). Contradictory, uncertain and inconsistent standards make self-regulation more difficult (Higgins, 1987). Koole (2009) assumes that goals are necessary for the emotion regulatory process and that it would not occur without them. For Thompson (1994) a major function or aim of emotion regulation is to achieve personal (long term) goals. Self-regulation takes effect on the behavioral system, self-leadership on the cognitive-behavioral system, self-control on the cognitive-behavioral and affective-emotional system, and emotion regulation on the affective-emotional system. To take active and effective influence on these systems, it needs *goals* (cf. Furtner, 2012; Lord et al., 2010).

(2) **Monitoring and (self-)observation.** For effective self- and emotion regulation, monitoring and self-observation are the second central key aspects. It is difficult to influence, regulate and control one's own thoughts, emotions, and behaviors specifically, if they cannot be observed and controlled (cf. Bandura, 1991; Baumeister & Vohs, 2007). Monitoring and self-observation are common key functions of self-leadership, self-control, self-regulation, and emotion regulation (cf. Bandura, 1986, 1991; Bracket et al., 2011; Carver & Scheier, 1998; Furtner, 2012; Manz, 1986; Thompson, 1994). For Bracket et al. (2011) monitoring is an advanced component of emotion regulation to reflect on personal emotions and those of others.

Emotion regulation aims to observe, evaluate and modify emotional reactions (Neubauer & Freudenthaler, 2006; Thompson, 1994).

Impulse control. Impulse control is a function that self-leadership, self-control, and self-regulation have in common (Baumeister, Heatherton, & Tice, 1994; Polivy, 1998): "Most, although not all, self-regulation can be understood as self-stopping"(Baumeister & Vohs, 2007, p. 118). Emotion regulation is associated with impulse control, too. For instance, within an alcohol or cocaine withdrawal both emotion regulation and impulse control are limited (Fox, Axelrod, Paliwal, & Sinha, 2007; Fox, Hong, & Sinha, 2008). Self- and emotion regulation show positive effects on impulse control. For example, disgruntled leaders try to control and regulate their thoughts, emotions, and behaviors, so that they do not regret any negative statement or behavior. Both self-leadership, self-control, self-regulation, and emotion regulation aim to control, restrain or inhibit thoughts, feelings and behaviors (Baumeister & Vohs, 2007; Gross & John, 2003; Thompson, 1994).

Why should individuals control and, if necessary, inhibit and retain their thoughts, emotions, and behaviors? Persons who can control and regulate their thoughts, emotions, and behaviors will be socially successful and will show higher effectiveness (Neck & Manz, 2010). By controlling one's thoughts, emotions, and behaviors a more effective performance behavior reveals. For example, negative thoughts and emotions inhibit the individual performance or a person can be too distracted or shows a lower work motivation and satisfaction. The influence of one's thoughts, emotions, and behaviors can have a positive effect on intrinsic motivation and flow experience (Furtner, 2012). At its core, the self-influencing strategies of self-leadership aim to increase task-related intrinsic motivation (Furtner et al., under revision). By using emotion regulation positive emotions can be generated. Positive (task-related) emotions (e.g., excitement, fun and enjoyment) are important features of intrinsically motivated behavior (cf. Deci & Ryan, 1987; Furtner, 2012). At the same time, negative thoughts, emotions, and behaviors can be attenuated or neutralized through monitoring and regulation. In social terms, control and regulation of one's own thoughts, emotions, and behaviors can also have a positive impact for individuals, groups, and societies (Baumeister & Vohs, 2007; Furtner et al., 2010). Often there is a conflict between egoistic and social interests. In short term, an egoistic interest can be successful. In medium to long term, egoistic persons are avoided by others (McClelland, 1975). Regarding to self-control, it is therefore advantageous to suppress and regulate egoistic tendencies (Baumeister & Vohs, 2007). Persons, who cannot regulate their emotions in a social context, are ignored or shunned. For instance, leaders who cannot control their thoughts, emotions, and behaviors are less successful. Their followers show a very high level of dissatisfaction, increased anxiety and provide a lower performance. In contrast, positive emotions can be transferred to the followers, if leaders can direct, control and regulate their thoughts, emotions, and behaviors (Furtner & Baldegger, 2013).

CONCLUSION

Self-leadership refers to the self-regulatory influence of one's own thoughts and behaviors (Neck & Houghton, 2006), self-regulation in its core to one's own behavior (Carver & Scheier, 1998), and emotion regulation influences one's own emotions (Gross, 1998a). Although there are partially different regulatory processes between self-leadership, self-regulation, and emotion regulation (Furtner, et al., 2010; Gross, 1998a; Hiller, 2011; Koole, 2009; Tice & Bratslavsky, 2000), the common core of any regulatory activity is a *goal* and an appropriate regulatory control function of *monitoring* and *self-observation* (Bandura, 1986, 1991). Considered from an evolutionary perspective, the effective application of self- and emotion regulatory mechanisms is a tremendous advantage for an individual, social groups and society. Future empirical studies should provide further insights into how the human self-influencing abilities for self-goal setting and self-observation (monitoring) positively influence emotion regulatory processes and how they interact with each other.

REFERENCES

Ashby, W. R. (1961). *An introduction to cybernetics*. London: Chapman.

Ashkanasy, N. M. & Draus, C. S. (2005). Rumors of the death of emotional intelligence in organizational behavior are vastly exaggerated. *Journal of Organizational Behavior, 26*, 441-452

Bandura, A. (1986). *Social foundations of thought and action: A social cognitive theory*. Englewood Cliffs: Prentice-Hall.

Bandura, A. (1991). Social cognitive theory and self-regulation. *Organizational Behavior and Human Decision Processes, 50*, 248-287.

Bandura, A. & Locke, E. A. (2003). Negative self-efficacy and goal effects revisited. *Journal of Applied Psychology, 88*, 87-99.

Barchard, K. A. (2003). Does emotional intelligence assist in the prediction of academic success? *Educational and Psychological Measurement, 63*, 840-858.

Bargh, J. A. (1997). The automaticity of everyday life. In R. S. Wyer, Jr. (Ed), *The automaticity in everyday life: Advances in Social Cognition* (Vol. *10*; 1-61). Mahwah, NJ: Erlbaum.

Bargh, J. A., Chen, M. & Burrows, L. (1996). Automaticity of social behavior: Direct effects of trait construct and stereotype activation on action. *Journal of Personality and Social Psychology, 71*, 230-244.

Baumeister, R. F., Heatherton, T. F. & Tice, D. M. (1994). *Losing control: How and why people fail at self-regulation*. San Diego, CA: Academic Press.

Baumeister, R. F. & Vohs, K. D. (2007). Self-regulation, ego depletion, and motivation. *Social and Personality Psychology Compass, 1*, 115-128.

Baumeister, R. F., Vohs, K. D. & Tice, D. M. (2007). The strength model of self-control. *Current Directions in Psychological Science, 16*, 351-355.

Boss, A. D. & Sims, H. P. (2008). Everyone fails! Using emotion regulation and self-leadership for recovery. *Journal of Managerial Psychology, 23*, 135-150.

Brackett, M. A. & Mayer, J. D. (2003). Convergent, discriminant, and incremental validity of competing measures of emotional intelligence. *Personality and Social Psychology Bulletin, 29*, 1147-1158

Brackett, M. A., Rivers, S. E., & Salovey, P. (2011). Emotional intelligence: Implications for personal, social, academic, and workplace success. *Social and Personality Psychology Compass, 5*, 88-103.

David, S. A. (2005). *Emotional intelligence: Developmental antecedents, psychological and social outcomes.* Doctoral dissertation. University of Melbourne, Melbourne, Australia.

Carver, C. S. & Scheier, M. F. (1981). *Attention and self-regulation: A control theory approach to human behavior.* New York: Springer.

Carver, C. S. & Scheier, M. F. (1998). *On the self-regulation of behavior.* Cambridge: Cambridge University Press.

Deci, E. L. & Ryan, R. M. (1987). The support of autonomy and control of behavior. *Journal of Personality and Social Psychology, 53*, 1024-1037.

Deci, E. L. & Ryan, R. M. (2008). Self-determination theory: A macrotheory of human motivation, development, and health. *Canadian Psychology, 49*, 182-185.

D'Intino, R. S., Goldsby, M. G., Houghton, J. D. & Neck, C. P. (2007). Self-leadership: A process for entrepreneurial success. Journal of Leadership and Organizational Studies, *13*, 105-120.

Driskell, J. E., Copper, C. & Moran, A. (1994). Does mental practice enhance performance? *Journal of Applied Psychology, 79*, 481-492.

Elliot, A. J. (2006). The hierarchical model of approach-avoidance motivation. *Motivation and Emotion, 30*, 111-116.

Elliot, A. & Church M. A. (1997). A hierarchical model of approach and achievement motivation. *Journal of Personality and Social Psychology, 72*, 218-232.

Elliot, A. J. & Fryer, J. W. (2008). The goal concept in psychology. In J. Shah & W. Gardner (Eds.), *Handbook of motivational science* (235-250). New York: Guilford Press.

Ellis, A. (1977). *The basic clinical theory of rational-emotive therapy.* New York: Springer.

Fox, H. C., Axelrod, S. R., Paliwal, P., & Sleeper, J. & Sinha, R. (2007). Difficulties in emotion regulation and impulse control during cocaine abstinence. *Drug and Alcohol Dependence, 89*, 298-301.

Fox, H. C., Hong, K. A. & Sinha, R. (2008). Difficulties in emotion regulation and impulse control in recently abstinent alcoholics compared with social drinkers. *Addictive Behaviors, 33*, 388-394.

Frijda, N. H. (1986). *The emotions.* Cambridge: Cambridge University Press.

Furtner, M. R. (2012). *Self-Leadership: Assoziationen zwischen Self-Leadership, Selbstregulation, Motivation und Leadership* [*Self-leadership: Associations among self-leadership, self-regulation, motivation and leadership*]. Lengerich: Pabst Science Publishers.

Furtner, M. R. & Baldegger, U. (2013). *Self-Leadership und Führung* [*Self-leadership and leadership*]. Wiesbaden: Springer Gabler.

Furtner, M. R., Baldegger, U. & Rauthmann, J. F. (2012). Leading yourself and leading others: Linking self-leadership to transformational, transactional, and laissez-faire leadership. *European Journal of Work and Organizational Psychology*, DOI:10.1080/ 1359432X.2012.665605.

Furtner, M. R. & Rauthmann, J. F. (2010). Relations between self-leadership and scores on the Big Five. *Psychological Reports, 107*, 339-353.

Furtner, M. R., Rauthmann, J. F. & Sachse, P. (2010). The socioemotionally intelligent self-leader: Examining relations between self-leadership and socioemotional intelligence. *Social Behavior and Personality, 38*, 1191-1196.

Furtner, M. R., Rauthmann, J. F. & Sachse, P. (2011). The self-loving self-leader: Examining relations between self-leadership and the Dark Triad. *Social Behavior and Personality, 39*, 369-380.

Furtner, M. R., Sachse, P. & Exenberger, S. (2012). Learn to influence yourself: Full-range self-leadership training. *Journal of the Indian Academy of Applied Psychology, 38*, 299-309.

Furtner, M. R., Rauthmann, J. F. & Sachse, P. (under revision). Unique self-leadership: A bifactor model approach. *Journal of Managerial Psychology*

Goldiamond, I. (1965). Self-control procedures in personal behavior problems. *Psychological Reports, 17*, 851-868.

Gross, J. J. (1998a). The emerging field of emotion regulation: An integrative review. *Review of General Psychology, 2*, 271-299.

Gross, J. J. (1998b). Antecedent- and Response-Focused Emotion Regulation: Divergent Consequences for Experience, Expression, and Physiology. *Journal of Personality and Social Psychology, 74*, 224-237.

Gross, J. J. (2001). Emotion Regulation in Adulthood: Timing is everything. *Current Directions in Psychological Science, 10*, 214-219.

Gross, J. J. (2002). Emotion regulation: Affective, cognitive, and social consequences. *Psychophysiology*, 39, 281-291.

Gross, J. J. & John, O. P. (2003). Individual differences in two emotion regulation processes: Implications for affect, relationships, and well-being. *Journal of Personality and Social Psychology, 85*, 348-362.

Gross, J. J. & Thompson, R. A. (2007). Emotion regulation: Conceptual foundations. In J. J. Gross (Ed.), *Handbook of emotion regulation*. (3-24). New York: Guilford Press.

Houghton, J. D. & Neck, C. P. (2002). The Revised Self-Leadership Questionnaire: Testing a hierarchical factor structure for self-leadership. *Journal of Managerial Psychology, 17*, 672-691.

Higgins, E. T. (1987). Self-discrepancy: A theory relating self and affect. *Psychological Review, 94*, 319-340.

Higgins, E. T. (1997). Beyond pleasure and pain. *American Psychologist, 52*, 1280-1300.

Hiller, L. N. (2011). *Relations between self-leadership, emotional intelligence, and mindfulness: Examining the effects on performance*. Unpublished Manuscript, University of Innsbruck.

Hopkin, D. V. (1995). *Human factors in air traffic control*. New York: CRC Press.

Hoyle, R. H. (2006). Personality and self-regulation: Trait and information-processing perspectives. *Journal of Personality, 74*, 1507-1525.

James, W. (1984). What is an emotion? *Mind, 9*, 188-205.

James, W. (1894). Physiological basis of emotion. *Psychological Review 1994, 101*, 205-210.

Johnson, R. E., Chang, C.-H. & Lord. R. G. (2006). Moving from cognition to behavior: What the research says. *Psychological Bulletin, 132*, 381-415.

Kee, K. S., Horan, W. P., Salovey, P., Kern, R. S., Sergi, M. J., Fiske, A. P., Lee, J., Subotnik, K. L., Nuechterlein, K., Sugar, C. A. & Green, M. F. (2009). Emotional intelligence in schizophrenia. *Schizophrenia Research, 107*, 61-68.

Koole, S. L. (2009). The psychology of emotion regulation: An integrative review. *Cognition and Emotion, 23*, 4-41.

Koole, S. L. & Rothermund, K. (2011). "I feel better but I don't know why": The psychology of implicit emotion regulation. *Cognition and Emotion, 25*, 389-399.

Kruglanski, A. W., Thompson, E. P., Higgins, E. T., Atash, M. N., Pierro, A., Shaw, J. Y. & Spiegel, S. (2000). To "do the right thing" or to "just do it": Locomotion and Assessment as distinct self-regulatory imperatives. *Journal of Personality and Social Psychology, 79*, 793-815.

Labordes, S., Brüll, A., Weber, J. & Anders, L. S. (2011). Trait emotional intelligence in sports: a protective role against stress through heart rate variability? *Personality and Individual Differences, 51*, 23-27.

Latham, G. P. & Locke, E. A. (1991). Self-regulation through goal setting. *Organizational behavior and Human Decision Processes, 50*, 212-247.

LeDoux, J. E. (1995). Emotion: Clues from the brain. *Annual Review of Psychology, 46*, 209-235.

Lewin, K. (1935). *A dynamic theory of personality: Selected papers.* New York: McGraw-Hill.

Locke, E. A. & Latham, G. P. (1990). *A theory of goal setting and task performance.* Englewood Cliffs, NJ: Prentice-Hall.

Lopes, P. N., Côté, S. & Salovey, P. (2006). An ability model of emotional intelligence: Implications for assenment and training. In V. Druskat, F. Sala & G. Mount (Eds.), *Linking emotional intelligence and performance at work* (53-80), Mahwah, NJ: Lawrence Erlbaum Associates

Lord, R. G., Diefendorff, J. M., Schmidt, A. M. & Hall, R. J. (2010). Self-regulation at work. *Annual Review of Psychology, 61*, 543-568.

MacCann, C. (2010). Further examination of emotional intelligence as a standard intelligence: a latent variable analysis of fluid intelligence, crystallized intelligence and emotional intelligence. *Personality and Individual Differences, 49*, 490-496.

Manz, C. C. (1986). Self-leadership: Toward an expanded theory of self-influence processes in organizations. *Academy of Management Review, 11*, 585-600.

Mayer, J. D., Roberts, R. D. & Barsade, S. G. (2008). Human abilities: Emotional intelligence. *The Annual Review of Psychology, 59*, 507-536.

Mayer, J. D. & Salovey, P. (1997). What is emotional intelligence? In P. Salovey & D. J. Sluyter (Eds.), *Emotional development and emotional intelligence: Educational implications* (3-31). New York: Basic Books.

Mayer, J. D., Salovey, P. & Caruso, D. A. (2004). Emotional Intelligence: theory, findings and implications. *Psychological Inquiry, 15*, 197-215.

McClelland, D. C. (1975). *Power: The inner experience.* New York: Irvington.

Miller, G. A., Galanter, E. & Pribram, K. H. (1960). *Plans and the structure of behavior.* New York: Holt, Rinehart, & Winston.

Muraven, M. R. & Baumeister, R. F. (2000). Self-regulation and depletion of limited resources: Does self-control resemble a muscle? *Psychological Bulletin, 126*, 247-259.

Neck, C. P. & Houghton, J. D. (2006). Two decades of self-leadership theory and research: Past developments, present trends, and future possibilities. *Journal of Managerial Psychology, 21*, 270-295.

Neck, C. P. & Manz, C. C. (2010). *Mastering self-leadership: Empowering yourself for personal excellence*. Upper Saddle River: Prentice-Hall.

Neubauer, A. C. & Freudenthaler, H. H. (2006). Modelle emotionaler Intelligenz [Models of emotional intelligence]. In R. Schulze, P. A. Freund, & R. D. Roberts (Eds.), *Emotionale Intelligenz: Ein internationales Handbuch* [*Emotional intelligence: An international handbook*] (39-60). Goettingen: Hogrefe.

O'Connor, R. & Little (2003). Revisiting the predictive validity of emotional intelligence: self-report versus ability-based measures. *Personality and Individual Differences, 35*, 1893-1902.

Phillips, J. M., Hollenbeck, J. R. & Ilgen, D. R. (1996). Prevalence and prediction of positive discrepancy creation: Examining a discrepancy between two self-regulation theories. *Journal of Applied Psychology, 81*, 498-511.

Polivy, J. (1998). The effects of behavioral inhibition: Integrating internal cues, cognitive behaviour, and affect. *Psychological Inquiry, 9*, 181-203.

Porter, S., ten Brinke, L., Baker, A. & Wallace, B. (2011). Would I lie to you? "leakage" in deceptive facial expressions relates to psychopathy and emotional intelligence. *Personality and Individual Differences, 51*, 133-137.

Powers, W. T. (1978). Quantitative analysis of purposive systems: Some spadework of the foundations of scientific psychology. *Psychological Review, 85*, 417-435.

Reeve, J. (2009). *Understanding motivation and emotion* (5th edition). Hoboken Wiley.

Riggio, R. E. & Carney, D. R. (2003). *Manual for the social skills inventory*. Redwood City, CA: Mind Garden.

Riggio, R. E. & Reichard, R. J. (2008). The emotional and social intelligences of effective leadership: *Journal of Managerial Psychology, 23*, 169-185.

Seligman, M. E. P. (1991). *Learned optimism*. New York: Knopf.

Shallice, T. & Burgess, P. (1993). Supervisory control of action and thought selection. In A. Baddeley & L. Weiskrantz (Eds.), *Attention: Selection, awareness, and control* (171-187). Oxford: Oxford University Press.

Stewart, G. L., Courthright, S. H. & Manz, C. C. (2011). Self-leadership: A multilevel review. *Journal of Management, 37*, 185-222.

Tangney, J. P., Baumeister, R. F. & Boone, A. L. (2004). High self-control predicts good adjustment, less pathology, better grades, and interpersonal success. *Journal of Personality, 72*, 271-322.

Tice, D. M. & Bratslavsky, E. (2000). Giving in to feel good: The place of emotion regulation in the context of general self-control. *Psychological Inquiry, 11*, 149-159.

Thompson, R. A. (1994). Emotion Regulation: A Theme in Search of Definition. *Monographs of the Society for Research in Child Development, 59*, 25-52.

Vancouver, J. B. (2008). Integrating self-regulation theories of work motivation into a dynamic process theory. *Human Resource Management Review, 18*, 1-18.

Vohs, K. D. & Heatherton, T. F. (2000). Self-regulatory failure: A resource-depletion approach. *Psychological Science, 11*, 249-254.

Wiener, N. (1948). *Cybernetics: Control and communication in the animal and the machine*. Cambridge, MA: MIT Press.

Wong, C. & Law, K. S. (2002). The effects of leadership and follower emotional intelligence on performance an attitude: An exploratory study. *The Leadership Quarterly, 13*, 243-274.

In: Handbook of Psychology of Emotions
Editors: C. Mohiyeddini, M. Eysenck and S. Bauer

ISBN: 978-1-62808-053-7
© 2013 Nova Science Publishers, Inc.

Chapter 24

IMPROVING EMOTIONAL COMPETENCE IN ADULTS

Moïra Mikolajczak[1,], Ilios Kotsou[1] and Delphine Nelis[2]*
[1]Université catholique de Louvain, Belgium
[2]University of Liège, Belgium

ABSTRACT

Emotional competence[1] (EC)— i.e. the ability to identify, express, understand, regulate and use one's own and others' emotions flexibly and constructively — has important consequences for adaptation. Specifically, people with greater EC have greater mental and physical well-being, better social relationships and greater career success. The current chapter focuses on what can be done for people suffering from a deficit in EC and answers the four following questions: (1) Is it still possible to improve one's competencies as adults? (2) How? (3) Do the changes last? (4) And, crucially, which benefits—in terms of well-being, health, social relationships and work success— can be expected from such EC improvement?

INTRODUCTION

Emotional competence[2] (EC)—also labelled "emotional intelligence" (EI) or "emotional skills"—refers the ability to identify, express, understand, regulate and use one's own and others' emotions flexibly and constructively. Individuals with high EC are able to identify their and others' emotions, express them in a socially acceptable manner, understand their causes and consequences, regulate them when there are not appropriate to the context or to

---

* Corresponding author: Université catholique de Louvain, Department of Psychology, Place Cardinal Mercier 10, B-1348 Louvain-la-Neuve, Belgium. E-mail: Moira.mikolajczak@ uclouvain.be..

[1] We use the term EC instead of EI to emphasize that, unlike IQ, these competences are subject to change after a psychological intervention.

[2] We use the term EC instead of EI to emphasize that, unlike IQ, these competences are subject to change after a psychological intervention.

their goals, and use them to improve their life. While those individuals take advantage of emotions without letting the latter lead them astray, individuals with low EC have a hard time taking into account the information emotions convey while at the same time being regularly overwhelmed by them (see Mikolajczak, 2009 for a review).

Individual differences in EC have far reaching consequences for adaptation. Specifically, a growing body of evidence indicates that the level of EC is a significant predictor of psychological, physical, social and work adjustment. At a psychological level, higher EC are for instance associated with greater well-being and higher self-esteem (Schutte, 2002), as well as a decreased risk to develop psychological disorders (Schutte, 2007) or burn-out (Mikolajczak, 2007). At a social level, higher EC lead to better social and marital relationships (e.g. Lopes, 2004; Lopes, 2005; Schutte, 2001); and, all things being equal, to a greater likelihood to be chosen as a romantic partner (Schutte, 2001). Workwise, EC have been found to be associated with superior academic achievement (Petrides, 2004) and higher job performance, especially—but not only—for jobs involving high levels of interpersonal contacts, such as service occupations (sales, nursing, call centers,...) (see Van Rooy, 2004 for meta-analyses; O' Boyle Jr, 2010). EC has also been associated with greater managerial competences, resulting in more efficient and less stressed teams (Mikolajczak, 2011). Finally, at a physical level, a deficit in some dimensions of EC (such as emotion identification or emotion regulation) is involved in the onset and/or severity of several somatic disorders, such as diabetes (Luminet, 2006), gastro-intestinal disorders (Porcelli, 2003), or coronary-heart diseases (Suls, 1995). Emotional competence also decreases the likelihood to adopt health-damaging behaviours, such as smoking, excessive drinking and reckless driving (Brackett, 2004; Trinidad, 2002).

Based on the foregoing results, interventions designed to help kids, students, managers or ordinary people to improve their EC bloomed over the past decade (Matthews, Zeidner & Roberts, 2002). The proliferation of those interventions was favoured by a zeitgeist which put socio-emotional learning to the foreground in both organizations and schools (Mayer, 2000). While validated programs for kids emerged with positive outcomes (see Zins, 2007 for a review) the literature on adult programs remained paradoxically scarce and much less convincing. Very few EC programs were based on a solid theoretical model and even fewer had been rigorously tested. The main problem with previous trainings is that they lacked of a clear theoretical and methodological rationale and employed a miscellany of techniques whose psychological bases were sometimes dubious (Matthews, 2002; Matthews, 2007). Another problem is that they targeted only some EC dimensions (e.g., emotion identification but not emotion management) and added a number of skills which are not considered as parts of EC, such as decision-making, or goal-setting making it difficult to know which component changes are attributable to. A third weakness of these programs is that their evaluations were most of the time limited to subjective evaluations right after the training, without considering objective or long-term effects. Finally, very few evaluations of EC trainings included a proper control group.

Thus, in spite of the proliferation of trainings, the most important questions remained unanswered until recently: Is it really possible to improve one's competencies as adults? Are the effect sizes meaningful? Do the changes last? And, crucially, which benefits—in terms of well-being, health, social relationships and work success— can be expected from such EC improvement?

A few years ago, my collaborators and I decided to attempt to answer those questions while avoiding the pitfalls that contaminated previous attempts in the field. This chapter aims to share the process and results of our endeavour.

1. CAN ADULTS CHANGE?

Theoretically speaking, there seemed to be as many arguments in favour as in disfavour of the possibility to improve EC in adulthood.

1.1. " What's Bred in the Bone Comes Out in the Flesh…": The Arguments against the Possibility to Improve EC in Adulthood

Three arguments plead against the possibility to improve EC in adulthood.

- First, the fact that EC are partially genetically determined (Vernon, 2008). One could argue that this genetic inheritability reduces change possibilities.
- Second, the fact that people's behavior in emotional situations is underlain by the brain functioning (Desseilles, 2012). One could argue that the velocity with which the brain processes information and generates emotional responses (a few milliseconds) may make it particularly difficult to alter these responses. This would be specifically true in adulthood, because emotional responses have been automated and reinforced for a long time.
- Third, the fact that personality (and specifically neuroticism) remains stable after 30 years old (McCrae, 1994). If personality is stable, there may be few change opportunities.

1.2. "Nothing is Impossible to a Willing Heart…": The Arguments in Favour of the Possibility to Improve EC in Adulthood

While there exists some reasons to doubt about the possibility to significantly improve EC in adulthood, there fortunately exist as many reasons to be optimistic.

- First, our genes do not entirely determine our level of EC (Vernon, Petrides, Bratko, & Aitken Schermer, 2008). On the one hand, the variance of EC explained by our genes varies between 25 and 50, thus leaving ample room for improvement. On the other hand, recent research in epigenetics show that environmental factors have the power to modulate the expression of our genes (Jaenisch, 2003; Krishnan, 2008), including the emotion-related genes (Krishnan, 2008).
- Second, our brain functioning is not rigid. Instead, research on neuroplasticity show that our brain changes and evolves in response to environmental demands, even in old age (Kempermann, 2002). These changes in the structure and/or functioning of our brain are made possible through two phenomena: neurogenesis (generation of

new neurons and/or new connections between existing neurons) and synaptic pruning (suppression of inefficient and/or unused connexions).

- Third, personality is stable, but certainly not fixed. Significant life events and/or environmental constraints can bring about selective and lasting personality changes (Caspi, 2001;Roberts, 1997).

Thus, if our genes only determine part of what we are, if our brain is flexible, and if life experiences have the power to change ourselves, there may be some hope that EC can evolve under certain conditions.

It is on the basis of this that we built our own training program. It took us several trials to finalize the training protocol. We started with a 10-hour protocol (Nelis, 2009), went on with an 18-hour protocol (Nelis, 2011) to end up with a final 15-hour protocol (Kotsou, 2011; Kotsou, Vermeulen, Grégoire & Mikolajczak, in preparation; Kotsou, Submitted). We will take stock of the findings in the next section.

2. How Can We Develop EC in Adults?

In this section, we share the main lessons that we have learned from our research program, in terms of prerequisite, content, teaching methods and transfer of newly acquired EC.

2.1. Prerequisites of the Training

As it has been repeatedly shown in education research, motivation, interest and self-efficacy are key predictors of learning success. A simple way to ensure sufficient **motivation** is to condition inclusion in the training to a motivation letter. In addition to increase the level of motivation (because participants face the risk of not being included if their motivation is deemed insufficient), the motivation letter helps participants to identify their main problems and to put words on them. It is then easier for them to recognize the changes that need to be brought into their life.

The importance of stimulating **interest** must not be underestimated, especially for men who are traditionally less interested in emotions than women. The introduction of the training will therefore need to be construed so as to boost the participants' interest for emotional matters. One way that my collaborators and I have found useful to this end is to introduce people to the adaptive functions of emotion (in order to show their functional nature) and to their biological correlates (in order to show that emotions are not vague and impalpable phenomena); we also explain what EC are, and which are their effects on mental and physical health, social relationships and work performance. This is usually sufficient to boost up participants' interest for emotions and consolidate their interest for emotional change.

However motivated and interested people are, no change can happen if people do not believe that they can change. Increasing **self-efficacy** is therefore a crucial prerequisite. It is also a sensitive one, because people have usually already attempted to change, without success. The way we have dealt with that issue so far is to explain people the rules of neuroplasticity. This contributes to show them that change is possible, but that it takes effort and time.

2.2. Content of the Training

The content of the training was based on hundreds of publications on emotions and EC in order to ensure its scientific relevance and content validity. Only empirically supported theories and methods were used to inform teaching modules (Mikolajczak, 2009) for a full description of the theoretical and empirical bases of the training). Modules were articulated around the five core emotional competencies: emotion identification, emotion understanding, emotion utilization, emotion regulation and emotion expression[3]. The goals of each module figure in Table 1. More about each module and examples of exercises can be found in Kotsou, Grégoire & Mikolajczak, in preparation (the pre-press paper can be requested from the authors).

Table 1. Goals of Each Module of the Louvain Emotional Competence Training

Identification
- Learn to welcome rather than suppress/repress emotions
- Learn to identify emotions and distinguish their various components (thoughts, bodily sensations, action tendencies, subjective feeling)
- Learn how to identify others' emotions

Understanding
- Understand the causes of one's emotions (e.g., . distinguish between the trigger and the profound cause; identify the unsatisfied needs which are potentially behind the emotion)

Use
- Learn how to use emotions as indicators of one's needs' level of satisfaction, as prompters to better know oneself and to take better care of oneself

Expression/listening
- Learn to express one's emotions (or needs) in a socially acceptable and functional manner (when? How?)
- Learn how to listen to others' emotions

Regulation
- Learn when an emotion should be regulated
- Learn how to down-regulate a depleasant emotion (or a stress) when necessary
- Learn how to up-regulate pleasant emotions (i.e., increase the frequency, intensity and duration of pleasant emotions)

---

[3] In Mayer & Salovey's model (1997), emotion identification and emotion expression are gathered in only one dimension. Because research shows that these are actually two distinct dimensions (they are underlain by different processes and one does not necessarily entail the other) and because their improvement requires different exercises, we have opted for a theoretical model that separates them.

2.3. Teaching Methods

The on-site part of the training lasted for 2 days and a half. The first two days (12 hours) consisted in an intensive training structured around the acquisition and/or the improvement of the five core emotional competencies (see table 1). The intervention focused on creating a context of learning where participants could understand the importance of emotional competencies, improve their self-awareness, as well as experience and practice several tools to develop these competencies. Our pedagogy was based on behavioral and experiential teaching methods (Bandura, 1997; Kolb, 1970) and was articulated around five axes:

- An informative dimension: Theoretical information about emotions (their origin, function, effects, correlates) and EC was provided.
- A reflective and reflexive dimension: Participants were led to question and discuss the purpose of emotions, the contexts in which they appear, the message they convey, the situations in which they need to be regulated and the various strategies to do so. They were also invited to reflect on the pros and cons of their own emotional habits.
- An implementation dimension: Concrete and practical tools to enhance emotional competencies were presented to the participants, who were encouraged to test their efficacy through exercises and role-plays.
- An interactive dimension: Interactions between the trainer and the participants as well as interactions between participants (through work in dyads and group discussions) were fostered in order to create the best dynamic for change.
- A customization dimension: Individual capacities were taken into account. Each participant was helped to identify their own ways of functioning and improve it according to their own resources.

Reminders and readings were given to the participants at the end of each day. This intensive training was followed with a one-month Internet follow-up (see below). Participants were also provided with a personal diary in which they were invited to daily report one emotional experience, which had to be analyzed in light of the theory presented in class. Two weeks after the beginning of the Internet follow-up, participants attended a half-day session (3 hours), where they received a reminder of the materials covered during the first two training days. Following this, team discussions were encouraged to identify things that were the most easy/difficult to apply and to find solutions where possible. These discussions allowed us to gauge the extent to which individuals attempted to use what they have learned.

2.4. Transfer of Learning Outcomes

Because the best trainings are useless if the newly acquired skills are not transferred into real life, we designed each and every module so as to maximize both near and far transfer of competencies (Barnett, 2002; Yamnill, 2001); for reviews and transfer guidelines). In addition to the careful choice of teaching aids, we appended a one-month Internet follow-up to the 15-hour on-site training. Twice a week, participants received an email encouraging them to apply a specific part of the intervention. All e-mails included a theoretical reminder of a notion discussed in class, accompanied with a practical exercise. E-mails were kept as short and simple as possible to increase the chances they were read and put into practice.

3. WITH WHICH BENEFITS?

As already mentioned earlier in this chapter, EC influences all the most important domains in people's life: psychological and physical well-being, social relationships (including marital ones), and work performance. An efficient EC training is therefore supposed to bring about not only a significant improvement in EC, but also a meaningful improvement in psychological, somatic, social and work adjustment.

The section below summarizes, for each criteria, the results of five studies, which rigorously tested the training efficiency (Nelis et al., 2009; Nelis et al., 2011; Kotsou et al., 2011; Kotsou et al., submitted; Kotsou et al., in preparation). Each study comprised a control-group, taking the form of either a waiting list or an active control group (i.e. same format but other content, such as drama improvisation or relaxation). Apart from the pilot study (Nelis et al., 2009), the evaluation relied not only on self-reported measures of EC and correlates, but also on peer-report measures (e.g., spouse-reported EC or spouse-reported relationship quality) and objective indicators (e.g., biological measure of stress; objective measure of employability). With the exception of one study, we also followed people for at least 6 months (sometimes a year) so as to ensure that the effects maintained across time.

3.1. Emotional Competence

As expected, the training led to a significant increase in EC in all studies. This effect manifested not only in self-reported measures of EC (TEIQue; TAS-20; ERP-R; EMA; DOE) but also in spouse reports (TEIQue-360) and ability measures (MSCEIT). The increase in self-reported EC turned around 5% in our first studies, and attained 12% in the last studies (i.e., using the last version of the protocol). The increase in peer-reports of EC (by best friend or spouse) ranged from 4% to 8%. Finally, the increase observed using ability measures turned around 9%. Although highly significant statistically speaking, the improvement may seem rather modest to a sceptical eye. Fortunately, the improvement in EC appeared significant enough to bring about meaningful changes in participants' adjustment.

3.2. Mental Adjustment

The training significantly enhanced psychological well-being. It first led to a significant drop in psychological symptoms[4]. The most spectacular decrease concerned perceived stress, which decreased by 25%. It also improved the positive/negative affect ratio (+30%), and led to a significant increase in happiness (+12%), optimism (+12%) and life satisfaction (ranging from 10 to 12% depending on the studies).

---

[4] As measured by the Brief Symptom Inventory (12% decrease).

3.3. Somatic Adjustment

In addition to improving psychological well being, the training also had a significant effect on physical symptoms (headache, stomach-ache, back-ache, etc). The drop in somatic complaints turned around 8% in our first studies, and attained 15% in the last studies. It is noteworthy that this improvement of somatic well being is associated with a 14% drop in diurnal cortisol secretion.

3.4. Social Adjustment

As expected given the influence of EC on social adjustment, participants' relationships with their friends and spouse got better after the training. While there was only a 5% improvement in the first studies, the enhancement reached 10% using the last version of the protocol. There was a remarkable agreement between participants and friend/spouse reports.

3.5. Work Adjustment

We currently lack of data on the effect of our training on work performance. Recent data (Kotsou, Grégoire et Mikolajczak, unpublished data) show that the EC training increases self-reported work performance. Yet, self-reported measures of performance are probably not a reliable indicator of true performance. Nelis & Hansenne (unpublished data) did collect some data on the effect of the training on objective indicators of *academic* performance (GPA and grade at the exam reputed to be the most difficult) but the results are inconclusive: there was only a marginal effect of the training on academic performance. It is difficult to know whether results are only marginally significant because the sample size is too small (less than 20 subject in each group) or because the effect itself is too small. Both reasons probably account for the findings. While we cannot yet draw conclusions regarding the benefits of the training on work performance, we do have interesting data concerning access to the work market. Our findings suggest that students who followed the training were then much more likely to be hired than students who did not (+ 18%; see Nelis, 2011 for the procedure).

While the foregoing sections support the efficiency and usefulness of EC trainings, an important question remains to be answered: do the benefits last?

4. How Long Do the Effects Last?

Whichever beneficial on the short-term, the effects of a training must be durable for the latter to be deemed useful. We currently have data up to a period of one year after the training. Both 6-month and 1-year follow-ups show that the benefits of the training persist with time.

Interestingly, changes in EC seem to bring about a significant decrease in neuroticism and a significant—although smaller—increase in agreeableness after 6 months (see Nelis et al., 2011). These changes in personality testify to the depth of the changes.

5. MODERATORS AND MEDIATORS OF THE TRAINING'S EFFECTS

5.1. Moderators

The benefits that people can expect from such training do not seem to depend on their sex, IQ, or even baseline EQ (see Kotsou et al., 2011). Although IQ and baseline EQ were not found to be significant moderators of change in our studies, we cannot formally claim that people with low IQ or very low baseline EQ would fully benefit of the training. The range of IQ and EQ was somewhat restricted in our studies (because we worked with educated people who were all university students or middle managers), so the results of our moderation analyses must be taken with caution. So far, only baseline motivation and regular practice of the exercises at home appear to moderate the effects.

5.2. Mediators

Why (how) does the training work? It is likely that the active ingredients, viz. the processes responsible for the beneficial effect of the training, vary from one person to another. However, a few common mechanisms can certainly be isolated.

First, the training increases emotional **self-efficacy**. Participants are more confident that they can change, both because we convince them that change is possible and because they are provided with concrete tools to do so.

Second, the training raises **self-awareness**. Participants are trained to observe themselves in emotional situation, and to draw lessons from it. They thereby better understand their emotional functioning and its drawbacks.

Third, the training augments **emotional acceptance** (thus decreases emotional avoidance). Distressing emotions are perceived as less threatening since participants know that there is a message to be drawn from every emotion—including so called "negative" ones—and since they are provided with tools to deal with them.

Fourth, the training increases **emotional flexibility**. Because participants are provided with new ways to react in emotional situations, their behavioural and cognitive repertoire broaden. They are less stuck in an automatic—therefore rigid—emotional functioning and regain some room for manoeuvre in emotional situations.

Fifth, the training improves participants' ability to **take care of oneself**. They are able to use emotions as indicators of unsatisfied needs and, as a result, take greater care of the latter, thereby improving life satisfaction.

CONCLUSION

The findings summarized in this chapter show that it is possible to improve EC in adults, with durable benefits in terms of well being, health, social relationships and work success. These results bear both theoretical and practical implications.

Theoretically speaking, these results first suggest that emotional competencies are somewhat malleable, even in grown-up adults. They confirm that even relatively stable traits are subject to change, under certain conditions. Our findings also show that, combined with proper teaching methods, fundamental research in affective sciences can be used to inform useful practices. The current training was informed by more than 500 scientific publications; it clearly disconfirms sceptical claims that fundamental emotion research is too disconnected from reality to provide practitioners with useful tools.

The average improvement across criteria was 12% (aggregated effect size: d = 0.64). This is significant for such a short intervention. It is certainly lower than the effect-size of short-term psychodynamic or cognitive behavioral psychotherapies—which turns around 0.95 (Butler, 2006; Leichsenring, 2004; Anderson, 1995), but the latter are assessed in the eyes of specific problems, while our focus is much wider. Nonetheless, there must be room for improvement in EC training effect size, and several related questions need to be addressed in future research: how wide is the room for EC improvement? Is it the same for all of us, or do our genes restrict or widen the room for manoeuvre? Besides participant motivation and trainer experience, what are the factors that most influence EC trainings' effect size? All these questions urgently need to find an answer, so as to improve our interventions and determine which percentage of improvement EC trainings should aim.

While our program raise a number of fundamental research questions, it already opens several exciting avenues for applied research. Our results suggest that EC interventions may be fruitfully applied in a number of settings. So far, we have tested its efficiency on stressed students and stressed employees. Research is in progress on specific populations in both clinical settings (migraines, depression and alcohol-dependence) and education ones (gifted students). Yet, there appear to be plenty of other possible applications in organizations (e.g. what are the effects on EC trainings for managers on their subordinates?), health care industry (e.g., can EC programs decrease the severity of some disease and/or help people to better cope with them?), and education domain (are teachers better able to handle difficult classes and less likely to burnout after an EC training?)? These all represent appealing questions, of which we are eager to see an answer.

REFERENCES

Anderson, E. M. & Lambert, M. J. (1995). Short-term dynamically oriented psychotherapy: A review and meta-analysis. *Clinical Psychology Review, 15*(6), 503-514.

Bandura, A. (1997). *Self-efficacy: the exercise of control*. New York: WH Freeman.

Barnett, S. M. & Ceci, S. J. (2002). When and where do we apply what we learn? A taxonomy for far transfer. *Psychological Bulletin, 128*(4), 612-637.

Brackett, M. A., Mayer, J. D. & Warner, R. M. (2004). Emotional intelligence and its relation to everyday behaviour. *Personality and Individual Differences, 36*(6), 1387-1402.

Butler, A. C., Chapman, J. E., Forman, E. M. & Beck, A. T. (2006). The empirical status of cognitive-behavioral therapy: A review of meta-analyses. *Clinical Psychology Review, 26*(1), 17-31.

Caspi, A. & Roberts, B. W. (2001). Personality development across the life course: The argument for change and continuity. *Psychological Inquiry*, 49-66.

Desseilles, M., Korb, S. & Vuilleumier, P. (2012). Les corrélats cérébraux de la régulation émotionnelle. In M. Mikolajczak & M. Desseilles (Eds.), *Traité de la régulation émotionnelle*. Bruxelles: DeBoeck.

Jaenisch, R. & Bird, A. (2003). Epigenetic regulation of gene expression: how the genome integrates intrinsic and environmental signals. *Nature Genetics, 33*, 245-254.

Kempermann, G., Gast, D. & Gage, F. H. (2002). Neuroplasticity in old age: Sustained fivefold induction of hippocampal neurogenesis by long term environmental enrichment. *Annals of Neurology, 52*(2), 135-143.

Kolb, D. A. & Boyatzis, R. E. (1970). Goal-setting and self-directed behavior change. *Human Relations, 23*(5), 439-457.

Kotsou, I., Grégoire, J. & Mikolajczak, M. (Submitted). Change processes in emotional competence improvement: the role of acceptance and need management.

Kotsou, I., Nelis, D., Grégoire, J. & Mikolajczak, M. (2011). Emotional plasticity: Conditions and effects of improving emotional competence in adulthood. *Journal of Applied Psychology, 96*(4), 827.

Krishnan, V. & Nestler, E. J. (2008). The molecular neurobiology of depression. *Nature, 455*(7215), 894-902.

Leichsenring, F., Rabung, S. & Leibing, E. (2004). The efficacy of short-term psychodynamic psychotherapy in specific psychiatric disorders: a meta-analysis. *Archives of General Psychiatry, 61*(12), 1208.

Lopes, P. N., Brackett, M. A., Nezlek, J. B., Schutz, A., Sellin, I. & Salovey, P. (2004). Emotional Intelligence and Social Interaction. *Personality and Social Psychology Bulletin, 30*(8), 1018.

Lopes, P. N., Salovey, P., Côté, S. & Beers, M. (2005). Emotion regulation abilities and the quality of social interaction. *Emotion, 5*(1), 113-118.

Luminet, O., de Timary, P., Buysschaert, M. & Luts, A. (2006). The role of alexithymia factors in glucose control of persons with type 1 diabetes: a pilot study. *Diabetes & Metabolism, 32*(5), 417-424.

Matthews, G., Zeidner, M. & Roberts, R. D. (2002). *Emotional intelligence: Science and myth*. Cambridge, MA, USA: MIT Press.

Matthews, G., Zeidner, M. & Roberts, R. D. (2007). *The Science of Emotional Intelligence: Knowns and Unknowns*: Oxford University Press.

Mayer, J. D. & Cobb, C. D. (2000). Educational policy on emotional intelligence: Does it make sense? *Educational Psychology Review, 12*, 163-183.

McCrae, R. R. & Costa, P. T. (1994). The stability of personality: Observations and evaluations. *Current Directions in Psychological Science, 3*(6), 173-175.

Mikolajczak, M., Balon, N., Ruosi, M. & Kotsou, I. (2011). Sensitive but not sentimental: Emotionally intelligent people can put their emotions aside when necessary *Personality and Individual Differences*, Article in press.

Mikolajczak, M., Kotsou, I. & Nelis, D. (2013). Efficient programs to improve trait and ability emotional intelligences in adults : Lessons learned from the Louvain Emotional Competence Training. In J. C. Pérez-González, S. Mavroveli & D. Anaya (Eds.), *Assessment and Education of Emotional Intelligence*.

Mikolajczak, M., Menil, C. & Luminet, O. (2007). Explaining the protective effect of trait emotional intelligence regarding occupational stress: Exploration of emotional labor processes. *Journal of Research in Personality, 41*, 1107-1117.

Mikolajczak, M., Quoidbach, J., Kotsou, I. & Nelis, D. (2009). *Les compétences émotionnelles*. Paris: Dunod.

Nelis, D., Kotsou, I., Quoidbach, J., Hansenne, M., Weytens, F., Dupuis, P. & Mikolajczak, M. (2011). Increasing emotional competence improves psychological and physical well-Being, social relationships, and employability. *Emotion, 2*, 354-366.

Nelis, D., Quoidbach, J., Mikolajczak, M. & Hansenne, M. (2009). Increasing emotional intelligence: (How) is it possible? *Personality and Individual Differences, 47*, 36-41.

O' Boyle Jr, E. H., Humphrey, R. H., Pollack, J. M., Hawver, T. H. & Story, P. A. (2010). The relation between emotional intelligence and job performance: A meta-analysis. *Journal of Organizational Behavior, 32*, 788–818.

Petrides, K. V., Frederickson, N. & Furnham, A. (2004). The role of trait emotional intelligence in academic performance and deviant behavior at school. *Personality and Individual Differences, 36*(2), 277-293.

Porcelli, P., Bagby, R. M., Taylor, G. J., De Carne, M., Leandro, G. & Todarello, O. (2003). Alexithymia as Predictor of Treatment Outcome in Patients with Functional Gastrointestinal Disorders. *Psychosomatic Medicine, 65*, 911-918.

Roberts, B. W. (1997). Plaster or plasticity: Are adult work experiences associated with personality change in women? *Journal of Personality, 65*(2), 205-232.

Schutte, N. S., Malouff, J. M., Bobik, C., Coston, T. D., Greeson, C., Jedlicka, C. & Wendorf, G. (2001). Emotional intelligence and interpersonal relations. *Journal of Social Psychology, 141*(4), 523-536.

Schutte, N. S., Malouff, J. M., Thorsteinsson, E. B., Bhullar, N. & Rooke, S. E. (2007). A meta-analytic investigation of the relationship between emotional intelligence and health. *Personality and Individual Differences, 42*(6), 921-933.

Schutte, N. S., Malouff, J., Simunek, M., McKenley, J. & Hollander, S. (2002). Characteristic emotional intelligence and emotional well-being. *Cognition and Emotion, 16*(6), 769-785.

Suls, J., Wan, C. K. & Costa, P. T. J. (1995). Relationship of trait anger to resting blood pressure: a meta-analysis. *Health Psychology, 14*, 444-456.

Trinidad, D. R. & Johnson, C. A. (2002). The association between emotional intelligence and early adolescent tobacco and alcohol use. *Personality and Individual Differences, 32*(1), 95-105.

Van Rooy, D. L. & Viswesvaran, C. (2004). Emotional intelligence: A meta-analytic investigation of predictive validity and nomological net. *Journal of Vocational Behavior, 65*, 71-95.

Vernon, P. A., Petrides, K., Bratko, D. & Schermer, J. A. (2008). A behavioral genetic study of trait emotional intelligence. *Emotion, 8*(5), 635.

Yamnill, S. & McLean, G. N. (2001). Theories supporting transfer of training. *Human Resource Development Quarterly, 12*, 195-208.

Zins, J. E., Payton, J. W., Weissberg, R. P. & Utne O'Brien, M. (2007). Social and emotional learning for successful school performance. In G. Matthews, M. Zeidner & R. D. Roberts (Eds.), *The sciebce of emotional intelligence: Knowns and unknowns*. Oxford: Oxford University Press.

In: Handbook of Psychology of Emotions
Editors: C. Mohiyeddini, M. Eysenck and S. Bauer

ISBN: 978-1-62808-053-7
© 2013 Nova Science Publishers, Inc.

Chapter 25

EMOTIONAL INTELLIGENCE

Marc Brackett and Nicole Elbertson

Yale Center for Emotional Intelligence, Department of Psychology,
Yale University

A book on the psychology of emotions would be incomplete without mention of emotional intelligence (EI). Though the specific concept of EI was introduced formally just over two decades ago, the idea that individuals vary in their ability to understand, leverage, and manage their own and others' emotions is common sense to many and something that ancient philosophers pondered well before the psychological sciences brought the issue to the fore.

The first formal and scientific introduction of EI occurred in 1990, when social psychologists, Drs. Peter Salovey and Jack Mayer, proposed a model of EI that delineated people's emotion-related abilities into four separate areas. This four-branch model described EI as the set of abilities required to perceive, use, understand, and manage emotions (Mayer & Salovey, 1997). Accordingly, *perception* of emotion involves identifying emotions in oneself, others, and even objects and processes. For instance, emotion may be perceived from one's own physiology, such as heart rate, breathing, or bodily tension; another's tone of voice or gestures; the sound of a symphony; or the colors and shapes in a painting. *Use* of emotion involves leveraging feelings to guide cognitive activities, including decision making, creativity, and communication. For instance, one may take advantage of upbeat, motivated feelings by seeing them as an opportunity to tackle a daunting task list, or one may wait until a calm and relaxed moment before dealing with an irritating coworker or family member. *Understanding* of emotion refers to knowing the causes and consequences of one's own and others' emotions. For instance, some people may be more attuned to and better able to predict how certain situations make them feel or how certain feelings may make them think or act. *Management* of emotion involves making conscious efforts to prevent, reduce, initiate, maintain, or enhance emotions in oneself or others. For instance, a friend's frustration may be reduced by offering to help; warm feelings toward loved ones may be maintained by focusing on their positive attributes.

The four EI abilities are interdependent and hierarchical to some extent, such that one must be able to perceive emotions in order to use them or understand them. Similarly, in order to manage emotion effectively, one must be able to perceive, use, and understand emotion well. EI develops over the lifespan and varies as a function of one's genetics and environment.

The general public as well as academics were mostly unaware of EI until 1995, when Daniel Goleman, writer for the New York Times, popularized the construct in his book, *Emotional Intelligence: Why it can Matter more than IQ*. With the release of this book, Goleman captured the attention of much of the world. Yet, within the book's pages were overzealous claims about EI, embellishing its importance and extending its definition to include a broad range of character traits and skills related to achieving success in life. Numerous self-help and professional development books as well as self-report measures of EI were developed based on Goleman's and many others' conceptualizations of EI. A number of studies have shown that self-report measures of EI are highly redundant with measures of personality and mostly unrelated to performance-based assessments of EI.

According to the ability model, individual differences in EI are measured best by performance tests. Performance tests address the limitations of self-reports of EI, which often are inaccurate (Brackett, Rivers, Shiffman, Lerner, & Salovey, 2006). The Mayer-Salovey-Caruso Emotional Intelligence Test (MSCEIT, V. 2.0; Mayer, Salovey, & Caruso, 2002) for adults and the Mayer-Salovey-Caruso-Emotional Intelligence Test, Youth Version (MSCEIT-YV) for adolescents (ages 12 to 17) are tests designed to measure the four abilities of EI. The MSCEIT is considered an objective, performance test because responses are evaluated based on comparison to responses made by either emotion "experts" or a normative sample. For example, the ability to manage emotions is assessed with vignettes describing emotion-laden situations. Participants read the vignettes and rate possible strategies for managing the emotional aspects of the situations on a scale ranging from "very ineffective" to "very effective." Their ratings are compared to responses made by a normative sample (of 5,000 individuals) or by a group of scientists and psychologists who have dedicated their careers to studying human emotion. MSCEIT scores are correlated somewhat with (correlations ranging from .3 to .4) but distinct from general and verbal intelligence.

EI, as assessed with MSCEIT scores, is associated with a wide range of outcomes. Individuals with higher MSCEIT scores report higher quality friendships and are rated as more socially skilled by peers. Dating and married couples with higher MSCEIT scores report having more satisfying and happier relationships with less conflict. College students with higher MSCEIT scores report lower levels of drug and alcohol use and less stealing, gambling, and fighting. Higher MSCEIT scores also are associated with decreased levels of anxiety and depression. In terms of workplace outcomes, MSCEIT scores are correlated positively with performance indicators such as company rank and merit pay increases. Business professionals with high MSCEIT scores are rated by their supervisors as effective at both managing stress and creating satisfying work environments (Mayer, Roberts, & Barsade, 2008).

With growing recognition of the potential role of EI in the success of individuals and organizations, questions have shifted from "What is EI and how can it be measured?" to "Can EI be taught, and if so, how?" As EI is a set of abilities associated with specific knowledge (e.g., one's ability to manage emotion likely depends on the repertoire of strategies one accumulates with experience), it is probable that EI is malleable and can be expanded with training. Indeed, increasing evidence indicates that emotional skills can be learned, in particular, in educational settings (Durlak, Weissberg, Dymnicki, Taylor, & Schellinger,

2011). In fact, over the last decade, a school-based program grounded in the ability model of EI has been developed and tested. This program, The RULER Approach, focuses on the development of EI skills in both the adult stakeholders in students' education (i.e., teachers, parents, administrators, and other school staff) as well as the students themselves. Adults are educated on the role of emotion skills in enhancing their own relationships at school and the academic, social, and personal lives of students. Adults develop their own EI and learn how to foster emotionally supportive learning environments. Then, classroom teachers are trained on a vocabulary-based program aimed at helping children from kindergarten through high school to identify, evaluate, and understand their own and others' feelings and behavior, and develop strategies for managing emotions in their lives (Brackett, et al., 2011). Research on RULER has shown that the program enhances academic performance, promotes well-being among teachers and students, and helps teachers to create more socially and emotionally intelligent classroom communities (Brackett et al., 2012; Rivers et al., in press).

Since its inception in 1990, EI has received much attention in scientific, educational, professional, and psychological communities. Research investigating its underlying theory and its application has shed light on the significance of EI in personal, professional, and social settings (Mayer, Salovey, & Caruso, 2008). Still, there is much to learn about the construct, its measurement, its development, and its impact.

REFERENCES

Brackett, M. A., Kremenitzer, J. P., with Maurer, M., Carpenter, M., Rivers, S. E. & Elbertson, N. (Eds.). (2011). *Creating emotionally literate classrooms: An introduction to The RULER Approach to social and emotional learning*. Port Chester, New York: National Professional Resources.

Brackett, M. A., Rivers, S. E., Reyes, M. R. & Salovey, P. (2012). Enhancing academic performance and social and emotional competence with the RULER Feeling Words Curriculum. *Learning and Individual Differences, 22,* 218-224.

Brackett, M. A., Rivers, S., Shiffman, S., Lerner, N. & Salovey, P. (2006). Relating emotional abilities to social functioning: A comparison of performance and self-report measures of emotional intelligence. *Journal of Personality and Social Psychology, 91,* 780-795.

Durlak, J. A., Weissberg, R. P., Dymnicki, A. B., Taylor, R. D. & Schellinger, K. B. (2011). The impact of enhancing students' social and emotional learning: A meta-analysis of school-based universal interventions. *Child Development, 82,* 405-432.

Goleman, D. (1995). *Emotional intelligence: Why it can matter more than IQ*. New York: Bantam Books.

Mayer, J. D. & Salovey, P. (1997). What is emotional intelligence? In P. Salovey & D. J. Sluyter (Eds.), *Emotional development and emotional intelligence: Educational implications* (4-30). New York: Basic Books.

Mayer, J. D., Roberts, R. D. & Barsade, S.G. (2008). Human abilities: Emotional intelligence. *Annual Review of Psychology, 59,* 507-536.

Mayer, J. D., Salovey, P. & Caruso, D. (2002). *The Mayer-Salovey-Caruso Emotional Intelligence Test (MSCEIT), Version 2.0*. Toronto, Canada: Multi Health Systems.

Mayer, J. D., Salovey, P. & Caruso, D. (2008). Emotional intelligence: New ability or eclectic traits? *American Psychologist, 65,* 503-517.

Rivers, S. E., Brackett, M. A., Reyes, M. R. & Salovey, P. (in press). Improving the social and emotional climate of classrooms: A clustered randomized controlled trial testing The RULER Approach. *Prevention Science.*

Salovey, P. & Mayer, J. D. (1990). Emotional intelligence. *Imagination, Cognition & Personality, 9,* 185-211.

In: Handbook of Psychology of Emotions
Editors: C. Mohiyeddini, M. Eysenck and S. Bauer

ISBN: 978-1-62808-053-7
© 2013 Nova Science Publishers, Inc.

Chapter 26

ADAPTIVE EMOTIONAL FUNCTIONING: A COMPREHENSIVE MODEL OF EMOTIONAL INTELLIGENCE

Nicola S. Schutte and John M. Malouff
University of New England, Australia

ABSTRACT

Emotional intelligence describes adaptive emotional functioning. Perceiving, understanding and managing emotions effectively in the self and others are core elements of emotional intelligence.

The model of emotional intelligence presented in this chapter organizes the numerous promising categories of research findings on emotional intelligence through a dimensional framework that describes aspects of emotional intelligence, possible antecedents of emotional intelligence, and likely consequences of emotional intelligence.

Aspects of emotional intelligence are the core dimension of the model and include ability emotional intelligence, emotional self-efficacy, and trait emotional intelligence. Ability emotional intelligence is the potential to show emotional competency. Emotional self-efficacy is the expectation that one can bring about good outcomes in emotional functioning.

Trait emotional intelligence describes the extent to which individuals actually show emotional competence in their daily lives.

The dimension of antecedents of emotional intelligence consists of the categories of individual difference characteristics and situational factors. Possible individual-difference antecedents of emotional intelligence include genetically and neurologically determined dispositions, cognitive abilities, emotion-related mastery experiences, processing style, characteristic states of consciousness such as mindfulness, and motivation. Antecedent situational factors include priming and social networks.

The dimension of consequences of emotional intelligence consists of categories reflecting functioning in different realms of life. These realms of life include subjective well-being, mental and physical health, relationships, work, and personality. Several intervention studies designed to increase emotional intelligence provide evidence for the causal role of emotional intelligence in bringing about improvements in these realms of life.

The dimensional model of emotional intelligence provides a framework for understanding discoveries already made regarding emotional intelligence as well as a guide for future research.

INTRODUCTION

Several models have attempted to define and operationalize emotional intelligence. These models focus on emotional abilities or competencies that group together and that involve drawing on emotion in adaptive ways.

Perceiving, understanding and managing emotions effectively in the self and others are competencies typically included in the models. Some models describe in detail aspects of perception, understanding and managing emotions; other models include in their conceptualization of emotional intelligence outcomes, such as stress management, that might arise from good perception, understanding and management of emotions.

A large number of findings on emotional intelligence have been published in the last two decades. At the end of 2011, over 7000 scholarly articles, chapters and books focusing on emotional intelligence were listed in the data base PsycINFO, which abstracts most, though not all, scholarly work relating to psychology.

Present influential models of emotional intelligence, such as those developed by Mayer, Salovey and Caruso, (2004, 2008) and Bar-On (2000) are useful, but do not provide comprehensive frameworks for organizing the many findings regarding emotional intelligence and do not provide a broad impetus for further research in the area.

The new model of emotional intelligence presented in this chapter organizes numerous categories of promising research findings on emotional intelligence through a dimensional framework that describes aspects of emotional intelligence, possible antecedents of emotional intelligence, and likely consequences of emotional intelligence.

INFLUENTIAL MODELS OF EMOTIONAL INTELLIGENCE

The four-branch model of emotional intelligence (Mayer, Salovey, & Caruso, 2004, 2008) holds that emotional intelligence is comprised of levels of competencies that build on each other.

The most basic competency is perception of emotion in the self and others. Accurate perception of emotion is the foundation for the second competency, using emotion to facilitate cognitive processes.

The next highest level involves understanding causes of emotion. Regulating emotion in the self and others is the highest-level competency and builds on the foundation created by the other emotional competencies.

The four-branch model of emotional intelligence is the most theoretically developed model of emotional intelligence and is the basis for much research in the area.

Bar-On's (2000) model of emotional intelligence exemplifies models that provide a broad definition of emotional intelligence. Bar-On's model posits that emotional intelligence consists of basic competencies such as perception and regulation of emotion as well as various skills or characteristics that may stem from the effective perception or regulation of emotions, such as good interpersonal relationships, problem solving, and stress tolerance.

As part of their presentation of the four-branch model, Mayer et al. (2004, 2008) maintained that emotional intelligence is best conceptualized as an ability similar in nature to cognitive intelligence.

They suggested that emotional intelligence is best assessed through performance measures that pose test-type problems to respondents. Other theorists and researchers (Neubauer & Freudenthaler, 2005; Petrides & Furnham, 2003) have argued that emotional intelligence can also be conceptualized and measured as trait (or typical) functioning.

Trait emotional intelligence has been assessed through self-report or reports by close others, in a manner similar to many personality inventories assessing other traits, such as the Big-Five Personality Factors.

A Comprehensive New Dimensional Model of Emotional Intelligence

Many studies provide information regarding variables associated with emotional intelligence, and several studies provide information regarding possible causes of emotional intelligence and consequences of emotional intelligence.

The following model of adaptive emotional functioning provides a theoretical model that organizes these findings in a dimensional framework describing aspects of emotional intelligence, possible antecedents of emotional intelligence, and likely consequences of emotional intelligence.

Aspects of emotional intelligence lie at the core of the model and include ability emotional intelligence, emotional self-efficacy, and trait emotional intelligence.

Possible antecedents of emotional intelligence include individual difference characteristics, such as cognitive abilities, and situational factors, such as social networks.

Possible consequences of emotional intelligence group into categories reflecting functioning in different realms of life, such as health and work.

The Dimensional Model of Emotional Intelligence helps organize existing research and stimulates ideas for future research. In the following sections relevant research is presented for each component of the model.

This is followed by an explanation of how the component relates to other components of the model and by suggestions for future research. Figure 1 shows the components of the Dimensional Model of Emotional Intelligence and the proposed relationships between components.

DIMENSIONAL MODEL OF EMOTIONAL INTELLIGENCE

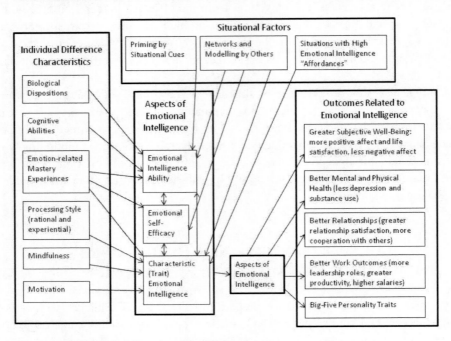

Figure 1. Dimensional Model of Emotional Intelligence.

RESEARCH ON THREE ASPECTS OF EMOTIONAL INTELLIGENCE: ABILITY, TRAIT AND SELF-EFFICACY

Even though the emotional intelligence literature has sometimes presented ability and trait functioning conceptualizations of emotional intelligence as mutually exclusive alternatives (e.g., Mayer, Salovey, & Caruso, 2000), they seem to be inter-related components of adaptive emotional functioning (Schutte, Malouff & Hine, 2011). Measures of ability and trait emotional intelligence tend to share moderate variance (Bracket & Mayer, 2003; Kirk, Schutte & Hine, 2008; Schutte et al, 2011). For example, Kirk et al. (2008) found an association of $r=.29$ between ability and trait emotional intelligence and Schutte et al. (2011) found an association of $r=.33$ between ability and trait emotional intelligence. In an additional test of the relationship between the two types of emotional functioning with each other and with alcohol problems, Schutte et al. (2011) found that trait emotional intelligence mediated between ability emotional intelligence and alcohol problems.

Neubauer and Freudenthaler (2005) have used the term trait emotional self-efficacy for self-report based assessment of emotional intelligence to indicate that this type of operationalization of emotional intelligence focuses on individuals' beliefs about their emotional abilities rather than a completely objective assessment of abilities. High self-efficacy for emotional functioning involves the belief that one can bring about good outcomes in the realm of emotional functioning. Kirk, et al. (2008) made explicit the notion of emotional self-efficacy through development and validation of a scale of emotional self-efficacy which asks respondents to indicate how confident they are that they can carry out adaptive emotional functions rather than asking them whether they typically show these functions as do trait measures. Kirk et al. (2008) found that emotional self-efficacy was significantly associated with ability emotional intelligence at r=.34 and with trait emotional intelligence at r=.73.

DIMENSIONAL MODEL INTERPRETATION OF THE RELATIONSHIPS AMONG THREE ASPECTS OF EMOTIONAL INTELLIGENCE

Emotional intelligence lies at the core of the model. Emotional intelligence may consist of three related aspects of adaptive emotional functioning: ability, self-efficacy and characteristic or trait functioning. The three aspects of emotional intelligence are related and influence each other. Emotional intelligence ability is an individual's actual current capacity for adaptive emotional functioning. The individual may or may not act on this capacity. Individuals with higher emotional intelligence ability are more likely to show good emotional functioning in daily life; this results in higher trait emotional intelligence. The finding that trait emotional intelligence mediated between ability emotional intelligence and alcohol problems (Schutte et al., 2011) suggests that ability emotional intelligence may be a latent function that when consistently expressed gives rise to trait emotional intelligence, which then influences outcomes such as alcohol problems. Whether abilities, such as cognitive intelligence, athletic ability, and emotional ability are consistently expressed as traits may depend on a variety of factors. Among the most important factors determining whether the ability is expressed may be an individual's motivation and situational factors.

Higher emotional intelligence ability along with the application of this ability in daily life may result in more confidence in the effectiveness of one's emotional functioning and thus in higher emotional self-efficacy.

Higher emotional self-efficacy may make it more likely that individuals will devote resources to developing their emotional abilities and also make it more likely that they will draw on emotional competencies in daily life, resulting in higher trait emotional intelligence. An intervention (Kirk, Schutte & Hine, 2011) designed to increase emotional self-efficacy resulted in an increase in both emotional self-efficacy and trait emotional intelligence, lending some support to the notion that emotional self-efficacy promotes trait emotional intelligence. Finally, individuals with higher trait emotional intelligence characteristically show competencies comprising emotional intelligence in daily life and thus have more opportunities to practice and receive feedback on these competencies. Such practice and feedback may influence both emotional intelligence ability and emotional self-efficacy.

CHARACTERISTICS ASSOCIATED WITH EMOTIONAL INTELLIGENCE THAT MAY GIVE INSIGHTS INTO THE ORIGINS OF EMOTIONAL INTELLIGENCE

A number of characteristics associated with emotional intelligence may provide preliminary insights into the origins of emotional intelligence. Most of the studies reviewed in this section on possible origins of emotional intelligence are correlational in design; thus identifying these characteristics as contributing to the development of emotional intelligence is speculative. Future experimental studies might further examine the direction of causality for the variables proposed as contributing to the development of emotional intelligence.

Some of the possible origins of emotional intelligence reviewed in this section can be described as individual-difference characteristics in that individuals differ in the extent to which they manifest these characteristics. For example, some individuals have greater cognitive ability than others. Other possible origins of emotional intelligence can be described as situational. Situational factors consist of conditions in the world that influence individuals in relatively similar ways. For example, most individuals are more outgoing when at a party than when attending a public lecture.

INDIVIDUAL-DIFFERENCE CHARACTERISTICS THAT MAY PROMOTE EMOTIONAL INTELLIGENCE

Research on Biological Characteristics. Research findings suggest that genetic influences may be related to the development of emotional intelligence. In two studies using family and twin designs respectively, Vernon, Petrides, Bratko, & Schermer (2008) found heritability estimates of .32 and .42 for trait emotional intelligence.

A separate line of research indicates that neurological functioning may play a role in emotional intelligence (Kruegera et al., 2009; Takeuchi et al., 2011). Kruegera et al. (2009) found that head injured veterans' prefrontal cortex functioning was associated with their trait emotional intelligence scores. Takeuchi et al. (2011) found that in healthy young adults gray matter density of various regions of the brain was associated with trait emotional intelligence. Such differences in neurological functioning might be in part genetically determined or might be shaped during individuals' development and interaction with the environment.

Dimensional Model Interpretation of Biological Antecedents. If emotional intelligence has a genetic component, as suggested by Vernon et al.'s (2008) research, future studies might explore which genes are involved in facilitating the development of emotional competencies, epigenetic factors, and how genetic predispositions unfold in the context of learning opportunities afforded by an individual's environment. Future studies might also build on the work of Kruegera et al. (2009) and Takeuchi et al. (2011) to further examine differences in neurological functioning and brain structure as determinants of emotional intelligence.

Research on Cognitive Ability. According to the four branch model of emotional intelligence (Mayer, Salovey, & Caruso, 2004, 2008), emotional intelligence involves an interplay of cognition and emotion. One would thus expect cognitive ability to be related to emotional intelligence. A meta-analysis by Joseph and Newman (2010) showed a moderate relationship between cognitive intelligence and ability emotional intelligence, with an r of .22 across 28 samples, and a smaller relationship between cognitive intelligence and trait emotional intelligence, with an r of .09 across 19 studies.

Dimensional Model Interpretation of Cognitive Ability. Moderate significant associations found across numerous studies examining the relationship between cognitive intelligence and ability emotional intelligence (Joseph and Newman, 2010) provide some support for the four branch model of emotional intelligence (Mayer et al., 2004, 2008) proposition that cognitive ability interacts with emotional processing in determining ability emotional intelligence. More conclusive support for the causal role of cognitive ability in facilitating emotional intelligence might come from future longitudinal studies examining whether increases in emotional intelligence follow increases in cognitive ability rather than the reverse. Across numerous studies there is a slight relationship between greater cognitive ability and trait emotional intelligence (Joseph & Newman, 2010). Future research might explore whether this relationship of cognitive intelligence and trait emotional intelligence is mediated by ability emotional intelligence to test the possibility that the relationship between cognitive ability and trait emotional intelligence occurs because cognitive ability influences ability emotional intelligence, which in turn influences trait emotional intelligence.

Research on Processing Style. Processing style is important in human perception and learning. Dual process models attempt to explain the basic mechanisms through which humans react to information and learn from experience. These models distinguish between two systems, one involving associative, experiential processes, and one involving analytic, explicit processes (Schroyens, Schaeken & Handley, 2003). The two systems operate together in guiding individuals' interpretations of the world and their ensuing reactions. Epstein's (1994) dual process model defines these processes as consisting of an experiential system that is effortless, rapid, and tied to emotion and a rational system that is intentional, logic-based, and relatively free of emotion. Schutte, Thorsteinsson, Hine, Foster, Cauchi, and Binns (2010) found that higher levels of both experiential and rational processing were associated with greater trait emotional intelligence. Rational processing was associated with emotional intelligence at $r=.38$ and experiential processing was associated with emotional intelligence at $r=.50$.

Dimensional Model Interpretation of Processing Style. Information processing style may provide a foundation for the development of emotional intelligence. The finding that both greater associative, experiential emotional processing and greater analytic, explicit cognitive processing are related to trait emotional intelligence (Schutte et al., 2010) is congruent with the notion that emotional intelligence is a function of emotion and cognition in combination (Mayer et al., 2004; 2008). The dimensional model of emotional intelligence proposes that a combination of high levels of basic processing styles promotes emotional intelligence. Schutte et al. (2010) found that high trait emotional intelligence mediated between high levels of the processing styles and greater subjective well-being, lending some support to the idea that processing styles are at a more fundamental level of functioning than emotional intelligence, and that emotional intelligence builds on processing styles. Future research might examine the relationship between processing style and ability emotional intelligence and emotional self-efficacy.

Research on Mindfulness. Aspects of consciousness may be related to emotional intelligence. Mindfulness is a state of consciousness that involves non-evaluative awareness and focus on the present. It is a flexible state of open attention to both one's inner state and the outside world (Brown & Ryan, 2003; Brown, Ryan, & Cresswell, 2007). Mindfulness has been found to be a generally beneficial state of consciousness in that it is associated with good outcomes such as greater well-being and better health (Brown et al., 2007). Brown et al. (2007) made the case that as well as being a state of consciousness, mindfulness is also an individual-difference characteristic in that some individuals are more typically in a mindful state than others. Greater typical mindfulness is associated with higher trait emotional intelligence (Baer, Smith & Allen, 2004; Brown & Ryan, 2003; Schutte & Malouff, 2011). For example, Schutte and Malouff (2011) found an association of $r=.65$ between mindfulness and trait emotional intelligence.

Dimensional Model Interpretation of Mindfulness. Individuals' preferred state of consciousness may influence emotional intelligence. A higher level of characteristic mindfulness may make it more likely that individuals show competencies, such as accurate perception of emotion and understanding of emotion, that comprise trait emotional intelligence. Aspects of mindfulness such as awareness may make it more likely that emotions are noticed, and other aspects, such as non-evaluativeness, may allow non-defensive emotional processing. In line with this notion, Schutte and Malouff (2011) found that greater mindfulness was related to more trait emotional intelligence and that trait emotional intelligence mediated between mindfulness and subjective well-being. The finding regarding the mediating role of trait emotional intelligence lends some support to the proposition that mindfulness is at a fundamental level of functioning and that emotional intelligence builds on mindfulness. Future research might explore the relationship between mindfulness and ability emotional intelligence and the effect of interventions aimed at increasing mindfulness on trait and ability emotional intelligence.

Research on Emotional Self-Efficacy and Emotion-related Mastery Experiences. Self-efficacy in a realm of life involves the expectation that one can bring about a good outcome in that realm (Bandura, 1997). A stronger sense of self-efficacy results in a greater likelihood of successfully carrying out an action (Bandura, 1997). Kirk et al. (2008) found that greater emotional self-efficacy was associated with higher trait emotional intelligence.

Each individual has a unique learning history. Actions that bring about desired or reinforcing results are likely to be repeated in the future, while actions that bring about undesired results are not likely to be repeated (Mazur, 2005). Competencies involved in emotional intelligence, such as attempting to understand the causes of others' emotions, may be learned just as many other cognitive and behavioral processes are learned.

As well as having a direct effect on the learning of competencies, successful emotional functioning may lead to an increase in emotional intelligence through personal mastery. Social Cognitive Theory (Bandura, 1984) examines cognitive and social aspects of learning. Bandura (1997) conceptualizes mastery experiences as performing a task or meeting a challenge in a manner the individual perceives as adequate. According to Bandura (1997) such successful personal mastery experiences are one of the most important ways to build a sense of self-efficacy, which in turn leads to a greater likelihood of showing a behavior related to this sense of self-efficacy. Kirk, et al. (2011) found that an intervention based on encouraging employees to reflect on personal mastery of emotional competencies as well as observation of emotional competency in others led to a rise in both emotional self-efficacy and in trait emotional intelligence in the employees who participated in the intervention.

Dimensional Model Interpretation of Mastery Experiences. An individual's learning experiences related to emotion are likely to influence ability emotional intelligence, emotional self-efficacy, and trait emotional intelligence. When individuals process emotions in an adaptive manner, for example by perceiving another person's emotion and helping that person regulate the emotion in useful way, this is likely to bring about desired outcomes, such as comforting a friend who is sad or helping a colleague down-regulate anger. The accumulation of such mastery experiences may influence emotional self-efficacy, ability emotional intelligence, and trait emotional intelligence.

Emotion-related mastery experiences may lead to new learning that increases emotional ability. Emotion related mastery experiences may also build confidence in being able to achieve good outcomes in the realm of emotional functioning and thus build emotional self-efficacy. Finally, such mastery experiences may make it more likely that individuals later show emotional competencies in daily life, and thus increase trait emotional intelligence. Emotional intelligence interventions (Kirk et al., 2011; Kotsou, Nelis, Grégoire & Mikolajczak, 2011; Nelis, Kotsou, Quoidbach, Hansenne, Weytens, Dupuis, & Mikolajczak, 2011) have tended to encourage practice of emotional competencies or reflection on successful emotional functioning, and thus have drawn on mastery-related learning. Such interventions have led to increases in trait emotional intelligence (Kotsou et al., 2011; Nelis et al., 2011) and in the case of the Kirk et al. (2011) study increases in both emotional self-efficacy and trait emotional intelligence.

Future experimental research might investigate the effect of mastery experiences on ability emotional intelligence. Future research might also examine specific aspects of mastery experiences that lead to the most pronounced increases in emotional intelligence.

Research on Motivation. Motivation initiates and maintains human functioning, including functioning related to emotions. Motivation can stem from goals an individual is attempting to reach, such as wanting to obtain a certain type of employment, intrinsic conditions, such as enjoyment of music, and external conditions, such as praise or monetary rewards. Being motivated to show competencies comprising emotional intelligence should make it more likely that individuals show higher trait emotional intelligence. Christie, Jordan, Troth and Lawrence (2007) examined the association between different motives such as need for achievement and need for affiliation with trait emotional intelligence. Some of these motivations were associated with components of trait emotional intelligence. For example, need for achievement was associated with regulation of emotion at $r=.66$ and need for affiliation was associated with appraisal of others' emotions at $r=.28$. Other research showed that individuals' moral identity and characteristics such as Machiavellianism can give rise to goals that then may influence how competencies comprising emotional intelligence are used (Cote, Decelles, McCarthy, Van Kleef, & Hideg, 2011).

Dimensional Model Interpretation of Motivation. Motivation may be a key element in determining trait emotional intelligence. Individuals have many abilities and behavior patterns upon which they can draw. Motivation helps determine which abilities or behavior patterns an individual will choose to show. Thus goals, such as wanting to understand another's emotions, as might be a goal of a therapist working with a client, intrinsic factors such as enjoyment that stems from fully experiencing positive emotions, and external factors, such as others reacting positively to an individual's attempt to regulate his or her emotions in a difficult situation, may prompt motivation to show competencies comprising trait emotional intelligence.

Some research (Christie et al., 2007; Cote et al., 2011) has started to examine how aspects of motivation, such as pro-social goals and achievement related goals, are related to emotional intelligence. The relationship of many other aspects of goals, intrinsic motivations and external motivators with emotional intelligence remains to be explored. Future intervention studies might examine the impact of modifying aspects of motivation on emotional intelligence.

Situational Influences that May Promote Emotional Intelligence Research on Priming. Environmental cues can prime or activate aspects of an individual's cognitive system and this in turn can influence performance. Environmental primes can result in changes in facial expressions, reaction time, performance on mathematics problems, and visual acuity (Dijksterhuis & Bargh, 2001; Langer, Djikic, Pirson, Madenci & Donohue, 2010). In two experimental studies Schutte and Malouff (2012) investigated the effect of priming individuals' emotion-related self-schemas and found that priming aspects of the self-schema related to high emotional self-efficacy resulted in significantly better performance on a measure of ability emotional intelligence.

Dimensional Model Interpretation of Priming. Aspects of the environment such as primes may determine whether individuals draw on their emotional competencies at a particular time. Such aspects of the environment might consist of others showing emotional competencies or reminders of times the individual has successfully shown emotional competencies. The active self-schema model (Wheeler, DeMarree, & Petty, 2007) provides a framework for understanding how aspects of the environment can activate emotional competencies.

According to this model, individuals have an active self-schema that is linked to the static self-schema. The static self-schema consists of a relatively stable representation of aspects of the self. The active self-schema is the individual's current state and draws on aspects of the static self-schema in response to primes. The active self-schema responds to external stimuli, such as primes, that relate to the static self-schema. Thus, when a prime relating to emotional competency activates aspects of the self-schema that relate to emotion processing, this may make more likely the display of emotional ability.

The finding that manipulation of primes can change performance on a test of ability emotional intelligence (Schutte & Malouff, 2012) provides preliminary support for the notion that transient aspects of the environment can influence emotional intelligence ability. If an individual often encounters such primes prompting display of his or her emotional intelligence ability, this may over time result in higher trait emotional intelligence. Future research might examine the relationship between primes and emotional self-efficacy and trait emotional intelligence.

Research on Transmission of Behavior Shown in Networks. Individuals learn much from observing others. Such learning has been termed vicarious learning (Bandura, 1984) and qualities of models which make it more likely that others will emulate the behavior shown by a model include higher status of models, more perceived observer-model similarity, and good outcomes for models showing the behavior. These processes may in part account for transmission or "contagion" of behaviors and emotions in networks. The spread of registering for an internet-based health forum (Centola, 2010) among individuals in contact with each other is an example of behavior contagion, and the spread of contentment through a network of relationships (Hill, Rand, Nowak & Christakis, 2010) is an example of emotion contagion.

Dimensional Model Interpretation of Emotional Competencies Shown in Networks. Parents can be important in modeling emotional competencies (Mayer et al., 2004) that children then may internalize through vicarious learning. Individuals' work and peer networks may also be sources of vicarious emotional learning opportunities. Further, such social networks may cue which learned abilities or competencies, including emotional competencies, might be appropriate in the context of the social network.

Two studies (Schutte, 2012) explored possible connections between emotional competency shown in an individual's social network and the individual's trait emotional intelligence. Individuals who gave high ratings to the emotional competence of the two adults with whom they spent the most time had higher trait emotional intelligence and more life satisfaction. In a second study with a longitudinal design, residents of colleges with higher composite emotional competency at the start of a semester showed greater increases in emotional intelligence from the start to the end of the semester and also showed greater increases in positive affect. These findings suggest that close others may indeed influence individuals' trait emotional intelligence and outcomes associated with emotional intelligence.

Future studies might examine what aspects of emotional intelligence displayed in social networks are most associated with an individual's emotional intelligence, the effect of qualities such as similarity of others in a social network, and the association between emotional intelligence displayed in a network and individuals' emotional self-efficacy and ability emotional intelligence.

Situationist and Interactionist Perspectives. The situationist perspective (e.g., Forgas & Van Heck 1992) holds that situations determine much behavior. Building on the situationist perspective, the interactionist approach (e.g., Hettema & Kenrick 1992) proposes that behavior is the result of interactions between situations and traits. Some of the ways in which situations and traits interact include some characteristics being more compatible with the requirements of a situation, individuals choosing to enter situations that will allow them to show characteristics that are strengths, and some situations having entry requirements that favor individuals with certain characteristics.

Dimensional Model Interpretation of Emotional Affordances of Situations through the Situationist and Interactionist Perspectives. Situations may influence whether individuals show competencies comprising emotional intelligence. Individuals can reliably rate the extent to which situations allow people encountering the situation to show emotional competencies (Schutte, Malouff, Price, Walter, Burke & Wilkinson, 2008). For example, raters agree that individuals have more opportunities to show emotional competency when at a dinner with friends than when watching television alone at home. Situations that allow or encourage expression of emotional competencies can be described as being high in "emotional affordances."

Individuals who frequently encounter situations with high emotional affordances may have more opportunities to observe others express emotional competencies and may have more opportunity to practice their own emotional competencies. These opportunities might lead to rises in ability emotional intelligence, emotional self-efficacy and trait emotional intelligence.

In line with this prediction, Schutte et al. (2008) found associations between individuals' trait emotional intelligence and the situations they chose to enter. They also found that observers rated as better the functioning of individuals high in emotional intelligence than those low in emorional intelligence in high affordance situations. Future research might examine more closely the nature of emotional affordances and different ways in which these emotional affordances interact with individuals' emotional intelligence to bring about various outcomes.

CHARACTERISTICS ASSOCIATED WITH EMOTIONAL INTELLIGENCE THAT MAY GIVE INSIGHTS INTO CONSEQUENCES OF EMOTIONAL INTELLIGENCE

Some characteristics associated with emotional intelligence may be the result of the competencies comprising emotional intelligence. Most of the studies reviewed in this section on possible consequences of emotional intelligence are correlational in design, so identifying these characteristics as resulting from emotional intelligence is speculative. A few studies have attempted to increase emotional intelligence through an intervention and then examined the effect of the intervention on characteristics thought to be related to emotional intelligence. Such experimental studies provide a stronger basis for inferring that emotional intelligence causes changes in these characteristics.

Research on Subjective Well-being. Ability emotional intelligence, trait emotional intelligence and emotional self-efficacy are all associated with indices of subjective well-being (Brackett & Mayer, 2003; Brackett, Mayer, & Warner, 2004; Ciarrochi, Forgas, & Mayer, 2006; Kirk, et al., 2008; Van Rooy & Viswesvaran, 2004). Positive affect, low negative affect, and life satisfaction are commonly used indicators of subjective well-being (Lyubomirsky, King & Diener, 2005). Examples of the relationship between emotional intelligence and subjective well-being include higher ability emotional intelligence being significantly associated with greater life satisfaction at $r=.12$ (Brackett, Rivers, Shiffman, & Salovey, 2006); higher trait emotional intelligence being associated with more positive affect at $r=.57$, less negative affect at $r=-.31$, and more life satisfaction at $r=.47$ (Schutte & Malouff, 2011); and higher emotional self-efficacy being associated with more positive affect at $r=.40$, and less negative affect at $r=-.35$ (Kirk et al., 2008).

Intervention studies provide preliminary information regarding the causal role of emotional intelligence in fostering subjective well-being. An intervention study designed to increase trait emotional intelligence (Kotsou et al., 2011) resulted in increases in self-reported as well as observer-reported trait emotional intelligence and also led to concomitant increases in life satisfaction. Another intervention intended to increase trait emotional intelligence (Nelis et al., 2011) resulted in increased self and other-reported trait emotional intelligence as well as increases in life satisfaction and happiness. A third intervention designed to increase trait emotional intelligence also led to increases in trait emotional intelligence as well as life satisfaction (Wing, Schutte, & Byrne, 2006). An intervention intended to increase emotional self-efficacy led to a significant increase in emotional self-efficacy and positive affect (Kirk et al., 2011).

Dimensional Model Interpretation of Subjective Well-being. Competencies, such as the ability to understand and regulate one's own emotions, comprising emotional intelligence theoretically should promote subjective well-being. For example, the ability to up-regulate positive emotions might be expected to lead to more characteristic positive affect, and the ability to down-regulate negative emotions might be expected to lead to less negative affect. Consistent with this prediction, research findings have shown associations of ability emotional intelligence, trait emotional intelligence and emotional self-efficacy with subjective well-being indices (e.g., Brackett et al., 2006; Kirk et al., 2008; Schutte & Malouff, 2011). Even stronger evidence for the causal role of emotional intelligence comes from experimental intervention studies aimed to raise emotional intelligence (Kirk et al., 2011; Kotsou et al., 2011; Nelis et al., 2011, Wing et al., 2006) that also increased subjective well-being.

Future experimental research might investigate the causal role of ability emotional intelligence in promoting subjective well-being. Future research might also investigate which emotional intelligence competencies are most important for raising subjective well-being and whether there is a feedback loop such that higher subjective well-being might facilitate further development of emotional intelligence.

Research on Mental, Psychosomatic, and Physical Health. Two meta-analyses (Martins, Ramalho & Morin, 2010; Schutte, Malouff, Thorsteinsson, Bhullar & Rooke, 2007) have reported effect sizes of the relationship between emotional intelligence and mental and physical health across many studies. In the Schutte et al. (2007) meta-analysis, which included 44 effect sizes and 7,898 participants, emotional intelligence had significant associations with health, with an average association of $r=.31$ with psychosomatic health, $r=.29$ with mental health, and $r=.22$ with physical health. Associations between trait emotional intelligence and health measures were stronger than associations between ability emotional intelligence and health measures. The later Martins et al. (2010) meta-analysis, which included 105 effect sizes and 19,000 participants, also reported significant associations of emotional intelligence with mental health, $r=.36$, psychosomatic health, $r=.33$, and physical health, $r=.27$. Again associations between trait emotional intelligence and health were stronger than those between ability emotional intelligence and health. An example of the relationship between emotional intelligence and health are the associations between lower ability emotional intelligence and more alcohol-related problems, $r=-30$, and between lower trait emotional intelligence and more alcohol problems, $r=-.27$, found by Schutte et al. (2011).

An intervention study designed to increase trait emotional intelligence (Kotsou et al., 2011) provides some preliminary information regarding the causal role of emotional intelligence in improving health. The intervention increased both self-reported trait emotional intelligence and observer reports of the emotional intelligence of participants (Kotsou et al., 2011). Accompanying the increase in emotional intelligence were lowered self-reported stress levels and better cortisol levels as measured by saliva assays (Kotsou et al., 2011). Another intervention intended to increase trait emotional intelligence (Nelis et al., 2011) resulted in increased self and other-reported trait emotional intelligence as well as in better mental health and fewer somatic complaints.

Dimensional Model Interpretation of Health. Competencies, such as the ability to perceive, understand and regulate one's emotions may facilitate mental, psychosomatic and physical health. Mood and anxiety disorders are characterized by maladaptive emotional states and other disorders, such as some personality disorders and impulse control disorders, are characterized by lack of awareness of emotion and inability to manage emotion (Schutte et al., 2007). Emotional intelligence may provide individuals with resilience in the face of adversity so that mental health problems are less likely to develop. Similarly, the awareness and understanding of emotional states that are components of emotional intelligence may make it more likely that individuals adaptively deal with life stressors resulting in fewer psychosomatic reactions. Finally, understanding and regulation of emotion may make it more likely that individuals engage in positive health behaviors, such as participation in sustained exercise programs.

The associations between emotional intelligence and mental, psychosomatic and physical health (Martins et al., 2010; Schutte et al., 2007) provide some support for the role of emotional intelligence in supporting health. Intervention studies aimed at raising emotional intelligence that improved mental and physical health at the same time as raising emotional intelligence (Kotsou et al., 2011; Nelis et al., 2011) provide even more convincing evidence of the causal role of emotional intelligence in promoting health.

Future studies might investigate the association between emotional intelligence and aspects of health not previously examined as well as possible mediators between emotional intelligence and health. For example, positive affect may mediate some of the relationships between emotional intelligence and health. Higher emotional intelligence is associated with greater characteristic positive affect. Positive affect in turn is associated with better health (Lyubomirsky et al., 2005). Future experimental research might investigate which aspects of emotional intelligence have the greatest impact on mental, psychosomatic and physical health.

Research on Relationships. Both higher ability emotional intelligence and higher trait emotional intelligence tend to be associated with better interpersonal relationships (Lopes, Brackett, Nezlek, Schutz, Sellin, & Salovey, 2004; Lopes, Salovey, Cote, & Beers, 2005; Schutte et al., 2001). A meta-analysis of 22 analyses involving 1188 individuals found an overall association of $r=.23$ between emotional intelligence and romantic relationship satisfaction (Malouff, Schutte & Thorsteinsson, 2012). The association between trait emotional intelligence and relationship satisfaction was stronger than the association between ability emotional intelligence and relationship satisfaction.

An intervention study designed to increase trait emotional intelligence (Kotsou et al. 2011) provides information regarding the causal role of emotional intelligence in improving relationships. The intervention resulted in increased self-reported and observer-reported trait emotional intelligence as well as self-reported and other-reported relationship quality. Another intervention intended to increase trait emotional intelligence (Nelis et al., 2011) resulted in increased self and other-reported trait emotional intelligence as well as in better social functioning.

Dimensional Model Interpretation of Relationships. Emotional intelligence includes competencies relating to perceiving and understanding the emotions of others and helping others regulate their emotions. Thus, one would expect that individuals higher in emotional intelligence would be able to build and maintain better relationships with others. The association between trait and ability emotional intelligence with more relationship satisfaction and better quality relationships (Lopes et al., 2004; Malouff et al., under review; Schutte et al., 2001) provides some support for this proposition. Even stronger support comes from intervention studies aimed at increasing trait emotional intelligence that also resulted in better general relationship quality and better social functioning (Kotsou et al. 2011; Nelis et al., 2011).

Future research might examine characteristics or behaviors that mediate between emotional intelligence and relationship quality or satisfaction. For example, individuals higher in emotional intelligence may use certain communication styles that in turn are associated with greater mutual satisfaction with a relationship. Future experimental research might also examine the effect of increasing ability emotional intelligence and emotional self-efficacy on relationship quality.

Research on Work. Ability emotional intelligence is related to work outcomes such as higher supervisor ratings, more merit-based increases in salary and a higher job rank (Lopes, Cote´, Grewal, Salovey, Kadis & Gall, 2006). Trait emotional intelligence is related to work outcomes such as work performance, work commitment and job satisfaction (Carmeli, 2003). In a comprehensive meta-analysis of emotional intelligence and job performance, both higher ability emotional intelligence and higher trait emotional intelligence were related to superior job performance (Joseph & Newman, 2010). The association between ability emotional intelligence and performance was $r=.18$ across 10 samples and the association between trait emotional intelligence and performance was $r=.47$ across 9 samples. Emotional intelligence is associated with aspects of work-related leadership, including leadership style (Harms & Credé, 2010). For example, across 62 samples, the association between ability and trait emotional emotional intelligence with transformational leadership was $r=.36$ (Harms & Credé, 2010).

An intervention intended to increase trait emotional intelligence (Nelis et al., 2011) resulted in increased self and other-reported trait emotional intelligence as well as in higher ratings of employability. An intervention designed to increase emotional self-efficacy (Kirk et al., 2011) resulted in increases in emotional self-efficacy and workplace civility.

Dimensional Model Interpretation of Work. Competencies comprising emotional intelligence may make it more likely that individuals have good work-related outcomes. For example, using emotion to facilitate cognitive processes may allow employees to more effectively solve work-related problems. Regulating emotions in the self and others may result in individuals creating more harmonious and productive relationships with co-workers. Associations between emotional intelligence and work-related outcomes and characteristics (Carmeli, 2003; Harms & Credé, 2010; Joseph & Newman, 2010; Lopes et al., 2006) provide some support for these propositions. Stronger evidence for the causal role of emotional intelligence comes from intervention studies aimed at raising trait emotional intelligence (Nelis et al., 2011) and emotional self-efficacy (Kirk et al., 2011) that found the respective interventions influenced work-related outcomes.

Future research might examine possible mediators and moderators that connect emotional intelligence and work outcomes. It may be that type of work is a moderator in that for certain types of work emotional intelligence is more beneficial than for other types of work, and that high emotional intelligence may even be a drawback for some types of work. For example, high emotional intelligence in a psychotherapist may be more important in allowing the therapist to bring about good outcomes for a client than high emotional intelligence might be for an engineer working on an intrinsically interesting project in bringing about a good outcome for the project. Future intervention research might also establish more firmly the causal role of emotional intelligence in determining various work outcomes.

Research on the Big Five Personality Characteristics. Conscientiousness, extraversion, emotional stability, agreeableness, and openness are the Big Five personality characteristics identified in many factor analytic studies, including cross cultural studies (McCrae & Costa, 1997, 1999). These characteristics are associated with a variety of life outcomes ranging from longevity, to mental health, to creativity (Costa & McCrae, 1996; McCrae & Costa, 1997, 1999; Malouff, Schutte & Thorsteinsson, 2005). A meta-analysis of associations of emotional intelligence with the Big Five characteristics (Joseph & Newman, 2010) found that higher levels of each of the characteristics were associated with both more ability emotional intelligence and more trait emotional intelligence. Across studies ranging from 58 to 60 samples for the five characteristics, r values ranged from .45 for the association between emotional stability and trait emotional intelligence to .12 for the association between conscientiousness and ability emotional intelligence.

In an intervention study designed to increase trait emotional intelligence, Nelis et al. (2011) found that the intervention increased trait emotional intelligence as well as extraversion, agreeableness and emotional stability.

Dimensional Model Interpretation of the Big Five Personality Characteristics. Emotional intelligence may be a partial foundation for the formation of personality characteristics. For example, being able to understand one's own and others' emotions may provide a platform for the development of agreeableness. The relationship between emotional intelligence and the Big Five personality characteristics has been much studied, with significant low to moderate associations found between a number of the Big Five characteristics and emotional intelligence (Joseph & Newman, 2010). An intervention study aimed to increase trait emotional intelligence that also increased the level of some of the Big Five characteristics (Nelis et al., 2011) provides support for the causal role of emotional intelligence in the development of these Big Five characteristics.

Future research might examine the role of emotional intelligence in the development of other individual-difference characteristics. Future research might also examine the possible reciprocal relationship between emotional intelligence and some of the Big Five characteristics. Strengthening of some of the Big Five characteristics might lead to increases in emotional intelligence as well as increases in emotional intelligence resulting in changes in Big Five characteristics.

CONCLUSION

The Dimensional Model of Emotional Intelligence provides a framework for discoveries already made regarding emotional intelligence and a guide for future research. The model delineates aspects of emotional intelligence, antecedents of emotional intelligence, and consequences of emotional intelligence. Much research can be placed into one of these dimensions. Some research spans dimensions of the model. For example, the finding that trait emotional intelligence mediates between mindfulness and subjective well-being (Schutte & Malouff, 2011) spans the dimensions of antecedents, aspects, and consequences.

Additional constructs can be incorporated into the dimensions of antecedents of emotional intelligence, aspects of emotional intelligence or consequences of emotional intelligence. For example, evolutionary psychology constructs might be incorporated in the antecedent dimension. Evolutionary psychology focuses on human characteristics that over time developed as a result of natural selection leading to optimal adaptation to natural and social environments. The genetic tendencies towards emotional competencies comprising emotional intelligence may have been shaped in part through such evolutionary processes.

Researchers have only recently begun conducting applied experimental research on interventions to increase emotional intelligence. These types of studies may soon increase in number because of their potential for practical benefits and because of the promising results so far. Intervention studies can provide more information regarding causal antecedents of emotional intelligence, the most effective ways of drawing on antecedents to maximize gains in emotional intelligence, and ways of optimizing emotional intelligence to facilitate beneficial life outcomes. By including possible mediators in intervention studies, researchers can help clarify the mechanism of effects. Much remains to be explored regarding the nature of aspects of emotional intelligence and the antecedents and consequences of emotional intelligence.

REFERENCES

Baer, R. A., Smith, G. T., & Allen, K. B. (2004). Assessment of mindfulness by self-report. The Kentucky inventory of mindfulness skills. *Assessment, 11*, 191-206.

Bandura, A. (1986). *Social foundations of thought and action: A social cognitive theory.* Englewood Cliffs, NJ: Prentice-Hall.

Bandura, A. (1997). *Self-efficacy: The exercise of control.* New York: W. H. Freeman.

Bar-On, R. (2000). Emotional and social intelligence: Insights from the Emotional Quotient Inventory, In R. Bar-On & J.D.A. Parker (Eds.), *The handbook of emotional intelligence* (pp. 363-388). San Francisco: Jossey-Bass.

Brackett, M. A., & Mayer, J. D. (2003). Convergent, discriminant, and incremental validity of competing measures of emotional intelligence. *Personality and Social Psychology Bulletin*, 29, 1147-1158.

Brackett, M.A., Rivers, S.E., Shiffman, S., Lerner, N., & Salovey, P. (2006). Relating emotional abilities to social functioning: a comparison of self-report and performance measures of emotional intelligence. *Journal of Personality and Social Psychology, 91*, 780–795.

Brown, K. W. & Ryan, R. M. (2003). The benefits of being present: Mindfulness and its role in psychological well-being. *Journal of Personality & Social Psychology, 84*, 822-848.

Brown, K. W. & Ryan, R. M., Creswell, J.D. (2007). Mindfulness: Theoretical foundations and evidence for its salutary effects. *Psychological Inquiry, 18*, 211-237.

Carmeli, A. (2003). The relationship between emotional intelligence and work, attitudes, behavior and outcomes. *Journal of Managerial Psychology, 18*, 788-813.

Centola, D. (2010). The spread of behavior in an online social network experiment. *Science, 329,* 1194–1197.

Christie , A., Jordan P. J., Troth, A. C., & Lawrence, S. A. (2007). Testing the links between emotional intelligence and motivation. *Journal of Management & Organization, 13*, 212 – 226.

Ciarrochi, J. Forgas, J., & Mayer, J. (2006), *Emotional intelligence in everyday life: A scientific inquiry (2nd edition).* New York: Psychology Press.

Costa, P. T.,& McCrae, R. R. (1996). Mood and personality in adulthood. In C. Magai & S. H. McFadden (Eds.), *Handbook of emotion, adult development, and aging* (pp. 369—383). San Diego, CA:Academic Press.

Cote, S., Decelles, K.S., McCarthy, J.M., Van Kleef, G.A., & Hideg, I. (2011). The Jekyll and Hyde of emotional intelligence: emotion-regulation knowledge facilitates both prosocial and interpersonally deviant behavior. *Psychological Science, 22*, 1073–1080.

Dijksterhuis, A., & Bargh, J. A. (2001). The perception–behavior expressway: Automatic effects of social perception on social behavior. In M. P. Zanna (Ed.), *Advances in experimental social psychology* (Vol. 33, pp. 1-40). San Diego: Academic Press.

Epstein, S. (1994). Integration of the cognitive and the psychodynamic unconscious. *American Psychologist, 49,* 709- 724.

Forgas, J. P., & Van Heck, G. L. (1992). The psychology of situations. In G. Caprara, & G. L. Van Heck (Eds.) Modern personality psychology (pp. 418–455). Hertfordshire: Simon and Schuster.

Grieve, R., & Mahar, D. (2010). The emotional manipulation-psychology nexus: Relationships with emotional intelligence, alexithymia and ethical position. *Personality and Individual Differences*, 48, 945-950.

Hatfield, E., Cacioppo, J. T., & Rapson, R. L. (1993) Emotional contagion. *Current Directions in Psychological Science, 2,* 96–99.

Harms, P. D., & Credé, M. (2010). Emotional intelligence and transformational and transactional leadership: A meta-analysis. *Journal of Leadership and Organizational Studies, 17,* 5–17.

Hettema, J., & Kenrick, D. (1992). Models of person–situation interactions. In G. Caprara, & G. L. VanHeck (Eds.) Modern personality psychology (pp. 393–417). Hertfordshire: Simon and Schuster.

Joseph, D. L., & Newman, D. A. (2010). Emotional intelligence: An integrative meta-analysis and cascading model. *Journal of Applied Psychology, 95,* 54–78.

Kirk, B.A., Schutte, N.S., & Hine, D.W. (2008). Development and preliminary validation of an emotional self-efficacy scale. *Personality and Individual Differences, 45,* 432–436.

Kirk, B.A., Schutte, N.S., & Hine, D.W. (2011). The effect of an expressive writing intervention for employees on emotional self-efficacy, emotional intelligence, affect, and workplace incivility. *Journal of Applied Social Psychology, 41, 179-195.*

Kotsou, I., Nelis, D., Grégoire, J., & Mikolajczak, M. (2011). Emotional plasticity: Conditions and effects of improving emotional competence in adulthood. *Journal of Applied Psychology, 96,* 827-839.

Kruegera, F., Barbeyb, A. K., McCabed, K., Strenziokb, M., Zambonie,G., Solomonf, J., Raymontg, V., & Grafma, J. (2009). The neural bases of key competencies of emotional intelligence. *Proceedings of the National Academy of Sciences of the United States of America, 106,* 22486 – 22491.

Langer, E., Djikic, M., Pirson, M., Madenci, A., & Donohue, R. (2010). Believing is seeing: Using mindlessness (mindfully) to improve visual acuity. *Psychological Science.* Published online in advance of print at *http://pss.sagepub.com/content/21/5/661.full.*

Lopes, P. N., Brackett, M. A., Nezlek, J. B., Schutz, A., Sellin, I., & Salovey, P. (2004). Emotional intelligence and social interaction. *Personality and Social Psychology Bulletin,* 30, 1018-1034.

Lopes, P. N., Coteˊ, S., Grewal, D., Salovey, P., Kadis, J., & Gall, M. (2006). Evidence that emotional intelligence is related to job performance, interpersonal facilitation, affect and attitudes at work, and leadership potential. *Psicothema, 18,* 132–138.

Lopes, P. N., Salovey, P., Cote, S., & Beers, M. (2005). Emotion regulation abilities and the quality of social interaction. *Emotion, 5,* 113–118.

Lyubomirsky, S., King, L. A., & Diener, E. (2005). The benefits of frequent positive affect: Does happiness lead to success? *Psychological Bulletin, 131,* 803-855.

Malouff, J.M., Schutte, N.S, &Thorsteinsson, E. (under review). The Association between Emotional Intelligence and Romantic-Relationship Satisfaction: A Meta-Analysis

Malouff, J.M., Thorsteinsson, E., & Schutte, N.S. (2005). The Relationship between the Five-Factor Model of personality and clinical disorders: A meta-analysis. *Journal of Psychopathology and Behavioral Assessment, 27,* 101-114.

Martins, A., Ramalho, N., & Morin E. (2010). A comprehensive meta-analysis of the relationship between emotional intelligence and health. *Personality and Individual Differences, 49*, 554–564.

Mayer, J. D., Salovey, P., & Caruso, D. (2000). Models of emotional intelligence. In R. J. Sternberg (Ed.), *Handbook of intelligence* (pp. 396-420). New York: Cambridge University Press.

Mayer, J. D., Salovey, P., & Caruso, D. R. (2004). Emotional intelligence: Theory, findings, and implications. *Psychological Inquiry, 15*, 197-215.

Mayer, J.D., Salovey, P. & Caruso, D.R. (2008). Emotional Intelligence: New ability or eclectic traits? *American Psychologist, 63*, 503-517.

Mazur, J.E. (2005). *Learning and behavior.* Prentice-Hall; New Jersey.

McCrae, R. R., & Costa, P. T. (1997). Personality trait structure as a human universal. *American Psychologist, 52*, 509–516.

McCrae, R. R., & Costa, P. T. (1999). A five-factor theory of personality. In L. A. Pervin & O. P. John (Eds.), *Handbook of personality: Theory and research* (pp. 139–153). New York: Guilford.

Nelis, D., Kotsou, I., Quoidbach, J., Hansenne, M., Weytens, F., Dupuis, P., & Mikolajczak, M. (2011). Increasing emotional competence improves psychological and physical well-being, social relationships, and employability. *Emotion, 11*, 354-366.

Neubauer, A.C., & Freudenthaler, H.H. (2005). Models of emotional intelligence. In R. Schultz & R.D. Roberts (Eds.), *Emotional intelligence: An international handbook* (pp. 31-50). Cambridge, MA: Hogrefe.

Pacini, R., & Epstein, S. (1999). The relation of rational and experiential information processing styles to personality, basic beliefs, and the ratio-bias phenomenon. *Journal of Personality and Social Psychology, 6*, 972-987.

Petrides, K.V., & Furnham, A. (2003). Trait emotional intelligence: Behavioral validation in two studies of emotion recognition and reactivity to mood induction. *European Journal of Personality, 17*, 39-57.

Schutte, N.S. (2012). Social contexts of trait emotional intelligence. Manuscript submitted for publication.

Schutte, N.S. & Malouff, J.M. (2002). Incorporating emotional skills in a college transition course enhances student retention. *Journal of the First-Year Experience and Students in Transition, 14*, 7-21.

Schutte, N.S., & Malouff, J.M. (2011). Emotional intelligence mediates the relationship between mindfulness and subjective well-being. *Personality and Individual Differences, 50*, 1116-1119.

Schutte, N.S., & Malouff, J.M. (2012). Priming ability emotional intelligence. Manuscript submitted for publication.

Schutte, N. S., Malouff, J. M., Bobik, C., Coston, T. D., Greeson, C., Jedlicka, C., et al. (2001). Emotional intelligence and interpersonal relations. *The Journal of Social Psychology, 141*, 523-536.

Schutte, N.S., Malouff, J.M., & Hine, D.W. (2011). The association of ability and trait emotional intelligence with alcohol problems. *Addiction Research and Theory, 19*, 260-265.

Schutte, N.S, Malouff, J.M., Price, I., Walter, S., Burke, G., & Wilkinson, C. (2008). Person-situation interaction in adaptive emotional functioning. *Current Psychology, 27*, 102-111.

Schutte, N.S., Malouff, J.M., Thorsteinsson, E.B., Bhullar, N. & Rooke, S.E., (2007). A meta-analytic investigation of the relationship between emotional intelligence and health. *Personality and Individual Differences, 42,* 921-933.

Schutte, N.S., Thorsteinsson, E.B., Hine, D.W. Foster, R., Cauchi, A., & Binns, C. (2010). Experiential and Rational Processing Styles, Emotional Intelligence and Well-Being. *Australian Journal of Psychology, 62,* 14 - 19.

Schroyens, W., Schaeken, W., & Handley, S. J. (2003). In search of counter-examples: Deductive rationality in human reasoning. *Quarterly Journal of Experimental Psychology: Human Experimental Psychology, 56,* 1129-1145.

Takeuchi H, Taki Y, Sassa Y, Hashizume H, Sekiguchi A, et al. (2011) Regional gray matter density associated with emotional intelligence: evidence from voxel-based morphometry. *Human Brain Mapping, 32,* 1497-1510.

Van Rooy, D.L., & Viswesvaran, C. (2004). Emotional intelligence: A meta-analytic investigation of predictive validity and nomological net. *Journal of Vocational Behavior, 65,* 71-95.

Vernon, P. A., Petrides, K. V., Bratko, D., & Schermer, J. A. (2008). A behavioral genetic study of trait emotional intelligence. *Emotion, 8,* 635–642.

Wheeler S.C., DeMarree K.G., & Petty R.E. (2007). Understanding the role of the self in prime-to-behavior effects: The active-self account. *Personality and Social Psychology Review, 11,* 234–261.

In: Handbook of Psychology of Emotions
Editors: C. Mohiyeddini, M. Eysenck and S. Bauer

ISBN: 978-1-62808-053-7
© 2013 Nova Science Publishers, Inc.

Chapter 27

REGULATING THE IMPACT OF EMOTIONS TO IMPROVE DECISIONS

Kathleen E. Darbor and Heather C. Lench [*]
Texas A&M University

ABSTRACT

Emotions influence decisions, often without our awareness. They affect how information is processed, whether a risk is perceived, the ability to regulate decisions and behavior, and the desire to act on a decision. Through these processes emotions impact almost every choice made in daily life. New research suggests that people have the ability to recognize and regulate the impact of emotions on their decisions, improving their choices, and that certain skills and knowledge are required in order to do so. This chapter will review recent evidence about the situations that encourage people to regulate the impact of emotions and the strategies that people employ to reduce emotional biases in decisions. We will also review evidence about the individual qualities that promote regulation. These findings have implications for helping people 1) make unbiased judgments of risk involved in future activities such as gambles and health choices, 2) avoid the use of stereotypes when evaluating new people and situations, and 3) improve their ability to make decisions by reducing tendencies to avoid the decision for fear of regretting the outcome.

INTRODUCTION

I shall never demand of you that you not grieve at all...Reason will have done enough, if it eliminates from grief what is excessive and overflowing. No one must hope or desire that it not allow grief at all.
—Seneca, Ad Polybium (referenced in Additional Essays on Seneca, 2009)

[*] Corresponding author: Department of Psychology, Texas A&M University, College Station, TX 77843-4235, email: hlench@tamu.edu.

Emotions are a part of everyday life, and they will inevitably influence the decisions people make. At times, emotions provide valuable information about our reactions to a situation that can improve decision making. Other times, emotions overwhelm attempts at rational processing and lead people to make detrimental decisions, including overindulgence, discriminating against others, attributing unwarranted blame, and acting selfishly. People can, and under some circumstances do, take steps to reduce the power that emotions hold over their choices and behavior. Indeed, the ability to recognize and control the potentially deleterious influence of emotions is a hallmark of optimal decision making. The focus of research in this area has typically been on how people reduce the intensity of their emotional experiences. However, as the above quote from the Stoic philosopher Seneca about grief suggests, people may also be able to reduce the impact of emotions by altering the way that they think about them, beyond the experienced intensity of those emotions. This chapter will explore recent theory and evidence suggesting how and when people can control the impact of emotions on their decisions.

IMPACT OF EMOTIONAL RESPONSES

What is an emotion? Two types of emotional experiences appear to be responsible for the majority of biases in decision-making: affective reactions to desirable or undesirable outcomes and overt emotional experiences. When referring collectively to both types of responses in the remainder of this chapter, we will use the term "emotional responses." Affective reactions are relatively automatic positive or negative responses to the evaluation of stimuli that reflect the perceived goodness or badness of the stimuli (e.g., Damasio, 2003; Lench, 2009; Slovic & Peters, 2006). Examples of affective reactions include the positive reaction you may feel to the idea of winning $20, or the negative reaction to the idea of losing $20. In contrast, an emotion is a brief and intense response to an experience or event that impacts an individual's goals that may last several seconds to several minutes (Clore, Schwarz, & Conway, 1994; Eich, Kihlstrom, Bower, Forgas, & Niedenthal, 2000; Ekman, 1992; Lench, Flores, & Bench, 2011; Russell, 1991). In other words, affective reactions reflect the desirability of different goals and stimuli, and emotions reflect the progress that one is making toward achieving (or failing to achieve) those goals. Examples of emotions include the anger you might experience when a computer crash prevents you from finishing a paper. Or the sadness after your paper is rejected from a top journal.

People are often unaware of the influence of their affect and emotions, but emotional responses are an integral part of judgments and decisions. Emotional responses are often a useful source of information and can improve decisions, but they can also exert a powerful influence that results in decisions that are biased and sometimes result in behaviors or choices that individuals regret. Biased decisions can be considered those that deviate from personal or objective norms, such that the decision is different from what the individual would rationally have chosen to do or different from what is objectively the best choice. For example, people may judge a new technology (e.g., nuclear power) to be more dangerous than it actually is because of their fear of what could happen if it fails rather than on the probability that it actually will fail (Lowenstein, Weber, Hsee, & Welch, 2001; Slovic & Peters, 2006).

Affective reactions bias judgment by changing the way that information is processed. First, people are motivated to arrive at conclusions that are consistent with their desires. They thus search for and are more easily convinced by information that is consistent with their desires, whereas they are more likely to avoid and be skeptical of information that is inconsistent with their desires (Ditto & Lopez, 1992; Kunda, 1990; Lench, Darbor, & Bench, 2013). For example, people spent more time and effort analyzing the results of a medical test when it indicated that they were at risk for a disease, as opposed to when it indicated that they were not at risk (Ditto & Lopez, 1992). Second, people tend to approach desirable situations and avoid undesirable situations and this tendency can bias judgments and choice (Lench, 2009; Lench & Darbor, 2013; Tversky & Kahneman, 1981). Negative outcomes are especially likely to motivate behavior and decisions. This influence can be seen in decisions under risk, as people become more risk seeking in order to avoid certain loss (Tversky & Kahneman, 1981). A classic example of this is the "Asian disease problem" (Tversky & Kahneman, 1981). Participants are asked to imagine that there is an outbreak of an unusual Asian disease, which is expected to kill 600 people. They are presented with programs of treatment, and given the expected outcomes in either lives lost or lives saved. In the lives lost frame, they are told that 400 people will die if they adopt the first program, and there is a 1/3 probability that nobody will die and a 2/3 probability that all 600 people will die if they adopt the second program. The majority of participants choose the second, more risk seeking option. However, this preference is reversed if the frame is changed to the number of lives saved (200 people will be saved; there is a 1/3 probability that 600 people will be saved and 2/3 probability that no people will be saved). The desire to avoid certain loss has also been shown to influence gambling behavior (Tversky & Kahneman, 1981), consumer preferences (Levin & Gaeth, 1988), voting decisions (Quattrone & Tversky, 2004), and medical screening and treatment choices (e.g., McNeil, Pauker, & Tversky, 1988).

Emotions such as anger and sadness can result in biased decisions through two paths: by changing 1) the type of processing or 2) the content of processing (Forgas & Vargas, 2000). When emotions bias the type of processing, they affect *how* people treat information when making a decision. When people experience many positive emotions, such as happiness, they tend to engage in broader thought that relies on more general knowledge (Bodenhausen, Kramer, & Susser, 1994; Fredrickson, 1998). Reliance on general knowledge structures can result in more bias, particularly biases that relate to the use of stereotypes or heuristics (cognitive shortcuts). In contrast, when people experience many negative emotions, such as sadness, they tend to engage in more systematic and detail-oriented thought (Bodenhausen, Sheppard, & Kramer, 1994). This analytic approach often results in a reduction in bias, although some research suggests that it can increase bias when the information that is considered in detail is misleading (e.g., anchoring, misleading memories; Bodenhausen, Gabriel, & Lineberger, 2000; Bodenhausen, Sheppard, & Kramer, 1994; Levine, Burgess, & Laney, 2008). Other negative emotions, such as regret (a cognitive emotion that is experienced when realizing a current situation might have been better with a different decision; Zeelenberg & Pieters, 2007) also result in a focus on what went wrong, as well as on the ways to improve future decisions (Zeelenberg, Inman, & Pieters, 2001). This focus increases information search (Shani & Zeelenberg, 2007; Summerville, 2011). Although such search may be beneficial in terms of future decisions, it can come at the cost of time, energy, and other information. Anger is frequently an exception to the impact of negative emotions on processing, as it leads to broader thought and use of more general knowledge, as is typically the case with positive emotions (Bodenhausen, Sheppard, & Kramer, 1994). There is some research that suggests, however, that anger may only broaden thinking in relation to information that is irrelevant to the source of anger, while at the same time narrowing focus to the blocked goal that elicited anger (Darbor, Lench, Davis, & Hicks, 2013; Levine & Pizarro, 2004). Thus emotions can result in biased decisions by changing how information is processed, with positive emotion and anger increasing biases that relate to broad thinking and negative emotions increasing biases that relate to analytic thinking.

When emotions bias the content of processing, they affect *what* information people consider when making a decision. Emotions can increase attention to different elements of an experience, depending on the motivational relevance of the information (Forgas, 1995; 2006; Levine & Pizarro, 2004). Happiness is associated with success in achieving a goal, indicating that the environment is supportive, and tends to result in a focus on opportunities, social relationships, and other positive experiences (Fredrickson, 1998). Happy people often view ambiguous situations (e.g., a picture of an animated conversation) as positive (e.g., two people telling a joke; Bower, 1981), and they tend to have enhanced memory for events as a whole (Levine & Burgess, 1997). Sadness is associated with the failure to achieve a goal (without hope of reinstating that goal), and tends to result in a focus on the outcomes and consequences of goal failure. Sad people are thus more likely to remember information related to the outcomes of an event, such as personal losses and defeats (Levine & Burgess, 1997; Levine & Pizarro, 2004). Anger is associated with the failure to achieve a still-attainable goal, and results in a focus on the causes of failure. Angry people tend to have better memory for their own and others' goals, with more intense anger resulting in greater recall of goal-related information (Levine & Burgess, 1997; Levine & Pizarro, 2004). This focus on goals has been shown to influence judgments of intent and willingness to punish wrongdoers (Ask & Pina, 2011). Finally, fear is associated with avoiding the threat of goal failure (Levine & Pizarro, 2004). Fearful people are thus more likely to have increased memory for threat-related information, and poorer memory for information irrelevant to the threat (Lowenstein et al., 2001; Wessel & Merckelbach, 1998). In criminal cases, this can be a problem, as people are more likely to remember the weapon used to commit the crime than the face of the culprit (e.g., Kramer, Buckhout, & Eugenio, 1990; Loftus, Loftus, & Messo, 1987; Steblay, 1992). Thus emotions can result in biased decisions by changing what information is processed, with specific emotions resulting in a focus on particular types of information that may be given too much weight in judgment.

EMOTION REGULATION

Emotion regulation is the process by which people influence the intensity of their emotional responses (Gross, 1988; Lench, Bench, & Davis, 2013; Koole, 2009). This general process is composed of many individual strategies that might be deployed by an individual to reduce their emotional responses. Regulation can result in an increase or decrease in intensity of both the experience and expression of positive and negative emotional responses, and it can be accomplished through either conscious or unconscious processes (Gross, 1998). For example, a woman might suppress her happiness over a promotion in front of a friend who recently lost her job. The extent to which people are able to regulate their emotional responses varies across individuals (John & Gross, 2004), and may depend on the strategies they choose and the time at which those strategies are implemented (Koole, 2009; Szczygiel, Buczny, & Bazinska, 2012).

Most research has focused on the regulation of the *intensity* of emotional responses, but recent theory suggests that people may also regulate the *impact* emotional responses have on subsequent decisions. According to this proposal, it is possible to experience an intense emotional response but control the extent to which the emotional response influences final judgments and behaviors. For example, a man may be furious with his wife, recognize the potential impact of this fury on his decisions, and engage in strategies to prevent himself from exploding at the first person he encounters, all the while remaining furious at his wife. The ability to control the impact of emotional responses on decisions is important because emotional responses are integral to the evaluative process of decision making, and thus influence many of the judgments and decisions people make every day.

CAN THE IMPACT OF EMOTIONAL RESPONSES BE REGULATED?

Emotional responses are often automatic responses to particular situations. As a result, people are frequently unaware of the influence they can have on judgments and decisions, particularly when the influence of emotional responses carry over to subsequent situations (Bechara & Damasio, 2005; Kahneman, 2003). For example, someone who just had an argument with a boss may not realize the impact that anger could have on how she drives on the way home. Despite the automatic way in which emotional responses often influence judgment, people may have the ability to recognize and regulate the impact of emotional responses on their decisions in some situations, which can lead to improved decision making. In a classic demonstration of this ability, Schwarz and Clore (1983) found that increasing attention to the source of an emotional response can eliminate the impact of that response. They contacted people on sunny or rainy days and asked them how satisfied they were with their lives. People typically are heavily influenced by the weather, judging that they are more satisfied with their lives on sunny days than rainy days. Yet this bias was drastically reduced when the person conducting the interview first asked about the weather, thus calling attention to the potential impact the weather could have on satisfaction. This finding suggests that people can reduce the impact of emotional responses on judgment if they attend to the potential source of their emotional responses.

Dual process theories of decision making propose that there are two ways to process information, through an experiential system that is rapid, automatic and based on emotional responses, and an analytic system that is slower, conscious, and based on logic (Epstein, 1994; Evans, 2008; Kahneman, 2003; Lench, Bench, Flores, & Ditto, 2009). Biased judgments are frequently the result of an error that is generated by experiential reactions and then not corrected by slower analytic processing (Kahneman, 2003). A person might have an intuitive fear that the airplane he is flying in will crash. If he does not remind himself that the probability of a crash is less than that of a car crash, his judgment of the risk involved in flying will be biased. The idea that analytic processing is often required to reduce bias is supported by research demonstrating that cognitive load, which limits the ability of people to think analytically, increases biased judgments that result from emotional processes (Lench & Ditto, 2008; Small & Lerner, 2008). For example, people make decisions biased in favor of their desires, judging positive outcomes to be likely and negative outcomes to be unlikely. This bias is increased when people are forced to make decisions quickly, which limits their ability to think analytically and encourages people to use experiential processes (Lench & Ditto, 2008). This suggests that, under normal circumstances, corrections for bias are indeed being made. Furthermore, it suggests that people have the ability to recognize the influence of emotional responses and regulate the impact on subsequent judgments and decisions.

Evidence from neuroscience research suggests that specific brain areas are activated when people attempt to regulate the impact of their emotional responses on decisions, and that these brain areas are slightly different from those activated during regulation of emotional response intensity (Beer, Knight, & D'Eposito, 2006). These studies focus specifically on affective reactions to stimuli rather than emotional reactions (such as anger or sadness). Generally, the orbitofrontal cortex has been implicated in the evaluation of contextual relevance for affective information when making decisions (Beer, 2009; Beer et al., 2006). In a study by Beer et al. (2006), participants were told to either focus on or ignore pictures that were negative or neutral in valence. They then selected how much money they would bet on a roulette game with specified odds and payoffs. It was found that there was less activity in the inferior frontal gyrus and lateral orbitofrontal cortex when participants focused on emotional responses, and that there was more activity when participants ignored emotional responses. This suggests these areas may represent a neural system (or at least part of one) that allows individuals to incorporate emotional responses into cognition when it is relevant, and reduce the influence of emotional responses when it is not relevant.

WHEN WILL THE IMPACT OF EMOTIONAL RESPONSES BE REGULATED?

The research reviewed thus far suggests that people can regulate the impact of their emotional responses on judgments and decisions. However, people frequently fail to do so or only partially reduce the impact and as a result still make biased decisions. Whether or not people regulate the impact of their emotional responses and the degree to which they are able to regulate likely depends on individual differences in the ability to implement regulatory strategies and situational factors that affect the attention given to decisions.

Although everyone has the capacity to implement emotion regulation strategies, there are likely individual differences in the extent to which people do so. The degree to which individuals are able to accurately identify and describe emotions in both themselves and in others is likely to determine whether they recognize the need to regulate the impact of emotion (Szczygiel et al., 2012). Such ability could allow them to better recognize and deal with their emotions, as well as provide compensatory resources to prevent impairment of functioning when highly arousing negative emotions are experienced (Szczygiel et al., 2012). For example, a man who can correctly identify that he is afraid of potential hazards associated with a new technology might regulate his reactions to decrease the impact of his fear on decisions, perhaps by also thinking about the potential benefits or objective risk. The ability to identify emotions could moderate the success of attempts to regulate the impact of emotion on judgment, as well as prevent mood congruent biases by increasing awareness of the source of emotional responses (Ciarrochi, Caputi, & Mayer, 2003; Szczygiel et al., 2012).

Individual differences that represent the ability to deploy analytic resources are also likely to influence the degree to which people successfully regulate the impact of emotional responses on judgment. These differences may reflect general cognitive capacity, with people who generally have more cognitive resources available better able to deploy regulatory strategies when they recognize the need. Indeed, higher scores on need for cognition, the self-reported degree to which people enjoy thinking carefully, is associated with reduced bias in judgment on a number of tasks, including loss aversion (Smith & Levin, 1996; but see also the failure to replicate these findings by LaBoeuf & Shafir, 2003). Differences in intelligence and working memory capacity may similarly impact the success of regulatory attempts (Mayer & Salovey, 1995; Schmeichel & Demaree, 2010). Recently research has focused on individual differences in the ability to regulate generally based on a strength model of regulation, in which willpower is like a muscle that improves with exercise (Muraven, Baumeister, & Tice, 1999). Although there is no evidence to date, individual differences in self-control abilities are also likely to predict individual ability to regulate the impact of emotional responses on judgment.

Situational factors are also likely to determine the degree to which people deploy analytic resources to reduce bias in judgment. As mentioned previously, the time that people have to make decisions can determine the degree to which they show bias, with more bias resulting when people are forced to make quick judgments (Lench & Ditto, 2008). People under pressure are unlikely to have the time necessary to engage in relatively slow analytic processing to recognize and regulate bias in judgment. Situational factors that determine the attention allocated to different features in the judgment context may also influence the degree of regulation and bias. In a recent series of studies on the tendency to make optimistic judgments consistent with desires, the strength of emotional response was found to determine attention to the judgment task and the degree of bias (Lench, Bench, Herpin, & Sweeney, 2013). It is commonly assumed that stronger emotional responses will result in greater bias; however, stronger emotional responses also capture attention and deploy more cognitive resources. In these studies, participants played a game with consequences that were strongly positive or negative (e.g., winning or losing $1 a hand) or weakly positive or negative (e.g., winning or losing 25 cents a hand). They showed less optimistic bias when the outcomes elicited strong emotional responses compared to weak emotional responses. Additional studies revealed that this correction only occurred when people had the time and resources necessary to carefully consider their judgments. These findings suggest that people engage in regulatory processes to decrease bias in judgment when they are prompted to pay more attention to their judgment.

HOW IS THE IMPACT OF EMOTIONAL RESPONSES REGULATED?

So, if people have the ability to regulate the impact of their emotional responses on decisions, what strategies do they use? Research suggests there are two general approaches people may take: regulation by controlling attention and regulation through cognitive control.

Both of these general approaches, as well as the strategies they entail, are discussed in this section.

Regulation by Controlling Attention

Many strategies have been proposed to reduce the impact of emotional biases on decisions, some of which have been shown to be more successful than others. Regulation can occur through controlling attention, either by attending to the source of a response or distracting attention from a stimulus or response. These strategies tend to be effective and appear to be less cognitively demanding than other regulation strategies (see Ochsner & Gross, 2005, for a review).

One strategy for reducing the impact of irrelevant affect is simply to call attention to the actual source of an affective reaction. An increase in attention to the emotional response can be prompted by external factors that encourage awareness (e.g., Schwarz & Clore, 1983) or internal factors that encourage additional thought (Lench et al., 2013). Similarly, research on persuasion suggests that calling attention to the content of an attitudinal message can result in less attitude change (e.g., Petty & Cacciopo, 1977; Quinn & Wood, 2004). People who are aware that the message will attempt to alter their attitudes are better able to resist this influence and their judgments are less influenced by viewing advertisements or political appeals (Quinn & Wood, 2004). It should be noted that this same strategy tends to be ineffective in improving decisions when affective reactions are relevant to the decision, suggesting that people are able to differentiate relevant from irrelevant affective reactions (see Wilson & Brekke, 1994). For example, positive affective reactions toward a particular car provide useful information when choosing to purchase a car, as those reactions reflect preferences. Positive affective reactions toward the car are not useful information for judging whether one should speed in the car, but may nevertheless have an influence on that behavior.

Another way to reduce the impact of emotional responses is through distraction (Lench et al., 2012). Distraction is a familiar experience that is often used in everyday life (both consciously and unconsciously). It alleviates unwanted emotional responses by diverting attention away from stimuli that elicit the response, and can be implemented either before or after an emotional response is experienced. Lench et al. (2012) found that the use of distraction ("avoid thinking about your feelings") can reduce several different forms of bias, including loss aversion, desirability bias, and optimistic bias. This reduction in bias was the result of more than just exposure control or regulation of the intensity of emotional response. For example, in one study, participants were told to avoid thinking about their feelings either prior to or following viewing neutral words and pictures that were subliminally paired with positive or negative words. They then rated the likelihood that they would experience various future life events, one of which was related to the conditioned word. It was found that the optimistic bias for these judgments (i.e., the tendency to judge an event as unlikely if it had been paired with negative stimuli and likely if paired with positive stimuli) was reduced when participants regulated their feelings immediately before making judgments, rather than before viewing the words/pictures.

Regulation through Cognitive Control

There are many different regulation strategies that involve the use of cognitive control. These strategies may be effective not only in reducing the intensity of an emotion, but also in reducing the impact of that experience on subsequent decisions. These strategies generally consist of deploying analytic resources to alter the way that decisions are made or the information considered when making a decision.

Simply devoting additional resources through attempts to engage in careful deliberation can reduce bias (Bodenhausen, Kramer, & Susser, 1994; Leith & Baumeister, 1996; Lerner, Goldberg, & Tetlock, 1998). This process can lead to less reliance on heuristic processing (Bodenhausen, Kramer, & Susser, 1994; Lerner et al., 1998). For example, when told that they will be held accountable for their judgments, happy people are less likely to rely on heuristic processing and as a result make less biased judgments in court cases (Bodenhausen, Kramer, & Susser, 1994). Careful deliberation can also lead to reduced loss aversion (Leith & Baumeister, 1996). For example, angry people tend to prefer risky gambles. However, when angry people are told to think carefully about their preference for gambles, they tend to choose less risky options (Leith & Baumeister, 1996). Of course, this strategy seems intuitively linked to the strategy mentioned above whereby increasing attention to the judgment can reduce bias. It is likely that these two strategies are linked, such that attending to a judgment also increases the likelihood that people engage in careful deliberation. However, there may also be circumstances under which these two strategies are not equivalent. For example, calling attention to the source of an emotional response might actually increase the impact of that response on judgment, and decrease careful deliberation, if that emotional response is believed to be relevant to the decision at hand.

Another way in which the impact of emotions on decisions can be reduced is through cognitive reappraisals (e.g., Heilman et al., 2010). Cognitive reappraisals involve changing thoughts about emotion-eliciting situations in ways that reduce emotional intensity and impact (Gross, 1998; Oschner & Gross, 2008; Szczygiel et al., 2012). It has been shown to lead to a reduction in both the emotional experience and the decisions that generally accompany that experience (Heilman et al., 2010; Szczygiel et al., 2012). Specifically, in studies examining risk preference, it was found that reappraisal of both fear and disgust led to less risk aversion (Heilman et al., 2010). It was proposed that the effective regulation of the experience of negative emotions increased people's sense of control, which has been shown to mediate the relationship between emotions and risk taking (Heilman et al., 2010; Lerner & Keltner, 2001). Other research suggests that reappraisal through perspective taking and imagery reduces loss aversion (Martin & Delgado, 2011; Sokol-Hessner et al., 2009). For example, when participants are told to imagine a relaxing scene, they are less likely to engage in risky behaviors (e.g., choose a riskier monetary lottery; Martin & Delgado, 2011).

A strategy that has not been shown to be as successful as the others at reducing the impact of emotional bias is suppression (Heilman et al., 2010; Szczygiel et al., 2012). Suppression is a behavioral strategy that works to inhibit the expression of emotion through constant self-monitoring and self-corrective actions (Szczygiel et al., 2012). It is generally effective for reducing the intensity of emotion (although it can backfire and result in more intense reactions in some situations), but is only effective in reducing the impact of positive emotions. It has no effect on the impact of negative emotions (e.g., fear, disgust), which may be due to the cognitive demand involved in suppression (Heilman et al., 2010). Indeed, research suggests that the cognitive demand of both suppression and exaggeration of emotions can lead to impaired performance and riskier behavior in subsequent tasks (Muraven, Tice, & Baumeister, 1998).

There may be additional cognitive strategies that are specific to particular emotional responses, although there is little research to date on some of these. In the case of regret, many strategies are used to reduce regret and other emotions, including reappraisal strategies (e.g., downplay the attractiveness of an alternative outcome, reframe as a learning experience), distraction (e.g., shift focus from imaginary outcomes to present reality), and suppression (e.g., "regret nothing"; see Fisher & Exline, 2010; Zeelenberg & Pieters, 2007). Yet some regulation strategies seem specific to the experience of regret and may be targeted to alleviate the particular circumstances that elicited regret. These strategies include attempts to undo/reverse the decision, justify the decision, and deny responsibility for the decision (see Zeelenberg & Pieters, 2007). To date, no research has examined how the impact of regret on decisions might be regulated. However, the similarities in regulation of intensity between regret and other emotions suggest that similar strategies may be used for regulation of impact. It is for future research to determine whether this is, in fact, the case.

CONCLUSION

For better or worse, emotions are an influential part of the decisions people make. Understanding more about how emotions bias decisions and how such biases can be regulated could thus have important implications for health, consumer behavior, and interactions with others. People could learn to 1) make unbiased judgments of risk involved in future activities such as financial and medical decisions, 2) avoid the use of stereotypes when evaluating new people and situations, and 3) improve their ability to make decisions by reducing tendencies to avoid those decisions for fear of regretting the outcomes.

REFERENCES

Ask, K. & Pina, A. (2011). On being angry and punitive: How anger alters perception of criminal intent. *Social Psychological and Personality Science, 2*, 494-499.

Bechara, A. & Damasio, A. R. (2005). The somatic marker hypothesis: A neural theory of economic decision. *Games and Economic Behavior, 52,* 336-372.

Beer, J. S. (2011). The neural basis of emotion regulation: Making emotion work for you and not against you. In M. S. Gazzinga et al. (Eds.), *The Cognitive Neurosciences 4ᵗʰ ed.* (961-972). Cambridge, MA: Massachusetts Institute of Technology.

Beer, J. S., Knight, R. T. & D'Esposito, M. (2006). Controlling the integration of emotion and cognition: The role of frontal cortex in distinguishing helpful from hurtful emotional information. *Psychological Science, 17,* 448-453.

Bodenhausen, G. V., Kramer, G. P. & Susser, K. (1994). Happiness and stereotypic thinking in social judgment. *Journal of Personality and Social Psychology, 66,* 621-632.

Bodenhausen, G. V., Sheppard, L. A. & Kramer, G. P. (1994). Negative affect and social judgment: The differential impact of anger and sadness. *European Journal of Social Psychology, 24*, 45-62.

Bodenhausen, G. V., Gabriel, S. & Lineberger, M. (2000). Sadness and susceptibility to judgmental bias: The case of anchoring. *Psychological Science, 11*, 320-323.

Bower, G. (1981). Mood and memory. *American Psychologist, 36*, 129-148.

Ciarrochi, J., Caputi, P. & Mayer, J. D. (2003). The distinctiveness and utility of a measure of trait emotional awareness. *Personality and Individual Differences, 34*, 1477-1490.

Clore, G. L., Schwartz, N. & Conway, M. (1994). Affective causes and consequences of social information processing. In R. S. Wyer & T. K. Srull (Eds.), *Handbook of Social Cognition* (323-417). Hillsdale, NJ: Lawrence Erlbaum Associates, Inc.

Damasio, A. (2003). *Looking for Spinoza: Joy, sorrow, and the feeling brain.* Orlando, FL: Harcourt.

Darbor, K. E., Lench, H. C., Davis, W. E. & Hicks, J. A. (manuscript under review). Speaking about emotions: Insight into the construction of emotional experiences. Ditto, P. H., & Lopez, D. F. (1992). Motivated skepticism: Use of differential decision criteria for preferred and nonpreferred conclusions. *Journal of Personality and Social Psychology, 63*, 568-584.

Eich, E., Kihlstrom, J. F., Bower, G. H., Forgas, J. P. & Niedenthal, P. M. (Eds.). (2000). *Cognition and emotion.*, New York, NY: Oxford University Press.

Ekman, P. (1992). Are there basic emotions? *Psychological Review, 99*, 550-553.

Epstein, S. (1994). Integration of the cognitive and the psychodynamic unconscious. *American Psychologist, 49*, 709-724.

Evans, J. St. B. T. (2008). Dual-processing accounts of reasoning, judgment, and social cognition. *Annual Review of Psychology, 59*, 255-278.

Fisher, M. L. & Exline, J. L. (2010). Moving toward self-forgiveness: Removing barriers related to shame, guilt, and regret. *Social and Personality Psychology Compass, 4*, 548-558.

Forgas, J. P. (1995). Mood and judgment: The Affect Infusion Model (AIM). *Psychological Bulletin, 117*, 39-66.

Forgas, J. P. (2006). Affective influences on interpersonal behavior: Towards understanding the role of affect in everyday emotions. In J. P. Forgas (Ed.), *Affect in social thinking and behavior* (269-289). New York: Psychology Press.

Forgas, J. P. & Vargas, P. T. (2000). Effects of moods on social judgment and reasoning. In M. Lewis & M. Haviland-Jones (Eds.), *Handbook of Emotions* (350-368. New York: Guilford.

Fredrickson, B. L. (1998). What good are positive emotions? *Review of General Psychology, 2*, 300-319.

Gross, J. J. (1998). The emerging field of emotion regulation: An integrative review. *Review of General Psychology, 2*, 271-299.

Heilman, R. M., Crisan, L. G., Houser, D., Miclea, M. & Miu, A. C. (2010). Emotion regulation and decision making under risk and uncertainty. *Emotion, 10*, 257-265.

John, O. P. & Gross, J. J. (2004). Healthy and unhealthy emotion regulation: Personality processes, individual differences, and life span development. *Journal of Personality, 72*, 1301-1333.

Kahneman, D. (2003). A perspective on judgment and choice. *American Psychologist, 58*, 697-720.

Koole, S. L. (2009). The psychology of emotion regulation: An integrative review. *Cognition and Emotion, 23*, 4-41.

Kramer, T. H., Buckhout, R. & Eugenio, P. (1990). Weapon focus, arousal, and eye-witness memory: Attention must be paid. *Law and Human Behavior, 14*, 167-184.

Kunda, Z. (1990). The case for motivated reasoning. *Psychological Bulletin, 108*, 480-498.

LaBoeuf, R. A. & Shafir, E. (2003). Deep thoughts and shallow frames: on the susceptibility to framing effects. *Behavioral Decision Making, 16*, 77-92.

Lench, H. C. (2009). Automatic optimism: The affective basis of judgments about the likelihood of future events. *Journal of Experimental Psychology: General, 138*, 187-200.

Lench, H. C., Bench, S. W., Herpin, R. E. & Sweeney, A. (under review). Affective processes that deploy analytic resources.

Lench, H. C., Bench, S. W. & Davis, E. L. (in preparation). Emotion regulation reduces bias in judgment.

Lench, H. C., Bench, S. W., Flores, S. A. & Ditto, P. H. (2009). Automatic optimism: The role of desire in judgments about the likelihood of future events. In E. P. Lamont (Ed.), *Social psychology: New research* (pp. 55-79). New York: Nova Science Publishers.

Lench, H. C. & Darbor, K. E. (in preparation). *Approach and avoidance tendencies in the creation of desirability bias in judgment.*

Lench, H. C. & Ditto, P. H. (2008). Automatic optimism: Biased use of base rate information for positive and negative events. *Journal of Experimental Social Psychology, 44*, 631-639.

Lench, H. C., Flores, S. A. & Bench, S. W. (2011). Discrete emotions predict changes in cognition, judgment, experience, behavior, and physiology: A meta-analysis of experimental emotion elicitations. *Psychological Bulletin, 137*, 834-855.

Lench, H. C., Darbor, K. E., & Bench, S. W. (under review). *Motivated use of probabilistic information: Why probabilities apply to you more than me.*

Leith, K. P. & Baumeister, R. F. (1996). Why do bad moods increase self-defeating behavior? Emotion, risk taking, and self-regulation. *Journal of Personality and Social Psychology, 71*, 1250-1267.

Lerner, J. S. & Keltner, D. (2001). Fear, anger, and risk. *Journal of Personality and Social Psychology, 81*, 146-159.

Lerner, J. S., Golberg, J. H. & Tetlock, P. E. (1998). Sober second thought: The effects of accountability, anger, and authoritarianism on attributions of responsibility. *Personality and Social Psychology Bulletin, 24*, 563-574.

Levin, I. P. & Gaeth, G. J. (1988). How consumers are affected by the framing of attribute information before and after consuming the product. *The Journal of Consumer Research, 15,* 374-378.

Levine, L. J. & Burgess, S. L. (1997). Beyond general arousal: Effects of specific emotions on memory. *Social Cognition, 15*, 157-181.

Levine, L. J. & Pizarro, D. A. (2004). Emotion and memory research: A grumpy overview. *Social Cognition, 22*, 530-554.

Loftus, E. G., Loftus, G. R. & Messo, J. (1987). Effects of ruminative and distracting responses to depressed mood on retrieval of autobiographical memories. *Journal of Personality and Social Psychology, 75*, 166-177.

Lowenstein, G. F., Weber, E. U., Hsee, C. K. & Welch, N. (2001). Risk as feelings. *Psychological Bulletin, 127*, 267-286.

Martin, L. M. & Delgado, M. R. (2011). The influence of emotion regulation on decision-making under risk. *Journal of Cognitive Neuroscience, 23*, 2569-2581.

McNeil, B. J., Pauker, S. G. & Tversky, A. (1988). On the framing of medical decisions. Decision making: Descriptive, normative, and prescriptive interactions. In D. E. Bell, H. Raiffa, & A. Tversky (Eds.), *Decision making: Descriptive, normative, and prescriptive interactions* (562-568). New York, NY: Cambridge University Press.

Mayer, J. D. & Salovey, P. (1995). Emotional intelligence and the construction and regulation of feelings. *Applied and Preventive Psychology, 4*, 197-208.

Muraven, M., Baumeister, R. F. & Tice, D. (1999). Longitudinal improvement of self-regulation through practice: Building self-control strength through repeated exercise. *The Journal of Social Psychology, 139*, 446-457.

Muraven, M., Tice, D. M. & Baumeister, R. F. (1998). Self-control as a limited resource: Regulatory depletion patterns. *Journal of Personality and Social Psychology, 74*, 774-789.

Ochsner, K. N. & Gross J. J. (2005). The cognitive control of emotion. *Trends in Cognitive Sciences, 9*, 242-249.

Ochsner, K. N. & Gross, J. J. (2008). Cognitive emotion regulation: Insights from social cognitive and affective neuroscience. *Current Directions in Psychological Science, 17*, 153-158.

Petty, R. E. & Cacioppo, J. T. (1977). Forewarning, cognitive responding, and resistance to persuasion. *Journal of Personality and Social Psychology, 35*, 645-655.

Quattrone, G. & Tversky, A. (2004). Causal versus diagnostic contingencies: On self-deception and on the voter's illusion. *Journal of Personality and Social Psychology, 46, 237-248.*

Quinn, J. M. & Wood, W. (2004). Forewarnings of influence appeals: Inducing resistance and acceptance. In E. S. Knowles, & J. A. Linn (Eds.), *Resistance and persuasion* (pp.193-213).

Russell, J. A. (1991). Culture and the categorization of emotions. *Psychological Bulletin, 110*, 426-450.

Schmeichel, B. J. & Demaree, H. A. (2010). Working memory capacity and spontaneous emotion regulation: High capacity predicts self-enhancement in response to negative feedback. *Emotion, 10*, 739-744.

Schwarz, N. & Clore, G. L. (1983). Mood, misattribution, and judgments of well-being: Information and directive functions of affective states. *Journal of Personality and Social Psychology, 45*, 513-523.

Shani, Y. & Zeelenberg, M. (2007). When and why do we want to know? How experienced regret promotes post-decision information search. *Journal of Behavioral Decision Making, 20*, 207-222.

Slovic, P. & Peters, E. (2006). Risk perception and affect. *Current Directions in Psychological Science, 15*, 322-325.

Small, D. A. & Lerner, J. H. (2008). Emotional policy: Personal sadness and anger shape judgments about a welfare case. *Political Psychology, 29*, 149-168.

Smith, S. M. & Levin, I. P. (1996). Need for cognition and choice framing effects. *Behavioral Decision Making, 9*, 283-290.

Sokol-Hessner, P., Hsu, M., Curley, N. G., Delgado, M. R., Camerer, C. R. & Phelps, E. A. (2009). Thinking like a trader selectively reduces individuals' loss aversion. *PNAS, 106*, 5035-5040.

Summerville, A. (2011). Counterfactual seeking: The scenic overlook of the road not taken. *Personality and Social Psychology Bulletin, 31*, 1522-1533.

Szczygiel, D., Buczny, J. & Bazinska, R. (2012). Emotion regulation and emotional information processing: The moderating effect of emotional awareness. *Personality and Individual Differences, 52*, 433-437.

Tvresky, A. & Kahneman, D. (1981). The framing of decisions and the psychology of choice. *Science, 211*, 453-458.

Wessel, I. & Merckelbach, H. (1997). The impact of anxiety on memory for details in spider phobics. *Applied Cognitive Psychology, 11*, 223-231.

Wilson, T. D. & Brekke, N. (1994). Mental contamination and mental correction: Unwanted influences on judgments and evaluations. *Psychological Bulletin, 116*, 117-142.

Zeelenberg, M., Inman, J. J. & Pieters, R. G. M. (2001). What we do when decisions go awry: Behavioral consequences of experienced regret. In E. U. Weber, J. Baron, & G. Loomes (Eds.), *Conflict and tradeoffs in decision making* (pp. 136-155). New York: Cambridge University Press.

Zeelenberg, M. & Pieters, R. (2007). A theory of regret regulation 1.0. *Journal of Consumer Psychology, 17*, 3-18.

SHORT COMMUNICATION ONE AND TWO

In: Handbook of Psychology of Emotions
Editors: C. Mohiyeddini, M. Eysenck and S. Bauer

ISBN: 978-1-62808-053-7
© 2013 Nova Science Publishers, Inc.

Chapter 28

SLEEP, MEMORY AND EMOTIONS

Małgorzata Wisłowska[1,2], Gabriela G. Werner[3], Tina Möckel[1],
Dominik P.J. Heib[1], Kerstin Hoedlmoser[1] and Manuel Schabus[1]

[1]Laboratory for Sleep, Cognition and Consciousness Research, Department of
Psychology, University of Salzburg, Austria
[2]Nicolaus Copernicus University, Toruń, Poland
[3]Division of Clinical Psychology, University of Salzburg, Austria

EMOTIONS, MEMORY AND SLEEP

Every day we learn. The question is how can we memorize and sort out the relevant bits of the vast amounts of information encountered each day. Today it is believed that sleep and "offline consolidation" do play a crucial role in this process (cf. Dang-Vu, Schabus et al. 2010). Consolidation is a process occurring as soon as fresh information has been encoded by the brain. It depends on the brain's plasticity that is the function to form new memories and integrate that new information into long-term memory according to subjective needs at a neuronal level. From everyday experience we know that emotional content has some advantage when it comes to forming a memory with specific "offline" benefits overnight. On average, people can remember almost twice as much of text when it is emotionally charged as compared to neutral information (Wagner, Degirmenci et al. 2005). The growing number of studies on sleep-dependent memory consolidation both confirm the benefits of various memory systems from specific sleep stages or sleep patterns but also reveal accumulating discrepancies and open issues (Schabus 2009). At the end, the success story of sleep and memory appears much less straightforward than originally believed.

The Role of Sleep for Emotional Memory

It has been reported that after a full-night sleep, in comparison to control day-time wakefulness, accuracy (d') in emotional picture recognition is improved (Hu, Stylos-Allan et al. 2006). In addition, Lewis and colleagues reported better declarative contextual memory performance after sleep compared to wakefulness, but in the same order for emotional and neutral material (Lewis, Cairney et al. 2011). In a study by Payne and colleagues it was shown that over daytime wakefulness both the features of objects and backgrounds of negative arousing scenes are being forgotten. Yet importantly, after a full night of sleep features of negative charged objects (but not backgrounds) are selectively preserved in memory (Payne, Stickgold et al. 2008). Latter effect could be interpreted in terms of the consolidation and preservation of important fragments of new experiences whiles irrelevant context information (such as the background) might be spared out. Also the authors reported in another study that sleep benefits consolidation of negatively charged stimuli over neutral ones (Payne and Kensinger 2011). Moreover, at least one study by Wagner and colleagues demonstrated that this consolidation is also relevant for long-term memory recall after years. In their study only emotionally arousing text material was better recalled after post-learning sleep as compared to periods of waking even when tested 4 years after learning (Wagner, Hallschmid et al. 2006). In this context it is also interesting to note that no difference was found between an early slow wave sleep (SWS) rich and a late rapid eye movement sleep (REM) rich sleep group with respect to the delayed memory recall. Yet, note that overnight emotional memory formation was more enhanced following REM-rich sleep (Wagner, Gais et al. 2001)

There is also evidence that in children (11-13yrs) emotional (declarative) memory benefits more from periods of sleep than wakefulness (Prehn-Kristensen, Göder et al. 2009) and furthermore that children might be using different sleep mechanisms in order to consolidate information. In children the great amount of SWS throughout early development seems to especially promote the consolidation of memories in the hippocampus-dependent declarative memory system (Backhaus, Hoeckesfeld et al. 2008; Wilhelm, Prehn-Kristensen et al. 2012). However, this slow-wave activity prevalence may counteract an immediate benefit from sleep for procedural memories, as typically observed in adults (e.g. Fischer, Wilhelm et al. 2007; for review see Wilhelm, Diekelmann et al. 2008; Prehn-Kristensen, Göder et al. 2009).

The mere presence of emotional stimuli during learning a procedural motor skill influences improvement of performance, in terms of accuracy and speed, both after sleep and after waking (Javadi, Walsh et al. 2011). Participants who learned this new skill with a negative image in the background demonstrated significantly greater enhancement of this skill across an offline retention interval than participant who trained with neutral or positive images in the background.

In general, a beneficial influence of sleep on emotional memory is evident. Yet it is to note that the picture is still ambiguous. While Walker and colleagues believe in a REM-dependent attenuation of emotional reactivity overnight, Baran and colleagues propose that the role of sleep for emotions is twofold. Besides the agreement that in general there is a beneficial effect of sleep for emotional memory the authors propose that sleep *protects* the emotional salience of a stimulus (Baran, Pace-Schott et al. 2012). Especially Baran and colleagues report that while emotional reactivity to negative pictures was greatly reduced over wake, the negative emotional response was relatively *preserved* over sleep and associated with greater time in REM.

In a next step we will consider the consequences of sleep deprivation on the formation and consolidation of newly acquired emotional material.

Sleep Deprivation

When participants are trying to form new memories following sleep deprivation, disturbances on encoding of especially positive and neutral stimuli is reported (Walker and Stickgold 2006). Moreover, Walker and colleagues indicated that there is a relative resistance of negative emotional memory even over sleep deprivation (for review see Saletin and Walker 2012). Interestingly a similar association had already been found earlier by Sterpenich and colleagues who reported no influence of sleep deprivation on recollection of negative arousing picture stimuli, but significant deterioration of positive and neutral stimuli following a lost night (Sterpenich, Albouy et al. 2007).

Altogether the results suggest that sleep deprivation profoundly destroys the ability to encode (especially not salient) material as well as to maintain freshly encoded (non-salient) memory traces. Whether negative stimuli are specifically less susceptible to forgetting or interference following sleep deprivation should be validated in future studies.

REM Sleep and Emotional Memory Consolidation

Without doubt, REMplays an important part in the consolidation of emotional memories (e.g. Greenberg, Pearlman et al. 1983; Wagner, Gais et al. 2001; Wagner and Born 2008; Nishida, Pearsall et al. 2009; Walker 2010; Payne 2011; Baran, Pace-Schott et al. 2012). When for example comparing 3 hours of REM-rich sleep versus early SWS-rich sleep or comparable times of waking, only the REM-rich condition facilitates the later recall of negative arousing narratives even if tested years thereafter (Wagner, Gais et al. 2001). Furthermore, after REM-rich sleep (relatively to SWS-rich sleep) subjects tend to rate emotional pictures seen before as more aversive (Wagner, Fischer et al. 2002). Latter finding stands in contrast to newer findings by Gujar and colleagues (Gujar, McDonald et al. 2011). Lately, it was demonstrated that emotional memory formation can also be manipulated pharmacologically. Wagner and colleagues (2005) tried to inhibit cortisol which usually is high in REM-rich sleep. The manipulation with metyrapone (a cortisol blocker) led to impaired consolidation of neutral but not emotional texts. Consequently, the authors speculated that the specific interaction between REM and the release of stress hormones like cortisol during post-learning sleep is adaptive and most critical for the consolidation of emotional memories (Wagner, Degirmenci et al. 2005). On the other hand Groch and colleagues blocked noradrenergic activity (primarily occurring during SWS and reported to be involved in linking the basolateral amygdala with the hippocampus) with clonidine and reported a disappearance of the retention advantage of emotional over neutral stories (Groch, Wilhelm et al. 2011). As clonidine is also known to have REM suppressive effects, it is difficult to assess whether an asscoiated mild REM suppression might have enhanced the pharmacologically induced attenuation of emotional memories.

Nishida and colleagues also reported that more REMand shorter REM onset latency in a nap is positively correlated with the extent of emotional (picture) memory enhancement (Nishida, Pearsall et al. 2009). Interestingly in that nap paradigm improvement in emotional memory was directly related to an increase in (right) prefrontal EEG theta activity during REM (Nishida and Walker 2007; Nishida, Pearsall et al. 2009). It is to note that besides the characteristic theta oscillations (4-7 Hz), an increase of the level of acetylcholine (particularly in limbic systems and the forebrain (Walker 2010)), and an enhancement in cortisol concentrations (Born and Wagner 2004) is characteristic for REM. Cortisol is known to influence the hippocampus through glucocorticoid and mineralocorticoid receptors. Wagner and colleagues believe that an increase of cortisol in REM-rich late sleep might reduce the emotional impact of memories (Born and Wagner 2004) similar to a currently proposed model by Walker and colleagues (Walker 2009; Walker 2010).

Next we will shortly review related neuroimaging findings which demonstrate brain plasticity changes on a cortical and subcortical level.

Neuroimaging and Emotional Memory Consolidation

In general, it is known that learning of emotional stimuli is accompanied by strong activation of the amygdala and hippocampus (for review see Walker 2010). It has been shown that the amygdala accompanies and facilitates memory storage in emotionally charged memory tasks (e.g. Cahill, Haier et al. 1996; Cahill and McGaugh 1998; Hamann, Ely et al. 1999; Hamann 2001; Paré, Collins et al. 2002; Kilpatrick and Cahill 2003; Born and Wagner 2004; Wagner, Degirmenci et al. 2005; Sterpenich, Albouy et al. 2007). Sterpenich and colleagues for example revealed that after a full-night of sleep, recollection of emotional stimuli elicits stronger response in hippocampus and the medial prefrontal cortex, as compared to neural stimuli. Yet, 6 months thereafter the hippocampus is not activated anymore when that information is retrieved. This is taken as evidence for a (declarative) systems memory consolidation process where information is transferred from the hippocampus to more permanent cortical storage sites. Moreover, recollection of negative stimuli was associated with a hippocampo-neocortical response pattern in all subjects, but with a stronger response in an amygdalo-cortical network in sleep-deprived subject (Sterpenich, Albouy et al. 2007; Sterpenich, Albouy et al. 2009). The authors interpreted their findings as a possible subcortical "backup mechanism" which keeps track of emotional relevant (negative) material even in the case of sleep deprivation.

Payne and Kensinger reported correlations between successful retrieval of negatively charged stimuli and activation in the hippocampus, yet, regardless of the presence or absence of sleep (Payne and Kensinger 2011). To-date it appears unclear how long amygdala activation is needed for recollection of emotional stimuli and how strongly this dependence is modulated by post-learning sleep (for review see Sterpenich, Albouy et al. 2007). It is therefore highly relevant to consider and control the time between encoding and retrieval of the information as there are highly diverging findings concerning the speed of "systems consolidation", or the transfer of initially hippocampus or amygdala driven responses to higher-cortical responses during retrieval.

As reviewed earlier, the amygdala has a strong modulating function in memory consolidation. When items are emotionally charged, the amygdala appears to facilitate hippocampal memory formation (e.g. Paré, Collins et al. 2002; Born and Wagner 2004; Wagner, Degirmenci et al. 2005). This widely held view builds upon the fact that the amygdala is involved in processing of emotions, whereas the hippocampus is known to be necessary for declarative and episodic memory formation. Since the participation of those two systems in the course of emotional memory consolidation is obvious, their reciprocal interaction is addressed in several neuroimaging studies. A recent study by Payne and

Kensinger using emotion-laden stimuli for example reported that after sleep the amygdala was more strongly connected to hippocampus and ventral medial prefrontal cortex as compared to a waking condition (Payne and Kensinger 2011). Importantly, connectivity changes were again specific to the retrieval of negative (but not neutral) study material.

It is known that in sleep-deprived subjects functional connectivity between amygdala and medial prefrontal cortex can be lost (see also Yoo, Gujar et al. 2007; Payne and Kensinger 2011). Yet, as seen in Sterpenich and colleagues (2007) there appears to be a kind of backup mechanism that prevents a complete deterioration of especially negatively charged emotional memories. In this case recollection might not depend upon hippocampo-neocortical networks but rather on alternative subcortical networks as also supported by Yoo and colleagues (2007). Specifically, the authors report greater connectivity between amygdala and the autonomic-activating centres in the locus coeruleus, as well as three times bigger extent of amygdala reactivity to aversive stimuli in the sleep deprived people (Yoo, Gujar et al. 2007). It can be speculated that after a sleep-deprived night a loss of mesial prefrontal mediated inhibition of the amygdala might lead to excessive emotional reactivityduring retrieval.

In summary it appears vital for us humans to memorize emotional material, specifically if of negative valence. Nature therefore seems to have come up with mechanisms to prevent forgetting of negatively charged information. With respect to brain plasticity changes, we generally agree with Diekelmann and colleagues (2009) who conclude and propose that "Patterns of emotional arousal that are induced during learning via amygdalar circuitry possibly become reactivated during REM sleep thereby strengthening memory traces and connectivity within hippocampo-neocortical networks."

THE INFLUENCE OF STRESSFUL EMOTIONS ON SLEEP

There is ongoing research concerning the influence of stress and emotions in general on sleep. In this context it is crucial to specify how exactly emotions or stressful events are elicited. Kim and Dimsdale (2007) distinguish three different types of stress, namely daily stressors, experimentally induced stress (like aversive films or simply a first night adaptation in the sleep laboratory) and real traumatic stress which is known to potentially even lead to severe psychiatric disorders such as posttraumatic stress disorder (PTSD) or major depression. In summary, very inconsistent results are evident in the literature, especially concerning the change of REM parameters following stress. Although Kim and Dimsdale (2007) could not reveal systematic differences between all of these different types of stressors in their systematic review (literature published between 1974 and 2004) they did find some consistent effects. Experimentally induced stress like first night adaptation or indwelling venous catheters resulted in less total sleep time (TST), less amount of SWS and REM , as well as longer sleep onset latencies together with a higher number of nightly awakenings. In contrast, experimental stress induced by aversive films appears to only cause marginal changes in (REM) sleep (Goodenough, Witkin et al. 1975; Levin, Strygin et al. 2002; Germain, Buysse et al. 2003). In people suffering from PTSD it seems that REM duration is decreased whereas REM latency is rather prolonged in most studies (Lavie, Hefez et al. 1979; Hefez, Metz et al. 1987). Interestingly, even sleep studies using experimentally induced stress - reviewed over the last 30 years – do not indicate consistent changes of sleep architecture.

Yet, it is to be noted that a recent study (Vandekerckhove, Weiss et al. 2011) does replicate early findings. The authors induced stress by provoking failure experience in different cognitive tasks (e.g. spatial abilities, counting or semantic tasks) using tasks which were impossible to solve (e.g., a related word had to be found for a group of three unrelated words). Participants were additionally told that they are doing cognitive tests which reflect their level of intelligence and their potential for future professional achievements. Moreover, the experimenter entered the experimental room during the tasks giving irritating comments and checking placement of electrodes. At the end of the task the experimenter explained, that the psychological measurements were erroneous and useless. After that kind of stress induction the authors found a significant increase in sleep fragmentation (higher amounts of number of awakenings and wake after sleep onset), decreased TST and sleep efficiency, REM duration decrease as well as enhanced latency to SWS.

Overall it can be concluded that sleep tends to be more fragmented after stress exposure which is reflected in higher number of awakenings, decreased TST and decreased sleep efficiency. Concerning REM parameters, the results are highly contradictory with studies indicating REM increases (Goncharenko 1979; Cartwright and Wood 1991; Engdahl, Eberly et al. 2000) as well as decreases (Lavie, Hefez et al. 1979; Hefez, Metz et al. 1987; Aber, Block et al. 1989; Vitiello, Larsen et al. 1996; Prinz, Bailey et al. 2001; Scholle, Scholle et al. 2003) following emotional stress. Furthermore, shortened (Goncharenko 1979; Cartwright and Wood 1991) as well as prolonged (Kupfer, McPartland et al. 1974; Lavie, Hefez et al. 1979; Hefez, Metz et al. 1987) latency to the first REM episode during sleep has been reported.

For future research it seems important to not only specify the eliciting type of stress or emotions but to also focus on the individual coping strategy. Not only the subjective intensity but also the quality of the stressor might be a crucial determinant for subsequent sleep architecture changes. Last but not least, it needs to be assessed more systematically how perceived stress is altered over the course of a single, or even the course of several nights.

DO EMOTIONS CHANGE OVERNIGHT?

Emotional reactivity specifies the intensity of subjective or physiological activation to an emotional event. As this reactivation is often investigated in combination with questions about emotional memory, studies typically use pictures, word pairs or texts as stimulus material.

An actual model of affective brain processing (Walker 2009) suggests a close connection between emotional memory consolidation and the level of emotional reactivity (Walker and Van Der Helm 2009). In his "Sleep to remember and sleep to forget" – hypothesis (SRSF) Walker claims that people sleep to remember the facts of an emotional event, but at the same time to "forget" the affective tone of this event. More precisely, Walker states that emotional memory consolidation is strengthened (during REM), whereas the subjective and physiological emotional reactivity is reduced over sleep. Consequently, it should be possible to retrieve emotional experiences without the affective tone after successful sleep. The theory predicts that this decoupling takes place overnight, especially during REM, as this sleep stage provides the best biological state with increased activity in the limbic and paralimbic structures, marginal amount of aminergic (e.g. adrenalin, dopamine and serotonin) transmitter concentration as well as theta waves for integration of the emotional event into longterm-memory. It has to be tested if such a dissociation of emotion and related memory is reliably to identify and whether subjective traits may differentially mediate these overnight changes in emotional valence.

A study by Van der Helm et al. (2011) adds weight on earlier interpretations. The authors investigated negative and neutral pictures of the International Affective Pictures System (IAPS; Lang, Bradley and Cuthbert (2005)). Using functional Magnetic Resonance Imaging it was revealed that amygdala activity as well as subjective ratings of valence and arousal decreased over sleep, but were enhanced over the same amount of time when filled with daytime wakefulness. In addition, this described decrease in emotional reactivity overnight was significantly correlated with the extent of prefrontal gamma activity during REM. The authors took the association of reduced prefrontal gamma activity during REM with a stronger reduction in emotional reactivity overnight as evidence for the reduced central adrenergic activity mediating a depotentiation of the emotional tone overnight.

Further support for a specific role of REM in processing emotional events comes from another study of Walker'sgroup using midday naps and an emotional face recognition task. Naps, especially if they contained REM, reduced on the one hand the subjective ratings of face expressions of fear and anger and on the other hand increased perceived valence of happy expressions (Gujar, McDonald et al. 2011). Given that and earlier findings it is likely that REM therefore is not only involved in emotion depotentiation, but probably all stages of consolidation, from supporting the consolidation of salient emotional events, to various degrees of potentiation and depotentiation of emotional quality over night. Future studies should strive to disentangle the relation of REM with emotional reactivity changes overnight versus over daytime and also adopt more find-grained analysis of the distinct sleep patterns prevalent in REM (e.g., number of rapid-eye movements, gamma oscillations, theta oscillations, connectivity changes).

Another related study which investigated emotional memory performance simultaneously to emotional reactivity revealed partly diverging effects. Specifically, Baran and colleagues found a significant negative association of REM percentage (in the third quarter of the night) and emotional reactivity change overnight (Baran, Pace-Schott et al. 2012). Participants with more REM showed less decrease in subjective valence ratings from evening to morning (same pictures and intermingled new ones for recognition test), although all subjects did show less emotional reactivity ("arousal") after sleep. Interestingly, also an earlier study by Wagner and colleagues (2002) reported enhanced emotional reactivity (only on 'valence', but not 'arousal' scale) to negative pictures after REM-rich sleep in contrast to SWS-rich sleep or wakefulness. Enhanced emotional reactivity was also found after a full night of undisturbed sleep (comparable to REM-rich sleep only).

Altogether, it appears inconclusive in which way emotions are processed or altered over periods of sleep. Evidence indicates that REM is playing a key role, yet the exact nature of the relationship is unclear as REM has been found associated with decreased as well as increased emotional reactivity overnight. Further research is needed in order to clarify the exact role of REM in emotional processing and reactivity overnight. In light of the contradictory results it is suggested to consider further modulating factors such as individual differences on the level of personality traits or reappraisal skills and measure subjective emotional reactivity after stress induction over various time spans.

CONCLUSION

In summarizing, it can be concluded that emotional material, and specifically negatively charged information is more likely to be consolidated over periods of sleep. Negative emotions also stand out in the respect that even under conditions of sleep deprivation alternative "backup systems" may help to keep track of such potentially vital experiences.

The effects of various emotions on sleep architecture and sleep patterns is much less well understood. REM appears to play a key role in this respect, yet the exact association is to be identified.

Also data about the change of emotional reactivity overnight is ambiguous. However, evidence appears to accumulate that perceived emotional reactivity is generally decreasing over time.

Surprisingly there is much left to do, when it comes to sleep, memory and emotions. We hope scientists will be stimulated by this review and follow up on raised questions from various angles.

ACKNOWLEDGMENTS

M. Wisłowska and D.P.J. Heib were supported by funds from the Austrian Science Fund (FWF; I-934-B23). D.P.J. Heib and G. Werner are associated to or financially supported by the Doctoral College ''Imaging the Mind'' (FWF; W1233).

REFERENCES

Aber, W. R., A. J. Block, et al. (1989). "Consistency of respiratory measurements from night to night during the sleep of elderly men." *Chest* 96(4): 747-751.

Backhaus, J., R. Hoeckesfeld, et al. (2008). "Immediate as well as delayed post learning sleep but not wakefulness enhances declarative memory consolidation in children." *Neurobiology of learning and memory* 89(1): 76-80.

Baran, B., E. F. Pace-Schott, et al. (2012). "Processing of Emotional Reactivity and Emotional Memory over Sleep." *The Journal of Neuroscience* 32(3): 1035-1042.

Born, J. and U. Wagner (2004). "Memory consolidation during sleep: role of cortisol feedback." *Annals of the New York Academy of Sciences* 1032(1): 198-201.

Cahill, L., R. J. Haier, et al. (1996). "Amygdala activity at encoding correlated with long-term, free recall of emotional information." *Proceedings of the National Academy of Sciences* 93(15): 8016.

Cahill, L. and J. L. McGaugh (1998). "Mechanisms of emotional arousal and lasting declarative memory." *Trends in neurosciences* 21(7): 294-299.

Cartwright, R. D. and E. Wood (1991). "Adjustment disorders of sleep: the sleep effects of a major stressful event and its resolution." *Psychiatry research* 39(3): 199-209.

Dang-Vu, T. T., M. Schabus, et al. (2010). "Functional neuroimaging insights into the physiology of human sleep." *Sleep* 33(12): 1589.

Diekelmann, S., I. Wilhelm, et al. (2009). "The whats and whens of sleep-dependent memory consolidation." *Sleep medicine reviews* 13(5): 309.

Engdahl, B. E., R. E. Eberly, et al. (2000). "Sleep in a community sample of elderly war veterans with and without posttraumatic stress disorder." *Biological psychiatry* 47(6): 520-525.

Fischer, S., I. Wilhelm, et al. (2007). "Developmental differences in sleep's role for implicit off-line learning: comparing children with adults." *Journal of Cognitive Neuroscience* 19(2): 214-227.

Germain, A., D. J. Buysse, et al. (2003). "Psychophysiological Reactivity and Coping Styles Influence the Effects of Acute Stress Exposure on Rapid Eye Movement Sleep." *Psychosomatic Medicine* 65(5): 857-864.

Goncharenko, A. M. (1979). "Electrophysiological investigation of sleep in shift workers exposed to emotional stress due to work." *Human physiology* 5(4): 468-474.

Goodenough, D. R., H. A. Witkin, et al. (1975). "The Effects of Stress Films on Dream Affect and on Respiration and Eye-Movement Activity During Rapid-Eye-Movement Sleep." *Psychophysiology* 12(3): 313-320.

Greenberg, R., C. Pearlman, et al. (1983). "Memory, emotion, and REM sleep." *Journal of abnormal psychology* 92(3): 378.

Groch, S., I. Wilhelm, et al. (2011). "Contribution of norepinephrine to emotional memory consolidation during sleep." *Psychoneuroendocrinology.*

Gujar, N., S. A. McDonald, et al. (2011). "A role for rem sleep in recalibrating the sensitivity of the human brain to specific emotions." *Cerebral Cortex* 21(1): 115-123.

Hamann, S. (2001). "Cognitive and neural mechanisms of emotional memory." *Trends in Cognitive Sciences* 5(9): 394-400.

Hamann, S. B., T. D. Ely, et al. (1999). "Amygdala activity related to enhanced memory for pleasant and aversive stimuli." *Nature neuroscience* 2(3): 289-293.

Hefez, A., L. Metz, et al. (1987). "Long-term effects of extreme situational stress on sleep and dreaming." *The American journal of psychiatry* 144(3): 344-347.

Hu, P., M. Stylos-Allan, et al. (2006). "Sleep facilitates consolidation of emotional declarative memory." *Psychological Science* 17(10): 891-898.

Javadi, A. H., V. Walsh, et al. (2011). "Offline consolidation of procedural skill learning is enhanced by negative emotional content." *Experimental brain research* 208(4): 507-517.

Kilpatrick, L. and L. Cahill (2003). "Amygdala modulation of parahippocampal and frontal regions during emotionally influenced memory storage." *NeuroImage* 20(4): 2091-2099.

Kim, E.-J. and J. E. Dimsdale (2007). "The Effect of Psychosocial Stress on Sleep: A Review of Polysomnographic Evidence." *Behavioral Sleep Medicine* 5(4): 256-278.

Kupfer, P. P. C., R. J. R. McPartland, et al. (1974). "Is there a first night effect? (a revisit)." *Biol Psychiatry* 9(2): 215-215.

Lang, P. J., M. M. Bradley, et al. (2005). *International Affective Picture System (IAPS): Affective Ratings of Pictures and Instruction Manual,* NIMH, Center for the Study of Emotion & Attention.

Lavie, P., A. Hefez, et al. (1979). "Long-term effects of traumatic war-related events on sleep." *The American journal of psychiatry* 136(2): 175-178.

Levin, Y. I., K. N. Strygin, et al. (2002). "Effect of Personality on Changes of Sleep Structure Caused by Emotional Stress." *Human Physiology* 28(3): 282-286.

Lewis, P., S. Cairney, et al. (2011). "The impact of overnight consolidation upon memory for emotional and neutral encoding contexts." *Neuropsychologia* 49(9): 2619-2629.

Nishida, M., J. Pearsall, et al. (2009). "REM sleep, prefrontal theta, and the consolidation of human emotional memory." *Cerebral Cortex* 19(5): 1158-1166.

Nishida, M. and M. P. Walker (2007). "Daytime naps, motor memory consolidation and regionally specific sleep spindles." *PLoS One* 2(4): e341.

Paré, D., D. R. Collins, et al. (2002). "Amygdala oscillations and the consolidation of emotional memories." *Trends in Cognitive Sciences* 6(7): 306-314.

Payne, J. D. (2011). "Learning, Memory, and Sleep in Humans." *Sleep Medicine Clinics* 6(1): 15-30.

Payne, J. D. and E. A. Kensinger (2011). "Sleep leads to changes in the emotional memory trace: evidence from fMRI." *Journal of Cognitive Neuroscience* 23(6): 1285-1297.

Payne, J. D., R. Stickgold, et al. (2008). "Sleep preferentially enhances memory for emotional components of scenes." *Psychological Science* 19(8): 781.

Prehn-Kristensen, A., R. Göder, et al. (2009). "Sleep in children enhances preferentially emotional declarative but not procedural memories." *Journal of experimental child psychology* 104(1): 132-139.

Prinz, P., S. Bailey, et al. (2001). "Urinary free cortisol and sleep under baseline and stressed conditions in healthy senior women: effects of estrogen replacement therapy." *Journal of sleep research* 10(1): 19-26.

Saletin, J. M. and M. P. Walker (2012). "Nocturnal Mnemonics: Sleep and Hippocampal Memory Processing." *Frontiers in Neurology* 3.

Schabus, M. (2009). "Still missing some significant ingredients." *Sleep* 32(3): 291.

Scholle, S., H. Scholle, et al. (2003). "First night effect in children and adolescents undergoing polysomnography for sleep-disordered breathing." *Clinical neurophysiology* 114(11): 2138-2145.

Sterpenich, V., G. Albouy, et al. (2007). "Sleep-related hippocampo-cortical interplay during emotional memory recollection." *PLoS biology* 5(11): e282.

Sterpenich, V., G. Albouy, et al. (2009). "Sleep promotes the neural reorganization of remote emotional memory." *The Journal of Neuroscience* 29(16): 5143-5152.

van der Helm, E., J. Yao, et al. (2011). "REM Sleep Depotentiates Amygdala Activity to Previous Emotional Experiences." *Current Biology* 21(23): 2029-2032.

Vandekerckhove, M., R. Weiss, et al. (2011). "The role of presleep negative emotion in sleep physiology." *Psychophysiology*.

Vitiello, M. V., L. H. Larsen, et al. (1996). "Objective sleep quality of healthy older men and women is differentially disrupted by nighttime periodic blood sampling via indwelling catheter." *Sleep* 19(4): 304-304.

Wagner, U. and J. Born (2008). "Memory consolidation during sleep: Interactive effects of sleep stages and HPA regulation." *Stress: The International Journal on the Biology of Stress* 11(1): 28-41.

Wagner, U., M. Degirmenci, et al. (2005). "Effects of cortisol suppression on sleep-associated consolidation of neutral and emotional memory." *Biological Psychiatry* 58(11): 885-893.

Wagner, U., S. Fischer, et al. (2002). "Changes in emotional responses to aversive pictures across periods rich in slow-wave sleep versus rapid eye movement sleep." *Psychosomatic medicine* 64(4): 627-634.

Wagner, U., S. Gais, et al. (2001). "Emotional memory formation is enhanced across sleep intervals with high amounts of rapid eye movement sleep." *Learning & Memory* 8(2): 112-119.

Wagner, U., M. Hallschmid, et al. (2006). "Brief sleep after learning keeps emotional memories alive for years." *Biological Psychiatry* 60(7): 788-790.

Walker, M. P. (2009). "The role of sleep in cognition and emotion." *Ann N Y Acad Sci* 1156: 168-197.

Walker, M. P. (2010). "Sleep, memory and emotion." *Progress in brain research* 185: 49.

Walker, M. P. and R. Stickgold (2006). "Sleep, memory, and plasticity." *Annu. Rev. Psychol.* 57: 139-166.

Walker, M. P. and E. Van Der Helm (2009). "Overnight therapy? The role of sleep in emotional brain processing." *Psychological Bulletin; Psychological Bulletin* 135(5): 731.

Wilhelm, I., S. Diekelmann, et al. (2008). "Sleep in children improves memory performance on declarative but not procedural tasks." *Learning & Memory* 15(5): 373-377.

Wilhelm, I., A. Prehn-Kristensen, et al. (2012). "Sleep-dependent memory consolidation–What can be learnt from children?" *Neuroscience & Biobehavioral Reviews.*

Yoo, S. S., N. Gujar, et al. (2007). "The human emotional brain without sleep--a prefrontal amygdala disconnect." *Current Biology* 17(20): R877-R878.

In: Handbook of Psychology of Emotions
Editors: C. Mohiyeddini, M. Eysenck and S. Bauer

ISBN: 978-1-62808-053-7
© 2013 Nova Science Publishers, Inc.

Chapter 29

Oxytocinergic Modulation of Emotional Processes in Social Interactions

Anthony Lane[*,1,2], Olivier Luminet[1,2] and Moïra Mikolajczak[1]

[1]Université catholique de Louvain, Belgium, Department of Psychology,
Louvain-La-Neuve, Belgium,
[2]Belgian National Fund for Scientific Research (FNRS),

ABSTRACT

Oxytocin (OT), a polypeptide hormone is, by far, one of the most studied hormones in the field of psychological science. For more than two decades now, many researchers have token, and still take, an interest in the effects of OT on human behaviours. Their findings show that OT is involved in many social and interpersonal processes. For those reasons, the scientific community has described OT as a social hormone *par excellence*, and as we will see in this chapter, OT influence social behaviours by acting on both emotions and cognitions involved in social interactions. Oxytocin does this particularly by acting on emotional recognition, on trust and on social sharing of the emotions.

Keywords: Oxytoxin, Emotions, Emotional recognition, Trsut, Social sharing of the emotions

1. INTRODUCTION

Oxytocin (OT), a polypeptide hormone is, by far, one of the most studied hormones in the field of psychological science. For more than two decades now, many researchers have token, and still take, an interest in the effects of OT on human behaviours. Their findings show that OT is involved in many social and interpersonal processes, from primal sexual behaviours (i.e. Ishak, Berman & Peters, 2008) to the regulation of complex intergroup relationships (i.e. De Dreu et al., 2010; De Dreu, Greer, Van Kleef, Shalvi & Handgraaf, 2011), influencing

[*] Corresponding author. E-mail. Anthony.Lane@uclouvain.be;n Fax. +32 10 47 48 34; Tel. +32 10 47 45 11.

mere social recognition (i.e. Domes, Heinrichs, Michel, Berger & Herpertz, 2007; Rimmele, Hediger, Heinrichs & Klave, 2009; Shamay-Tsoory et al., 2009) to the regulation of parent – infant bonding (i.eFeldman, Weller, Zaggory-Sharon & Levine, 2007; Van Ijzendoorn & Bakermans-Kranenburg, 2011). For those reasons, the scientific community has described OT as a social hormone *par excellence* (for a review, see IsHak, Kahloon & Fakhry, 2011; Lane, Luminet, Mikolajczak, 2012), and as we will see later on in this chapter, OT influence social behaviors by acting on both emotions and cognitions involved in social interactions.

In 1906, Sir Henry Dale, a neuroscientist from the University College of London, worked on a post-pituitary extract and its effect on cats. He noticed that an injection of this substance into females' blood circulation induced the same uterine contractions than during the labour and the delivery. Therefore, he named this extract from two Greek words: *"Ôkus"* and *"Tokos"* which literally mean *"quick delivery"*. The word Oxytocin was born! But we had to wait until 1954 and Vincent du Vigneaud, an American biochemist, to discover the molecular structure of OT: a polypeptide hormone made of 9 animo-acides[1].

Oxytocin may be defined as a neurohormone because it is synthesized by nervous cells, namely the magnocellular neurones located in the supraoptic and the paraventricular nuclei of the hypothalamus. In response to specific stimuli (see Campbell, 2008), OT will be released in the cerebrospinal fluid and into the blood circulation through the neurohypophisis (posterior part of the pituitary gland). Once released, OT will bind to a specific receptor : the OTR, which is, up to now, the only receptor known for OT. Those OTR can be separated in two groups.The first one is the central OTR, located in several brain areas, like the amygdala, the septum, the hippocampus, the insula, the acumbens nuclei, and the frontal cortex, will play an essential role in the behavioural effects of OT (Landgraff & Neumann, 2004). The second one is the peripheral OTR located in the digestive tract, the kidneys, the heart, the uterine muscles, the nipples, the *corpus cavernum* and the epididymis, will get involved in the physiological effects of OT. Given these physioanatomic facts, we can easily understand why OT is described either as a neurohormone for its central and behavioral effects or as a hormone for its peripheral and physiological effects.

In this chapter, we will focus on the role of OT in modulating three emotional processes that play a crucial role in social interactions: recognition and discrimination of others' emotions, feelings of trust (an emotion of higher order according to Di Simplico, Massey-Chase, Cowen & Harmer, 2008), and the social sharing of emotions.

2. OXYTOCIN AND RECOGNITION OF EMOTIONS

To interact in a social world, individuals have to adapt their behaviours to the characteristic of the situation and to the mood of their partners. In order to adopt an adaptive behaviour (or a conscientiously chosen non-adaptive behaviour) people need to recognize the emotion which is currently lived their interlocutor. Indeed, it would be detrimental or even dangerous to annoy someone who is angry or if you want to carry on talking to someone, you have to ensure that this person is interested by what you say. For these reasons, human beings need to correctly recognize and discriminate the emotions displayed by others. According to

---

[1] There is the animo-acides sequence of OT : H3N+—Cys—Tyr—Ile—Gln—Asn—Cys—Pro—Leu—Gly—COO (-)

the literature, OT seems to be one of the central pieces of the emotions recognition jigsaw puzzle.

Schultze and colleagues (2011) have first demonstrated that OT plays a role in the mere detection of emotional expressions. Using a morphing paradigm where emotional expressions were shown for a very short time (between 18 and 53 ms) before faces turn neutral, they asked the participants to spot those "emotional faces" out in the middle of a set of "always neutral" faces. The OT group (24 IU nasal administration of OT) performed significantly better that the control group (nasal administration of a placebo). They concluded that OT positively influences our ability to recognize an emotional state, even at very early stages of the emotions recognition process.

Then, there is strong evidence than OT increases the gaze toward the eye region of the interlocutor. This is particularly adaptive because the eye region is a key area for the recognition of the emotions (Guastella, Mitchell & Dads, 2008). Domes and colleagues (2007) have shown that the individuals under the influence of OT perform better at the *Read the Mind in the Eyes Test* [2](Baron-Cohen, Wheelwright, Hill, Raste & Plumb, 2001) than the control group. So OT seems to orient individuals' focus to relevant area in emotional recognition, thereby enhancing their ability to figure out if their interlocutor presents an emotion and then to correctly identify it.

Those findings also apply to people suffering from a severe emotion recognition disability (such as people suffering from autistic spectrum disorder or alexithymia). Guastella and colleagues (2010) showed that the performance of youth suffering from autistic disorder on the *Read the Mind in the Eyes Test* (Baron-Cohen et al, 2001) (see figure 1. for an examples) is enhanced after administration of exogenous OT. On their side, Hollander and colleagues (2007) demonstrated that administration of OT enhances the ability of people suffering from autistic disorder to recognize the emotion expressed in the prosody of an interlocutor, even when the prosody was not congruent with the content of the sentence (i.e. "My house is beautiful" said in an angry tone). Those findings are very relevant for two reasons: firstly, they show that OT possesses a potentially strong therapeutic effect for people suffering of a major emotional recognition deficit. Secondly, they suggest that the effect of OT on emotional recognition may be moderated by individual patterns such as a pathological state or individual differences in the ability of recognizing others' emotions. In accordance with this idea, Luminet and colleagues (2011) found that OT enhances emotion recognition ability in people presenting high, but not low, degree of alexithymia (high scorer on the Toronto Alexithymia Scale (TAS-20), Bagby, Parker & Taylor, 1994).

Even if the whole scientific community agrees on the fact that OT enhances emotion recognition, there is a lack of consensus about the kind of emotion whose OT promotes the detection and recognition. According to some authors, OT would only ease the detection and recognition of positive emotions such as joy (i.e. Di Simplico et al, 2010; Marsh, Yu, Pine & Blair, 2010; Van Ijzendoorn & Bakermans-Kranenburg, 2011). For some other authors, OT would only affect the detection and recognition of neutral or negative emotions like fear or anger (i.e. Guastella, Carson, Dadds, Mitchell & Cox, 2009; Fischer-Shofty, Shamay-Tsoory, Harari & Levkovitz, 2010). However, it is very difficult to draw a conclusion from this puzzling inconsistency across those studies. Although the paradigms used across the different

---

[2] The Read the Mind in the Eyes Test aims to mesure participant accuracy to recognize an emotional state by correcty indentifying an emotion (out of 4 possibilities) from a picture of an eye region.

studies are quite similar[3], we have no information about several parameters like personal variations in some personality traits or a possible covered pathological state (i.e. autistic tendency or a high degree of alexithymia) across the participants. Moreover, OT's effects may be moderated by some contextual differences across the studies like the attitude of the experimenter toward the participant for instance (i.e. the bad mood of the experimenter may have induced a bias toward a specific detection and recognition of negative emotions). It is therefore possible that OT facilitates emotion recognition *in general*, regardless of the emotional valence, as found by Shamay-Tsoory and colleagues (2009). According to these authors, OT would produce a general enhancement of our capacity to detect and recognize emotions by increasing the salience of social clues allowing this detection and recognition.

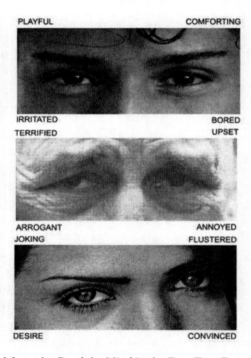

Figure 1. Examples of a trial from the *Read the Mind in the Eyes Test* (Baron-Cohen et al., 2001).

In conclusion, we can see that OT promotes both emotion detection and recognition. Studies examining the mechanisms underlying this effect are very recent and limited, so more research is needed to understand how OT exerts its effects. The only things we know at this stage is that OT facilitates emotion detection and recognition by increasing the gaze toward the eyes region and by enhancing the salience of social clues. Importantly, the effect of OT on the emotional recognition ability is advantageously moderated by the personal capacity to recognize other's emotions: the less the individual is competent in emotional recognition, the stronger the effect of OT will be!

While emotion detection and recognition are essential to the construction and maintenance of social relationships, they are far from being sufficient. One also needs to feel

---

[3] Intranasal administration of exogenous OT, emotional faces vs neutral faces dispalyed on a computer where the participant were asked to determine if the face showed an emotion and what kind of emotion it was.

that s/he can trust the interlocutor, and it seems that OT modulates trust feelings and behaviors as well.

3. OXYTOCIN AND TRUST

The findings on the relation between OT and trust are probably some of the reasons why this hormone received such great attention from the media. Since Kosfeld and colleagues have published their article about the effect of OT on trust in 2005, an enormous number of press articles about OT have sprout up, presenting this hormone as a miraculous one. *"Trust in bottle", "A sniff of trust", "The hormone of trust"*. The descriptions aren't lacking! So much so that a parapharmaceutical lab has developed a perfume made of OT to increase the trust of our interlocutor when you wear it. But is this reputation, describing OT as a miraculous hormone, scientifically established?

Kosfeld and colleagues (2005) showed that OT has a general effect on trust as far as the interaction linked an individual with another person, meaning that OT does only work during social interactions. They found that, during a computerized trust game (Berg, Dickhaut & mccabe, 1995), participants under OT (intranasal administration of 24 IU of exogenous OT) showed more trust toward their partner than those under PL. However, this effect was only significant when they played with a virtual *human* partner and not when they were told to play against a computer. Furthermore, Baumgartner and colleagues (2008) interestingly demonstrated that OT enhances the ability to rebuild confidence toward an individual (i.e. to a partner X) after a betrayal (i.e. from a partner Y). However, in this study, the participant interacted with a different partner after the betrayal. So we cannot infer that OT allows the rebuilding the trust toward a traitor. But it made way for future research that will attempt to find out whether OT effect is driven by memory processes (i.e. OT fosters oblivion of a past betrayal) and/or by motivational ones (i.e. OT enhances the motivation to reengage in a trustful relationship).

While the foregoing studies suggest a relatively *general* effect of OT on trust, other studies suggest that this effect may rather be *context-dependent*. Zak, Kurzban and Matzner (2005) have demonstrated that OT increases individual trustworthiness toward a partner only if the partner has previously shown an intentional mark of trust toward the individual. That may mean that OT drives the individual to look for a relevant clue, here a mark of reliability in the partner, to affect the trusting process. Should this mark be disconfirmed, the person would not be trusted. This is exactly what Mikolajczak, Lane and colleagues (2010) found. Thus, even if OT drives the individual to be more trustful, it doesn't make them gullible. Mikolajczak, Lane et al. (2010) brought the proof that, under OT, individual preserve their discriminative capacities between reliable and unreliable partners. Those findings boost the idea that OT orient individual to focus on relevant clues for their action. In this study, participants, after an administration of 32 IU of exogenous OT or a placebo, received instruction for an adapted computerized trust game. Each participant assumed the role of an investor and could transfer money to a virtual partner, in whose hands the amount would triple. The partner would then back transfer any amount of money. The back transfer could thus be either advantageous (more than the invested amount), neutral (the initial invested amount) or unfair (less than the initial invested amount, even nothing). Each participant played 10 trials with 10 different partners, and also played 10 rounds with the computer, which would randomly determine the back transfer (as a fully neutral condition). Before the investment, the participants received some information about the partner, playing on stereotypes about the trustworthiness emanating from various academic choices and hobbies. The aim of those information was to present the partner as reliable or not (i.e. "reliable partner" → academic field: nursing study, hobby : volunteer in an orphanage; "unreliable partner" → academic field : marketing, hobby: playing poker). The results indicated that the experimental group showed more trust toward the "reliable partners", by investing more money, comparing to the placebo group but wasn't more trustful with "possibly unreliable partners" than the placebo group. It is noteworthy that, contrary to Kosfeld et al. (2005) this study also found OT to have a statistically significant stronger effect on trust in the computer condition, where the participants know that computer won't try to betray them. This underlines the fact that the human versus nonhuman nature of the partner may not moderate OT's effect on trust, but this relation may rather be moderated by the perceived risk inherent to the interaction. And so, once again, OT drive the individual to spot out the relevant clues in an interaction to ensure their interest by making them behave in an adaptive way.

Invested Amount (0 – 50€)	Final Amount (I.A. x 3)	Back Transfert		
		ADVAN-TAGEOUS	NEUTRAL	UNFAIR
10	30	15	10	0
25	75	32,5	25	5
50	150	75	50	10

Figure 2. Adapted trust game examples.

The hypothesis here is participants may infer that a reliable partner would be more inclined to do an advantageous back transfer while an unreliable partner would be more incline to do an unfair back transfer. So participants should invest a higher amount when they interact with a reliable partner and invest a lower amount when they interact with an unreliable partner.

Although most studies have used a monetary paradigm, it has been shown that OT does not only influence our trust behaviour when money is at stake, but also when confidential information is in the balance. Mikolajczak, Pinon and colleagues (2010) have investigated this. When a reliable looking experimenter asked participants to fill out a very confidential questionnaire (asking questions on participant's sexual behaviours and fantasy notably) and, once finished, to put it in an envelope and close it, they noticed that 80% of the participants under the influence of OT left the envelop open while 93.3% of the placebo group closed it (60% of whom even closed the envelope with paper tape)[4]. Those findings are very interesting because they clearly show that OT's effect on trust is not limited to a specific topic of interaction, like monetary transfer, but extends to a wilder kind of interaction including the ones happening in our everyday life, like sharing a secret for example.

---

[4] This effect must be attributed to an increase in trust (and not to a loss of inhibition) because questions about sexual fantasies were asked twice (before and under OT administration, both questionnaire being put in the same envelope until completion of the second one) and OT does not remove inhibitions.

So, to conclude, we have to remember that if OT enhances our level of trust toward others, this action will be moderated by the perceived reliability of the interlocutor. It is also crucial to keep in mind that this effect is not specific to a particular kind of topic and seems to work for every kind of interaction where trust comes into play.

3. Social Sharing of Emotions

While emotion recognition and trust are preconditions of social interactions, the latter must then be fed to go on. Emotion sharing plays a crucial role in this. The construction of intimacy, whether in friendship or marital interactions, involves indeed a disclosure-counter-disclosure cycle: Each partner must disclose in turn elements of his private life, i.e. emotions or intimate facts (Van den Broucke, Vandereycken, & Vertommen, 1995). Intimacy grows as cycles develop, with an increment in self-disclosure at each new cycle (Reis, 2001). Beyond trust, social sharing is therefore crucial to the construction of relationships. In this process, the disclosure of emotions is more important than the disclosure of facts because emotions are considered as more intimate than facts. Lane and colleagues (2012) have recently demonstrated that OT increases the readiness to share one's emotions with others. In their study, they asked participants to write about their most painful experience lived. Firstly, they were asked to name this experience (the most recurrent topics were loss of a close person, romantic break-ups and abuse), then they were asked to write about the factual aspect and about the emotions they felt and still feel about this event. Finally, they were asked to rate on a 10 points Likert scale their readiness to talk about either the fact or the emotions related to the event with someone. The results first showed that OT doesn't make people more talkative (the general word count does not differ from one to the other condition) and the two groups had the same propensity to write about facts and emotions. But when the willingness to share facts and emotions orally with another person was evaluated, they found out that participants under OT were more incline to share their emotions with someone comparing to the placebo group (actually, people under OT were as inclined to share about the emotions as they were about the facts while participants under placebo preferred to share about the fact comparing to the emotions). So OT seems to increase the willingness to share our emotions. In doing so, this hormone, through the emotional disclosure, reinforces the bonds with the listener (Laurenceau, Barrett & Pietromonaco, 1998). OT, trust, and self-disclosure seem to feed on each other within a positive loop: OT would increase trust, thereby decreasing privacy protection and facilitating self-disclosure. This would result in an increase in reciprocal trust (Rimé, 2009), which would in turn prompt OT release (Zak, Kurzban, & Matzner, 2005). A new cycle would then occur, resulting in increased trust, attachment and intimacy.

Conclusion

In this chapter, we have seen that Oxytocin, a polypeptide neurohormone, significantly influenced three emotional processes that play a crucial role in social interactions: emotion identification, trust, and emotion sharing. In addition to uncovering the other emotional processes that are under oxytocinergic influence, future research will have to take the wraps off the mechanisms underlying those effects. Is the increased gaze toward key areas or the salience of the positive clues the only reason why OT enhances the emotional recognition? Does OT turn us just a bit more conscious of the perceived reliability of a partner and of the subsequent risk to promote our trusting behaviours? Is the increased willingness to share our emotions due to a crossed-over effect of OT on emotional recognition and trust? Maybe or maybe not! There is still lot to do in order to perfectly understand how this hormone drives our behaviors.

REFERENCES

Bagby, R.M., Parker, J.D.A., & Taylor, G.J. (1994). The Twenty-Item Toronto Alexithymia Scale -- I. Item selection and cross-validation of the factor structure. *Journal of Psychosomatic Research,* 38, 23-32.

Baumgartner, T., Heinrichs, M., Vonlanthen, A., Fischbacher, U., and Fehr, E. (2008). Oxytocin shapes the neural circuitry of the trust and trust adaptation in humans. *Neuron,* 58(4), 639-650.

Baron-Cohen, S., Wheelwright, S., Hill, J., Raste, Y., & Plumb, I. (2001). The "Reading the Mind in the Eyes" test revised version: A study with normal adults, and adults with Asperger syndrome or high-functioning autism. *Journal of Child Psychology and Psychiatry and Allied Disciplines,* 42, 241–251.

Berg, J., Dickhaut, J., and McCabe, K. (1995). Trust, reciprocity, and social history. *Games and economic Behavior,* 10, 122-142.

De Dreu, C.K.W., Greer, L.L., Handgraaf, M.J., Shalvi, S., Van Kleef, G.A., Bass, M., Ten Velden, F.S., Van Dijk, E., and Feith, S.W.W. (2010). The neuropeptide oxytocin regulates parochial altruism in intergroup conflict among humans. *Science,* 328(5984), 1408-1411.

De Dreu, C.K.W., Greer, L.L., Van Kleef, G.A., Shalvi, S., and Handgraaf, M.J. (2011). Oxytocin promotes human ethnocentrism. *PNAS,* 108(4), 1262-1266.

Di Simplico, M., Massey-Chase, R., Cowen, P.J., and Hamer, C.J. (2009). Oxytocin enhances processing of positive versus negative emotional information in healthy male volunteers. *Journal of Psychopharmacology,* 23(3), 241-248.

Domes, G., Heinrichs, M., Michel, A., Beger, C., and Herpertz,S. (2007). Oxytocin improves "mind-reading" in humans. *Biological Psychiatry,* 61(6), 731-733.

Feldman, R., Weller, A., Zagoory-Sharon, O., and Levine, A. (2007). Evidence for a neuroendocrinological foundation of human affiliation: Plasma oxytocin levels accross pregnancy and the postpartum period predict mother-infant bonding. *Psychological Science,* 18, 965 – 970.

Fischer-Shofty, M., Shamay-Tsoory, S.G., Harari, H., and Levkovitz, Y. (2010). The effect of intranasal administration of oxytocin on fear recognition. *Neuropsychologia,* 48(1), 179-184.

Guastella, A.J., Mitchell, P.B., and Dadds, M.R. (2008). Oxytocin increases gaze to the eye region of human faces. *Biological Psychiatry,* 63(1), 3-5.

Guastella, A.J., Carson, D.S., Dadds, M.R., Mitchell, P.B., and Cox, R.E. (2009). Does oxytocin influence the early detection of angry and happy faces? *Psychoneuroendocrinology*, 34(2), 220-225.

Guastella, A.J., Einfeld, S.L., Gray, K.M., Rinehart, N.J., Tonge, B.J., Lambert, T.J., and Hickie, I.B. (2010). Intranasal oxytocin improves emotion recognition for Youth with autism Spectrum Disorders. *Bilogical Psychiatry*, 67(7), 692-694.

Hollander, E., Bartz, J., Chaplin, W., Anagnostou, E., and Wasserman, S. (2007). Oxytocin increases retention of social cognition in autism. *Biological Psychiatry*, 61(4), 498-503.

IsHak, W.W., Berman, D.S., and Peters, A. (2008). Case report: Male anorgasmia treated with oxytocin. *The Journal of Sexual Medicine*, 5(4), 1022-1024.

IsHak, W.W., Kahloon, M., and Fakhry, H. (2011). Oxytocin role in enhancing well-being: A litterature review. *Journal of Affective Disorder*, 130(1-2), 1-9.

Kosfeld, M., Heinrichs, M., Zak, P.J., Fischbacher, U., and Fehr, E. (2005). Oxytocin increases trust in humans. *Nature*, 435, 673-676.

Landgraf, R., and Neumann, I.D. (2004). Vasopressin and oxytocin release within the brain: A dynamic concept of multiple and variable modes of neuropeptide communication. *Frontiers in Neuroendocrinology*, 25 (3-4), 150-176

Lane, A., Luminet, O., Rimé, B., Gross, J.J., de Timary, P., and Mikolajczak, M. (2012). Oxytocin increases willingness to socially share one's emotions. *International Journal of Psychology*, In press.

Lane, A., Luminet, O., and Mikolajczak, M. (2012). Psychoendocrinologie sociale de l'ocytocine : Revue d'une littérature en pleine expansion. *L'Année Psychologique*, In press.

Laurenceau, J.P., Barrett, L.F., Pietromonaco, P.R. (1998). Intimacy as an interpersonal process: The importance of self-disclosure, partner disclosure, and perceived partner responsiveness in interpersonal exchanges. *JPSP*, 74, 1238-1251.

Luminet, O., Grynberg, D., Ruzette, N., and Mikolajczak, M. (2011). Personality-dependent effects of oxytocin: greater social benefits for high alexithymia scorers. *Biological Psychology*, 87(3), 401-406.

Marsh, A.A., Yu, H.H., Pine, D.S., and Blair, R.J.R. (2010). Oxytocin improves specific recognition of positive facial expressions. *Psychopharmacology*, 209(3), 225-232.

Mikolajczak, M., Gross, J.J., Lane, A., Corneille, O., de Timary, P., and Luminet, O. (2010a). Oxytocin makes people trusting, not gullible. *Psychological Science*, 21(8), 1072-1074.

Mikolajczak, M., Pinon, N., Lane, A., de Timary, P., and Luminet, O. (2010b). Oxytocin not only increases trust when money is at stake, but also when confidentiel information is in the balance. *Biological Psychology*, 85(1), 182-184.

Reis, H. T. (2001). Psychology of love and intimacy. In *International Encyclopedia of the Social and Behavioral Sciences* (pp. 9091-9094).

Rimé, B. (2009). Emotion elicits the social sharing of emotion : Theory and empirical review. *Emotion Review*, 1, 60 -85.

Rimmele, U., Hediger, K., Heinrichs, M., an Klaver, P. (2009). Oxytocin makes a face in memory familiar. *The Journal of Neuroscience*, 29(1), 38-42.

Schulze, L., Lischke, A., Greif, J., Heprterz, S.C., Heinrichs, M., and Domes, G. (2011). Oxytocin increases recognition of masked emotional faces. *Psychoneuroendocrinology*, 36(9), 1378-1382.

Shamay-Tsoory, S.G., Fischer, M., Dvash, J., Harari, H., Perach-Bloom, N., Levkovitz, Y. (2009). Intranasal administration of oxytocin increases envy and schadenfreude (gloating). *Biological Psychiatry,* 66(9), 864-870.

Van den Broucke, S., Vandereycken, W., & Vertommen, H. (1995). Marital intimacy: Conceptualization and assessment. *Clinical Psychology Review, 15,* 217-233.

Van Ijzendoorn, M.H., and Bakermans-Kranenburg, M.J. (2011). A sniff of trust: Meta-analysis of the effects of intranasal oxytocin administration on face recognition, trust to in-group, and trust to out-group. *Pychoneuroendocrinology,* In press.

Zak, P.J., Kurzban, R., and Matzner, W.T. (2005). Oxytocin is associated with human trustworthiness. *Homones and Behavior,* 48(5), 522-527.

INDEX

#

20th century, 361
21st century, 232

A

abstraction, 435
abuse, 65, 66, 179, 182, 373, 523
academic performance, xxii, 149, 150, 154, 157, 344, 351, 441, 460, 464, 467
academic progress, 148
academic success, 145, 344, 441, 446
accelerometers, 317
access, xvi, xix, 20, 23, 28, 47, 235, 238, 290, 377, 382, 383, 385, 386, 389, 391, 393, 395, 399, 400, 460
accommodations, 301
accountability, 500
accounting, xv, 211
acetylcholine, 507
achievement test, xiii, 115, 134
acid, 177, 185
acquaintance, 51
acrophobia, 440
ACTH, 346
action research, 228
activation state, 437
activism, 216
activity level, xix, 307, 315
acts of aggression, 333
AD, 193, 209, 251, 252
adaptability, x, 4, 444
adaptation(s), x, xv, xvi, xx, 7, 9, 13, 37, 57, 60, 156, 206, 211, 212, 222, 231, 256, 287, 326, 328, 332, 341, 355, 403, 436, 249, 453, 454, 484, 509, 524
adipose, 240
adipose tissue, 240

adjustment, xv, 65, 66, 67, 68, 113, 181, 204, 211, 213, 214, 216, 221, 223, 227, 228, 230, 231, 244, 280, 294, 396, 397, 404, 405, 443, 450, 454, 459
administrators, xxii, 467
adolescents, xiii, xxii, 76, 107, 140, 143, 144, 147, 150, 151, 152, 154, 165, 204, 214, 229, 240, 241, 244, 274, 304, 316, 320, 323, 375, 466, 514
adult obesity, 246
adulthood, 64, 72, 73, 74, 75, 76, 77, 135, 137, 165, 243, 419, 455, 463, 485, 486
adults, ix, xx, xxi, 40, 60, 76, 82, 84, 116, 117, 123, 133, 134, 138, 148, 188, 189, 199, 200, 205, 222, 226, 230, 239, 245, 280, 294, 305, 315, 316, 320, 321, 323, 356, 416, 453, 454, 461, 463, 466, 478, 506, 513, 524
advancement(s), 179, 298
adverse conditions, 113
adverse effects, xii, 87, 88, 89, 90, 92, 93, 95, 97, 214, 242
advertisements, 496
advocacy, 116
aerobic exercise, 322
affect intensity, 58
affective dimension, 310
affective disorder, xviii, xx, 180, 243, 253, 297, 299, 300, 303, 304, 305, 306, 377, 378, 395, 396, 397, 399, 421
affective experience, 45, 53, 54, 55, 59, 184, 198, 332, 385, 395, 405
affective meaning, 23
affective reactions, ix, xviii, 116, 120, 122, 126, 307, 308, 309, 310, 311, 312, 313, 314, 315, 316, 318, 319, 490, 494, 496
African Americans, 46
African-American, 130, 140
age, xii, 63, 64, 65, 72, 73, 74, 75, 77, 82, 118, 124, 133, 147, 156, 163, 165, 213, 216, 217, 218, 223, 224, 226, 253, 257, 274, 275, 290, 294, 295, 317, 320, 335, 416, 417

aggression, xi, 5, 7, 11, 14, 28, 29, 30, 31, 32, 33, 34, 37, 197, 202, 276, 277, 281, 282, 290, 352
aggressive behavior, 27, 28, 29, 197, 198, 212, 342
aggressiveness, 290, 333, 352
agonist, 181
agoraphobia, 239
AIDS, 426
alcohol abuse, 398
alcohol problems, 472, 473, 481, 487
alcohol use, xxii, 198, 464, 466
alcoholics, 447
alcoholism, 404
alertness, xviii, 297, 298, 300, 302, 303, 306, 311
alexithymia, 48, 56, 58, 163, 463, 486, 519, 520, 525
algorithm, 401
alienation, 69, 70, 71, 72
allele, 177, 178
alters, xix, 325, 498
altruism, 524
ambiguous events, 42
ambivalence, 69, 70, 221
American culture, 48
American Psychiatric Association, 162, 201, 254, 269
American Psychological Association, xii, 9, 63, 64, 78, 169, 293, 370, 401
amplitude, 46, 84, 280, 342
amygdala, 132, 139, 175, 178, 182, 183, 184, 301, 401, 410, 507, 508, 509, 511, 515, 518
amylase, 349
ancestors, 13
anchoring, 491, 499
anorexia, 161, 164, 419, 420
anorexia nervosa, 161, 164, 420
anorgasmia, 525
ANOVA, 224, 225, 280
ANS, 52
anterior cingulate cortex, 131, 136, 178, 384
anthropologists, xi, 39, 40, 43
anthropology, 57
antibody, 410
anticipatory control, xi, 11, 12
antidepressant, 178, 180, 184, 240, 299, 300
antidepressant medication, 240, 300
anxiety disorder, xiv, 161, 163, 164, 168, 191, 192, 193, 195, 196, 201, 202, 203, 205, 209, 236, 243, 244, 251, 252, 254, 255, 270, 271, 373, 374, 375, 481
anxious mood, 191, 192, 196, 202
anxiousness, 176, 178
APA, xii, 63, 64, 69, 135, 188, 193, 195
apathy, 70, 116
appeasement, 9

appetite, 237, 239, 241, 242, 243, 254, 299
appraisals, 15, 27, 31, 43, 49, 75, 145, 310, 328, 353, 354, 363, 365, 367
Aristotle, x, 3, 7, 64
arithmetic, 120, 122, 123, 126, 127, 128, 131, 135, 137, 138, 139
armed conflict, 229
armed groups, 231
arousal, 15, 30, 32, 44, 45, 46, 48, 50, 55, 75, 173, 194, 199, 207, 276, 278, 279, 280, 282, 284, 285, 286, 295, 310, 311, 316, 319, 335, 338, 339, 350, 353, 355, 383, 390, 395, 400, 437, 500, 509, 511, 512
Asian Americans, 48
Asian countries, 45
assessment, xix, xx, 30, 109, 110, 164, 166, 167, 168, 169, 203, 208, 271, 274, 275, 276, 291, 294, 303, 307, 315, 316, 319, 320, 321, 322, 323, 324, 338, 349, 370, 392, 404, 407, 412, 413, 414, 415, 435, 436, 437, 443, 472, 526
assets, 269
asthma, 239, 245, 246
athletes, 326, 331, 333, 334, 336, 337, 341, 342, 343, 347, 349, 350, 351, 352, 353, 354
atmosphere, 108, 109, 112
attachment, 8, 368, 374, 523
attacker, 37
attentional bias, 90, 98
attitudes, xiii, 8, 43, 49, 53, 111, 115, 116, 117, 118, 120, 134, 135, 139, 140, 151, 167, 228, 326, 328, 355, 396, 413, 423, 425, 485, 486, 496
attribution, 56, 57, 77, 158, 310, 375
attribution theory, 77, 158
Austria, 297, 407, 431, 505
authenticity, 47
authoritarianism, 413, 500
authority, 113
autism, 84, 179, 181, 183, 184, 524, 525
autobiographical memory, 60, 205, 369
automaticity, 237, 356, 446
autonomic nervous system, 58, 339, 340, 424
autonomy, 204, 309, 345, 395, 426, 447
aversion, 70, 274, 414, 421, 426, 495, 496, 497, 502
avoidance behavior, 279, 393, 412, 436
avoidance motivational system, 279
awareness, xix, xxiii, 45, 52, 59, 103, 131, 144, 164, 172, 203, 213, 238, 254, 255, 359, 360, 361, 363, 365, 366, 367, 389, 450, 475, 476, 481, 489, 495, 496, 499, 502

B

babbling, 19

backlash, 116
bacteria, 419
bargaining, 35
barriers, 243, 499
basal ganglia, 201
base, xi, xiv, 5, 112, 161, 167, 177, 393, 470, 500
base rate, 500
base rate information, 500
basic competencies, 117, 471
basic research, xiv, 161
Beck Depression Inventory, 259
behavior therapy, xiii, 101, 102, 104, 107, 109, 112, 361, 374
behavioral approach system, 184, 279
behavioral change, 12, 44, 136, 434
behavioral disorders, 204, 372
behavioral dysregulation, 208
behavioral inhibition system, 279, 285
behavioral intentions, xi, 5
behavioral medicine, 169, 372
behavioral sciences, 371
behaviorism, 19
Belgium, 37, 453, 517
belief systems, xiii, 101, 102, 107
beneficial effect, 265, 461, 506
benefits, xx, xxiii, 21, 28, 119, 238, 266, 323, 343, 360, 361, 370, 372, 373, 377, 378, 395, 453, 454, 460, 461, 484, 485, 486, 505, 506
bias, 41, 166, 168, 175, 181, 204, 207, 228, 264, 275, 317, 338, 360, 402, 487, 491, 492, 493, 495, 496, 497, 498, 499, 500, 520
binge eating disorder, 164, 169, 170
biochemistry, 177
biofeedback, 343, 345
biological rhythms, 301
biopsychology, 323
bipolar disorder, 198, 199, 203, 204, 280, 395, 397, 404
births, 54
blame, 105, 148, 150, 153, 490
blind spot, 289
blindness, 32
blood, xx, 56, 197, 201, 301, 407, 409, 411, 418, 419, 420, 464, 514, 518
blood circulation, 518
blood flow, 56
blood pressure, 197, 201, 301, 418, 464
blood pressure reduction, 418
BMI, xvi, 235, 317
body dissatisfaction, 169
body fat, xvi, 235
body image, 375
body mass index, xvi, 235, 244

body weight, 236, 420
bonding, 13, 518, 524
bonds, 523
borderline personality disorder, 166, 168, 198, 292, 420
boredom, 15, 50, 70, 103, 277, 278
Bosnia, 216, 229
bottom-up, 435
brain activity, 172, 301, 315, 423
brain functioning, 93, 455
brain structure, 181, 410, 474
brainstem, 178, 306
brainstorming, 391, 392
Brazil, 414
breakdown, 352
breast cancer, 205, 318, 321
breathing, xxi, 45, 310, 314, 370, 465, 514
breeding, 173, 174, 176, 412
Britain, 253
Buddhism, 361
bulimia, 164, 166, 169, 300, 419, 420
bulimia nervosa, 164, 166, 169, 300, 419, 420
bullying, 148, 150, 154, 155, 157, 205
burn, 454
burnout, 462
Butcher, 355

C

CAD, 426
call centers, 454
cancer, xv, 29, 191, 202, 235, 315, 318, 361, 368, 369
candidates, 179
carbohydrate, 237, 246, 247, 299
carbohydrates, 237
carbon, 314
carbon dioxide, 314
cardiovascular disease(s), xv, 235, 240, 315
cardiovascular system, 339
career success, xx, 453
caregivers, 82, 84, 374, 416
cartoon, 54, 393
cascades, 208
case study(s), 158, 348, 352
castration, 20, 33
catecholamines, 346
categorization, xiii, 44, 48, 101, 102, 383, 385, 403, 404, 426, 501
category a, 384
category b, 391
catharsis, 28, 37
catheter, 514

Caucasians, 46, 47, 56, 130

causal antecedent, 484

causal attribution, 75

causal relationship, xi, xiii, 11, 12, 115, 119, 236

causality, 88, 329, 369, 425, 474

causation, 30, 134, 145, 239, 240

CDC, 324

central executive, xii, 87, 89, 90, 91, 93, 97, 99, 122, 123, 125, 135, 140

cerebral asymmetry, 422

cerebrospinal fluid, 177, 180, 518

certificate, 104, 106

CFI, 260

challenges, x, xix, 4, 12, 109, 119, 165, 166, 168, 256, 342, 359, 366, 436, 437

changing environment, x, 4, 436

character traits, xxi, 466

cheese, 393

chemical, 410, 427

Chicago, 7, 58, 157, 270, 290, 372

child abuse, 230

child development, 58, 136, 404

childhood, xii, xx, 63, 64, 72, 73, 75, 76, 77, 78, 134, 179, 182, 200, 215, 246, 397, 407, 416, 417, 419, 425

China, 140

chromosome, xiv, 171, 174

chronic diseases, xv, 235

chronic fatigue, 239

chronic illness, 243

cigarette smoke, 27

circadian rhythm(s), xviii, 297, 298, 299, 300, 301, 303, 306

citizens, 227

City, 216, 450

civil society, 228

clarity, 108, 394, 402

classes, 105, 106, 108, 411, 462

classical conditioning, 25, 132

classification, xii, 63, 64, 65, 66, 68, 70, 78, 260

classroom, xii, xxii, 101, 102, 109, 110, 113, 128, 134, 141, 467

classroom environment, 141

classroom management, xii, 101, 102, 113

classroom teacher, xxii, 134, 467

classroom teachers, xxii, 467

cleaning, 409, 418

clients, 57, 357

climate, 105, 468

clinical application, 371, 375

clinical depression, 98, 190, 205, 241, 369

clinical disorders, 486

clinical interventions, xviii, 223, 228, 251

clinical psychology, 69, 162, 168

clinical trials, xviii, 297, 298, 300

close relationships, 54, 59, 153, 205

closure, 202

clustering, 52

clusters, 52

CNS, 183, 305

coaches, 345

coal, 287

cocaine, 445, 447

coding, 16, 22, 23, 32, 34, 35, 36, 173, 179, 185

cognition, x, xviii, 4, 6, 9, 23, 57, 58, 75, 78, 99, 122, 126, 135, 137, 139, 144, 157, 183, 251, 271, 297, 298, 301, 303, 327, 381, 384, 400, 401, 402, 404, 416, 437, 438, 442, 443, 448, 474, 475, 494, 495, 498, 500, 501, 515

cognitive abilities, xxiii, 344, 469, 471

cognitive ability, 379, 474, 475

cognitive activity, 436

cognitive associations, 144

cognitive capacity, x, 3, 495

cognitive construction(s), 42

cognitive development, 102, 103, 416

cognitive dimension, 310

cognitive flexibility, xix, 377, 383, 385, 387, 391, 404

cognitive function, 92, 176, 334

cognitive level, 433

cognitive load, 97, 99, 494

cognitive models, xiii, 101, 102, 104

cognitive performance, ix, 88, 89, 90, 98, 127, 137, 301, 330, 349

cognitive perspective, 251

cognitive process, x, xix, 4, 23, 43, 75, 94, 97, 122, 126, 192, 196, 314, 315, 359, 374, 378, 400, 437, 438, 470, 475, 483

cognitive processing, xix, 97, 122, 126, 192, 359, 475

cognitive psychology, 19, 331

cognitive research, 195

cognitive science, 133

cognitive style, 371, 379

cognitive system, 97, 126, 478

cognitive tasks, xii, 87, 92, 301, 302, 510

cognitive theory, 397, 424, 436, 446, 485

cognitive therapy, 361, 373, 374, 375

cognitive-behavioral therapy, 361, 364, 462

collage, 213

collectivism, 49, 60

College Station, 489

college students, 50, 54, 130, 382

colleges, 479

color, xix, 301, 304, 325, 335, 383

common sense, xxi, 465
communication, xxi, 7, 10, 81, 82, 85, 105, 107, 350, 438, 441, 450, 465, 482, 525
communication patterns, 441
community(s), xxii, xxiv, 64, 69, 153, 172, 189, 212, 213, 223, 227, 228, 231, 233, 236, 241, 243, 244, 294, 368, 426, 467, 513, 517, 518, 519
comorbidity, 204, 251, 252, 255, 259, 260
Comparative Fit Index, 260
comparison task, 134
compassion, 326
compatibility, 22, 23, 33, 34, 37
compensation, 76, 77, 280
competition, 128, 309, 327, 328, 329, 330, 331, 334, 337, 338, 341, 343, 349, 352, 353, 356
competitive sport, 331, 343, 351
compilation, 103
complement, 442
complexity, x, 3, 16, 55, 118, 144, 229, 274, 276, 340, 387, 395
compliance, 301, 302, 317, 369
complications, 242
composition, 298, 301
compounds, 427
comprehension, xix, 121, 325
compulsion, 273
compulsive behavior, 201, 244
computation, 117, 121, 125, 131
computer, 124, 134, 166, 401, 490, 520, 521, 522
computing, 119, 121
conception, 16, 20, 28, 31, 64, 76, 274, 275, 281, 403, 426
conceptual model, 203
conceptualization, xi, xviii, 18, 39, 52, 69, 168, 203, 254, 273, 274, 290, 333, 470
conditioned stimulus, 25, 26
conditioning, 33, 34, 37, 75, 201, 416, 417, 427
conductance, 21, 46, 172, 278, 282, 290, 339
conduction, 108
confidentiality, 286
configuration, 52, 150, 179
conflict, xv, xxii, 47, 53, 94, 96, 105, 190, 211, 212, 214, 215, 226, 229, 230, 231, 389, 445, 466, 524
conformity, 113
confrontation, 46
congruence, 138, 326
connectivity, 132, 509, 511
conscientiousness, 333, 483
conscious awareness, 290, 389, 435
consciousness, xxiii, 10, 12, 184, 302, 346, 372, 428, 469, 475, 476
consensus, x, 4, 40, 51, 82, 90, 172, 277, 329, 362, 378, 392, 395, 396, 519

consent, 216, 231
consolidation, xxiii, 78, 505, 506, 507, 508, 510, 511, 512, 513, 514, 515
construct validity, 313, 421
construction, 36, 43, 47, 55, 59, 180, 292, 421, 499, 501, 520, 523
consulting, 204
consumers, 500
consumption, xv, xvi, 235, 236, 237, 238, 242
contamination, 274, 341, 411, 412, 413, 414, 415, 416, 417, 418, 419, 420, 422, 426, 428, 502
contingency, 25, 384
continuous data, 308
contradiction, 28
control condition, 26, 94, 96, 123, 130, 383
control group, 131, 236, 280, 283, 284, 285, 319, 369, 386, 387, 454, 459, 519
controlled research, 375
controlled studies, 369
controversial, x, 4, 116, 243, 299
convergence, 291
conversations, 360, 364
cooperation, 105
coordination, 125
coping strategies, 255, 265, 285, 286, 287, 289, 290, 333, 336, 366, 368
core assumptions, 313
correlation, xvii, 45, 88, 119, 147, 149, 176, 218, 222, 250, 251, 260, 263, 264, 279, 280, 288, 292, 329, 414, 415, 420
correlation analysis, xvii, 250
correlation coefficient, 251, 260
correlational analysis, 224
correlations, xxii, 120, 217, 218, 260, 275, 280, 281, 282, 285, 288, 386, 415, 420, 466, 508
cortex, 238, 294, 301, 410, 414, 418, 494
corticosteroids, 298
cortisol, 139, 196, 203, 237, 240, 341, 349, 350, 351, 354, 356, 371, 410, 460, 481, 507, 508, 512, 514
cost, 121, 162, 166, 213, 330, 338, 491
Council of Europe, 309, 320
counterbalance, 280
country of origin, 45
covering, 326, 369
craving, 246, 247, 299
creative functioning, 396, 399
creative outcomes, 397
creative potential, xix, 377, 381, 397, 400
creative process, xx, 377, 378, 382, 385, 394, 396, 398, 403, 404
creative thinking, 378, 380, 381, 384, 390, 398, 399, 400, 402

creativity, xix, xxi, 216, 301, 345, 348, 377, 378, 379, 380, 381, 382, 383, 384, 385, 386, 387, 388, 389, 390, 391, 392, 393, 394, 395, 396, 397, 398, 399, 400, 401, 402, 403, 404, 405, 465, 483
creativity tests, 386
critical thinking, 391
criticism, 174, 436
cross-cultural differences, 46
cross-cultural literature, xi, 39, 40
cross-validation, 317, 524
crystallized intelligence, 449
CT, 32, 137, 187, 229, 405, 421, 425
cues, 26, 27, 28, 29, 31, 36, 96, 175, 237, 239, 243, 254, 279, 283, 367, 402, 416, 438, 442, 450, 477
cultivation, xviii, 251, 264, 374
cultural beliefs, 43
cultural differences, xi, 7, 39, 40, 41, 44, 46, 47, 48, 53, 54, 55, 56, 58, 133, 241, 422
cultural heritage, x, 4
cultural influence, 416
cultural norms, 46, 240, 241
cultural practices, 49
cultural values, 41, 42, 45, 48, 216, 416
culture, ix, x, xi, 4, 9, 39, 41, 42, 43, 44, 46, 47, 48, 49, 51, 52, 53, 54, 55, 57, 58, 59, 60, 117, 137, 152, 216, 378, 392, 423, 425
cycles, xvii, 250, 253, 256, 523
cytokines, 411

D

daily living, 308
damages, xv, 188
dancers, 354
danger, 12, 13, 195, 252, 277, 279, 283, 301, 310, 386, 398
Darwin, Charles, 12
data analysis, xvii, 228, 250
data collection, 166, 167, 228
data set, 280, 317, 363
database, xii, 63, 64, 65
decay, 412, 414
declarative memory, 506, 512, 513
decoding, xi, 5, 184, 410
decoupling, 510
defecation, 173
defensiveness, 356
deficiency(s), 133, 134, 244, 308
deficit, xx, 69, 127, 129, 134, 135, 280, 300, 314, 418, 453, 454, 519
degradation, 238
dehumanization, 423
delinquency, 156, 320

dementia, xviii, 297, 300
dendritic spines, 175
denial, 242, 412, 421
Denmark, 235
deoxyribose, 185
Department of Education, 139, 143
Department of Health and Human Services, xv, 235, 246
dependent variable, 90, 96, 97, 224, 289
depressive symptomatology, 320, 425
depressive symptoms, 162, 169, 177, 188, 189, 194, 196, 199, 200, 204, 205, 206, 207, 236, 239, 240, 241, 246, 259, 280, 281, 300, 320, 368, 373, 396
deprivation, 507
depth, 46, 137, 212, 460
desensitization, 365, 367
destruction, 28, 215
detachment, 360, 366
detection, 45, 60, 177, 179, 180, 410, 519, 520, 525
devaluation, 20, 27, 30, 31, 32
developmental process, 77, 83, 417
developmental psychology, ix, xii, 63, 64, 65, 67, 68, 69, 71, 72, 73, 74, 75, 77
deviation, 54
diabetes, xv, 235, 240, 454
Diagnostic and Statistical Manual of Mental Disorders, 162, 165, 269
diagnostic criteria, 254, 397
diastolic blood pressure, 410
dichotomy, 28, 31, 329
diet, 242
dieting, 237
diffusion, 366
digestion, 411
dignity, 6
dimensionality, 202, 308, 311
direct action, 342, 436
direct measure, 93, 383
disability, 135, 271, 357, 519
disappointment, 70
disclosure, 523, 525
discomfort, 52, 193, 316, 382
discriminant analysis, 419
discrimination, 37, 46, 240, 243, 278, 518
discrimination learning, 37
diseases, xviii, 271, 297, 307, 309, 315, 355
disgust, xviii, xx, 14, 41, 46, 70, 75, 163, 273, 276, 283, 310, 395, 407, 408, 409, 410, 411, 412, 413, 414, 415, 416, 417, 418, 419, 420, 421, 422, 423, 424, 425, 426, 427, 428, 497
disorder, 7, 57, 120, 163, 164, 168, 193, 198, 199, 200, 202, 207, 215, 252, 254, 270, 299, 300, 372,

395, 397, 401, 418, 419, 420, 422, 423, 427, 509, 513, 519
displacement, 148
disposition, 14, 88, 105, 118, 149, 342
dissatisfaction, 69, 70, 71, 72, 76, 437, 443, 445
dissociation, 36, 113, 131, 146, 511
dissonance, 113, 240, 382
distortions, 290, 367
distress, 69, 70, 71, 75, 153, 166, 190, 194, 195, 230, 237, 239, 240, 241, 264, 300, 304, 360, 365, 371, 386
distribution, 302, 341
divergent thinking, 379, 384, 386, 391, 392, 393, 394, 400, 405
diversity, x, 4, 98, 99, 413
dizygotic, 176
dizygotic twins, 176
DNA, 173, 176, 177, 183
dogs, 26, 36
DOI, 139, 447
dominance, 52
dopamine, 179, 181, 185, 238, 279, 293, 299, 384, 391, 511
dopaminergic, xix, 179, 377, 384
dorsolateral prefrontal cortex, 94
Down syndrome, 84
down-regulation, 194, 198
drawing, 21, 103, 470, 484
dreaming, 513
drug abuse, 238
drug discovery, 183
drugs, 180, 242, 274, 277
dual task, 33, 122, 123, 138
dualism, 364
dynamical systems, 158
dysgraphia, 224
dyslexia, 224
dysthymic disorder, 253, 255

E

East Asia, 46
eating disorders, xiv, 161, 162, 164, 168, 170, 242, 244, 324, 368, 372, 419, 422
ecology, 232
economic crisis, xvi, 249, 251
economic status, 226, 253
economics, 182
education, ix, xxii, 102, 107, 108, 109, 110, 111, 112, 117, 126, 144, 146, 149, 151, 152, 154, 345, 456, 462, 467
educational research, xiii, 143, 144, 145, 148, 150, 154

educational settings, ix, xiii, xxii, 115, 129, 466
EEG, 45, 57, 94, 99, 172, 180, 278, 410, 507
egocentrism, 292, 374
elaboration, 119, 205, 379, 389
electrodes, 510
electroencephalogram, 322, 410
electroencephalography, 172
electromyography, 282, 342
elementary school, 77, 116, 134, 136, 140, 402
e-mail, 249, 458
EMG, 428
emotional action, xi, 11, 12, 13, 14, 16, 17, 18, 21, 25, 26, 29, 30, 33
emotional bias, xxiii, 489, 496, 497
emotional disorder, xvi, 204, 249, 253, 271
emotional dispositions, 332, 344
emotional distress, xvi, 15, 53, 236, 239, 240, 241, 243, 264
emotional experience, 6, 12, 44, 45, 46, 47, 48, 49, 50, 52, 53, 57, 59, 60, 144, 154, 158, 194, 196, 198, 277, 320, 327, 332, 337, 338, 339, 341, 350, 378, 389, 395, 397, 399, 458, 490, 497, 499, 510
emotional information, 12, 163, 170, 498, 502, 512, 524
emotional intelligence, ix, xxi, xxiii, 66, 333, 348, 351, 353, 354, 357, 363, 440, 441, 442, 446, 447, 448, 449, 450, 451, 453, 463, 464, 465, 467, 469, 470, 471, 472, 473, 474, 475, 476, 477, 478, 479, 480, 481, 482, 483, 484, 485, 486, 487, 488
emotional problems, 52, 241, 244, 259
emotional processes, ix, 256, 280, 403, 494, 518, 523
emotional reactions, 13, 35, 79, 104, 126, 132, 310, 437, 443, 445, 494
emotional responses, x, 4, 16, 66, 340, 437, 438, 455, 490, 492, 493, 494, 495, 496, 498, 515
emotional stability, 66, 483, 484
emotional state, xv, xix, 12, 15, 17, 18, 65, 66, 67, 68, 69, 71, 73, 76, 188, 196, 198, 200, 217, 258, 276, 290, 325, 327, 329, 333, 336, 340, 347, 378, 380, 381, 382, 393, 395, 438, 443, 481, 519
emotional stimuli, 25, 172, 178, 184, 301, 339, 506, 508
emotional valence, 339, 511, 520
emotional well-being, 375, 464
emotionality, ix, xiv, xx, 59, 66, 82, 84, 132, 135, 171, 176, 177, 178, 179, 181, 183, 377, 398, 428
empathy, xi, 5, 75, 105, 355
empirical studies, xix, 164, 257, 377, 384, 412, 446
employability, 459, 464, 483, 487
employees, 275, 387, 393, 397, 462, 476, 483, 486
employment, 116, 477
encoding, xi, 5, 11, 23, 36, 507, 508, 512, 514
endurance, 313, 349

energy, xvi, 44, 235, 236, 238, 239, 240, 241, 242, 243, 254, 309, 313, 316, 319, 320, 328, 395, 491
energy consumption, 239, 313, 319
energy expenditure, 239, 241, 243, 309
engineering, 116, 138, 378
England, 7, 9, 10, 30, 57, 203, 295, 306, 347, 348, 355, 356, 401
enrollment, 118
environment(s), x, xii, xiv, xxi, 4, 6, 12, 17, 23, 37, 78, 81, 82, 83, 84, 103, 117, 166, 168, 169, 172, 173, 175, 178, 187, 201, 225, 232, 238, 244, 301, 309, 316, 326, 331, 353, 360, 363, 367, 392, 419, 466, 474, 478, 492
environmental conditions, 228
environmental factors, 176, 214, 228, 455
environmental resources, 271
enzyme, 179
epidemic, xv, xvi, 235, 236, 243, 246
epidemiology, 305
epididymis, 518
epigenetics, 178, 455
episodic memory, 508
epistasis, 179, 181
equality, 263
equilibrium, xvi, 212, 249, 255
erosion, 366
ERPs, xii, 87, 93, 97, 410
erythrocytes, 176
estrogen, 514
ethical standards, 174, 413
ethics, 64
ethnic background, 257
ethnic diversity, 178
ethnic groups, 46, 241
ethnicity, 39, 130, 178, 241, 243, 257
ethnocentrism, 524
etiology, xvi, 170, 174, 249, 252, 254, 255
euphoria, 70, 276
Eurasia, 141
Europe, 59, 239
evaluative thought, 189
event-related potential, xii, 87, 93, 94, 95, 410, 424
everyday life, 113, 166, 168, 310, 312, 315, 316, 317, 319, 321, 446, 485, 490, 496, 522
evoked potential, 278
evolution, x, xi, 4, 6, 8, 9, 31, 39, 40, 69, 137, 144, 291, 340, 413, 420
evolutionary psychologists, 13
exaggeration, 498
excess body weight, xvi, 235
exclusion, 336
excretion, 408, 411
execution, 11, 20, 22, 23, 35, 125, 354, 392

executive function, 91, 92, 93, 96, 98, 99
executive functioning, 91, 98
executive functions, 91, 92, 93, 99
executive processes, 93
exercise, xviii, 6, 307, 308, 309, 311, 313, 314, 315, 316, 317, 318, 319, 320, 321, 322, 323, 324, 338, 341, 346, 347, 349, 350, 354, 391, 400, 437, 459, 462, 481, 485, 495, 501
exercise programs, 481
exertion, 239, 391
experimental condition, 283
experimental design, 165, 285, 289, 392, 399
expertise, 126, 131, 357
exploitation, 228
exposure, xviii, 27, 117, 212, 221, 222, 297, 298, 300, 302, 304, 305, 306, 365, 373, 410, 418, 421, 424, 496, 510
expressivity, 423, 442
external validity, 82
extinction, 20, 25, 26
extraversion, 181, 184, 291, 327, 356, 428, 483, 484
extreme poverty, 226
extrinsic motivation, 433
eye movement, 55, 511
eye-tracking, 175, 184

F

facial expression, xi, 6, 7, 35, 39, 40, 41, 45, 46, 48, 54, 56, 57, 58, 175, 181, 231, 310, 409, 417, 418, 422, 423, 425, 440, 450, 478, 525
facial responses, 425
factor analysis, 189, 363
faith, 362
false positive, 178
families, 216, 223, 228, 344
family life, 398
family members, 153, 215
fantasy, 386, 522
fat, xvi, 235, 237, 238, 242
fear response, 14, 132
fears, 36, 112, 133, 351, 420, 421, 425, 428
feces, 414, 416, 417
fever, 411
fibromyalgia, 369, 373
fights, xix, 325
films, 47, 60, 423, 509
financial, 283, 498
Finland, 245
fires, 19
first generation, 46
fitness, 12, 309, 315
five-factor model, 182, 208, 346

fixation, 96
flavor, 26
flaws, 195
flexibility, 12, 379, 391, 392, 395, 402, 461
flight, xi, 11, 12, 13, 14, 15, 27, 201, 351
fluctuations, 166
fluid, 121, 412, 441, 449
fluid intelligence, 121, 449
fMRI, xii, 35, 87, 93, 94, 97, 131, 132, 133, 137,
    172, 175, 178, 279, 341, 348, 410, 414, 415, 420,
    427, 514
food, xvi, 20, 52, 235, 237, 238, 239, 242, 243, 244,
    245, 246, 408, 409, 410, 411, 412, 413, 414, 416,
    417, 418, 419, 425, 426, 427
food intake, 237, 239, 412
force, 41, 327, 329, 333, 336
forebrain, 508
formal education, 117, 135
formation, 237, 239, 243, 245, 380, 405, 484, 506,
    508
formula, 176
foundations, 102, 103, 371, 374, 446, 448, 450, 485
fragility, xv, 136, 211
fragments, 506
framing, 185, 367, 500, 501, 502
France, 78, 325
free recall, 512
free will, 6, 10
freedom, 214, 221, 366
freezing, 15, 33, 437
Freud, 408, 416, 423
Freud, Sigmund, 423
friction, 191
friendship, 208, 523
frontal cortex, 201, 498, 518
frontal lobe, 99
functional analysis, 13
functional MRI, 179, 180
fundamental needs, 275, 310
funds, 512

G

gambling, xxii, 292, 373, 466, 491
ganglion, 298, 302
garbage, 411
gastrointestinal tract, 410
Gaza Strip, 215
gender differences, 217, 226
gender identity, 130
gene expression, 463
gene promoter, 184
general adaptation syndrome, 355
general knowledge, 491, 492
generalized anxiety disorder, 139, 163, 193, 202,
    203, 207, 209, 251, 252
genes, xiv, 171, 173, 174, 175, 176, 179, 181, 455,
    456, 462, 474
genetic code, 176
genetic factors, 174
genetic information, 178
genetic predisposition, 474
genetics, ix, xiv, xxi, 171, 173, 174, 176, 178, 179,
    181, 184, 466
genome, 176, 463
genotype, 180
Georgia, 171
Germany, 3, 11, 63, 77, 78, 79, 101, 109, 110, 148,
    161, 171, 273, 286, 307, 325, 407, 414
gerontology, 8, 309
Gestalt, 76
Gestalt psychology, 76
gestures, xxi, 82, 409, 465
gifted, 462
glucocorticoid, 508
glucocorticoids, 346
glucose, 463
goal setting, 257, 331, 432, 433, 434, 437, 446, 449
goal-directed behavior, 208
goal-setting, xvii, xviii, 250, 251, 264, 265, 454
GPA, 460
grades, 104, 118, 120, 139, 154, 286, 344, 450
graph, 68, 390
gray matter, 185, 474, 488
grazing, 242
Greece, 438
grounding, 34
group identity, 130
group membership, 122
grouping, 217
growth, 71, 222, 228
guidelines, 231, 342, 369, 380, 458
guilt, xi, xiii, 5, 15, 35, 70, 75, 143, 144, 145, 146,
    147, 148, 151, 152, 153, 154, 155, 156, 157, 158,
    228, 326, 499
guilty, 144, 146, 152, 153
Guinea, 41
gymnastics, 339
gymnasts, 356

H

habituation, 313
harmony, 59
hazards, 436, 494
headache, 460

healing, 231
health care, 462
health effects, 287
health problems, xv, xix, 235, 359
health promotion, 165
health psychology, 69, 308
health risks, 240, 243
health services, 230
heart disease, 454
heart rate, xxi, 28, 46, 172, 199, 278, 290, 302, 339, 340, 349, 351, 355, 356, 409, 414, 415, 418, 449, 465
height, xvi, 235, 244, 420
helplessness, 70, 214
hemisphere, 315
heritability, 173, 176, 474
herpes, 421
herpes labialis, 421
heterogeneity, 178, 314
heuristic processes, 129
heuristic processing, 497
high fat, 238
high school, xxii, 120, 139, 286, 354, 386, 467
high school grades, 120
higher education, 116
hippocampus, 301, 506, 507, 508, 518
Hispanics, 54
history, x, 4, 6, 12, 27, 37, 46, 171, 199, 200, 205, 287, 300, 301, 392, 401, 402, 476, 524
HM, 244
Hmong, 47, 60
hobby, 522
homeostasis, 313
homes, 302
homework, 116
homogeneity, 314, 321
homosexuality, 413
Hong Kong, 59
hopelessness, 70, 76, 206, 208, 284
hormone(s), xviii, xxiv, 237, 240, 297, 298, 341, 346, 349, 507, 517, 518, 521, 524
hormone levels, 298
host, 43, 44, 120, 399
hostility, xiv, 187, 284, 395
House, 7, 370
HPA axis, 237, 240
hue, 310
human actions, 437
human behavior, 173, 181, 279, 320, 401, 422, 436, 447
human body, 176
human brain, 7, 32, 33, 172, 178, 183, 305, 513
human condition, 223

human development, 69, 78
human existence, 6
human motivation, 447
human nature, x, 4, 6, 8
human perception, 475
Human Resource Management, 450
human right(s), 216, 230
human security, 216, 229
humanistic psychology, 69, 77
husband, xiv, 17, 187
hybrid, 263
hygiene, 412, 413, 414, 418, 419
hyperactivity, 255, 300
hypersensitivity, 284
hypersomnia, 299
hypochondriasis, xx, 407, 418, 419, 422, 428
hypothalamus, 301, 518
hypothesis test, 29

I

Iceland, 304
ideal(s), 10, 103, 127, 241
identical twins, 176
identification, 24, 133, 140, 153, 256, 397, 399, 454, 457, 523
identity, 53, 130, 144, 157, 158, 227, 352
ideology, 71
idiosyncratic, 327, 337, 355
illumination, 300, 304
illusion, 42, 501
image(s), xi, 5, 45, 54, 84, 111, 148, 189, 193, 194, 241, 244, 293, 368, 371, 427, 506
imagery, 10, 122, 124, 204, 208, 343, 354, 357, 428, 497
imagination, 395, 404
imitation, 416
immediate situation, 365
immersion, 27
immigrants, 413
immigration, 233
immune function, 371, 411
immune system, 361, 368
immunization, 76
immunoglobulin, 410
impairments, 96, 126, 128, 129, 252
implicit association test, 131, 137
imprisonment, 222, 226, 284
improvements, xxiii, 110, 361, 369, 383, 469
impulses, 24, 162, 281, 298, 331, 365
impulsive, 29, 31, 37, 244, 277, 281, 282, 283, 286, 293, 294, 396
impulsiveness, 276, 277, 281, 282, 374

impulsivity, 274, 291, 292, 397
in vitro, 183
inattention, 361
incidence, 134, 395
income, 230
increased access, 394
independence, 49, 395
independent variable, xvii, 217, 224, 226, 250, 262
indexing, 24
indirect measure, 172
individual character, 395
individual characteristics, 395
individual development, 69, 416
individual differences, xii, xiv, xvi, xxi, 44, 81, 83, 87, 88, 97, 137, 139, 171, 173, 174, 176, 177, 179, 180, 188, 197, 212, 236, 287, 327, 333, 351, 380, 415, 466, 494, 495, 499, 511, 519
individual perception, 434
individual students, 149, 153
individualism, 60
individualistic values, 54
individuality, 49
individuation, 141
Indonesia, 57, 232
induction, 46, 189, 190, 192, 196, 199, 370, 382, 383, 384, 385, 386, 387, 389, 391, 395, 399, 400, 408, 410, 415, 463, 487, 510, 511
industry(s), 378, 462
inefficiency, 88
infancy, ix, 40, 64, 72, 75, 81, 84, 85, 137, 395, 425
infants, xii, 40, 81, 82, 83, 84, 85, 117, 141, 423
infection, 75, 411, 412, 414, 426
inferiority, 66
inflammation, 411
information processing, 122, 381, 383, 487
informed consent, 216
infrared spectroscopy, 320
infrastructure, 214, 215
ingestion, 242, 408, 411
ingredients, 26, 461, 514
inhibition, xii, 87, 91, 92, 93, 94, 95, 96, 97, 98, 99, 125, 204, 279, 291, 450, 509, 522
initiation, xi, 5, 18, 26, 35, 253
injury(s), 28, 271, 294, 412, 413, 414, 418, 419, 425
inmates, 374
inoculation, 343, 352, 356
insecurity, 112, 195
insertion, 177
inspectors, 111
instinct, 14, 35
institutions, 216
insulin, 237

integration, 12, 23, 31, 76, 121, 168, 270, 291, 326, 345, 405, 498, 511
integrity, 416
Intellectual Disability(s), 181, 184, 357
intelligence, xxii, xxiii, 37, 132, 285, 380, 405, 440, 441, 442, 447, 448, 449, 450, 462, 463, 464, 466, 467, 468, 469, 470, 471, 472, 473, 474, 475, 476, 477, 478, 479, 480, 481, 482, 483, 484, 485, 486, 487, 488, 495, 501, 510
intelligence scores, 474
intentionality, 7, 77
interaction effect(s), 177, 179, 284, 289
interdependence, xiii, 49, 101, 102
interface, 12, 102
interference, 24, 89, 91, 99, 122, 124, 128, 133, 139, 140, 507
interference theory, 89
internal consistency, 188, 258, 270, 274
internal processes, 25, 93
internalised, xiii, 143, 144, 145, 146, 147
internalization, 75
internalizing, 208
interpersonal attitude, 426
interpersonal conflict, 60
interpersonal contact, 454
interpersonal interactions, 52, 75
interpersonal processes, xxiv, 517
interpersonal relations, 52, 54, 146, 154, 155, 157, 253, 464, 471, 482, 487
interpersonal relationships, 52, 54, 146, 154, 155, 157, 253, 471, 482
interpretability, 174
interrelations, 76
intervention, xiv, xv, xxiii, 9, 88, 161, 165, 166, 174, 211, 213, 217, 218, 221, 223, 224, 226, 236, 242, 246, 335, 344, 361, 368, 370, 373, 374, 401, 402, 403, 453, 458, 462, 469, 473, 476, 477, 480, 481, 482, 483, 484, 486
intervention programs, xv, 211
intimacy, 523, 525, 526
intrinsic motivation, xx, 265, 323, 377, 379, 398, 432, 433, 442, 443, 445, 477
intrinsic value, 151
introspection, 52, 149
introversion, 185, 395
intrusions, 270
investment, 522
Iowa, 21
IQ scores, 176
Iraq, 374
irritability, 299
isolation, 122, 240
Israel, 214, 224, 225, 227, 293

issues, ix, xix, xxiv, 52, 147, 178, 228, 274, 321, 344, 351, 359, 368, 369, 505
Italy, 211, 414

J

James-Lange theory of emotion, 42, 180
Japan, 45, 50, 57, 59, 414
job insecurity, xvi, 249, 251
job performance, 354, 454, 464, 483, 486
job satisfaction, 153, 483
joints, 17
Jordan, 477, 485

K

kidneys, 518
kill, 28, 491
kindergarten, xxii, 117, 146, 467
kindergartens, 231
Kosovo, 214, 232

L

labeling, 14, 164, 364
laboratory studies, 383, 387, 389
lack of control, 281, 370, 415
lack of opportunities, 222
landscape, 331
language processing, 133
languages, 64, 69
latency, 22, 96, 300, 342, 509, 510
laws, 33, 426
leadership, ix, xii, xx, 101, 102, 109, 111, 112, 431, 432, 441, 442, 443, 444, 445, 446, 447, 448, 449, 450, 451, 483, 486
leadership style, 483
leakage, 450
learners, xiii, 143, 154, 344
learning difficulties, 135
learning environment, xxii, 467
learning process, 37, 112, 119, 158
left hemisphere, 315
leisure, 315, 320
leisure time, 315
lending, 473, 475
lens, xi, 39, 40
leptin, 237
lesions, 33
levator, 413, 419
level of education, 117
liberation, 361

life changes, 293, 294
life course, 462
life cycle, 230
life experiences, 456
life satisfaction, xv, xviii, 76, 211, 212, 213, 214, 217, 218, 219, 220, 221, 222, 223, 225, 226, 227, 230, 232, 251, 310, 459, 461, 479, 480
Life Satisfaction Scale, 216, 224
light, ix, x, xvi, xvii, xviii, xxii, 3, 29, 88, 123, 195, 196, 249, 250, 251, 263, 264, 265, 274, 297, 298, 299, 300, 301, 302, 303, 304, 305, 306, 367, 378, 395, 458, 467, 511
light-emitting diodes, 303
Likert scale, 275, 286, 523
limbic system, 173, 508
liquids, 242
literacy, 156
living conditions, 213, 214, 215, 221, 223, 226, 227
living environment, 227
locomotor, 83
locus, 49, 126, 173, 284, 509
loneliness, 68, 69, 70, 71, 72
longevity, 483
longitudinal study, 231, 241
long-term memory, xxiii, 126, 391, 505, 506
love, 42, 43, 47, 56, 69, 70, 310, 326, 395, 525
lying, 309

M

Machiavellianism, 477
machinery, 16
Mackintosh, 193, 209
magazines, 318
magnetic resonance, xii, 87, 93, 138, 172, 279, 341, 410
magnetic resonance image, 341
magnetic resonance imaging, xii, 87, 93, 138, 172, 279, 410
magnets, 116
magnitude, 127, 139, 141, 408
major depression, 163, 182, 199, 202, 203, 207, 375, 509
major depressive disorder, 190, 203, 204, 207, 209, 244, 251, 253
majority, xix, 94, 95, 123, 153, 163, 165, 172, 176, 197, 212, 229, 236, 259, 282, 360, 377, 386, 387, 389, 399, 408, 409, 415, 419, 441, 490, 491
malnutrition, 226
mammalian brain, 172
mammals, 13, 173, 302
man, 7, 8, 12, 32, 421, 426, 493, 494

management, xii, 41, 78, 101, 102, 148, 150, 155, 156, 167, 371, 432, 454, 463, 470
mania, xx, 68, 69, 70, 199, 204, 377, 378, 396
manic, 198, 199, 200, 204, 280, 392, 396, 404, 405
manic episode, 392
manic symptoms, 199, 204
manipulation, 120, 121, 122, 125, 129, 130, 184, 192, 285, 334, 335, 336, 338, 344, 478, 486, 507
MANOVA, 289
manufacturing, 394
mapping, 426
marijuana, 274
marketing, 116, 522
married couples, xxii, 466
masking, 46
mass, xvi, 204, 235, 237, 244
mass media, 204
materials, 313, 396, 411, 458
mathematical knowledge, 139
mathematics, xiii, 115, 116, 117, 118, 119, 120, 125, 128, 130, 134, 135, 136, 137, 138, 139, 140, 141, 478
matter, 14, 27, 88, 107, 119, 121, 136, 138, 173, 265, 267, 328, 354, 372, 467
measurement(s), xviii, xxii, 46, 47, 55, 60, 172, 205, 223, 256, 259, 270, 273, 275, 284, 287, 289, 290, 301, 308, 312, 313, 316, 317, 319, 320, 321, 322, 341, 347, 350, 351, 369, 402, 421, 467, 510, 512
meat, 411, 413
media, 240, 242, 244, 521
median, 289
mediation, 16, 442
medical, 191, 216, 341, 344, 356, 369, 374, 392, 491, 498, 501
medical expertise, 341
medication, 237, 244
medicine, xviii, 180, 183, 297, 314, 346, 351, 356, 378, 513, 515
melatonin, xviii, 297, 298, 299, 300, 302, 304, 305, 306, 368, 371, 374
mellitus, 240
memory biases, 363
memory capacity, 129, 137, 391, 501
memory formation, 506, 507, 508, 515
memory function, 129, 373
memory performance, 506, 511, 515
memory processes, 134, 521
memory retrieval, 317
mental arithmetic, 121, 124, 135, 137, 138
mental capacity, 126
mental disorder, xiv, xvi, xx, 69, 161, 163, 165, 167, 201, 249, 251, 253, 290, 407, 417, 418, 420

mental health, xiii, xvi, xix, 161, 168, 193, 212, 214, 215, 229, 230, 231, 232, 236, 245, 251, 322, 359, 367, 369, 374, 441, 481, 483
mental illness, 161, 162, 164, 165, 270, 369, 378, 395, 400
mental model, 43
mental processes, 13, 348
mental representation, 44, 394
mental state(s), 284, 300
messages, 167
meta-analysis, xix, 29, 41, 57, 60, 88, 99, 139, 168, 177, 192, 203, 206, 244, 303, 322, 323, 348, 350, 354, 359, 363, 369, 371, 372, 393, 395, 400, 401, 462, 463, 464, 467, 474, 481, 482, 483, 486, 487, 500
metabolism, 172, 309
metacognition, 255, 259
Meta-Cognitions Questionnaire, xvii, 250, 252, 258, 265
methodology, 47, 89, 166, 327, 330, 369
methylation, 178
mice, 28, 175
migraines, 462
military, ix, xv, 211, 212, 215, 216, 222, 223, 226, 228, 232, 233, 344, 353, 356
military occupation, 215, 226
mimicry, 408
mineralocorticoid, 508
Ministry of Education, 224
Minneapolis, 79
miscarriage, 109
misuse, 328
mobile device, 166
mobile phone, 166, 167
moderates, 140, 181, 313, 321
moderators, 165, 200, 201, 241, 285, 291, 327, 329, 378, 387, 399, 461, 483
modernism, 404
modules, 55, 166, 457
molecular structure, 518
monozygotic twins, 176
mood change, 299
mood disorder, xviii, 168, 182, 203, 204, 206, 253, 297, 303, 304, 375, 395, 397, 400
mood states, xx, 199, 200, 311, 318, 322, 346, 377, 379, 389, 391, 392, 394
moral behavior, xi, 5, 158
moral code, 426
moral development, 8, 147, 150, 152
moral identity, 147, 477
moral imperative, xiii, 143, 145
moral judgment, 78, 185
moral reasoning, 146, 147, 154, 157

moral standards, xiii, xx, 143, 144, 407
morale, 64, 66
morality, 52, 64, 413, 423, 428
morbidity, xv, 208, 235, 242
morphology, 184
mortality, xv, 235, 242, 243, 271, 283, 294, 412, 414, 415
mother tongue, 224
motor actions, 85, 401, 402
motor activity, 19, 342
motor behavior, 32, 342
motor skills, 83
motor task, 355
MRI, 179
mucus, 411
multidimensional, 52, 327, 354
multiplication, 96, 122, 124, 125, 126, 138, 140
multivariate analysis, 245
muscles, 45, 518
museums, 293
music, 274, 344, 345, 350, 353, 477
mutilation, 414, 419

N

naming, 94
narratives, 52, 155, 213, 398, 507
National Academy of Sciences, 136, 486, 512
National Health and Nutrition Examination Survey, xvi, 235
natural selection, 13, 484
nausea, 20, 409, 418
negative affectivity, 236
negative attitudes, 116, 134, 413
negative consequences, 118, 436
negative effects, xviii, 89, 96, 251
negative experiences, 201
negative mood, xv, xix, 164, 169, 176, 188, 190, 192, 208, 377, 385, 386, 387, 392, 394, 396, 399, 400, 405
negative outcomes, 146, 193, 195, 212, 364, 494
negative reinforcement, 28, 433
negative relation, 256, 441
negative stimulus, 24
negative valence, 44, 193, 315, 395, 509
neglect, xii, 63, 64
Nepal, 231
nervous system, 7, 340, 422
nervousness, 120
Netherlands, 51, 303, 414
neural network(s), 132, 238, 390, 410
neural system, 298, 494
neurobiology, 463

neurogenesis, 455, 463
neuroimaging, 19, 99, 131, 175, 180, 207, 420, 508, 512
neuronal circuits, 172
neurons, 298, 456
neuropathy, xv, 235
neuropeptides, 179, 183
neurophysiology, 514
neuroscience, 31, 56, 184, 347, 348, 401, 494, 501, 513
neurotransmission, 173, 177, 299
neurotransmitters, 178, 391
neutral, xiv, xxiv, 21, 22, 24, 25, 29, 45, 46, 53, 55, 83, 84, 96, 111, 130, 131, 187, 189, 335, 362, 367, 383, 384, 385, 386, 387, 390, 395, 396, 410, 414, 416, 494, 496, 505, 506, 507, 509, 511, 514, 519, 520, 521
New England, 428, 469
New Zealand, 31
NGOs, 213
nicotine, 368
Nomothetic, 337
non-clinical population, 192, 209, 422
nondysphorics, 190
norepinephrine, 178, 513
North America, 134, 149, 207
Norway, 400
novelty seeking, 294
nuclei, 518
nucleic acid, 185
nucleus, 132
nurses, 300, 303
nursing, 454, 522
nutrition, xvi, 235

O

obesity, ix, xi, xv, xvi, 5, 235, 236, 237, 238, 239, 240, 241, 243, 244, 245, 246, 247, 309, 322
obsessive-compulsive disorder, xx, 201, 203, 207, 251, 407, 418
obstacles, 267
occupied territories, 231
OCD, 251, 252, 253, 418, 419, 427
offenders, 292
old age, 64, 75, 280, 455, 463
omission, 18
one dimension, 310, 457
onset latency, 507
open spaces, 227
openness, 275, 333, 360, 395, 415, 483
openness to experience, 275
operant conditioning, 252

operations, 16, 117, 125, 126
opponent process theory, 322
opportunities, xii, xiv, 81, 107, 109, 110, 112, 116, 161, 166, 212, 230, 437, 455, 473, 474, 478, 479, 492
optimism, xv, 69, 70, 72, 73, 76, 211, 213, 214, 223, 225, 226, 227, 229, 230, 232, 443, 450, 459, 500
optimization, 76, 77
organ, xxiii, 343, 344, 469, 470, 471
organism, x, 4, 43, 172, 313, 314, 332, 340, 408, 419
organizational behavior, 402, 446
organizational development, 345
organizational stress, 350
organize, 55, 103, 112, 471
originality, 379, 391, 392
outpatient(s), 371, 372
overlap, 23, 34, 92, 188, 193, 195, 263, 332, 412, 442
overrepresentation, xii, 63, 64
overweight, xvi, 235, 236, 240, 241, 242, 243, 246, 309
oxygen, 172, 309, 314, 319
oxygen consumption, 172

P

pagers, 316
pain, xix, 29, 31, 34, 37, 57, 314, 323, 324, 341, 344, 359, 361, 364, 365, 368, 369, 371, 372, 448
painters, 378
panic attack, 201
panic disorder, 163, 200, 201, 239, 271, 361
parallel, 33, 166, 194, 198, 382
parallel processing, 33
parasite, 412
parasympathetic activity, 340
parental care, 14
parenting, 216
parents, xxii, 48, 53, 76, 84, 118, 174, 216, 238, 397, 403, 416, 467
parietal cortex, 98, 131, 139, 410
passive-aggressive, 196, 197
path analysis, 353
pathogenesis, 172
pathogens, 414, 415, 416, 419
pathology, 170, 450
pathways, xvi, 177, 205, 229, 236, 237, 238, 239, 256, 298, 397
Pavlovian conditioning, 36
Pavlovian learning, 26, 29, 32
PCM, 37
PCR, 173
peace, 212, 232

pedagogy, 458
peer group, 227
peer relationship, 154
PEP, 195, 196
perceived control, 293, 330
percentile, 280
perceptual processing, 410
performance effectiveness, xii, 87, 90, 93, 94, 95, 97
performance indicator, xxii, 152, 466
performance-based assessments, xxi, 466
performers, 350, 353
permit, 92, 441
perpetrators, 212
perseverance, 391, 392, 399
personal choice, 147
personal control, 76
personal goals, 444
personal hygiene, 309
personal life, 153
personal qualities, 396
personal relations, 144, 145, 153
personal relationship, 144, 145, 153
personal relevance, 147, 278
personal values, xiii, 143
personality characteristics, 214, 293, 483, 484
personality dimensions, xiv, 171, 333, 351
personality disorder, 291, 481
personality inventories, 177, 471
personality test, 460
personality traits, 99, 174, 178, 182, 183, 185, 241, 244, 291, 333, 415, 511, 520
persuasion, 496, 501
pessimism, 70, 214, 223, 225, 226, 230
PET, 91
pharmacogenetics, 182
pharmacotherapy, 299
phase shifts, 298
phenomenology, 144, 205
phenotype(s), 174, 176, 181, 183
Philadelphia, 401, 402, 404, 405
phobia, 203, 418, 419, 420, 422, 424, 425
phonemes, 44
photographs, 41, 413
physical activity, ix, x, xvi, xviii, 4, 235, 236, 239, 242, 244, 245, 307, 308, 320, 321, 322, 323, 324, 331, 356
physical education, 355
physical environment, 305
physical exercise, 213, 300, 304, 323, 349, 383, 391
physical fitness, 309
physical health, xix, xxiii, 359, 361, 368, 456, 469, 481, 482
physical inactivity, 240

physical well-being, xx, 162, 453, 459, 487
Physiological, 30, 32, 33, 36, 46, 278, 448
physiological arousal, 46, 48, 52, 195, 197, 389
physiology, xxi, 8, 35, 46, 47, 48, 49, 55, 59, 60,
    300, 338, 347, 349, 422, 423, 427, 465, 500, 512,
    513
pilot study, 320, 356, 401, 459, 463
pineal gland, 298, 305
PISA, 138
pituitary gland, 518
placebo, 519, 521, 522, 523
planned action, 22
plasticity, xxiii, 463, 464, 486, 505, 508, 509, 515
platform, 484
playing, 178, 380, 511, 522
pleasure, 15, 28, 69, 70, 72, 73, 75, 237, 238, 247,
    254, 264, 275, 277, 311, 312, 323, 355, 387, 396,
    398, 448
poetry, 343, 380
Poland, 505
polar, 40, 43
police, 344, 356
policy, 243, 463, 501
policy makers, 243
politics, 413
polymerase, 173, 183
polymerase chain reaction, 173, 183
polymorphism(s), 176, 177, 178, 179, 180, 181, 182,
    183, 184, 185
polypeptide, xxiv, 517, 518, 523
poor performance, 136
population, xv, xvi, 84, 176, 178, 211, 215, 235, 236,
    244, 270, 284, 293, 294, 299, 369, 395
portfolio, 111
portraits, 229
positive attitudes, 117
positive correlation, 118, 151, 152, 218, 226, 254,
    264, 416, 418, 419
positive emotions, xv, 33, 50, 69, 71, 73, 76, 153,
    188, 211, 213, 214, 218, 221, 222, 223, 227, 279,
    287, 292, 318, 330, 332, 333, 334, 349, 384, 385,
    390, 395, 398, 399, 401, 436, 443, 445, 477, 480,
    491, 492, 497, 499, 519
positive feelings, xix, 310, 316, 377, 398
positive influences, 111
positive mood, xix, 198, 199, 200, 201, 204, 290,
    308, 317, 318, 319, 377, 383, 384, 385, 386, 387,
    391, 392, 393, 394, 396, 399, 402
positive regard, 385
positive relationship, xiv, 119, 187, 415
positron, 91
positron emission tomography, 91
posttraumatic stress, 163, 168, 207, 215, 509, 513

post-traumatic stress disorder, 252
potential benefits, 400, 494
poverty, 215, 226, 227
predictive validity, 450, 464, 488
prefrontal cortex, 21, 31, 91, 95, 131, 132, 181, 474,
    508, 509
pregnancy, 415, 422, 524
prejudice, 365, 413
preparation, 11, 24, 112, 132, 139, 199, 203, 278,
    285, 456, 457, 459, 500
preschool, 60, 72, 75, 231, 401
preschool children, 60, 401
preschoolers, 146, 428
preservation, 436, 506
prevention, xx, 135, 162, 165, 167, 168, 361, 374,
    393, 394, 399, 402, 407, 412, 436
primary school, 152, 153, 155, 156
priming, xxiii, 22, 24, 25, 26, 29, 37, 383, 469, 478
principles, 13, 34, 107, 108, 109, 116, 117, 434
proactive behavior, 365
probability, 13, 191, 381, 437, 490, 491, 493
probe, 35
problem solving, ix, x, xiii, 4, 8, 115, 125, 126, 129,
    130, 132, 133, 136, 137, 138, 162, 163, 189, 190,
    195, 196, 205, 209, 382, 384, 385, 386, 389, 394,
    401, 403, 444, 471
problem-solving, xiv, xv, xvii, xviii, 13, 187, 188,
    189, 190, 191, 193, 203, 208, 249, 251, 343, 378,
    380, 383, 386, 389, 391, 395, 399, 400, 402
problem-solving skills, 343
problem-solving strategies, 391, 395
problem-solving task, 386, 399
producers, 76, 78
professional achievements, 510
professional development, xxi, 112, 466
professionalization, 109, 110, 111, 352
professionals, xxii, 110, 165, 228, 243, 466
profit, 131
prognosis, 251
project, 78, 103, 105, 107, 152, 228, 298, 330, 483
proliferation, 454
promoter, 181, 182, 185
prophylaxis, 422
proposition, 149, 153, 475, 476, 482
prosocial behavior, xi, 7
prosocial children, 146, 157
prostate cancer, 371, 374
protection, 109, 173, 227, 229, 410, 411, 412, 413,
    420, 523
protective factors, xv, 211, 216, 223, 227, 228, 232
protective role, 351, 449
protein structure, 173
proteins, 411

prototype, 405
pruning, 456
psoriasis, 368, 369, 373
psychiatric disorders, 161, 172, 300, 421, 463, 509
psychiatry, 9, 57, 162, 425, 513
psychobiology, 421, 425
psychological distress, xvii, 162, 250, 368
psychological health, 404
psychological phenomena, x, 4
psychological problems, 52, 242, 424
psychological processes, xi, 39, 303
psychological states, 313, 318, 339
psychological well-being, 232, 246, 251, 255, 264, 321, 322, 370, 459, 485
psychologist, 148, 311, 349, 361
psychometric properties, 258, 259, 363
psychopathology, xi, xiii, 5, 7, 69, 161, 162, 164, 165, 166, 167, 168, 169, 170, 191, 196, 201, 202, 206, 244, 245, 397, 404, 417, 422
psychopaths, 283
psychopathy, 276, 292, 293, 450
psychosis, 368
psychosocial stress, 285
psychosomatic, 245, 481, 482
psychotherapy, 162, 165, 168, 361, 372, 373, 374, 404, 419, 462, 463
psychoticism, 415, 428
PTSD, 232, 252, 284, 375, 509
public health, 162, 308, 315
punishment, 17, 18, 21, 32, 393, 432, 433
purity, 424
Pyszczynski, 187, 190, 204, 207

Q

qualitative differences, 342
quality of life, 213, 214, 240, 242, 243, 246, 251, 270, 304, 371
quantitative research, 157
questionnaire, 50, 54, 105, 106, 147, 178, 199, 202, 205, 207, 260, 264, 265, 266, 267, 270, 271, 286, 287, 303, 311, 332, 337, 342, 363, 413, 414, 418, 420, 522

R

race, 46
radiation, 301
radio, 269
rapid eye movement sleep, 506, 515
rating scale, 140, 338

rational-emotive behavior therapy, xiii, 101, 102, 104, 107, 109, 112
rationality, x, 3, 57, 488
reaction time, 125, 132, 172, 478
reactivity, 56, 178, 182, 194, 197, 198, 201, 282, 293, 355, 365, 366, 417, 419, 420, 487, 506, 509, 510, 511, 512
reading, 116, 132, 134, 276, 301, 524
real time, 166
reality, 42, 47, 56, 85, 113, 256, 267, 356, 362, 363, 364, 365, 366, 367, 462, 498
reasoning, x, 3, 16, 88, 127, 129, 146, 367, 391, 488, 499, 500
recall, 45, 123, 124, 127, 166, 168, 196, 197, 290, 328, 384, 492, 506, 507
recalling, 197
reception, 283
receptors, 179, 238, 294, 508
reciprocity, xi, 5, 524
recognition, xi, xxii, xxiv, 39, 40, 41, 55, 57, 118, 181, 193, 231, 365, 394, 412, 423, 466, 487, 505, 511, 517, 518, 519, 520, 523, 524, 525, 526
recognition test, 511
recommendations, 216, 300, 387
reconciliation, 382
recovery, 165, 197, 201, 284, 292, 308, 318, 319, 369, 446
recreation, 318
recreational, 274
recurrence, 253, 375, 421
referees, 345
reflexes, 342
reform(s), 153, 156, 158
refugee camps, 215, 216
refugees, 227, 231, 232
regression, 50, 217, 221, 404
regression analysis, 217, 221
regulations, 75, 76
regulatory systems, xx, 431, 432, 436
rehabilitation, 212
reinforcement, 20, 33, 34, 107, 228, 279, 292
reinforcement learning, 20
reinforcers, 276
rejection, 53, 131, 140, 396, 409, 412, 413, 414, 415
relational concerns, 51
relational theory, 9, 326
relationship quality, 459, 482
relationship satisfaction, 482
relatives, 396, 400, 404
relaxation, 343, 374, 386, 391, 394, 459
relevance, xii, xiv, 69, 95, 101, 102, 111, 145, 161, 166, 263, 326, 419, 457, 492, 494
reliability, 217, 259, 288, 380, 414, 521, 523, 524

relief, 137, 190, 237, 276, 290, 326, 332, 333, 397, 398

religion, 413

REM, 506, 507, 509, 510, 511, 512, 513, 514

remission, 299, 303

repair, xiv, 28, 146, 187, 327, 384, 385

repellent, 408

replication, 133, 202, 209, 271, 411

repression, 360

reproduction, 310, 410

repulsion, 414

reputation, 521

requirements, 228, 301, 309, 314, 479

researchers, ix, xi, xix, xxiv, 15, 25, 39, 40, 41, 43, 45, 46, 48, 50, 53, 55, 82, 83, 84, 87, 91, 93, 120, 121, 130, 134, 145, 162, 165, 171, 172, 174, 193, 216, 243, 259, 316, 317, 318, 325, 330, 334, 336, 337, 341, 342, 343, 345, 385, 386, 387, 410, 411, 471, 484, 517

resilience, xv, 211, 212, 229, 231, 232, 233, 269, 481

resistance, 112, 113, 212, 228, 339, 365, 501, 507

resolution, xvii, 13, 92, 180, 212, 250, 256, 330, 512

resources, xii, 85, 87, 90, 97, 122, 123, 125, 126, 127, 128, 129, 130, 133, 137, 138, 222, 227, 328, 330, 389, 436, 449, 458, 473, 494, 495, 497, 500

respiration, 301, 318

response time, 131

responsiveness, 20, 276, 277, 281, 282, 283, 286, 360, 367, 525

restrictions, 22

restructuring, 256, 364, 366

retardation, 243

retention interval, 506

retirement, 182

retrospection, 13

rewards, 17, 20, 21, 156, 436, 477

rhythm, 304, 306

right hemisphere, 315

rings, 12

risk assessment, 290

risk aversion, 394, 497

risk factors, xvi, 235, 242, 271

risk-taking, 292, 294, 342, 347, 398, 399

RMSEA, 260

rodents, 173

rods, 298

ROI, 131

role of culture, xi, 39, 40, 41, 55, 57

romantic relationship, 368, 482

room temperature, 27

root(s), 10, 204, 340, 437

routes, 16

routines, 361

Royal Society, 36, 181, 421

rugby, 342, 352, 357

rules, xi, 5, 41, 42, 48, 56, 58, 105, 108, 456

rural areas, 225

S

sadness, xv, 15, 41, 42, 46, 48, 53, 54, 55, 69, 70, 71, 72, 144, 188, 190, 196, 200, 201, 214, 217, 218, 221, 222, 254, 287, 326, 364, 389, 393, 394, 395, 398, 408, 409, 490, 491, 494, 499, 501

safety, 209, 214, 305

saliva, 410, 412, 420, 481

sanctions, 108

savings, 182

scaling, 52

scene perception, 184

schema, 14, 478

schemata, 42

schizoid personality disorder, 397

schizophrenia, 161, 397, 420, 441, 449

school, xii, xiii, xviii, xxii, 72, 101, 102, 103, 104, 105, 106, 107, 108, 109, 111, 112, 113, 133, 134, 140, 143, 146, 148, 150, 152, 153, 154, 155, 156, 157, 158, 181, 213, 216, 218, 221, 223, 230, 232, 297, 301, 305, 318, 344, 454, 464, 467

school interaction, xiii, 101, 102

school performance, 464

school psychology, 230

science, xxiv, 34, 56, 77, 116, 140, 169, 178, 180, 308, 310, 311, 321, 326, 351, 355, 356, 370, 402, 434, 447, 517

scientific publications, 462

scientific theory, 382

scope, xviii, 64, 111, 173, 250, 264, 265, 345, 384, 394, 395

scripts, 41

search terms, 308

seasonal changes, 303

secondary schools, 155, 244

secretion, 178, 181, 237, 240, 304, 412, 460

security, 65, 66, 68, 215, 436

sedentary lifestyle, 308

selective attention, 92, 99, 293, 391

selective serotonin reuptake inhibitor, 177

self esteem, 50, 151

self-actualization, 264, 265

self-assessment, 436, 443

self-awareness, 113, 335, 361, 433, 434, 444, 458, 461

self-concept, 8, 78, 119, 138, 140, 147

self-confidence, 395

self-conscious emotions, ix, xiii, 143, 144, 145, 147, 150, 152, 154, 155, 156, 158
self-consciousness, 208
self-control, 363, 365, 432, 441, 443, 444, 445, 446, 449, 450, 495, 501
self-efficacy, xxiii, 113, 117, 118, 119, 120, 136, 138, 140, 328, 330, 343, 443, 446, 456, 461, 469, 471, 472, 473, 475, 476, 477, 478, 479, 480, 482, 483, 486
self-enhancement, 501
self-esteem, 199, 222, 240, 241, 327, 454
self-image, 148, 156
self-interest, 370
self-knowledge, 433
self-monitoring, 434, 437, 497
self-observation, 432, 433, 437, 444, 446
self-perceptions, 76, 240, 333, 423
self-reflection, 113, 433
self-regulation, xi, xvi, xx, 5, 157, 189, 193, 202, 249, 269, 347, 360, 372, 402, 431, 432, 433, 434, 435, 436, 441, 442, 443, 444, 445, 446, 447, 448, 450, 500, 501
self-report data, 166
self-reports, xxi, 47, 168, 284, 285, 290, 466
self-understanding, xiii, 143, 154
SEM model, xvii, 250, 260
semantic information, 122
sensation(s), ix, xviii, 19, 20, 42, 45, 46, 48, 51, 53, 154, 191, 273, 274, 275, 276, 277, 278, 279, 280, 281, 282, 283, 284, 285, 286, 287, 288, 289, 290, 291, 292, 293, 294, 295, 314, 328, 347, 360, 415, 419
sensation seeking, ix, xviii, 273, 274, 275, 276, 277, 278, 279, 280, 281, 282, 283, 284, 285, 286, 289, 290, 291, 292, 293, 294, 295, 347, 415
senses, 44, 274
sensitivity, xiii, 45, 55, 56, 57, 101, 102, 208, 238, 278, 279, 281, 283, 284, 292, 302, 304, 360, 398, 413, 414, 415, 416, 417, 419, 420, 421, 422, 423, 424, 425, 426, 427, 428, 442, 513
sensitization, 244
sensors, 348, 355
sensory experience, 274
September 11, 229
septum, 518
sequencing, 164
serotonin, 177, 178, 182, 184, 185, 237, 246, 247, 279, 511
serum, 180, 411
services, 57, 232, 246
severe stress, 212
sex, 136, 137, 139, 275, 294, 295, 413, 415, 421, 428, 461

sex differences, 139, 275, 294, 415
sexual activities, 412
sexual behaviour, 517, 522
sexual experiences, 274
sexual motivation, 20
sexuality, 411, 412, 414, 423
shame, xi, xiii, 5, 47, 50, 52, 70, 75, 112, 143, 144, 145, 148, 149, 150, 151, 152, 154, 155, 156, 157, 158, 228, 310, 326, 415, 428, 499
shape, x, xi, 4, 5, 44, 55, 200, 201, 214, 389, 501
shelter, 12, 173
shock, 14, 21, 22, 24, 25, 26, 28, 33, 34
shortage, 369
short-term memory, 92, 122
showing, 28, 48, 117, 119, 122, 171, 174, 179, 236, 239, 242, 279, 299, 301, 393, 397, 414, 476, 478
sibling(s), 150, 412
side effects, 35, 104, 305
Sierra Leone, 230
signalling, 240, 313
signals, x, xi, 4, 5, 21, 175, 386, 407, 463
signs, 72, 145, 299, 397
skills training, 335
skin, 21, 46, 172, 278, 282, 290, 339, 349, 373
sleep deprivation, 506, 507, 508, 512
sleep disorders, xviii, 297
sleep disturbance, 300
sleep fragmentation, 510
sleep physiology, 514
sleep spindle, 514
sleep stage, xxiv, 505, 510, 514
smoking, 271, 372, 454
smoking cessation, 372
snakes, 411
SNP, 177, 178, 179
soccer, 309, 346, 350
sociability, 180, 182
social adjustment, 460
social anxiety, 35, 192, 194, 196, 200, 202, 203, 207, 208, 372
social behavior, xi, 5, 37, 174, 175, 176, 196, 407, 446, 485, 518
social behaviour, xxiv, 154, 294, 517
social benefits, 525
social cognition, 85, 183, 401, 402, 499, 525
social competence, 8
social conflicts, 231
social consequences, 448
social construct, xi, 39, 40, 42, 43, 55, 56, 57, 59, 85
social context, 6, 204, 213, 277, 320, 378, 445
social desirability, 264, 294, 338
social development, 69, 75, 323
social deviance, 275

social distance, 50
social environment, x, xi, xiii, 4, 5, 101, 102, 246, 484
social exclusion, 232
social group, 55, 223, 446
social hormone, xxiv, 517, 518
social identity, 130, 131
social image, 156
social influence(s), 156
social information processing, 499
social institutions, 396
social integration, 229
social interactions, ix, xi, xiii, xxiv, 5, 42, 43, 53, 143, 195, 196, 300, 517, 518, 521, 523
social interests, 445
social learning, 139
social learning theory, 139
social life, 59, 413
social network, xi, xxiii, 5, 191, 240, 469, 471, 478, 479, 485
social norms, 41, 42, 413
social order, 45, 413
social perception, 485
social phobia, 163, 200, 203, 208, 239, 271, 420
social psychology, 30, 35, 37, 103, 113, 356, 378, 485
social relations, x, xv, xx, 4, 42, 43, 144, 150, 151, 152, 154, 157, 188, 222, 309, 441, 453, 454, 456, 459, 461, 464, 487, 492, 520
social relationships, xv, xx, 43, 144, 150, 151, 152, 154, 188, 222, 309, 441, 453, 454, 456, 459, 461, 464, 487, 492, 520
social resources, 227
social roles, 42, 52
social rules, xi, 5
social sciences, 78
Social Security, 182
social situations, 154, 195, 196, 204, 240
social skills, 301, 450
social standing, xi, 5
social status, 51
social stress, 347
social structure, 49
social support, xv, 188, 191, 206, 280, 284, 293
social support network, 206
socialization, 42, 48, 58, 77, 417
society, 45, 49, 52, 57, 378, 413, 420, 446
software, 167
solution, x, 3, 103, 121, 123, 129, 190, 212, 332, 379, 392, 414
somatic activation, xx, 407
somatization, 57
Southeast Asia, 47

Spain, 133
spatial information, 124
spatial processing, 89, 98
species, 12, 30, 172, 173, 184, 310
specific knowledge, xxii, 110, 466
speech, 192, 285, 286, 287, 288, 289, 290
spiders, 418, 419
Spring, 183, 270
SS, 289
SSS, 274, 275, 277, 278, 280, 281, 286, 287, 288, 289, 292
stability, xvi, xvii, 188, 202, 249, 250, 251, 264, 436, 463, 483
stakeholders, xxii, 467
standard deviation, 54, 261, 288, 340
standardized testing, 133
stars, 378, 396
statistics, 178, 217, 260
stereotypes, xxiii, 116, 130, 416, 489, 491, 498, 522
stigma, 240, 241
stigmatized, 241
stimulation, 19, 28, 37, 172, 274, 275, 276, 277, 280, 286, 294, 395
stimulus, 11, 13, 17, 20, 22, 23, 24, 25, 26, 27, 34, 36, 37, 51, 83, 185, 202, 278, 279, 283, 299, 313, 324, 330, 365, 405, 409, 412, 436, 496, 506, 510
stock, 403, 456
stomach, 45, 242, 268, 460
storage, 89, 92, 121, 122, 124, 125, 508, 513
storytelling, 343, 380, 400
stress factors, 109
stress reactions, 285, 290
stress response, 367
stressful events, 284, 340, 367, 509
stressful life events, 284
stressors, 281, 283, 284, 285, 286, 334, 336, 481, 509
striatum, 238, 418
stroke, 315
structural equation modeling, xvii, 250, 259, 270
structure, 7, 13, 14, 20, 32, 36, 37, 46, 173, 175, 177, 180, 181, 183, 185, 227, 259, 270, 275, 291, 323, 324, 332, 363, 372, 405, 414, 415, 424, 426, 427, 434, 448, 449, 455, 487, 524
structuring, 364
style(s), xiv, xxiii, 188, 191, 192, 196, 204, 230, 231, 232, 274, 275, 294, 368, 379, 381, 393, 404, 415, 469, 475, 488, 513
subgroups, 163, 222, 223, 224, 225, 226
subitizing, 127, 134, 139
subjective experience, 42, 43, 338
subjective well-being, xxiii, 227, 230, 469, 475, 476, 480, 481, 484, 487

substance abuse, xx, 274, 377
substance use, 293
substrate(s), 35, 98, 410, 425
subtraction, 117, 123, 124, 126, 128, 129, 132, 140, 141
successful aging, 76
suicidal behavior, 180
suicide, 177, 180, 244, 253
suicide attempts, 244
sulfate, 371
Sun, 52, 59
supervision, 105, 108, 224
supervisor(s), xxii, 108, 380, 466, 482
suppression, 24, 25, 45, 125, 138, 163, 168, 169, 170, 191, 194, 205, 287, 300, 303, 305, 356, 363, 365, 423, 456, 497, 498, 507, 514
suprachiasmatic nucleus, 298, 305
survey design, 149, 264
survival, xix, 13, 69, 310, 325, 344, 407, 415
survival value, 407
susceptibility, 87, 182, 201, 278, 398, 499, 500
suspense, 276
sustainability, xi, 5
sweat, 339, 351, 411, 420
Sweden, 231, 414
Switzerland, 306
sympathetic nervous system, 133, 197, 339
sympathy, xi, 5, 70
symptomology, 361
synchronization, xviii, 180, 297
syndrome, 84, 85, 174, 180, 181, 182, 183, 184, 185, 244, 253, 305, 419, 524
synthesis, 10, 337, 351, 385, 400
systematic processing, 386

T

talent, 379
target, x, 5, 17, 47, 94, 162, 166, 177, 243, 275, 277, 346, 375
task conditions, 92
task demands, 327
task interference, 36
task load, 351
task performance, 22, 34, 89, 93, 98, 122, 127, 294, 304, 330, 351, 389, 392, 449
taxonomy, 34, 254, 426, 462
teacher training, xii, 101, 102, 109
teachers, xii, xiii, xxii, 101, 102, 103, 105, 106, 107, 108, 109, 110, 111, 113, 118, 129, 134, 136, 143, 144, 145, 152, 153, 154, 155, 156, 157, 223, 344, 462, 467
teaching abilities, 109

teaching evaluation, 109
teams, 228, 344, 454
techniques, 166, 172, 173, 174, 179, 213, 259, 264, 334, 343, 389, 394, 454
technology, 116, 131, 166, 169, 490, 494
teens, 116
temperament, x, 4, 8, 83, 180, 348, 403
temperature, xviii, 297, 298, 301, 303
temporal lobe, 175
tension, xxi, 17, 28, 44, 59, 120, 311, 342, 382, 397, 465
territory, 229, 230
terrorism, 233
terrorist attack, 229
test anxiety, 88, 90, 99, 144
test scores, 134, 397
testing, 64, 94, 120, 128, 129, 133, 177, 313, 337, 468
testosterone, 33, 341
text messaging, 167
textbook, 321
thalamus, 201
theatre, 213
theoretical approaches, x, 3, 163, 321
theoretical assumptions, xi, 39, 40, 90
therapeutic approaches, 165
therapeutic interventions, 162, 228
therapeutic practice, 148
therapist, 477, 483
therapy, xviii, 103, 264, 292, 297, 298, 299, 300, 301, 303, 304, 305, 306, 361, 365, 367, 370, 371, 372, 375, 418, 424, 428, 447, 514, 515
thermoregulation, 302
theta waves, 511
thinking styles, 366
threats, xix, 7, 195, 222, 359, 366, 411
time frame, 287, 289
time periods, 6, 302, 308
time pressure, 287
timesharing, 34
tissue, 240
TNF, 411, 423
tobacco, 26, 464
toddlers, 84, 85, 145, 157
toilet training, 416
tones, 125
tonic, 339
top-down, 392, 434, 435
torture, 14
toxin, 20
tracks, 14
trade, 16
traditions, 64, 216, 361

trainees, 104, 113

training, xix, xxii, 20, 26, 102, 106, 109, 112, 116, 117, 309, 331, 343, 344, 349, 352, 353, 356, 359, 361, 362, 364, 365, 366, 368, 369, 370, 371, 372, 374, 375, 448, 449, 454, 456, 457, 458, 459, 460, 461, 462, 464, 466

training programs, xix, 359, 362

trait anxiety, 87, 88, 92, 94, 95, 96, 99, 259, 333, 349, 415, 419, 422, 428

traits, xvii, 6, 8, 182, 250, 256, 259, 281, 292, 333, 392, 396, 397, 398, 404, 420, 461, 468, 471, 473, 479, 487, 511

trajectory, 66, 68, 69, 71, 73, 212

transformation, 124, 125, 365

transgression, 152, 156, 196, 197, 198

translation, 12, 22, 34, 223

transmission, xx, 13, 46, 112, 255, 407, 412, 415, 416, 419, 478

trauma, xv, 70, 211, 212, 214, 216, 223, 226, 227, 228, 229, 230, 368, 372

traumatic events, xv, 211, 222, 227, 230, 252

traumatic experiences, 214, 228

treatment, xiv, xvi, xviii, xix, 27, 69, 88, 99, 135, 146, 161, 162, 165, 167, 168, 170, 180, 203, 204, 236, 242, 244, 291, 297, 299, 300, 301, 302, 303, 304, 305, 318, 357, 359, 362, 369, 371, 372, 373, 374, 375, 413, 422, 428, 491

treatment methods, 69

trial, 24, 96, 236, 299, 304, 375, 468, 520

triggers, 127, 408, 411, 413, 443

Trinidad, 454, 464

true/false, 126, 131

trustworthiness, 521, 526

tryptophan, 237, 303, 304

tumor, 411

tumor necrosis factor, 411

turnover, 436

twins, 176, 317

type 1 diabetes, 463

type 2 diabetes, 309, 315

U

UK, 78, 87, 114, 139, 143, 155, 161, 246, 249, 271, 422

unconditioned, 25

underrepresentation, xii, 63, 64

unhappiness, 225

uniform, 13

United, xv, 57, 59, 115, 140, 235, 245, 249, 414, 486

United Kingdom, 249

United States, xv, 57, 59, 115, 140, 235, 245, 414, 486

universality, 41, 55, 56, 57, 59, 415

universities, 257

university education, 107

unusual perceptual experiences, 396

updating, 20, 91, 92

urban, 223, 224, 225, 227, 320

urban areas, 225

urine, 408, 411, 420

US Department of Health and Human Services, 324

USA, 39, 184, 270, 463

V

vacuum, 17

valence, 15, 32, 44, 50, 52, 144, 166, 168, 189, 279, 311, 312, 314, 315, 319, 326, 329, 330, 335, 338, 339, 410, 494, 511

validation, 207, 208, 231, 259, 264, 270, 294, 306, 321, 322, 324, 352, 372, 421, 472, 486, 487

variables, 83, 120, 173, 214, 217, 221, 224, 227, 228, 240, 241, 245, 257, 259, 260, 261, 262, 263, 264, 284, 298, 316, 328, 330, 339, 345, 363, 369, 378, 380, 382, 394, 471, 474

variations, 10, 56, 103, 145, 151, 173, 174, 176, 177, 520

vasopressin, 179, 181, 183

vegetables, 238

vehicles, 419

vein, 360, 365

velocity, 455

verbal report, xx, 407, 408

victimization, 240, 243

victims, 212, 226

videotape, 386

violence, ix, xi, xv, 5, 211, 212, 214, 216, 221, 222, 223, 226, 227, 228, 229, 230, 231, 232, 233, 282

violent entertainment, 292

vision(s), 78, 351

visual acuity, 478, 486

visual attention, 329, 333, 346, 350

visual cliff, 81, 85

visual stimuli, 277, 282, 295, 421

visual system, 410

vocabulary, xxii, 42, 467

vocalizations, 180, 409

volleyball, 349

vomiting, 169, 283, 409

voting, 491

vulnerability, xv, xx, 179, 199, 211, 223, 231, 241, 252, 254, 284, 285, 343, 396, 400, 407, 412, 416, 417, 420

vulnerability to depression, 179

W

waking, 506, 507, 509
walking, 82, 309, 315, 316, 320, 321
war, xv, 211, 212, 213, 214, 223, 227, 228, 229, 230, 232, 284, 293, 294, 513
Washington, 9, 78, 99, 139, 169, 201, 269, 324, 370, 401, 427
waste, 360, 408
water, 27, 412
wavelengths, xviii, 297
wavelet, 348
weakness, 48, 254, 266, 369, 454
wear, 412, 521
weight control, 245
weight gain, xvi, 236, 238, 243, 246, 299
weight loss, 237, 239, 242, 243, 245, 246, 317
weight reduction, 236
welfare, 146, 153, 501
West Bank, 215, 216, 230
western culture, 41, 117
WHO, 251
Wilhelm Wundt, 311
William James, ix, 3, 19, 361
wires, 19
withdrawal, 109, 172, 254, 395, 410, 412, 422, 445
work environment, xxii, 300, 302, 466
workers, 257, 356, 381, 394, 398, 483, 513

working memory, xii, xiii, 87, 89, 91, 97, 98, 99, 115, 120, 121, 122, 123, 124, 125, 126, 127, 128, 129, 130, 131, 132, 133, 134, 135, 136, 137, 138, 139, 140, 141, 189, 298, 306, 330, 368, 391, 400, 495
workload, 284
workplace, xxii, 157, 300, 303, 306, 380, 386, 387, 388, 393, 400, 401, 403, 447, 466, 483, 486
World Health Organisation, 271
worldwide, xvi, 235, 249, 253
worry, xvii, 89, 96, 99, 127, 133, 134, 193, 194, 195, 196, 202, 203, 205, 206, 208, 209, 250, 252, 253, 254, 255, 256, 263, 265, 266, 268, 270, 282, 286, 289, 314, 368, 419

Y

Yale University, 32, 137, 187, 421, 465
yield, 21, 83, 133
young adults, 147, 154, 274, 474
young people, 165, 212, 275, 320
young women, 116
youth populations, 368

Z

zeitgeist, 454

Due Date	Date Returned
ILL/Feb 12, 15	FEB 1 9 2015
T/Jan. 21, 16	APR 1 5 2016
www.library.humber.ca	